SAINT FRANCIS XAVIER

SAINT

FRANCIS XAVIER

(1506-1552)

by

JAMES BRODRICK, S. J.

✝

THE WICKLOW PRESS
41 EAST 50TH STREET
NEW YORK 22, NEW YORK

DE LICENTIA SVPERIORVM ORDINIS S.J.

———

NIHIL OBSTAT: HVBERTVS RICHARDS, S.T.L., L.S.S.
CENSOR DEPVTATVS

IMPRIMATVR: E. MORROGH BERNARD
VICARIVS GENERALIS

WESTMONASTERII: DIE XVIII FEBRVARII MCMLII

Library of Congress Catalog Card Number: 52-9459

Manufactured in the United States of America

PREFACE

Papist and Jesuit of the old Spanish vintage, Francis Xavier might not at first sight seem a promising subject for modern consideration. Though his dates are Renaissance he was mediaeval to the core, and confident of his world in a way difficult for us, heirs of uncertainty, even to understand. An effort is made in this book to picture him with all his limitations—which he so magically transcends. No one reading the book will progress far without discovering that it owns to a presiding genius, a scholar of the great tradition who has devoted more than thirty years of unremitting and sacrificial labour to the task of finding the real Xavier under the great pyramid of pious accretion built upon his humble bones by the mistaken reverence of biographers and editors throughout four centuries. Now growing old and grey, Father George Schurhammer, S.J., is still busily wielding his pick. Few of the archives and great libraries of Europe but have known his genial presence, and it can be revealed that he once tracked a lost letter of St. Francis even into a bookshop in Berkeley Square, London, W.1., the famous house of Maggs Brothers. He has followed on his own feet every league of sea or land traversed by the sublimest of the world's globe-trotters, from the green pastures of Spanish Navarre to the sacred city of Kyoto, once the capital and still the artistic heart of Japan. It has ever been the delight of Father Schurhammer to share the fruits of his incessant toil with even the least of the camp-followers who hang around the tents of the learned. That is why this book was possible. My good friend and brother made it possible, and all but its blemishes are more his than mine. The outstanding natural virtue of St. Francis Xavier was gratitude, which is a comforting reflection for one as hopelessly indebted to Father Schurhammer as I am.

To the staff of the publishers, experts in the mysteries of book-production, the volume owes such seemliness as it possesses. No bibliography is needed, as the title and author of every work cited is given in full, and repeated wherever necessary to avoid a rash of *loc. cit.'s* and other such annoyances. The capitals MHSJ prefixed to a title stand for *Monumenta Historica Societatis Jesu*, a collection of letters and documents on early Jesuit history which has now reached its sixty-sixth huge volume but is still a long way from reaching the end of the sixteenth century. St. Francis Xavier's Letters first appeared in this series in 1912, and were re-edited in a most thorough and scholarly fashion by Fathers Schurhammer and Wicki in 1943-1944. Their two volumes, *Epistolae S. Francisci Xaverii*, are the basis of the present work.

JAMES BRODRICK, S.J.

CONTENTS

TO

THE CATHOLICS OF ASIA

"Xavier the magnanimous, the holy and the gay; the canonized saint, not of Rome only, but of universal Christendom."—*The Edinburgh Review*, 1842, p. 335.

"Le pèlerinage de François Xavier demeure un des plus héroïques efforts de la nature humaine. Son rêve a agrandi le monde. Il y a mis une fièvre immortelle."—*Revue des Deux Mondes*, 1924, p. 338.

CHAPTER I

SHADOWS IN ARCADY

THE mediaeval stronghold in Spanish Navarre which gave its Basque name of Xavier[1] to the subject of this book was never of much importance in either war or peace, and ended its uneventful existence by having its few remaining relics incorporated in a massive modern structure designed for the accommodation of ecclesiastical students. It stands or stood close to the swiftly flowing little river Aragon, a boundary of the once famous kingdom christened by its waters, and its function, during the centuries of Navarre's independence, seems to have been to dispute the passage of this trivial obstacle. There is no record that it was ever called upon to exercise its function. At least since Chaucer's age, building castles in Spain has been regarded as equivalent to daydreaming, or planning something otiose or futile, such as bringing coals to Newcastle (once upon a time!), because Spain is the most be-castled land on earth.[2] Birth in such a place cannot therefore have been any great distinction, and Xavier besides ranked very low in the hierarchy of Spanish castles, a mere unblooded corporal among magnificent battle-scarred generals and field marshals. But in renown the little sentinel of Navarre has outstripped all the hoary giants of the Spanish hills. Very few people except Spaniards or inveterate travellers in Spain will have heard of cloud-capped Peñafiel or tremendous Coca, but everybody has heard of Xavier. It would hardly be an exaggeration to say that the name has become a household word the world over, a magic evocative name, conjuring up visions of

[1] The name as traditionally spoken in English rhymes with saviour, but in Spanish has the sound of Have-ee-air, with the accent on the last syllable. It means nothing more romantic than New House, like Casanova in Italian or Maisonneuve in French.

[2] Brewer's *Readers' Handbook* informs the untravelled that the proverb derives from the fact that ' Spain has no Castles '.

galleons, catamarans and brown junks tossing on tropical seas, of hot Indian plains and stifling Malayan jungles, of explosive, sun-drenched Indonesian islands, of a China and Japan as un-mapped and mysterious as the dark side of the moon. A child born within the gloomy battlements of Xavier on April 7, the Tuesday of Holy Week in the year 1506, was to make all that difference. He was christened Francis, a name before unused in his family of habitual Michaels, Jeromes, Martins, Peters and Johns, perhaps because his arrival in Holy Week reminded his devout mother of the saint who had borne the wounds of Christ in his living flesh.[1]

Navarre at the time of Francis Xavier's birth was a united kingdom, though divided geographically by the mighty barrier of the Pyrenees. Four-fifths of it lay in Spain, immediately south of the mountains, and the other fifth in France, *ultra-puertos*, beyond the few passes through them. The French fifth provided the ruling dynasty, the House of Albret, which afterwards in the person of Henry of Navarre did the same service for the whole of

[1] During the last quarter of the seventeenth century, a very lively, not to say heated, controversy flared up between two eminent Jesuits, Pierre Poussines and Daniele Bartoli, concerning the year of Francis Xavier's birth. On the strength of some oral evidence provided by an old gentleman of ninety-two, a distant relative of the Saint, Francis's first biographer, Orazio Tursellini, who published his book in 1594, plunged for 1497 as being the momentous year, principally, according to Poussines, because that was the year when Vasco da Gama set out on his tempestuous and epoch-making voyage to India. Bartoli, a man of prodigious literary fecundity, championed the same date, partly for the same romantic reason, but the more austerely minded Poussines could not see what the great Admiral had to do with the matter. He pointed out that if Francis was born when Bartoli wanted him born, he must have spent twenty years at the University of Paris, an unconscionably long time to acquire an M.A.—if he ever did acquire it. Then, in 1677, he published at Toulouse a Latin dissertation of 137 pages, *De Anno natali S. Francisci Xaverii*, in which he finally demolished Bartoli and all the romantics. Bartoli, a good scholar, with a small but secure niche of his own in Italian literature, refused to capitulate and maintained his wrong date to the end of his long life in 1685. An interested spectator of the fray in which quotations from the ancient poets were freely used as ammunition was the future Jesuit General, Charles de Noyelles. To him, in 1676, Poussines wrote a long and trenchant letter from which the facts given here are derived. There is no longer the slightest doubt that Francis Xavier was born in 1506. Poussines produced the written evidence of the Saint's elder brother Juan to that effect.

France. At the time now in question all the fifths spoke the enigmatic Basque language and belonged to the patriarchal Basque world where everything was on a modest scale, except the Pyrenees and the hearts of the people. Long afterwards, when he was among the pearl-fishers in the region of Cape Comorin, the apex of the immense Indian triangle, St. Francis wrote somewhat despondently to his Jesuit brethren in Rome that he could not hold converse with his humble neophytes and had to employ such interpreters as knew a little Portuguese, ' because their mother tongue is Tamil and mine is Basque '.[1] Basque is no longer spoken in the part of Navarre where he was born, but he used it during his home-keeping years and babbled in it when dying off the coast of China. Francis was never a great linguist, though he learned to speak and write, serviceably, if not elegantly, Portuguese, Spanish, French and Italian. Latin of the workaday order he acquired in abundance, but apparently no Greek at all. His family, like that of his King, who held court at Pamplona, originated on the French side of the Pyrenees, a fact which, at the time of his canonization, inspired the children of St. Louis to agitate mildly for his inclusion in the Roman Martyrology and Breviary as of their nation. But the wary authorities, with half an eye on the children of St. James, evaded the issue by enrolling him as ' Francis, born of noble parentage at Xavier in the diocese of Pamplona '.

It would be possible at this point to expatiate on the racial characteristics of St. Francis, which were strongly marked, but he can safely be left to disclose them personally as the narrative proceeds. His parents bore elaborate Basque names ringing with pride of race and place—Don Juan de Jassu y Atondo and Doña Maria de Azpilcueta y Aznarez de Sada. All of these except the John and Mary were derived from hamlets and moated granges unknown to any but the most extravagantly hospitable maps. In the later Middle Ages, the farming family of Jassu, a speck of a village in French Navarre from which Don Juan derived, became prosperous and urbanized at Saint-Jean-Pied-de-Port. As a consequence of the rise in fortune, the father of Francis was

[1] Schurhammer, *Epistolae S. Francisci Xaverii*, i, 162.

enabled to proceed to Bologna and acquire a doctorate in law at the university there. Law was the surest ladder to success in a land as feudalized, and so as litigious, as Navarre. He was a gifted man and rose high in the service of the Lilliput Kingdom whose brave and glorious centuries of independence were then rapidly drawing to a close. In some undetermined year of the decade 1470–80, Dr. Juan márried Maria de Azpilcueta, who brought to him as part of her dowry the Castle of Xavier. He was of peasant stock, but she claimed descent from a certain mediaeval duke reputed rightly or wrongly to have been an ancestor also of the kings of Aragon. The men of her family showed an addiction to the profession of arms, though the only one of them in the least known to fame, her cousin, Martin de Azpilcueta, commonly called the Doctor of Navarre, was a priest and professor of canon law. This good and genial man, who was much sought after by universities, had a few proclivities in common with his second cousin once removed, St. Francis Xavier, though a passion for canon law was not one of them. He had a roving disposition and a great gift for living contentedly among foreign peoples. Indeed, he was much criticized in Spain for his determined cosmopolitanism. When challenged on the point of his nobility, he replied that his and Maria's family had come out of two *palacios*, Azpilcueta and Jaureggiuçar, which were standing long before the days of Charlemagne.[1]

[1] Cros, *Saint François de Xavier: sa vie et ses lettres*, Paris, 1900, i, 20. Père Leonard Cros, a Jesuit and the son of a notary, spent twenty years scouring all the likely archives of Europe for any scrap of a document which bore, however remotely, on the life of St. Francis Xavier. He projected three volumes of his finds, but after the first one, which appeared at Toulouse in 1894 under the title, *Saint François de Xavier, son pays, sa famille, sa vie*, his publishers refused to indulge his magpie instincts any further. Let him, they said, write a proper consecutive biography of the Saint rather than bury him under an avalanche of papers referring only to his remote ancestors or to his immediate aunts, uncles and cousins. The result was the work in two volumes cited above, itself much cluttered with Xaverian minutiae of no importance whatever. But Père Cros's passionate and obstinate labours, which he applied also to the history of St. Ignatius Loyola, were not in vain, for they helped greatly to outmode the older pietistic and often purely imaginary type of saint's life, and to start a better tradition, represented, for instance, by Alexandre Brou's massive *Saint François Xavier* (1911) and Paul Dudon's *Saint Ignace de Loyola* (1934).

Doña Maria, a matron sketched to the life in the thirty-first chapter of Solomon's *Proverbs*, had no need to stress the glories of her birth and state, for her husband was only too ready to assume the office of family trumpeter, especially when in litigation with his humbler neighbours. Navarre was a pastoral country and merino sheep constituted the principal element in its economy. So much was this the case that the whole land south of the Pyrenees had been divided for administrative purposes into five *merindades*, or areas under the jurisdiction of *merinos*, who were not only sheep but royal judges appointed to superintend sheep-walks. Sheep have often been a source of contention among men ever since Abram and Lot had their argument on the subject. In Navarre, the creatures were always putting neighbours at sixes and sevens, in fact, eating men, just as in England, though much more humanely. Thus, the *ciudadani* or burghers of the very old, picturesque and tired little town of Sangüesa, adjoining Castle Xavier, maintained that they had a right to drive their flocks to pasture across any private property whatsoever. Juan de Jassu not only denied this right but seized as toll one head in every five of the flocks that trespassed on his land, for which cause the outraged Sangüesans brought him to law and produced twenty-three witnesses. On his side Dr. Juan produced sixty. The case lasted six months and gave the defendant occasion for such lofty assertions as the following:

The House of Xavier is one of the most ancient and free in the Kingdom of Navarre. Its Lord enjoys sovereign seignorial rights, without other obligation to the King and Crown of Navarre than to make war or peace at his command. From time immemorial the House of Xavier has enjoyed the right of sanctuary, ... and not infrequently have the citizens of Sangüesa fled to its shelter to escape the penalties of the law. At various periods this same House has been ruled by lords of great distinct-ion, several of whom rose to be governors of the Kingdom or held other eminent posts under the Crown. . . . Xavier has always had vassals, serfs and taxpayers subject to its seignorial jurisdiction. . . .[1]

[1] Cros, *Saint François de Xavier, son pays, sa famille, sa vie*, III-12.

Another instance of the same baronial demeanour occurred as far back as the year 1478 when, newly married and capped a doctor of Bologna, Juan was promoted to high office by his sovereign. On that occasion the King granted his ' illustrious, faithful, and well-beloved counsellor and finance minister, Don Johan de Jassu ', civil jurisdiction over a *palacio* or manor-house called Ydocin, and transferred to him all the curious feudal rights attaching to the place and its lands, homicides, demi-homicides, sixantenas, and calonyas,[1] which had hitherto apper-tained to the Crown. Juan accordingly thought himself entitled to graze his numerous flocks on the Ydocin pastures which adjoined those of Xavier, but a swarm of village Hampdens immediately sprang to their crooks to resist the woolly invasion. They also brought their overlord to law and went on fighting him in the courts for years with the greatest enthusiasm. Theirs was the spirit of the vassals of Aragon whose oath of allegiance to their feudal lord began with the words: ' We who are as good as you, swear to you who are no better than we. . . .' After its fashion, little Navarre was the perfect democracy. In spite of all protestation and litigation the people of Sangüesa continued to drive their sheep across the Xaverian domain, and the people of the Castle continued to impound one sheep in five of the trespassing flocks, whenever they could catch them. It is recorded that the mother of St. Francis used regularly to hand back the confiscated beasts to their owners, being content to maintain her rights by keeping them for a short while in captivity, and it is recorded also that Francis himself, at the age of thirteen, helped his two brothers and the family bailiff to round up one of the contumacious flocks. In fact, that incident is half of his boyhood's story, as documentary evidence knows it.[2] The rest is deduction and conjecture.

One perfectly safe deduction is that he was bred in an atmo-sphere of austere Catholic piety. There still exists a little leather-bound volume containing the regulations which Doña Maria and her husband had drawn up for the better ordering of divine

---

[1] These were fines or tribute that had to be paid by the families of murderers, libellers, etc.

[2] Cros, *Saint François de Xavier: sa vie et ses lettres*, i, 80.

worship in their secluded home. The grandiloquence of Navarre is very evident in the brown pages, for the little Castle church of Santa Maria looms in them as though it were some mighty cathedral or vast Cistercian abbey. The ordinances, as they are called, run to fourteen chapters and not only prescribe a daily sung Mass and solemn High Mass every Sunday and feast, but require that the Divine Office be always said in choir and that the *Salve Regina* be chanted each evening at the sound of the Castle bell. The chaplains involved are given minute instructions on the deportment expected from them. They must strive to imitate the ascetic and other-worldly lives of the primitive saints and hold all their conversation in Heaven. No woman under the age of sixty was to be allowed across the threshold of their *abbadia*. Study is to be their chief recreation, and the most that is permitted to them of any other kind is to fish, like the Apostles, or to dig in their garden, like Adam. So the ordinances go on, citing St. Augustine and St. Ambrose, but more obviously inspired by a third Doctor, held in chiefest honour at Xavier, the intense and somewhat ruthless Jerome. Little could a reader unacquainted with the spirit of Navarre have guessed that the whole brave show was for the sake of three humble priests and a sacristan, probably the most obscure ecclesiastics to be found within the four corners of Spain. There is something truly impressive about this, an indication of religion pure and undefiled, with God the first and last of its considerations. It was in keeping with the same spirit that the chief object of worship at Xavier should have been one of those terrifyingly realistic Spanish crucifixes, a relic preserved from Moorish times, which bring home the tragic sense of life so much more tellingly than the words of philosophers.

Tragedy was to be the portion of Navarre and Xavier. Francis, born in his parents' middle age, had been preceded into the world by two sisters and two brothers. One of the girls, Magdalena, became a lady-in-waiting to Queen Isabella of Castile, but soon exchanged her court robes for the habit of a Poor Clare at Gandia and died prematurely through the excess of her austerities. The two brothers of Francis had little chance of being anything but *guerrilleros*, the same style of men who centuries later, in the

Peninsular War, won the unstinted praises of a man slow to praise, the Duke of Wellington. Of Juan, the nearest to Francis in age though nine years his senior, it is recorded that he held the national sport of bull-fighting in contempt, because he judged it to illustrate the art of evading a foe, rather than of pursuing him or of meeting him face to face in good soldierly fashion. Francis, the baby of the family, seems to have shared with the toreadors a certain amount of this almighty Juan's disdain. How the children obtained an education in that isolated chessboard world, which, for all the rustling and crackling of ancient parchments, was built mainly on sheep and cheese, is not indicated in the blizzard of family papers let loose on our heads by the devotees of Francis. Perhaps the three chaplains took the boys in hand, possibly helped out by some university-bred miscreant in sanctuary at the Castle. Or they may have attended the school at Sangüesa where their mother owned a house. Whatever the process of his initiation into the world of mediaeval learning, Francis emerged from it sufficiently equipped with Latin and other lore to be able to face undismayed the very mild scholastic requirements of the most famous university on earth. His father, Dr. Juan, can have had little influence on his development, for he was away nearly all the time during the boy's formative years, striving pathetically to prop up the tottering independence of Navarre. The print of Navarre, its intensity of religious feeling, its spirit of loyalty, its sense of human dignity, its high seriousness, its courage, its profound contentment with life as God arranged it, its reserve and taciturnity, even its obstinate prejudices, would be deep on Francis Xavier to the day he died, and it was altogether in keeping that he should mutter in his last delirium at the end of the world snatches of the Basque prayers which he had learned at his mother's knee.

Some modern delineations of Francis in youth are charming, though purely conjectural. Thus, one of his numerous Protestant lovers pictured him in the following way:

Many a day of wild sport and adventure must the boy have passed among his native mountains, bracing his nerves and hardening his frame for the labours of his manhood, climbing the cliffs to find the eagle's nest, tracking the wolf by torch-light over the blood-stained snow, fishing for his Lenten fare in the dark lakes that lie in the heart of the hills, or rambling on some long summer day by pine forest and winding stream, even to where the rocky ramparts of France are cleft as with Titan sword at the far-famed Brêche de Rolande, or scaled by the sacred pass of Roncesvalles.[1]

It may very well have been so, for Francis afterwards acquired some reputation as an athlete at Paris, but strict documentary history obliges us to point out that the solitary recorded exploit of his boyhood was a successful chase of sheep rather than of wolves. He had reached only the age of six when, despite anything that his unhappy father could do to prevent it, his country lost its age-long independence and was forcibly incorporated into the dominions of Ferdinand, King of Aragon, perhaps the most crafty and unlovable of all the murky Renaissance princes.[2] All that the Lord of Xavier received for his unremitting labours to stave off the evil day was a grant from King Henri d'Albret entitling him to extract one log or beam from each raft of timber which some forest magnate used to float down the Aragon, with damage to a mill on its banks part-owned by the Doctor. But after his death in 1515 the King, then in exile, very creditably sent his widow a sum owing to him of 791 pounds, 13 shillings, and 4 pence. The poor lady, part of whose remaining property had been confiscated by the despot of Aragon, signed her acknowledgement, ' La tryste Marya d'Azpylcueta '.

That was only the beginning of sorrows for the stricken family. The death of King Ferdinand in 1516 was the signal for an abortive rising in Navarre, which brought on the country the

---

[1] Mary Hall McClean, *Life of Francis Xavier, Apostle of the Indies*, London, 1895, p. 2. As for the sacred pass of Roncesvalles, it is well known now that, not the Moors, as the great epic pretends, but the Catholic Basques defeated the raiding Charlemagne's rearguard and slew Roland.

[2] Requiem Masses are still regularly sung for El Católico in the splendid crypt where he lies at Granada, looking so pious in effigy. One is tempted to think that he must still sorely need them, even after four hundred years.

vengeance of his great and terrible regent, Cardinal Ximenes. Demolition squads arrived at Xavier, as at other fortresses, and proceeded to destroy methodically its age-old bravery of towers and walls, until little was left intact but the living quarters or *casa*, which the viceroy of Navarre, the Duke of Nájera, spared out of pity for Maria and her children. Even the moat was filled up and the drawbridge dismantled.[1] If Francis, aged ten, had conceived any views on those proceedings, he refrained from expressing them. Not only is he scarcely visible at Xavier up to the age of nineteen, when he left it for good, but he gives the impression throughout life of having been extraordinarily detached from his own kith and kin. One solitary letter from him to a member of his immediate family has come down, and it is written in a style so coldly courteous and ceremonious that it might have been addressed to a perfect stranger rather than to his blood brother. The people of his country never did wear their hearts on their sleeves, but we could wish for an occasional flash of family affection in the one of them who was most prodigal of love for all mankind. His negative attitude has disconcerted biographers of other nations who felt compelled to supply from their own resources the *pietas* so strangely missing in the files of their hero. No doubt, they had every justification, except such as may be found in *pièces justificatives*.

In 1520, when Francis was sufficiently advanced in years to appreciate the dramatic events, the *Comuneros* of Castile staged their famous and sanguinary rebellion against the authority of their new and very foreign ruler, Emperor Charles V, grandson of King Ferdinand. One consequence was that Navarre had to be largely denuded of its occupying troops, and that gave the brave indomitable people the chance of which they had been dreaming for five black years. The King of France, debonair and dissolute François I, born rival of the Emperor whom he fought through four successive wars, dispatched a large army across the Pyrenees to the assistance of the patriots, not, of course, that he

[1] Cros, *Saint François de Xavier, son pays, sa famille, sa vie*, 175–82. The damage done to the Castle was reckoned at 2,500 gold ducats and there was no compensation, though Xavier had not been involved in the rising.

cared a straw about the independence of Navarre except as an embarrassment to the hated Charles. Miguel de Jassu, the new lord of Xavier, and his brother Juan promptly sallied forth from the Castle, or what was left of it, to join the invaders under the command of André de Foix, a relative of Catherine de Foix, the exiled Queen of Navarre.[1] A report from Sangüesa, dated May 17, 1521, gives a vivid picture of the hopes and fears that must have been prevalent at adjoining Xavier:

> The French are swarming through Roncesvalles, Maya, and San Juan in numbers beyond counting. Sangüesa, Caseda and Gallipenzo rose today for King Henry. The Duke of Nájera has fled from Pamplona and the City is again free. The French army will be there tomorrow, and I am told that they will hardly have to dismount to capture the citadel. Like the mountain regions, the whole Kingdom is in revolt, and I think that the Duke of Nájera will have cause to thank God if he succeeds in reaching Castile. God grant that all this may be for His service and the good of the Kingdom, for we have suffered enough misfortune and humiliation to want no more.[2]

The French began the bombardment of Pamplona's citadel on April 20. One of the defenders, a Basque soldier from the province of Guipúzcoa, destined for great subsequent fame, obloquy and passionate devotion under the name of Ignatius Loyola, has left a dictated account of the event, pithy but revealing. He speaks of himself in the third person and is not inhibited by any false modesty from telling the plain truth as he knew it, whether it did him credit or showed him in a less favourable light:

> Up to the twenty-sixth year of his age, he was a man addicted to the vanities of the world, and took his chief delight

---

[1] Her husband, Jean d'Albret, had died and their son, Henri d'Albret, was claimant to the throne of Navarre at this time. Henri also married into the wide-spreading Foix family and had for daughter Jeanne d'Albret, Queen of French Navarre, who enthusiastically embraced the doctrines of Calvin and became the mother of Henry of Navarre, later the great French monarch, Henri Quatre.

[2] Cros, *Saint François de Xavier: sa vie et ses lettres*, i, 84.

in the exercise of arms, with a great and vain desire of gaining renown. So, being in a fortress besieged by the French, and all the others of the opinion that they ought to surrender if granted their lives, as it seemed clearly impossible to hold out, he urged so many reasons on the commander that, in spite of the contrary judgment of the other cavaliers, it was decided there should be no capitulation. Indeed, those others took new heart from his spirit and exertions. When the day came for the bombardment, he made his confession to one of his companions-in-arms. After the bombardment had lasted a good while, he was struck on one of his legs by a cannon ball which smashed it completely and badly damaged the other leg also. When he fell, the garrison of the citadel surrendered to the French, who treated the wounded man very well, with all courtesy and friendliness. They kept him twelve or fifteen days in Pamplona and then sent him on a litter to his own country. There he became so extremely ill that all the doctors and surgeons of the country around were summoned, who decided that the leg must be again dislocated and the bones re-set, as they were out of position and could not heal, owing either to bad setting at first or to disturbance on the journey. And so that butchery began anew, and during it, as during all the torments he had already endured and was still to endure, he never uttered a word nor showed any other sign of suffering, except by tightly clenching his fists.[1]

[1] Zapico et Dalmases, *Fontes narrativi de S. Ignatio de Loyola*, vol. i (Vol. 66 of the series MHSJ), Rome, 1943, pp. 364, 366. The translation is from the Spanish original, which has been variously expanded and embellished in other versions. The soldier turned saint who gave those reminiscences was not the type of man to write a formal autobiography. It needed a great deal of persuading to get them out of him but, in sheer kindness, he agreed during the last years of his life to give a broad account of it orally to a Portuguese Jesuit then resident in Rome, Luis Gonzalez da Camara, who was reputed to have an excellent memory. After each of the very irregular sessions with Ignatius, Gonzalez went straight off and dictated what he had learned to an amanuensis. The very first line of the little record has caused much controversial ink to flow. If Ignatius was twenty-six in 1521, he must have been born in 1495, but the Roman Jesuits, his intimates, who composed his epitaph immediately after his death in 1556, said in it that he was sixty-five years old, making the year of his birth 1491. Other considerations, including the evidence of his nurse as a

That little story needed to be reproduced as it had a more intimate bearing on the fortunes of Francis Xavier than any other event in his meteoric passage through this world. Some writers have toyed with the possibility that the fateful shot which laid Ignatius low and completely revolutionized his existence, as well as so many other people's existences, may have been fired by one of the brothers of Francis, and good men have reflected with melancholy, in the spirit of Pascal on Cleopatra's nose, that, given a gunner drunk or less accurate a marksman, the world need never have been troubled with Jesuits. In Navarre the war pursued its course much in the fashion of English summer weather—three glorious days and a thunderstorm. A battle fought at Noain near Pamplona resulted in heavy defeat for the French and the insurgents. Miguel de Jassu then took to the hills as a *guerrillero*, but was eventually captured and cast into a dungeon in Pamplona, once more in Castilian hands. After a while, he made a brilliant escape to join his brother Juan in the historic old fortress of Fuenterrabía, frowning over the sea opposite Hendaye, the last despairing gamble of Navarre. This was a nut which even the

---

child in Loyola Castle, render this latter date almost certainly the right one. Ignatius was not good at dates, and should have said his thirtieth year rather than his twenty-sixth. His confession of his sins to a lay person, there being no priest at hand, was in accordance with a pious custom of the Middle Ages, approved by St. Thomas Aquinas. It may be as well to explain here that he was baptized, not Ignatius but Iñigo (*Latine* Enecus), in honour of a local Basque Benedictine saint, but appears to have had imposed on him by the university registrar of Paris the better-known name of Ignatius, possibly under a mis-apprehension that it was the Latin form of Iñigo. He adopted the new name and used it in signing his numerous Latin letters, but continued until 1543 to employ Iñigo when he wrote in Spanish. Eventually Ignatius ousted Iñigo altogether. Sometimes, usually in hostile books such as the late H. G. Wells's preposterous *Crux Ansata*, he is found written Iñigo Lopez de Recalde, which is much funnier than its users imagined. During the early period of his con-version Iñigo made three close friends or disciples, Juan Lopez, a young Frenchman Jean Reynald, and Lopez de Cáceres. All four of them fell under the ban of the Inquisition at Alcalá de Henares, but the notary appointed to draft the sentence got the names hopelessly muddled, massacred the French-man's name, and seems to have thought that only Iñigo was involved. So, instead of writing, 'To Iñigo, to Lopez, and to Reynald', he wrote, 'To Inigo Lopez de Recalde', thus providing Mr. Wells and others with an oppor-tunity to display their erudition.

might of Emperor Charles, master of half the western world, could not so easily crack, and the brothers with their companion patriots defied him from its ramparts for two years more. Miguel and Juan were only minor characters in the drama of a nation's downfall, but yet important enough for Charles to condemn them to death by name and to declare confiscated whatever remained of their property. During three hopeless, hapless years, the men from Xavier, both still in their twenties, had certainly done enough to satisfy that soldierly honour which their stricken enemy, Iñigo de Loyola, so greatly prized, and when guaranteed their lives and liberty by the frustrated besiegers could return to their mother and brother at the dilapidated Castle by the Aragon without needing to blush for their existence.[1]

The Francis who greeted them was eighteen years old and had had himself tonsured as a cleric of the diocese of Pamplona. The gesture committed him to nothing and exempted him from whatever military service the Emperor might impose. One who knew him well in youth observed that he was decidedly ambitious, though for what nobody as yet could say. Presently, he made his second and last appearance in the huge family register as agent for his mother in the lease of half a share owned by her in a certain mill. The transaction took place with the ceremony characteristic of all business dealings in Navarre at a spot near Roncesvalles, before a notary and two witnesses, a harness-maker and a black-smith. The lessee, a carpenter, pledged his word to the cadet of Xavier that he would pay the Señora de Azpilcueta an annual rent of 120 bushels of wheat or its market value in money.[2] That little rustic negotiation between good people as homely on the one side as on the other takes us very far away from the sound of Roland's horn or other echoes of the knightly world. Shortly after its conclusion, in September, 1525, Francis, the homespun youth, set off over the Pyrenees in a cloud of mystery to an assigna-tion at the University of Paris, arranged by the providence of

[1] Père Cros might have been projecting a large history of the War of Navarre, so copious are the details about it which he copied from the municipal archives of Pamplona. Those given above are from his dossier (*Saint François de Xavier, son pays, sa famille, sa vie*, 196–233, 244–9).

[2] Cros, *Saint François de Xavier: sa vie et ses lettres*, i, 100–1.

God, from which he would have fled in as much dismay as Jonah did to Tarshish, had he had the slightest inkling of it. He was going to Paris because the university there offered wider scope than any in Spain for his rosy dreams. There is no evidence that he ever saw Xavier or his family again, but presumably they sanctioned his departure and provided him with enough money to live frugally as a student. The five hundred miles of dangerous travel in a foreign land, on horse or foot or somehow, passed without a syllable of comment to his mother or anybody. So far as is known, he did not then or ever write to his mother, and when she died four years later, he discovered no grief. Even by Basque standards, which are notoriously high, he had a phenomenal capacity for saying nothing.

CHAPTER II

YOUNG AMBITION'S LADDER

FRANCIS XAVIER spent eleven consecutive and, so far
as is known, unbroken years in Paris (September, 1525–
September, 1536), but for the greater part of that long time
his history remains almost as much a blank as it was in Navarre.
Hardly a sight or sound of him has rewarded the patient search
of a multitude of his lovers, and they have been reduced in their
frustration to the dreary task of reconstructing the frame of his
life, empty of picture though it be. One resourceful modern lady
shepherded the evasive man up the towers of Notre-Dame and
pointed out to him with Scottish determination the beauty in
stone and garden and misty hill of which he never chose to
speak. 'Yes, Francis, that is *Mons Martyrum*. And there, at the
close of your student life, you will take the cup of salvation and
pay your vows unto the Lord.'[1] For anything known to the
contrary, Francis may have had the same poor opinion of Paris
as St. Thomas Aquinas, who is reported as saying that he would
willingly exchange all its pomp for ' a codex containing some lost
homilies of St. John Chrysostom '. Though the University had

[1] Stewart, *The Life of St. Francis Xavier, Evangelist, Explorer, Mystic*, London,
1917, pp. 46–7. Miss Stewart, a member of the Church of Scotland, was not too
sympathetic in her attitude towards the specifically Catholic aspects of her hero,
but apart from that, and from a certain amount of fancifulness in the narrative,
her book is one of the best attempts made in English to portray him. A special
and valuable feature of it is that many of the Saint's letters are cited extensively
in uncommonly faithful translations made from the original Spanish texts
published in MHSJ by the Rev. David Macdonald. The letters given in such
older biographies as those of Bouhours (Englished by the poet Dryden in 1688)
or Coleridge (two volumes, 1872), are translations of Latin versions made early
on by Jesuits who, in all good faith, evidently thought that the best way to
honour St. Francis was to put his hurried, repetitive, and often ungrammatical
sentences into fine, expansive, Ciceronian prose. Francis, who cared nothing
for style and hadn't any, would have been astonished at the magnificent flowing
robes wherein they dressed him.

28

sadly declined from its zenith of fame in St. Thomas's time, it still attracted students from all quarters, even Arabs and Persians. They numbered about four thousand and continued to be divided for administrative purposes into the traditional four nations, the French Nation, whose King was a prisoner in Madrid, oddly including both Spaniards and Portuguese. In theory, social and academic relations presented no special difficulty to the polyglot throng, as all were obliged by statute to converse and imbibe knowledge through the medium of Latin. In practice, their man-handling of that venerable instrument would certainly have startled a ploughboy of Latium. Upwards of fifty colleges, huddled together on the south bank of the Seine, each autonomous and with its own teaching staff, constituted the University, which, like all mediaeval universities, cherished learning, not for its own sake, but as a means of providing Church and State with sound God-fearing theologians, lawyers, schoolmasters and doctors of medicine.[1] Humanism brought in a different ideal which Paris only reluctantly and half-heartedly accepted.

The college chosen by Francis Xavier for his nursing mother was the only one named after a saint, famous Barbara, the lady of so many legends. It used to stand in the present Boulevard St. Michel, and is still commemorated by the building that took its place, the modern lycée Sainte-Barbe. Old Sainte-Barbe enjoyed a good deal of prestige owing to the patronage of the King of Portugal and to the possession of some distinguished professors who had gone over enthusiastically to the flag of the humanists. St. Francis was no humanist, and it was not the presence of those bright spirits immersed in *hoti*'s business which attracted him to their college, but the presence of many Spanish and Portuguese students. He could feel at home in Sainte-Barbe and better able to cope with problems of articulateness beyond the range of his slender Latinity. He must have rated as a relatively elderly under-graduate, for the universities liked to catch their hopefuls young in those days and there were plenty of mere boys to brighten the academic scene. One of them, an infant prodigy named Henri

[1] Irsay, *Histoire des Universités Françaises et Etrangères*, vol. i, Paris, 1933, pp. 267-8.

de Mesmes, had proceeded Master of Arts and Doctor of Law by the time he was nineteen, and has left a revealing account of the merciless régime which made such a result possible:

> We were up at 4 a.m., and, having said our prayers, trailed an hour later to the hall of studies, with our big books under our arms and our inkpots and candlesticks in our hands. There was no break in the lessons until 10 o'clock, when we were given something to eat. After dinner, we read by way of recreation Sophocles, Aristophanes or Euripides, and sometimes Demosthenes, Cicero, Vergil and Horace. At 1 o'clock, we began private study. We had supper at 6 o'clock and then read more Greek or Latin.[1]

There is some doubt as to whether Francis Xavier ever attained even the first of Henri's distinctions, though he is often called Master in the records. He had a gift at this time for evading the more onerous requirements of university life and seems to have found his mind's delight anywhere but in books.

Excessive study did not exhaust the rigour of undergraduate existence, as may be seen from the extant dietary of Sainte-Barbe's neighbour and rival, the stern old Collège de Montaigu, where John Calvin excogitated some of his ideas about predestination. The younger scholars were given a roll and water for breakfast, and half a herring or an egg for dinner. Older men received a whole herring or two eggs, a pint of inferior wine among each three, a stew of cheap vegetables unfortified by meat,[2] and to round off the banquet a small piece of cheese. All the masters carried canes and used them on their charges in a way that disgusted, not only Rabelais who probably deserved his thrashings, but the humane and fair-minded Montaigne. One young professor at Sainte-Barbe in Francis Xavier's time, George Buchanan, famous afterwards in many fields—as the best Latin poet ever produced by Britain, as tutor of Mary Queen of Scots and her

---

[1] Franklin, *Paris et les Parisiens au seizième siècle*, Paris, 1921, pp. 158-9.

[2] *Offa ex leguminibus quae vili poterunt pretio comparari, sine ulla carnium pinguedine. . . .*

son James, as Presbyterian leader, as propagandist of democratic ideas, and as writer of a history of his native land designed in its author's words ' to purge it of some English lies and Scottish vanity '—complained bitterly that his pupils, including very possibly Francis himself, fell asleep while he sweated to improve their minds, or stared listlessly at their dilapidated boots, or pretended to be ill, or absented themselves altogether, or drifted in late with much clatter, or drifted out again bored across the the filthy Street of the Dogs to the rival halls of Montaigu, a place ' for ever steeped in the odour of cheap vegetable soup '. As a final comment on his defeat, this great teacher and humanist declared sadly that the rod was the only sure begetter of scholars.[1] The drifters mentioned in the gloomy report would have been the non-resident students, nicknamed martinets[2] or birds of passage, who had an evil reputation at the University. One of them, a strange and dangerous character named Miguel Landivar, was taken into his service as a sort of valet by Francis Xavier who thus hoped, despite his chronic impecuniosity, to assert his *hidalguia* before the world.[3] The sinister Landivar will re-enter the story at a later stage. The employment of the man and other extravagances almost drove his relatives to the point of peremptorily summoning him home, but they were deterred by his sister Magdalena, the saintly Poor Clare Abbess, who apparently saw more in him than did his mother and brothers.[4] But even she could not have divined the tremendous hidden depths under the surface frivolity which were waiting for an angel to trouble them.

Besides Buchanan, there were other humanists at Sainte-Barbe in St. Francis's time who later passed over to the camp of Calvin. Calvin himself used to pay occasional furtive visits to the College

[1] Quicherat, *Histoire de Sainte-Barbe*, vol. i, Paris, 1860, pp. 163–4. A deadly dull production by a violent anti-clerical.

[2] The Concise Oxford French Dictionary has a sign attached to this word meaning, ' Pitfall! Beware of apparent analogy! ' The French martinet was the precise opposite of a strict disciplinarian. He flouted discipline.

[3] The word *hidalgo* is an abbreviation of *hijo de algo*, literally, ' son of something ', the something being good blood.

[4] Cros, *Saint François de Xavier: sa vie et ses lettres*, i, 112–13.

where he won two notable recruits, Nicholas Kopp and Mathurin Cordier. But he failed to capture William Postel, an engaging lunatic, deeply versed in Oriental lore and stormy champion of universal federation, who preferred to become a Jesuit for a while and nearly drove his superiors out of their senses. With such people under its roof, it is plain that Sainte-Barbe, unlike the Sorbonne and Montaigu, was no citadel of reaction, and there are indications, supplied by himself for once in a way, that Francis from Navarre did not altogether repudiate the radical ideas whispered into his ear.[1] In the dirty malodorous streets beyond the College portals, where exits and entrances were checked by a formidable one-eyed giant nicknamed inevitably Polyphème, the newly won disciples of Luther and Calvin did not content themselves with verbal propaganda, but outraged Catholic feeling by stealing and profaning the Sacred Host, by smashing a popular statue of the Madonna and Child, by posting in public places insulting placards about the Mass, and by other such provocative nocturnal activities. The King, recently returned from his pleasant captivity in Madrid where he had earned great repute and popularity as a healer of scrofulous Spaniards, behaved well in face of the sacrilegious hooliganism. After replacing the broken statue by a copy of it in solid silver at a magnificent ceremony attended by the whole student body, he ordered a procession of reparation to Notre-Dame, in which he walked with his family and entire court, preceded by the ambassadors of all Christian nations and a great part of the nobility. But, influenced to some extent by his sister, Marguerite de Valois, an overt patron of the new thought, he

---

[1] But it is wholly gratuitous to assert that Francis ' read the writings of Luther and loved the Lutherans ' (Stewart, *The Life of St. Francis Xavier*, p. 57). The most that can be said is that he frequented company in which Lutheran ideas may have been given an airing. He was an easy-going, companionable person, ready to think the best of everybody, but belonged in every fibre of him to the nation which ' put herself at the head of Southern Europe and fought, not for gain but to her impoverishment, in Flanders, in Germany, on the English seas, with fortunes prosperous or adverse, but always holding back the Northern flood within those dykes it has never since overpassed, leaving her poor, spent, defenceless, . . . thus showing examples of self-abnegation and heroic self-sacrifice for an idea as splendid as any in history ' (Menéndez y Pelayo, *Teatro selecto de Calderón*, vol. i, pp. xxvii sq.).

showed irresolution in his attitude to individual heretics and
endeavoured mercifully to shield them from the lightnings of the
Sorbonne and the Parlement or High Court of Paris, the two
sturdiest and most ruthless defenders of the ancient faith. He
frequently failed, and then would follow terrible burning ceremonies in the Place de Grève, at which Francis Xavier and all his
fellows were required to be present, for the good of their souls
and bodies.[1]

To compensate for the rigour of life and letters at the University, there were plenty of such diversions as pageants,
masquerades, fairs, public dances in the streets, sports on the Ile
aux Vaches, and free fights open to all. Though to have been young
in the circumstances could not exactly be described as heaven,
neither was it the complete hell painted by Rabelais, Ramus,
Vives and other malcontents. Apart from the perennial difficulty
of making ends meet, Francis must have enjoyed the Parisian life
or he would not have stayed at the University for eleven years.
He took a special delight in the sporting activities, and was
accounted by a famous witness who knew him intimately at
Paris ' one of the finest high-jumpers on the island '.[2] As will be
seen, his addiction to that form of athleticism and the pride he
took in his success afterwards caused him acute remorse. But he
had more serious things on his conscience than the vanity of an
outstanding jumper. Many years later, when in India at the shrine
of the Apostle St. Thomas, hard by modern Madras, he fell into
one of his very rare reminiscent moods and told his Portuguese
host, Gaspar Coelho, some few details of his past life, especially
in Paris. After his death, Coelho communicated what he had
learned to the Jesuits in Goa, who transmitted a copy of his letter
to their European brethren in December, 1554.

He related to me [wrote the witness] the story of his life
from its beginning up to that time of our conversation and

[1] Cros, *Saint François de Xavier, son pays, sa famille, sa vie*, 269–90.
[2] ' *Era en la isla de Paris uno de los mayores saltadores.*' The witness was
Ignatius Loyola (*Fontes narrativi de S. Ignatio de Loyola*, i, 705). The island, then
called ' Aux Vaches ', is the present Saint-Louis.

friendship, the country of his birth, who his father and mother were, the age at which he went to Paris, and what befell him there. Speaking of the life of the students, he said that they, and his master also, were given to debauchery. Often they would steal from the College at night under the leadership of the master and take him, Francis, with them. But terrified by the loathsome ulcers which he saw both master and pupils contract, he did not dare to continue associating with them. This fear sustained him until the master died from the effects of his profligacy a year or two later, and was succeeded by a chaste and virtuous man, whose example he determined to follow. So, for that reason, never in his life up to the moment of telling me the story had he committed sin with a woman.[1]

Very soon after taking up residence at Sainte-Barbe, Francis Xavier found himself sharing a room with a new arrival from Savoy named Pierre Favre, his junior in age by exactly one week. Favre, the son of poor peasants who must have stinted themselves for years to enable him to go to the University, confessed at a later time that in boyhood, while tending his parents' few sheep, he used to weep with longing for an education—*flebam desyderio scholae*. A kindly country priest coached him for nine years until he was ready to try his humble fortunes in the Quartier Latin. He has been beatified by the Catholic Church and was regarded during his brief life as a saint by several canonized saints, as well as by an enormous mob of sinners who had found peace and new hope from his charity in France, Germany, Italy and Spain. Even among the saints with all their wideness of heart, few have been

---

[1] MHSJ. *Monumenta Xaveriana*, ii, 947–8. The Portuguese of the original is execrable. The last sentence runs: '*De donde nunca em seus dias conhecera molher até presente hora que elle contava aquilo.*' The older biographers averted their eyes from the confession altogether, and the moderns, such as Cros, Michel, and even Brou, render the final words thus: '*De sorte que jamais, jusqu'à ce jour, je m'eus de telles accointances*'!! The illiterate '*de donde*' might possibly be rendered 'from which time' and that would raise a fresh question. But there is much good evidence that Francis always maintained his integrity complete, however near he came to losing it in Paris. cf. p.225 *infra*.

known to pray habitually for such enemies of the Catholic and
Roman name as Luther, Henry VIII, and the Terrible Turk,
Suleiman the Magnificent. But this rustic Good Samaritan did,
because, as he said, ' so many people judged them harshly, it was
impossible not to pity them '.

Long after his student days, Favre kept for one year a diary of
his spiritual experiences for the profit of his own anxious soul. It
survived and, though never meant for such a fate, has been translated from its unstudied Latin into many languages and published
as his *Memorial*. A qualified critic, no less than the secretary of the
Académie Française, has expressed the following opinion of the
little book: ' It is one of the tenderest confessions of interior
lyricism in the whole range of mystical literature. . . . No book
conveys a more vivid spiritual impression. Here a soul is shown in
its incorporeal nudity, with its tremors of light and blushes of
shame under the delicate operations of grace. It still feels the chains
of the flesh, and sometimes in an anguished word recalls that in
other years they weighed more heavily.'[1] Among the things for
which Favre begged God to make him everlastingly grateful was
his early association with Francis Xavier. But practically nothing
is known of their life together, nor whether Pierre made any
attempt to keep Francis out of bad company. There was one
subject on which both men could have talked with some authority,
namely sheep, but its possibilities as a conversational topic are
limited. At the time when they first met, neither of them, it seems,
had made any definite plans for the future, beyond the attainment
of their degree. Favre confessed to much vacillation of mind, and
the modest ambitions which kept competing within him may very
well have troubled the soul of his companion also, only that, by
all the indications, the ambitions of Francis were not modest.
' I used to be constantly agitated and blown about by varying
winds,' wrote Pierre, ' proposing to myself one day to get married,
and other days to qualify as a physician, or lawyer, or school

[1] Bellessort, *Saint François Xavier*, 13ième éd., Paris, 1937, p. 30. The book
first appeared in serial form in the *Revue des Deux Mondes*, when M. Bellessort
was its editor. Long experience of Asiatic countries, especially Japan, roused
his interest in St. Francis and gave birth to a little masterpiece.

teacher, or doctor of theology, or just as a plain priest. Occasionally I had thoughts of being a monk.'[1] Years later, when he had completely found his feet, Favre told a group of young Jesuit students in Paris that Francis and he in their day had followed the line of the purely secular humanists with their philosophy of letters for letters' sake. 'We hampered and obstructed ourselves gravely, or at least I did, by refusing to admit that the Cross of Christ had any claim to a place in our studies, either at the beginning or in the middle or at the end.' It is more likely that Francis followed no line at all, but just drifted along, with his heart much more on the cross-bar of the high jump than on any of the old fogies of antiquity. Pierre became a good Greek scholar, but his friend appears to have by-passed that department of learning completely and to have done his minimum of philosophy out of an Aristotle in ragged Latin weeds. Three years slid away thus indeterminately when all of a sudden destiny climbed the stairs of Sainte-Barbe in a shape as strange and unrecognizable as it ever has taken.

Iñigo de Loyola, aged thirty-six, arrived in Paris on February 2, 1528, having limped the whole way from Barcelona, all alone except for a little donkey loaded with his books. At the time, France and Spain were again at war, and the French, as the traveller knew well, had contracted the habit of burning alive any enemy nationals who fell into their hands. His total fortune was a bill of exchange for twenty-five crowns, given him by a kind working-woman of Barcelona named Inés Pascual. It is necessary to explain briefly the chain of events which had launched him on his perilous journey. After 'fearful suffering caused by repeated and clumsy operations on his broken leg at the gloomy old castle of his ancestors in Guipúzcoa, he began to mend and asked for romances of chivalry to while away the tedious hours of convalescence. The entire castle library was put at his disposal without difficulty, for it consisted of exactly two books, Ludolph of Saxony's *Life of Christ* and a Spanish version of *The Golden*

[1] MHSJ, *Fabri Monumenta*, Madrid, 1914, p. 495. For some inscrutable reason, nearly all writers who cite this passage omit the reference to matrimony. Did they think it an idea unworthy of the great man Favre became?

Legend. While drowsing over the extravagant mediaeval tales of the saints, he gradually came to see that there might be other fields of glory to shine in than those of courtly love and war, closed to him permanently by his disablement. 'How would it be,' he used to wonder naïvely, 'if I were to do what St. Francis did or St. Dominic did?' Then, stirred by the spirit of emulation which was strong in him, he reached a conclusion : 'St. Dominic did that; so must I do it.'[1] It was the oddest motive, hardly more spiritual than the fear for his skin which deterred Francis Xavier, to initiate a conversion as momentous as any in the history of Christianity. But God from such stones can raise up children to Abraham.

Able to walk again, Iñigo, dressed like a mendicant and as penniless, had sought his dimly discerned grail for seven crucifying years of intermittent darkness almost to the point of despair and of sudden heavenly light, in the towns of Spain and as far afield as Rome and Jerusalem. Those latter journeys are among the most affecting incidents in his extraordinary pilgrim's progress. At Venice he looked so pale and emaciated from hunger and exposure that people who encountered him fled in horror as from one stricken with the plague. At last, after innumerable trials and errors, during which he had put together in a Catalonian cave or monastery his *Spiritual Exercises*, a little manuscript as disconcerting and alarming to religious complacency as its author, he was given relative peace and a clue to the labyrinth of the divine purposes in the thought that if he acquired some education he would be able to do more to win souls to God, an aim that had become the passion of his existence. Accordingly, in his thirty-third year, shortly before Francis Xavier set out for Paris, he took his place with a class of boys at Barcelona to learn the rudiments of Latin, and that laboriously done, trudged alone and destitute to the new University of Alcalá, hoping to glean a few sheaves of philosophy. But the love of God burned so ardently in his heart that he could not refrain from speaking about it publicly and so was arrested by the Inquisition, which august body, reasonably enough in those precarious times, entertained a profound suspicion

[1] MHSJ, *Fontes narrativi de S. Ignatio de Loyola*, i, 372.

of itinerant preachers. After six weeks' detention he was released but strictly forbidden to carry on his humble apostolate. He therefore moved on to Salamanca where he met with an even frostier welcome, for he was not only gaoled but chained by his leg to a stake. To a visitor who expressed sympathy with him in that predicament, he replied: ' I assure you that there are not so many gyves and shackles in Salamanca as I would be glad to wear for the love of God, ay, and more of them.'[1] But the word of God is not bound, and it was the inhibition from speaking it in Spain that led Iñigo to turn his thoughts towards Paris.

In Paris, the ex-patriate obtained a lodging at a hostel frequented by his fellow-countrymen and entrusted to one of them for safe keeping the twenty-five gold crowns which he had received against his bill of exchange. That wretch dissipated the entire sum on his private pleasures within a month, thus leaving Iñigo destitute once more and obliged to resort to street begging, with serious hindrance to his studies. After the hostel had thrown him out because he could not pay for his keep, he found a refuge in the Hospice of St. James, a charitable institution which used to stand in the present rue Saint-Denis, a long way from his chosen college, the much berated Montaigu. This most unusual *martinet* had put his name down for the class of grammar composed of mere boys, with a view to improving his still uncertain Latinity. But Montaigu began operations at five in the morning, and St. James's, miles away, would not let him out before dawn, so what was he to do? He tried very hard to obtain work as servant to one of the Montaigu masters, but nobody wanted a middle-aged cripple such as he. Then, in his sore perplexity, a kindly priest advised him to visit Bruges and Antwerp during the vacations to see whether the wealthy Spanish merchants resident in those cities might not be willing to help him. He went, and even extended the expedition to England, with results that not only freed him from the necessity of street begging, but enabled him to assist other students hampered by poverty. When he learned that the

---

[1] MHSJ. *Fontes narrativi de S. Ignatio de Loyola,* i, 460. ' *Yo os digo que no hay tantos grillos ni cadenas en Salamanca, que yo no deseo más por amor de Dios.*'

Spaniard who had robbed him of his twenty-five crowns lay ill and friendless at Rouen, he was moved to pity and, in his own words, ' felt constrained to visit and help him '. He made the journey of eighty-four miles barefooted and fasting to obtain the mercy of God for the sick and sinful man.

To appreciate the quality of Iñigo, sublime and dedicated vagabond, it is necessary to know that at this time he was already suffering intermittent agonies from the gall-stones which eventually killed him, though none of the many doctors consulted by his friends ever suspected the true nature of his malady until an autopsy revealed it.[1] Each morning at the first blush of dawn, he used to limp the long way to Montaigu and squat among the boys on the hay-strewn floor of the classroom. As in Spain, his peculiar way of life puzzled the watch-dogs of orthodoxy and he was submitted to a number of interrogations. Sometimes he may have brushed shoulders with Francis Xavier in the narrow street separating Montaigu from Saint-Barbe. Francis must inevitably have known who he was, as so many people were talking about him, a soldier who had contributed in his measure to the downfall of Navarre, a gentleman of Spain who had demeaned his quality by vagrancy and mendicancy, a Catholic whose orthodoxy had been called in question. Francis definitely did not like him nor want to have anything to do with him, an attitude heartily shared a little later by another Spaniard destined for great things named Jerome Nadal. Much more inconvenient than the critics were the enthusiastic admirers who took to imitating Iñigo's ascetical way of life in a fashion that aroused the indignation of the authorities. The principal of Sainte-Barbe, one of a dynasty of Portuguese principals, named Diogo de Gouvea, even threatened Iñigo with a public flogging if he did not stop turning the heads of the young men. But something mysterious occurred between the two elders, some sudden change of heart which caused Diogo to welcome Iñigo as a boarder at Sainte-Barbe when he had completed his Latin studies at Montaigu. To the hardly concealed disgust of Francis

---

[1] The anatomist who performed the post-mortem on Ignatius in 1556 testified that he had extracted ' innumerable stones ' from the kidneys and other organs (*Fontes narrativi de S. Ignatio*, i, 769, n. 16).

Xavier, the newcomer was assigned the same room as himself and Favre, and there at last did the long, patient providence of God, working with a cannon ball and a few tawdry human ambitions, bring about the encounter of Basque with Basque which was destined to have consequences more surprising than anything told in a fairy tale.

It was autumn of the year 1529 when Iñigo de Loyola, aged thirty-eight, began his arts course at Sainte-Barbe, and, according to one reading of Favre's *Memorial*, to Francis Xavier, who had practically finished his course, was assigned by authority the task of guiding the intruder's first steps in Aristotle. If that reading is accurate, Xavier very quickly and smartly shuffled the distasteful burden on to Favre, who gladly accepted it. But it is much more likely that Favre, a far better scholar, was appointed from the first.[1] At this time, Pierre was so heavily assailed by scruples of conscience and carnal temptations that to be rid of them, he said, he would willingly have gone into a desert and lived on roots. He told his troubles to his pupil whose eyes alone were a sufficient invitation to such confidences. Once, in Padua, a possessed man whom Iñigo, or Ignatius as he may now be called, had helped in some way was asked what he looked like and answered: 'He is a little bit of a Spaniard, slightly lame, and he has bright friendly eyes.'[2] His rapt soul sat in his eyes. One who was very close to him related that when his eyes rested on anybody in need of comfort they would light up as though he yearned to draw the sad person into his very soul. Such was the experience of Pierre Favre. He tells very simply how Ignatius brought peace to his troubled heart, taught him how to master his many temptations, and gently stilled the agitation caused in him by the sight of his neighbour's defects. Pierre names no names, but the neighbour

---

[1] Biographers alive to the drama of the situation are all for the Franciscan theory. Brou devotes nearly a whole page to its possibilities. But the Petrine theory, apart from its inherent probability, has twice as much support in the manuscript variants (*Fontes narrativi de S. Ignatio*, i, 32, n. 14).

[2] '*Un espannoleto, picolo, un poco zopo, che he l'ochi alegri*' (*Fontes narrativi de S. Ignatio*, i, 637). *Allegro*, an adjective that combines a number of attractive ideas, gladness, vivacity, contentment, cordiality, is used many times in the *Fioretti* to describe the eyes of St. Francis of Assisi.

nearest to him and most likely to rile him was the man from Navarre. On him the bright eyes smiled in vain for more than two years. There is even a possibility that to escape their troubling radiance Francis obtained permission to live in a different room for a while.[1] A Spaniard named Juan Polanco who knew both men well probably understated the case when he wrote that Francis was not at first much taken with Ignatius—*non ei admodum addictus*—for there is some evidence that he regarded the new lodger as a joke and was sarcastic about his efforts to bring souls nearer to God. But Ignatius had the patience of a good angler and, through long experience, was an expert in the use of bait. The really strange, unaccountable thing is that he should have set his heart, almost from the first hour, on the capture of this particular fish which nobody else at the time believed to be worth the taking. There is a story repeated in all the biographies of Francis from the first printed[2] to the very latest, that Ignatius broke down his resistance by constantly dinning into his ear the text: ' What shall it profit a man if he gain the whole world and lose his own soul?' Such a frontal method of attack is quite uncharacteristic of the great spiritual strategist to whom it is attributed, and not a shred of real evidence exists that he employed it at all.[3]

Six months after the arrival of Ignatius in their midst, Xavier and Favre won their second university degree, the licentiate, by successfully defending a variety of scholastic theses before a jury of masters in the church of Sainte-Geneviève. They were then

[1] MHSJ. *Epistolae PP. Paschasii Broeti . . . et Simonis Rodericii*, Madrid, 1902, p. 454.

[2] By a Jesuit named Orazio Tursellini, published in Latin at Rome in 1594. Orazio's style would not have shamed the original Horace, but his history is of the gilded imaginative kind, with fact and fiction in about equal proportions.

[3] We have only the word of Tursellini, a born romancer, and it is a pity that he should have been copied without question by all subsequent writers, including, alas, even Father Schurhammer. Ignatius does not use the text anywhere in his *Spiritual Exercises*, but Francis himself used it once in a letter to his great friend Simon Rodriguez, whom he asked to suggest to the King of Portugal, John III, that his Highness should ' occupy himself for a quarter of an hour daily begging God to give him a better understanding and deeper realization of the meaning of Christ's words : What shall it profit a man . . . ? ' (Schurhammer, *Epistolae S. Francisci Xaverii*, i, 421). That circumstance probably gave Tursellini his inspiration.

given a diploma entitling them to teach the arts course, which included Aristotelian philosophy, 'anywhere in the world'. To become a master no further examination was required, but only to pay a heavy fee for the privilege. Favre waited six years before taking his biretta, and it may reasonably be doubted whether the impecunious Xavier took it at all. He found a teaching post at the obscure College of Dormans-Beauvais, but continued to reside at Sainte-Barbe, and consequently must often have felt resting on him the friendly appealing eyes of Ignatius. He needed pupils in order to pay his way, and these Ignatius, whose influence mounted all the time, discreetly directed to him. He was often by his own confession in desperate need of money, and that difficulty, too, Ignatius met, not once but again and again, with a delicacy of consideration for the other's natural pride that softened without disarming him.[1] Francis was still a long way from becoming, as Favre had quickly done, 'one in will and aspiration with Ignatius '. In February of the year 1531 he made a last pathetic attempt to assert his importance by applying through a public notary for testimonials from Spain that he was a descendant in direct line of ancestors ' all nobles and persons of great distinction and pre-eminence in the Kingdom of Navarre '.[2] Nothing came of the move for several years, either because his brothers, whom he had constituted his attorneys, ignored it, or because he himself had lost interest and did not press the futile business. There was no longer a Kingdom of Navarre, and soon, through the death of his mother and eldest brother, there would be no Xavier, as his second brother, Juan, married an heiress and went to live elsewhere.

[1] Schurhammer, *Epistolae S. Francisci Xaverii*, i, 9–10.

[2] Cros, *Saint François de Xavier, son pays, sa famille, sa vie*, p. 309. A rare little Latin booklet called *Hispania* was published at Louvain in 1542 by a certain Damian de Goes. In part it takes the form of a bijou Debrett and gives lists of the noble families of Spain, Navarre included, and Portugal. No ancestor or relative of St. Francis figures among them. Goes, himself a Portuguese, carries on a lively and amusing contention with the famous German Lutheran, Sebastian Münster, who in his *Cosmographia* had cast aspersions on the learning and moral qualities of the Iberians. Let Münster, says he, show in his abominable Germany men of the stature of Juvenal, Seneca, Lucan, Trajan, Quintilian, Martial, Theodosius the Great, etc., all good Spaniards, even if they did live a while back.

For seven months during the year 1533 Francis and Ignatius had the room at Sainte-Barbe to themselves owing to the absence of Favre in Savoy, and it must have been then that the Basque fortress hauled down its tattered flag and capitulated to the Basque besieger. Nothing whatever is known of the process by which Ignatius finally weaned Francis from his worldly dreams, but only that his young ambition's ladder turned during those momentous months into a Jacob's ladder, pitched between Heaven and the rue des Chiens. When Favre reappeared at the beginning of the year 1534, he found Francis as resolved as himself to cleave henceforth to Ignatius. It had been a hard struggle on both sides, for Ignatius afterwards confessed in the hearing of Polanco, who remembered the forcible kitchen metaphor, that Francis ' was the lumpiest dough he had ever kneaded '.[1]

---

[1] The words occur in a dialogue on the ancient model, written in French by the first Jesuit confessor to the kings of France, Emond Auger, who had the detail from Polanco directly. They run : ' *J'ai ouï dire à notre grand mouler d'homme, Ignace, que la plus rude pâte qu'il ait oncques maniée c'était au commencement ce jeune François Xavier* ' (Tournier, *Saint François Xavier d'après un manuscrit inédit du P. Auger,* in *Études,* December 9, 1906).

CHAPTER III

THE ROADS OF ITALY

THOUGH the initial impulse came from Spain, it was really France and her Paris that, quite unconsciously and afterwards most regretfully, prepared the way for the Society of Jesus. Even Ignatius himself, during his Paris days, was wholly unaware of how time and God would shape his strange eventful history. The idea of founding a new religious order had never crossed his mind, and the only ambition he cherished was to gather round him a small group of like-minded men to help in the apostolate of souls which he had been carrying on single-handed ever since he issued, with his *Spiritual Exercises*, from the cave of Manresa. All of those first enlisted in Spain and in Paris had fallen out to become monks or men of the world, and not till Favre appeared was he sure of a permanent disciple. Then, while he wooed Xavier, others had been won or had come spontaneously to offer their adhesion. First on the scene were two young students of Alcalá who had been attracted to Paris, not only because it still remained the most celebrated of universities, but also by reason of what they had heard of the extraordinary Ignatius in their native land. The names of the resolute pair were Diego Laynez, a man of Jewish extraction, aged twenty-two, and Alfonso Salmeron, aged eighteen. On arrival in intimidating Paris, not knowing where to go or what to do, they heard themselves saluted in their own tongue by the very man whom they had come so far to seek. They made easy conquests for Ignatius and were among his greatest.[1] A young Portuguese gentleman named Simon Rodriguez, studying at Sainte-Barbe on a scholarship

[1] There is now available in Spanish a very fine and scholarly biography of Laynez who became famous at the Council of Trent and was a central figure in the Catholic revival of the sixteenth century—*Diego Lainez en la Europa Religiosa de su Tiempo*. Por Feliciano Cereceda, S. J. Two vols, Madrid, 1945-6.

granted by his country's King, was the next to be attracted, and after him came an eccentric Spaniard, Nicholas Alonso, commonly called Bobadilla from the small Palencian town of his birth. Both of those recruits were pronounced individualists who caused much trouble one way or another and did a great deal of good by fits and starts. That made seven, including Ignatius, and at seven the little circle remained for two years more.

At Easter of the year 1534, an *annus mirabilis* in Jesuit chronology, Ignatius, aged forty-three, graduated as a master of arts at Paris. The fee for it was high, but since degrees began no student ever paid such a price as did he. By a strange reversal of rôles, Francis Xavier at this very time contemplated renouncing whatever little distinction attached to his modest function of lecturer at Dormans-Beauvais. He wanted to devote himself entirely to prayer, but the others pointed out that he must also eat and have a roof above his head, to which ends his explications of Aristotle were not wholly irrelevant. Under the guidance of Ignatius, whom the others revered and loved as the captain of their souls, each went separately through the fiery ordeal of the *Spiritual Exercises* for thirty days, as circumstances permitted, but St. Francis had his turn relegated to the end of the queue, probably because Ignatius feared that his ardour would outrun his discretion, as indeed happened.[1] To strengthen the bond between them, the seven friends held reunions from time to time at their various lodgings, when their studies, all now dedicated to theology, gave them leisure. From those meetings came the resolution to bind themselves irrevocably to the service of God and their neighbour by private vows of chastity unconditionally, as they all purposed to be priests, of evangelical poverty, as soon as their university course ended, and of making a pilgrimage to Jerusalem. The nostalgia for Jerusalem was strong in Christian hearts from the earliest ages. It led to the Crusades and created, as a consolation for those unable through age or infirmity to make the long

---

[1] MHSJ. *Epistolae PP. Paschasii Broeti . . . et Simonis Rodericii,* 454. In the lives of St. Francis it is usually stated that his lectures caused the postponement of his retreat, but were not the vacations, longer at Paris than now at Oxford or Cambridge, available for the purpose?

journey, one of the most appealing of Catholic devotions, the Stations of the Cross, by which the Via Dolorosa came, as it were, to ramble through men's hearts all the world over. Ignatius had himself done the pilgrimage in circumstances of appalling hardship, and treasured to his dying day every memory of the Holy Places. It may well have been thoughts of Palestine which, as Bobadilla remembered more than half a century later, caused Francis Xavier to dream one night in Paris ' that he had abducted a small Turk and baptized him '. Eight months before he passed to God, Francis was still dreaming of the golden road which he had not been privileged to travel, and sending Japanese converts to Europe that they might visit Jerusalem as his proxies.[1] It was entirely natural, then, that such an undertaking should have been part of the programme set for themselves by the seven men, though, with Ignatius for informant, they were perfectly well aware of its difficulties.

To give solemnity to their resolution, the little group, in which all were equal and Salmeron's vote as weighty as Ignatius's, decided to pronounce their vows in a simple corporate ceremony on August 15, 1534, the feast of the Assumption of the Blessed Virgin Mary. Not a trace is to be found in their deliberations of morbid excitement. They went about their business in as practical and sober a fashion as a meeting of company directors and reached their conclusions only after much earnest debate—*longam post disputationem*. The pilgrimage to Jerusalem, for instance, was not conceived exclusively as a means to satisfy their private devotion, but also as a first step in their apostolate, for ' they were filled with an ardent and eager longing to bring the light of the Gospel to the heathen, and resolved, if need be, to sacrifice their very lives for any cause redounding to the greater worship and reverence of God '. Arrived in Palestine, they would reconsider their position and decide by a majority vote whether to stay for good working among the Turks, or to return to Europe. But what if they could not get to Palestine, through the incidence of war or other obstacles? For that contingency also they made careful provision, agreeing that, if after waiting one entire year

[1] Schurhammer, *Epistolae S. Francisci Xaverii*, ii, 358.

at Venice and using all possible diligence to find passage on some ship, they completely failed, they would then proceed to Rome, as was the custom of returned pilgrims, and leave their future to the arbitrament of the Pope, as men ' prepared to preach the Gospel anywhere in the world at his discretion, including the lands of the Turks and other tyrants hostile to the Christian name '.[1]

The spot chosen for the ceremony of the vows was an isolated chapel on the slopes of Montmartre, traditionally believed to mark the place of martyrdom of Saint Denis, first bishop of Paris, and his companions.[2] At the secluded rendezvous, Pierre Favre, who had been ordained priest shortly before, said Mass and each of the men pronounced his vows separately before receiving Holy Communion. It was the simplest of ceremonies, unwitnessed by anybody except the seven, and even they, at the time, had no remotest idea that they were making history. Many writers have regarded it as the foundation of the Society of Jesus, and a tablet was erected on the spot asserting the claim of Paris to be considered the mother of that order: *Societas Jesu quae Sanctum Ignatium Loyolam Patrem, Lutetia Matrem, Anno salutis MDXXXIV, Aug. XV, hic nata est.* The claim is as unwarranted as the iden- tification of Saint Denis of France with Dionysius the Areopagite. Nobody but the Pope can call a new religious order into existence, and the Pope then reigning had not as yet the faintest suspicion that there was such a person as Ignatius Loyola on this earth.

Shortly after the ceremony of the vows Francis Xavier made his belated retreat at some quiet suburban place which Ignatius

---

[1] Simon Rodriguez is the source of the quotations given above (*Epistolae PP. Paschasii Broeti . . . et Simonis Rodericii*, 457–8).

[2] The origin of the name Montmartre is much disputed and it may have come from the pagan *Mons Mercurii* rather than from the Christian *Mons Martyrum*. There is no real proof that Saint Denis was martyred there. The Saint Denis of the Roman liturgy is a composite of Dionysius the Areopagite, Dionysius of France, about whom hardly anything is known, and pseudo- Dionysius, the fifth-century mystical writer. A French prelate named Hilduin, abbot of the monastery of Saint-Denis near Paris in the ninth century, was responsible for turning the three men, separated by centuries, into one. French vanity has contributed more than its fair share to the bedevilment of Church history !

had found for him. Never did the *Spiritual Exercises* prove more effectually their power to transform a man than during that September of 1534 when Francis wrestled in solitude with angels of light and darkness.[1] Even Ignatius, who visited and counselled him all the time, was unable wholly to control the sort of forest fire kindled by meditation in his ardent Spanish soul. To expiate the vanity of the past, ' he not only fasted severely, but, mindful of the satisfaction which he used to get out of his jumping on the Island of Paris, roped his upper limbs in so tight a manner that he could no longer move, and thus trussed up made his meditations '. To that account coming from Ignatius himself Simon Rodriguez made the following addition:

So thoroughly and inextricably did he do the binding that his limbs swelled and covered the cord which he had used beyond any possibility of cutting it. His companions, full of sorrow for him, gave themselves to prayer, fearing that at least one of his arms would have to be amputated. But after causing him two days of terrible agony the cord embedded most deeply in his flesh broke, and by the singular mercy of God, in a way

[1] ' This little book, one of the great books of the Renaissance, . . . is personal to the last degree. . . . Stretched on a bed of torture, Loyola had lived powerfully by his imagination and learned that this faculty, so easily suborned by the devil, might also be an instrument of salvation. But for this it has to be denied its vagabond habits, assigned fixed hours, and forced to veil its terrestrial charms, as were those beautiful lady professors of Bologna who used to put screens before their faces while they lectured in order to spare the men in their auditory from distractions. There is plenty besides in the *Exercises*, but this to begin with, that never was a stricter method conceived for disciplining the imagination and making it yield all that it is capable of bringing to the perfection of a man's soul and to the triumph of his faith. Let those who feel so inclined complain that the method too cleverly mechanizes the theatre of the soul. Such criticism will appear valid only to one who does not know the difference between day-dreaming and meditation' (André Bellessort, *St. François Xavier*, 37–8. M. Bellessort's fellow Academician, Henri Bremond, used to maintain that the *Exercises* were a school of spiritual energy, the best ever, but not at all a school of prayer. What he meant by the distinction he never explained. It was one of the famous *boutades* that caused a critic to wonder which part of the genial Abbé's anatomy would wear out first, his tongue or his cheek. Anyhow, twenty-six Jesuit saints, bred on the *Exercises*, did not get canonized without knowing something about prayer).

utterly beyond my comprehension, he became completely well.[1]

In the case of the saints, as of other men, the process of conversion and self-mastery is usually gradual and never quite so absolute as pious writers would have us imagine. God's mercy to Saul of Tarsus on the road to Damascus was but the culmination of other secret and less dramatic mercies which also went to the making of St. Paul.[2] It was Paul for whom to live was Christ who, long years after his absolute surrender to that Divine Master, cried out in agony: ' The good that I would I do not, but the evil that I would not, that I do. Unhappy man that I am! Who will deliver me from this body of death?' Very few of the saints, perhaps a boy or girl martyr here and there too young to feel the bondage, but could have echoed that terrible and comforting cry. Certainly, Francis Xavier could and did. He became a mighty saint, but he remained to the end a man, a passionate, obstinate man, capable at times of fierce resentments and highly autocratic actions, which, however, did not prevent him from being one of the most generous, large-hearted, lovable human beings this sad world has ever known. To complete the picture, it has to be said that he once burst a blood-vessel in the violence of his efforts to repel a carnal temptation, which assailed him when he was well away towards the summits of sanctity.

The first extant letter of Francis, written just six months after his emergence from the heroic retreat, to his brother Juan, then head of the family and living with his aristocratic wife in wealth and leisure at a manor-house called Obanos a little south of Pamplona, is by no means a great spiritual document. In fact, it is mainly a begging letter, but relieved from being commonplace by the deep love and reverence for Ignatius which shine through its stiff ceremonious sentences, as also by a sudden flash of the

[1] MHSJ. *Fontes narrativi de S. Ignatio de Loyola*, i, 705; *Epistolae PP. Paschasii Broeti . . . et Simonis Rodericii*, 454.

[2] St. Augustine and others of the Fathers would not allow that *both* thieves began by reviling our Lord on the Cross, notwithstanding the obvious meaning of Matthew xxvii, 44 and Mark xv, 32, because it would make the conversion of the Good Thief appear too sudden.

unregenerate hidalgo touched on the point of honour.[1] Ignatius himself was its bearer, as well as one from Laynez to his relatives at Almazán in the province of Soria, for he had been at last persuaded by the doctors to seek his native air, that wonderful remedy for the stone, and left Paris for good, astride a pony, the gift of his companions, on March 28, 1535. It would be tedious to reproduce the letter in full as it is entirely devoid of literary attractiveness, but the gist of it was as follows. It opens with the frosty word, *Señor*, and is peppered throughout with the expression, *V. Merced*, meaning Your Honour or Your Worship. Francis has written to his brother several times recently by various routes but has received no answer, a fact which he blames, not on Juan, but on the bad postal service between Spain and Paris. His Worship is irreproachable all along the line: ' On your part there is no lack of love, but rather love grown warmer, since in your comfortable home you are as keenly alive to the poverty and hardship of my existence, as I am here in Paris where I daily lack for everything.' The next sentence is in flat contradiction with its predecessor, but Francis never worried about a little thing like that: ' This my necessity has come about only because your Honour is not thoroughly conversant with my difficulties, which I support in the certain hope that, once made fully aware of them by careful inquiry, your Honour's great liberality will bring them to an end.' There follows a paragraph which so much disconcerted the early Jesuit copyists of the letter that they either omitted it

[1] In his contention with Poussines over the date of St. Francis's birth, Bartoli denied the authenticity of this letter as being unworthy of a nobleman, to which Poussines replied that he knew in Rome the eldest son of one of the richest and most aristocratic families of France who was also reduced to dire straits through the failure of those at home to send him supplies. There is no doubt whatever about the authenticity of the letter, as Father Schurhammer has abundantly proved. But is the same scholar correct in his statement, for which he gives no grounds, that the eldest brother of Francis, Miguel, died as late as 1542? Why, then, did Francis not apply to him, the head of the family, in 1535, and why does he address Juan throughout as his ' Lord ' and use more deference, not to say obsequiousness, with him than even the strictest Spanish etiquette can have required towards anybody except the acknowledged head of the family? It is surely simpler to assume that Miguel was dead by the time the letter was written. These puzzles of chronology constantly crop up in the life of Francis and are a weariness to the flesh.

altogether or contracted it in such a way as to remove what they considered to be its unsaintly virulence:

> Señor, the Reverend Friar Vear has recently been at this University and informed me at great length of certain complaints which your Honour holds against me. If what he told me of the complaints is true, your feeling them so acutely is a sign and great proof of the very warm love and affection you bear to me. What troubled me so much in the matter was thought of the pain caused your Honour by the tittle-tattle of some vicious and despicable fellows whom I long to identify in order to pay them out as they deserve. As everybody here is very friendly to me, it is difficult to discover who they are. God knows what I suffer in having to delay my revenge on them. My only comfort is in the thought that a matter postponed is not a matter abandoned.[1]

Plainly, Francis was not a saint made to any pious biographer's measure! The completeness of his conquest by Ignatius, if not yet by the Sermon on the Mount, is indicated in the next paragraph:

> That your Honour may know clearly how greatly our Lord has favoured me in giving me the acquaintance of Señor Maestro Iñigo, I here pledge you my word that never will it be possible for me to repay my full debt to him, both for having often helped me with money and friends, and for having been the cause of my separation from bad company, which in my inexperience I did not recognize as such. Now that those heresies are discovered at Paris, I would not for anything in the world have been associated with those holding them. For this reason alone I owe Iñigo a debt beyond my power to repay that he kept me from intimacy with persons outwardly of good behaviour, but inwardly, as is now known,

[1] Père Cros, using one of the ' improved ' texts, translated the final sentences as follows: ' God knows what I have suffered, above all at seeing the name of Master Iñigo involved in those accusations '!

full of heresies. I accordingly beg your Honour to receive him, to whose goodness I am under such heavy obligation, as you would myself. . . . I beg you most earnestly not to fail to consult and commune with him, and to trust his advice. Believe me, his counsel and conversation will profit you greatly, so much is he a man of God and of all virtue. Again, I entreat your Honour to do this. As for anything he shall say to you concerning myself, favour me by giving him as much credence as you would to me speaking to you personally. From him you will be able to learn of my necessities and hardships, for he is better informed about them than anyone else on earth. If your Honour wishes to do me the kindness of alleviating my great poverty, you can entrust to Señor Iñigo whatever you propose to send me. . . . So I finish by kissing the hands of your Honour and those of the Señora a thousand times. May our Lord increase your lives by as many years as your noble hearts desire. Your Honour's trusty servant and younger brother, Francés de Xavier.[1]

There is no indication how the cold-blooded hero of Navarre received St. Ignatius nor whether he parted with a single one of his superabundant *cruzados* to relieve the indigence of his student brother. It may have been the receipt of Francis's letter that stirred Juan a few months later to take a belated interest in his request for a certificate of nobility four years earlier. At all events, the family suddenly became very busy with the question, consulted lawyers, hunted up witnesses, and produced sheaves of domestic records. The great name of Xavier, distinguished through the centuries for its orthodoxy and *limpia sangre*, meaning blood untainted with the racial blood which redeemed the world, must not be allowed to become contaminated through the association of the madcap Francis with persons imprisoned by the Inquisition, or, like Laynez, whom he had mentioned in the letter as

---

[1] Schurhammer, *Epistolae S. Francisci Xaverii*, i, 8–12. Francis mentioned that he had gone after a ' dear cousin ' of theirs, a fugitive from the University, for thirty-four leagues, but failed to catch him up. He was anxious about him, fearing that he would never come to any good.

' mui amigo mío ', of Jewish extraction.[1] Unaware of the flutter in Navarre, Francis and his five friends went on peaceably with their study of theology and their daily meditations and examinations of conscience, under the guidance of their one priest, Pierre Favre. It had been settled among them before Ignatius left that they would all quit Paris on January 5, 1537, to rejoin him at Venice in preparation for their pilgrimage to the Holy Land. The doctorate in theology, most honorific of the University's degrees, at which they were aiming would have to be sacrificed if they kept to their date, but they did not mind. Theology without its laurels would serve them well enough. Together they renewed their vows in the chapel on Montmartre when the feast of the Assumption came round, and the second time, in 1536, had their number increased to eight by the adhesion of three excellent French students recruited by Pierre Favre named Claude Le Jay, Paschase Broet, and Jean Codure. Like Favre, Le Jay and Broet had already been ordained priests and that was a great advantage. Meantime Ignatius was turning his Spanish holiday into one of the most intensive spiritual campaigns of his whole existence. First, by example and counsel he completely reformed the Laodicean clergy of his native place, Azpeitia, and then, in the words of one who observed his activities, ' did all in his power for the poor folk of those parts who were suffering grievously from hunger and other numerous necessities '. A hundred days he spent among his own people, tirelessly catechizing

[1] The entire *Inquisitio de Xaverii Nobilitate* is given in *Monumenta Xaveriana*, ii, 34–88. Miguel de Jassu, the eldest brother, figures prominently in the affair, but that may have been, as Père Poussines believed, because the documents were drawn up before the year 1535, and then relegated to some pigeon-hole until retrieved in 1535 in order possibly to divert Francis from his new loyalties and unworldly aims. It is difficult to agree with this, as the dates given are quite specific, Friday, August 13, Friday, October 1, Saturday, October 2, Friday, October 29, Wednesday, November 3, etc., so the puzzle remains why Francis, in March, 1535, should seemingly have regarded Juan as the head of the family, while as late as December of that year Miguel, according to these papers, is bearing witness at the Castle of Xavier to his nobility and licensing him to use the family coat of arms. The present unworthy investigator is convinced that Miguel died before March, 1535, but is wholly unable to prove it except by psychological arguments. In his *Vie de Saint Ignace* Père Dudon boldly cuts the Gordian knot by making Francis address the letter to Miguel!

children, preaching, serving the sick in the public hospital where he had his own humble billet, and feeding the poor with the bread he had begged for them. Loyola, the castle of his birth and subsequent agonies, tried to claim him, but he preferred the company of the dispossessed, while showing no lack of love and courtesy towards his own proud kith and kin. When all was done that man could do, he set off on a wider apostolate and, though sick and suffering, undertook journeys, embraced hardships, and faced perils that might have daunted the Cid Campeador. He walked the whole way to Almazán, the home of Laynez, from there to Madrid, where he was greeted by the boy of eight who became King Philip II, from Madrid to Toledo to visit the relatives of Salmeron, and from Toledo the two hundred miles to Valencia, merely in order to cheer and fortify a Carthusian monk of that city whose vocation he had nurtured in Paris. Then he embarked for Genoa and nearly lost his life three times over before reaching his goal of Venice towards the end of the year 1535.

Another war between Charles V and Francis I burst on the world in the summer of that year and made Paris forthwith a place dangerous for Spaniards, even such pacific ones as battled only with Peter the Lombard or Thomas Aquinas. Nothing remained for the eight friends but to anticipate the order of their going and go at once. They sold whatever small possessions remained to them, except their books, gave the proceeds to the poor, and slipped quietly out of Paris before daylight on November 15. Just at the moment of departure, there arrived from Navarre that solemnly attested certificate of his nobility for which Francis Xavier had applied five years earlier.

We, the Emperor, Queen and King [it ran], by this present definitive sentence pronounce and declare Don Francisco de Jassu y Xavier to be a nobleman, hidalgo, and gentleman of ancient lineage, and as such empower him and his sons and descendants in direct line to use and enjoy all the prerogatives, exemptions, honours, offices, liberties, privileges, landed property, and duelling rights which appertain to gentlemen, hidalgos, and noblemen in our Kingdom of Navarre and everywhere else.[1]

The appearance of the Emperor in the document was, of course, a mere legal technicality, and nobody would have been more astonished than Charles V could he have had just then five minutes' converse with the ' hombre noble, hijodalgo y jentilhombre' entitled to fight duels in his name. With the parchment came an official notification from the Chapter of Pamplona Cathedral that Francis had been elected as a canon into their high company. He wrote to thank all concerned for their friendly intentions, which were too late, not by five years, but by an eternity.

As they judged the journey into Italy by the direct route through Savoy to be too dangerous owing to the war, Francis and his seven companions decided to go the long way round by Lorraine, Germany and Switzerland. They travelled on foot, each wearing the cassock and broad-brimmed hat of a Paris student and carrying in a knapsack on his back a change of linen and a Bible and Breviary. They used staffs in pilgrim fashion and wore their rosaries round their necks as badges of faith and of devotion to the Mother of God. It rained and rained all the way to Metz, and then, right up to the Italian frontier, they had frost and snow. But they were glowing within at the prospect of rejoining Ignatius, ' so winged with happiness that their feet seemed not to touch the ground at all', as their historian, Simon Rodriguez, recorded. Each day they halted at some town or village so that the three priests among them might say Mass and give the others Holy Communion. When held up by marauding soldiery they stuck to the one answer, given in Spanish or French as the occasion demanded, that they were students from Paris on pilgrimage to a popular shrine near Nancy. They had enough money between them to pay for a frugal supper at the inns and for a little space in which to lie down at night, but not enough to hire

[1] MHSJ. *Monumenta Xaveriana*, ii, 83–4. People who complain of Whitehall's jargon ought to read some Spanish legal documents, at any rate of the sixteenth century, to see how lucid and succinct our English bureaucrats are.

a private room. So they were obliged to say their prayers in
public, to the accompaniment of popping corks and hearty
drinking, a habit that involved them in wordy battles with
various types of more or less inebriated Protestants. They took
up the challenges with alacrity and enjoyed themselves, for the
Protestants handsomely kept the rules and showed no disposition
to denounce them. Only once, at an inn near Constance, did they
encounter a pastor who had reached the bellicose stage in his cups
and sought to have them imprisoned. But they escaped, and
reached Venice safe and sound on January 6, 1537, after being
nearly eight weeks on the road.

Quickly the nine, as they had now jubilantly become, discovered that there was no chance of a ship sailing to the Levant
before June, so by common accord they decided to offer their
services during the first months of waiting to the two great
hospitals of the city, those of SS. Giovanni e Paolo and the
Incurabili. Francis Xavier made one of the group at the Incurabili,
a charity already doubly hallowed by the labours of two great
men, both canonized and founders of religious orders, St. Cajetan
and St. Jerome Aemiliani. Simon Rodriguez, a narrator often
tiresomely garrulous as well as foolishly credulous, is at his best
in describing the routine of himself and his companions at the
hospitals:

> We made the beds, swept the floors, emptied and scoured
> utensils, cleaned up the wards generally, carried the bodies of
> the dead reverently to the graves we had dug for them, and
> day and night attended hand and foot on the sick, with so much
> satisfaction and joy that we astonished those living at the
> hospital and even attracted the attention of eminent persons
> in the city, who came to stare at our activities as at something
> wonderful.

Then the useful Simon proceeds to tell a story of his good
friend Francis Xavier:

> In the hospital of the Incurabili there was a leper or a man
> very like a leper, as he was covered all over with foul suppu-

rating sores. As my friend one day was passing by, this unfortunate man cried out to him, ' Ho, there ! Pray, rub my back ',
which he at once turned to do until suddenly overcome by
sensations of horror and nausea, fearing that he might catch
the loathsome disease himself. But desiring rather to crush his
rebellious feelings than to avoid the contagion, he scraped some
of the pus together with his fingers and swallowed it. Next
morning, he told me with a smile how he had dreamt in the
night that the leprosy of the afflicted man remained stuck in
his throat and that he could not get rid of it by coughing or
other means, short of being very sick. In fact, however, it
happened with him as our Lord said, ' If they drink any deadly
thing it shall in no wise hurt them.'[1]

After two months of nursing and charing, the companions,
with the exception of Ignatius, turned their feet towards Rome
in order to obtain the sanction of Pope Paul III for their projected
pilgrimage. Ignatius held back because of the presence in Rome
at that time of two excellent and important men whom he
suspected of being hostile to him, Cardinal Gian Pier Carafa, a
future Pope and one of the most explosive good men known to
history, and a certain Dr. Pedro Ortiz, an emissary of Charles V.
Ortiz, later one of his most devoted friends, had been a little
critical of Ignatius in Paris, and Ignatius in Venice had incurred
quite innocently the lifelong resentment of the sensitive, fiery
Carafa. The others hoped for the best should they encounter the
formidable pair. They had thought to have become experts in
the endurance of bad weather, but Italy, the fabled land of sunny
skies, added to their education. All the way to Rome they squelched
along wet to the skin, covered with mud, and ravenously hungry.
They chose to travel completely unprovided, as the Apostles had
done, only to discover when too late that Lombardy and Umbria
were by no means Palestine. During the three days it took them
to reach Ravenna, they did not meet a soul from whom they

[1] MHSJ. *Epistolae PP. Broeti . . . et Rodericii*, 475; *Fontes narrativi de S.
Ignatio*, i, 110. Laynez in the second source says that the man's disease was the
' *mal francés* ', which had already given Francis the horrors in Paris.

could have begged a mouthful of food, and 'were often so exhausted that they could neither go on nor go back, and sank to the drowned earth in utter weariness, but in those straits each was more concerned for the plight of the others than for his own'. The Po, over its banks for a mile on either side, barred their way, but they plunged in and managed to cross its bed at a ford, with the water up to their necks. 'On emerging, they found themselves in a wood of pine trees and were so hungry that they plucked the cones, extracted the seeds, and ate them. And so they came to Ravenna.'

The next stage of their journey, to Ancona, they made in a coastal ship, having had enough of the misnamed dry land for a while. A day and a night they tossed on the sea, 'without food or drink or money to pay their passage'. Not unnaturally, the captain of the ship became very angry when they told him their predicament, but relented to the extent of allowing one of them ashore at Ancona to pawn his Breviary for a few hours and thus obtain their quittance. They then split into little groups to quest for alms, and 'a man among them who might have acquired name and glory in the world for the greatness of his learning and other gifts was to be seen barefooted in the market-place accepting humbly and thankfully from the *contadine* now a radish, now an apple or some other fruit'. The hero of the radish was undoubtedly Laynez. Ancona treated them all very nicely, and by their united efforts they obtained enough food and money, 'not only to have a merry though frugal meal together which banished their hunger, but to redeem the Breviary from the pawnbroker'. From Ancona they walked to the famous shrine of Loreto and spent three happy days of prayer and contemplation at the Holy House, entirely unvexed by any of our modern doubts about its authenticity.[1] Then they struck across country to Rome, traversing

---

[1] Not that the doubts nor even the certainty of its being unauthentic need trouble a man's devotion. It is, at least in the intention of those who originally built it, a replica of the Holy House of Nazareth, a memorial of it, as a statue is of a saint or other great man. By the love and piety of pilgrims throughout centuries, including a long list of canonized saints, it has acquired a kind of secondary authenticity, which no legend of angelic house-removers is needed to support.

the Apennines and the Sabine Mountains. On this stretch, the incessant rain, the ubiquitous mud and the pangs of hunger tested them almost to breaking point. In the towns they made straight for the poorhouse and spent the night in one of its casual wards. In the open country they slept in whatever shelter offered, sometimes with cattle in their byres, sometimes in barns, sometimes in abandoned, tumbledown shacks. All in all, it can fairly be maintained that they made an honest pilgrimage. Most of them had something to say about it afterwards, but from Francis Xavier there was never a word.[1]

The sight of Rome, the ' clean brown city of memories which was once the world ', made up to the stained and weary pilgrims for all they had been through. It was only ten years since the city had been sacked by the German Lutherans in the service of the Catholic Emperor, but the great churches remained and the shrines of the saints to thrill the eyes and heart of Francis Xavier. As for the dreaded Dr. Ortiz, it was he who brought them to the notice of the Pope, and in such eulogistic fashion that they were all invited to the Vatican on April 3 to entertain his Holiness with a theological disputation while he dined. They pleased him at any rate to the extent of sixty ducats, which he contributed with his warm blessing to the expenses of their voyage to Palestine. At the same time, he expressed to them his gravest doubts of their ever getting there, owing to impending trouble between Venice and the Sublime Porte. What was more important for their immediate future, he granted them a faculty, signed and sealed by his Cardinal Penitentiary, empowering them to be ordained priests by any bishop of their choosing who resided not less than forty miles from Rome.[2] Altogether, their hard pilgrimage had great rewards, materially as well as spiritually, for they made their way back to Venice enriched by the lordly sum of 260 ducats,

[1] The details and quotations given above are entirely from the pen of Simon Rodriguez (*Epistolae PP. Paschasii Broeti . . . et Simonis Rodericii*, 479–87).

[2] MHSJ. *Scripta de S. Ignatio de Loyola*, i (Madrid, 1904), 543–6. Special provision was made in the faculty for Salmeron, the youngest of the group, as he had not attained the canonical age of ordination by a year. This wanting year was graciously remitted so that he might be ordained when he became twenty-three, shortly after the others.

every one of which they returned to the several donors when it became plain some months later that the Mediterranean was to be a theatre of war.

Ignatius, Francis Xavier, and the others not yet priests were ordained in Venice on June 24, 1537, by a Dalmatian bishop who charged them, as Laynez put it, not so much as the price of a candle. Their hard work at the two hospitals, to which they had immediately reverted, raised a problem, for it left them no time to prepare, as men such as they would want to prepare, for the solemn occasion of their first Mass. They accordingly decided to disperse in groups throughout the territory of the Republic, which was not so serene just then, and to spend forty days in prayer and penance. It was probably at Venice before they left that a significant incident occurred which Laynez afterwards related to Pedro Ribadeneira, the intimate friend and first biographer of St. Ignatius. According to Ribadeneira, ' Father Francis and Father Master Laynez were sleeping one night side by side when Father Francis suddenly awoke and cried to the other: " Jesus, how crushed and fatigued I feel! Do you know what I dreamt?—that I was trying to hoist an Indian on my shoulders, and he was such a deadly weight I couldn't lift him ".'[1] In the dispersion, Francis took for companion the youthful Salmeron, still short by six weeks of his twenty-third year and ordination. They made their residence in an abandoned and ruinous hut on the outskirts of Monselice, a little town about ten miles south of Padua. What passed there and how they subsisted during the forty days of solitude is entirely unknown. Presumably they went into the town each day to beg for some food. When the time of retreat was over, Ignatius invited all the companions to join him in the ruins of a monastery a mile outside Vicenza, where he was living in great contentment with Favre and Laynez. For bedding they had some loose straw begged from the local peasantry, and for a roof, the canopy of heaven, which enabled him to indulge

---

[1] *Scripta de S. Ignatio de Loyola*, i, 382. It is a small point but it may be noticed that Ribadeneira, who was a careful and well-informed writer, gives Laynez the title of Master and denies it to Francis. Still, Francis himself assumed the title in a letter to Ignatius from India, January 27, 1545.

in his hobby of contemplating the stars.[1] Here at Vicenza it was
that Francis Xavier said his first Mass, and here he and Rodriguez
fell so ill that they had to be removed from the open-air monastery
to the city's hardly more comfortable hospital.

We were obliged to share the same bed [wrote Rodriguez]
and one so narrow that it barely accommodated the two of us.
This was a source of much suffering, for it often happened that
my companion, burning with fever, would desire to be relieved
of the coverings, while I, shivering with cold, as the place was
full of draughts, would hanker for their warmth. But each
consulted the need of the other rather than his own and gladly
put up with the consequences. One night, my bedfellow, when
he believed he was awake, had a vision of St. Jerome, to whom
he was greatly devoted. The Saint, grave and venerable in
appearance, consoled him lovingly and told him that he would
pass the winter in Bologna and there endure many and great
sufferings, which is exactly what happened.

The intervention at this point of the learned and combative
Dalmatian Doctor who shared with St. Michael Archangel the
patronal superintendence of Castle Xavier is not without significance. He certainly helped to mould the spirit of Francis, the
Castle's child. If Jerome's erudition and delight in battle be
excepted, and it is a huge exception, a most interesting comparison might be instituted of his character with that of his devoted
client more than a millennium later. In both there may be observed
the same loving ardent hearts which made their lives a long
procession of friendships, in both the same sort of divine restlessness allied with a craving after solitude, the same frank, loyal
nature, the same strongly ascetical bent, the same devouring
passion for work, though such different work, which made them
achieve results apparently beyond the capacity of human nature.

[1] From the time of his conversion at Loyola Castle Ignatius became an
inveterate star-gazer. About those early days he told Gonzalez da Camara :
' *La mayor consolación que recibía era mirar el cielo y las estrellas, lo qual hacía
muchas veces y por mucho espacio, porque con aquello sentía en sí un muy grande
esfuerzo para servir a nuestro Señor* ' (*Fontes narrativi de S. Ignatio*, i, 376).

They wrote nearly the same number of letters, best mirrors of their souls, but Jerome loved style and ensued it while Francis cared nothing for it at all. In one respect Francis parted company with Jerome completely. Though like the other a deeply sensitive man and one who often felt hot anger blaze in his heart, he never once allowed himself to get into a rage.

As the winter of the year 1537 drew on, it became obvious to St. Ignatius and his companions that their prospects of sailing to Palestine by the date stipulated for in their vow, January 6, 1538, were over. Reluctantly they turned their faces, so long set towards Jerusalem, in other directions, and dispersed once more. Ignatius, Favre and Laynez went to Rome, where one of the feared lions, at least, had proved himself a lamb, and the others visited in pairs various university cities of northern Italy, in hopes of attracting some students to join their small band. They were still without the least ambition to found a new religious order. Such a thought does not seem to have occurred to any of them, even Ignatius, but they felt that before separating they ought to choose a name for themselves corporatively, so as to be able to answer questions about their affiliation. ' They therefore began to pray about the matter and to think hard what name would be most fitting. Considering among themselves that, as a group, they had no other head than Jesus Christ whom alone they desired to serve, they concluded that they should take His name and call themselves the Company of Jesus '.[1] Ignatius himself was the most eager of them for the adoption of the title because

[1] MHSJ. Polanco, *Vita Ignatii Loiolae et Rerum Societatis Jesu Historia*, i (Madrid, 1894), 72. Juan Polanco was for many years the secretary of St. Ignatius. His history of the first Jesuits, commonly called the *Chronicon*, runs to six printed volumes. The name *Jesuit* in both its friendly and abusive meanings was being employed many years before there were any Jesuits as the world now knows them. Thus, in a little book of devotion, published at Basel in 1470, a Carthusian monk of Saxony supplicated the Blessed Virgin ' that as from Christ we are called Christians, so from Jesus we may deserve to be called Jesuits '. On the other hand, the author of a *Confessionale* printed at Antwerp in 1519 invited his reader to examine his conscience as to whether he omitted any good works ' for fear of being derided as a Pharisee, a Jesuit, a hypocrite '. The name in both its senses was first attached to the sons of St. Ignatius in Germany in the 1540's, but the more truculent Protestants preferred to alter it scriptually into Jebusites, those accursed children of Canaan.

it wounded all that was unassuming and lowly in his nature to hear his friends called, as they often were, *Iñiguistas*. The decision was reached in that same wreck of a monastery outside Vicenza, with the winds from the Alps whistling about the poor men's heads, as they crouched frozen and semi-starved on the straw. But in their hearts there was great exultation.

This time in their humble Diaspora, Francis Xavier had Bobadilla, the incalculable, for companion and Bologna for his field of activity. Person and place were decided by a drawing of lots, in which St. Jerome must obviously have had some say. St. Dominic also came into the picture, for when Francis offered Mass at his magnificent shrine in Bologna a lady present was so profoundly moved by his devotion that she waylaid him afterwards and besought him to visit her uncle, rector of the parish of Santa Lucia. The rector in his turn underwent the spell and prevailed upon Francis to stay with him, an offer gratefully accepted, but only on condition that the lodger be permitted to seek the little food he needed from charitable people in the streets. The kind priest and others who knew Francis intimately in Bologna have left their impressions of him.

He was a man [they said] slow to speak, but whose words when he did speak went straight to people's hearts. At Mass, and particularly if it was a Mass of the Passion of Christ, he wept abundant tears. One Friday, while saying Mass in the church of Santa Lucia, he was rapt out of himself for more than an hour at the Memento, though the server tried hard to rouse him by tugging at his vestments. After Mass he would spend the entire day hearing confessions, visiting the sick in the hospitals and prisoners in the gaols, serving the poor, preaching in the piazzas, and teaching children or other un-instructed persons Christian doctrine. Though very ill all the while, he never omitted his early morning prayer, or his Mass, or any of his daily avocations.[1]

The question arises, how was Francis the Spaniard able to

[1] *Monumenta Xaveriana*, ii, 115–17, 824.

communicate with the Italians at all? The answer might almost be, by main force. He had been in Italy nearly a year, which was time enough for one as quick-witted as he and as gifted with a magnificent memory to pick up sufficient of the language for his purposes. He never had any inhibitions about speaking a new and unfamiliar tongue. His accent might be execrable and his grammar deplorable, but he made no apologies and went brazenly ahead, without a trace of the hangdog, furtive look which is said, according to good authority, to come upon the faces of Englishmen abroad, indicating that they are about to launch into French. In Bologna's squares Francis attracted an audience by standing on a vacant bench, waving his big hat, and shouting to loungers and marketing folk to come and listen to the Word of God. Perhaps they laughed at him to start with, perhaps they understood little of what he was trying to say, but soon a hush would fall upon them because the love that shone in his dark bewitching eyes and burned on his stammering lips spoke to their hearts so eloquently. At Bologna, for the first time, he was able to give free vent to that passion for the salvation of souls which soon afterwards drove him to the ends of the earth and, at forty-six, out of this world altogether. No saint ever more flagrantly burned the candle at both ends, and the marvel is that he lasted as long as he did. ' He had a terrible bout of the quartan ague at Bologna,' wrote one of his intimates, ' and through cold and want became so pale and wasted that he seemed no longer to be a living man but a walking corpse. When I saw him afterwards in Rome, a mere shadow of his former self, I judged that he would never recover his health nor be able to do a day's work again in his life.'[1]

---

[1] MHSJ. *Epistolae PP. Broeti . . . et Rodericii*, 491. The agues were of various kinds, *quotidian* when the attack occurred daily, *tertian* when it came on every second day, and *quartan* when the victim had two days' relief between his bouts. The affliction, which killed people by the million all over Europe, was supposed to be caused by ' bad air ', hence the name malaria. The Anopheles mosquito had a grand time until Sir Ronald Ross detected its abominations.

CHAPTER IV

JESUIT BEGINNINGS

IN accordance with their third vow, all the companions of Ignatius Loyola began to converge on Rome as soon as the date set for the beginning of their pilgrimage to Palestine had passed. Francis Xavier arrived late, towards Easter, which in 1538 fell on April 21, but the wonder is that he arrived at all. Even for a crow there are 180 miles between Bologna and Rome, and he walked every foot of them, with another hundred added for the twists of the roads, though he was suffering from fever and exhausted from work. Rodriguez was not the only one to have a sorrowful conviction that this must inevitably be the last of the well-beloved Francisco's earthly journeys, leading forthwith to a premature Roman grave. But he had some unaccountable spring of vitality in him which it would require fourteen more years of direst hardship and superhuman labour to quench for ever. Reunion with his brethren that Easter soon restored his usual buoyancy and eagerness for a part in their multifarious activities. They lived together at first in a wretched little house near the Trinità dei Monti, but later found more ample and central quarters in a building that nobody else would enter because it was reputed to be haunted. Rodriguez, who had courage, spent a troubled night alone in the place as caretaker before the others moved in. He was wakened suddenly in the small hours by a fearful din, whereupon he argued with himself bravely: ' If these be robbers, there is nothing for them to steal; if they be demons, they can do me no harm except by the permission of God; if they have permission to kill me, the will of the Lord be done. So despising whatever it was that made the disturbance, I turned over and resumed my slumbers.' The clatter continued after the coming of his brethren, and there was much crashing of pots and pans, movement of furniture, rapping on doors, and

65

other phenomena usually associated with poltergeists, but they
soon got used to the noises and did not give them much thought,
especially as their modest household equipment seemed to be none
the worse in the morning for its nocturnal gambols. Here it was
among the spooks that St. Francis had a notable duel with the
demon of the flesh. ' He sprang from his couch one night,' relates
Rodriguez, ' crying aloud and with the blood streaming from his
nostrils. The others thought that a demon must have tried to
strangle him, as he would not explain, but a few days later he
confided to me that it was his violent efforts to repel a sensual
dream which caused the haemorrhage.'

The Church of Saint-Louis, frequented by the French colony,
became the scene of the Saint's new labours, probably because his
knowledge of their language, after eleven years in Paris, was more
adequate than his hit or miss Italian. His friend Laynez had been
appointed by the Pope lecturer at the Sapienza, but made little
impression owing to his shyness and dryness, for he was as dry as
the hills around Almazán in June. His day was still to come,
though even then the genial Pope, very much of a Renaissance
man, admired the subtlety of his mind and had him in twice a
month to argue with other theologians, as a condiment for his
dinner. No one thought of inviting Francis Xavier to enter the
lists because no one considered him to be an intellectual. Nor was
he either, thanks be to God. While he worked quietly at Saint-
Louis, mainly hearing confessions, a terrible storm broke on the
heads of himself and his companions. Ignatius said that it was the
worst storm in the whole of his agitated existence. ' Many believed
that we would be burnt at the stake or condemned to the galleys.'
It all came about because a popular preacher in Rome named
Mainardi seemed to them to be airing views of a Lutheran trend,
and they felt that charity required them to remonstrate, as well
as to refute the dangerous opinions in their own sermons. Now,
Mainardi had a wide circle of admirers, particularly two influential
Spanish priests named Mudarra and Barrera who, greatly an-
noyed by the criticism of their hero, determined to turn the tables
on Ignatius and his men. For this purpose they enlisted the
services of Miguel Landivar, the rolling stone who had attached

himself to Francis Xavier in Paris. Landivar was an extraordinary person, one blown about by every wind of passion. In Paris he seriously considered murdering St. Ignatius when he withdrew St. Francis from his worldly ambitions. Then, by a rebound, he begged Ignatius to take him into his circle and was for a time at Venice numbered among the companions. But he proved himself impossible and Ignatius had to tell him to go.[1] Now in Rome the occasion had come for his sweet revenge. Through his propaganda, the encounters of Ignatius with the Inquisition or its equivalent in Alcalá, Salamanca, Paris and Venice soon became known all over the city until people began to murmur that not the preacher, but those foreigners, his self-appointed censors, were the real heretics. The impulsive, not to say imprudent, charity of Francis Xavier counted for something in the campaign of slander, for he was watched and seen to visit the house of an unmarried woman of scandalous reputation whom he was endeavouring to reform. That was a chance in a thousand for the enemy and they seized it with enthusiasm. Things came to such a pass that Ignatius, who personally did not care a Spanish fig what the world thought of him, felt compelled, if his efforts through seventeen tormented years to promote the glory of God were not to be completely ruined, to take strenuous counter action. The spirit of Pamplona flared up in him again. If they all must die, then they would die fighting for their ideal. Through Dr. Ortiz, now his devoted friend, he obtained an audience with the Pope and laid before him the whole course of his life in detail. He even begged the Holy Father to put himself and his companions in prison while investigations into their opinions and conduct were being made, lest any should suspect them of planning to take flight from Rome. He prosecuted Landivar before the Governor of the city, and secured against him a sentence of banishment. And finally,

[1] Landivar's name figures with those of St. Francis and the others in the ordination faculty granted to them by the Pope. The complexion of the man, his inconstancy, his show of penitence which so easily changed to viciousness, his humility all moth-eaten with jealousy and pride, are revealed by himself in a letter which he wrote to St. Ignatius after his dismissal at Venice (MHSJ. *Epistolae Mixtae*, Madrid, 1898, i, 11–14. He concludes the letter thus: ' *El que desea ser comendado en vuestras oraciones, su minimo, Miguel.*')

he canvassed by letter prominent men in all the towns and cities where his companions had laboured.

It was eight months before the storm blew itself out. During that time Ignatius had two great allies, first the Pope himself who never doubted of him, and then the second most influential figure in Italian ecclesiastical affairs, Cardinal Gaspar Contarini. Contarini might be described as a Venetian rendering of St. Thomas More. He had made the *Spiritual Exercises* under the guidance of Ignatius and became so smitten with them that, though a humanist born, he copied out in his own hand every word of the dry, inelegant text, under the crust of which lay banked such tremendous fires.[1] The testimony supplied by the vicar-general of Bologna in answer to the appeal of Ignatius gives a clue to the calumnies that were spread about him and his companions:

> By these presents we solemnly bear witness in the Lord that Francis Xavier and Nicholas Bobadilla, priests, did preach in this city of Bologna with our full sanction true and Christian doctrine, in no wise savouring of the errors of Luther. Rather did they strive with all their might to extirpate those errors, thus doing this our City an immense service. Their lives and conduct, in tune with their words, were the admiration of all, and it is a false and lying tale that they had to flee this City as fugitives from justice, for they left on their lawful occasions to sow elsewhere the good seed which they had sown here.[2]

Similar testimonies came from other places, and there came too, simultaneously and, as it were, fortuitously, the very three judges before whom Ignatius had been arraigned in Alcalá, Paris and Venice. Their witness in his favour ruined the adversaries' main contention, and the whole case was wound up by the Governor of Rome in a final judgment, dated November 18, 1538, which

[1] MHSJ. *Scripta de Sancto Ignatio de Loyola*, ii (Madrid, 1918), 872–3. Though a cardinal, Contarini was a layman and, like St. Thomas More, keenly concerned for ecclesiastical reform. Among his writings was an admirable little treatise *De Officio Episcopi*.

[2] *Monumenta Xaveriana*, ii, 133–4.

declared the accused men to be, not only absolutely innocent of the charges brought against them, but priests of the highest probity and orthodoxy.[1]

The fierce Roman winter of 1538–39 put a frosty crown on their rehabilitation. Never had there been known such a winter, never anything more like the ghastly weather conditions imagined by Dante as prevalent in the Third Circle of Hell. Up to a tenth of the population died of sheer starvation and cold, and hundreds of poor wretches were to be seen daily collapsed on the frozen pavements. That was a challenge such as the ten pilgrim priests who so clearly saw God in their neighbour had been born to meet. Expert and unabashed beggarmen that they had become, they soon had large quantities of hay or straw for beds, wood for fires, and bread for empty stomachs accumulated, and then they one and all scoured the sodden streets at sunset to bring in their guests. Sometimes by miracles of planning they crowded as many as four hundred homeless, hungry, frost-bitten wrecks of humanity into their ramshackle but roomy house, washed them, fed them, consoled them, and made them as comfortable as the rough circumstances permitted. Those activities did not go unnoticed. The contagion of their example spread into high circles, until many rich and noble persons were to be found vying in works of mercy with the poor priests who owned little except the shabby clothes on their backs. A secular canon of ample means named Pietro Codazzo was so much impressed that he gave himself over entirely to Ignatius and became the first Italian Jesuit.[2]

It appears that at this time the brethren were not as yet entirely weaned from their project of making a pilgrimage to Palestine, though no longer bound to it by vow. It seems, too, that the Pope had divined the thought in their hearts, for one day, after a particularly successful prandial disputation, he suddenly asked the four of them present: ' Why are you so anxious to go to Jerusalem? Is not Italy a good and true Jerusalem if you desire

[1] *Scripta de S. Ignatio*, i, 627–9; *Sancti Ignatii Epistolae et Instructiones*, i (Madrid, 1903), 137–44.
[2] MHSJ. Polanco, *Vita Ignatii Loiolae et Rerum Societatis Jesu Historia*, 65–6.

to bear fruit in the Church of God?' Bobadilla, who probably
made one of the four as he was powerful in argument, relates
the incident, and goes on to say that the Holy Father's question
was the immediate cause of their beginning to deliberate seriously
whether they ought not to shape themselves into a body more
tightly knit and highly organized than their then loose association.[1] At all events, about the middle of Lent, 1539, they began
to hold nightly meetings to discuss the grave question, when
their hard day's work was over. Often they prolonged their
consideration of it far into the night, until at last, after three
months of intensive study and prayer, they had hammered out
the basic principles by which their future lives and activities should
be guided. It was easy and pleasant for them to agree unanimously
to maintain their corporate unity, even though the Pope might
choose to disperse them far and wide throughout the world, but
it was far from easy to decide how the unity should be conserved
and fortified. Ought they to elect a common superior and add a
new vow of obedience to those of poverty and chastity taken at
Montmartre? It seemed the only way, and yet they hesitated in
great perplexity, fearing, as one of them recorded, that if they
took such a vow ' they would be obliged by the Pope to live
according to some existing religious rule, which would preclude
them from working directly for the salvation of souls, the one
and only aim of their aspirations, after their personal sanctifi-
cation '.[2]

Other objections to the proposed new vow were discussed
with similar thoroughness and seriousness, and then its advantages
came under review, one being that ' nothing is so effective as
obedience to overthrow all pride and pomposity.' So, weary,
hungry and cold, after many days and great argument, Ignatius,
Francis Xavier and the others reached their fateful decision:
' We concluded, not by a majority of votes, but unanimously,
that the best and most essential thing for us was to vow obedience
to one of our number, for we considered that to be the soundest

[1] MHSJ. *Bobadillae Monumenta* (Madrid, 1913), 616.
[2] MHSJ. *Sancti Ignatii de Loyola Constitutiones Societatis Jesu*, i (Rome,
1934), 5–6.

and safest means of achieving our primary aims, the fulfilment of the divine will in all things and the conservation of our unity.' That was how the Society of Jesus, as an idea, came to be born. There were many more nightly sessions to debate other features of the life which the companions proposed for themselves, but the determination concerning obedience, taken on April 19, proved decisive. It was a leap in the dark, but a darkness not without stars. The confidence of Ignatius in the issue never wavered, and some scholars both ancient and modern were so much impressed by his serene assurance as to maintain that he must have had the idea of founding a new religious order in mind from the first days of his conversion.[1] But the immediate companions and early disciples of the Saint are explicit that such was not the case.

In August, 1539, Ignatius condensed into five chapters all the conclusions, including two revolutionary ones, which he and his friends had reached, as, for instance, that the superior to be elected should hold office for life, that they should recite the Divine Office privately, ' not in choir, lest we be drawn away from the duties of charity to which we have wholly dedicated ourselves ', and that there be a special, explicit fourth vow of obedience to the Pope, binding them, beyond the obligations of Catholics in general, to undertake promptly and with alacrity whatever missions or tasks he might choose to assign them, no matter how distant or dangerous. The little document, packed with canonical dynamite, was first submitted to the judgment of Father Thomas Badia, O.P., Master of the Sacred Palace, who must have been an extraordinarily broad-minded man, for he commented on it very favourably, and then was read aloud to the Pope at Tivoli by Cardinal Contarini. Contarini, the good friend who might be described as the godfather of all Jesuits, wrote immediately and joyfully to tell Ignatius the result: 'His Holiness was greatly pleased with all five chapters, and has most bene-

---

[1] The eminent historian of the Spanish Jesuits, Antonio Astrain, was of that opinion and contended for it with a certain warmth (*Historia de la Compañía de Jesús en la Asistencia de España*, i, Madrid, 1902, 102–23). Astrain completed seven volumes of his work before he died.

volently approved and confirmed them. When I return to Rome with him on Friday, instructions will be given to the Most Reverend Ghinucci to draft the brief or bull.' Ghinucci, however, refused point blank to perform the service, and he could hardly be blamed. A strict canonist, he was unable to stomach such innovations in the religious tradition as private recital of the Office and the election of a superior for life. No order in the Church, not even the recent ones of clerks regular, had such novel features. The Pope then turned to Cardinal Guidiccioni, one of the most venerable and respected members of the Sacred College, for his opinion, but he showed even more fight than Ghinucci. No plea nor argument of Contarini and other eminent men had the least effect on him, for he held almost as an article of faith, and wrote an incisive tract to enforce his conviction, that the Church already was plagued with far too many religious orders.[1]

The Cardinal's opposition led to an impasse which lasted for more than a year from the date of Contarini's optimistic announcement, but St. Ignatius was not unduly dismayed. Long afterwards, when his Society had become solidly established and was vigorously growing, he confessed to one of his men that he thought a quarter of an hour in prayer would reconcile him to its complete destruction and leave him as cheerful as he had been before.[2] He and his companions turned to prayer in the emergency of 1539, agreeing among themselves to offer three hundred Masses apiece, three thousand in all, that God might effect a

---

[1] Tacchi Venturi, *Storia della Compagnia di Gesù in Italia*, i, parte 2a, Documenti, ed. 2a (Rome, 1939), 197–200, 207–14. Having compared religious orders to the many heads of the fabulous Hydra which, when lopped off, immediately grew again, Guidiccioni continued : ' As all secular clergy serve, subject to Christ, under one leader, St. Peter, in a dress and manner of life common to all, so let all regulars serve God and Christ under St. Paul, or some other chosen leader. Diversity thus abolished, the abominable strife among regulars for preferment, their brawls and contentions among themselves and with the seculars, the anti-clerical attitude which they cause in the laity, and many other grievous scandals would, perhaps, cease and be removed from the Church.' The good old man exaggerated, and his policy of amalgamation would undoubtedly have led to a great impoverishment of the Church's spiritual life.

[2] *Fontes narrativi de S. Ignatio*, i, 638.

change in the attitude of Guidiccioni. While carrying on their work as usual, they were heartened by the encouragement of the Pope, who had begun to use them as though that fourth vow of theirs, to which Ghinucci had strongly objected, was already in operation. He had already sent Broet, and for a time Rodriguez, on a special mission to Siena, and presently dispatched Favre and Laynez to see what they could do with that nest of brigands, Lutherans, and dissolute humanists, Parma. Bobadilla received a brief in March, 1540, instructing him to make Calabria his Palestine, and of the six who then remained in Rome, two, Codure and Salmeron, were at that time marked out by His Holiness for adventures in Ireland. Why was Francis Xavier overlooked in this papal general post? It is difficult to say. Perhaps he was ill, but much more likely God had marked him out and reserved him, as He once did Paul and Barnabas.

In a letter of December, 1538, to one of his faithful friends in Spain, Isabel Roser, Ignatius mentioned that he and his companions were being 'much importuned'[1] by various prelates and others to come and work in their dioceses or dukedoms. Even Majesty itself applied, in the person of King John III of Portugal, on whose conscience an empire weighed. King John has been much maligned, especially in English books unable to forgive him for having introduced the Inquisition into Portugal, but he was substantially a good man and a good Catholic, who showed throughout his long reign (1521–57) the sincerest concern for the welfare, temporal as well as eternal, of the many new peoples subjected to his sway during that brilliant period of Portuguese oversea expansion.[2] Nothing did he more earnestly desire than to have good priests who would bring the knowledge

---

[1] *Infestados*, harassed, pestered, was the strong term he actually used, somewhat to the embarrassment of his modern editors.

[2] Almeida, *História de Portugal*, ii (Coimbra, 1923), 301–71. Also, Ameal, *História de Portugal* (Porto, 1942), 285–311. Maurice Collis's snarl at the King (*The Grand Peregrination*, 1949, 14) is so biased as to be funny. John would have done better for his own good name and for his country's fortunes, if he had managed to carry on without the Inquisition, as Pope Paul III frequently and urgently advised him, but he was in great difficulties with the Jews and ' New Christians ' who swarmed into Portugal when Spain became too hot for them, and made themselves extremely obnoxious (Almeida, l.c., 320–2).

and salvation of Christ our Lord to those peoples, and at the same time keep his own doughty conquerors in the paths of righteousness, a task even more difficult than the other. It was primarily to secure such priests that he had so liberally endowed the Collège de Sainte-Barbe in Paris. On every ship that sailed from Lisbon to India and Brazil there went some Franciscans, Dominicans, Augustinians, or secular priests, but the field was vast, and those good, devoted men were too few to cultivate more than the microscopic portion of it where Portuguese garrisons had established their fortresses. The population of Portugal in those days cannot have been much more than that of Middlesex today. The little country had strained her human resources to breaking point in her tremendous leap over the oceans and could not possibly supply from her private treasure all the missionaries needed. So the cry was always for volunteers from other nations, but Portugal did not make it too easy for them by her insistence, so long as she had the power, that they must invariably travel east or west from Lisbon and in none but Portuguese ships.

In 1538 Diogo de Gouvea, principal of Sainte-Barbe, Paris, drew King John's attention to his former charges, Favre, Xavier, Rodriguez and Ignatius, of whose activities in Italy he had been receiving glowing accounts. He also made a direct appeal to Favre, who replied that he and his companions, one and all, would be delighted to go to India, provided that the Pope, to whom they had vowed their services, approved. ' Should he send us whither you call us, we shall go rejoicing.'[1] Nine months later, in August, 1539, King John wrote to his ambassador in Rome:

Dom Pedro Mascarenhas, my friend. I, the King. As you know, my principal purpose, as that of my Father before me, God reward him, in the enterprise of India and the other conquests which I made and maintain with so much peril, toil and expense, has ever been the increase of our holy Catholic

[1] MHSJ. *Sancti Ignatii de Loyola Epistolae et Instructiones*, i, 132–4. There are twelve volumes in this series, a fact which illustrates the literary fecundity of Ignatius.

faith. For this I have gladly borne everything, and it has been my constant preoccupation to secure for my dominions lettered and virtuous priests to exhort and instruct those newly converted to the faith. This by God's grace I have been enabled to do so far,[1] but now that the work is developing I feel it my bounden duty to obtain new workers. I was recently informed by Mestre Diogo de Gouvea that certain clerics of good attainment and virtuous life had departed from Paris, after vowing themselves to the service of God, and that, living solely on the alms of the faithful, they went about preaching and doing a great deal of good. One of them wrote to the same Diogo at Paris on November 23 last, saying that, if it should please the Holy Father, to whom they have vowed their services, they would go to India. I enclose you a copy of the letter, . . . and commission you with all earnestness to inquire into the lives of those men, their learning, their habits, their aims, letting me know the result, so that I may be sure whether their purpose is to increase and profit the faith by their prayers and example. As the sanction of the Holy Father is necessary in the case, you will petition him in my name to have the goodness to issue the order required. . . .[2]

After diligent investigation, Mascarenhas reported to his royal master on March 10, 1540, that the men answered entirely to his Highness's hopes, that the Pope had told him ' a thousand good things about them ', and that they were eminently qualified for the Indian mission field. In view of the perils and length of the journey, however, the Holy Father felt reluctant to issue an order until the Ambassador had sounded the priests on their willingness

[1] A wild exaggeration, as the story will show. The King had little true information about his Eastern Empire, as the reports from India were written by megalomaniacs anxious to create an impression of vast achievement.

[2] *Sancti Ignatii de Loyola Epistolae et Instructiones*, i, 737–8. The principal business of Mascarenhas in Rome was to press for the *de jure* recognition of the Inquisition, which King John had set up on his own account. He had to plead for fifteen years before the Pope gave in. It is an interesting story, well told in an appendix to an earlier edition of the letters of St. Ignatius (*Cartas de San Ignacio de Loyola*, i, Madrid, 1874, 496–509).

to go. ' I had little trouble in this respect,' Mascarenhas continued, ' for they accepted the proposal with great contentment, though they could offer me only two men owing to their number in Rome being reduced to six, of whom two are destined by the Pope for Ireland and Scotland. One of the men offered is a Portuguese and your Highness's vassal; the other is a Castilian.' By his last sentence the Ambassador meant Rodriguez and Bobadilla, neither of whom ever came within ten thousand miles of India. Francis Xavier does not seem to have been in the running at all, in spite of his dreams and his known eagerness, though a perfect stranger, a young priest named Paul of Camerino,[1] is mentioned as having volunteered and been accepted. It is not a mere surmise that the thoughts and desires of Francis strayed constantly Eastwards. ' He used to talk frequently and fervently about the affairs of India and the conversion to our holy faith of its great gentile population,' related a young Spanish priest named Doménech who had formed a profound attachment to him in Bologna. ' He had his heart set on making the voyage and was all afire to accomplish it before he died.'[2] After the nomination of Rodriguez and Bobadilla, his chances must have seemed very remote. At the time, he was occupied helping Ignatius with his growing correspondence, and in that secretarial capacity drew on his head the raillery of a young recent recruit named Estrada. Writing to Ignatius and Francis from Montepulciano in November, 1539, this worthy said:

I have told you in other letters the particular fruit derived from the purgations or, as you call them, exercises. It astonishes me that I have received no reply. If I felt so inclined I could impute this delinquency to Señor Maestre Francisco, who took

---

[1] This devoted priest who became a Jesuit in India does not appear to have owned a surname and is called after the town of his birth, a small but very ancient place, forty-one miles south-west of Ancona. It boasts a bishopric dating from the third century, a remarkable cathedral, and a most peculiar patron martyr named Venantius, a youth of seventeen, who got into the Roman Martyrology and Breviary by the strangest chance (cf. Thurston, *Lives of the Saints*, v, 225).

[2] *Monumenta Xaveriana*, ii, 832.

it upon himself to answer for you all. But I'll be kind and excuse his remissness so far, while praying him to remember that if the wintry cold has rendered his hands too numb to write, the heat of a fire, which possesses the property of bànishing cold, would make them again fit for the business of clutching a pen. Thus I write, teasing Maestre Francisco, as though I were talking to him face to face. As a matter of fact, owing to the intense cold here I have been obliged myself to light a little fire to get my hands sufficiently thawed out for this letter.[1]

At the moment now reached in this story, March, 1540, unexpected things began to happen in the little circle of Ignatius Loyola. His handy man, tough, stout-hearted Nicholas Bobadilla, arrived back from Naples a wreck of his former self through grave illness. Willing though he was, he would obviously never do for the impending Indian expedition. Rodriguez, his elected partner, had also been ill, but recovered sufficiently to set off by sea for Lisbon on March 5, accompanied by Paul of Camerino and travelling in great state with some of the Ambassador's gentlemen. The Ambassador himself was about to return home by the long land route, and impatiently awaited the second man promised to him. Ignatius, in bed and greatly suffering at the time, hardly knew what to do. Claude Le Jay, the penultimate of the nine on whom he might have called, had just recently been appropriated by the Pope for a mission in Tyrol. So there was only Francis left, Francis the half of his soul, who so short a time before had seemed at the end of his earthly tether. The Ambassador was leaving on March 15. Not until the 14th did Ignatius summon up resolution to make the fateful plunge. ' Francis,' he said, ' you know that by order of his Holiness two of us have to go to India, and that we chose Bobadilla as one of the two. He cannot go now owing to his illness, nor can the Ambassador wait until he gets better. This is your enterprise.' Such was the unemotional scene, a truly Basque picture, etched in the heart's blood of two fast friends who were to part for ever on the morrow. It is recorded

[1] MHSJ. *Epistolae Mixtae*, i, 40–1. Estrada became the most eminent pulpit orator among the early Jesuits.

by Ribadeneira, the man so close to Ignatius, so much of a miser of every detail of his sayings and doings. He goes on to relate the reaction of Francis: 'That Father of blessed memory instantly replied with great joy, " *Pues, sus! héme aquí* ", and there and then set to work patching some old pair of trousers and nondescript soutane.'[1]

On March 15, the day he left Rome for Lisbon in the Ambassador's train, Francis signed and sealed three short secret papers, to be opened if and when his brethren were at length granted the bull then being held up by the opposition of Cardinal Guidiccioni. The first signified his assent to every decision which his companions might take thereafter about their manner of life, ' even if only two or three of them found it possible to come together in Rome '. The second was his vote for Ignatius as superior of the Company, should it receive canonical approval, and the third ran as follows: 'After the Company shall have met and elected a superior, I hereby promise perpetual obedience, poverty and chastity, and I ask my dear Father in Christ Laynez for the service of God our Lord to make this my will known, and to pronounce in my name the three vows of religion before the superior elected.' The parting of Ignatius and Francis was probably as undemonstrative as their Basque natures could make it, but that did not deter romantic biographers from investing the occasion with high ceremony and abundant emotion.[2] Of the journey to Bologna nothing is known beyond a few generalities reported long afterwards by the Ambassador's secretary. Francis

---

[1] MHSJ. *Scripta de S. Ignatio de Loyola*, i, 381. The words of Francis are interjectional and untranslatable. *Sus* is an interjection used ' to move another to the prompt execution of some activity ', while ' *He*, joined with the adverbs *aqui* and *alli*, or with the pronouns *me, te, la, le, lo*, etc., is an adverbial expression used to point out some person or thing ' (*Diccionario de la Lengua Castellana por la Academia Española*, Madrid, 1824, *sub verbis*). Perhaps it is permissible to say that the Spanish expression closely corresponds in meaning with the traditional reply of a subordinate instructed by a superior in the Senior Service of another country, ' Aye aye, Sir ', pronounced with enthusiasm.

[2] Tursellini mentions a visit of Francis to the Pope to obtain his blessing, and that is likely enough. But it is in the last degree unlikely that the Pope made him a long speech in Ciceronian Latin, mainly about the problematical activities of the Apostle St. Thomas in India.

·was ' always at his prayers ', this man told a Jesuit in India. ' He
was very pleasant and genial in his intercourse with others, and
had a way of being the first to saddle and feed the horses in our
cavalcade. His conversation was of God and moved the hearts of
those who heard him to sorrow for their sins and amendment of
their lives. Wherever he passed, he left the remembrance of his
sanctity, above all of his charity, as I myself had good reason to
know.'[1]

The party reached Bologna towards the end of March, and
on the last day of that month Francis happily became his own
historian, though as always a reserved one, in a letter to Ignatius
and Pietro Codazzo:

I received your letter on Easter Sunday, enclosed in a packet
addressed to the Lord Ambassador. Our Lord knows how much
joy and comfort it gave me. As I think that it is only through
the medium of letters we shall see one another again in this
life—in the next it will be face to face with many embraces—
it remains for us during the little time left here below to secure
these mutual glimpses by frequently writing. This is what you
tell me to do, and I shall see to it, as well as to your instructions
about the *hijuelas*.[2] I had a long and pleasant interview, as you
advised, with the Cardinal of Ivrea, who received me with the
greatest kindness and offered to help us by every means in his
power.[3] . . . The Lord Ambassador has provided me with so
many luxuries that I could never finish recounting them. I do
not know how I could endure them were it not for the thought
that in India I may well have to pay for them with my life.
Indeed, I am certain of it. At the shrine of our Lady of Loreto

[1] *Monumenta Xaveriana*, ii, 832–3.
[2] The primary meaning of *hijuela* is little daughter, but it has a dozen
secondary meanings, one of them being a piece of cloth for widening a garment.
The early Jesuits imposed a private meaning on it, namely, a separate sheet,
enclosed with an ordinary letter, containing information not meant for the
general eye.
[3] Cardinal Ferreri, papal legate to Bologna, had been Bishop of Ivrea in
Piedmont for twenty-eight years, and so obtained his title. The help wanted
from him was to intercede with his obdurate brother in the purple, Cardinal
Guidiccioni.

on Palm Sunday, his Lordship and many of his suite made their confessions to me, and the good man arranged that all his retainers might be able to receive Holy Communion with him at my Mass in the Holy House. . . . Would you give my compliments to the Lady Faustina Ancolina, telling her that I have said Mass for her Vincent and mine, and shall say another for herself tomorrow. She can rest assured that I shall never forget her. Remind her from me, Micer Pietro, *hermano mio carissimo*, to keep the promise she made me of going to confession and Holy Communion, and to let me know if she has done so and how often. If she wishes to please Vincent, hers and mine, tell her from me to forgive his murderers, as he is praying much for them in Heaven. I am busier with confessions here than I was at San Luigi dei Francesi. My kindest remembrances to all. Truly, it is not for want of thinking of them that I do not mention them by name.[1]

From Bologna the Ambassador and his retinue wound their way north-west via Modena and Reggio to Parma, where a disappointment awaited Francis. As usual, he says nothing about it, but Favre, recently at work in Parma, does, in a letter to Ignatius of April 16: 'Master Francis arrived here the very day that I left for Brescia. He deliberated about following me to my new destination, but the rest of his party and the Ambassador were against it, and they were right. May the Lord by His grace

[1] Schurhammer, *Epistolae S. Francisci Xaverii,* i, 29–31. The Lady Faustina mentioned at the close of the letter belonged to the high Roman aristocracy and appears to have been a penitent of St. Francis, who, as was his unfailing habit, writes the name incorrectly. He must have had a great deal of trouble with her, for she had become thoroughly embittered by the violent death of her only son and child, as may be seen in the epitaph which she composed for his tomb: ' To Vincenzo Ubaldi, the Roman, knight designate, foully slain in the flower of his youth by Alpine soldiery while collecting a debt, but not unrevenged [*non inultus tamen*], his loving inconsolable mother Faustina Jancolina erected this monument to her darling only child, the last vanished hope of the Ubaldi line.' This rather formidable matron, a Renaissance Cornelia, bequeathed to St. Ignatius and his men her house on the Piazza Colonna, but attached such a multitude of impossible conditions that the gift had to be declined (Tacchi Venturi, *Storia della Compagnia di Gesù in Italia*, i, parte 2a, 15, 223–8).

bring it about that if we are not to see each other again in this world we may rejoice together in the next, not only over our reunion, but over these partings which we endure solely for His love.'[1] Francis, writing to Ignatius and Bobadilla, mentions ' the great toil and hardship' of the journey beyond Parma, and then goes on to extol the Ambassador: ' God's hand was with us in every danger, and He enabled the Ambassador so to rule his family that they seemed more like monks than lay persons. He often went to confession and Holy Communion, as did his servants, inspired by his example. I could find no place in the inns where we put up to hear their confessions, so it became my custom, there being no other way, to ride ahead with my penitent of the moment, dismount, and hear his confession in the open.'

Francis loved to praise other people whenever they gave, or seemed to give, him the opportunity. This was a pronounced trait in his character. He tended to see all his geese as swans, until they forced on him by their conduct compelling evidence to the contrary, and then he would not recriminate but only fall sadly silent about them, which, however, is not in the least to suggest that Pedro Mascarenhas was a goose. For a professional diplomat he appears to have been a singularly upright and devout man, even if much too inclined to identify *Império* with *Fé*, the glory of Portugal with the glory of God. Herein he resembled his sovereign, King John, whose viceroy in India he became at a later date, and it has to be said for both of them that their nationalism was a general plague of that age, except among saints. Francis thought Mascarenhas such a wonder that he believed him capable of working miracles. As the travellers pursued their way towards the Italian frontier, they came to a river in spate from recent rains. An equerry of the Ambassador who had gone to Rome with the idea of becoming a monk and changed his mind determined to display his mettle by fording the swollen torrent on horseback, against all advice and expostulation. Both he and his mount were swept under before he was half-way across, and seemed doomed. Francis when reporting the incident to

[1] MHSJ. *Fabri Monumenta*, 29–30. Brescia is a good hundred miles by road north of Parma.

Ignatius opined, with a sardonic touch not uncommon in his letters, that the swaggering hero ' would have been much better contented, while under the water, had he been in the monastery, but it pleased God our Lord to hear the devout prayers of His servant the Ambassador and to save him, more by a miracle than by human means '. The man profited from his dowsing, for Francis says that he afterwards made a great impression on the company ' by speaking of the pains of Hell as feelingly as if he had been through them '.

Little else is known of the journey into Portugal except that it was through Lyons to Fuenterrabía, the fortress town in which the Xavier brothers had made their last stand for the independence of Navarre. Why did Francis not turn aside to Navarre to say good-bye to those who remained of his family? There is no telling. Perhaps he did turn aside and said nothing about it. It is almost certain that he visited the relatives of St. Ignatius in Guipúzcoa, but he says nothing about that either. Perhaps, on the other hand, Mascarenhas, who was in a hurry, would not have liked the delay caused by a diversion to Navarre. Or perhaps, again, Francis had good reason to know that proud Juan would not want to see him at Obanos after his rejection of the Pamplona canonry. His first biographer, of imagination so compact, propounded a most original solution of the problem. The Ambassador urged Francis with all his might to pay a last visit to his *mother* (who was then eleven years dead!), but the resolute rock-like man steadfastly refused, ' lest some Jesuit of later times be deflected from the straight path of duty by his example '. A more sentimental story is that he climbed some craggy eminence from which he could obtain a last glimpse of Castle Xavier,[1] and that people afterwards named it *La Peña del a Dios*, Farewell Rock, just as they are supposed to have named another hill in the far south of Spain *El Ultimo Suspiro del Moro*.[2] The trouble

[1] He would have needed wonderful sight as Xavier is sixty miles and more from Fuenterrabía. Besides there are no sufficiently lofty crags in the district.

[2] The Moor's Last Sigh, the Moor being poor soft King Boabdil, who was reputed to have wept as he looked back from the hill-top on his lost Granada, shimmering golden in the distance, on his way to African exile in 1492.

with such attributions is that Spaniards are notoriously unsenti-
mental. The ride of Francis from beginning to end was certainly
not less than two thousand miles, no kind of record, but a fair
effort for a man quite unused to the saddle.

CHAPTER V

THE GATEWAY TO THE EAST

LISBON can be a terrible city in summer for a man who has to go about on his feet, for its seven hills are real hills, not just slight rises in the street level, like some of the famous Seven in Rome. Francis Xavier reached his destination towards the end of June, half baked by the fierce Iberian sun. ' He was appalled and daunted by the heat,' wrote Simon Rodriguez, who himself had gone down with a quartan ague almost immediately after his arrival in April and was still in the grip of the disease. Francis went straight to his bedside and found him, despite the utmost efforts of the King's own physician, disconsolately awaiting that very day a fresh onset of his *quartana*. ' But he was so delighted to see me and I to see him,' wrote the visitor afterwards, ' that our united joy expelled the fever and he has not now had an attack for a month. He is very well and doing great work.' Simon much appreciated the honour of having been attended by the King's physician. He liked the company of the illustrious, and seems to have been slightly jealous of Bobadilla who also was addicted to titles. ' Among the many clients on whom we exercise our little talent,' he tells St. Ignatius at this time, ' there are persons of great importance, such as Bobadilla would plume himself on knowing. . . . I have myself given the Exercises to a duke, very fruitfully too, and he one of the principal grandees of the land.'[1] Francis, the hidalgo born, much preferred

---

[1] Schurhammer, *Epistolae S. Francisci Xaverii*, i, 61. Simon's standards could sometimes be a little odd. Reporting to Ignatius the death of the King's brother, the Cardinal Archbishop of Lisbon, he said that this prelate had set a wonderful example of humility, ' for he stooped so low as even to go personally and give Viaticum to the sick ' (l.c., 34). St. Francis seems to have been amused by Bobadilla's capers. That Father, who lived to be eighty-two, prided himself somewhat on having a number of mysterious diseases such as are not given to baser clay. He had no faith in doctors, and used to say that

the company of simple men, and the poorer they were the better he seemed to like them.

Four days after his arrival in Lisbon, he and Rodriguez were commanded to a private audience with the King and Queen, which lasted more than an hour. ' His Highness questioned us in great detail about our manner of life, how we came to know one another and to form our union, our principal desires and aspirations, and the nature of the persecution that befell us in Rome.' So wrote Francis to Ignatius. The King expressed himself as well satisfied with all that he was told, and there and then appointed the two priests confessors of the hundred pages at his court, with general supervision over their conduct. Before the audience closed, he sent for his young son and daughter that the Fathers might greet them, and spoke with feeling about his seven other children, all of whom had died in infancy or when only just out of it.[1] Francis must already have possessed a smattering of Portuguese, picked up, perhaps, from his companions at Sainte-Barbe, for, at the King's request, he began boldly to preach in that difficult language, which was to become to him a second mother tongue. The King, always generous, offered him and Rodriguez comfortable rooms and fare from his own kitchen, but they asked, with all thankfulness, to be allowed to follow their old custom of living at a hospice for the poor and finding their bread in alms. This shows that at heart Simon Rodriguez was as sound as a top. After a while, the two men discovered that the quest for their daily bread took too much time, and agreed to accept the King's dishes on five days of the week, which brought

---

' the subject of medical science is the human body, except the body of Boba-dilla '. He even composed a little tract entitled: *Justa et legitima causa quare Mag. N. Bobadilla non facile credit medicis.* Francis invented the mock term *merachya* for his condition. It is in no dictionary but may, perhaps, have been derived from the Spanish verb, *merar,* to mix liquors.

[1] Even the two brought in that day died at seventeen and eighteen respectively. The King probably did not mention that he had two illegitimate sons, neither of whom survived very long. To have had eleven children but no immediate heir was almost as tragic a record as that of England's Queen Anne. The King's youth had been dissipated, and that may account for the high mortality among his offspring.

great rejoicing to their fellow-guests at the hospice, the chief beneficiaries.

Up and down the precipitous streets that would tire a hardy Alpinist went the indomitable pair on their crowded errands of mercy, rubbing shoulders with Cingalese princes, Indian rajas, even an occasional Negro bishop, not to mention hordes of bewildered African slaves, torn up by the roots as though they were not human beings at all, but some exotic species of useful vegetable. It has been brought against St. Francis that he never fulminated, at least in writing, against the institution of Negro slavery, which Catholic Portugal was the first country to set up in modern times. It is difficult to see what protest he, a stranger and unknown, could have made, and it is a little anachronistic to want him to have been a Wilberforce, in addition to all else great and beautiful that he was. The Portuguese conquerors suffered from divided minds, as did the English conquerors, and all other conquerors. They were as sincerely religious as they were heartily imperialistic, and when they seized unfortunate Africans and brought them to Lisbon or to Goa, it was not entirely for the sake of cheap labour. They genuinely wanted to Christianize the heathen, even when often badly in need of being Christianized themselves. They had no colour prejudice, treated their slaves humanely, and frequently intermarried with them. But the fundamental objection remains, and it would have been pleasant to be able to record that St. Francis Xavier had shot three centuries ahead of his time and condemned the whole abominable practice.

Another charge against the Saint, one that might be lodged against a hundred saints, is that he did not openly condemn the Inquisition. It is tempting to answer that, had he done so, there would be no saint to criticize, for the Inquisition would inevitably have burnt him. But the problem cannot be met by any such smart retort. In October, 1540, Francis wrote to Ignatius as follows:

The Infante Dom Henrique, brother of the King and chief Inquisitor of the Kingdom, has exhorted us on numerous occasions to look after the prisoners of the Inquisition. We visit them every day and do our best to help them to recognize that it is the mercy of God which has put them where they are. On each visit, we preach to them collectively and give them meditations from the first 'week' of the *Spiritual Exercises*, from which they have derived no small profit. Several of them have told us that God our Lord has done them a great favour by thus bringing them to a knowledge of many things necessary for the salvation of their souls.

To that brief reference, Simon Rodriguez added a lurid detail: 'One day recently I clothed a dozen of the prisoners in the *san benito*. Two were burned at the stake, and the chief Inquisitor ordered us to go with them and stand by them to the end, which we did. Others of the twelve were condemned to life imprisonment.'[1] It is really distressing to find a man as tender-hearted and pitiful as St. Francis involved in such merciless doings, but he

[1] Schurhammer, *Epistolae S. Francisci Xaverii*, i, 62, 67. The two unfortunate men burned were a relapsed French cleric and a Portuguese Jew. King John's father, Dom Manuel I, began his reign by showing much clemency and even favour to the Jews and Moors resident in Portugal, but changed completely in 1496, when he saw a chance of marrying the daughter of Ferdinand and Isabella. This unlovable princess refused to have him except on condition that he took a leaf from her father's book and expelled the Jews from his kingdom. He may have sighed as a statesman, but he obeyed as a suitor, and, perhaps to win another of his lady's frosty smiles, even out-Heroded Herod by ordering the forcible seizure and baptism of the Jewish children. When the bishops of Portugal urged on the infatuated man that such baptisms would be invalid by the law of the Church, he answered that he cared nothing for their laws and was acting out of the piety of his heart. The deed brought a curse on Portugal from which she never recovered. Manuel knew right well that the 'New Christians', as the forcibly baptized were called, would be Christians only in name, while faithful to Moses in heart and secret practice. The affront to their consciences and the sacrileges that would necessarily be involved did not trouble him. He wanted the pseudo-Christians for the sake of their financial ability, and made a ruling that, provided they conformed externally, they were not to be molested or called to account for whatever they chose to do behind the scenes. But public opinion, which the Judaizers, wealthy, arrogant and oppressive, did little to placate, eventually forced the King to seek a remedy at the hands of the Pope in the shape of the Inquisition. The Pope refused his consent, and so it came about that Manuel's son, John III, established the tribunal without any sanction from Rome (Almeida, *História de Portugal*, ii, 203–9).

had no choice, and in any case it is highly probable that he considered the sentences just. To his way of thinking heresy was the worst evil in the world, for it involved the ruin of souls. He could stand anything but that, and so was ready even for burnings to prevent it. His attitude was the obverse of the passionate love for souls that consumed him, a love the modern unbelieving liberal or humanitarian could never so much as guess at. Rather than judge St. Francis by the Inquisition, it would be much more sensible to judge the Inquisition by St. Francis. That men such as he and St. Ignatius, its frequent victim, saw no injustice in the tribunal's proceedings is an argument not to be despised by those who seek the truth rather than the legends of history.

An autumn and a winter still separated Francis from the goal of his desires, as no ships sailed East before March 25. A time came when it looked as if he might not be permitted to sail at all. Many important people, including the King's chaplain, started a little plot to retain his services for Portugal where, they maintained, he and Rodriguez could accomplish more for the service of God than would be possible beyond the seas. The King himself came round to that point of view for a while and contemplated writing to the Pope for permission to keep them. But India had influential champions, too, who eventually succeeded in forcing a division of the spoils. Portugal secured her child Simon who, with dukes in profusion to be evangelized, did not break his heart over India, while the gentiles, to his infinite satisfaction, got Francis. He strove with all his might to win others for the great enterprise, but was strangely unsuccessful. In fact, besides a boy named Diogo Fernandes, a relative of Simon Rodriguez, he obtained only one volunteer, a young man at a loose end named Francis Mansilhas, who had little or no education and even less capacity to be educated. This half of a broken hope became the prop and comfort of St. Francis's existence. He dared not put him forward for the priesthood in Portugal, for he would surely have been rejected, but hoped that in India, where standards were more adjustable, the Bishop of Goa, a kindly man, would oblige by ordaining the good fellow on the title, as he put it, ' of voluntary poverty and abounding simplicity'. As for Diogo, he was too young to be of any help, but sturdily went forward and became a Jesuit later on in Goa.

Suddenly one day there came to Francis an offer from a very different type of volunteer, a man of European reputation, even his illustrious second cousin once removed, the Doctor of Navarre. He had recently been secured for the University of Coimbra by the good offices of King John's sister, the Queen of Spain, and very proud Portugal was to possess such a renowned professor. But the good Doctor must have grown tired of teaching canon law, for as soon as he learned that the child he had known long ago at Xavier was in Lisbon, a priest, and bound for India, he conceived a great longing to go with him. He even had the temerity to write to the King, asking him to press his suit with Francis. Genial, boyish-hearted man, he was ever an optimist, and the only result of his moves must have been a royal injunction on Francis to refuse him. It was an embarrassing situation for India's apostle, sweltering in his stuffy confessional ' all the day long and part of the night ', but he liked his distant, distinguished cousin, and dealt very gently with the dreams which he had spread under his feet.

Since my arrival here [he wrote from Lisbon to the Doctor] I have received two letters from you, full of tenderness and affection. May Christ our Lord who moved you to address me reward you for the great kindness and benevolence you have shown. With all the will in the world, I could never myself thank you adequately. Knowing what a sorry creature I am in the expression of gratitude, I comfort myself with the thought that God, in whom I have put all my trust, can answer for me to you and other generous souls. . . . I would be delighted if given a chance to meet you, and may it please God to bring us together before my companion and I set out for India. I could then, much better than through the post, satisfy your wishes by telling you all about myself and the way of life I have embraced. You mentioned that our manner of living has been the subject of much dispute but, Doctor, we are not greatly perturbed by what men think of us, especially when they deliver judgment without really knowing us at all. The bearer of this letter, Blasio Gomez, is anxious to become your servant and disciple. He and I are great friends, so I beg you to take him out of your kindness and the love you bear me. I shall be most grateful, and you will do a service to our Lord by directing his studies. He is entirely devoted to you and wants to consecrate his youth to the pursuit of learning. See how the great talent God has given you finds you out, and clamours to be shared! May God our Lord ever have us both in His keeping. Thine in Him to the end.

The next extant letter of Francis to the same address went off in November, just as he was about to move with King John and his court to the winter palace of Almeirim, eighty leagues north from Lisbon:

Your letter of October 25 was such a joy and consolation to me that nothing short of seeing you face to face, as I ardently desire, could have given me greater refreshment. How good it is to know of your holy labours and employments, teaching those who pursue learning only in order to use it in the service of Christ our Lord. So I haven't the pity for you that I would feel if I thought you a less faithful servant of God, knowing, as I surely do, that the crown of your hard work will be great. . . . I am writing to the Prior of Roncesvalles as you requested. I shall say nothing more until we meet, which may be when you least expect it. The great love for me shown in your letters demands my compliance with your wishes. I say nothing of my love for you. The Lord, the searcher of hearts, knows how dear you are to me.[1]

Was ever a suppliant more sweetly and deftly side-tracked than the good Doctor? Francis obviously expected and desired to meet him, but he never got to Coimbra, though it is only a matter of seventy miles or so from Almeirim, nor did the Doctor, for all his laurels, receive an invitation to court. What other

[1] Schurhammer, *Epistolae S. Francisci Xaverii*, i, 57-9, 71-2.

explanation for this can there be but that the King feared to lose his regius professor and so kept the two friends apart? It may well have been also at his prompting that Francis sorrowfully quenched the professor's missionary hopes by a gentle hint that he was too old at forty-eight for the rigours of India. The Doctor, who outlived him by thirty-four years to become a hale and hearty nonagenarian, probably saw the King's hand in the business and dutifully acquiesced.

As the letters cited and many others yet to be given show, Francis really believed himself to be deficient in a sense of gratitude. The reason of it was his feeling that he could never do enough to repay the kindnesses which he had received, and consequently he experienced a sense of frustration in dealing with his friends, and mistook it for ingratitude. Pedro Mascarenhas had been good to him and his companions, so we find him begging those in Rome to write to the Ambassador, or at least to mention him and send him wishes in other letters addressed to Portugal, which he could be shown. He understood his grandees and knew that they appreciated a little notice. '*Acá son mucho de cumplimientos*,' he said. The grateful heart in him was utterly untainted with the cynical ' lively sense of favours to come '. It was the past favours done him by God and by man which he could never get over. Like St. Teresa, he could be bribed with a sardine. Above all, his love went out to Ignatius and others of the little Company who had cured his blindness and given him so great a vision. In Portugal, he worked for the Company might and main, still thinking it menaced by the august shadow of Cardinal Guidiccioni. The King, Mascarenhas, and other men of power were petitioned to bring their influence to bear on his obstructive Lordship, and willingly did so out of regard for the petitioner. In a letter to Le Jay and Laynez written in March, 1541, just before he sailed for India, he mentioned that he and Paul of Camerino had offered 250 Masses for the Cardinal since leaving Rome and proposed to continue offering them for him every alternate day as long as they lived. The Masses, he said, gave him great comfort, as though he had had some intimation from God of happenings in Rome six months earlier. Guidiccioni and his supporters had withdrawn their opposition to the extent of approving the establishment of the Society of Jesus as a new order in the Church, provided it remained confined to sixty professed members. As they numbered nothing like sixty at the time, Ignatius and his men did not greatly worry about the restriction, which God, if He willed them to expand, could remove at any moment. The bull, *Regimini militantis Ecclesiae*, which gave the Jesuits the freedom of the Church, was signed and became law on September 27, 1540, but that good news did not reach St. Francis until long after his arrival in India. More than three years later, he and the priest from Camerino were still cheerfully saying a daily Mass for the old Cardinal, whose name Francis never learned to spell. ' To all intents and purposes,' he reported, ' Father Paul and I have become El Reverendissimo Guidation's perpetual chaplains.' ' Guidation ' had been kind, even if a little slow about it, so he must be remembered in perpetuity.

King John was another enrolled into the ever-growing order of merit instituted by Francis. He had promised to establish a college for the new Company in Coimbra, as well as residences in Lisbon and Evora. He is the finest King in the world, Ignatius is told, and ' we would fall into the sin of ingratitude if we did not pray for him all the days of our lives '. Francis was not so good a judge of character as Ignatius. He tended to jump to conclusions on too little evidence, and consequently suffered disappointments which a more cautious estimate of human nature, particularly the nature of Portuguese imperialists, might have spared him. The governors of Portuguese India were changed every three years, and a new one, Martim Affonso de Sousa, was in Lisbon, preparing to sail at the same time as Francis and his companions. It is difficult to get at the truth of this highly complex and many-sided man, already famous for his prowess on the Indian seas and in Brazil. The historians of his own country paint him in very gloomy colours, and a classic English authority, taking his cue from them, blackened him still further. ' In Martim Affonso de Sousa,' wrote this good scholar, ' Portuguese India had one of the worst governors that up to that date had afflicted it. The government, if such it could be called, became little more than an organization for robbery.' After that general introduction, the reader is regaled for twelve pages with accounts of the ogre's iniquities.[1] Now let us hear St. Francis Xavier on the same man.

> The Governor [he tells St. Ignatius] is taking us with him on his flagship, and shows us so much love that he will not have anybody else but himself concerned with our embarkation. He is personally providing for all our needs, and has even invited us to his table. He is well acquainted with India, as he was out there many years and much beloved by everybody, as he is at this court. He told me the other day that in an island of India where there are no Moors nor Jews, but only heathen, we are sure to gain a great harvest and to convert without difficulty the king of the said island and all his people.[2]

St. Francis will pay yet warmer tributes to de Sousa, and de Sousa will show himself deserving of them. He had an element

[1] Whiteway, *The Rise of Portuguese Power in India* (London, 1899), 279-90. Whiteway was a retired Indian civil servant and a man of much learning. But his book is very one-sided, though he occasionally finds something good to say about a Portuguese official. He maintained the proposition, surely odd when everything is taken into account, that the Portuguese were much less civilized than the Indians whom they despised and plundered. Did they worship cows and monkeys in Portugal ? Had they there the cruel institution of child-marriage ? Were widows in Lisbon encouraged, even compelled by custom, to commit suicide when their husbands died? Was temple prostitution ever a feature of Portuguese religion? India did indeed produce great sages and artists, but until a few years ago a considerable proportion of her population, the untouchables, were not regarded as having any human rights at all. The Portuguese Albuquerque suppressed suttee wherever he found it in the sixteenth century, but the English authorities tolerated the abominable practice until the governorship of Lord William Bentinck in the second quarter of the nineteenth century.

[2] Schurhammer, *Epistolae S. Francisci Xaverii*, i, 79-80. The island in question was Ceylon and the king, a certain Bhuvaneka Bâhu. When Captain of the Seas in those parts in 1536 and the following years, de Sousa came to the assistance of the King against his enemies, and Portugal's enemies, the Moslems, whom Spaniards and Portuguese, knowing them chiefly as such, invariably called Moors, though they were practically all from Arabia. Bhuvaneka Bâhu was genuinely grateful to de Sousa for his protection, and gave that warrior reason to believe that he might turn Christian, which in fact he never had any intention of doing.

of the pirate in him undoubtedly, but the same is to be said of all the great sea captains of the sixteenth century, particularly the English ones. Moreover, he confined his occasional depredations to the heathen world and never warred on his fellow-Christians, as did the English, the French and the Dutch. Finally, during his brief term of office he tried very earnestly, according to his lights, to propagate the Christian faith, which was not exactly the motive behind the splendid exploits of, say, Sir Francis Drake. But Martim Affonso was by no means the sound authority on India which Francis Xavier imagined him to be. None of the Portuguese conquerors had much understanding of the real India that lay beyond the reach of their coastal guns. Their gift was rather for exploitation than for exploration, and they moved about, brave fellows, with immense self-confidence, in worlds completely unrealized. What they lacked in knowledge they made up for by imagination, and the result was a sad amount of delusion for St. Francis, who had his innocent head stuffed with travellers' tales before he left Lisbon at all.[1]

As so often in his life, he turned for guidance to St. Ignatius, and wrote in the plural because thinking also of his two companions· on the journey into the unknown:

For the love and service of God our Lord, we beg you to write and tell us at great length how you consider we ought to deal with the infidels. . . . We pray and beseech you again and again, by the friendship which unites us so intimately in Christ Jesus, to give us your ideas and counsels as to the way we should proceed in order the better to serve God our Lord. We long with all our hearts to have the will of our Lord made known to us by you. We beseech you to give us a special remembrance in your prayers, seeing that the length of the voyage and the littleness of our ability to deal this first time with the heathen plead for much more of your charity than usual. . . . In conclusion, we pray Christ our Lord that you

[1] The Portuguese had no monopoly of misinformation. Two hundred years after the death of St. Francis, travellers home from India, English, French, Dutch, Italian, were still regaling an open-mouthed Europe with the most fantastic nonsense about the beliefs and customs of the Hindus.

and we may be reunited in Heaven, since I doubt whether in this world we shall see one another again. . . . Let the first of us to go to God beg Him to bring together once more in His glory the brethren He loved here below.[1]

St. Ignatius's knowledge of non-Christians was extremely slender. In the early days of his conversion he had met a Moor in Spain and wondered whether it was not his duty to slaughter the dog. In Palestine, he had encountered a number of Saracens who may well have wondered whether it was not their duty to do the same by him. That was the extent of his experience, so he had nothing to offer his friend Francis but his prayers. At any rate, Francis escaped the kind of briefing which poor Ignatius, misled by Roman pundits, gave to Broet and Salmeron when Pope Paul, in the innocence of his heart, sent those brave, unfortunate men off on their wild-goose chase in Ireland.

King John, in spite of his seeing and hearing so much of them, appears to have been a little puzzled as to the status of Francis, Simon and Paul. Monks he knew, friars he knew, secular priests he knew, but the mysterious three fitted into none of those categories. He would therefore invent a title for them himself. In a letter to his majordomo and favourite, the Conde de Castan-heira, he said: 'Conde, my friend, as you are aware, Mestre Francisco and Micer Paulo, clerics of the order of St. Peter, are going this year to India. I strongly commend them to you, and request you to issue orders concerning their embarkation and hospitable reception aboard ship. See that each of them is given two suits of clothes, one for the voyage and one for use in India.

[1] Schurhammer, *Epistolae S. Francisci Xaverii*, i, 80–2. Speaking of his farewell audience with the King, Francis wrote: ' His Highness is very sorry for the unhappy state of the Indians and deeply anxious that God should not be continually offended by those souls He created, and redeemed at so dear a price. His zeal for the honour of Christ our Lord and the salvation of his neighbour should cause us to give infinite praise and thanks to God. Had I not witnessed it, I could hardly have believed it. . . .' The genuineness of the King's zeal is beyond question, but it may well be doubted whether it was a zeal according to wisdom, for some of the measures he ordered, the destruction of temples on the island of Goa, for instance, were more calculated to antagonize the Indians than to convert them. Besides, it was unjust ; not only a blunder but a crime.

Let them have such books as they request and need, and also give instructions for the provision of medicines and everything else requisite for their journey.'[1] The Count strongly pressed Francis to take with him a valet or *moço de camara* whom the King would provide, but Francis begged the Count for the love of God to spare him such an encumbrance. ' Well, then,' the great man insisted, ' you must at least take an ordinary servant to attend to your wants on the voyage, for it would diminish your credit and authority with the other passengers, whom it will be your duty to instruct, were they to see you washing your clothes at the side of the ship, and preparing your meals, just like themselves.' To which argument Francis replied with some heat: ' Señor Conde, it is credit and authority acquired by the means you suggest which have reduced the Church of God and her prelates to their present plight. The right way to acquire them is by washing one's own clout and boiling one's own pot, without being beholden to anybody, while at the same time busying oneself in the service of souls.'[2] The reply so stunned the Count that he had not another word to say. Francis did, however, accept for himself and his companions three *bernias* or cloaks of coarse wool, ' against the cold of the Cape of Good Hope, and also a few books necessary in India but not obtainable there '. The only book, besides his Breviary and a species of catechism, which he is known for certain to have taken still exists, a little thick volume (an 18mo.), published at Cologne in 1531, containing excerpts from the Scriptures, St. Jerome, St. Gregory the Great, Eusebius, Cassian, and other ecclesiastical writers. Possibly, it was St. Jerome's contributions which attracted Francis to the anthology.[3]

[1] MHSJ. *Documenta Indica*, ed. Wicki, i (Rome, 1948), 3–4.

[2] MHSJ. *Monumenta Xaveriana*, ii, 836–7.

[3] He is known to have carried the book about with him in India, but unlike his junior contemporary, St. Teresa of Jesus, who heavily annotated her copy of Osuña's *Third Spiritual Alphabet*, now one of the chief treasures of San José, Avila, he made no mark of any kind on the pages. Père Cros admired the virgin condition of the little volume, and stated primly that Francis thus kept by anticipation the rule later imposed on Jesuits of not writing in the margins of books provided for their use. The true reason was probably that Francis most unfortunately never had enough spare time to set down his thoughts in the blank spaces.

The voyage to India in the sixteenth century was regarded as a very desperate undertaking by all those who went on it and survived to tell their experiences. If Camoens, who kept his life though he lost his entire fortune on the hungry seas, is to be trusted, the departure from Lisbon resembled in many respects a funeral:

The multitude already deemed us lost
In the long mazes of a barren chase.
The wails of women saddened all the coast,
Mixed with the groans of men, a dismal bass.
Brides, mothers, sisters, as they loved the most,
With deepest anguish sought a last embrace. . . .

Old men that creep as if they read the ground,
And little children, tottering as they go,
In imitation of the mourners round
Lament for sorrows deeper than they know.
The neighbouring mountains murmured back the sound,
As if to pity moved for human woe,
Uncounted as the grains of golden sand
The tears of thousands fell on Belem's strand.[1]

Among the earliest detailed accounts of the voyage is one by an Italian Jesuit named Alexandro Valignano who left Lisbon for India in March, 1574, and travelled thence to Malacca, Macao, and Japan. He had a relatively good journey and reached India in the excellent time of five months and sixteen days, whereas Francis Xavier took one whole year and twenty-nine days to attain the same goal. It is in a manuscript biography of St. Francis that Valignano, the greatest organizer of missions

[1] *The Lusiads*, canto iv, stanzas 89, 92. Camoens is describing the scene at the sailing of Vasco da Gama in 1497, but as he was not born at the time he must have drawn on his own later experience. He was a boy of fourteen in Lisbon when St. Francis Xavier went off. The Tower of Belem (Bethlehem) with the great Hieronymite monastery and church were begun in A.D. 1500 as a monument to the Portuguese discoverers. The Tower stands at the spot from which Vasco da Gama—and Francis Xavier—sailed. Lisbon let Camoens die in a poorhouse, but gave him a magnificent tomb in Belem church.

the Jesuits have produced, ventilates his opinions of life on the ocean waves in the brave old times when ships were ships and men were men.

The perils and hardships suffered on this expedition [he says] are very extensive and terrifying. The first hardship is lack of accommodation. True, the ships are large and powerful, but so packed with passengers, merchandise and provisions that there is little room left for any one to move about, and the ordinary people aboard, for whose comfort there is no arrangement whatever, must stand all day on deck in the blazing sun and sleep there somehow all night in the cold. On the other hand, the berths put at the disposal of noble or wealthy persons are so low, so narrow, so confined, that it is all a man can do to fit himself into them. The second hardship has to do with food and drink. Though his Highness the King provides daily rations of biscuit, meat, fish, water and wine sufficient to keep the passengers alive, the meat and fish are so salty, and the provision of utensils to collect the rations so inadequate, that the suffering on this account, especially among the soldiers, beggars description. The third hardship among the general run of the voyagers is due to their being poor and happy-go-lucky. They set out with insufficient clothing, the little they bring soon rots on their backs, and they suffer dreadfully in lower latitudes, both from the cold and from the stench of their rags. The fourth hardship is caused by the calms off the Guinea Coast, which may last for forty, fifty or sixty days. During that time the passengers almost sweat their souls out and suffer torments from the heat beyond the power of my pen to set forth. The fifth hardship, and the worst of any, is the lack of water. During much of the voyage, the water doled out in the daily ration is so foul and malodorous that it is impossible to bear the stench of it, and the passengers have to put a piece of cloth before their mouths to filter off the corruption. This liquid is distributed only once a day, and many fail to get their portion through having no jugs in which to collect it. Others drink their entire ration at one gulp, the result being that large numbers die of thirst.[1] The sixth hardship results from disease of every description among the passengers, who suffer a thousand miseries before dying or recovering. The King appoints a surgeon to each ship, but he and his remedies soon cease to be of any use.

Having thus listed six typical *incomodidades*, Valignano proceeds to make a parallel inventory of the perils which the passengers on the coffin-ships had to face. The first, of course, came from the elements, especially tempests in the region of the most famous of the world's capes, which its Portuguese discoverer, Bartholomew Diaz, named feelingly Cabo de Todos os Tormentos, Cape of all the Storms.[2] The second peril was from shoals and reefs ' which keep all souls aboard in a continual state of alarm ', the third peril was from fire, ' always possible owing to the amount of gunpowder, bitumen, pitch and tar in the holds '. The fourth peril was from French corsairs lurking off the Azores, the fifth, from the exhaustion of the filthy water in the tanks, and the sixth, the ever imminent one of death:

It often happens that the majority of the passengers die, sometimes two hundred, sometimes three or four hundred, on a single ship, and it is the most heart-rending thing to watch each day the poor inflated bodies being committed to the sea. With all these and other perils, it is extraordinary that so many Portuguese should seek to come to India every year. Yet they

[1] Valignano afterwards reverts to the question of thirst, mentioning that the water, such as it was, usually gave out altogether before the end of the voyage, and that the gums of many passengers became ' so swollen and ulcerated from the saltiness of the food that they could no longer eat at all '. Twenty-seven years later, the well-known French traveller, François Pyrard de Laval, confirmed every detail of the Jesuit's report. ' The water,' says he, ' becomes putrid and full of big worms.'

[2] It was Bartholomew's sovereign, King John II, who rechristened the fateful promontory Cabo de Boa Esperança, by reason of the hope which it gave of reaching India by sea, and so of outflanking the Moslem monopolists of eastern trade. Diaz rather than his jealous rival and supplanter, Vasco da Gama, was the real epoch-maker. He had turned the Cape without knowing it, and might have discovered India ten years before the other man did, had not his frightened crew rebelled and forced him sorrowfully to go back to Lisbon.

do, and as cheerfully as though India was only a league from Lisbon. They embark with no other linen than the shirts on their backs, with a couple of loaves in their hands, a cheese, a pot of marmalade, and nothing else whatever.[1]

Owing to spring gales along the Portuguese coast in 1541, the little fleet of five ships, including the carrack or larged armed merchantman *Santiago* which was to take the Governor and the three Jesuits, could not set sail until April 7, a crucial fortnight late that would add six months to the duration of the voyage. St. Francis mentions that upwards of seven hundred men embarked with him on the *Santiago*. They were from all classes of society and walks of life: the Governor and his retinue of officials, rich merchants bent on becoming richer, a large contingent of good-natured, hard-drinking and hard-swearing soldiers, Portugal's unemployed, the men with one shirt which they were putting on India as the dark horse that would bring them fortune, the black cargo of African slaves taken from Lisbon's forty thousand of such poor wretches, and finally a choice collection of Portugal's criminal population, the *desesperados*, being shipped to perish in such infernos as Mozambique and Ormuz. No women were permitted to go, in accordance with Albuquerque's policy of persuading soldiers and deportees to find Indian spouses.[2]

[1] MHSJ. *Monumenta Xaveriana*, i, 10–13. One of the great collections of Portuguese literature, a very encyclopedia of disaster, is called *Historia Tragico-Maritima*. That work and the relevant volumes of the Hakluyt Society, still happily flourishing, are the chief sources for seafaring conditions during the century of Portuguese expansion. There are two moving accounts of wrecks on the Indian route during the sixteenth century in *Portuguese Voyages*, published in Everyman's Library in 1947. For Jesuit maritime adventures in general, there is no better book than *Jesuiten zur See: Der Weg nach Asien*, by F. A. Plattner, S. J., Zurich, 1946. The *Roteiro de Lisboa a Goa* of João de Castro, who set out on the journey in 1538, is sadly disappointing, except for people interested in the science of navigation. John could think of nothing but his nautical tables, though he does admit to having been badly scared off the Cape by a sudden squall ' which lasted the space of three Credos '. The Cape had the effect of making even mathematicians reckon in pious terms.

[2] Camoens nicknamed Albuquerque ' the Terrible ', and with reason. After his second and final conquest of Goa from the Moslems in 1510, he wrote as follows to King Manuel : ' In the capture of Goa our Lord did much for

It was on his thirty-fifth birthday that St. Francis Xavier sailed down the Tagus to the first of the three oceans on which he was so often to be tossed and tormented. In his valedictory letter to St. Ignatius, he said: ' Please let your annual letter to us in India be a very big one, so big that it may take us eight days to read it, and give us detailed, specific news of each and all of the brethren.' Just one day later, April 8, 1541, Ignatius had the generalship of the diminutive Society of Jesus thrust upon him by every vote except his own, but official news of that event did not reach St. Francis in India for two and a half years more.[1] His first letter back to his Roman brethren was written on New Year's Day, 1542, from Mozambique, the miasmal coral island off the east coast of Africa which Albuquerque had wrested from its Arab sheik and fortified:

We left Lisbon on April 7 last year, and I was seasick for two months. It was miserable off the coast of Guinea owing to prolonged calms. We had forty days of them, and the weather was no help,[2] but God in His great mercy brought us to an

---

us. . . . Afterwards, I burnt the City and put all to the sword. For four consecutive days your soldiers slaughtered the Moors, not sparing a single one. They herded them into mosques and then set those buildings on fire. We reckoned that six thousand Moors had been slain. Sir, it was a great deed, well fought and well finished, the first time that vengeance has been taken in India for the treacheries and villanies perpetrated by the Moors against your Highness and your people. I am not leaving a single Moorish tomb or building standing, and the Moors captured I have caused to be burned alive. . . . I am giving the property and lands of the Great Mosque as an endowment for the church in honour of St. Catherine which I am building, for it was on her day [November 25] and on account of her merits that our Lord gave us the victory ' (*Cartas de Affonso de Albuquerque*, six volumes, Lisbon, 1884 sq., i, 26). The mixture of piety and ferocity in that letter reminds one forcibly of Oliver Cromwell, but Albuquerque possessed qualities of loyalty and disinterestedness which the dour Protector lacked. He did not make war on women, and married 450 captive Moslem belles to those of his soldiers who would have them. He abolished suttee, but showed himself greatly tolerant of Hindu custom and religion.

[1] Ignatius flatly refused the honour, so there had to be another election four days later. The result was the same, but he again refused and persisted in refusing until his Franciscan confessor warned him that he must stop resisting the Holy Spirit (*Fontes narrativi de S. Ignatio*, i, 16–22).

[2] One of St. Francis's habitual understatements. François Pyrard is more explicit about weather in the doldrums: ' The heat is violent and stifling in

island where we now are. As I am sure that you will like to know whether the Lord made use of us to serve His servants, I shall tell you what we have done. Immediately on arriving at this island, we took charge of the poor sick folk who came out on the ships. I heard their confessions, gave them Viaticum, and helped them to die holily, while Micer Paul and Micer Mansilhas attended to their temporal needs. I granted them those plenary indulgences which the Pope conceded to me for the Eastern world, and practically all of them died very happily when they knew how fully I was empowered to absolve them. All three of us share our lives and take our rest with the poor people, doing what we can for them materially as well as spiritually, according to our limited and feeble capacity. As for the good results, they are God's secret, seeing that He is the cause of them all. The Governor and his gentlemen are well aware that we are not here for any personal advantage, but for God's sake alone, and we derive no little consolation from this circumstance. As for myself, the hardships of the voyage were of such a kind that otherwise I would not have faced them during a single day for the whole world.[1] . . . We beg you all for the love of our Lord to remember us specially in your prayers and Masses, knowing as you so well do of what base metal we are made. One of the things which greatly comforts us and makes us hope increasingly for the mercy of God is the complete conviction we have of lacking every talent necessary for the preaching of the Gospel in pagan lands. As anything we do is done for God our Lord alone, our hope and confidence

---

the extreme; it destroys most of the provisions: all kinds of meat and fish go bad, even the most carefully salted; all the butter we had was melted to oil and so were the tallow candles. The ships began to split in those parts which were not under water, the pitch and tar likewise melted, and it was as impossible to remain below as to stay in a red-hot oven.' Pyrard then goes on to speak of sudden and fearful thunderstorms, of great whirlwinds and waterspouts, and of cruel warm rains which rotted clothing and covered men's skins with tumours and boils (*The Voyages of François Pyrard de Laval*, London, the Hakluyt Society, 1887, i, 11–12).

[1] '*Los trabajos eran de tal calidad, que yo no me atreviera sólo un dia por todo el mundo.*' That generalization, coming from whom it did, must surely be regarded as the most fearful of all comments on the voyage to India.

grow greater daily that He will give us abundantly in His own good time whatever we need to promote His service and glory. If you know any men in Rome who are keenly desirous of serving God, you would do a good and fruitful deed by directing them to Portugal, whence they could come out on the annual sailings to India. During the voyage, I preached every Sunday, and here in Mozambique I do so whenever I can. The good will, the affection, the love shown us by the Governor assures us that whatever favour we need for the service of God we can obtain at his hands. I would love to be able to go on writing to you, but at present sickness makes it impossible. They bled me for the seventh time today, and I am middling well, praise be to God. My best wishes to all our acquaintances and friends. Francisco.[1]

The ship's surgeon provided for the *Santiago* was a man named Cosme Saraiva. At a judicial inquiry made by order of the King of Portugal in Goa four years after the death of St. Francis, this man was summoned as a witness and gave the following sworn testimony:

I came out from Portugal on the same ship as Father Francis, and often watched him at his charitable occupations and while he taught Christian doctrine. He used to beg alms from other passengers for the poor and sick persons. He took personal charge of such as were ailing or prostrated by illness. From this work of mercy, and from his hearing of confessions, he allowed himself never a moment's respite, but cheerfully

[1] Schurhammer, *Epistolae S. Francisci Xaverii*, i, 91–3. About Mozambique François Pyrard, who arrived there from St. Malo in 1604, had the following remarks to make : ' From thence very rich cargoes are brought to Goa, chiefly of slaves or Cafres, which are carried everywhere. . . . It is an island, a fortress and a haven, well adapted for a refuge to ships after they have passed the Cape of Good Hope. You might call it . . . a kind of hostelry for the refreshing of the Portuguese, worn out with a long, toilsome voyage amid such heats and calms as attend the passage of the line. Hence are produced the many ailments of scurvy and pestilential fevers, whereof full many die. It is no wonder they are glad enough to fetch some port, and there is none nearer than Mozambique. It is a very small island, low-lying, and the air very unwholesome ' (*Voyages*, ii, 224).

accomplished it all.[1] Everybody held him for a saint, and that was my own fixed opinion. At Mozambique, the Father gave himself so completely to the service of those who were taken from the five ships already ill, and to those who fell ill afterwards during the winter spent on the island, that only forty or forty-one of the sufferers died. Everybody regarded this as a marvellous thing, indeed as a real miracle due under God to the devotedness and goodness of the Father. He fell sick himself in consequence of his crushing labours, and I took him to my lodging to care for him. So bad did he become that I had to bleed him nine times, and for three whole days he was out of his senses. I noticed that while in delirium he raved unintelligibly about other things, but in speaking of the things of God was perfectly lucid and coherent. As soon as he was convalescent, he resumed his former labours with all his old enthusiasm.[2]

Another witness cited by the same Goan tribunal was a certain Mestre João, a married man who, like Dr. Saraiva, had come East with de Sousa's fleet. After taking his oath on the Gospels, Master John testified in the following terms:

Padre Francisco laboured so hard for the sick at the hospital in Mozambique where he had installed himself, as well as for many other fever-stricken persons on the island, that he became dangerously ill. I visited him and begged him to moderate his activities while he was so sick, if he did not want to kill himself. He could return to them, I told him, when he had recovered somewhat. He answered me that throughout the following night he had a little business to do with a poor fellow who was at death's door and astray in his mind. When he had finished

---

[1] ' Nunca seçava hum momento, e tudo fazia com muita alegrya.'

[2] Monumenta Xaveriana, ii, 187–8. The passage is given in indirect speech in the original. Francis himself reported in a letter to Europe that eighty persons had died, but he was probably referring to the voyage as a whole, and not, like the Doctor, to Mozambique alone. Both numbers, forty or eighty, were relatively very small. Jean Moquet who sailed to India seventy years later reported that 755 persons died at Mozambique on that occasion.

it he would relax. The man he referred to was a deck-hand and had been delirious for some days. Next morning, I went to the hospital again and visited the Father in the cell which he occupied. I found the sailor lying in his bed, an affair made out of thongs with nothing over them but a scrap of old cloth and a pillow. Up against the bed was a piece of wood taken from a gun-carriage, and on this the Father himself lay, conversing with the sailor, who had completely recovered his senses as soon as he was put into the bed. He died that evening, after making his confession and receiving holy Viaticum, and his good end caused the Father great happiness. Indeed, he always looked happy, no matter what his sufferings and burdens.[1]

That last sentence was echoed by several different people who either knew Francis on the voyage or learned about him afterwards from others on board. Their favourite adjective for him is *alegre*, meaning cheerful, merry, gay, in both Spanish and Portuguese. It was this trait and his unalterable friendliness that brought the sinners and tough customers spontaneously to his feet. 'May God be praised,' he wrote later on, 'who was so good to me, so merciful as to use me to interpret His word according to each one's need, while we sailed through the realm of the fishes.'[2]

---

[1] *Monumenta Xaveriana*, ii, 211–12. Francis performed all the functions of a real nurse for the sick, washed them and their clothes, fed them, gave them their medicines with his own hands, and emptied and cleaned the commodes—*los servicios*—which they used (*Monumenta Xaveriana*, i, 15 ; ii, 838).

[2] ' *Navegando por el señorio de los peces* ' (Schurhammer, *Epistolae*, i, 120).

CHAPTER VI

ISLAM AND VISHNU-LAND

ST. FRANCIS had been six months on his coral island (August, 1541, to February, 1542), waiting with the Governor and the other voyagers for the April monsoon to waft them all to their destination across the Indian Ocean and the Arabian Sea. For obscure reasons, of which Francis says nothing but which historians with none of his facilities declare confidently to have been disreputable, de Sousa suddenly elected to make use of a ship recently arrived from India named the *Coulam*[1] and to sail to Goa ahead of his fleet, without the help of the south-west monsoon. But he would not venture on the risky voyage without the help of Francis, to whom naturally he had become much attached. The *Coulam*, a small, unarmed and unescorted merchantman, might easily run into a fleet of Turkish galleys, in which case it would be a great comfort to have a priest, and such a priest, at one's side .So Francis had to go, leaving the sick to the care of Paul of Camerino and Mansilhas. He expected

[1] A Portuguese trading-station, now Quilon in Travancore. In his book, *Os Portugueses no mar* (Lisbon, 1926), Quirino da Fonseca states that of 1,344 old Portuguese ships whose names are known 1,203 were called after the Blessed Virgin, the saints, and mysteries of the Catholic faith. According to the contemporary historian Gaspar Correa, the reason for de Sousa's hurry was that he hoped to catch his predecessor, Estevam da Gama, in some misdemeanour and thus gain credit for himself with King John. Whiteway, who appears to have swallowed Correa whole, says that he behaved ' rather as if he were in pursuit of a fraudulent bank clerk than as if he were a new governor taking over charge from a retiring one ' (*The Rise of Portuguese Power*, 278). One thing de Sousa seems certainly to have done which recoiled on the head of St. Francis Xavier long afterwards. He arrested at Mozambique Estevam's brother, Alvaro da Ataìde da Gama, third son of the great Vasco, took him prisoner to Goa on the *Coulam*, and kept him in durance for several months. Francis had nothing whatever to do with this affair, but his friendship with the Governor appears to have damned him irretrievably in the embittered Alvaro's eyes. Anyhow, at a critical juncture in the Saint's life Alvaro made himself as unpleasant and obstructive as he possibly could, a sad story that will be told in its own place.

to welcome those good companions at Goa in September but, through various chances, did not set eyes on them again for well over a year. As the unfriendly north-east monsoon still blew when the *Coulam* weighed anchor, de Sousa, though in such an unchristian hurry, was obliged to hug the African coast right up to the Gulf of Aden, but saved time by calling at only two places, Malindi in Kenya and a harbour near Suk on the north side of Socotra.[1]

At Malindi, Francis made his first acquaintance with the Moslem world, that great and powerful polity of Islam which had been and was still so fearful a menace to Christian civilization. But trade relations often had the effect of softening religious asperities, and such was the case in fortunate Malindi, as Francis himself, who loved not Moors, reported.

> Portuguese merchants are usually to be found in the place [he wrote] and when they die they are buried in fine tombs, with crosses over their remains. Close to the city, the Portuguese have erected a great stone cross, gilded and very beautiful. God our Lord knows the consolation which the sight of it gave me, standing there, alone and victorious, in the land of the Moors. . . . I went into the city to bury a man who had died on our galleon, and the Moors were edified by seeing how we Christians lay our dead to rest. One of them, a man highly respected in the city, asked me whether our churches were much frequented, and if our people prayed with fervour. He said that devotion had declined markedly among his own community, and wondered if the same thing had happened to the Christians. He told me that there were seventeen mosques in Malindi, but that not more than three had now any worshippers, and these few in number. He could not understand why there had been such a serious falling-off in devotion, and

[1] It was from Malindi that Vasco da Gama, helped by the right monsoon, made his famous dash across the unknown ocean to Calicut. In his account of the exploit, Correa says that Malindi was then, what it certainly is not now, ' a great city of noble buildings, and surrounded by walls ', the capital of a benign old Moslem king who swore eternal friendship with the Portuguese. That child of Allah had little option, with Vasco's big guns trained on his walls.

gave as his opinion that it must have resulted from some great sin. We argued the point a long while, but he was not satisfied with my solution, that God, the all-faithful, abided not with infidels and took no pleasure in their prayers. . . . A priest of Mohammed in this city, very learned in the law, has said that if the Prophet does not return to visit his people within two years, then they may as well give up believing in him and his sect. It is natural that infidels and great sinners should live in fear and distrust, a state which is a mercy of God to them, without their being aware of it.[1]

That passage reveals one of the serious limitations of St. Francis as a preacher of Christian truth to non-Christians. In his dealings with sinners within the fold, sailors, soldiers, slaves, traders, officials, he could be and was the very soul of pity and understanding. The Jesuit provincial superior in India at the time of his death, Padre Antonio de Quadros, admitted to having been astonished and even a little frightened by the daring of some of his manoeuvres to rescue men from their vices. 'Truly,' wrote this good authority in 1555, 'he was, like St. Paul, all things to all men, with Lascars a Lascar, and with other types, completely one of themselves.'[2] But a change came over him when his inter-

---

[1] Schurhammer, *Epistolae S. Francisci Xaverii*, i, 122–3. The stone cross which thrilled Francis at Malindi was erected by Vasco da Gama in 1498. It was one of many *padraões* planted by the Portuguese conquerors wherever their ships touched, to signify that the adjacent territory had come under the *padroado* or patronage of the Portuguese Crown. The crosses bore the royal arms of Portugal and an inscription. This *padroado* was recognized by the Popes, who had little option but to recognize it, and has been a bone of contention between Portugal and other countries through all subsequent centuries. As already mentioned, it led to such intolerable requirements as that all missionaries, no matter what their nationality, must travel East via Lisbon and on Portuguese ships. In our own time Portugal graciously abandoned her *padroado* rights in India and other Eastern lands. Francis probably misunderstood the reference to Mohammed, the one in question being most likely, not the founder of Islam, but the twelfth Imâm of the Shiite sect, who bore the same name and disappeared mysteriously as a boy in A.D. 879. The Shiites, who were mainly Persians, are traditionally supposed to have established Malindi. They believed that their long lost Imâm would return as Mahdi, or Moslem Messiah, to restore all things and convert the world to Islam.

[2] '*Com os lascarins lascarim, e com todos todo*' (*Monumenta Xaveriana*, ii, 953).

locutor happened to be a Moslem or a Brahman. He stiffened and
fell back on the old slogan, ' the Christians are right, the Pagans
are wrong ', which is perfectly true, but not the best way to win
the attention or the sympathy of the pagans. Not sober Catholic
theology but an overwhelming prejudice bred in his Spanish
bones dictated his hard answer to the Moslem doctor, who was
so plainly an earnest searcher after God. How could Francis be so
sure that the prayers of such a one were not pleasing to God? At
any rate, they were very pleasing to Him when He was visible
on earth, a man amongst men, and worked miracles for the pagan
Centurion and the pagan Woman of Syrophoenicia. The mercy
of Christ our Lord is not limited by the Seven Sacraments which
He instituted to be the normal channels of sanctifying grace. He
can produce in men's souls the effects of the Sacraments without
the Sacraments, and may have seventy times seven other and secret
channels to bring His salvation to millions of human beings the
world over who worship Him as the unknown God and believe
in His justice. Contrary to civil codes, the code of the Catholic
Church declares that ignorance of the law, provided it be incul-
pable ignorance, is a complete excuse for the law-breaker.[1] The
law in the present case is that outside the Apostolic Roman Church
no one can be saved, ' but it is to be maintained as equally certain
that those who are invincibly ignorant of the true religion are
in no way held accountable for this in the eyes of the Lord '.[2]
St. Francis Xavier appears to have overlooked that second
principle in his overwhelming concern with the first, but it may
be taken to condone his harsh pronouncement at Malindi, for

[1] ' *Violatio legis ignoratae nullatenus imputatur, si ignoratio fuerit inculpabilis*'
(*Codex Juris Canonici*, canon 2202).
[2] Words of Pope Pius IX to a great concourse of Catholic bishops assembled
in Rome in 1854. The Holy Father's allocution continued: ' Now, who could
claim to be able to trace the limits of such ignorance, taking into consideration
such an immense variety of circumstances as affect the lives of peoples in their
physical environment and intellectual endowment? When, after death, we
shall see God as He is, we shall in very truth understand by what a close and
beautiful bond the divine mercy and the divine justice are linked together. . . .
The hand of the Lord is not shortened, and the gifts of His heavenly grace will
by no means be wanting to those who sincerely desire and petition for
them. . . .' (*Pii IX Pontificis Acta*, i, Rome, 1854, 623 sqq.).

he was as much and as invincibly ignorant of Islamic theology and piety as any Moslem ever was of Catholic theology and piety. It must also be said for him that his ignorance was shared by practically every Christian alive at the time, whether Catholic or Protestant.[1]

After Malindi, the *Coulam* called for water and other supplies at the island of Socotra, from which it is a fairly straight run across the Arabian Sea to Goa. St. Francis was unusually informative about that present humble and disregarded step-child of the British Commonwealth, which never seems to evoke a question in the Mother of Parliaments. After a description of the sterility and poverty of the island whose chief product was dates, he continued:

The natives esteem themselves to be Christians and are very proud of it. They can neither read nor write, possess no books nor other sources of information, and are extremely ignorant. But they have churches, crosses, and ritual lamps, and in each village there is a *caciz*, who corresponds to a priest among us. Though, like the rest, unable to read or write, those functionaries know a great number of prayers by heart, and officiate in the churches four times a day, at midnight, in the morning, and at the hours of Vespers and of Compline. Having no bells,

---

[1] The shining exception was the Flemish secular priest, Nicholas Cleynaerds, who died at Granada in 1543, aged fifty. This great forgotten man rediscovered the true method of Christian approach to the problem of Islam, so marvellously championed in the Middle Ages by the invincible Don Quixote of God, Blessed Ramón Lull. Briefly, it was to master Arabic and make a profound study of Islamic theology in the Koran and its several supplements and commentaries. By dint of cultivating the friendship of Moors who had been held in Spain and Portugal as slaves after the general expulsion in 1492, Cleynaerds became extraordinarily proficient in Arabic, but all his efforts to obtain a private copy of the Koran were frustrated by the Inquisition, which promptly burned every copy that came to light. Not a single chair of Arabic was to be found in the universities of Europe at the time, and try as he might Nicholas was unable to persuade the authorities to establish one for his apostolic purpose. But though so long dead and forgotten, Cleynaerds has won his battle, and Islamic theology and spirituality are now intensively studied in their Arabic sources by Catholic scholars and missionaries. Cf. *Introduction à la théologie musulmane*, par Louis Gardet et M.-M. Anawati, Paris, 1948 ; *Aspects intérieurs de l'Islam*, par Jean Abd-el-Jalil, O.F.M., Paris, 1949.

they summon the people to services with wooden clappers, such as we use during Lent. They do not understand the meaning of the prayers which they recite because they are in a language not their own. I think it is Chaldean. On my two visits to the island, I wrote down three or four of those prayers. The people are devotees of the Apostle St. Thomas and claim to be descendants of the Christians he converted in that part of the world. While reciting the prayers, the priests exclaim Alleluia! Alleluia! every now and then, pronouncing the word as we do. They do not baptize nor even know what baptism is. When I was on the island, I baptized a large number of children, to the great satisfaction of their fathers and mothers. With much kindness and good-will, they tried to make me accept such presents as their poverty afforded, and I was touched by the way they pressed me to take a quantity of their dates. They begged me very earnestly to stay with them, promising that if I did they would all, old as well as young, come to be baptized. I asked the Señor Gobernador to let me stay, for I wanted to do so, having there a harvest ready to my hand, but he refused permission on the ground that the Portuguese had no garrison on Socotra, and I would run the risk of being captured by the Turks, who came there from time to time. He also objected that there were other Christians as much in need of instruction as those of Socotra, if not more so, and that I would do God better service by going on to them.[1]

[1] Schurhammer, *Epistolae S. Francisci Xaverii*, i, 123–5. The other Christians to whom de Sousa referred were the pearl-fishers of Southern India, in whom, for reasons that will appear, he took a fatherly interest, entirely unconnected with personal advantage. The people of Socotra have a peculiar language of their own, but some of them must have known sufficient Portuguese to be able to enter into relations with St. Francis. Albuquerque and his captain, the fierce buccaneer Tristan da Cunha, had thrown out the Arabs in 1507 and maintained a fort on the island for four years. Even after abandoning it, their ships paid frequent visits to Socotra. Francis was correct in his surmise that the language of the prayers was Chaldean, a fact which lends support to the conclusion that the people of the island were not descendants of converts made by St. Thomas but of those brought to Christianity by the very remarkable Nestorian missionaries who had turned eastwards after the Council of Ephesus in A.D. 431 and made large groups of converts in both India and China before the ninth century. Those random baptisms of St. Francis are somewhat puzzling at

Francis never forgot his visit to the forlorn island, lost in the Islamic Sea. Other missionaries had twice gallantly attempted to establish themselves on its shores, but were forced to retire through Moslem persecution. He, too, would want to make the desperate gamble. Thus, in 1549, with a team of not more than ten men to supply all the needs of India, Malacca, the Moluccas and Japan, he proposed to send two Jesuit priests and two lay assistants to the succour of the unhappy Christians whose children were being seized by a Moslem tyrant for education in the religion of the Koran. But the Portuguese navy would have to help if the little mission was to have the slightest chance of becoming established. ' For the love of our Lord,' he wrote, begging Simon Rodriguez to be urgent with King John, ' do what you can to deliver those poor miserable captives from the tyranny of the Moors. Not more than eight days would be necessary for the ejection of the tyrants, if the fleet took the matter in hand. It is heart-breaking to hear the lamentations of those Christians of Socotra. Six years ago I was among them and conceived the greatest compassion at seeing them so cruelly persecuted by the Moors from the coast of Arabia.'[1] But the enemy was more solidly entrenched than Francis imagined, and in the opinion of experts it would have required a force of from fifteen to twenty thousand men to wrest the island from his grip. That was an expedition beyond the resources of Portugal, so the poor Christians had to be abandoned and the twelve thousand protégés of England on Socotra today are all Mohammedans.

St. Francis Xavier's knowledge of Hinduism was, if possible,

---

first sight, but he administered them only because he hoped to be allowed to stay to instruct the neophytes, or to return or send others for that purpose. He tells the following story against himself : ' I was anxious to baptize two little boys here, never suspecting them to be sons of Moslem parents. They ran off and told their mother, who came to me making an outcry and saying that I was not to baptize them, as she was a Moor and had no desire to be a Christian. Upon this, the Christian islanders told me that, even should the woman change her mind and seek baptism for herself and her children, I must on no account grant it. They are great enemies of the Moors and will never acquiesce in their being made Christians, maintaining that they are unworthy of it.'

[1] Schurhammer, *Epistolae S. Francisci Xaverii*, ii, 39–40.

even less adequate than his few biased notions of Mohammedanism. Though the Portuguese had been in India for over forty years, none of them appears to have made the slightest attempt to understand the venerable civilization, so much more ancient than their own, on which they had violently intruded. Indians were just pagans and idolaters, superior to similar breeds only in that they grew the pepper which the housewives of Europe in those days greatly coveted. It was the vision of pepper and souls that launched the Portuguese armadas, with the accent on pepper. The curious kind of megalomania which had taken hold of the Portuguese authorities at home is reflected in the papal bull constituting St. Francis ' Apostolic Nuncio to the islands of the Red Sea, the Persian Gulf, and the Indian Ocean, as well as to the provinces and places of India this side the Ganges and the promontory called the Cape of Good Hope, and beyond '. Francis bore a letter of greeting from the Pope to the princes and rulers of those various localities which might just as well have been written for Lemuel Gulliver on his travels into several remote nations of the world. Needless to say, the Pope personally had nothing whatever to do with the composition and peculiar geography of the documents. They were drafted by his secretariate under Cardinal Ghinucci in response to requests from Lisbon and according to information supplied by that city of legends. So Francis, the victim of romancers in life as after death, found himself furnished with such odd faculties as those of commuting imaginary vows made by Red Sea islanders to go on pilgrimage to Compostela, and carried a letter from the Pope to Prester John, recently discovered to be the Negus of Abyssinia, in which that heretical barbarian was addressed as 'dearest son in Christ' and exhorted to give the Nuncio his royal support.[1]

The *Coulam*, with the new governor and Francis aboard, reached Goa on May 6, 1542. To expect a description of the place from a man on whom the beauty and historic interest of Paris, Venice, Bologna, Rome and Lisbon appear to have made little impression would be to misjudge his character. Beauty, whether created by God or fashioned by the genius of man, seems never

[1] *Monumenta Xaveriana*, ii, 119–33.

to have touched his preoccupied soul. He was not Franciscan at all, in that sense. It was a defect in his nature, but one to which may fairly be applied the remarks of an illustrious authority on the prose of the Saint's good client, John Dryden: ' That there are purposes for which it does not suffice, charms which it does not possess, atmosphere which it cannot give, is all perfectly true. But Dryden does not pretend to give us these things. He gives us what he has to give and we go elsewhere for what he has not. He could never have had what he has in such abundance, had he not lacked what he lacks so reprehensibly.' Of poetry's silver and gold Francis might own hardly a sixpence, but he had other riches to spend on men with an almost divine extravagance, and there grew in him a beauty of holiness, often a terrible beauty, more thrilling than the pastels of sunrise and sunset, or the pomp of the stars, or mountain glory, or the loveliest of men's master-pieces. Where art stops short, unable to say anything more, there the grandeur of the saint begins.[1]

Francis did admit to his Roman friends that Goa, reckoned by the widely travelled Tavernier the finest port in the world after Constantinople and Toulon, was a *cosa para ver*, but he had his special non-aesthetic reasons for the judgment. Goa was a sight to be seen because it was ' a city wholly Christian, with a populous Franciscan friary, a cathedral of much distinction and many canons, as well as numerous other churches '. That was as far as he was prepared to move in the realms of Baedeker, and a quarter

---

[1] The narrowness of the specialist is, to some extent, in all the saints, even such ones as Francis of Assisi and Thomas More, for the life of prayer, lived as intensely as they lived it, necessarily involves a detachment comparable with that involved in the process of dying. ' *La prière est vraiment l'ombre de la mort : elle en a la forme et toutes les exigences. Les anciens Juifs avaient bien vu que nul ne peut voir Dieu sans mourir. C'est vrai ; on n'entre pas en présence de Dieu sans mourir. Le détachement de la mort est préfiguré dans celui qu'impose la prière. Il faut abandonner les biens extérieurs, les amis, les êtres les plus chers ; et puis le corps lui-même s'ob-scurcit, se refroidit, on abandonne son corps ; l'âme elle-même est livrée à l'inconnu, elle est précipitée de tout son haut dans l'abîme vertigineux de l'au-delà. Nous appelons cela mourir. Je crois que c'est aussi prier et que, dans la prière, il faut se résoudre à faire tous ces abandons volontairement, en détournant notre affection de tous ces objets, comme en mourant on le fait par force. Si les saints d'ailleurs meurent si facilement, c'est qu'en priant de tout leur coeur et depuis longtemps, ils ont pris l'habitude de mourir* ' (Bruckberger, *Rejoindre Dieu*, Paris, 1939, p. 18).

of the information is incorrect. Goa at that date was by no means entirely a city and island of the baptized. Like Sheppey and Thanet, it is an island only by courtesy of the two rivers which encircle it, Mandovi and Juari, and in those days their blue waters still served the ancient gods. The Moslems were back also for trade, undeterred any longer by the menacing ghost of Albuquerque. Francis neither knew nor probably cared to know that for more than a millennium Goa had been a centre of Hindu learning, wealth and splendour, and then, falling to the Moslems, had become one of the leading markets of the East from whose quays thousands of devout souls departed annually on the pilgrimage to Mecca. Such a place was not to be easily Christianized, as Francis himself quickly discovered. The Goa he knew did not during his lifetime put on her golden robes to vie in magnificence with such fabled emporia as Isfahan and Samarkand. Of his Goa not a trace remains, and of the Goa Dourado which replaced it, the proudest jewel in Portugal's imperial crown, there still stands intact only the majestic cathedral and the great church that for centuries has been his shrine. The rest is ruin and desolation, an Indian Ephesus or Pompeii given over to the mocking commentary of frogs and jackals.[1]

[1] It was the humble mosquito, the contriver of St. Francis's own agues, which wrought the destruction. Old Goa, with all its glory, had to be abandoned in 1759. New Goa or Panjim, a charming city laid out amidst luxuriant vegetation, three miles from the mouth of the Mandovi, then became and remains the capital. Buses, with small pictures of St. Francis Xavier or Krishna over the driver's seat, according to his religion, run daily to the deserted city, taking visitors and the diocesan canons to sing Mass and the Divine Office in the cathedral. The French traveller Thévenot who saw Old Goa before the mosquito got to work noticed that the island, facing the Indian mainland, was walled, ' with Towers and great Guns, to hinder the slaves from running away'. Perhaps that fact, too, had something to do with the destruction that came upon the golden, heartless city. ' It is a great town,' Thévenot continued, in a quaint old English translation, ' and full of fair churches, lovely convents, and palaces well beautified. There are several orders of religious, and the Jesuits alone have five publick Houses' (*The Indian Travels of Thévenot and Careri*. Ed. Surendranath Sen, Delhi, 1949, p. 129). Of course, Old Goa, dead Goa, with the palms for its funeral plumes, has been the subject of many Portuguese elegies. The following quatrain is a good specimen of the *genre* which has the advantage of not needing a translation, except, perhaps, the words *Eis* (behold !) *alvejando* (whitening), and *jazigo* (a sepulchre):

As the legions, the walking walls of Rome, had built the roads for the hurrying feet of St. Paul, so did Albuquerque, as ruthlessly as Caesar himself, prepare the way for St. Francis. But though a pious man in his moments and particularly devout to the Passion of our Lord, that was not the great conqueror's primary consideration. He and his men hated the Moslems not only as the traditional enemies of the Cross, but far more as trade rivals, whose monopoly of the Indian export markets they were determined to smash. And smash it they did by a combination of superlative courage, magnificent seamanship, colossal bluff, and basest treachery. Besides his conquest of Goa, Albuquerque wrested the island state of Ormuz, gateway to the Persian Gulf, from the Turks,[1] made Cochin permanently safe for Portuguese trade, neutralized the Moslem opposition in Calicut, one of the few places which he tried but failed to capture, and finally crowned his extraordinary exploits by the seizure of Malacca, a city of a hundred thousand Moslems commanding the Straits by which the products of the Far East reached the West. This would be Francis Xavier's gateway to the Indonesian Islands and Japan. No Albuquerque, no Xavier, is a fair conclusion. Why were they so ruthless, those Christian conquerors, precursors of the Gospel of mercy ? Why did they kill or mutilate their captives, women sometimes as well as men? How did one of them, Albuquerque's predecessor, reconcile it with his humanity to fire the dismembered bodies of his prisoners limb by limb from his cannon into Moslem strongholds as he sailed defiantly past? The answer is surely fear.

> Eis a cidade morta, a solitaria Goa!
> Seis templos alvejando entre um palmar enorme!
> Eis o Mandovy-Tejo, a oriental Lisboa!
> Onde em jazigo regio immensa gloria dorme.

The area was recently drained and cleansed of the malarial pest, and the city is now used to quarter troops.

[1] He first attempted to subdue Ormuz in 1507, with only 450 men at his back. These he marched up and down and about, as if on the stage, so as to create the impression among the Turks of a considerable army. When they delayed to surrender, he sent their chief officer a message : ' If you interfere with me in any way, I will build the walls with Mohammedans' bones. I will nail your ears to the door and erect the flagstaff on your skull ' (Whiteway, p. 121).

Outnumbered ten to one, they felt, as did Cortes and Pizarro on the other side of the world, that only by a policy of terrorization could they hope to survive. This does not condone their atrocities, but it helps to explain them, as does also the judgment of the ' Livy of Portugal ', excellent João de Barros, who propounded calmly in his celebrated *Decades da Asia* that, ' though the Moors and Gentiles are certainly rational creatures and so potential converts to Christianity, yet since they show no disposition to be converted, we Christians have no duties towards them.' Any man anxious to understand why Asia is so little Christian today after the missionary labours and sacrifices of centuries, might find in such deeds and such an attitude at least one clue to the dark mystery.

In Goa, the child of his heart, Albuquerque built greatly and among other things a hospital that was to become in time one of the finest in the world.[1] To that hospital, as by a kind of homing instinct, St. Francis Xavier repaired and made it the centre of his activities. Most of the patients were victims of the sea and dying men, of whom Francis became at once the absolute slave. He admitted himself that had it been possible to be in ten places simultaneously, he would in each of them have been fully engaged. The governor of the hospital, a grandee named Luis Ataíde who was afterwards appointed viceroy of Portuguese India, marvelled at his custom of lying on the floor, after his hard day's work, ' by the bed of the man most dangerously ill, so as to be able to help the poor fellow at a moment's notice '.[2] Another witness, familiar with the scene, reported that the least moan of a patient—*un minimo gemito*—would start Francis from his light slumbers on the floor and bring him like a flash to the sufferer's assistance. That was his way at the hospital, but many besides the sick in body

[1] In the sixteenth and seventeenth centuries the Portuguese built and equipped forty hospitals in Africa and Asia for the benefit of pagans and Christians alike. As one of their great preachers, Vieira, said, God gave them only a little country for their birth but all the world to die in. Wherever they strayed they also established the remarkable *Casas da Misericordia* for the assistance of the poor, the sick, orphans, and distressed people generally, which were a feature of their Catholic life at home.

[2] *Monumenta Xaveriana*, ii, 842.

needed his ministrations, and for these too his limitless charity found some means to provide. After midday, he made it his custom to go the round of the city's three prisons where were locked away in fearful conditions such types as even the very indulgent colonial laws could not tolerate. More than half a century later, the eminent and eloquent François Pyrard was committed for a while to one of those places on a misunderstanding. ' It is the filthiest, foulest den on this earth,' he wrote feelingly in his *Travels*, ' a place reeking with infection, where as many as two or three hundred slaves, galley-birds, and other scum are herded together anyhow.' But ordure and infection had no terrors for St. Francis. Perhaps some may think that he ought to have set about establishing a sort of Howard league for the betterment of prison conditions instead of trying to get the poor devils of convicts to repent of their crimes by a good confession. At any rate, the convicts listened to him, poured out their hearts to him, and felt, perhaps for the first time since childhood, that there was at least one man in the bleak hostile world who cared for them and whom they could be certain of as a friend.

Near the hospital in Goa, Albuquerque had built also a small church dedicated to Nossa Senhora do Rozario, and there Francis started the course of simple, solid religious instructions which, perhaps, more than anything, more certainly than the many miracles attributed to him, gave his apostolate its enduring quality. He appears to have based his method on a little book of devotions, a Portuguese *Garden of the Soul*, compiled by the great historian João de Barros, which he had taken with him to India. His report of his activities to Rome was as matter of fact as something from a stockbroker's diary. He mentioned his visits to the prisons but nothing about his relations with the prisoners. He told of his instructions at the Rosary Church, which for some reason he called a hermitage, but omitted to say how he attracted an audience. He made no allusion at all to his dealings with the Bishop of Goa, another Albuquerque, elderly and kind, but unsuited to rule the most extensive diocese in the world, which sprawled for thousands of coastal miles from Mozambique to Malacca. Luckily there was a Jesuit in India who, as a young man and his novice, once saw Francis plain and ever after worshipped his memory. This man, Manuel Teixeira, might have been a modern Bollandist, so painstaking and rigorous was he in investigating the claims made for his hero, and his sketch of Francis is in consequence the best of the kind that has survived the centuries. He was impatient of Roman exaggerations, and when sent in 1584 an advance or manuscript copy of the official *Life of St. Ignatius* by Pedro Ribadeneira for his comments, wrote a charmingly tactful letter to the author pointing out certain mistakes into which he had inadvertently fallen in his references to Francis Xavier. Pedro would forgive his impertinence, he hoped, as during his thirty-three years in India he had been over all the ground traversed by Francis and knew most of the men associated with him. He then continued:

In Book IV, Chapter 7, which deals with the death of Father Francis, you say that he founded more than forty churches on the Fishery Coast. But on both Coasts, the Fishery and Travancore, there are not today so many churches as that, and several were built after the time of Father Francis. He did not establish a single church in Travancore, and the credit for the ones now there belongs to Father Henriquez. All that he did on the Fishery Coast was to have some wattle structures roofed with straw put up to serve as churches.[1]

One warms to the honest Teixeira, but he made no impression on Ribadeneira, whose *Vida de San Ignacio de Loyola*, a classic of Spanish literature, still continues (latest edition Madrid, 1945) to inform the world that St. Francis founded more than forty churches in Southern India.

Speaking of the interview granted to Francis by Bishop Albuquerque immediately after his disembarkation, Teixeira writes:

Father Francis explained that he had been sent by the Pope and the King of Portugal to help the colonists in India, to

[1] *Monumenta Xaveriana*, ii, 801.

instruct the newly converted Indians, and to work for the salvation of the unbelievers, but that he committed himself unreservedly into the hands of his Lordship and desired to do nothing except with his permission and approval. He showed him the letters of the Pope accrediting him as Apostolic Nuncio and said that he had no intention of using the powers which they conferred otherwise than as might seem good to his Lordship. Thereupon, the Bishop, a virtuous man, embraced him with great love, told him that he knew well who he was and his quality, and bade him use the Papal briefs in any way that the goodness of his heart might direct.

In the same place, Teixeira tells of the method adopted by Francis to attract an audience:

He went up and down the streets and squares with a bell in his hand, crying to the children and others to come to the instructions. The novelty of the proceeding, never seen before in Goa, brought a large crowd around him which he then led to the church.[1] He began by singing the lessons which he had rhymed and then made the children sing them so that they might become the better fixed in their memories. Afterwards he explained each point in the simplest way, using only such words as his young audience could readily understand. By this method, which has since been adopted everywhere in the Indies, he so deeply engrained the truths and precepts of the faith in the hearts of the people that men and women, children and old folk, took to singing the Ten Commandments while they walked the streets, as did the fisherman in his boat and the labourer in the fields, for their own entertainment and recreation.[2]

[1] The precise words used by the combined muffin-man and Pied Piper were : ' Faithful Christians, friends of Jesus Christ, send your sons and daughters, and your slaves of both sexes, to the *Santa Doctrina*, for the love of God.' Francis appears to have used a sort of ' pidgin ' Portuguese, which was the most that the swarming half-castes (the result of Albuquerque's marriage policy) and other illiterates could understand of that language.
[2] *Monumenta Xaveriana*, ii, 842, 843–4.

We are not told from what source Francis drew his music, but he must have used catchy tunes, perhaps remembered from his boyhood in the land of bells and songs. It is recorded that he, normally so quiet, was very free with gestures and practically dramatized the catechism, to the delight of the brownies in front of him.

The sick and dying, the sinners of high and low degree who came for his absolution at all hours of the day and night, the neglected slaves and mestizos, the children, was there any other class for Francis to think of and comfort? Yes, the most shunned and abandoned class, the living corpses who reminded people too forcibly of the grave for their presence in society to be tolerated. ' Each Sunday,' wrote the Saint, ' I went to a lazaretto outside the city to say Mass for the lepers, and gave them every one the Sacraments and a sermon. They have become my very good and devoted friends.'[1] There he was, then, *El Divino Impaciente*, the inspired hustler, who could never stay still in one place, but must ever be restlessly traversing new ground, new seas, new lands, driven on by what an admiring French misinterpreter of him called *le vertige de l'inconnu*. It is true that on this first occasion he spent less than five months in Goa, where there was ample scope for the zeal of five or even fifty years among the thousands of Hindu idolaters and Moslem traders still on the island, among the half-baked, semi-pagan Eurasian converts, among the Kaffir slaves, among the Portuguese fidalgos who kept whole harems of Indian mistresses.[2] But Francis did not leave the island of his own volition, any more than he did Mozambique and Socotra. Again, it was Governor de Sousa who directed him to pastures new.

[1] Schurhammer, *Epistolae S. Francisci Xaverii*, i, 126.
[2] Numerous tales are told of his methods in dealing with gross sinners. We hear of him playing cards or pitch-and-toss with disreputable characters, of his financing a gambler to enable him to recover his losses at the table, of his habit of inviting himself to dinner at the houses of Portuguese dandies notorious for their loose living. Even if not strictly true in every detail, and of that there is no judging owing to the failure of such old writers as Tursellini and Bartoli to supply any references, those stories do seem to have been at least well invented. The Padre de Quadros mentioned earlier cannot have been awed and even frightened by the daring methods of Francis unless he was in the habit of taking such risks as the stories would have involved.

In the year 1513, a high-caste Hindu of Calicut had been sent
by the local ruler or Zamorin to represent him at the court of
King Manuel in Lisbon. While there, the man became a Catholic
and was knighted by the King under the new name of John of the
Cross. On his return to Calicut two years later, the Christian
knight was dismissed by the Moslem Zamorin and fell upon very
evil days, during which he clung steadfastly to his faith and
endeavoured to spread it. When John III succeeded to the
Portuguese throne he made efforts to compensate the Crown's
good servant for his many tribulations by granting him a
monopoly of the horse trade at Quilon and stewardship of the
pearl-fishery beyond Cape Comorin, both of which valuable
sources of revenue the Portuguese had succeeded in wresting from
Mohammedan control.[1] While at the Cape in 1539, vainly hoping
to obtain payment for twelve horses which he had sold to the
local Raja, it occurred to the zealous John that it would be a
great thing if he could persuade the pearl-fishing caste, or Paravas
as they were called, to accept the Christian faith. For generations
those lowly and pacific villagers had been victimized and exploited
by both Hindus and Moslems so, as John pointed out to some of
their headmen, they had nothing to lose and much to gain by
accepting baptism, seeing that it would bring them automatically
under the powerful protection of Portugal. The Paravas agreed,
whereupon a small band of apostles, Franciscans and secular
priests, came from Cochin to visit their thirty villages along the
Coromandel Coast, and within two years, 1535–37, baptized
practically the entire caste. When news of this event reached Goa,
the vicar-general, a man of fertile imagination named Miguel
Vaz, composed a glowing letter to the Pope reporting that half
a million pagan pearl-fishers had been added to the number of
his children. Now, it is quite certain from the reports of Jesuits
working among them fifteen years later that the number of
Paravas baptized did not much exceed twenty thousand, and

[1] The horse not being indigenous to India, the many independent rulers of
the sub-continent who prized the animal, particularly for use in their interminable petty wars, were obliged to import it. The Arabs had the trade entirely
in their hands until the Portuguese came and beat them off the field.

these had received no instruction in Christianity whatever because the priests from Cochin could not speak Tamil, their native language. After baptism and the acceptance of a Portuguese name as a talisman, the new Christians carried on cheerfully in their old ways, invoking gods and goddesses or placating demons, as they judged to be most expedient. The Arabs returned with a large fleet to harass the unfortunate pearl-fishers in 1538, and then they discovered the value of their baptism. At the time, Martim Affonso de Sousa was ' Grand Captain of the Sea ' in the Malabar area. He had not a tenth of the enemy's ships, but pursued them without hesitation, and by a combination of skill and daring won a resounding victory at Vêdâlai near Ramnad, which Camoens celebrated in the national epic. From that glorious day dated Martim Affonso's interest in the Paravas, and it says much for him that he willingly surrendered to them the priest he so much admired, to deliver them from the thraldom of the Indian gods and demons as he had himself delivered them from bondage to Islam.[1]

Shortly before he departed from Goa, St. Francis wrote three letters to his Roman brethren, all bearing the same date, September 20, 1542. The second of them dealt with the vitally important question of a native clergy for India. Portugal, with huge, undeveloped Brazil on her hands in the West, and a home population of little more than a million which was being constantly further depleted, could not supply more than a trickle of white priests for her African and Indian conquests. The Franciscans and other religions had come out at an early date, not to engage in missionary work among the pagans, but to minister to the Portuguese soldiers and settlers at the widely flung fortresses and trading-stations or ' factories ' which had been established by fair means or foul at Sofala, Mozambique, Ormuz, Diu at the entrance of the Gulf of Cambay, Daman on the opposite shore,

[1] Schurhammer, *Die Bekehrung der Paraver*, in *Archivum Historicum Societatis Jesu*, Rome, 1935, 201–33. This admirable study of how the Paravas came originally to be baptized supersedes everything else written on the subject. It was the news of their conversion which primarily inspired the movements in Paris and Lisbon to seek the assistance of the former students of Sainte-Barbe (l.c., 220–1).

Bassein just north of Bombay, Salsette Island, Cochin, Quilon, San Thomé close to Madras, Colombo, Malacca, the Moluccas. They were far too few even for that limited apostolate, yet such was their spirit that several of them made valiant attempts to bring the Syro-Malabar or so-called St. Thomas Christians, who were Nestorians, into the Catholic fold, and at least one brave Franciscan, Luis de San Salvador, ventured right into the great Hindu kingdom of Vijayanagar to preach the Gospel to the Brahmans, paying for his charity with his life. Another grave consequence of the fewness of priests was the inadequate instruction of such converts from heathendom as were made in the various Portuguese settlements. The first Jesuit martyr in history, Antonio Criminali, pioneer of a very long line, who came out to Goa in 1545, was appalled by the ignorance of the faith which he found among the nominally Christian half-castes. Since St. Francis had left the island three years before, nobody seemed to have done anything for those wretched and degraded folk, repudiated by Mother India and despised by Father Portugal. None of the many whom Padre Antonio met and interrogated was able to say the *Pater Noster*, the *Ave Maria* or the Creed. The language learned from their Indian mothers would have been the Dravidian Konkani, and that the European priests neither knew nor troubled to learn. Criminali told St. Ignatius that baptism was given to any who asked for it, without instruction either before or after. Being young and full of theology, Antonio argued the point with an excellent and experienced secular priest named Diogo de Borba. At the very least, he maintained, the prospective Christians should be required to remain catechumens for forty days, if not for the six months which St. Thomas Aquinas advocated. On those conditions, Borba retorted, there would be no baptisms at all, for the pagan relatives of the candidates would thus be given time to dissuade them, and besides they might die during the interval.[1]

---

[1] Criminali had a ready answer for that last objection. He was butchered for his faith in southern India only four years later, at the age of twenty-nine. Another Italian Jesuit who had come with him to Goa gave St. Ignatius an even gloomier account of the situation. ' The people of this country who become

Despite his defence of automatic baptisms, into which he may have been provoked by the criticisms of a young man new to the problems of India, Diogo de Borba was well aware of the need for reform. A year before the arrival of Francis Xavier, he had organized an association of Portuguese gentlemen to look after the interests of the Goan Christians, who suffered a good deal of veiled oppression from the forty thousand Hindus and Moslems living under the flag of Portugal. It was named the Confraternity of Holy Faith and had for patron the Apostle St. Paul. An immediate result was the foundation of a small school for non-European boys, which Borba hoped might later develop into a seminary dedicated to the production of an indigenous clergy, as that seemed to be the only way of meeting the man-power problem. Boys offered themselves in every shade of the human skin, Paravas, Malays, Bengalis, Cingalese, Malagasies, Ethiopians, and even Kaffirs from Mozambique, but it was another and much more difficult matter to find a staff. Who would want to be a master in such a menagerie, and not of malleable babes either, but of precocious lads, none under thirteen? Nobody wanted, and the good Borba had to keep his sixty young barbarians together almost single-handed until St. Francis Xavier brought him succour.

Governor de Sousa took a lively interest in the school, and it was probably he who inspired Borba to seek the help of St. Francis. Borba desired to put the college entirely into his hands, but Francis, with only two lieutenants and they still marooned in Mozambique, could not assume the responsibility for some

---

Christians,' he wrote, 'do so purely for some temporal advantage, as is inevitable in a land where slavery reigns. Slaves of the Moors or Hindus seek baptism in order to secure their manumission at the hands of the Portuguese. Others do so to get protection from tyrants, or for the sake of a turban, a shirt, or some other trifle they covet, or to escape being hanged, or to be able to associate with Christian women. The man who embraces the faith from honest conviction is regarded as a fool. They are baptized whenever or wherever they express a wish for the sacrament, without any instruction, and many revert to their former paganism. . . . This country is so vast that a hundred thousand priests would not be sufficient to evangelize all of its population. . . .' (Wicki, *Documenta Indica*, i, 82–4. The writer was Nicholas Lancillotto, a man of very bad health and melancholy temperament, but a zealous missionary.)

years to come, though he immediately wrote to enlist the sympathy of his great stand-by in every emergency, St. Ignatius.

God our Lord [he said] moved some men here in Goa to found a college for His service. Of all things it is the most necessary, and every day the need for it increases. Thanks be to God, the material buildings are being constructed which will lead to the making of many spiritual temples by the indoctrination and conversion of great numbers of un-believers. The Lord Governor has given the project his completest support.[1] The church within the college which is now being roofed is very beautiful and about twice the size of the church of the Sorbonne. It has already enough income to support a hundred students. Within six years or so I believe it will have passed out some three hundred men of different tongues, races and nations to multiply, please God, the number of Christians. We live at war out here all the time, and the Governor has won many and resounding victories. I trust that God will grant him even greater ones. For the love of our Lord and His service, I beg you and all of our Company to reserve a special place in your prayers for Martim Affonso de Sousa that he may be given grace to govern this great India well, and so to order temporal affairs that he may not let slip the things of eternity. I commend him to you as I would my own soul, so much do I stand indebted to him, and so truly is he my friend. If I should ever forget him, which God forbid, I think our Lord would have to punish me for so great a sin of in-gratitude. He is writing to the King about the college so that his Highness may apply to the Pope for some men of our Society to be its spiritual sinews. . . . He tells me that he intends to write to you also about the whole affair, and feels that an appeal should be made by you to all of our Society, your

[1] De Sousa applied to the support of the college some of the loot obtained by his raids on Indian temples, much as his admired predecessor, Estevam da Gama, had done. Both were not only encouraged but commanded by their royal master to destroy the shrines of the idols whenever they could. De Sousa does not seem to have needed much encouragement. Idolatry, or what the Conquistadors conceived to be idolatry, was judged to have no rights whatever.

spiritual sons, putting before them the needs of this college and asking for volunteers. . . .[1]

In his letters, Francis begged Ignatius to obtain if possible from the Pope a number of favours on which de Sousa had set his heart. They were peculiar favours for a bloodthirsty, avaricious scoundrel, such as the Governor is represented by historians, to want. The first was for a privileged altar in the chapel of the new college, at which all Masses for the dead should be said gratis. The second was for plenary indulgences to be granted to the sick and their nurses, and to members of the Confraternity of Mercy, each time they went to Holy Communion and at the hour of death. The third was for the same privilege to be conceded to the faithful in general on the feast of the Apostle St. Thomas, and on the titular days of the eleven shrines of the Blessed Virgin which flourished on the Goan territory. The fourth was for a pair of indulgenced rosaries for the Governor and his wife, and the privilege of gaining the indulgences attached to the Seven Stations in Rome each time that he, his wife and their seven children went to confession and Holy Communion together. Finally, the Governor greatly desired that the vicars appointed by the Bishop of Goa in the widely separated Portuguese settlements should be empowered to administer the Sacrament of Confirmation, and that Rome might enable the Indian Christians to observe the Lenten fast and make what Catholics call their Easter duties with less hardship by moving both fast and feast forward from the unbearably hot months of the year to a more merciful part of the calendar. In the summer months, Francis explained, ' fish putrefy as soon as taken out of the sea '. He concluded his long appeal to Ignatius with a little touchingly human consideration: ' It would be a great charity on your part to obtain those privileges for the Governor, and I might go up in his estimation, for he would reflect that I must be a person of some credit in your eyes if by merely writing to you on his behalf I was the means of securing such favours from the Holy Father.'

Now that he was about to launch out into the unknown,

1 Schurhammer, *Epistolae S. Francisci Xaverii*, i, 132–4.

Francis gives the impression in his letters of feeling a little lonely and intimidated, almost like a child who has lost his bearings and cries for the reassurance of familiar voices and faces. He had already learned and told Ignatius that life even in Goa, which aimed to be a Lisbon transplanted, was only for the robust and young. Life in the new college, named indifferently St. Paul's or Holy Faith, would be very hard for men unused to the rigours of India and would test their quality to the utmost. What, then, would life be like in the wild, scorched, devil-haunted places that had never heard of Navarre or Lisbon or Paris or Rome?

The Lord Governor [he wrote] has posted me to a territory in which, by all accounts, the prospects are bright for winning men to the faith. I am taking three Indian clerics with me, two of them deacons and the other in minor orders. The Governor has promised to send Father Paul of Camerino and Francisco Mansilhas after me, directly they arrive from Mozambique, to the place where I am going. It is six hundred miles away and called Cape Comorin. May God our Lord through your devout prayers forgive me my infinite number of sins and grant me His holy grace to serve Him well in that country. The hardships of the long voyage there, the charge and care of so much spiritual infirmity when a man has all he can do to remedy his own personal miseries, the life in a land given over to idolatry and under a killing sun—all these things turn to refreshment and consolation when borne for Him to whom our duty is absolute. . . . For His love and service I beseech you, dearest brothers, to write to me in long detail about all of our Company. In this world I have no hope of ever seeing you again, except as in a glass darkly through the medium of your letters. Do not deny me this favour, all unworthy of it though I am. Remember that your great merits were given you by God that through them even I might be refreshed and have hope of attainment. In God's name and for His glory, tell me fully and clearly what ought to be my method of approach to the pagans and Moors of the country to which I am now going. It is my hope that by means of you God will teach me

how I must proceed in order to convert them to His holy
faith. Your letters will show me the blunders to avoid, the
wrong methods which I must change. I trust in Christ our Lord
that by the merits of Holy Church whose living members
you are He will give His grace to even such a broken reed as
I to plant His faith among the Gentiles. That would bring
confusion to those slow ones who hold back, though having it
in them to do so much, and would be a mighty encouragement
to eager timid souls. Dust and ashes as I am, and made to feel
still more puny and despicable by witnessing with my own eyes
the need of priests out here, I would be for ever the slave of all
who had the the heart to come and labour in this vast vineyard
of the Lord.[1]

---

[1] Schurhammer, *Epistolae S. Francisci Xaverii*, i, 126–8.

CHAPTER VII

A MERCHANT SEEKING FINE PEARLS

FROM Goa to Cape Comorin is a longer stretch of the sea than from the Orkney Islands to the Straits of Dover. When Francis went aboard his ship towards the end of September, 1542, he appears to have carried with him, besides his Breviary and Mass equipment, only some kind of umbrella or parasol as a protection against the dreaded sun. Friends at Goa had offered to equip him handsomely for the expedition, but all that he could be persuaded to accept was a piece of leather with which to cobble his one pair of boots. He liked to go barefooted when he could, but must have been told that boots or thick-soled sandals were an essential of travel in the south, unless one happened to possess the special gifts of a fire-walker. He had no word to say of the long tedious voyage which he was to repeat in one direction or the other thirteen times in ten years. He does not even mention where he disembarked, and the student of his life can take his choice of three landing-places, Cochin, the thriving Portuguese centre of the pepper trade, which would have meant a highly improbable journey over mountains and through deserts, or Cape Comorin, called after the goddess Kumari, one of the numerous names of Siva's principal wife and to this day a place of Indian pilgrimage and riotous paganism, or Manapad, an oasis town about forty miles up the East Coast, where there was an anchorage off-shore. Manapad, the most likely of the three, is still, after four hundred years, dreaming of St. Francis, and shows with pride a little grotto lapped by the sea where, according to cherished tradition, he used to retire for communion with God to the diapason of the waves.

Fortunately, we are not dependent on Francis for a description of the scene of his new labours. It is still there, tidied up somewhat and made more habitable, but substantially as he knew it. Since the dawn of history, it has been the home of a lowly, indigenous, non-Aryan tribe who made their scanty living by diving for the pearl-producing oyster in famous beds lying in the Gulf of Manar, between the Carnatic and Northern Ceylon. Of course, never in their humble history were they permitted to keep the pearls for which, every March, they risked their lives. In the Indian caste system they figured low down among the many divisions of the Sudras, the fourth and last estate, the hewers of wood and drawers of water of Hindu religion and civilization, beyond which lay the untouchable mass of humanity, the pariahs. It seems to have been the Portuguese who christened the habitat of the pearl-divers or Paravas the Fishery Coast, a name never recognized by Indian geographers. It is a hot and barren strip of coast, consisting mostly of sand, and stretches north from Cape Comorin for about fifty miles, between the sea and the fertile land three or four miles to the west. But for the grace of numerous small streams, fed by the monsoon rains, which make a difficult journey to the sea through the envious sands, the area would not be habitable at all. The streams create oases at intervals, studded with palmyra palms, and on the products of the palms, supplemented by fish and rice, the Paravan villagers eke out their modest, cheerful existence, in which song, dance and mime have never failed, in spite of centuries of exploitation and the great hazards of their calling. Marco Polo came upon the pearl-divers at work during the course of his travels, and mentions that they used to give a twentieth of their catch to a sorcerer, whose office it was to cast a spell upon the sharks, 'depriving them of power to injure the divers'. The Paravas dived naked, with no other equipment than a net for the oysters and a knife for the sharks. Owing to the necessity of holding their breath for a minute or more on the ocean bed, the poor fellows acquired an 'occupational disease' of the lungs from which they died young.

When St. Francis Xavier came among them, the Paravas numbered about thirty thousand, living close to the sea in some thirty wretched villages. Like several million other non-Aryan Indians their mother tongue was Tamil, a venerable and poetic language of which St. Francis neither understood nor spoke a single word. But the three clerics accompanying him were themselves Paravas who had been sent to Goa for education in hopes that they might return as priests to minister to the spiritual needs of their baptized fellow-tribesmen. Though the hopes were not fulfilled, they performed a useful service by interpreting for Francis in his new and incomprehensible environment. Except possibly on a few very rare occasions, and these perhaps explicable by the now scientifically accredited hypothesis of telepathy, it is a mere legend that God endowed him with a miraculous ' gift of tongues '. He learned such smatterings of Eastern languages as he knew the hard way, and was dependent to the end of his apostolic course on such poor collaborators as could boast a little Portuguese. Translator and traitor never came nearer to being the same word than in the case of many of them, as will luridly appear later in these pages. In a letter to St. Ignatius written shortly after his arrival among the pearl-fishers, Francis explained the difficulties and told how he was endeavouring with the aid of his three mildly westernized clerics to teach the young Paravas the bare bones of Christian doctrine.

No Portuguese live among the villagers [he wrote] because the country is so utterly sterile and poor. The Christians here were baptized eight years ago, but owing to their having had no priest to say Mass for them, or to teach them the Creed, the Pater Noster, the Ave Maria and the Commandments, they know nothing whatever of their religion except to say that they are Christians. As soon as I had disembarked on the Coast, I proceeded to the various villages where they live and baptized all the children who had not yet received the sacrament, as well as a large number of babies. The children besieged me in such crowds that I had no time to say my Office or to eat or sleep. They clamoured to be taught some prayers and I then began to understand that in very truth of such is the Kingdom of Heaven. It would have been a crime to deny them, so I started by getting them to confess Father, Son and Holy Ghost, and then taught them the prayers. They are very quick and bright, and if they only had someone to instruct them properly I am sure they would make fine Christians.[1]

No doubt, the Sign of the Cross, the Creed, the prayers and the Commandments, as translated by the rusty clerics, were not in the most elegant Tamil nor pronounced in the best of accents, but the children picked up something of the new learning and passed it on to their parents. So Francis, drenched by the monsoon rains, ploughed his way through the glutinous sands from one village with a tongue-twisting name to another, Alantalai, Periyatalai, Tiruchendûr, Vîrapândyanpattanam, Talambuli, Punnaikâyal, Palayakâyal, Kâyalpattanam, Kombuturê.[2] In each place except the last two where there were no Paravas, he went without food or sleep to speak his poor lesson to a swarm of excited children, and thus he progressed north, confronted all the way with the grotesque and often obscene idols of popular Hinduism. Francis was not so broadminded about the statuary as the Italian Catholic traveller, Pietro della Valle, in the following century. ' Some of these Idoles,' wrote Pietro in an old English translation, ' sat upon sundry Animals, as Tygers and the like, and even upon Rats ; of which things the foolish and ignorant Indians tell ridiculous stories. But I doubt not that, under the Veil of these Fables, their ancient Sages had hid from the vulgar many secrets of either Natural or Moral Philosophy, and perhaps also of History. And I hold for certain that all these so monstrous figures have secretly some rational significance, though expressed in this uncouth manner.'[3] For Francis, as for the Psalmist, all the

---

[1] Schurhammer, *Epistolae S. Francisci Xaverii*, i, 147–8.

[2] *Talai* is the Tamil name for a white flower common on the Coast (the *Pandana odorifera* of the botanists, perhaps so called because like ' Panda's Gate ' always open). The Sanskrit suffix *patam, patna, pattanam*, simply means town or village). *Ur* or *urê* is a Tamil suffix meaning village. Palayakâyal on the Tâmbraparni River was described by Marco Polo who twice visited it, as ' a great and noble city ', the busy and wealthy port of the Pândya Kingdom. The site is now occupied by a few miserable fishermen's huts, all the former glory having been devoured by the sands.

[3] *The Travels of Pietro della Valle*, ed. Grey, the Hakluyt Society, London, 1892, i, 73. As is well known, the worship of the cow in India with its attendant superstitions which Europeans and Americans find disgusting originated in the

idols of the Gentiles were demons which might and ought to be destroyed without scruple as occasion offered. While passing through a completely pagan place on his route, probably Kombuturê, he learned that a woman there had been three days in labour and was likely to die. He was told also that she was being treated with those *mantrams* or magical invocations to the use of which Indian villagers have always been addicted. 'There is no moment, according to Hindu superstitions, when *mantrams* are more needed than at the birth of a child. Both the new-born infant and its mother are peculiarly susceptible to the influence of the evil eye, the inauspicious combination of unlucky planets or unlucky days, and a thousand other unpropitious elements. A good midwife, well primed with efficacious *mantrams*, foresees all these dangers, and averts them by reciting the proper words at the proper moments.'[1]

Moved by compassion for the pagan woman's suffering and

---

wise foresight of the ancient Indian sages. They knew that cattle, as the only animals available for the tilling of the soil and transport, as also for the production of milk and butter, were absolutely essential to the life of the people. They knew also that they would be slaughtered indiscriminately in times of drought or famine unless protected by a religious taboo, and accordingly declared the animals sacred, the killing of them a heinous crime, and the eating of their flesh the worst of all defilements. Other Indian religious customs repugnant to Western minds have had origins similarly dictated by necessity and enlightened self-interest, which is not to say that they have not become associated with grave abuses during the course of the centuries.

[1] Dubois and Beauchamp, *Hindu Manners, Customs, and Ceremonies*, Oxford, 1897, p. 143. Though the Abbé Dubois's book is now nearly 150 years old, the judgment pronounced on the Clarendon Press edition of it in 1897 by Sir Friedrich Max Muller, the German scholar who spent the best part of a lifetime expounding Hinduism to the English and defending it from criticism, still holds good. He wrote that the work 'has always continued to be read and to be quoted with respect, and will always retain its value, as containing the views of an eye-witness, of a man singularly free from prejudice, and of a scholar with sufficient knowledge of Tamil, both literary and spoken, to be able to enter into the views of the natives, to understand their manners and customs, and to make allowance for many of their superstitious opinions and practices as mere corruptions of an originally far more rational and intelligent form of religion and philosophy.' All the same, the book throughout is a terrible indictment of Brahmanism, and nothing that Francis Xavier has to say about the Brahmans matches the singularly unprejudiced Abbé's denunciations of their conduct.

by horror of the superstitions practised on her in her helplessness, St. Francis decided, without a thought of the danger into which he might be running, to pit his Christian invocations against the *mantrams* of the midwives and sorcerers. Describing the scene afterwards to St. Ignatius, he wrote:

All the invocations of the pagans are hateful to God because all their gods are devils. Accompanied by one of the native clerics I went to the house where the dying woman lay and began confidently to call upon the great name of Christ, nothing caring that I was in a strange land, but remembering only that the whole earth is the Lord's and all that dwell thereon. I began with the Creed which my companion translated into Tamil: By the mercy of God the woman came to believe in the articles of faith. I asked her whether she desired to be a Christian and she replied that she would most willingly become one, upon which I read excerpts from the Gospels in that house where, I think, they were never heard before. I then baptized the woman, and no sooner was that done than she who confidently hoped and believed in Christ Jesus brought forth her child. I afterwards baptized her husband, sons and daughters, as well as the infant just born and all others in that house. The news of what God our Lord had accomplished there spread through the whole village, so when I had finished I went to the headmen of the place and intimated to them in the name of God that they must believe in Jesus Christ His Son, the sole source of salvation. They replied that they dare not become Christians without the permission of the raja, their overlord. There was an official of that ruler in the village who had come to collect taxes for his master, and him I sought out. When he had heard what I had to say, he agreed that to be a Christian was a good thing and gave the villagers leave to accept the faith, but he would not follow his counsel to others and embrace it himself. I thereupon baptized the chief men of the place and their families, and afterwards the rest of the people, young and old. Then I continued on my way to Tuticorin, where my companions and myself were received with much kindness and charity. We are hoping through the goodness of God our Lord to do great things here. . . .[1]

That letter raises once again the question of automatic baptisms, about which St. Francis appears, at first sight, to have had as little scruple as any of his predecessors. What can Christianity have meant to those simple villagers sunk in age-old superstitions who found themselves rushed into it in such a cavalier fashion? The action of Francis has caused comment and criticism ever since, even by those who revere him with all their hearts. Thus, Dr. Louis Mylne, Anglican bishop of Bombay for twenty-one years, wrote in 1908:

> It would not, I believe, be untrue to say that, since the days of St. Paul, no grander or more fascinating personality has been brought to bear upon the heathen than that of St. Francis Xavier. . . . He ranged over provinces and kingdoms, preaching with a fervour and winningness unsurpassed, one might say unrivalled; sweeping converts by the thousand into his net. . . . The magic of his apostolic personality broke through all barriers of language, all strangeness of foreign thought; so that opponents gave way before him, and bystanders were converted by his arguments, when they were totally incapable of understanding them. Yet what is the result today? That the conversion of the country to Christianity is no nearer than it was when he left it, for anything that his followers have done; that they form but a Christian caste, unprogressive, incapable of evangelizing, observing distinctions of caste within the body of the Christian Church; holding their own with a pathetic faithfulness among people of other creeds. . . . Xavier would preach to crowds of heathens, attract them by his personal magnetism till they were ready for anything he might propose, teach them the Commandments, the Creed, and some other verbal devotions, chiefly to the Mother of our Lord. And then, when they knew these by heart, he would admit them to the Church by baptism, and leave them to the care of others who

[1] Schurhammer, *Epistolae S. Francisci Xaverii*, i, 148–50.

had none of his own unique force. . . . One would have thought that the most fervid enthusiast, with the profoundest faith in the sacraments, would have made some allowance at least for the circumstances of the country in which he was; that he would have asked whether the character of the people, their surroundings, their training, their beliefs, were such as to justify the assumption that such preparation was sufficient. But as far as his history shows, Xavier was never troubled with such a thought. . . .[1]

The Bishop goes on to compare the methods of St. Francis with those of two noble and saintly Protestant missionaries, the Danish Lutheran Schwartz who died in 1798, and the famous and lovable Baptist ex-cobbler, William Carey, who died in 1834. He contends that their methods were wiser than those of St. Francis in that they concentrated on small areas and did not spread themselves all over the map. There is much to be said for the contention, except that men like Paul of Tarsus and Francis Xavier are laws unto themselves and conceived their rôle to be openers of doors, blazers of trails, spearheads, forerunners. That certainly was the rôle intended by the Pope for Xavier when he appointed him nuncio to the islands of the Red Sea and the provinces lying to the east and west of the Ganges. Now, though it is by no means the purpose of this book to seek to justify or find excuses for everything said and done by Francis, his holy memory may fairly claim consideration for the following facts. Bishop Mylne, the fairest of critics, admits that Schwartz with his consuming zeal and carefully planned policy left behind no results comparable to those obtained by the unmethodical Jesuit, nor did the great-souled Carey, though backed by powerful organizations in England, make in India in forty years anything like the permanent impression which Xavier made in two years. The Fishery Coast, so to call it, from Cape Comorin to its chief town, Tuticorin, sixty miles away, is a very small strip of the mighty bulk of India, so small as to be barely descriable on an ordinary map. The whole of it is less in area than Surrey, yet Francis spent nearly

[1] *Missions to Hindus*, London, 1908, 114–18.

two years of the ten remaining to him in this world, ceaselessly moving backward and forward over its desolate sands. Surely that was concentration of heroic quality? Again, he stuck doggedly to his Paravas whose vices and stupidity at times nearly drove him to despair. He said once in a vivid phrase that they were *todos pegados con el mar*, all clamped to the sea, but he knew perfectly well that a short distance inland among the palm groves there lived another caste, the Shânars, akin to his fisher-folk and as ripe for Christianity as they, tree-tappers by calling and among the most intelligent of the Southern Indian tribes.[1] Then as today, groups of Shânars lived apart in the Paravan villages, so Francis must often have come in contact with them. But he made no endeavour to bring about their conversion, at least in a large way. When they became Christians later on, it was not through his ministry. He kept his love and devotion for the Paravas, much in the spirit of the Gospel merchant who spent all that he possessed on a single pearl. As for his not having been troubled with a thought about their conditions, their temptations, their education in the faith, the qualifications of the men whom he appointed to carry on his work among them, it would be more according to the evidence of his letters to say that he never stopped troubling, even when he was three thousand miles away in Japan.

The purpose of Francis in hurrying to Tuticorin was to come to grips in his own determined way with the formidable Tamil language. He had no intention of trying to acquire it as a spoken tongue, since that would have demanded a great deal of time which he could not afford, and high linguistic ability which he did not possess. But he had every intention of getting a simple course of Christian instruction and prayer into its difficult vocabulary and of then committing the whole range of sounds to memory. What a task he had set himself may be realized to some extent by a glance at the first few articles of the Apostles' Creed transliterated from their strangely beautiful Tamil characters:

[1] Thurston and Kangachari, *Castes and Tribes of Southern India*, vol. vi, Madras, 1909, 363–78. So skilled are the Shânars at climbing the palmyra palms to extract the juice from which toddy and sugar are made that their name has been conferred by naturalists on the Indian woodpecker, *shanara kurivi*.

VISUVASA—MANTHIRAM
Faith   Prayer

PARALOGATHIYUM   PŪLOGATHIYUM   PADAITHA
Heaven (and)   earth (and)   Him who created

SARVATHUKUMVALLA   PITHĀVAGYA   SARVESAR-
all-powerful   Father   God

ANAI   ATHIOKIA   BAKTHIYĀGA   VISUVASIKIRAIN.
with reverential   piety   I believe (in)

AVARUDYA   YEGA   SUTHANAGYA   NAMUDAYA
His   only   Son   our

NĀTHAR   YESU   CHRISTUVAYUM   ATHIOKYA
Lord   Jesus   Christ (and)   with reverential

BAKTHIYĀGA   VISUVASIKIRAIN.   IVAR   ISPIRITHU
piety   I believe (in)   He   by the Ghost

SANTHUVINALAI   KARPOMAI   URPAVITHU   ARCH-
Holy   conceived

AYASISHTHA   KANNI   MARIYAIYIDATHILAI   NINDRU
the holy   Virgin   Mary   (from)

PIRANTHU, PONCHU PILATHINKIZHAI PĀDUPATTU
born,   Pontius   Pilate under   suffered

SILUVAIYLAI   ARAIYUNDU   MARITH - ADAKAP -
on the Cross   fixed,   dead,   was

PATTAR.   AVARUM   PĀTHĀLAMGALILAI   IRANGI.
buried.   And He   into lower regions   descended.

MOONDRAM   NAL   MARITHAVARGAL   IDATHILAI
On the third   day   the region of the dead

NINDRŪ   ŪYIRTHU   YEZHUNTHARULINAR.   PAR-
from   raised   He came forth.   Into

AMANDALAMKALILAI   YERI   SARVATHUKUMVALLA
the Heavens   having ascended   the all-powerful

PITHAVĀGYA SARVESARANUDYA VALATHU PARIS-
Father   God (of)   the   right

ATHILAI   UTKĀRNTHIRUKIRAR.
side (on)   He is sitting.

When he had thus set down on paper brought from Goa the
lesson to be learned by heart, St. Francis was only at the beginning

of his difficulties. The Portuguese-speaking Tamils who had
helped him so far could not have been much assistance with the
problem of syllabic stresses on which the meaning of the spoken
word depended. On this subject a celebrated authority, the Italian
Jesuit, Giuseppi Beschi, writer of a pioneering Tamil grammar,
has the following observations:

The Tamils assign a measure of time to the sound of each
letter; to a long syllable they give a double measure, to a short
one a single measure, and to a consonant half a measure. Thus,
when they pronounce the word of six syllables, *pâttirattinôdê*
(which is the ablative of the noun meaning a vessel), it is well
distinguished from another *pattirâttinôdê* (ablative of the noun
meaning caution) by the sole fact that the first syllable of the
latter word is in itself short. This is usually a hard task for
beginners, and yet the exact observance of it is so indispensably
necessary in this language that if it be not carefully attended to
we will never be able to explain our ideas, and whilst we
endeavour to say one thing, the Tamils will understand it
quite the contrary way.[1]

[1] Beschi, born at Chatillon in Piedmont in 1680, went out to the Madura
Mission twenty years later and remained there amongst the Tamils for the rest
of his life. He died in 1746. Following the example of Robert de Nobili, he
lived outwardly according to the strictest requirements of Brahmanism, in
hopes of winning some of the proud priestly caste to the Christian faith. His
grammar appeared in print at Tranquebar in 1732, under the auspices of the
Danish Lutheran missionaries there, and with the title, *Grammatica Latino-
Tamulica ad Usum Missionariorum Societatis Jesu.* The good Danes, whose mission
the great Schwartz afterwards joined, faithfully reproduced Beschi's A.M.D.G.
He and they carried on some lively controversy in their spare moments. The
Grammar was published in English at Madras in 1806. A modern university
professor of Tamil, S. S. Bharati, has paid Beschi the following tribute: ' His
versatile genius and erudition have left an indelible impress on Tamil literature. . . . He avoided Father Robert de Nobili's blinding passion for Sans-
kritizing Tamil; he is rightly called the father of Tamil prose; he was the
pioneer in the field of Tamil fiction; he was also the pioneer Tamil lexico-
grapher, compiling the first Tamil dictionary . . . which still holds the field as a
standard authority ' (*Modern India and the West*, ed. O'Malley, Oxford, 1941,
509–10). He also contributed to Tamil literature a long religious poem (3,615
verses) called *Tembavani*, in honour of his patron St. Joseph, which still ranks
with Hindus and Christians alike as a classic.

Tuticorin today can boast of being the third most important port in Southern India, after Madras and Cochin. It is largely a cotton city, a miniature Manchester, with a population of seventy-five thousand Hindus, Moslems, Catholics, Protestants, Jews and men of other faiths. Though it can no longer display its former pride of pearls which attracted the Portuguese like moths to a flame, it still is a rendezvous of the palms that made it beautiful in the days of St. Francis. Francis told his Roman brethren how he went to work under their shade so as to make himself as independent as was feasible of interpreters in his missionary rovings:

I sought out men who had an understanding of my Portuguese as well as of their own Tamil. Then, after many days and meetings, we got the prayers into Tamil, beginning with the manner of making the Sign of the Cross as a profession of faith that there exists one only God in three Divine Persons. After that, we set forth the Creed, the Commandments, the Pater Noster, the Ave Maria, the Salve Regina and the Confiteor in the same language. I then learned the translated formulae by heart and, taking a bell, went ringing it right through the town to collect as many children and adults as I could. Having gathered my audience, I held forth to them twice each day until, at the end of a month, they had learned the prayers. I then arranged for the children to teach their fathers, mothers, sisters, brothers, and neighbours the lessons which they had acquired at my school. On Sundays I assemble all the people, men and women, young and old, and get them to repeat the prayers in their language. They take much pleasure in doing so and come to the meetings gladly. We begin with a profession of faith in the unity and trinity of God, I first saying the Creed in stentorian tones and then they all together in mighty chorus. That done, I go through the Creed article by article. . . . As they confess themselves to be Christians, I require them to tell me whether they firmly believe each and every one of the articles, and they reply in loud chorus, with their arms folded on their breasts in the form of a cross, that they do. I make them repeat the Creed more often than anything else because only a man who believes in the twelve articles has a right to call himself a Christian.

Francis next goes on to explain how he rubbed the Ten Commandments into those Indian heads, hitherto so full of strange gods, *mantrams,* and the fear of demons:

I give out the First Commandment which they repeat, and then we say all together, *Jesus Christ, Son of God, grant us grace to love Thee above all things.* When we have asked for this grace we recite the Pater Noster together, and then cry with one accord, *Holy Mary, Mother of Jesus Christ, obtain for us grace from thy Son to enable us to keep the First Commandment.* Next we say an Ave Maria, and proceed in the same manner through each of the remaining nine Commandments. And just as we said twelve Paters and Aves in honour of the twelve articles of the Creed, so we say ten Paters and Aves in honour of the Ten Commandments, asking God to give us grace to keep them well. . . . I require all of them to say the Confiteor, especially those about to be baptized, and then we have the Creed. I question the candidates individually about each several article to see whether they believe it firmly. If they reply that they do, I go on to explain to them the law of Christ which must be observed in order to save one's soul, and then I baptize them.[1]

Day after day for four months St. Francis thus exerted himself at Tuticorin. He must have had a very remarkable memory to be able to learn and carry such a burden of strange sounds, some entirely foreign to European languages, and all full of delicate nuances of pitch and duration. Did he understand the meaning of the separate words or was each for him a case of *vox et praeterea nihil*? It is impossible to say, but very certainly his task was much harder than that of the Apostles and other preachers of the Christian faith in the first age, as they had the advantage of a common language throughout the Roman Empire, the popular Greek which they understood and could adapt to Christian uses.

[1] Schurhammer, *Epistolae S. Francisci Xaverii,* i, 162–4.

He had to take everything on trust from his Indian translators, who meant well but were themselves constantly baffled by their imperfect knowledge of Portuguese and their inability to find in their own language exact terms for such leading Christian ideas as creation, redemption, the remission of sin, the resurrection of the body, life everlasting, the Catholic Church, the Holy Ghost, and so on. It is a sad familiar story that the word chosen by the Catholic missionaries in India, China and Japan to represent the idea of God in the languages of those countries was the cause of endless controversy and frustration. Even a man as profoundly versed in Tamil as Robert de Nobili found the problem beyond him and toyed with the solution of Christianizing the Indians' great Shiva, just as the early Church had taken over and Christianized the pagan *deus*. In the West, the difficulty had been to cleanse the word of its polytheistic taint ; in the East, both polytheism and pantheism had to be extruded from the selected term. It is not surprising, then, that the translators at Tuticorin made many mistakes and used inexact or ambiguous expressions which had afterwards to be corrected. Francis himself strongly suspected that all was not well, and took such pains as were in his power to remedy the situation. When, a few years later, he found that one of his men on the Fishery Coast, Padre Henriques, was showing a distinct aptitude for Tamil, he bade him re-write all the Christian doctrine lessons and prayers. The work of the gifted Padre then became the authorized version on the Coast, but, like a more famous Authorized Version, it also abounded in mistakes. It was more the phonetics of the language than its vocabulary that defeated the missionaries. ' We say one thing to them,' wrote Henriques despondently to St. Ignatius, ' but they take us to mean something else.' All the more extraordinary is it that Francis Xavier, with so poor an instrument as his painfully memorized lessons and little sermon on Heaven and Hell, achieved such remarkable and enduring results. Something went out from him when he spoke besides the badly rendered Tamil vocables, and in that sense he may very truly be said to have possessed the gift of tongues.

The native boys in particular were fascinated by the great

swamiyar from over the seas, and he by them. In the letter cited above he wrote:

> They are full of love and desire for the faith, keen to learn the prayers and to teach them to others. They detest the idolatries of their people and get into fights with them on the subject. They tackle even their own parents if they find them going to the idols, and come to tell me about it. When I hear from them of some idolatrous ceremonies in the villages adjoining Tuticorin, I collect all the boys I can, and off we go together to those places, where the devil gets from them more despiteful treatment than their worshipping parents had given· him of honour. The little fellows seize the small clay idols, smash them, grind them to dust, spit on them and trample them underfoot.

That particular activity of St. Francis will not appeal to all tastes, and it may fairly be questioned whether the boys, in their orgy of destruction, were actuated simply and solely by hatred of idolatry. It is fun to knock things about, especially under the approving eye of a well-loved friend. On the other hand, the figurines may well have been instruments of sympathetic magic, used to bring death or disease to rivals or enemies, and that superstition, still surviving in the backward areas of even Christian lands, is not deserving of much regard.[1] Besides, if the Englishman St. Boniface, Apostle of Germany, can rightly be regarded as a hero for hewing down the great oak of Geismar, sacred to Thor, it would not be fair to blame St. Francis, Apostle of India, for destroying the idols which his Christians had openly renounced and continued secretly to worship.

His grim struggle with the language and daily teaching were far from exhausting the activities of Francis in the town of pearls and palms.

[1] The custom of burning unpopular persons in effigy is a lingering shadow in civilized places of the old superstition. In his book, *Omens and Superstitions of Southern India* (London, 1912), Edgar Thurston devotes a long chapter to 'Magic and Magicians' which has horror enough in it to justify much stronger measures than those taken by Francis Xavier.

During my stay there [he wrote] I was besieged by crowds of people who wanted me to come to their huts and pray for their sick. So numerous were the petitioners that merely to read an excerpt from the Gospels over their stricken relatives would have taken all my time, and besides, I had the children to teach, baptisms to administer, prayers done into Tamil to memorize, and the dead to bury. It was an endless round, but I had not the heart to deny any of those sacred requests lest my people's faith should suffer injury. As it was impossible for me to meet personally the ever growing volume of calls, or to counter the little jealousies that arose among the good people in their competition to have me in their homes, I resorted to the following expedient. I told the children who had memorized the Christian doctrine to betake themselves to the homes of the sick, there to collect as many of the family and neighbours as possible, and to say the Creed with them several times, assuring the sick persons that if they believed they would be cured. . . . In this way I managed to satisfy all my callers, and at the same time secured that the Creed, the Commandments, and the prayers were taught in the people's homes and abroad in the streets. Moreover, owing to their faith and the faith of their families and friends, God has shown great mercy to the sick, healing them in both body and soul. . . .

The last sentence of that excerpt is the only reference in the entire extant correspondence of St. Francis to the subject of miracles. There is no telling what kind of diseases afflicted the sick, but surely they were not all merely such functional or nervous disorders as could be cured naturally by the working of a strong faith. From all that is known of them, the pearl-fishers were an uncommonly stolid, unemotional tribe. Their trade might and did drive them to drunkenness as an anodyne, but it certainly did not make them hysterical, and the only conclusion that can be drawn is that the cures wrought among their sick by the instrumentality of St. Francis were, at least in some instances, miracles in the fullest theological sense of the word.

The programme which Francis had set himself in Tuticorin

he repeated in the thirty places north and south of that town where the pearl-fishers maintained their separate and precarious existence. It meant endless journeyings to and fro between Vêdâlai, near Ramnad, in the north and Cape Comorin, a hundred and forty miles to the south, and no sooner had he completed the circuit than he started it again. Never did he show himself more heroic than on those dreadful perambulations, which in the hot season were like walking mile after mile on live coals, and in the rainy time, like floundering through a sea of mud. When a high wind from the Indian Ocean blew over the waste in summer it brought with it vast clouds of grit and dust, dust to eat and to breathe and to dream of, inescapable, all-pervading dust. And the fauna of that eerie, dangerous tip of India ought not to be forgotten, venomous snakes of every variety, cobras, hamadryads, kraits, vipers innumerable ; crocodiles and pythons ; jackals that made the night hideous with their howling; bandicoot rats, the biggest of their abominable kind on earth; vampire bats and water scorpions; tigers, leopards and wild elephants. Francis must have spent many nights in such company, but if he ever had a contest with the frightening creatures he kept the shiver of the experience to himself. As for his diet on the incessant journeys, the possibilities were lavish according to a Jesuit writing from Goa to his young brethren in Portugal four years later and mentioning beef, pork, goat-flesh, fowl, eggs, honey, butter, fruit, vegetables, ' all very cheap '.[1] But that was mere mission propaganda, bait for healthy appetites, because, to mention only one point, cattle are sacred animals in India and beef is never marketed or eaten. No; rice in one dreary form or another, supplemented in good times with fish, was the regular fare, which the Paravas countered by getting heartily drunk on toddy made from the juice of the Palmyra palms. St. Francis did not find his monotonous rations a hardship. He never seemed to care or even to know what he ate, or how little of it. One who observed him closely on the Fishery Coast reported that ' sometimes he would go two days without partaking of two farthings' worth of sustenance '. The same man, who used to accompany him on his rounds, has a like tale to tell

[1] Wicki, *Documenta Indica*, i, 459.

about the indifference of Francis to the second of nature's fundamental needs. ' It was a great thing,' says he, ' when sheer exhaustion from unremitting labour forced him to snatch two or three hours of sleep.'[1] He begrudged even that small alms to the body, it seems, for, according to the testimony of many witnesses, it was his habit to spend most of the night in prayer, as often as not under the stars.

On all his wanderings, but especially at the coastal town of Tiruchendûr, twenty miles south of Tuticorin, where there is a great Hindu temple built out into the sea, Francis encountered the Brahmans and soon conceived a hearty dislike of them. It is true that the southern priests were not the best types of their caste and only poorly educated, but even so the animus of Navarre must seem a little extravagant.

> There is a class of men out here called *bragmanes* [he explained to his Roman brethren, as usual in his devil-may-care orthography]. They are the mainstay of heathenism, and have charge of the temples devoted to the idols. They are the most perverse people in the world, and of them was written the Psalmist's prayer : *De gente non sancta, ab homine iniquo et doloso eripe me.* They do not know what it is to tell the truth but for ever plot how to lie subtly and deceive their poor ignorant followers. . . . Thus, they make the simple people believe that the idols require food, and many bring an offering before sitting down to table themselves. They eat twice daily to the din of kettle-drums and give out that the idols are then feasting. . . . Rather than go short, these *bragmanes* warn the wretched credulous people that if they fail to provide what is required of them, the idols will encompass their deaths, or inflict disease, or send devils to their houses. They have little learning, but abundance of iniquity and malice. They regard me as a great nuisance because I keep on exposing their wickedness all the time, but when I get one or other of them alone they admit their deceptions and tell me that they have no other

[1] *Diversi Avisi particolari dall' Indie di Portogallo*, Venice, 1568, 206. These are letters from the first Jesuits in India, translated into Italian.

means of livelihood than those stone idols and the lies they
concoct about them. They really think that I know more than
all of them put together, and they request me to visit them and
take it ill when I refuse the gifts they send me to keep my
mouth shut. They tell me that they know right well
there is only one God and that they will pray to Him
for me. In exchange, I let them have my views of their
behaviour; and I expose their impositions and trickeries
to the poor simple folk, who out of sheer terror alone
remain attached to them, until I become tired out with the
effort. As a result of my campaign, many lose their devotion
to the devil and accept the faith. Were it not for these *bragmanes*
all the heathen would be converted. . . . Since I came here
only one *bragmane* has become a Christian, a fine young
fellow, now engaged in teaching the children Christian
doctrine.[1]

Tantaene animis coelestibus irae! After that explosion, who will
say that St. Francis was not a man of temper and spirit, as well as
of woefully inadequate views about Indian religion and civilization? For him, the old slogan always seemed to suffice, the
Christians are right, the pagans are wrong, which, while being
perfectly true, by no means precludes the existence of partial, frag-
mentary truth, of deep spirituality, of genuine holiness, in such
a non-Christian religion as Brahmanism. It has to be said for him,
though, that his indictment of the Brahmans was subsequently
endorsed in every particular by the Abbé Dubois and others of
equal authority and impartiality. The head and front of their
offending in the eyes of Francis, himself the least Brahmanical of
men, was their lofty disdain of the lower orders, the Sudras, to
which caste his pearl-fishers belonged. ' The Sudra was relegated
to the lowest stratum of humanity . . . pushed more and more into
the abyss of degradation. He was held to have been doomed to
serfdom. He must not acquire wealth, lest he should thereby
cause pain to the Brahman. So physically unclean was he believed
to be that a householder was warned not to sip water brought by

[1] Schurhammer, *Epistolae S. Francisci Xaverii*, i, 170–1.

him for purification. Members of the superior castes were not to travel in his company. . . .'[1]

Still, all allowances made for Francis, it is impossible not to feel a little sorry for the Brahmans whom he trounced so mercilessly. For one thing, it was their country, not his, and the religion which they professed and served had a title to some respect from a foreigner, if only by reason of its venerable antiquity, so much more impressive even than that of the Holy Catholic Church. Besides, it has a metaphysic, a philosophy of being, as profound in its own way as any of which the Western world can boast, but of that St. Francis was completely ignorant. He does not seem ever to have heard of such deep-rooted and cherished doctrines as those of *karma, maya, bhakti,* and *yoga.* From all appearances he looked upon India as though it were a huge Navarre gone wrong, not as a land utterly new and strange and exciting, and it would have astounded him could he have known that millions there, including many of the Brahmans whom he despised, were as hungry for God as himself, as full of mystical tenderness, of genuine piety towards the Author and Ground of all being, as ready to sacrifice themselves and to practise the most stringent of disciplines in order to attain to unity with the Source of their existence.[2] Even the idolatry which he execrated is not so theologically absurd as he imagined, for eminent Catholic theologians, Capreolus, Cajetan and Billuart among them, have maintained that ' God of His absolute power could assume the nature of a stone or other inanimate object, nor would it be more incongruous to say that God is a stone than to say that He is a

---

[1] R. Masani in *The Legacy of India,* the Clarendon Press, 1937, 137–8. Masani cites the sage Apastambha: ' A Sudra attempting to hear the sacred texts shall have his ears filled with molten tin or lac; if he recites the Veda, his tongue shall be cut off; and if he remembers it, he shall be dismembered.'

[2] A sympathetic Catholic directive on this and allied subjects will be found in *Littérature Religieuse: Histoire et Texts Choisis,* Publiée sous la Direction de Joseph Chaine et René Grousset (Paris, 1949, pp. 649–54). Also in Otto Karrer's most learned and appealing book, published in English under the title, *The Religions of Mankind* (London, 1936), especially the Introduction and the whole of Part IV.

man, because He is infinitely above both natures.'[1] Idolatry as
practised so widely in India, and also the whole mythology of
avatars, is a pitiable attempt to render the Absolute more accessible, a first arrested stage of a journey towards the true God
incarnate in Jesus Christ.[2] Had St. Francis seen it that way he
might not have been so free with his very Spanish anathemas, and
a little closer in spirit to his great Italian brethren of a later time,
de Nobili, Ricci and Beschi, who approached the age-old pagan
religions of India and China with the humility and reverence
surely due to the world-wide and world-old striving of men after
God and salvation, however misguided, purblind or even blotted
with pride and cruelty might be the outcome. Of course, St.
Francis was not alone or singular in the hastiness and superfici-
ality of his views. They were shared by all Western men of his
time, and we too would have shared them, had we been alive
then, so there is no particular reason why we should imagine
ourselves to be superior. Even now, how few there are in the
West who have the remotest understanding of the rhythm of
Indian life or any feeling at all of the pulsations of its yearnings
and its prayer.[3]

---

[1] *F. Joannis Capreoli in Tertio Libro Sententiarum Amplissimae Quaestiones . . .
Nuper castigatae Auctore F. Matthia Aquario Dominicano. Venetiis, 1588. Distinctio
ii, Quaestio i: 'Utrum persona divina posset assumere entitatem totius . . .
lapidis?' Respondendum: 'Deus de potentia sua absoluta posset assumere naturam
lapidis aut aliam naturam irrationalem. . . .' 'Christ méconnu, Christ outragé
extérieurement, il est présent quand même. Il habite au désert et il bénit la ville. Il est
à Bénarès, à La Mecque, et à Rome, ici chez lui, là comme chez l'étranger. Il parle au
Vatican, et le muezzin sonore, voix de néant par elle-même, peut prononcer des mots qui
seront efficaces de par lui. . . . Il fait vivre ceux qui le tuent. Il accueille mystérieusement
ceux qui ne le blasphèment que des lèvres. . . .'* (Sertillanges, L'Église, 1921, ii, 120–1).
[2] There is an admirably lucid discussion of the whole question in *Missio-
logie*, by Pierre Charles, S.J. (Paris, 1939, pp. 14–29).
[3] The Protestant missionaries, Dutch and English, very much including the
great William Carey, showed as little understanding of, and as much hostility
to, Indian religion, as ever did St. Francis, though they lived in the enlightened
eighteenth and nineteenth centuries. Of Carey another eminent Protestant
missionary, Marshman, wrote: 'He exposed the absurdities of Hindooism
and the pretensions of its priesthood to ridicule in the most poignant language.'
As a rule, those missionaries respected the memory of St. Francis, though they
strongly criticized his methods. One of them, the Hollander Philip Baldaeus,
paid him the following tribute in an old book about the Malabar and Coro-

If the contention of Francis with the Brahmans lacked urbanity, it could not be held wanting in picturesqueness, to judge by what happened one day in the great temple at Tiruchendûr. Let Francis himself tell the story, in another excerpt from the huge letter which he addressed to Europe on January 15, 1544 :

As I go my rounds visiting the Christian villages, I pass many pagodas. One of those places contained more than two hundred *bragmanes*. They came out to see me, and among many other matters discussed between us I put to them the following question, 'What do the gods and idols whom you adore command you to do in order to attain salvation?' There was much dispute among them as to who should answer me. It fell to one of the oldest, an octogenarian, who asked me to tell him first the demands made of His followers by the God of the Christians. Perceiving his malice, I refused to say anything until he had dealt with my question, and thus he was forced to exhibit his ignorance. He answered that the gods had two commandments for all men desiring to attain to their heaven, the first being not to kill cows but to adore in them the gods themselves, and the second, to give alms to the *bragmanes* who served the pagodas. On hearing this I was overcome with sadness that the devil should so lord it over our neighbour as to draw to himself the adoration due to God alone. So I jumped up and, bidding the *bragmanes* to remain seated, I gave out to them at the top of my voice the Creed and the Commandments in their own tongue, pausing a little after each Commandment. Then, also in their language, I delivered an exhortation on the subject of Heaven and Hell, and told them who go to the one place and who to the other. After the sermon, the *bragmanes* all rose and embraced me warmly, saying that the God of the Christians was indeed the true God, since His Commandments

mandel Coasts: 'If the religion of Xavier was ours, we would feel constrained to venerate him as another St. Paul. He has hardly an equal. I find it difficult to elevate my thoughts to the stature of such a man, and my pen is powerless to express his greatness. When I think of his courage, his patience, his endurance in the midst of tribulation, I find myself saying with St. Paul, Who is capable of such things?'

are so conformable to all right reason. They asked me whether our souls died with our bodies, like those of brute animals, and God gave me arguments suitable to their capacity to prove clearly the immortality of the soul. They seemed to be highly pleased and satisfied on this score. One must avoid scholastic subtleties in reasoning with such simple folk. Another thing they wanted to know was by what orifice the soul issued when a man died, and whether when a man was asleep and dreamed that he stood in a land with his friends and acquaintances, his soul went there and ceased for a time to inhabit his body (I often dream that dream myself, you dear ones, and think I am in the midst of you).[1] Still another of their questions to me was whether God was black or white, according to the diversity of colours seen on human faces. As all the people of this land are black and like the colour, they maintain that God too is black. Most of the idols are black.[2] They anoint them constantly with oil and they stink abominably. They are also appallingly ugly. The *bragmanes* seemed satisfied with my answers to all their questions, so I wound up the discussion by saying that, since they knew the truth, they ought to become Christians. But they answered in the fashion so common even in Christian lands—What would the world think of them if they were to make this change in their way of living? They were also deterred by the consideration that it would mean the loss of their only means of subsistence.

The scene in the pillared courtyard of the temple that day, among the weird, malodorous effigies of the Hindu gods,[3] was

[1] ' *Quando un hombre dormía, que soñava estar en una tierra con sus amigos y conoscidos (lo que me a mí muchas vezes acaesce, estar con vosotros charíssimos).* . . .'

[2] But Shiva is always represented as white. The people of the Fishery Coast are not coal black like negroes, and their faces are usually as well moulded as those of Europeans.

[3] Speaking of the Indian temples, in particular those of Benares, Francis Yeats Brown, well known for his deeply sympathetic attitude towards Hinduism which even misled him into an attempt to reinterpret the New Testament according to Brahmanical teaching, wrote as follows: ' The temples are terrible. . . . There is a worship of foetus-like figures, smeared with red, that lurk amidst the acrid corruptions of milk and wilted flowers, and cattle-ordure, and bats and blood. . . . I turned away from these squalid

one for the brush of a great artist. Francis, thin and prematurely aged, in his shabby black cassock to which he had sewn a small hood as some protection from the sun, stands in vivid contrast to the smiling tolerant priests of Vishnu in their white muslin robes, with the trident of their divinity, emblem of generative power, painted on their foreheads. Did the Brahmans understand more than a word here and there of the memorized Tamil which he recited to them *a grandes vozes*? And was the curiously acquiescent demeanour of the audience due to courtesy on their part or to diplomacy on the part of the Saint's interpreter? The priests were probably not so simple as the ex-professor of Paris imagined, for the Abbé Dubois who knew the Southern Brahmans well regarded them as the perfect counterparts of the Pharisees denounced by our Lord.

Francis might dislike the Brahmans and fight them, but he could not help being interested in their beliefs. He looked about for an instructor better schooled in the lore of the caste than the rustic priests of Tiruchendûr and was pleased to hear at some coastal village that a *Sannyasi*, or Brahman hermit, who had attended a famous place of learning, possibly the monastery of Vyasaraya in southern Kanara, was living his solitary life in the area. ' I took steps to bring about a meeting with him,' Francis told his Roman brethren. ' He confided to me as a great secret that the first thing done by the teachers in the schools is to exact an oath from their pupils that they will not reveal certain matters taught to them. We became friendly and he let me know in confidence what those matters were. Among them was the following—never to disclose that there exists one only God, Creator of the heavens and the earth, who dwells in Heaven, but to adore Him and not the idols, which are demons.'[1] Again,

---

sanctuaries. Corruption stank in my nostrils, but my soul smelt something different . . .' (*Bengal Lancer*, 1930, Chapter IX). Perhaps Francis Xavier may be excused after all for his inability to catch that other smell or to find the meanings which came to Colonel Brown ' from far away, along pathways my brain had never used '.

[1] Dubois when describing the investiture of young Brahmans with the triple cord gives, but only on hearsay, a precisely similar formula, except that there is no mention of the idols being demons (*Hindu Manners, Customs and Ceremonies*, p. 168). Some wild Indian tribes do indulge in devil-worship, but the Brahmans represent the demons as attendants on the god Shiva.

remembering the inveterate pantheism and syncretism of Hindu theology, we are compelled to wonder whether the Brahman said anything half as definite as the interpreter of the dialogue, no doubt a Christian, allowed St. Francis to understand. From his new friend Francis learned, apparently for the first time, that the Indians possessed a sacred Sanskrit literature of great antiquity, which contained commandments resembling those of the Decalogue. ' It is almost incredible,' he continued, ' but the wise among them actually observe the Lord's Day and repeat many times that day this prayer, *Om cirii naraina noma*, which is to say, *I adore Thee, O God, with Thy grace and help, for ever.*'[1]

The remainder of the story is not without pathos. The friendly hermit evidently thought that the religion of Francis, like his own, would have esoteric doctrines communicated only to a privileged circle of initiates, and promised faithfully to keep them secret if his Christian visitor would kindly let him know what they were:

I replied that, on the contrary, I would tell nothing of the principal Christian tenets unless he agreed *not* to keep them hidden, and to this he readily assented. I then with the greatest pleasure pronounced and expounded those important words of our faith, *He who believes and is baptized will be saved*. He wrote down the words and the commentary in his own language, together with the Creed and the Commandments which I had similarly expounded. He told me how he dreamed one night, to his great joy and contentment, that he had to become a Christian and be my companion on my journeys. He begged me to make him a Christian secretly, but under

[1] This is a common invocation of the Vishnu sect of Brahmans and not at all reserved for Sundays, which are no more sacred to Hindus than other days. The accurate text of the Sanskrit incantation runs: *Om* (the secret mystical name of the Absolute) *Sri* (holy) *Narâyana* (a name of Vishnu regarded as an ocean city)' *namah* (adoration), and the translation would be something like: ' OM! Hail holy Narâyana! ' Francis added that ' they repeat the invocation slowly and quietly, so as not to violate their oath '. They need not have taken the precaution, as Sanskrit had long centuries earlier become a dead language, understood only by learned people. Very many of the Brahmans did not understand it, and repeated formulae from the Vedas by rote, as St. Francis did his Tamil formulae.

conditions that were neither honest nor licit, so I had to refuse
him. I trust in God that he will become a Christian without
any of those reservations. I counselled him to teach the simple
people to adore one only God, the Creator of heaven and earth,
but he was reluctant to do so on account of his oath and for
fear that a demon might kill him.

At that point, Francis ran out of news for the dear men far
away who came close to him only in dreams, but he would not
end his enormous letter on a note of sadness.

I know not what more I can tell you [he continued] except
this. So great are the consolations given by God our Lord to
those working out here for the conversion of the heathen that
if there be joy on earth, this is it and no mistake. Many a time
do I hear one such person cry out, ' O Lord, give me not so
much solace in this life, or since of Thy infinite goodness and
mercy Thou dost comfort me thus, take me to Thy holy glory
because it is an agony to live without seeing Thee after ex-
periencing Thy interior consolations.'[1] . . . My recreation out
here, dearest Brothers, is to think of you constantly, recalling
the times when by God's good mercy I came to know you and
have your intimacy. I feel keenly how much, through my own
fault, I then missed by not profiting far more from the wisdom
which God had communicated to you. May He have mercy
on me and grant me through your faithful prayers to perceive
and grieve for the infinite number of my sins, as well as strength
to hold on my way among the heathen. I am so grateful to
Him, and to you, too, dearest Brothers. . . . So I end by praying
that as in His mercy He brought us together, and then for His
service separated us so far from one another, He may again
unite us in His holy glory. That that joy may be ours, let us
take for intercessors and advocates, all those holy souls, more
than a thousand, I think, whom I baptized in these parts and

[1] The person, of course, was St. Francis himself, and the passage is the origin
of the exclamation often attributed to him in books and paintings, *Satis est,
Domine, satis est* !

whom God called to Himself before they lost the state of innocence. May they obtain for us in this world of exile to know His holy will and to fulfil it perfectly. Your loving brother, Francis.[1]

---

[1] Schurhammer, *Epistolae S. Francisci Xaverii*, i, 171–7. The reference of the Saint to the thousand Indian babies whom he had baptized before they died shocked one of his Protestant admirers. Francis seemed to be glad that the children had died and become advocates of the Society of Jesus in Heaven, ' instead of being sorry that human stupidity and carelessness had deprived them of life ' (Stewart, *The Life of St. Francis Xavier*, p. 186). As an apology for him the writer urged that his words ' were the feverish utterance of a fine imagination, hurt and bruised with the sight of over much sorrow '. The words bear no such interpretation. St. Francis was not glad that the babies had died, but that he had been able to baptize them before death and so ensure for them the immediate vision of God. He could not have saved the children's natural life except by a thousand miracles, but he did them a far greater, an altogether incommensurable service, by obtaining for them, at a terrible cost of personal suffering, eternal life.

CHAPTER VIII

ALARMS AND EXCURSIONS

FOR more than a year, St. Francis remained completely alone at his post, the only white man in that black or brown world of sand and sun where even the hardiest Portuguese traders hesitated to poke their covetous noses. A percentage of the revenue on pearls went to Goa and Lisbon, and that seemed to be all that Lisbon and Goa cared. As for the three indigenous clerics who were to help the lonely missionary, they appear to have quickly faded into their background, and Francis, ever eager to praise, has nothing for them but the charity of silence. He had been promised that Paul of Camerino and Francis Mansilhas would be sent to him as soon as they arrived from Mozambique, but month after weary month he watched for them and longed for them in vain. It must have seemed to him such ages ago since he had had his dream or nightmare in Venice of the Indian too heavy for him to carry on his back, though he endeavoured so desperately to raise him. Well, the dream was being starkly fulfilled. Despite the divine consolations at the peak of his spirit, which in any case are compatible with an extremity of suffering, as St. Teresa is witness, he felt crushed and bewildered. Thirty villages, a language he never could learn, twenty thousand Christians, and only himself to dispense to them the Word of Life and the Bread of Life, therein lay his agony. In a famous passage of his letters, he wrote:

> Multitudes out here fail to become Christians only because there is nobody prepared for the holy task of instructing them. I have often felt strongly moved to descend on the universities of Europe, especially Paris and its Sorbonne, and to cry aloud like a madman[1] to those who have more learning than good

[1] '. . . *como hombre que tiene perdido el juizio.* . . .'

will to employ it advantageously, telling them how many souls miss Heaven and fall into Hell through their negligence! If, while they studied their humanities, they would study also the account which God will demand of them for the talent He gave, many might feel the need to engage on spiritual exercises that would lead them to discover and embrace the divine will, as against their own proclivities, and to cry to God, ' Lord, here I am. What wouldst Thou have me to do? Send me where Thou willest, yea, even to India.' Ah, then, with how much more peace would they live and with how much more hope in the mercy of God would they die, being able to plead at their Particular Judgment, which every man born has to face, *Domine, quinque talenta tradidisti mihi, ecce alia quinque super-lucratus sum.* But I fear that many university men pursue their studies and conform to regulations purely in order to attain to dignities, benefices, bishoprics, which gained, they say, it will be time enough to serve God. So their choice of a career is determined by their own disordered inclinations, for they are afraid lest God's will for them might not coincide with their own will, and they consequently refuse to leave to Him the disposition of their lives. I really feel tempted to write to our friends at Paris, Maître Pierre de Cornes and Dr. François Le Picard, telling them what vast multitudes—*mil milares*—of gentiles would become Christians if only there were priests to help them. . . . Out here, people flock into the Church in such numbers that my arms are often almost paralyzed with baptizing, and my voice gives out completely through repeating endlessly in their tongue the Creed, the Command-ments, the prayers, and a sermon on Heaven and Hell. . . .[1]

[1] Schurhammer, *Epistolae S. Francisci Xaverii*, i, 166–8. This also is an excerpt from the letter of pamphlet size (about 4,400 words) which Francis addressed to his Roman brethren on January 15, 1544. When translated into Latin, printed, and widely diffused throughout Europe, it contributed greatly to the encouragement of missionary enterprise. An outstanding Spanish preacher of the time maintained that the *carissimo Francisco* ' was doing as much good in Spain and Portugal by his letter, as he was in India by his teaching ' (MHSJ. *Epistolae Mixtae*, i, 225). It served the infant Society of Jesus royally as the best answer to frequent and virulent criticism, and as an agent for winning recruits. Among others into whose hands a copy of the letter fell was a certain Majorcan

At the end of October, 1543, Francis decided to go in search of the two companions who had been promised to him but had so unaccountably vanished into thin air. Leaving his flock momentarily to the care of trained and trustworthy catechists whom he had appointed in the various communities to baptize infants and others in danger of death, and to teach the Christian doctrine daily, he made his way somehow to Goa, eight hundred miles distant, taking with him a few promising Paravan boys for education at the College of St. Paul. Throughout his missionary life, he cherished the project of a native clergy, Asia to evangelize Asia, but his experience of Indians already in orders had not been reassuring, and he felt the need of great reserve and caution in approaching a problem so beset with difficulties of ethnology, ethology and theology. As for his journey, perhaps a Portuguese ship had put in at Manapad, though it was not the season for such visits, or perhaps he sailed in one of the small local fishing craft called *tônis* to Quilon or Cochin and caught a larger vessel there. However he travelled, he must have spent Christmas at sea, without Mass or carol, except for the *Benedicite* of the winds in the rigging.

At Goa he learned to his passing wonder that the two henchmen he sought had been there for more than a year, adscripted by the Governor's orders to the rapidly developing and all-absorbing College of St. Paul. So much for promises to apostles at a convenient distance. It never occurred to Francis to complain. On the contrary, he expressed his delight at the progress made, even though the whale had swallowed his Jonah. Paul of Camerino had became a main prop of the College, with its miscellany of races and languages, but the Bishop, good, honest man, was

---

named Dr. Jerome Nadal. This eminent and learned priest had known Ignatius Loyola and Francis Xavier during their student days at Paris but determinedly refused to join their circle, though Ignatius, with his uncanny power of discerning greatness, wooed him assiduously. Ten years later, a friend in Rome sent Nadal, then living a retired life on his native island, a copy of the letter. It overwhelmed him, and he not only joined Ignatius, but became, after him, the greatest single influence in the building up and diffusion of the Society of Jesus. The Spanish of the letter is more than ordinarily involved and repetitive, but the spirit of the man shines and flames in it, like the sun among the clouds.

willing to sacrifice Mansilhas. Anybody was welcome to
Mansilhas, the poor well-meaning dunce who could not learn
enough Latin to say Mass or Office, and so remained forlornly
unordained. A Jesuit who came across him some time later, after
he had been eventually made a priest, expressed strong views to
St. Ignatius on the subject. ' May God be merciful to those who
gave him orders,' he wrote. ' He cannot read his Office and it is
doubtful whether he will ever acquire enough Latin to say Mass.
I asked the Bishop straight out how he could bring himself to
ordain men as ignorant as that, and his answer was : What am I
to do when there are no better educated candidates? '[1] Mansilhas
became something of a legend among his brethren as a Boeotian,
and legends always tend to be larger than reality. Boeotians are
not fools all round the compass. Anyhow, Francis the Great
was exceedingly glad to have the services of Francis the Little.
The good fellow had bravely joined his adventure when the
bright spirits of Portugal, the ecclesiastics of light and leading,
had looked in the other direction. He conceived a deep affection
for this man whom nobody wanted and, as time showed, the
affection, except possibly for one unhappy piece of recalcitrance,
was honestly returned. Two secular priests, Juan de Lisano, a
Spaniard, and Francis Coelho, an Indian, also volunteered for the
Cape Comorin Mission, simple, faithful men who had little to
contribute except the great gift of the Mass. Finally, John Artiaga,
a Portuguese gentleman who had come to India on the same ship
as St. Francis and was then at a loose end, offered his doubtful
services. Thinking of that forlorn quartette, the best muster he
could make for the conversion of India, it is little wonder that
Francis felt like returning to Europe and storming into the ivory
castles of the universities.[2] But Goa held for him a thrill out-

---

[1] Wicki, *Documenta Indica*, vol. i, p. 138. The writer's own Latin was not
so wonderful. He was the Nicholas Lancillotto whose pessimistic habit of mind
has already been indicated.

[2] There is a highly interesting parallel to the outburst of St. Francis in a
letter of St. Jean Eudes written just on a hundred years later (October, 1641),
while he was preaching in Normandy: ' *Que font à Paris tant de docteurs et
tant de bacheliers pendant que les âmes périssent par milliers faute de personnes qui
leurs tendent la main pour les retirer de la perdition et les préserver du feu éternel?*

weighing many disappointments, the news, then more than three years old, that the redoubtable ' Reverendissimo Guidatión ' of his daily Mass had withdrawn from the lists and permitted the Society of Jesus to take its place as a new religious order in the Church. How he felt about it is plain in a passage of the big letter which he dispatched to Rome from Cochin on his hurried return journey to the Fishery Coast:

> Among God's many mercies to me present and past there is one I longed for with all my heart, that I might see before I died the confirmation of our rule and manner of life. Thanks and unending thanks to God our Lord that He has seen good to make publicly known what He secretly gave His servant and our father Ignatius to understand. For two years now, I think that all Father Paul's Masses and mine have been for the Most Reverend Cardinal Guidatión.[1]

Back again with his four acquisitions in the region of goddess Kumari's Cape, there began for Francis the crowded and critical year, 1544. It plunges us for a while into a minor labyrinth of Indian history with outlines as shifting as the sands in a monsoon, and long strange native names that suffered fearful mutations at the hands of a saintly heterographer. Besides Francis himself and his squire Mansilhas, there are five principal actors in the drama about to be unfolded. First, in dignity as in asserted power, must be named Sada Siva, titular ruler of the once great Hindu empire

---

Certainement, si je m'en croyais, je m'en irais à Paris crier dans la Sorbonne et dans les autres collèges—Au feu! au feu de l'enfer qui embrase tout l'univers! Venez, messieurs les docteurs; venez, messieurs les bacheliers; venez, messieurs les abbés; venez, messieurs les ecclésiastiques, nous aider à l'éteindre ' (Joly, *Le Vénerable Jean Eudes*, 1907, p. 63; Père Eudes was canonized in 1925). The challenge, the desperate urgent appeal of the two Saints has a power as of massed trumpets to stir Christians from their complacency. It might be said with little exaggeration that no man nor woman can be the Christian, the Catholic, God meant them to be unless the need of the vast shadowed pagan world is part of their consciousness and substance of their prayer. *Adveniat regnum tuum!* comes easily to the lips, but if it be not also an agony in the heart, a terrible sigh of the soul to God, it means nothing.

[1] Schurhammer, *Epistolae S. Francisci Xaverii*, i, 175–6. Guidatión, it may be remembered, is the Saint's version of Guidiccioni.

of Vijayanagar, who claimed suzerainty over the whole of southern India.[1] Next, and the star of the entire piece, is a raja named Rama Varma, whose dominions, based on Quilon, stretched round Cape Comorin right up to Punnaikâyal at the mouth of the river Tâmbraparni. This personage, inheritor from his marauding ancestors of the title of Maharaja or Great King, though they and he were in fact mere vassals of Vijayanagar, boasted a second handle to his name, Unni Kêrala Tiruvadi, meaning ' Son of the Prince of Travancore '. That was too much of a mouthful even for Indians who shortened it to Unnikêla Tiruvadi. The good convert John of the Cross, himself a Malabar, made identification easier for the Portuguese by writing it Unique Trebery, and so it reached St. Francis who, taking one of his usual pot shots at transliteration, metamorphosed the Raja into Iniquitriberim. Iniquitriberim, with minor variations, the potentate has remained in books of the Western world. He is going to play quite a startling part in the missionary career of the man who thus massacred his patronymic. Two more Indian rulers remain to be mentioned, Mârtanda Varma, Raja of coastal Travancore and brother of Iniquitriberim, for whom his affection oscillated considerably, and Vettum Perumâl (Betebermal to St. Francis) who held sway over the town of Tuticorin and part of the Tinnevelly district, last remnants of the once extensive and powerful Pândya kingdom. He is the bad man of the story, but not the only one, for with him unfortunately must be linked the official representative of Portugal in the south, Captain Cosmas de Paiva, a predatory creature who made his lair in Tuticorin and from thence plundered and oppressed Christian and heathen alike.[2]

[1] In its heyday, Vijayanagar City almost stunned fifteenth and early sixteenth-century European travellers by its wealth and magnificence. One worthy, familiar with splendid cities, declared that ' eye hath not seen nor ear heard of any place resembling it on the whole earth '. It was completely overrun and erased from history by Moslem hordes in 1565, who turned it into a wilderness of ruins nine square miles in extent. These, one of the most impressive sights of India, are at Hampi, about 140 miles east of Goa.

[2] A glance at the map provided, which assigns to those several rajas their approximate spheres of control, will do more than a narrator's best efforts to make the situation seem a little less involved. The map also shows in their

The country was still at peace when St. Francis arrived back among the sand dunes during February, 1544, though Iniquitriberim and Vettum Perumâl had already begun to glance balefully in each other's direction. A few months' respite remained before his shoulders would be called upon to keep the local heavens suspended, and he employed them *à toute outrance*, to the last limit of human endurance. Other horizons were beckoning, and he could hear in his soul an insistent knocking on other doors of the unknown which had never yet been opened to Christ his Lord, his Life, his love, his everything. Therefore, during such brief time as God would let him stay among the pearl-fishers, he must spend himself mercilessly in order so to root the faith in their hearts that it would never wither. He had no illusions about his Christians, and was well aware that they still felt strongly attracted to the idols and superstitions which they had verbally abandoned, as well as to the highly intoxicating arrack or toddy distilled from palm tree sap by their tree-climbing neighbours, the Shânars. The severe measures which, as will be seen, he took to suppress drunkenness were accepted in a docile spirit, itself a proof of the virtue that went out from him. If his catechists and interpreters, on whom so much depended, were to be full-time workers, he must be able to support them, as well as his four recruits. For this purpose Governor de Sousa had put at his disposal an annual sum of four thousand *fanams*, the value of which may be estimated by the fact that one *fanam*, the smallest of Indian gold coins, made of very base metal, was the current price of three plump chickens.[1] Among the catechists none had

---

Indian dress the towns and villages of the Cape Comorin area associated with the labours and sorrows of St. Francis. It is principally the fruit of Father George Schurhammer's investigations, and the history given, which renders obsolete all other accounts in lives of St. Francis, is largely derived from a learned article entitled *Iniquitriberim and Beteperumal*, which the same great scholar contributed to the *Journal of the Bombay Historical Society*, vol. iii (1930), 1–40.

[1] Apparently the Governor had the privilege of bestowing the money in charity during his three years of office, but it was really a perquisite of the Queen of Portugal, her 'slipper-money', a tax *para seus Chapins*. Padre Teixeira, who knew St. Francis in India, states that he wrote to the Queen begging her to make the concession permanent and that she graciously con-

more of his love than a quick-witted Paravan lad, baptized
Matthew, to whom he had taught sufficient Portuguese to qualify
him as Mansilhas's interpreter, for that good soul would certainly
never be able to learn any Tamil, whether like a parrot or a
pundit.

Francis Mansilhas, the Wanting and Unwanted, now suddenly
becomes the second self of Francis Xavier, the intimate of his
soul's secrets, his stay and confidant in all the fluctuations of
sorrow, as never was another, not even Ignatius Loyola. To him,
at this period, Francis wrote or hastily scribbled twenty-six little
Portuguese letters which bring him closer to our understanding
than almost anything else said or done by him in the whole of
his martyred existence. It is to the everlasting credit of Mansilhas
that he carefully treasured those bits and scraps of correspondence,
and when dying, long after the death of their writer, bequeathed
the collection to the Jesuits of Cochin.[1] The first of the series,
dated from Punnaikâyal, February 23, 1544, and addressed to
Mansilhas at Manapad, where he was stationed with the boy
Matthew and John Artiaga, runs as follows:

May the grace and love of Christ our Lord befriend us and
stand by us always. Dearest Brother, I have a great yearning
to know your news. I beg you earnestly for the love of Jesus
Christ to give me a long account of yourself and your companions. I shall let you know when I am due to arrive in Manapad. Keep in mind the instructions which I gave you in writing,
and pray God to endow you with an abundance of patience in
relation to your flock. Imagine to yourself that you are in
Purgatory expiating your sins, and reckon that you are very
highly privileged to be able to pay your account in this world.

sented. The letter is not extant but Teixeira gives the gist of it: ' The Father
suggested to Her Highness that she could have no better slippers in which to
climb to Heaven than the Christian children of the Fishery Coast, supported
and taught out of the funds derived from such an exchange' (*Monumenta
Xaveriana*, ii, 852–3).

[1] The originals perished when the Dutch besieged Cochin and destroyed
the Jesuit college there in 1663, but many copies had been made and sent to
Europe long before that year.

Captain de Paiva has written to say that he gave John Artiaga ten *pardaus* for me. Would you tell John this, and that I have let the Captain know that we are none of us, neither you nor John nor I, in need of money until he returns from the pearl-fishing.[1] I said that the sum would be returned at once, so John must see that this is done. If the Captain had given him the ten *pardaus* in the shape of an official money-order from the Governor, he might have used them to hire an interpreter, but, unless he received them in this authoritative form, tell him to return them at once. May our Lord give you grace to serve Him, and as much of it as I could wish for myself. I do not write to John Artiaga separately, as this letter is for both of you. Your loving brother, Francis.

Loving he certainly was, but, as the next letter shows, Francis could also breathe fire at times and use stern measures to bring offenders to their senses. It is plain that he already suspected Captain de Paiva and was not going to be bribed by him into holding his tongue. Meantime, he had changed Mansilhas and his company to Punnaikâyal and himself moved into Manapad, from which place the second letter went off on March 14, the height of the pearl-fishing season, when few but women and children were left on the Coast:

Dearest Brother in Christ, Your letter gladdened my heart. I earnestly beg you to comport yourself with your people as a good father does with naughty sons. Do not weary of them because of the many evils you see. God whom they offend so gravely does not destroy them, though He so easily could, nor deprive them of the necessities of life, which also are in His power to withdraw. Do not give way to vexation and heaviness of heart. You are bearing more fruit than you imagine, and if you cannot achieve all that you would like, be content with

[1] A *pardau* was an Indian coin worth ten *fanams*. De Paiva sailed with the fleet of *tônis* and catamarans, the latter more in the nature of rafts than boats, to supervise the pearl-fishing in the interest of Portugal. He appears to have had the administration of the Queen's 'slipper-money'.

what you are able to do, the difference being no fault of yours. I am sending you a person to act as policeman[1] until I arrive. I shall give him a *fanam* for every woman he catches drinking arrack, and, what is more, the offender may be put in a lockup for three days. Have this proclaimed all over the area, and tell the headmen that if from now on I hear of any more arrack being drunk in Punnaikâyal, they will have to pay me dearly for it. Give Matthew a message from me that he is to be a very good boy and I shall look after him more solicitously than his own kith and kin could. Before I come to join you, make those village officials change their ways. Otherwise, I shall have to send them all prisoners to Cochin, without hope of return, as they are the cause of all the mischief in Punnaikâyal. Be very diligent in baptizing the new-born babies; teach the children in the way I recommended; on Sundays, gather all the people together to learn the prayers and give them a little sermon; and finally stringently prohibit any making or worshipping of idols. Keep the letter which Alvaro Fogaça has addressed to me until I come. May God our Lord give you as much consolation in this life and the next as I desire for myself. Your loving brother in Christ, Francis.

The next letter, also from Manapad and dated March 20, gives some obscure hints of tragedies and triumphs impending:

My dearest Brother in Christ, It was a great joy to me to hear that you are happy. Since God is so mindful of you, do you remember Him, and never weary of going on and on with the work you have begun. Thank Him unceasingly because He chose you for so great a charge as yours is. I do not wish to burden you with suggestions other than those which I set down in my memorandum. Remember me, for I never have you out of mind. Tell Matthew to be a good boy and I will be a good father to him. Watch over him well. Tell him

---

[1] *Meirinho*, literally, a tipstaff or sheriff's officer. The word derives from those same merino sheep which were so much a part of Francis's boyhood and constituted a large part of the economy of Portugal as well as of Spain.

to speak out loudly when he is interpreting for you on Sundays so that everybody may hear him, so that he might even be heard here in Manapad![1] Let me have news of the Christians in Tuticorin and whether the Portuguese who stayed there did them any harm. Also, is there any news as to whether the Governor is going to Cochin, to put things in order there? Here, an affair of great importance for the service of God is gradually unfolding. Pray to the Lord that it may have effect and come to light. I entreat you to bear yourself very lovingly towards those people, the ones with authority among them in the first place, and then all the rest, for if they love you and get on well with you, you will do God great service. Learn to pardon and support their weaknesses very patiently, reflecting that if they are not good now, they will be some day. If you fail to accomplish with them all that you might wish, be satisfied with such results as you can bring about, which is what I do myself. May the Lord God always be with you, and may He give us both His grace to serve Him to the end. Your brother in Christ, Francis.

He asked about Governor de Sousa in that letter because he was very anxious to discuss with him the *couza muito grande de serviço de Deos*. Iniquitriberim, the Great King or Maharaja, had begun hostilities with the Pândyan Prince, Vettum Perumâl, whom he had displaced and who was supported by certain unsubmissive tribes of the other man's jurisdiction. Both parties courted the Portuguese, whom at heart they despised and hated, because those Western barbarians were lords of the sea and in control of the horse-trade. Likewise, the dogs possessed gunpowder. Here, thought the sanguine Francis, was a chance to obtain favourable concessions from the Maharaja for the subject Paravas, but, as will be seen, his hopes jumped a good deal ahead of events, and he did not reckon on stabs in the back from the money-grubbing white men. A week after the dispatch of his last letter he writes to Mansilhas again, still from Manapad:

[1] Manapad is nearly nineteen miles south of Punnaikâyal.

Dearest Brother, I rejoiced to hear what you had to say of yourself, and was delighted with your letter and the good results you are obtaining. God give you strength always to go on from good to better.[1] It is impossible for me not to feel cut to the heart by the harm which heathen and Portuguese alike are doing to those Christians. I have good reason to be troubled, as I am now so used to witnessing the aggressions, without power to intervene on the Christians' behalf, that the whole thing has become a permanent bruise on my soul, an over-whelming sorrow ever with me. I have already written to the vicars-general of Quilon and Cochin, telling them about the women whom the Portuguese snatched as slaves at Punnai-kâyal, that by threat of major excommunication they may be able to learn the identity of the ravishers and their Christian victims. I took this step three days ago, immediately on receiving the headmen's note. You must give Matthew everything he needs in the way of clothing, and be a good companion to him, so that he may not leave you, as he is free to do. Treat him very lovingly as I used to do when he was with me, so as to keep him attached. When you repeat the Creed in Tamil, you ought not to start by saying *enaquvenum* but *enaquvichuam*, because *venum* means ' I wish, will, desire ', while *vichuam* means ' I believe ', and it is better to say ' I believe in God ' than ' I wish in God '. Similarly [in the Fourth Article] do not say *Vampinale*, because that means by constraint or necessity, whereas Christ suffered voluntarily. When the folk return from the pearl-fishing be sure to visit the sick among them, and get some of the children to recite the prayers over them, as I explained in the memoran-dum. Finish off by reading some verses of a Gospel yourself. Always deal very lovingly with your people, and take pains to

---

[1] That simple sentence, *Deos vos dê força para sempre perseverar de bem em melhor*, is rendered in the old Latin versions and in Coleridge as follows: ' May our Lord whom we serve prosper your diligence in the future also, and give you in His mercy sufficient strength to make you equal to a continuance of your exertions, so as to bring always to greater and greater perfection the good you have done, and, in short, to persevere courageously to the end, and so entirely overcome the obstacles and troubles which you may have to meet ' ! !

win their love. I would be greatly pleased to know that they are avoiding arrack and the idols, and that they hasten every Sunday to the prayers. If at the time when they were baptized they had had some one to teach them as you are doing now, they would today be better Christians than they are. May our Lord give you as much consolation in this life and glory in the next as I could desire for myself. Your loving brother in Christ, Francis.[1]

The two men are still in the same places when Francis writes to Mansilhas once more on April 8:

Dearest Brother, I was greatly pleased to hear of your visits to the Christian villages, and still more delighted with the grand results everybody tells me you obtained. I am hoping for a message from the Governor today or tomorrow. If it arrives I shall come to you without fail, as I am most anxious to see you in the flesh as I always see you in spirit. I have dismissed John Artiaga, as he is full of temptations which he fails to recognize, and does not take the right way to find out what is the matter with him. He says he is going to Kombuturê to teach the people there, and to be near you, but I haven't much faith in his proposals because, as you know well, he is very inconstant. If he turns up, do not waste much time with him. I have written to the Captain to supply you with whatever you

[1] According to informants born to the language, the Tamil corrections of Francis were sadly out of order. They say that *enakku vênhum* (the correct transliteration) does not mean, as he thought, ' I wish or desire ', but ' I have need of ', and *vichuam* does not mean ' I believe ', but the noun belief. ' I believe ' in good Tamil is *visuvasikiran*. So much for poor Francis and his alleged miraculous gift of tongues ! Yet there *was* a miracle and a great one, for with his pathetic little stock of ill-understood Tamil words, like the seven loaves that fed four thousand in Galilee, he somehow succeeded in impressing the Catholic faith so indelibly on the souls of that primitive tribe that no manner of violence or cajolery has ever been able to erase it. When the Dutch conquered the Fishery Coast in the seventeenth century, they used every kind of persuasion in their power to win the Paravas to Calvinism, but they failed egregiously and, when they pressed too hard, came near to bringing about a general insurrection (Thurston, *Castes and Tribes of Southern India*, vi, 146). The same is to be said of the English Protestant missionaries, good earnest men and women, with all

need, and have asked Manuel da Cruz[1] to lend you money whenever you require it. He has very readily promised me to do so. Take great care of your health, since with it you are doing the Lord God such fine service. Tell Matthew from me to serve you well, and let him know that if you are satisfied with him he can count on me as both father and mother. But if he fails to be very obedient to you I won't want to see him or have anything to do with him. Give him whatever he needs for his wardrobe. In the villages you visit, assemble the men one day in one place, and the women another day in another, and see to it that they say the prayers daily in their homes. Baptize those who have not received the sacrament, both children and adults, remembering the adage that, if the water does not come to the mill, the miller must go to the water.[2] May our Lord always help you and have you in His keeping. Your loving brother, Francis.

The next letter, dated April 23, was written from a little place adjoining Manapad named Levadhi:

Dearest Brother, I am very anxious to see you. Please God it may be soon, though every day I do not fail to see you in spirit, nor you me. So we are always together, as you might say. As you love God, write me news of all the Christians, and about yourself, how you are faring. Be very circumstantial, please!

---

their abundant resources of schools, orphanages, hospitals, etc. The Paravas, though still as always poor, remain the staunchest Catholics in India. The illness among them to which Francis referred was caused, partly by the nature of their work, and partly by the effluvia of the oysters laid out on the shore to putrefy that the pearls might be the more easily seen and extracted. The people could not eat them for the simple reason that, unlike their Whitstable cousins, they are inedible.

[1] Owing to the leading part played by the Hindu convert, John of the Cross (see above, p. 122), in bringing about the baptism of their caste, the name Cruz became a very popular one among the Paravas. The Manuel da Cruz referred to was a comparatively rich Paravan in Punnaikâyal and a very good friend of St. Francis, who often borrowed money from him.

[2] The text of this sentence about mills and water is corrupt, and it is not clear what St. Francis meant. The idea seems to have been that Mansilhas must search for the unbaptized if they did not come to him spontaneously.

I am expecting the *Pula* from Travancore this week, as he wrote to say that he would come for certain. I hope in God that some service will be done to His Divine Majesty through this, and will let you know all that happens so that you may render Him your thanks.[1] I have already written to the headmen about the oratory to be made of entwined boughs and thatched with palm-leaves. It might be better for the women to come to church on the Saturday mornings, as they do at Manapad, and the men on the Sundays.[2] Do as you think best about this. When you need to write to the Captain about provisions of any kind, do so in good time so that you may not run short.[3] Let me know where John Artiaga has got to and whether he is serving God, for I fear very much that he will not keep it up, being so unstable, as you know. The Indian Father [Francis Coelho] and myself are well. Tell Matthew to be a good child and to speak up and in good style when he translates what you say. When I reach you, I will give him something that will please him immensely. Tell me whether the children come to the prayers and how many now know them by heart. Write to me in detail about everything by the first messenger that comes this way. May our Lord be with you as much as I would like Him to be with myself. Your loving brother, Francis.

The next communication is a mere note from some small unidentifiable village which he calls Nar, situated somewhere

[1] The Pulas were a superior class, a sort of aristocracy, of the Sudra caste. The branch of them living on the Malabar Coast, especially at Quilon, were the subjects and allies of Iniquitriberim, but those settled on the other side of the mountains, towards the Fishery Coast, though also his subjects, were in a constant state of rebellion and aided his enemy Vettum Perumâl. It is some indication of the wide repute in which St. Francis was held that the proud Maharaja, Iniquitriberim, should now be sending an envoy to him in hopes of obtaining his intercession with the Portuguese authorities.

[2] This may partly have been because the small wattle and daub structures, which were all that Francis could run to in the way of churches, would not have accommodated the entire congregation at any one time, but he also seems to have had a definite policy of keeping the men and women apart during their devotions, for undisclosed reasons.

[3] The Captain always in question was Cosmas de Paiva, Portuguese representative in Tuticorin, who, though a knave, had the administration of the Queen's 'slipper-money', granted annually to St. Francis.

near Manapad. What brought him there is not indicated, but it probably had to do with his negotiations on behalf of Iniquitriberim:

Dearest Brother, Today, the first of May, I got a letter from you which brought me such comfort that I could go on telling you about it endlessly. For you must know that I have been down with fever four or five days and was bled twice. Now I am better, and hope by God's goodness to see you in Punnaikâyal next week. I am expecting the envoy from Travancore today or tomorrow. When we meet, we shall have a chat about what is going on up here. May it please God to grant that some service to Him may result from it. Father Coelho is sending you two sombreros. Since we shall see you soon, I conclude by praying that God our Lord may give us His holy grace to serve Him. Your loving brother, Francis.

It was a fortnight before he wrote again, during which he had travelled far to the north, beyond Tuticorin. On his way south to join Mansilhas at Manapad, he was detained at Tuticorin by a split among the Christians there. Francis had been busy endeavouring to obtain for Iniquitriberim the alliance which he coveted with Governor de Sousa, and his activities, if they became publicly known, might mean serious danger for the neophytes of Tuticorin and of Palayakâyal, a village just north of the river Tâmbraparni, as both places were subject to the Maharaja's sworn enemy, Vettum Perumâl. The Saint therefore wanted to remove his exposed children south of the river, into the territory of Iniquitriberim, but a section of them in Tuticorin strongly objected to being moved, and were backed up in their opposition by the scheming Captain de Paiva who was feathering his nest by selling horses, the real sinews of Indian war, to the rampaging Vettum Perumâl. The man was thus doubly a traitor, to the Government at Goa and to the Catholic mission which he had been officially appointed to protect. The Peter and Antony mentioned in the letter were native catechists and interpreters:

Dearest Brother in Christ, God knows how much better pleased I would be to spend a few days with you than to stay on in Tuticorin, but I am obliged to remain awhile in order to pacify the people here, and console myself with the thought that this is the best way I can serve God our Lord. I do beg you not to let yourself become provoked by those very troublesome people, no matter how much cause they give you. When you see yourself burdened with engagements too many to be met, keep a good heart and do whatever you can, at the same time thanking the Lord that you are in a place where you couldn't take things easy even if you wished it, so much, so very much, is there to be done and all for the service of God. I am sending you Peter, and as soon as Antony is well again, which may be in six or eight days, you shall have him also. I am writing to Manuel da Cruz, asking him to get the church up for you soon. Would you send me my little trunk by the first *tôni* that sails this way. When I finish matters here I shall come to see you immediately. You might be surprised to know how anxious I am to spend a few days with you. Whenever you have need of anything, send me a line by somebody coming from your direction. Try always and as well as ever you can to bear with your people very patiently, and when they refuse to be good, exercise on them the merciful injunction which says, Punish him that stands in need of punishment. May our Lord be your helper as I desire Him to be mine. Your loving brother, Francis.

Nearly a month, May 14 to June 11, now passes before Mansilhas receives another note, and there is no means of telling how Francis was occupied during that time, beyond the ordinary routine of baptizing, teaching, attending the sick and burying the dead. When he wrote he was at a small place called for its sins Vîrapândyanpattanam, close to Tiruchendûr:

Dearest Brother in Christ, I announce to you that by the help of God I am in very good form. May it please Him from whom my health comes to give me grace to use it in His service. Keep on sending me news of yourself and of your

Christians, and get the church up soon, and tell me when it is finished. I enclose letters for the Captain which you must transmit to him by some very dependable messenger. I earnestly recommend to you the teaching of the children, and be very diligent about the baptism of newly born babies. Since the grown-ups have no hankering for Paradise, whether to escape the evils of life or to attain their happiness, at least let the little ones go there by baptizing them before they die. My warmest wishes to Manuel da Cruz, and wishes also to Matthew that he may be a good boy, or rather I should say, a good man. Let your attitude to the people be always one of love, and treat their headmen in the same kind way. May our Lord ever be with you. Your loving brother, Francis.

At the point now reached in the correspondence, calamity supervened. Francis was making his way over the sand to pay his promised visit to Mansilhas when, at Kombuturê on June 13, he learned that troops of the Emperor Sadâ Siva, ruler of great Vijayanagar, had descended on Cape Comorin and were slaughtering, pillaging and enslaving the defenceless Christians of that region. A proud and fierce class of warriors, something like the cavalry of Genghis Khan, those Badagas or Men of the North, as they were called, seized the opportunity of hostilities between Iniquitriberim, nominally their suzerain's vassal and ally, and Vettum Perumâl, his enemy, to avenge themselves on the unhappy Paravas for having, by becoming Christians, gone over to the detested Portuguese. And it was on swift Arab horses supplied by the Portuguese that they made their raids. Immediately on hearing the terrible report, Francis hastened back to Manapad to organize relief, as he explains in a hasty note sent off to Mansilhas, then at Punnaikâyal, just before he sailed for the Cape:

Dearest Brother in Christ, I arrived back in Manapad on Saturday evening [June 14], having heard very bad news in Kombuturê about the Cape Comorin Christians. The Badagas, I learned, were carrying them off as slaves, and the Christians, to save themselves, had taken refuge on some rocks out in the sea, where they are now dying of hunger and thirst. Tonight, June 16, I go with twenty *tônis* of Manapad to their rescue. Pray for them and for us, and above all get the children to pray. They promised me at Kombuturê to construct a church and Manuel de Lima offered to give a hundred *fanams* towards the cost. Would you go to Kombuturê on Wednesday or Thursday and give instructions how the church is to be made. Next week, God willing, you should visit the Christians from where you are at Punnaikâyal southwards to Alantalai, baptizing those not yet baptized, especially babies, and calling on the people in their own homes, door by door. Keep your eyes open to see whether those who teach the children, and the others charged with getting them together, are doing their duty well. Will you tell Manuel da Cruz who is at Kombuturê to watch carefully over the two villages of Carean Christians to see that they live in concord, do not frequent idols, avoid the drinking of arrack, and meet on Sundays to say their prayers, the men in the morning and the women in the evening. If Francis Coelho is around, would you tell him from me to come to me soon. May God protect you. I have paid the Moor who is taking this letter to you what he needed to get him to Kâyalpattanam. Your loving brother, Francis.[1]

A fortnight goes by before another letter is dispatched to Mansilhas, with its tale of disaster:

Dearest Brother, I arrived back at Manapad on Tuesday the 24th, after God knows what tribulations on the sea. The winds were so contrary when I set out with the twenty *tônis* to the succour of the Christian fugitives dying of hunger and thirst on the rocks off Cape Comorin, that neither by rowing nor by towing the boats with ropes from the shore could we reach the Cape. When the winds subside we shall have another try, and I shall do all in my power to help the poor souls whom it

---

[1] So Francis trusted a 'Moor', i.e. an Arab Moslem, with his correspondence. Kâyalpattanam is a Mohammedan town a little south of Punnaikâyal. The Manuel de Lima in the text was a Paravan convert.

is the most pitiful thing in the world to see in such dire straits. Many of them arrive daily in Manapad, despoiled of everything and without food or clothing. I have written to the headmen of Kombuturê, Punnaikâyal and Tuticorin asking them to send alms for the unhappy Christians, but have told them that they are not to exact any contributions from poor people. Let the small ship-owners who spontaneously desire to help do so, but nobody is to be forced. Do not permit anything to be taken from the poor by the headmen. I look for no good from those fellows. Our hope is in God rather than in them, so do not let them bring pressure to bear on anybody, whether rich or poor, to contribute. I beg you most earnestly to write me a long letter saying if the church in Kombuturê is now up, if Manuel de Lima gave the hundred *fanams* towards it, how you got on while visiting those villages, and if the children in them are receiving instruction. I paid all the catechists their salaries, but do not know how they behaved in my absence. Write to me at good length about everything, as I am anxious for news of you and of your Punnaikâyal. I was eight days at sea, and you know what it is like in one of those *tônis* with a gale blowing all the time. May our Lord have you always in His keeping. Your loving brother, Francis.

The contrary winds experienced on that occasion would have been the tail end of the south-west monsoon which blows from mid-June to October and brings with it, not only heavy rains, but great clouds of red dust fifty or sixty feet high, picked up in the flat lands east of the Ghats and driven out to sea over the Fishery Coast. Francis, therefore, was modest in his reference to the miseries of life in a small open boat, full of provisions, which could neither be sailed nor rowed nor pulled along by main force. Mansilhas received no letter from him during the grim July of 1544 because he had turned beggarman and spent the month going from village to village the whole length of the Coast seeking food and clothing for the Badagas's victims. After his death, Mansilhas solemnly testified that ' he was an utterly fearless man, and not only confronted the Badagas, but denounced them to their

faces, while he went around from village to village collecting
alms for their victims, marooned on rocks in the sea '. During
breaks of quiet weather in the monsoon, he would ' load the food
and drink thus obtained into boats and take them himself to the
starving Christians '.[1] Having devastated the villages near the
Cape, and being unable through lack of shipping to reach the
Christians on their rocky islands, the Badagas turned north to
become a menace to Punnaikâyal, as Francis mentioned to the
other Francis stationed there, in a letter sent off from Manapad
on August 1. Apparently he had succeeded in bringing about the
evacuation of the Christians from Palayakâyal, though not from
Tuticorin owing to the manœuvres of Captain de Paiva. He would
save what remnant he could of his people, and was determined
that the evacuees should not again put themselves under the jurisdiction of Vettum Perumâl while that violent person remained
on the war-path, even if their headmen, no doubt hankering
after arrack, tried to force them to return. The letter was in the
following terms:

Dearest Brother, May our Lord continually protect you and
give you ample strength to serve Him. I was delighted with
your letter, seeing from it how carefully you are watching
over your people so that the Badagas may not take them
unawares. I have been along the land route to the Cape to
meet the stricken Christians. They made the most lamentable
sight you could imagine, here a group perishing for lack of
food, there some old men vainly endeavouring to keep pace
with the others. And the dead were all about, and husbands
in mourning, and wives bringing babies into the world by the
roadside, and many other sights to move one to tears. If you
had seen what I have seen, you would be as much heartbroken.
I directed all the poor souls to Manapad and now the place is
full of them. Oh, beg the Lord God to move the hearts of the
rich so that they may have pity on those hapless ones. I hope to
set out for your Punnaikâyal on Wednesday [August 6]. Keep
careful watch and ward until those Badagas return to their own

[1] *Monumenta Xaveriana*, ii, 318.

country. Tell Antonio Fernandez the Fat[1] and the headmen of Palayakâyal that I forbid them to try to get the people back there, and will demand heavy payment if they disobey me. Remember me very kindly to Manuel da Cruz and to Matthew. May our Lord be with you, and grant us both grace to be His good servants. Your brother in Christ, Francis.

Only two days later he wrote again, alarmed by further news of the Badagas's progress:

Dearest Brother in Christ, May God always be with you. The part of your letter telling of the consolation you derived from your visitation of the Christian villages gave me much joy, but I was very sorry to hear of the oppression you are suffering and will continue to be sorry until God delivers you. Neither of us lacks such tribulations, praise be to God. I have sent instructions to Father Coelho to get the boats launched and in readiness to embark all the villagers of your area, in case of emergency, for I am sure the Badagas will attempt to surprise you and capture the Christians. According to news given me by a revenue collector from Malabar, an important man who is friendly to the Christians, the marauders are bound to make for the Coast. This Kanakkar is also my very good friend, so I sent him a letter for King Iniquitriberim, with whom he is intimate, asking that monarch to control the Badagas and prevent them from doing us harm, seeing that he is on good terms with Governor de Sousa and that the Governor would take it very badly did he hear of the Christians being maltreated. The Kanakkar came to see me and to offer his assistance, as he has numerous Christian relatives and appreciates my friendship with them. I wrote to him subsequently asking to be kept posted on all developments and to be advised when the raiders approached the Coast, so that

[1] To distinguish him from slimmer Paravas with the same name. The Indian name for the headmen of a Paravan village was *patangatims*. They were an oppressive and usurious class, the gombeen men of the Fishery Coast.

we might have time to withdraw to the security of the sea. I have also written to the Captain requesting that a small armed ship should be sent for the protection of you and your people. Make the people keep a vigilant watch on the mainland,[1] as those Badagas, who are mounted, pounce at night and capture the folk before they have time to get into their boats. Keep a close eye on your Christians, for they have so little sense that to save two *fanams* they would abandon their sentry duties. Make them launch all their boats at once and put their belongings into them, and get the women and children to pray, now as never before, for we have none to help us but God. Send me at once by a coolie whatever writing-paper remains in the box, as I have nothing left for letters to you, and let me know the news, if the boats are being launched and the good placed in them, and how diligently this is being done. Tell Antonio Fernandez the Fat that he is to keep most careful watch for the people, if he wishes to be my friend. Those Badagas do not make prisoners of the lowlier poor folk, but take away only such as they expect to be ransomed. Above all, see to it that a most vigilant watch is maintained at night and that spies are posted on the mainland. I greatly fear that with the moon now at the full they may come to the Coast by night on a foray, so mind that your people are on the alert during the night hours. May our Lord be your protector. Your loving brother, Francis.

Our man was plainly not one to take chances or to leave anything undone which human foresight could suggest. But for his precautions and diplomatic moves, it seems certain that the Paravas would have been completely exterminated, for Vettum Perumâl, enemy though he was of the Badagas, now also moved against the luckless tribe. Obviously, he had got wind of the negotiations proceeding between Iniquitriberim and Governor de Sousa, and proposed to make the native Christians and the Portuguese in Tuticorin pay dearly for whatever advantage the Maharaja might gain. So Cosmas de Paiva's horse-trading, his

[1] Punnaikâyal is situated on an island at the mouth of the Tâmbraparni.

cavalerias, as St. Francis called it, was to recoil on his own head. Francis writes from Manapad on August 19:

Dearest Brother, Stand by the people and fortify them in their tribulation, and also have the goodness to let me know any certain news from Tuticorin. I fear that the *cavalerias* of that town may bring the poor folk into trouble. I couldn't describe to you the terror that has seized on them here. I never thought that your idea of leaving them [temporarily to administer baptism in another place] was a good one, so do not go away with John Artiaga until the country is free from the Badagas's persecution. Please, I beg you to tell me immediately when you have trustworthy news. Here in Manapad just now is a Brahman sent by Iniquitriberim to negotiate terms of peace with [Vettum Perumâl or his delegates]. Captain de Paiva's interpreter is with him and they are both leaving by sea immediately. I have no notion what they will achieve. As soon as you have any news of the Portuguese in Tuticorin, please send me a detailed report to relieve my great anxiety. Tell me whether any of them have been wounded or killed, and also whether the same has happened to the native Christians. As for your going from Punnaikâyal, we shall see. I shall write to you about it when this fury of the Badagas is past. May our Lord be always with you. Amen. There has just arrived a palm-leaf note from the Kanakkàr, telling me, your *charissimo Irmăo*, that the Christians have fled into the woods, and that the Badagas have plundered them, killing one Christian and one heathen. From all sides bad news pours in, praise be to the Lord for ever. Francis.[1]

Next day, August 20, there is another letter to Mansilhas who seems to have been complaining of the conduct of the wretched de Paiva, official protector of the Christians:

[1] The mutable Artiaga, we see, is still around, and it may have been he who suggested to Mansilhas that they should go to the island of Manar off the north-west coast of Ceylon to baptize the people of a village called Patim there, who seem to have appealed for help. Francis gave his blessing to this project a little later, and also received Artiaga back into favour for a while.

Dearest Brother, God always be with you. Amen. From the saying of our Lord, *He who is not with Me is against Me*, you can see how many friends we have out here to help us make this people Christian ! But let us not be discouraged, for God at the end will requite every man according to his due. If it please Him, He can be served just as well by few as by many. I have pity for those opposed to God rather than desire to see them punished, since heavy chastisement will be their portion at the end, as we know from the condition of God's enemies in Hell. The Brahman I mentioned is going on to you with a dispatch from the Badagas to King Vettum Perumâl.[1] For the love of God order a boat immediately to take him to Tuticorin. Let me have news of that town, of the Captain, of the Portuguese, and of the native Christians, for I am greatly worried. My warmest wishes to John Artiaga and Manuel da Cruz. Tell Matthew not to grow weary, that he is not labouring in vain, and that I will reward him more handsomely than he imagines. As you love God, be instant in helping the Brahman on his way, and say a word to the Captain that he may at least treat him respectfully. Your loving brother in Christ, Francis.

The Captain did not at all sympathize with the Brahman's mission, since peace between the Princes and the cessation of the Badagas's raids would have meant a drop in the demand for horses, with consequent damage to his prospects as a business man. Francis writes next time, August 29, from Punnaikâyal, to Mansilhas at Tuticorin:

Dearest Brother in Christ, May God be ever your helper. Amen. Your letter gave me great pleasure. Let me know when the Tuticorin area is safe from the Badagas, so that without

[1] As the Brahman was also the envoy of Iniquitriberim, it is plain that that potentate was allied with the Badagas against Vettum Perumâl. This fragment of history has been muddled and misinterpreted in all books about St. Francis Xavier until the matter was straightened out at last by Father Schurhammer in his great edition of the Xaverian letters. The reason that Iniquitriberim could not keep his allies in order was that he had not the power, since they were part of the army of his suzerain, the Emperor of Vijayanagar.

offence to your people I may send Father Coelho to take your
place. You will thus be able to do God the great service of
baptizing the people at Patim on Manar island, as also the
Careas of Vêdâlai and their chieftain.[1] The Portuguese Captain
at Negapatam has a good deal of influence with the Raja of
Jaffna who rules the islands off the coast, and is in duty bound
to help the people in their relations with that person.[2] Immediately that your territory is free of the Badagas, dispatch a
courier so that I may send you Father Coelho with money,
letters, and instructions for your work in Manar. I commend
our brother, John Artiaga, to you very warmly. Let me know
whether he is in need of anything, so that I may provide it,
as is only reasonable. Here, I am going about among the people
all alone, without an interpreter, as Antony is sick in Manapad,
and I am left with Rodrigo and the other Antony, neither of
whom understands what I say, nor I, even less, what they say.
So you can imagine the sort of life I am leading and the exhortations I deliver! And you can see me trying to converse with
the people! However, I baptize the new-born babies and such
others as I find ready for baptism. I have no need of an interpreter for that, and the poor make me understand their necessities without an interpreter, for I can see them and appreciate
them all unaided. The big things in life don't need interpreting.
The Badagas who were here have all now decamped to
Kalakkâd,[3] and the country is safe again, except that the local
pagans are doing what mischief they can until Iniquitriberim

[1] Vêdâlai is a small town on the Indian coast opposite to the island of
Râmesvaram, where stands one of the most massive and venerated of all
Hindu shrines, with pillared corridors nearly four thousand feet in length.
The Careas were a pearl-fishing caste similar to the Paravas. A section of them
had crossed Adam's Bridge from Vêdâlai and made new homes on the island
of Manar.

[2] The Captain at Negapatam was Antonio Mendes de Vasconcellos. Jaffna
is a peninsula at the north of Ceylon and has a large and flourishing city of
the same name, now the see of a Catholic bishopric. The Raja of Jaffna and
Vasconcellos were engaged in some shady private transactions advantageous to
both. The Captain was not the man to allow consideration for the Christians
to interfere with his business prospects.

[3] A provincial capital of Iniquitriberim, between Cape Comorin and
Tinnevelly.

brings about a settlement. I leave tonight for Alantalai where there are many poor people. May our Lord be ever with you. Your loving brother, Francis.

The seventeenth letter from the one Francis to the other went off on September 5, the address being Alantalai, which the Saint wrote in the English-looking form of Alendale. Mansilhas at that time had returned to Punnaikâyal:

Dearest Brother in Christ, God our Lord be your helper always. Amen. I am very anxious about the Christians of Tuticorin, as they have no one to look after them. For the love of our Lord, let me know at once what is happening, and if you think it to the service of God, assemble all the *tônis* you can from Kombuturê and Punnaikâyal, take the people from those islands they are on, and bring them to Kombuturê, Punnaikâyal and Tiruchendûr. Leave immediately with all the *tônis* available at Punnaikâyal, and send orders to Kombuturê that the ones there are to sail after you without delay. Don't allow those poor refugees on the islands to perish of hunger and thirst for the sake of Vettum Perumâl and his horses. It would be better for the Captain's reputation if he concerned himself with the Christians rather than with trading horses to that personage. I am sending you a written order for the head-men of your place and of Kombuturê that they are to make ready their *tônis* to go with you immediately to rescue the starving Christians. If you think it unnecessary to join the expedition yourself, stay where you are. I leave the matter entirely to your discretion. But see that the boats take water and food. Let me know how Manuel da Cruz and Matthew are feeling, as they were disconsolate when I parted from them. Your loving brother, Francis.

There are three islands off Tuticorin, the largest of them Pândyan Tivu, two and a half miles out, being called Hare Island by the British because that animal and other game, such as partridges, may be shot there. A certain sea-slug, highly appreciated by the Chinese as an article of diet, is to be found in abundance on the coral-girt shores at low tide, so, even if they could not trap hares or partridge, the Christian refugees need not necessarily have starved. The fact that they were obliged to abandon their homes in Tuticorin is proof of Vettum Perumâl's unwillingness to come to terms with Iniquitriberim. He might pay good prices for horses to Captain de Paiva and his kind, but he loathed the Portuguese in other respects, and was bent on wiping out the unoffending Paravas because of their connection with them. The same day that he dispatched his last letter, Francis heard of the Raja's assault on Tuticorin and of de Paiva's misfortunes, so he hastily penned another note to Mansilhas at Punnaikâyal:

Dearest Brother in Christ, I have been given sad news of the Captain, that they have burnt his ship and houses. He is now a refugee on the islands. For the love of God, go at once with your people of Punnaikâyal, and take all the water which a complete muster of *tônis* will carry. I am writing in strong terms to the headmen, telling them that they are to go with you at once to see the Captain and to take plenty of boats well supplied with water to bring away the refugees. If I thought that the Captain would like me to accompany the expedition myself, I would go and you could remain in Punnaikâyal, but he has written me a letter saying that he could not, without great scandal, put down in set terms the harm I had done him. God and all the world knows where the scandal lies. I do not think he would be pleased to see me, and for this and other reasons refrain from going. As well as to your headmen, I am writing to those of Kombuturê and Vêmpâr[1] to go at once with all their *tônis* to where the Captain is, taking water and food. For the love of God, use all your diligence in this matter, for you can see that the Captain is in great distress, as are all the Christians. Please, for the love of God, hurry, hurry. Our Lord be with you always. Your loving brother, Francis.

[1] The last Paravan village, to the north of Tuticorin.

The political situation has now become so involved that a little further elucidation may not be considered superfluous. The part of India south of the river Tâmbraparni used at one time to be ruled by the Pândya dynasty, to which Raja Vettum Perumâl belonged, but this territory was wrested from its overlords in the fifteenth century by the ancestors of the Maharaja Iniquitriberim, to keep to the name fastened on that monarch by St. Francis. The nobles of the territory, the Pulas, whom St. Francis designates as *os da terra*, the People of the Land, never became reconciled to the new situation and backed Vettum Perumâl in his efforts to regain the lost dominion. Iniquitriberim did not want war, but had it forced on him by the other man, who rejected his peace overtures. The Portuguese captain at Tuticorin, de Paiva, was all for war because it promoted his horse-trading, and he hotly resented the interference of St. Francis on the side of Iniquitriberim and peace. The Badagas incursion was merely an incident in the long struggle and ceased as soon as St. Francis had brought his influence to bear on the Maharaja, who had called in the raiders, not to persecute the Christians, but to help him against Vettum Perumâl. Francis discovered that the Pulas, who were wealthy miscreants, had started bargaining on their own account with Governor de Sousa, but Iniquitriberim outbid them and in the long run prevailed. De Sousa does not appear in too favourable a light in this business, but he continued to have the trust of Francis and to be, on the whole, a good friend of the missions. The next letter to Mansilhas, sent from Tiruchendûr on September 7, shows that the Portuguese traders on the Coast did not much care whom they injured, and least of all the Christians, provided that they were enabled to line their own pockets:

Dearest Brother in Christ, May God give us His holy grace, for in this country we have no other help but His. I have been in Tiruchendûr on my way to visit the Christians of Vîra-pândyanpattanam, as I had already done those of Alantalai and Pudikudi.[1] All three communities, as well as that of Tiru-chendûr itself, badly need attention. Just as I was about to

[1] This is the name of two small villages between Manapad and Âlantalai.

leave, I was brought news that the people of the land were staging a revolt because some Portuguese had carried off a brother-in-law of Vettum Perumâl, and that, as a reprisal, the natives designed to seize the Christians from Cape Comorin [now in Manapad]. Father Coelho writes that I ought to return at once to Manapad, for if I am not with them the Cape Christians there may suffer terrible harm. The Father also says that a prince, the nephew of Iniquitriberim, has arrived in the district, on business concerning those unhappy people, and that he may do them much mischief if I am not there to prevent it. He further reports that Iniquitriberim has sent three or four of his servants with a letter for me. Exhausted with their journey, they are resting in Manapad, but the contents of the letter have been given to me. It is an invitation from Iniqui-triberim to visit him at the place where he now is, as he is very anxious to discuss with me some business of high importance to him.[1] I imagine that he is greatly in need of Governor de Sousa's favour, as his enemies the Pulas are very prosperous and have plenty of money. Perhaps he fears that they will outbid him for the Governor's assistance. He assures me that the Christians in his dominions may regard themselves as secure, and as certain to receive the kindest treatment at his hands. I am leaving tonight for Manapad, and from thence, out of my love for the Christians of Tuticorin and Vêmpâr, I shall go to the Great King and concert measures with him for their safety also, under his jurisdiction.[2] You will see to it that the Tuticorin Christians on the islands, now near death from exposure and want, are brought to Kombuturê and Punnaikâyal. Let me have detailed news of all the Christians, but I especially want to know how the Captain and the Portu-guese are faring. If you can find time to visit the Christians of

[1] The Maharaja was in camp at the time in the Tinnevelly area, a long and weary way from Manapad.

[2] Namely, by transferring them south of the Tâmbraparni, out of Vettum Perumâl's reach. Francis was going to present the Maharaja with a *fait accompli*, as we have already seen him pressing Mansilhas to bring the island refugees at once to places south of the river, and so into Iniquitriberim's territory.

Kombuturê, and the Carean converts, and those at Kâyal-pattanam, I should be very pleased, as they greatly need your presence. I'd love to go to those places myself, if I could. Borrow a hundred *fanams* from your friend Manuel da Cruz and use it to pay those who teach the children. You can find out from them the rates I used to pay. You will be doing God good service by this transaction. I am sending you a very good man, who is anxious to serve God. Give him a warm welcome and hospitality until I return from my visit to Iniquitriberim. If you find him adapted to the work, keep him there permanently. Send me all your news by some boatman, as I have the Portuguese and native Christians very much on my mind. May our Lord grant you and me more rest and tranquillity in the next life than we have in this. Your loving brother, Francis.

It seems that Captain de Paiva, in spite of his rough treatment by Vettum Perumâl, still nursed a grievance against St. Francis, who was so ready to forgive and forget all the mischief he had done. At any rate, he refused to be evacuated south with the poor native Christians, for whose plight he was so largely responsible, and Mansilhas had to leave him alone, Achilles sulking on his rock. The sigh of Francis at the end of the last letter is suspended momentarily in the next, which went off from Manapad on September 10:

Dearest Brother, I couldn't express to you the relief your letters brought me, as I had been so anxious about the Captain and the others. May our Lord always be with them as I desire Him to be with me. Yesterday, two hours before dawn, I sent Father Coelho to visit the Prince, Iniquitriberim's nephew, who is at Periya Tâlai, two leagues from here. The Father was very well received. I thought this move necessary in order to bring back peace to the country, which was in a state of semi-rebellion. I hear that Vettum Perumâl is hastily organizing an expedition by sea against the Maharaja. Your letters reached me on Tuesday afternoon, and I at once dispatched a man with a note for Father Coelho, telling him to send written orders to

the Adigas of the region[1] that they must permit the free flow
of rice and other foods from the interior to Punnaikâyal and
behave in a friendly way towards the Christians. It would be
a satisfaction for me, before I go on to Iniquitriberim, if by
some means or other I could bring peace to this Coast. From
Iniquitriberim's camp, I hope to be able to go with authority
to resist those Adigas. I shall write to the Captain tomorrow,
being unable to do so now owing to the great hurry the messenger is in. I expect Father Coelho back tonight and will
write you tomorrow more fully. Give Paul Vaz[2] my warm
good wishes, and tell Matthew that I am asking Manuel da
Cruz to let him have the twelve *fanams* which he wants for his
father and a poor brother. May our Lord bring us together in
His Kingdom. Your loving brother, Francis.

What sad stuff from a literary point of view those letters are,
of what trifles composed, and how abominably repetitive!
There is hardly a grace of style or a profundity of observation in
them from beginning to end. They are letters in overalls, poor
workaday things, almost smelling of the grime and sweat of the
Fishery Coast. Again and again, Francis trots out his stale clichés
such as *Nunca acabaria de vos escrever*, ' I could never stop writing
to you ', or his very unoriginal invocation, *Nosso Senhor seja sempre comvosco*. And the people mentioned, except for the shadowy
majesty of Iniquitriberim, are the humblest folk in the world, the
dimly descried Indian priest Coelho, Artiaga the inconstant, the
interpreters who could not interpret, the young villager Matthew,
the voice of Mansilhas, and Mansilhas himself, dull of wit,
irritable, obstinate, what a gallery of nonentities they make!
As for the Portuguese appearing, they are the disgrace of their
nation, murky renegades, prepared to sell out to the devil for a
fanam. Yet, read one after another, the letters, so clumsy and
unstudied, seem somehow, like the oyster, to leave a deposit that

[1] The Adigas were Iniquitriberim's local collectors of revenue, and an
oppressive set who mulcted the Paravas unmercifully.
[2] Probably the good unnamed man whom Francis sent to Mansilhas shortly
before.

in the end becomes a shining pearl. In them Francis unconsciously paints his own portrait, and who will deny that it is among the loveliest of all things under heaven, the picture of a completely selfless man? He has often been likened to St. Paul, and indeed his next letter to Mansilhas, dated September 11,[1] has in it more than a touch of Second Corinthians:

> Dearest Brother, I could go on writing to you for ever of the desire that burns in me to be at your point of the Coast. The truth is, I assure you, that if I could find a boat to take me today I would be off at once. Just now, three of the Maharaja's men came to see me with complaints that a Portuguese in Kâyalpattanam had seized a servant of the Prince, Iniquitriberim's nephew, carried him off prisoner to Punnaikâyal, and announced his intention of dragging him along to Tuticorin.[2] When you know the full facts, write to the Captain. If the Portuguese person is still in Punnaikâyal, and I don't care what his importance, you are to give him orders in my name to set his prisoner free immediately. If the Hindu owes him anything, he can seek justice from the Prince. He must not cause more commotion in the country than we are having already. It is because of such occurrences that we never make any progress. If the man is not released, I think I shall have to give up the idea of going to see Iniquitriberim. The people are indignant that they should be so dishonoured and abducted in their own country, a thing that never happened when the Pulas had power. I know not what to do, if it be not to stop wasting our time among these reckless Portuguese who are allowed to commit their atrocities with impunity. If those of them who tried to steal the ship you mentioned had been punished, the rest would not now be behaving as they are. It will not be a matter for much surprise if the Prince avenges himself on our Christians

[1] The letter is wrongly dated March 21 in all editions earlier than Schurhammer's, with disastrous consequences for biographers dependent on them.

[2] That is, straight into the hands of Vettum Perumâl. In spite of all that had happened, the Portuguese, bent on resuming their horse-trade, continued to play up to the enemy of the Christians.

for the seizure of his servant. Would you write and tell the Captain the great grief this event has caused me. I shall not have the heart to write myself any longer to men committed to evil-doing and so brazen about it. If the man seized by the Portuguese has been taken to Tuticorin, go at once, for the love of God, to where the Captain is, and get the prisoner released. If it is justice the Portuguese wants, let him come here to demand it. It would not look good if a Hindu, ignoring the presence of the Captain, were to seize a Portuguese on the islands and forcibly carry him off to the mainland, and neither does it look good to the Indians when one of their own people is seized by a Portuguese on Indian soil and taken to the Captain, especially as there are courts of justice for the redress of wrongs, and the two peoples are at peace. If you are unable to approach the Captain yourself, send Paul Vaz to him with a letter. I can tell you that the suffering I have endured over this business is greater than I have words to describe. May God give us patience to put up with such folly. You must let me know immediately what happens about the servant of the Prince, whether my information is accurate that the Portuguese did, in fact, abduct him to Tuticorin, and if so why? Should it be true, I have made up my mind not to visit Iniquitriberim. Tell me, too, as well as you can judge, what the heathen Indians feel about the incident, and what they are saying about ourselves. To get away from the very rumour of such happenings, and also to go whither my heart calls me, namely, to the land of Prester John where a man can serve God our Lord royally without being hounded for his pains, I have a good mind to take a *tôni* here in Manapad and make for the west coast of India at once. May our Lord assist you and give you His grace. Amen. Your loving brother, Francis.

That was only one of many occasions when European Catholics, building their fortunes in the East, almost drove Francis to despair. But his contemplated refuge from their iniquities, Abyssinia, was not the missionary paradise he imagined, as his persecuted and slaughtered brethren who went there were soon

to discover. The letter shows a Francis very different from the
all-conquering human phenomenon, the mighty wonder-worker,
the Alexander Magnus of the missions, pictured in the imaginative old and new books, and he is a greater Francis in every way,
and altogether more lovable, and a far better advertisement for
God. In his next letter, sent from Manapad on September 12,
he has recovered his poise:

Dearest Brother in Christ, The Prince, Iniquitriberim's
nephew, who is at Periya Tâlai, has become so much our
friend that, when he heard of the wrongs done to the Christians
by the Adigas, he at once dispatched a messenger with a
mandate ordering those people to permit shipments of food
and other necessaries from the mainland,[1] and to behave properly towards the Christians. The messenger is to find out for
me the names of the oppressive Adigas, so that if I go to the
Great King I shall be able to give him a truthful account of
what happened. As the man is the Prince's representative, and
engaged on work for the Christians, make sure that the headmen show him every mark of honour and also, as is only right,
pay his expenses. The money they waste on dancing-girls
would be better spent in such ways as this, sensible ways and
to the general advantage. You, too, must give him a present,
so that he may the more readily check the Adigas and bring
them to a friendlier mind towards the Christians. Let me know
about that servant of the Prince said to have been carried off
prisoner to Tuticorin by a Portuguese. Is the story accurate and
if so why was the aggression committed? The people in general
believe it and make the case look very ugly. They are full of
resentment. I had much better stay where I am than go to
Iniquitriberim if all is as they say. The Prince, his nephew,
greatly honoured Father Coelho and arranged with him everything to the advantage of the Christians. As a mark of special
esteem, he nominated four of them at Manapad headmen,
without imposing on the people the tax that used to be de-

[1] To Punnaikâyal which, as already mentioned, is on an island. The place
was full of refugee Christians, hungry and destitute.

manded for such appointments when the Pulas were in power. He created headmen in several other places also, entirely gratis. For the love of God will you write to the Captain on my behalf and say that I beg him from the bottom of my heart not to command or permit any harm to be done to the heathen of the Great King's dominions throughout the whole of this month of September. As they are all so friendly to us in connection with Christian affairs, it is excusable to ask that they should not be injured. If I am to visit Iniquitriberim, my going and returning and subsequent departure for Cochin would all be accomplished within this month, and I am anxious that there should not be a breath of complaint against us to the King during the whole of the time. Let me know here in your own hand why you said that you could not write [again] without first seeing me.[1] If there is any matter of grave importance bearing on the service of God with which I could help— whether it has to do with the Captain or the Portuguese generally or the native Christians—I shall certainly not go to Iniquitriberim or to Cochin without seeing if the trouble may possibly be remedied. May our Lord always help us and be gracious to us. Your loving brother, Francis.

The next brief note to Mansilhas came from Tuticorin on September 20, showing that Francis had in fact betaken himself north to investigate the trouble weighing on the mind of his lieutenant. He obviously went by sea, but owing possibly to weather difficulties or to the urgency of his business with Iniquitriberim he found himself unable to put in at Punnaikâyal en route, for the much desired and long postponed visit to the other Francis:

Dearest Brother in Christ, Antonio [my interpreter] is still

---

[1] This is one of Francis's numerous maddening sentences: ' *Escrever-me heis por vossa mão, porque me escrevestes que sem vissemos não podieis escrever.*' The Rev. David Macdonald who translated a good number of the letters in whole or in part for Miss Stewart's biography tried to be literal, with the following fearful result: ' Write me by your own hand why you wrote that you would not write without our seeing each other.'

unwell. Would you send the other Antony to Manapad at once, as he is needed to act as cook. Write to me here at Tuticorin directly, as I am very anxious about all these people. As soon as I get to wherever Inquitriberim is,[1] I shall set about obtaining orders from him to the Adigas, requiring them to permit food to go to the refugee Christians, and to show a friendly attitude towards them. These I shall dispatch to you immediately. Pray for me, and tell the children to remember me in their prayers. I am enclosing a note for Manuel da Cruz, asking him to give you a hundred *fanams* with which to pay the children's instructors. May our Lord help you and be gracious to you. Your loving brother, Francis.[2]

Seven weeks were to pass before the one Francis heard from the other again. It is certain that during October Xavier repaired to the camp of Iniquitriberim, but not a detail of his adventures escaped on to paper. It is known only that the Maharaja, a proud, sensual man who probably believed in nothing, not even Vishnu, was pleased with him to the extent of two thousand *fanams*, given entirely unsolicited to help him contrive his humble oratories in any place he pleased. More than that, Iniquitriberim's brother, Mârtanda Varma, conferred on Francis the freedom of his steaming-hot and insalubrious coastal dominion west of Cape Comorin, inhabited by a tribe of primitive men who lived on the undependable mercies of the sea. Among those Tamil-

[1] The Maharaja moved his camp from place to place, as the necessities of the war demanded. Francis could not be sure from day to day where he was bivouacking. It was typical of the Saint's cool courage to walk unconcernedly into the land of the enemy, Vettum Perumâl, who would certainly have had him slaughtered, did he know of his presence.

[2] The Portuguese text of the letters to Mansilhas so far reproduced is in Schurhammer, *Epistolae S. Francisci Xaverii*, i, 178–239. Those who wrote about St. Francis in the dark ages before Schurhammer (1944) were at a heavy disadvantage, which is not to say that all is now plain sailing in Franciscan studies. In India nothing ever is. One weary Jesuit who had lived the best part of his long life in that country advised newcomers to Vishnu-land to believe nothing that they heard there and only half of what they saw.

speaking, idol-worshipping Macuas he was at liberty to preach and proselytize to his heart's content, as they were outside the Brahman pale and of no interest whatever to their flashy Raja. The consequences of the licence were surprising, but then St. Francis was a man of surprises.

Chapter IX

SANGUIS MARTYRUM SEMEN CHRISTIANORUM

I N his letter of August 29 from Punnaikâyal to Mansilhas at Tuticorin, St. Francis spoke of the Careas, another humble piscatorial caste akin to the Paravas, who inhabited places at both ends of the island bridge between India and Ceylon. This exposed and exploited people had obviously heard great tales of the wonderful white *swami* in the south, and they appear to have sent a deputation to beg him do for them what he had done for the Paravas. Doubtless, their motives were mixed and baptism may have seemed to them a cheap price to pay for the protection of Portugal's ships. But given any kind of foothold, the grace of God can work marvellous transformations, as of water into wine or a poor human bargain into shining heroism. As he explained later to his brethren in Rome, Francis could not himself go to the Careas at their two miserable villages of Vêdâlai on the Indian mainland and Patim on the island of Manar, up against Ceylon, owing to the urgency of his business with Iniquitriberim, nor could Mansilhas be spared while the Badagas still threatened the Paravan Christians. Nothing for it then but to send the best substitute available and that was an unnamed Indian *clerigo* whose identity has not been established. Having no suspicion whatever of his own importance or of his future fame, Francis naturally did not realize the amount of trouble he would give in future times by his scanty regard for names and dates and geographical realities. The cleric, possibly one of the two deacons whom he had brought with him originally from Goa, proved to be a very remarkable man, for within a matter of weeks he not only instructed and made Christian close on a thousand of the Careas, but so marvellously inspired them that six or seven hundred were found ready and even eager, on the morrow of their baptism, to suffer torture and violent death for their new faith.[1]

The massacre brought to the front of Xavier's preoccupations

[1] Dr. P. E. Pieris, a Sinhalese Protestant of Cambridge and Inner Temple education, displays in his massive work, Ceylon: the Portuguese Era, a great deal of anti-Portuguese and anti-Catholic bias, even justifying the slaughter of the Manar Christians, and this though his three portly volumes, published at Colombo in 1913, are largely a mere paraphrase or, one might even say, plagiarization, with vitriol added, of a huge history of The Temporal and Spiritual Conquest of Ceylon written in the last quarter of the seventeenth century by Father Fernão Queyroz, a Portuguese Jesuit who spent no less than fifty-three years in India. Father Queyroz proved himself a most able and admirable historian who took infinite pains to assemble and test his authorities. He was extremely critical of his fellow-countrymen in the East, and he was gifted with a saving sense of humour. His work, translated into English at the request of the Ceylonese Government in 1930 by Father S. G. Perera, S.J. (like Pieris a Sinhalese, but a much more urbane and genuinely learned one), is now regarded as second only to the great Sinhalese Chronicle, the Maha-wansa, in its value for the history of Ceylon. How and why Queyroz came to write it, immediately after laying down his office as Provincial or general superior of the Jesuits in India is an interesting and little known story. He was commissioned to write the biography of a saintly Portuguese Jesuit lay brother named Pedro de Basto who died at Cochin in 1645 and was famed far and wide for his holiness and gift of prophecy. At that time the Portuguese had conquered Ceylon. Father Queyroz found in the personal papers of Brother Pedro many predictions that they would not be permitted by God to retain their conquest, that, in punishment for their misdeeds, they would be thrown out by another European people, as happened many years later when the Dutch wrested the island from them. The number and accuracy of the Brother's prophecies, which all came to pass exactly as he said they would, greatly impressed Queyroz and induced him to investigate the history of the Portuguese in Ceylon from the beginning, as a background for his biography of Basto. But the material, printed, manuscript, or obtained, as was frequently the case, from persons who had taken part in the events, grew so enormously under his diligent and capable hands that he felt constrained to write two books instead of one. The biography was published at Lisbon in 1689, just a year after its author's death in Goa, but the Conquista, partly, perhaps, because of its great length, 1,054 pages, and partly, it may be, because of its incisive criticism of Portuguese administration in Ceylon, did not receive the honour of print until our own times. The original manuscript found its way long ago into the Royal Library, Rio de Janeiro, where it still remains. The purpose of Queyroz in writing the book was to animate Portugal to recover Ceylon from the heretical Dutch who were savagely persecuting the very numerous Catholic converts of the island. But it must be a new Portugal that undertook the crusade, a repentant and chastened Portugal, made wise by the lessons of history, by the tragic results of tyranny and exploitation in the past, which the good Father is at pains to lay before his countrymen in all their hatefulness.

Ceylon, the island supposedly ' without Moors or Jews ' of which he had wistfully dreamed as a missionary Utopia before leaving Lisbon. Starkly different did he find the reality. When the Portuguese first stumbled on Ceylon in 1505 by the luck of a typhoon, the island, though only half the size of England, was parcelled out among at least seven rulers, each more or less at daggers drawn with the rest. But of this unloving heptarchy only three kingdoms really counted, a Tamil one in the far north, based on Jaffna, a Sinhalese one in the low country to the south, based on Kottê, which is now a mere outer adjunct of Colombo, but once claimed to be the imperial capital of the whole country, and a second Sinhalese one in the hills, based on Kandy. For the moment our concern is only with the Tamil kingdom. The Aryan conquerors of India had also established themselves in Ceylon centuries before the Christian era, but the Tamil peoples of the south who were non-Aryan entered into contest with them for the rich prize almost from the start. By the thirteenth century A.D. the persevering Tamils were safely ensconced in the north and in the islands off the western coast, the largest of which is Manar. In religion they remained Hindus, partly perhaps because their Aryan enemies to the south had long since taken to Buddhism. The king or raja of Jaffna in 1544 was a man of blood and guile named Chekarâsa Sêkaran, known to the Portuguese as Sankily. According to St. Francis, he was a usurper who had dethroned his Brahman brother, the rightful king, and forced him to flee for his life to India, where he made contact with the brave Mansilhas. The reasons why Sankily decided to eliminate the new Christians in Manar are obscure, as he was on excellent terms, of the kind that subsist between two like-minded thieves, with Antonio Mendes de Vasconcellos, the Portuguese Captain at Negapatam. Probably the converts provoked the wrath of the Hindu priests by destroying the shrines of the idols which they had formerly worshipped, and the priests may well have incited the Raja to avenge this insult to his religion.[1] He had little to fear from Portuguese intervention, as Governor de Sousa was pre-

[1] This is the explanation given by Padre Queyroz (*Conquest of Ceylon*, i, 243).

occupied at the time with affairs in far-off Cambay, and the man
on the spot, Vasconcellos, could be trusted to regard the slaughter
of some obscure fishermen as all in the day's business. Whatever
may have been the precise circumstances, the Raja gathered a
force of five thousand warriors and descended on Manar. Some of
the Christians succeeded in escaping to India across Adam's
Bridge, but at least six hundred were surrounded and, on steadfastly refusing to abandon Christianity, put to death in the most
cruel and barbarous fashion. Not even children and babes in arms
were spared.[1]

Meantime St. Francis had returned to Manapad after his visit
to Iniquitriberim, from which place he resumed on November 10
his interrupted correspondence with Mansilhas. He said that he
had to go on his travels again immediately, as a Portuguese envoy
was waiting for him at Ovari, a village fifteen miles to the south,
with a letter from the Governor's Comptroller of Revenue,
Aleixo de Sousa, and certain other dispatches which would entail
another weary journey to the camp or court of the Maharaja.[2]
'I am going to Cape Comorin by the land route,' Francis continued, ' and shall visit all the Christian villages and baptize any

[1] Schurhammer, *Ceylon zur Zeit des Königs Bhuvaneka Bâhu und Franz
Xavers* (Leipzig, 1928), 135–6, 142, 263–4, 290. In this scholarly work, Father
Schurhammer has collected and edited all the Portuguese documents bearing
on the history of Christianity in Ceylon during the period 1539–52. His two
volumes completely supersede and make look absurd the biased account of
events given in such works as Pieris's *Ceylon: the Portuguese Era*. They also
supersede a great deal in Brou and other biographers of St. Francis Xavier.
Speaking of Sankily, the historian Diogo de Couto, who resumed the un-
finished work of the great Barros and was a soldier well acquainted with India,
says in his Seventh Decade *da Asia*: ' At the gate of his palace our people
found a very large block on which he ordered many of his vassals to be be-
headed; and to do this it was not necessary to have many trials or proofs of
crimes, since there sufficed a very little story, or even suspicion, imagination
or dream.'

[2] The presence of Aleixo de Sousa in the Cape Comorin district is evidence
of the dirty politics in which poor Francis, concerned only for the safety of
his Christians, had become involved. De Sousa had been negotiating with the
Pulas, the local robber barons and declared enemies of Iniquitriberim, to see
whether he could get a better price from them for Portuguese support than
their overlord, the Maharaja, was willing to pay. He did not find their offer
satisfactory, and the Governor, for whom he was acting, accordingly declared
for Iniquitriberim.

children who have not yet received the Sacrament.' There were ten villages involved and a distance of about seventy miles which very likely the wayfarer covered barefooted, as was his habit when the sun and the sand permitted such a liberty. Mansilhas was to assemble as best he could the displaced Christians of Tuticorin who, in obedience to Francis, had fled from their poor homes in order to escape the tyranny of Vettum Perumâl. But there were gainsayers and petty mutineers among the Tuticorin flock, partisans of Captain de Paiva, who defied the Saint's orders and even seized the huts and other little properties of his obedient children. Their action, apparently instigated by a mysterious Portuguese miscreant of official standing named Nicholas Barbosa, greatly depressed and angered Francis. In his letter, the spirit of feudal Navarre flashed ominously for a moment. It was November, the season when the Paravas dived for the spiralled conch shell, ' old Triton's wreathed horn ', which was valued by the Indians as both an ornament and ceremonial trumpet. ' Tell Nicholas Barbosa in my name,' the letter continued, ' that he is not to call the Christians of Tuticorin who took possession of the houses of the refugees to the conch fishing. Not if I can help it will those rebels and renegades enjoy the fruit of our sea. . . . Warn Barbosa to mind his step and say that his past misdeeds are beyond counting.'[1]

The journey before St. Francis, two hundred miles and more

[1] The phrase, *fruito de nosso mar*, gravely shocked M. André Bellessort who commented as follows: ' *De notre mer! Mais à qui appartenait-elle, cette mer? Aux Portugais ou à ces pêcheurs qu'il prétendait exclure de la pêche des perles (sic), parce qu'ils avaient abandonné une foi dont ils n'avaient encore qu'une imparfaite connaissance? Si même le châtiment n'étaient point excessif, l'expression nous parait fâcheuse, comme d'un conquérant plutôt que d'un missionnaire. Seulement ce missionnaire est excédé. Ses nerfs le trahissent* '(*Saint François Xavier*, p. 138). Surely that censure is a little heavy-handed? The Gulf of Manar *was*, in fact, a Portuguese sea and the pearl-fishers had derived considerable benefit from the expulsion of its former lords, the merciless Moslems. There is no reason to think that the Tuticorin Christians had really reverted to paganism. They were behaving like fractious children and needed a good rap on the knuckles, which Francis gave them. What other sanction had he to apply except this temporary exclusion from the fishing grounds ? If they would misbehave and occupy other people's property, they could hardly complain when given a dose of the same medicine themselves.

of the hardest going, from Manapad to Cochin, through trackless deserts and over mountains, in the rains and winds of the north-east monsoon, would have been a terrifying prospect for anyone but a man on familiar terms with check and accident. He knew perfectly well that he was heading into danger, not only from wild beasts but from wild men, and he didn't care on two accounts, because he was very brave, and because he had become weary of life anyhow, as he confessed to Mansilhas:

> I earnestly commend myself to your prayers and to those of the children. With such help, I have no fear of the terrors with which the Christians here try to inspire me. They urge me not to go by land because all who are hostile to them nurse a far bigger grudge against me. I am so out of humour with life that I prefer to die in the attempt to promote the faith, rather than witness the wrongs done before my eyes, without my having any power to redress them. My only sorrow is that I could not do more to stop those men known to you who so cruelly injure God. . . .

But the dark moods never lasted long with the born optimist that was Francis. No sooner had he rounded the Cape and dis-covered the primitive and piratical Macuas or Mukkavans at their idolatries and other questionable occupations than his spirit soared and sang. Those children of nature, those outcasts and oft-scourings of mankind, were his very own to groom for the Kingdom of God, without interference from white men bent on plunder, because there was nothing to plunder, or from Indians zealous for their deities, because the brief, forgotten slip of sand and hillock between Trivandrum and Comorin held none but accursed untouchables.

Mass conversions have always been regarded by thoughtful Christians with a certain feeling of suspicion or even aversion, though something of the kind certainly happened at Jerusalem on the morning of the first Whitsunday. However, let the facts of the humbler Indian Pentecost speak for themselves as St. Francis summarily related them, immediately to Mansilhas and six weeks later to the Roman Jesuits.

I reached Cochin on December 16 [he told his man on the opposite coast] having baptized [nearly] all the Macuan fishermen who inhabit the Kingdom of Travancore. God knows how delighted I would be to return immediately to baptize the rest, did not the Vicar-General[1] consider that I would serve God better by going to see the Governor at the place where he is now sojourning. . . . I most earnestly beg you for the love and service of God our Lord to make ready, as soon as you get this letter, to go and visit the Christians of the Travancore shore whom I recently baptized. In each village set up a school for the children with a master to teach them. Take with you money up to 150 *fanams* for the payment of all the masters along the coast as far as the Cape. Ask the Captain for the sum needed to cover your expenses.[2] Take a *tôni* at Manapad . . . to bring you to Momchuri which is a village of Macuas about a good league from Cape Comorin. They have repeatedly asked for baptism, but I was prevented from going to them, so do you give them the Sacrament. Antonio Fernandez, a Malabar Christian and very fine man, zealous for God's honour, knows those people and is experienced in dealing with them. He will seek you out in a *catur*[3] and keep you company until you have finished all the baptisms. Do exactly as he tells you, without argument, and you will find, as I did, that

---

[1] Miguel Vaz Coutinho. Strange to say, this dignitary, who in effect ruled the Church in Portuguese India, was a layman. St. Francis held him in the highest regard and so did the King of Portugal. A zealous and honest man, ' the true father of the Indian Christians ', as the Saint described him, he was yet narrow-minded and very oppressively hostile to the native religion. It was not, as he imagined, by destroying Hindu sanctuaries in Portuguese territory and applying their revenues to the building of churches that the Indians would be won to Christianity. No Hindu in Goa, Cochin, Malacca and other centres was ever forced by that policy to accept the faith, but a great deal of pressure, social and financial, was exercised to ' persuade ' them to do so. Of course, it had exactly the opposite effect and bred a hatred of Christianity. All said, however, it was but the application in India of the accepted motto of European politics, *Cajus regio, illius religio.*

[2] Cosmas de Paiva, who as official representative of Portugal in Tuticorin had charge of the sum assigned by the Governor to St. Francis.

[3] A light, swift vessel used on the Malabar coast. It was usually propelled by oars, but sail could be hoisted in favourable circumstances.

invariably things work out well. Take Matthew with you, and the police official, and a scribe to write out the prayers for each village, so that they may be learned by young and old. . . .

The village close to Cape Comorin named by St. Francis Momchuri was known to its own people as Manakkudi, and is now called Agastisvaram Taluk. His reference to it seems to show that he began his work of evangelization in the northern part of the Macuan territory and worked his way southwards through thirteen villages, till only Manakkudi remained. At that point, he appears to have learned, with conflicting emotions of exultation and sorrow, the tragically glorious news of the martyrdoms on Manar Island, and felt that he must hurry at once to Cochin to seek retribution on the murderous Raja. Swift vengeance for so great a crime as the slaughter of six hundred defenceless and unoffending human beings seemed to him the only way to assure the safety of his present and future converts.[1] Nevertheless, he did not desire the death of the sinner, but rather that he should do penance and live. By the first boat sailing he was away to Goa, prepared for the much longer journey to Cambay. But he was spared the extra ordeal, as the Governor had returned from his expedition to the north. He poured forth his tragic tale and was assured with loud protestations of wrath and grief that the hell-hound of Jaffna would pay dearly for his deed of blood. With that promise as his viaticum he returned post-haste to Cochin, after a miserable month on the sea, in order to get off a letter to the King of Portugal by the ships soon sailing thence to Lisbon. The letter is extant only in a grandiose Latin translation, ludicrously unlike the Saint's own simple, unstudied style. Except in the last paragraph where he expresses a hope that he may be permitted to live out his days in the Indies, it is entirely about other people, good men and men not so good. The Vicar-General, Miguel Vaz, going home on a brief visit to his native land, is extolled in the

[1] Padre Queyroz represents St. Francis as arguing with Governor de Sousa in the following vivid fashion: ' If we do not defend those who are baptized, it will henceforth be necessary to preach Martyrdom along with Baptism, and we shall have to look for those with enough courage to offer themselves to the Sacrifice as well as to the Sacrament' (Conquest of Ceylon, i, 247).

warmest terms. So is the old Bishop of Goa, a man of consummate virtue, but needing help in his office, now that the years are heavy on his head. So is Cosmas Anes, the faithful friend of the College of St. Paul, whom the King might honour with a personal letter in recognition of his services. So is the devoted Capuchin, Frei Vicente de Lagos, who founded the admirable college in Cranganore, an institution deserving of every assistance the King can give it. Very different, very Hildebrandine, is the tone when Francis comes to speak of the royal representatives in India. His Highness is hastening to his Judgment, so let him beware lest he hear an angry God demanding why he did not control his officials who by their misdeeds hampered the spread of the faith, when he was so careful to punish the same men if they happened to be found guilty of negligence or peculation in the matter of his revenue. Yes, and what a tiny fraction of that rich revenue derived from India is returned by Portugal to help towards India's salvation! It did honour to King John that he accepted such straight speaking in good part and respected his admonitor all the more for his bluntness.[1]

His letter dispatched, Francis suddenly found himself dreaming happily of new horizons and fresh worlds to conquer, though a good deal of unsuspected mirage was mixed up in the vision. First, a ship put in at Cochin from Malacca on January 26, 1545, having as passenger a certain remarkable person named Antonio de Paiva. This man thrilled Francis with the news that at the town and seaport of Macassar on the island of Celébes in the East Indies

[1] Schurhammer, *Epistolae S. Francisci Xaverii*, i, 244–7 (Mansilhas), 248–54 (the King). Other items of information in the two letters are that Mansilhas is to be ordained at long last in Goa, that the two Indian clerics, Gaspar and Manuel, have recently been ordained and are hastening back to help Mansilhas, that a Portuguese and an Italian Jesuit, the latter being Antonio Criminali, the first of his order's martyrs, are on their way out, that the University of Coimbra has already sixty Jesuit students, practically all Portuguese, ' which pleases me greatly ', says Francis, that when writing to the King in January the Saint expected to make a hundred thousand converts in Malabar and Jaffna before the close of the year, a wildly optimistic estimate, that Malacca is crying out for evangelists, and that King Bhuvaneka Bâhu of Ceylon, notwithstanding much Portuguese help and favour, is showing himself very hostile to Christianity.

two native rulers had recently been baptized and were anxious for missionaries to instruct their peoples. Next day, a ship arrived from Ceylon bringing no less a person than Prince John, nephew of the little loved King of Kottê, Bhuvaneka Bâhu, who also had become a Christian. In 1543 the Portuguese had been very hopeful that Bhuvaneka himself would renounce Buddhism, but his promises to that effect were merely a ruse to obtain military assistance against his numerous enemies. In fact, he caused his own son, Prince Jugo, to be executed because he showed a disposition to embrace Christianity. Still, the faith of Prince John compensated for the duplicity of his uncle, though the honest pessimist, Nicholas Lancillotto, S.J., who was standing by, appears to have had some doubts about the genuineness of the two conversions. He represents Jugo as ' reflecting astutely ' to the following effect: ' I shall surrender to the Christian persuasion, for once a Christian, the King of Portugal will be propitious to me and, after my father's death, will constitute me his heir and successor. So I shall be a Christian King in my father's Kingdom.'[1] St. Francis would have nothing to do with such an interpretation. He believed what Prince John and his Portuguese sponsor, André de Sousa, told him, that Jugo was an authentic martyr and that great heavenly portents had taken place at his grave. He could hardly contain his excitement, and on one day, January 27, dashed off three letters home, to St. Ignatius, to Simon Rodriguez, and to the Roman Jesuits in general. The first two were largely appeals for more labourers in the huge Indian vineyard, with its promise of magnificent returns. Let all the unwanted ones come, he said to Ignatius, the men with no talent for hearing confessions or preaching or other ministries of the Society, provided only that they be strong of body and spiritual of soul.

In these heathen places the only education necessary is to be able to teach the prayers and to go about baptizing little ones,

[1] Wicki, *Documenta Indica*, i, 44. Lancillotto added dryly: ' When his father perceived what was in the wind, he promptly had the young man slain.' Jugo was the son of a concubine, and not the legal heir to the throne. Polyandry was practised by Bhuvaneka, which makes his family relationships exceedingly difficult to disentangle.

who now die in great numbers without the Sacrament because we cannot be everywhere at once to succour them. . . .[1] I say that the volunteers must be such as can stand hardship and drudgery, for living out here is far from comfortable owing to the great heat, the lack of good water in many places, and the poorness and monotony of the food. Rice, fish and [occasional] fowl, that is the menu, without bread or wine or the other good things so abundant in Europe. This is not a country for the infirm or the old. There is too much to be done and to be endured by those who come, ay, even the divine privilege of risking their lives for their Lord and Redeemer, the end for which they were born. . . . That is why they must have spiritual valour, and because I lack it on journeyings where it is vitally necessary, I implore you for the love and service of God our Lord to keep my need in special memory and to commend it to all of the Society. I have not the slightest doubt that God's protection of me in danger so far was due to your prayers and those of the brethren. . . .

At that point in his letter Francis appears to have thought that he might be losing some useful men by painting their prospects on the mission in colours too dark, for he went on to assure Ignatius that there *were* places in India *en las quales no ay peligros de muerte*, and in such the less valiant brethren could do God great service. Even talented men whose health was poor might be sent out, because they would be assigned to Goa or Cochin where everything was to be found in abundance, including medical attention, just as in Portugal itself, and by giving the Spiritual Exercises in those cities they could serve God splendidly. He concluded on a touching note:

I have been four years out here now, and during all that time I have received only one letter from Rome and two from Master Simon in Lisbon. Every year, I long to have news of you all. I know that you write to me annually, as I do to you,

[1] St. Francis entirely changed this mistaken view of the qualities of mind necessary in missionaries later on, as the result of wider experience.

but I fear that as I receive no letter from you, so you get none from me. The ship bearing those of the Society destined for India this past year has not arrived, and I know not whether they were taken back to Portugal or are wintering in Mozambique.

The letter ended lightly, with a joking reference to a well-loved physician named Dr. Inigo Lopez who lived in the Jesuits' house and dosed them when necessary, but was himself always full of aches and pains. Francis wanted to know whether he still as of old had to employ a mule or horse to get about, and had not, with all his medicines and treatments, learned the art of using shanks's mare! ' God grant,' he finished, ' that if we are not to see each other again in this life we may do so in the next, with greater peace than is now our portion. *Vester minimus filius, Magister Franciscus.*'[1]

In his letter to Rodriguez, the old friend whom he so greatly loved, Francis wore his heart on his sleeve unashamedly. It would give him inexpressible joy were Father Simon to come out to India, but he must not do so unless his bodily health matched the virtue and goodness of his soul, and unless, of course, Ignatius so decided. Almost as if anticipating the darkened future when Simon would prove temporarily a rebel, Francis added: ' Ignatius is our Father to whom we owe obedience, and without whose counsel and command we must make no move.' If Simon himself is unable to write reams about all the brethren in particular and general, would he for the love of God get some one more at leisure to do so, ' because there is no greater consolation for us in India than to receive your letters '. But let the same Simon beware of permitting any friend of his to sail East in the guise of a royal office-holder, ' for to such might fairly be applied the text: Let them be blotted out of the book of life and not be written with the righteous '. Coming from one so gentle and generous, that

[1] Schurhammer, *Epistolae*, i, 257–60. Ignatius *did* write annually, but, so to put it, there was in those days many a slip twixt the pen and the ship. Letters from Rome had to go to Lisbon by courier and couriers made a habit of being late for the yearly sailings to India.

savage judgment on Portuguese officialdom is all the more terrible, and Francis gives his reasons:

> However confident the newcomers may be of their own integrity, unless confirmed in grace like the Apostles they need not hope out here to do their duty. Evil-doing is so much a matter of course that I see no remedy whatever for it. All go the same road of 'I plunder, thou plunderest', and it terrifies me to witness how many moods and tenses and participles of that miserable verb *rapio* those who come to India discover.

The third letter of January 27 is the one that roused and enthralled, not only the Roman Jesuits to whom it was addressed, but also wide circles of Catholic Europe. Francis begins it in his familiar, deeply affectionate way:

> God knows how much more solace I would obtain from a sight of you than from writing this letter whose fate is so uncertain owing to the vast distance between here and Rome. Though our Lord has put us so far apart, yet, if I am not mistaken, the sundering miles cause no lessening of love, no forgetfulness, in those who love one another in Him and are united in charity. In my opinion, we see one another all the time, though we are no longer able to have the old companionable relations. . . . You and all of our Society are a continuing presence in my soul, and this my unfailing remembrance of you is due to your dear selves, to the prayers and Holy Masses which you say so faithfully for me, the *triste peccador*. May God our Lord whom you love reward you for me, since I am so powerless myself to requite your charity. . . . As for news of these parts, I must tell you how in a kingdom out here which I traversed God moved many persons to become Christians. It was so that in a single month I baptized more than ten thousand men, women and children. My method, on arriving in a heathen village, was to assemble the men and boys apart, and to begin by teaching them to make the Sign of the Cross three times as a confession of faith in Father, Son and Holy

Ghost, three Persons in one only God. I then recited in a loud voice the General Confession, the Creed, the Commandments, the Pater Noster, the Ave Maria, and the Salve Regina. Two years ago, I copied out those prayers and formulae in the Tamil language which is spoken here, and know them by heart. I put on a surplice for the occasion. All, little and big, then repeated the prayers after me, and that done I gave them an instruction on the articles of faith and the Commandments, in Tamil. Next, I required them one and all to ask pardon from God for the sins of their past lives, and that publicly and loudly, in the presence of heathens who did not desire to become Christians.[1] This was done for the confusion of bad men and the consolation of the good. . . . When they had finished, I asked them severally, young and old, whether they believed sincerely each article of the Creed, to which they replied that they did. I then went again through the Creed article by article, asking after each if they believed it, and they answered me, with their arms folded on their breasts in the form of a cross, ' I do believe '. Thereupon I baptized each one, and handed him his new Christian name written on a slip of paper. It was next the turn of the women and girls, and these I instructed and baptized in the selfsame way. The baptisms over, I told the new Christians to demolish the shrines of the idols, and saw to it that they crushed the images into dust. I could not express to you the consolation it gave me to watch the idols being destroyed by the hands of those who so recently used to worship them. I went thus from village to village making Christians, and in each place I left a written copy of the doctrine and prayers in their language, with instructions that they were to be taught daily, each morning and evening. My joy in doing all this was greater than I could ever tell you by letter or even explain to you, were we face to face.

The story of the conversions as thus told by St. Francis is extraordinary enough, but, as might be expected, it has received

[1] There is no record of Francis ever having heard the *private* confession of any Asiatic person, again an indication of his poverty as a linguist.

many embellishments at the hands of his biographers. Thus, we
are informed on the sole authority of a stupid, self-contradictory
person named João Vaz, who claimed to have gone about with
the Saint though Francis never once mentions him, that the Raja
of Travancore, Mârtanda Varma, issued a proclamation throughout his cramped dominions ordering all ' to obey the Great
Father, his Brother, as they would obey himself in person '.
Moreover, says this witness of imagination all compact, ' the
Great Father founded forty-four or forty-five churches along the
coast, knew the language very well, and used to climb into a tree
to preach to people gathered in the open to the number of two,
three, four, and six thousand souls '.[1] The most distinguished
of the Saint's modern biographers labours through six pages to
establish that Francis *must* have worked numerous miracles in
Travancore to achieve such amazing results, while admitting
that the only evidence for *any* miracles at the time, dated from
the year 1616, a mere seventy-two years after the event. Surely
it was a mistake to attach much importance to the vague childhood reminiscences of ancient Indians, uneducated and credulous,
who regarded marvels as essential to the make-up of a holy man,
be he a yogi or a Christian. In India signs and wonders have
always been two a penny, and it was not by such things but by
the miracle of his personality that St. Francis drew so many of
her humblest children away from her gods to the only God.[2]

---

[1] MHSJ. *Epistolae Mixtae*, i, 231–2. As already mentioned, St. Francis did
not set up a single church on the Travancore coast. He left the coast for good
almost immediately after baptizing the Macuas. And, of course, there was no
proclamation. From the little known of him, we can safely say that Mârtanda
Varma was not that sort of person. Again, imagine what it would entail to
preach to six thousand people from a tree in the open. A man would need the
lungs of the strong bulls of Bashan! Yet both Brou and Bellessort take Vaz
seriously.

[2] Very much to the point are the following gracious words of André
Bellessort: ' *Sa tâche eût été bien aplanie s'il avait eu le don [des langues] de son
prédécesseur saint Thomas; et les conversions qu'il a faites paraîtraient moins
surprenantes. Pourquoi lui retirer un mérite en lui prêtant une faveur divine? Il tient
à tous les clous de sa croix. Ils sont tous joyaux pour lui. Et puis la question est moins
de savoir si les miracles qu'on lui attribue sont indiscutables que de savoir pourquoi on
y crut. On y crut parce que sa vie était un perpétuel miracle. . . .*' (*Saint François
Xavier*, pp. 119–20).

The Macuas, now a highly respectable Indian community under another name, have maintained the Catholic faith delivered to them by St. Francis through all the vicissitudes of the centuries, which is miracle enough of itself. They had heard of the foreign *swami* from their neighbours the Paravas. News had trickled round the Cape of the strange white man so different from the other white men they knew, those barking, peremptory men of Quilon, merciless to their little delinquencies in the matter of piracy, and to their furtive dealings with Moslem smugglers. This white man seemed unaccountably, as by a kind of good magic, to want to treat them as his friends and brothers. And perhaps, too, there was healing in the touch of his gentle hands, a power over their many diseases such as the proud Brahmans who despised them never wielded. He did not speak their Tamil tongue at all fluently or well, but he had enough of it, at least by heart, to convey to them the most extraordinary story of a supreme God utterly unlike their familiar capricious gods, a God all goodness and mercy who made them and loved them so well that He actually, and not in any myth, became a man like them, one as lowly and despised as themselves, and died a dreadful death to deliver them from the power of demons, and to open to them prospects of glorious personal immortality. All that was certainly part of the process of conversion, but just as certainly not the whole of it. It is safe to say that motives were mixed, and that the converts prized the scraps of paper on which Francis had written their new Christian names as talismans against molestation by either Portugal or Islam. Men, themselves detached from all religion, have reproached the Saint for thus allowing dross to debase his gold. An ironist has genially commented on that selective indignation of the agnostics who cry scandal when they observe religion to have commerce sometimes with poor dust, who are so sensitive about purity of intention, while themselves never hesitating on the hustings 'à suborner l'électeur et à lui promettre le paradis dans ce monde et des bureaux de tabac dans l'autre'. Opportunist Francis may have been, but neither the benevolence of an obscure Indian raja nor the official pressure of a Portuguese captain, supposing him to have exerted it, come anywhere near to explaining that extraordinary month in Travancore. Other evangelists, American for choice, appeared later on with incentives at their disposal such as Francis never enjoyed:

In India, in China, in Korea they poured out money, medicines, expectations, but not one of them achieved in thirty years what Francis did in thirty days. They were rich, well dressed, well accommodated. They went about on horseback or in fine coaches, and they had behind them a government infinitely more imposing than that of Portugal. No man dare touch a hair of their heads. But he, alone, trudging on tired feet, his features worn with fasting, at the mercy of any insolent or brutal fellow, with his few phrases painfully learned, astounded and carried away thousands, who may have believed that it was their interest to follow him, but who in fact obeyed the promptings of the grace that shone in his eyes.[1]

It was a foible of St. Francis in his letters to suppress geographical names. Perhaps he did not know them or how to spell them, even according to his own liberal orthography; perhaps he felt that the dear brethren in Rome and Lisbon would not be much the wiser were he to mention them. So the derelict fag-end of Travancore where the Macuas lived becomes ' a kingdom where I move about ', Manar Island is ' a land fifty leagues from here ', Kottê in Ceylon is ' a kingdom of this part of the world forty leagues from where Francis Mansilhas and I live ', and Macassar in Celébes is ' a very distant land, perhaps five hundred leagues from here '. It is all so beautifully vague, a kind of dream-geography that leaves the imagination ample scope to build cloud-capped towers and gorgeous palaces out of sand and Palmyra palms. It has been hinted that that may have been the very purpose of the wily Francis, to fill young, brave, zealous hearts with the seduction of the illimitable and the unknown. But it is impossible to think of him in the mantle of Prospero, and anyhow the dreams were his own before he sent them sailing to

[1] Bellessort, *Saint François Xavier*, pp. 141–2. As mentioned before, M. Bellessort was secretary of the Académie Francaise.

Europe. Referring to the massacre of Manar, he thanked God for the martyrs, the martyrs that never fail, and went straight on to speak of the great expedition against their murderer, and of his brother who had fled to India and promised the Governor to become a Christian and to make all his people Christian, if granted the vacant throne.[1] Francis believed the bland deceiver implicitly and already saw Jaffna as a new bright jewel in the Church's crown. Ceylon is a land of jewels and for him they had come to be prophetic of the rubies and pearls of the Kingdom of Heaven. An old Portuguese chronicler, Ribeiro, described Ceylon as ' the loveliest parcel of land God had put in this world ', and in the Middle Ages the Florentine Franciscan, John of Marignoli, turned aside there on his way back from China to search for traces of the Garden of Eden, but the politics of the demi-Paradise were as hideous and entangled as the locks of the Medusa. At the centre of the vast web of intrigue and treachery was King or Emperor Bhuvaneka Bâhu VII of Kottê, who claimed the independent states of Jaffna, Kandy and Sitavaka as his rightful inheritance. The rulers of all four states had waded through slaughter to their respective thrones and were as select a band of schemers as the sixteenth century anywhere, even in Portugal or England, produced. As for the others, the traders, Jews, Moslems, Christians, an ironic Hollander said later on that ' cinnamon was the bride around which they all pirouetted '. After his great victory over the Moslems at Vêdâlai in 1538, Martim Affonso de Sousa, later governor of India and friend of St. Francis, reasonably enough demanded tribute from Sankily, the Raja of Jaffna, whose skin he had saved. The proud blood-thirsty Raja grudgingly agreed to pay, but hated the Portuguese in consequence and massacred the helpless fishermen of Manar when, by becoming Christians, they thought to find shelter from his tyrannies under the great

---

[1] Writing to the new Governor, Dom João de Castro, from San Thomé on June 17, 1546, Miguel Ferreira, a distinguished and honest soldier, said: ' According to your Lordship's instructions, I spoke at Kâyalpattanam with the Brahman who is the heir of Jaffna. . . . He expressed willingness to become a Christian at once, together with his grown son, and his grandsons and grand-daughters, and several of his Brahman kinsmen. . . . But I had nobody to instruct and baptize them. . . .' (Schurhammer, *Ceylon*, i, 382).

Red Cross of the Conquerors. He seems to have understood the nature of the Conquerors much better than St. Francis Xavier did.

> I have often told you [wrote Francis in his letter to the Roman Jesuits] what a devoted friend of mine and of the whole Society the Governor of India is. He took the deaths of the Manar Christians so much to heart that, just as I recommended, he is ordering a great expedition by sea to capture and kill that King. This he did in such a way that I found it necessary to calm down his godly anger. The brother of that King is the rightful heir to the throne but had to fly for his life from the country. He says that if the Governor sets him up in power, he and his nobility, with the rest of the Kingdom of Jaffna, will become Christians, so the Governor has instructed his captains to hand over the country to him as soon as he has fulfilled his promise. He is also ordering the execution of the King who killed the Christians, or rather the disposal of him according as I, speaking for his Lordship, may direct. I trust in the infinite mercy of God our Lord that through the prayers of those he martyred he will come to a true recognition of his crime, beg God's forgiveness, and do salutary penance.

From those lines it is plain that St. Francis believed in the protestations of the offending Raja's brother, just as he hoped for the Raja's own repentance. His was the charity that bears with all things, believes all things, hopes all things, endures all things, and by it St. Paul did not mean foolish credulity or irrational optimism, nor in his practice of it was St. Francis merely the victim of delusion. By the year 1556, only four years after his death, a devoutly Christian king, grandson of Bhuvaneka Bâhu, reigned in Kottê, and the Church began to make rapid strides through the zeal and heroism of the Friars Minor who, with a price on their heads and the prospect of martyrdom in the terrible shape of dismemberment by savage elephants always hanging over them, had been biding their great chance for half a century.[1]

[1] Bhuvaneka Bâhu, at continuous war with his brother Mayadunnê, ruler of Sitavaka, thirty miles inland from Kottê, and with Karalliyeddê Bandara,

But what happened to Sankily, the mass-murderer of Jaffna and rouser of Governor de Sousa's holy wrath ? The answer is, nothing at all. St. Francis, bent only on preventing him from doing further mischief, made the long penitential journey by sea to Negapatam, one of the earliest Portuguese settlements on the Coromandel coast, expecting to find assembled or assembling there the grand armada promised by the Governor. But he found business as usual and not the slightest indication that Sankily was other than a valued customer of King John's representative at that outpost of empire and trade, Captain Mendes de Vasconcellos. What that man's game was Francis learned before he had been long ashore. A richly laden Portuguese merchantman from Pegu, fifty miles north of Rangoon, had come to grief off the Jaffna coast and had been seized by Sankily as surety that its

---

Prince of Kandy, over whom he claimed suzerainty, sought help from the Portuguese, as also did his two enemies. Both the King of Kottê and the Prince of Kandy gave the Portuguese to understand that they would be willing to abandon Buddha for Christ in exchange for military assistance (Schurhammer, *Ceylon zur Zeit des Königs Bhuvaneka Bâhu*, ii, 588 ; i, 166) and the latter actually did so, being baptized in his capital by a Franciscan on March 9, 1546. Bhuvaneka, though he readily accepted the overlordship of the King of Portugal, managed to evade the religious issue to the end of his life, a fact which did not endear him to St. Francis Xavier. On the other hand, Padre Queyroz, while recognizing the pusillanimity of the ' extremely cheerful ' old gentleman, took up the cudgels in his defence and castigated the proud Viceroy of India from 1550 to 1554, Dom Affonso de Noronha, for the rude way in which he had treated the King. He denounced the Portuguese contempt for Asiatics in general, and speaking of Ceylon in particular wrote: ' That island . . . is little inferior in size to the Kingdom of Portugal; its riches have been explained; the antiquity of its Kings . . . is unequalled in Europe. The people are noble, cultured, and by no means barbarous; well-featured and olive complexioned, which is the common colour of India as far as the Ganges. . . . It is a wonderful thing that we seek to improve the works of God and fancy that only Northern people are to be esteemed, because they are white ' (*The Temporal and Spiritual Conquest of Ceylon*, i, 297–8). The Padre, who appears to have modelled himself on Livy, though he is much livelier, especially in his quite exciting battle pieces, than that Ancient, is never able to refrain from praising a good quality when he sees it, even in the worst of men. Thus, he again and again expresses his admiration for the military valour of Vidiye Bandara, the father of Dharmapala, Kottê's first Christian king, though he was the most ferocious enemy of the Sinhalese Christians and martyred five Franciscans, one ' worthy of eternal remembrance ' being torn to pieces by elephants. ' In his heart reigned Hell ', wrote the Jesuit, 'but he was very brave'.

owners would not attempt any forcible measures against him. The miscreant calculated shrewdly that such eager traders as the men of Negapatam would be ready to do a deal, and they were, and St. Francis knew himself to be defeated. He confessed as much to friends in Goa a little later. ' Jaffna has not been taken,' he wrote in execrable Portuguese, ' nor has the brother of the King who was to become a Christian been placed on the throne.' Then he reported the incident of the ship from Pegu as explanation of the failure to carry out the Governor's orders, and added : ' Please God, they will be carried out some day, if it be to His divine service.'[1] He was to be in his grave eight years before the punitive expedition eventually sailed, and even then the crafty Raja, with the blood, not only of the Manar martyrs, but of thousands of others, on his hands knew how to outwit the avengers.

The abortive armada, which there is some reason to believe Sousa, in spite of his *ira sancta*, never seriously intended,[2] marked a crisis in the life of Francis Xavier, but, before dealing with it, we may be permitted to seek a moment's refreshment in Europe, away from the chaotic politics and baffling family relationships of fair Ceylon. The letter of St. Francis to the Roman Jesuits telling of the Travancore conversions, of the Manar martyrs, of the Prince of Ceylon fresh from the waters of baptism, and of the bright prospects in Indonesia, the world's largest archipelago, was meant for general consumption and therefore copied by assiduous pens in Portugal before being sent on its way over the Pyrenees. When thus circulated widely in both Portugal and Spain, it caused an immense stir. Simon Rodriguez heard rumours of its contents even before its arrival in Lisbon, possibly from the courier who usually went ahead with dispatches for the King when the fleet

---

[1] Schurhammer, *Epistolae S. Francisci Xaverii*, i, 291.

[2] He had a problem of which Francis knew nothing. Besides the brother of Sankily who considered the throne of Jaffna worth a Mass, there were two other contenders for the same prize, namely the two boys, one a nephew and the other a son of Bhuvaneka Bâhu who had fled to India and become Christians under the names of Prince John and Prince Luis. They were genuine Christians, but died of cholera at Goa in 1546, leaving all the bright hopes centred on them unfulfilled.

reached the Azores. His excitement is apparent in a few lines of a letter addressed to Rome: 'We must come to the rescue of Master Francis, as according to news reaching me he has converted countless numbers of infidels. In those parts of India three kings have likewise been converted to the faith of Christ our Lord, by what means we know not, as the ships have not yet arrived.' When the King, then at Evora, was shown the letter, he said that nothing else in the world could have given him so much satisfaction and directed that the marvellous news was to be proclaimed from all the pulpits of the land. This was no mere airy, romantic gesture of his much maligned Highness, for at the same time he ordered provision to be made in hard cash from his treasury for the support of a hundred students at the Jesuit college in Coimbra, of whom twelve would go to India at his expense the following year.[1] The Rector of Coimbra wrote to Pierre Favre of the soul-stirring effect the letter had on his young men. ' I think,' he said, ' that I would have little difficulty in transferring the whole of this college to India ! ' None was more profoundly moved than Favre himself, the old room-mate and intimate friend of Francis. He was in Madrid when copies of the letter reached him and promptly showed one to King Philip II, whose ships at that very moment were causing grave concern in Portugal by their intrusions into the Moluccas, in contravention of the Treaty of Tordesillas. Favre became, as it were, an apostle of the epistle, spreading it far and wide in Spain and beyond. ' God knows,' he wrote to Simon Rodriguez, ' how gladly I would send helpers to Master Francis, and how still more gladly I would myself make one of them. . . . I think it would not be unreasonable if our whole Society and each of its members were to dedicate themselves to the task of producing missionaries for India. . . . I am unable to express what I felt in my soul when I heard of the six hundred martyrs there. It would give me great contentment to have a relic of them. . . .' The letter laid a spell upon Favre's young companion, Juan of Aragon, who was very ill and pined to die in India. ' The Lord knows,' said Pierre, ' how pleased I

[1] Schurhammer, *Epistolae*, i, 262; *Ceylon zur Zeit des Königs Bhuvaneka Bâhu*, i, 266 ; MHSJ. *Monumenta Ignatiana*, i, 392–3.

would be if, in a cause so dear, he had the strength to go and be my ambassador with my brother Francis.'[1]

Meantime, while the hastily written letter, which was to run to and fro like a spark among the reeds, setting so many hearts aflame, sped over the seas, its writer underwent a period of spiritual desolation and uncertainty at Negapatam. What was he to do next? His hopes for Ceylon seemed to have foundered with that ship from Pegu whose salvaged cargo of silks and lacquer and rubies had put the Raja of Jaffna in such a strong bargaining position. March, when Francis was in Negapatam, is the season of hot weather when humid and enervating long-shore winds blow from the south along the Coromandel Coast, making it perilous for a small sailing ship to set course for the Cape. As he could do little good where he was and might not return to his Christians on the sand dunes, Francis began to think in his perplexity of the small Portuguese settlement about 160 miles to the north which bore the name and was reputed to contain the shrine of the Apostle St. Thomas. Who better qualified than that dear Doubter to help a soul unsure of its direction? A ship bound for San Thomé on Passion Sunday, March 22, carried him among its few passengers. He shared a cabin of sorts with a man named Diogo Madeira and his servant, besides whom there appears to have been tucked away in some corner a little girl of eight, perhaps Madeira's daughter. On their very first night at sea the wind veered and blew so strongly against them that they could make no headway and were obliged to clew up their sails. There they remained, at the mercy of wind and waves, for six days, as Madeira afterwards testified. During the whole of that time, he said, the Father ate absolutely nothing, a fact vouched for also by his servant and the child, who had him always in sight. ' I asked him a number of times whether he would not like something to eat and suggested that he should at least take some chicken broth. He declined, but on the Saturday of that Passion Week he agreed to take a little soup made with onions, which I immediately

---

[1] MHSJ. *Fabri Monumenta*, 372–3. St. Ignatius saw in the Manar martyrdoms God's way of comforting the Church for the rebellion of Luther and Melanchthon.

ordered to be prepared. That was all the nourishment he had during those six days, and I was greatly astonished.'[1] Francis's fast can hardly be put down to seasickness due to the rolling and pitching of the ship, as there would then have been no reason for the astonishment of the good Diogo. He further reported that when they set sail again and resumed their voyage, Francis asked him if the ship was in good condition, to which he replied that she had seen the best of her days. ' In that case, the Father replied instantly, I beg you to put back to Negapatam. We consulted about the matter and decided to proceed, but had not gone far when a terrible gale suddenly came down on us and obliged us willynilly to put about and run before it to the shelter of Negapatam. I took note of the matter because it seemed to me a mystery that the Father should have spoken as he did before the gale began to blow.'

So there he was, back again in the town of the hucksters. To console himself Francis wrote to Mansilhas, recently ordained priest in Goa:

Dearest Father and Brother mine,[2] God knows how much better pleased I would be to see you than merely to send you a letter. With regard to the Christians on your Coast, I want to explain the method to be observed in the service of God our Lord. I tell you this because I do not know at present what is to become of me. May God our Lord grant us in His chosen time knowledge of His most holy will, and, whatever it prove, readiness to comply with it as soon as plainly manifested and felt within our souls. To be good in this life we have to be pilgrims prepared for journeys to any and all places where we can best serve God. I am convinced from reliable news I received that in countries [beyond] Malacca there is a strong movement towards God and that only the lack of someone to promote it prevents many from becoming Christians and increasing the spread of our holy faith. I don't know what is to be the outcome with regard to Jaffna, and for that reason

[1] MHSJ. *Monumenta Xaveriana*, ii, 214. Madeira told the little story at Goa in 1556, four years after the Saint's death.
[2] *Charissimo Padre e Irmão meu.*

am not yet decided whether to go to Malacca or to remain in India. I am going to devote the whole of the month of May to the question. Should it be that God wants me to serve Him by proceeding to Macassar, I shall send a messenger overland to Goa to inform the Governor and ask for his good offices on my behalf with the Captain of Malacca. A king of Macassar applied to Malacca for priests, but I do not know whether any were sent to instruct the people. If I decide to go myself I shall write to tell you. I earnestly beg you not to relax or grow weary in your labours for your people. Preach continually in all the villages, baptize the new-born babies with great diligence, and see that the prayers are taught in each place. . . . Do not fix your residence in any one spot, but go round all the time from village to village visiting each and every one of the Christians, as I did when I was there. In this way you will best serve God. . . . And don't omit to visit similarly the Travancore Christians, distributing among them the native priests as seems best to you. But see to it that those priests lead upright and chaste lives, working hard in the service of God and setting a good example. . . . These two things I specially commend to you, to keep moving round baptizing and procuring that the prayers are assiduously taught; to keep careful watch on the native priests, lest they go to perdition and bring others with them. If you discover them doing wrong, reprehend and punish them, for it is a serious matter not to mete out punishment to those who deserve it, especially if their conduct gives much scandal. Help Captain Cosmas de Paiva to unburden his conscience of the many robberies he has committed on that Coast, as well as of the mischief and murder which his greed brought to pass in Tuticorin. As a friend of his honour, counsel him to return the money which he took from the shedders of Portuguese blood, for it was a foul and shameful thing to sell that blood for gold.[1] I do not write to him myself because I have

---

[1] The reference is to de Paiva's horse-trading with Vettum Perumâl. That despot used the horses so acquired to invade Tuticorin and make war on Iniquitriberim, in the course of which operations some Portuguese lives were lost.

no hope of his amendment, but you can tell him from me that
I am minded to write an account of his misdeeds to the King,
to the Governor that he may punish him, and to the Infante
Dom Henrique that by means of the Inquisition he may bring
to book those who persecute converts to our holy law and
faith. Let that be a warning to him to amend! . . . Write to
me here telling me all about yourself and your Christians, as
also about Captain de Paiva, whether he shows himself repentant and is restoring what he wrested from those Christians.
May our Lord be your help always, as I desire Him to be mine.[1]

Shortly after dispatching that letter, its writer made a second
attempt to reach San Thomé by sea, but his ship was again driven
back by a storm. Nothing for it then but to traverse the 160 miles
of unknown country on foot in the deadly heat of May. It is easy
to picture him toiling over the difficult tracks, begrimed and
sweating, often losing his way, begging the little food he needed
from kind-hearted Indians, or subsisting in the divine way of
birds and wild flowers, but never daunted or tempted to give up
because there beckoned to him welcoming in the distance fingers
that had once been put into the wounded side of his Lord and his
God. Some who are tender to all the miracle stories told of him
and determined to uphold the legend of his gift of tongues would
deny outright that he was led on by any such attraction of a
doubtful shrine, probably invented by the Nestorians.[2] He says
himself that he ' was compelled to go to San Thomé ', and what
other compulsion could there have been to seek so remote a place
where a mere hundred Portuguese and their half-caste children
eked out a precarious existence? St. Francis added the name of St.

---

[1] Schurhammer, *Epistolae S. Francisci Xaverii*, i, 284–8. Francis was certainly
on the war-path, but he had every justification, as the documents in Schurhammer's *Ceylon* luridly show (e.g., i, 223–34, 244–5, 367, 373). Among his
other iniquities, Paiva monopolized the entire harvest of conch shells which
the Paravas won from the sea at the risk of their lives. He paid them a mere
pittance, and then sold the shells to Hindu traders, especially from Bengal, at
a handsome profit (l.c. 244, 330).
[2] Such, to a large extent, is the position taken by Père Brou, *Saint François
Xavier* (1922), i, 328–9.

Thomas to the others in the *Confiteor* when he taught it to his Indian children, and a little relic of the Apostle's tomb, acquired at the end of his journey, was found about his neck at the end of all his journeyings. Marco Polo who roamed to San Thomé in the thirteenth century had no misgivings about the presence of Messer St. Thomas. ' Both Christians and Saracens,' he wrote, ' greatly frequent it in pilgrimage, for the Saracens also do hold the Saint in great reverence. The Christians who go thither take of the earth of the place where the Saint was killed, and give a potion thereof to any one who is sick of a quartan or a tertian fever; and by the power of God and of St. Thomas the sick man is incontinently cured. The earth, I should tell you, is red. . . .' Marco goes on to retail the singularly beautiful local tradition of the Saint's death, which is still held in those parts, though it tends to deprive the Apostle of the glory of martyrdom: ' They tell that the Saint was in the wood outside his hermitage saying his prayers; and round about him were many peacocks, for these are more plentiful in that country than anywhere else. And one of the idolaters of that country having gone with his bow and arrows to shoot peafowl, not seeing the Saint, let fly an arrow at one of the peacocks; and this arrow struck the holy man in the right side, insomuch that he died of the wound, sweetly addressing himself to his Creator.'[1] Mylapore, the ancient and still

[1] Yule, *The Book of Ser Marco Polo, the Venetian* (London, 1871), ii, 290–1. Both of the valiant Franciscan missionaries, John of Monte Corvino, who became Archbishop of Peking (Cambaluc in those days) under Kublai Khan, and John Marignoli, give the same local account of St. Thomas's death. In our time, Bishop Medlycott, a Catholic and strong defender of the Indian apostolate of St. Thomas, and of his proper martyrdom, was told the same story when he visited Mylapore, but regarded it as merely an application of the principle of face-saving, so much practised in the East. The people of Mylapore would be the last to deny that St. Thomas was a true martyr but, as he understood them, they meant to avert by their version of his death the slur, the shame, and the dishonour that would fall on their town and people did they openly avow to the stranger that the Apostle had been done to death by their forefathers (*India and the Apostle Thomas*, London, 1905, p. 128). It may reasonably be doubted whether the good people of Mylapore at the beginning of the twentieth century were as sensitive as all that about something that had happened in the middle of the first! The tradition that St. Thomas preached in India and was martyred there, no matter in what way, was known to St. Ephraem, St.

alternative name of San Thomé, is said to be derived from the Tamil *Mayil*, a peacock, and *pura*, the Sanscrit for a city or town.

Mylapore-San Thomé is now only a suburb of great, upstart Madras, but the memory of St. Thomas remains as green and revered as ever, and with it is linked indissolubly in Indian love and gratitude the memory of St. Francis Xavier. Only one of the three letters which Francis is known to have written from Peacock Town is extant, and in that he says very little about either town or shrine, but when did he ever say much about any place of his sojourning?

Ambrose, St. Jerome, St. Paulinus of Nola, and numerous other Fathers or ecclesiastical writers, and is startlingly vouched for by the existence in India from the third or fourth century of a considerable body of native Christians on the Malabar coast. Only arrogance or ignorance would dismiss such evidence lightly. Why should St. Thomas not have preached in India, and in Southern India at that? If travellers and traders from ancient pagan Rome got there by the overland route, and by sea from the Gulf of Aden, as they certainly did, there is no reason at all for coolly assuming that one of the Apostles, who was of the Jews, the most widely roving race in history, and halfway there already, was somehow precluded from performing the feat. The evidence for the Saint's death in Mylapore or San Thomé, now included in the boundaries of Madras City, is good and nobody's fabrication. The Portuguese, when they came to Mylapore in 1516, did not invent the Apostle's tomb; they found it or what they genuinely believed to be it, as the historian Correa, who was one of the party, movingly testified. They were mistaken in thinking that the sacred remains of the Saint were in the tomb complete, as it is almost certain that the greater part was removed to Edessa in the third century and thence eventually to Ortona in Italy. The case for the South Indian tradition is excellently stated by M. F. A. D'Cruz, in his small but meaty book, *St. Thomas the Apostle in India* (Madras, 1929). Though a firm believer himself, Mr. D'Cruz, once superintendent of the Government Secretariate in Madras, is conspicuously moderate in statement, as the following words show: ' Catholics who venerate the tomb (now in the Cathedral of San Thomé, Madras) are not compelled to believe in its genuineness; and they know well that it is a question of evidence and that they may be mistaken as to the fact. They regard it, in any case, in the light of a memorial whereby the Saint is remembered and honoured. If miracles are said to have occurred, they understand . . . that, if genuine, they are the result of faith excited by the memorial ' (p. 112). The evidence is splendidly marshalled in *Die Thomas-Legende*, by Joseph Dahlmann, S.J. (Freiburg, 1912), who, however, is hesitant to admit the claims of Mylapore, while entirely endorsing those of the Malabar Christians. On the main point Father Dahlmann convinced even such a reluctant critic as Father Herbert Thurston.

In the holy house of St. Thomas [he told his Goan friends Diogo de Borba and Paul of Camerino] I made it my office to pray without intermission that God our Lord would grant me to perceive and feel in my soul His most holy will, with firm resolution to fulfil it. . . . It pleased Him to remember me with His wonted mercy and I felt and knew, with great interior consolation, that it was His will I should go to those parts of Malacca where Christians have lately been made, with a view to teaching the people there the truth of our holy faith and putting into their language a statement of its articles and commandments duly expounded. As they show spontaneously such a good disposition towards the faith, it is only right, dearest Brothers, that we should give them all the help in our power. That they may know how to beg of God an increase of faith, and grace to keep His Commandments, I shall translate for them the Pater Noster, the Ave Maria, and other prayers such as a general confession of their sins to be made daily to God. That will serve instead of sacramental confession until God provides priests who understand their language.[1] Father Francis Mansilhas and the Malabar priests remain with the Cape Comorin Christians and so they are provided for. . . . I have good hope that God will be very merciful to me on my voyage, as He was in showing me, to my immense consolation, His holy will that I should go to Macassar. I see it so clearly that were I not to fulfil it, I should meet with God's displeasure in this life and the next. I am so determined to fulfil it that if no

---

[1] Francis was thinking of Macassar rather than of Malacca. All the peoples of the East Indies speak languages belonging to a single linguistic stock, the Malayo-Polynesian, which is one of the most widespread linguistic families in the world. But the scores of Indonesian languages are as mutually incomprehensible as the Romance and Germanic languages of Europe. Intercommunication among the islands is rendered possible by the general use of a sort of ' basic Malay ', but such a lingua franca only partially existed in the time of St. Francis (Kennedy, *Islands and Peoples of the Indies*, Washington, 1943, p. 31). He, as usual, depended on the services of some native who had learned Portuguese. The fact that he is never known to have even attempted to hear the confession of any person in the East, except such as had a smattering of Portuguese or Spanish, is plainly indicative that he had no miraculous command of languages.

Portuguese ships sail to Malacca this year,[1] I shall go in some Moorish or heathen ship. Indeed, I have so much faith and hope in God our Lord, dearest Brothers, for whose love alone I make this journey, that if I could find no ship of any kind to take me but only a catamaran, I would set out confidently in that.[2] Remember me, a sinner, in your prayers and Masses. I hope to leave for Malacca at the end of August, as the ships bound thither must wait till then for the monsoon winds. I am writing to the Governor to obtain a patent for presentation to the Captain of Malacca that he may provide me with means of transport and all else necessary to get to the islands of Macassar.[3] For the love of our Lord will you see to it and send it to me by the present messenger, together with a small Roman Breviary. Give my kindest wishes to our great friend Cosmas Anes, to whom I do not write separately as this letter is meant for all three of you. Should any of our Society come out unable to speak Portuguese, they must learn that language, for otherwise they will not find an interpreter capable of understanding them. I shall write to you again from Malacca at much greater length, telling you about the prospects for the faith in those parts, so that you may provide the man-power. As your house is called Holy Faith, its works must correspond to its name! By the messengers that go your way in July, I shall send you another and longer letter. May our Lord bring us together in

[1] He is writing on May 8, 1545. A prosaic reason for his stay in San Thomé was that the vessel known as ' the Coromandel Ship ' plied between that small port and Malacca.

[2] A catamaran is the most primitive type of boat used by Indian fishermen, and is made by lashing three or four logs together. The name is from the Tamil *kattu*, ' binding ', and *maram*, ' wood '. To keep one's perch in this contraption requires much practice and skill.

[3] Malacca, a city of a hundred thousand souls, was captured from its Moslem Sultan in 1511 by one of Albuquerque's most daring exploits. He had precisely eight hundred Portuguese soldiers and sailors at his back. In those days, the Portuguese and other Europeans thought that Celébes, on which stands Macassar, was a group of islands rather than one island, shaped oddly enough to satisfy the cravings of the most advanced modern art. They called the imaginary group by the name Macassar or Celébes indifferently. Many highly respectable English dictionaries, e.g., Wyld's (1934), still think Macasssar is an island.

His holy glory, as I know not whether in this life we shall see one another again. Your least brother, Francis.[1]

The Portuguese found the chapel and reputed tomb of St. Thomas in a very dilapidated condition when they first established themselves at Mylapore and were at pains to rebuild the little sanctuary, as well as a small cottage alongside for a resident priest. Between the cottage, which appears to have had nothing but a kitchen and bedroom, and the chapel there lay a garden on the same modest scale, containing a tiny outhouse used to store candles. These details are provided by the good vicar of San Thomé, Gaspar Coelho, who acted as host to St. Francis during his four months in the town. Coelho seems to have been a worthy but earthy type, with a strong belief in the prevalence of demons in his garden after dark. Francis obviously liked him and was not above teasing him, though the honest soul did not perceive the banter in his guest's eyes. They became very intimate, as how could they not sharing the same kitchenette and bed-sitting-room? For the only time in his life the Saint indulged in reminiscences of his youth, and confessed to the Vicar, as mentioned above,[2] how far from edifying had been his early years in Paris. Those years obviously still lay heavy on his conscience and may very well be the explanation of something that Coelho, who slept soundly, believed to be devilry pure and simple in his compound.

It was his habit almost every night [wrote the Vicar] to slip out of the house without disturbing me, except on a few occasions, and to make his way across my garden to the hut adjoining the sanctuary of the Blessed Apostle. He said nothing about these nocturnal expeditions, but I could guess that he went to pray and scourge himself. One day, I spoke to him on the subject. ' Father Francis,' said I, ' please don't walk in that garden alone any more. There are devils about there o' nights

[1] Schurhammer, *Epistolae S. Francisci Xaverii*, i, 292–4. The word Francis uses for an interpreter is *topaz* and was applied in Asia to Christians of mixed breed, perhaps because they had the usually yellowish complexion of the precious stone.

[2] Pp. 33–4.

and they may do you harm.' He laughed at that, but all the same took with him on subsequent occasions a Malabar of his acquaintance, a simple soul, whom he used to leave stretched full length outside the door of the hut. One night, while he was praying within, he began to shout and cry many times, ' Lady Mary, will you not protect me?' and that so loudly that he waked his sleeping guard who heard the sound of blows issuing from the hut for some time. Afterwards, Master Francis returned to his bed at the cottage, but I myself never even knew that he had gone out. Next morning he did not come to say Matins on his knees before the altar of the Apostle, as was his invariable practice, so after finishing Matins I sought him out and found him still in bed. ' Is your Reverence unwell?' I asked, to which he answered, ' Padre mio, I am very unwell.' At that point the Malabar appeared and beckoned me outside, where he told what had happened in the night. I spoke to Father Francis about it. ' Wasn't I right,' I said, ' when I warned you not to go to the chapel at night?' But he only smiled. He remained prostrated for two days, but not a word did I get out of him about the happenings. Afterwards, for the fun of it, I used sometimes to say to myself aloud at the end of our meal, ' Senhora, surely you must protect me!' at which sally he would smile, and give himself away by blushing all over.[1]

Coelho is not a witness to be taken too seriously, and Francis may well have been merely chaffing him in return when he said to him one Saturday after their modest evening meal: ' Does your Reverence know what befell me last night? I went to the hut as usual, and what should I hear but Matins being said in the choir of St. Thomas's chapel! I could distinguish some parts of the

---

[1] MHSJ. *Monumenta Xaveriana*, ii, 946–7. ' *François avait la pudeur de ses austérités. Ce n'étaient point les diables qui l'avaient flagellé, ni contre les diables qu'il appelait Notre-Dame à son secours. Honnête Gaspar Coelho, tous les diables de l'Inde diabolique lui étaient moins redoutables que les souvenirs dont il avait distrait votre veille avant de traverser d'un pas furtif les allées de votre jardin* ' (Bellessort, *Saint François Xavier*, p. 156). Francis may have brought with him from Negapatam as interpreter and bodyguard the mysterious Malabar, to whom there is no other reference.

Office given out in a loud voice. All the chapel doors were locked from the inside, so I returned to the house astonished and not knowing what to make of the affair.' Devils might be up to most things, but it was new to the Vicar that they should come together to say Matins, so he was properly impressed. ' Father Francis mentioned the matter lightly and off-handedly,' he reported, ' and I could not get him to discuss it any further.' Father Francis had had his revenge ! We are given only vague generalities about his occupations during the day: ' By his teaching and holy life he did great good and our Lord Jesus Christ great service in this town. He drew many out of mortal sin, regularized illicit unions, and brought peace and the fear of God among us. Almost every-body became his disciple through witnessing his goodness. His was the life of the Apostles down to the last detail.' Francis himself tells of one of his conquests during that only respite and breathing-time which he allowed his hard-driven limbs in the whole of his career:

> While I was at San Thomé awaiting the day of embarkation, a merchant arrived in the port with his ship and asked me to hear his confession. He had long been unable to make up his mind, but I talked to him of the things of God and God taught him that there is other merchandise in which he had never dealt. With great violence he achieved victory over himself and chose the road of Heaven. By God's mercy he made his confession one day and the following day decided, in that same place where St. Thomas was slain, to sell his ship and all else he possessed and give every penny of the proceeds to the poor. Then we set off together for Macassar. His name is Juan de Eiro and he is thirty-five years old. Since he grew up he has been a soldier, and now he is a soldier of Christ. He commends himself very earnestly to your prayers.[1]

[1] Schurhammer, *Epistolae S. Francisci Xaverii*, i, 300, 320–1. Juan de Eiro subsequently became a Franciscan and gave evidence at the canonical investiga-tion at Goa in 1557 into the life of his Jesuit friend. From this it appears that he first met St. Francis in Ceylon, which is the only indication that Francis ever set foot on the island's shores (*Monumenta Xaveriana*, ii, 378–82). It is probably incorrect, as the good Friar was a very muddled and muddling witness.

It would be good to know something about the mind of a great mystic as he communed with God nightly in that little garden under the Indian stars, but, alas, Gaspar Coelho, snoring on his mat, was not the man to seek or convey the information. We are left to our own conjectures. One seems safe enough, that St. Francis was becoming more and more obsessed and tormented by the thought of the myriad souls to whom the love and mercy and glory of Christ his Master had never yet been told. The world was expanding daily, and hardly a sea remained without some ship of the West ploughing its unfamiliar wastes in search of new lands and peoples. Spain had dropped the negative from the inscription traditionally supposed to mark on the Pillars of Hercules the confines of the world (impassable, as Pindar had said, for wise men or fools), and proudly took *plus ultra*, ever onwards, for her national motto. Francis, the child of Spain, had the words incised in his heart. As has been made abundantly clear from his own letters, he never abandoned the Christians he had won. He made all the provision in his power for them before moving on, and, in a very real sense, carried their burdens of sin or sorrow with him to the ends of the earth. But he could just as little forget the others, the unknown ones on the ' further shore ' whose yearning outstretched hands filled his dreams and waking thoughts with their irresistible appeal. Above Macassar there shone in his mind a light like the Magi's star. There also, as on the sand-dunes of Cape Comorin, must be born the King of the Jews, the King of his heart. In his two tired arms he would enfold half of the world. Could he only blaze the trail, others, he felt certain, would follow to build a highway for God, and they did in their thousands, drawn by his magnetic example.

CHAPTER X

THE GREAT ARCHIPELAGO

THE small vessel on which Francis Xavier departed from India probably sailed south-east through the Sombreiro Channel of the Nicobar Islands into Malacca Strait. The voyage lasted about a month and was diversified by the storms of the south-west monsoon, by the constant peril of running aground on hidden shoals, and by the prevalence of pirates. Francis has a few bald words to say on the subject:

What between storms and pirates, I encountered many dangers on that voyage. I remember one in particular. Our ship of four hundred tons ran before a violent wind for more than a league, and during the whole of the time the rudder was scraping the ocean floor. Had we struck a rock, the ship would have gone to pieces, and had the depth decreased at any point, we would have been stranded. Then did I see tears flowing freely aboard. God our Lord wished to prove us by those dangers and to bring home to us our inadequacy when we rely on our own strength or put our trust in created things, as also to show us how powerful we become by abandoning false hopes and confidently turning to the Creator of the world who makes us strong to meet dangers encountered for His love. Those who, placed in such dangers, meet them for His love alone, believe without a shadow of doubt that all creation is in obedience to the Creator, and know clearly that the consolation of the critical moment prevails over the natural fear of death, since men's days must come to a close. When the trials are over and the dangers past, it is not possible to tell or describe how they affected one at the time, but they remain scored in a man's memory to prevent him from ever wearying in the service of so good a Master, and to encourage hope

for the strength necessary from Him whose mercies are
without end.[1]

That was unusual language from a man quite prepared to
affront the Indian Ocean on a raft, and the danger must indeed
have been extreme, not so much because it made the tears of
Portugal's tough old sea-dogs flow, as because it made the most
reticent of far-ranging travellers unveil a tiny corner of his heart.
We may leave him for a moment to the monsoon and shallows
in order to take a quick glance at the strange new world to which
he was perilously proceeding. Malaya's history is so ancient and
complicated that hardly any two modern books, even when
written by learned Malays, agree about its details. Some maintain,
for instance, that Malacca as a great city, which it no longer is,
dated only from the fifteenth century, when an astute Javanese
pirate made it his lair and took so much toll of Indian shipping in
the Strait that the merchants were driven to calling voluntarily
at his fever-ridden cove and paying whatever dues he exacted.
It had a splendid harbour, and they soon discovered it to be a much
more suitable site for an emporium than the remote place at the
far end of Sumatra, which had been their resort until then.[2]
That is one story, but a rival to it put forward by a formidably
learned French scholar on the basis of Chinese documents would
add no less than seven hundred years to the age of Malacca, and
it seems certain in any case that it was a well-known port at the
close of the thirteenth century.[3] In the second century A.D.,
Ptolemy of Alexandria referred to Malaya at large as the
' Golden Peninsula ' and averred that there were cannibals in the
islands beyond, accurate if not very complete information. Those
islands, comprising the three monsters, Sumatra, Java and Borneo,

---

[1] Schurhammer, *Epistolae S. Francisci Xaverii*, i, 326–7.

[2] That is the view to which Professor Vlekke of Harvard inclines in his
learned and attractive book, *Nusantara: A History of the East Indian Archipelago*
(Harvard University Press, 1943, pp. 27–49). Nusantara is a Malay word
meaning ' Empire of the Islands '. A Javanese patriot of modern times endeavoured to popularize it as a general name for the Archipelago, but he had
little success.

[3] So M. Gabriel Ferrand in his *Malaka*, a splendid anthology of sources
contributed to the *Journal Asiatique* in 1918.

jointly larger in area than England, France and Italy put together, whirligig Celébes which, with its satellites, could easily embrace two unpartitioned Irelands in its four fantastic arms,[1] the equally oddly shaped but smaller Halmaheira or Gilolo, Timor and Ceram, each bigger than Belgium, and hundreds of lesser fry, many at least as substantial as the Isle of Wight, were all colonized from Asia via the Malay Peninsula in prehistoric times.

Sumatra made a brief appearance in Chinese annals during the life of our Lord, when the Emperor Wang Mang of the Han dynasty dispatched an embassy there to procure him a rhinoceros for his zoological garden. But from time out of mind Java has been the most civilized and progressive of the islands. Immigrants from India established kingdoms on it during Europe's Dark Ages and sedulously propagated Hinduism and Buddhism, as the still existing ruins of magnificent temples attest. One of them, the Borobudur, might be described as the Chartres of Buddhism, with its four hundred finely sculptured statues and four thousand bas reliefs depicting the life and teaching of the Enlightened, who, however, showed a distinct tendency to adopt characteristics of the Hindu Shiva. Besides the Indian kingdoms, there were also numerous small native ones with picturesque and bloody histories. In the fourteenth century A.D., a very remarkable Javanese conqueror named Gajah Mada succeeded in bringing the whole mighty Archipelago under one central authority, so creating the Empire of Madjapahit as a new Asiatic great power, the peer of China herself. China in those days was extremely active in Indonesian and Malay affairs, just as she still is. Among other things, she protected the Raja of Malacca from the encroachments of Siam and so enabled him to flourish in relative independence. But already in the thirteenth century the inevitable Moslem traders had established a headquarters in Sumatra, to await larger opportunities. Their zeal for their religion burned as steadily as their determination to amass wealth, and they possessed one enormous advantage over Christian missionaries in dealing

[1] The Portuguese thought that the four arms must be four separate islands, for they did not penetrate inland to discover the hub. That was why St. Francis always pluralized Celébes (or Macassar) in his letters.

with pagan peoples, namely, that chapter of the Koran which not only permitted but strongly counselled the use of the sword for the propagation of the Word. Soon they were to be found everywhere in coastal Malaya and in almost all parts of the Archipelago. When the Empire of Madjapahit dissolved in anarchy after the death of its Napoleon, they stepped softly or with murderous noises, as the case might be, into the vacancies created, so that native princelings who gloried in the title raja one day blossomed out into sultans the next. The Indonesians at large made little difficulty about exchanging the coalesced Shiva and Buddha for the more rewarding Allah, and by the end of the fifteenth century the green Crescent flew proudly throughout the islands, except in rude mountainous places of the interior where there was no trade to attract it.

Then Albuquerque arrived, to open a new chapter in the long history of Malaya and the Moluccas. Avenger is a more accurate word to apply to that portentous man than aggressor. Duarte Barbosa, the most delightful and informative of Portuguese travel writers, who reached Malacca shortly after its capture, explains the situation:

The King our Lord sent an order to have this land [of Malacca] explored by Diogo Lopes de Sequeira, a gentleman of his household; and after he had discovered it the King [Sultan] and the Moors thereof took by treason certain of our men and much merchandise, and slew many of them. Affonso D'Alboquerque who at that time was Captain General of India came up against the city with his fleet to demand a reckoning of him for this, and not being willing to discuss terms with him he attacked the city and took it by force of arms, driving the King out from it; who defended himself with his folk and fought very bravely with abundance of artillery, guns, poisoned arrows and excellent long spears, also with valiant men of Java, and many elephants equipped with wooden castles containing fighting men therein after the custom of India. In this assault a great number of Moors was slain, and the King and his surviving warriors fled, but the merchants submitted to remain in the city in subjection to the King our Lord, and no injury whatsoever was done unto them. . . . To this City and Kingdom of Malacca is subject the province of Pam [Pahang], having its own individual king, who, perceiving that Malacca had become subject to the King our Lord, sent an embassy and presents to Affonso D'Alboquerque, as he wished to follow the same course.[1]

The defeated Sultan took refuge in what then existed of Singapore and Johore and from those outposts harassed the Portuguese to the best of his ability. He had a strong and fierce ally in the Sultan of Achin or Atcheh at the western tip of Sumatra whose doughty Moslems never became reconciled to European domination and remained, until Indonesia recently became an independent republic, a perennial nuisance to the Dutch authorities.

There, then, was Malacca, one of the world's greatest centres of trade, a seething, sweltering, terrible place, not much more than a degree above the Equator, and with an atmosphere as stuffy and heavy as that of the palm-house at Kew. As his little battered ship sailed into the great crowded harbour towards the end of September, 1545, St. Francis Xavier could see the cross-crowned steeples of Catholic churches appealing to Heaven above mosques and synagogues and heathen temples. The garrison of the strong citadel built by Albuquerque,[2] partly out of Moslem tombstones, must have been an exceptionally brave and resourceful body of men. They rarely numbered more than five hundred, and yet held on gamely to their magnificent prize for 130 years in the

[1] *The Book of Duarte Barbosa*. Translated by Mansel L. Dames, London, the Hakluyt Society, 1921, vol. ii, pp. 178–9.

[2] They called it *A Famosa*, 'The Famous', and with some reason, as its walls were 32 feet high and 24 feet thick. It took the Dutch over five months to reduce it in 1641, though there were only 260 Portuguese defenders. ' The bastions of *A Famosa* were given new names. San Domingo became Victoria, Madre de Dios was changed to Emilia, St. Jago to Wilhelmus. The bastions no longer bore witness to the glory of God but to the glory of the sponsors of unmitigated trade, and the walls of *A Famosa*, ceasing to breathe the enchantment of Rome and the Middle Ages, became a stronghold for ledgers ' (Sir Richard Winstedt, *Malaya and its History*, London, 1948, p. 49).

teeth of incessant attack, siege and pestilence. But considering the
..ture of the climate which, according to a Dutch sufferer, no
European could long survive without having to thank God for
a major miracle, considering likewise Portuguese colonial nature,
and considering most of all the nature of Malayan womanhood,
charming and accommodating, it is no great surprise to be told
by Padre Valignano, who knew it well, that the holy land of
commerce was a sink of all iniquity. International ports usually
are, but Valignano, who was familiar with many of them,
thought that Malacca topped the list in those days for ' abomi-
naciones, dissoluciones, toda immundicia y maldad'. The white men
and their numerous dusky progeny and slaves plainly had need
of St. Francis Xavier, and realized their need, for they gave
him a rousing welcome. A large crowd of men, women and
children flocked to the quay when the arrival of the ship was
announced to greet the ' Holy Father ', of whom they had heard
many wonderful things. Nothing is more certain than that the
reputation of Francis as a saint and thaumaturge was very widespread during his lifetime. He was the kind of man to whom
people would almost instinctively have attributed the power of
miracles, and it can safely be said that they did not invariably
labour under illusions. A small European boy named Paul
Gomes was present when Francis stepped ashore,[1] and treasured
to his dying day one little memory of the occasion. ' The Father
beckoned to us boys, greeted each of us by our own name, and
asked us how our fathers and mothers were. He had never seen
us before and there were quite a few of us, and certainly no one
had told him our names. So how could he have known them,
except, as I and many others believed, miraculously? '[2]

[1] The great bay is very shallow, that being one of the reasons why it was
eventually abandoned by shipping in favour of Singapore, created by the genius
and foresight of Sir Stamford Raffles out of a derelict mangrove swamp. The
Queen Elizabeth would certainly have to give Malacca a wide berth, but the
400-tonner of St. Francis may have been able to creep cautiously to the quays.

[2] MHSJ. Monumenta Xaveriana, ii, 483. The little story, which is so perfectly
in keeping with the character of St. Francis, does not seem to be explicable by
any of the various forms of what is called extra-sensory perception. Paul Gomes
became very intimate with Francis and when grown up entered the Society of
Jesus. His report is given in indirect speech in the original.

There appears to have been only one priest in Malacca, a sort of chaplain to the forces, before the arrival of Xavier, and he evidently had despaired of being able to cope with the harems of Malay beauties kept by the Portuguese officers and merchants. But all was not bad within that enclave of European pride and passion. The conquerors had built a hospital and a refuge for the poor, tended by the Confraternity of Mercy to which even the worst of them were proud to belong. In so far as it was compatible with their trading and their pleasures, they strove in their own queer, inconsistent way to spread the faith, at least among their Malay slaves and mistresses. The Eurasian population which resulted from their illicit unions became to a large extent Catholic, and has remained so through the centuries, principally owing to the labours of St. Francis Xavier and his successors. For Francis, Malacca was merely a stage on his route to Macassar and farther east, but it became a very busy stage.

Every Sunday [he wrote to his Jesuit brethren in Europe] I preach at the principal church, Our Lady of the Assumption, but am not as satisfied with my sermons as are my audience, judging by the patient way they listen to me. I teach the children the prayers for an hour or more every day. At the hospital, where I have a room, I hear the confessions of the poor sick people, say Mass for them, and give them Holy Communion. I am so greatly importuned to hear confessions that it is simply impossible to meet all the demands. My principal task is an endeavour to interpret the prayers and doctrine in a language that will be understood in the Macassars. It makes things very difficult and troublesome not to know the language. . . . Since my arrival in Malacca I have received several letters from Rome and Portugal which gave, and still give me every time I read them, the greatest comfort. I read them so often that I feel myself to be at home again, or that you, dearest Brothers, are with me out here. The Fathers who came out this year with Dom João de Castro have written to me from Goa. I am instructing two of them to join dear Francis Mansilhas and his three priest helpers at Cape Comorin, and telling the third to remain as a teacher at the College of Holy Faith. . . . Next year, I shall give you a full account of the heathen peoples of the Macassars. Above all things, dearest Brothers, I beg you for the love of God to send out many of our Society every year. They are sorely needed, and for work among the heathen it is not essential that they should be highly cultured, provided they are thoroughly grounded in the spiritual life. So I stop, praying our Lord to give us a realization of His holy will and strength to fulfil it. Your least brother and servant, Francis.[1]

Many witnesses came forward in 1556, four years after the death of Francis, to give their impressions of him during the months he stayed among them at Malacca. Their various reports, which have a very definite stamp of authenticity, were summarized by the careful and level-headed Valignano in 1574 as follows:

So lax and corrupt were morals in Malacca that the Father had great difficulty in bringing about reform, but here more than at any other place of his sojourning his prudence and charity became evident. Seeing that there was nothing to be hoped from mere exhortation or denunciation, he set himself deliberately to win the hearts of the sinners, and with such success that the City, to this day, is still marvelling at his memory. By his charming address and conversation he made them his friends and regularly came to watch them at their amusements and games, which he obviously enjoyed. Even their gambling did not deter him. If, out of respect for him, they stopped some game they were playing at his approach, he would pleasantly invite them to resume and even join in the amusement himself. ' You are soldiers,' he would say to them, ' so there is no reason why you should live like monks. To be merry without offending God is better any day than grumbling and quarrelling.' In the same spirit, he used to invite himself to

[1] Schurhammer, *Epistolae*, i, 299–301. Dom João de Castro was the new governor of India, in succession to de Sousa, and one of the best ever sent out. The three Jesuits accompanying him were Juan Beira, a Spaniard from the Galician coast, the young Italian Antonio Criminali, Jesuit proto-martyr, and Nicholas Lancillotto from Urbino.

dinner with one or other of the merchants, would highly praise
the dishes, and be the life and soul of the party. Afterwards, he
would ask his host who was his excellent cook and might he
see her. He would greet her very sweetly, tell her how much
he had enjoyed her delicacies, and bid her good-bye remarking
that she must be sure to become a saint. . . . So it came about
that not only the Portuguese but their Malay concubines and
slaves learned to love the Father greatly. . . . When he had thus
won all hearts he would say to a selected officer or merchant
that such and such a girl in his house was very beautiful and
deserved a good husband. The man would be led to confess that
he loved her very much, whereupon the Father would say,
' Why, then, not marry her, honestly and holily, instead of
living in sin with her and damning both her and yourself ? '
The result would be a wedding ceremony. With others he took
the opposite line, asking a man, for instance, why on earth he
made himself a laughing-stock in the community by living
sinfully with an ill-favoured native woman, when he could do
so much better for himself. ' If you like,' he would continue,
' I can find you a wife beautiful and good enough to be the
consort of a king.' He would be as good as his promise and
marriage would follow in those cases also. . . .[1]

Francis was not content to remain cooped up in the Portuguese
quarter of Malacca. In one of his letters he mentions casually that
as night approached he used to collect a flock of children and sally
forth with them into the city, ringing a bell and praying aloud for
the souls in Purgatory. No doubt, the idea was to impress the
Malay and Javanese residents, Moslems to a man, and Francis did
not know what Duarte Barbosa had to say about a little habit of
the men from Java: ' If any one of these *Jaos* falls sick, he makes a
vow to his god that if he restores him his health he will seek out
another more honourable death in his service; and after that he
is whole he takes a dagger in his hand with certain wavy edges

[1] *Monumenta Xaveriana*, i, 67–9. Francis stuck to a certain individual until
he had persuaded him to dispense one by one with a harem of six. Then he
married him to the last lady left.

which they have among them of very good quality [the kris],
and going forth into the places and streets he slays whomsoever
he meets, men, women or children, letting none go.'¹ This was
the practice of running amuck, not a speciality of the Javanese
but widespread at that period in Malaya and the East Indies
generally. Back from the evening excursions, Francis had his own
way of spending the best part of the night. A Portuguese official
named Rodrigo de Sequeira shared with him for a time a bamboo
hut, roughly partitioned to afford a little privacy. The good
Rodrigo, who loved and deeply reverenced Francis, confessed
in 1556 that he used sometimes to spy on him in the middle of
the night through chinks in the partition. It was always the same
scene, Francis on his knees, arms uplifted, before a little crucifix
made of wood from the shrine of St. Thomas at Mylapore. Beside
the small table, the only piece of furniture, lay an oblong black
stone. ' On the two or three occasions when I watched him at last
lie down for a little rest, he used the stone as a pillow. Then he
would be up before dawn to say his Office and his Mass.'²

The good physician Dr. Cosmas Saraiva, who had come to
India with Francis, was stationed at Malacca the same time as he.

I was medical officer at the hospital where the Father lived
[he testified] and had such a profound reverence for him that I
never missed attending his daily Mass. One day, after he had
pronounced the words of consecration, he seemed to me to be
raised in the air, his feet not touching the ground at all. I
wondered at the time whether I was not suffering from an
hallucination brought on by my intense love and veneration
for the Father as a saint, so I cannot definitely say whether my
experience was a fact or a trick of my imagination. One thing
I do know is that a certain Jew, learned in his law, used to
come to the Father's sermons and make a mock of his teaching.

¹ Schurhammer, *Epistolae S. Francisci Xaverii*, i, 322; *The Book of Duarte
Barbosa*, ii, 177.
² *Monumenta Xaveriana*, ii, 213. Two brothers or cousins named Pereira,
merchants and devoted friends of St. Francis, bore a like testimony from their
own observations at Malacca. ' The Father,' said they, ' wasted very little time
in sleep ' (l.c. 201).

This man was so solidly established in his errors that if other Jews showed a disposition towards Christianity he would go out of his way to dissuade and prevent them from becoming Christians. But the Father somehow won his friendship, so that the Jew began to invite him to his house to dine. The upshot was that the Father received him into the Church and he remained an excellent Christian for the rest of his days. His conversion was regarded as a mystery throughout Malacca, because he was so well known as a learned and obdurate person.[1]

Mention of that Jew requires it to be said that Francis wrote from Malacca to the King of Portugal advocating the establishment of the Inquisition at Goa. The letter is not extant and may never have reached its destination, but it is certain that Francis sent it off from Malacca on November 10, 1545, as he refers to it in a later letter to King John:

Senhor, I have already written to your Highness by another route concerning the great need of preachers in India, for lack of whom many among our Portuguese lose the faith. From much experience gained in the fortified places I have visited, I can say that continual trafficking with the infidels and our own deplorable lack of devotion cause temporal advantages to be more highly esteemed than the mysteries of Christ our Redeemer and Saviour. The native women, wives or mistresses of the merchants, and their half-caste sons and daughters, are content to say that they are Portuguese by blood but not by religion, and this because of the dearth of missionaries to teach them the law of Christ. Another need in India to protect the Christian life of those who have been baptized into the faith is that your Highness should order the establishment of the

[1] *Monumenta Xaveriana*, ii, 236–7. The original Portuguese is, as usual with the testimonies taken at Goa in 1556, in indirect speech, put into this form by the Bishop's notary for transmission to the authorities in Rome. The reports are given with a very correct Latin translation, except for minor changes of emphasis such as the translation, in the story of the Jew, of the phrase ' *cousa misteriosa* ' by the word ' *miraculum* '.

Holy Inquisition. Many nominal Christians, dispersed widely through the various fortresses, live openly as Jews or Mohammedans, without any fear of God or shame before men.[1]

From those lines it seems clear that Francis wanted the Inquisition, not in the least to bring about the forcible conversion of Jews or Moslems, but to keep the Christians up to the mark and to protect them from the ceaseless and ruthless propaganda of those unitarians, as well as from the oppression of unscrupulous Portuguese traders. Some may be found to regret that a man as sympathetic and lovable as Xavier should have had recourse to the secular arm, but a little experience of Moslem truculence and barbarity on Allah's behalf might quickly bring them round to his point of view. The riots at Singapore as recently as December, 1950, when a Dutch child was taken out of Moslem hands and restored to her Catholic parents, threw a revealing light on Koranic ideas of justice, even in our enlightened times.[2]

St. Francis was well aware of the confusion of tongues in ' the Macassars ' and other strange places he was going to, but he had been told also that Malay was generally understood in the islands, even if each island had its own language or, in some cases, several languages. So it was into Malay that he translated ' with great labour ' the Creed, with an exposition of each article, the General Confession, the Our Father, the Hail Mary, the Salve Regina,

---

[1] Schurhammer, *Epistolae S. Francisci Xaverii*, i, 346–7. The letter was written from Amboina on May 16, 1546.

[2] The technique of lavish promises, infiltration and terror by which Islam gained so much of India and almost the whole of Indonesia, where today ninety per cent of the peoples are nominally Moslems, bears a striking resemblance to the methods of modern Communism. In Protestant and liberal circles clever propaganda has brought it about that the very name of the Inquisition arouses instinctive repugnance, but real students of the tribunal's history are inclining more and more to compare it very favourably with other governmental instruments of control, such as the Star Chamber under the Tudors and Stuarts. The Inquisition became almost wholly a state institution in Catholic countries, and any Catholic is entitled to regret that bishops and priests should have become involved in its proceedings, though the cruelties attributed to it are to a large extent purely mythical. There will be more on this topic, in so far as it concerned St. Francis Xavier, later on.

and the Commandments.[1] Malay, a soft, harmonious tongue, was written at that time only in Arabic characters, which did not render the task of Francis any easier, but he persevered, inspired by his dreams, and no doubt helped by the courteous native people in their magnificent sarongs. 'Those Macassars,' he informed the Jesuits of Europe, 'are a long way from Goa, more than a thousand leagues.[2] Men who have been there say that it is a promising land for the propagation of the faith, as it has no temples for idols nor false priests to hold the inhabitants in heathenism. They adore the sun at its rising, and that is the extent of their religion. They are at war among themselves all the time.' Only the last sentence of that bulletin is entirely accurate. Far from being just elegant sun-worshippers, the people of Celébes fed their immortal souls on primitive magic, involving head-hunting, fetishism, the propitiation of demons, and other super-stitious practices. Today they are all nominally Mohammedans, and head-hunting, as in Borneo, has long been suppressed, but in the wild interior of Celébes, still largely unexplored, paganism holds its own.

[1] There are five distinct languages in southern Celébes and nine more in the north. In his classical work, *The Malay Archipelago*, the great naturalist, Alfred Russel Wallace, gives nine words (nouns and adjectives) in fifty-nine languages, and 117 words in thirty-three languages, which he had collected in his famous wanderings through the islands in search of new species of beasts, birds, beetles and butterflies. He collected a few Jesuits also at the same time, the years 1854–62, and liked them. 'No wonder they make converts,' he wrote of the French Fathers working among the Chinese in the interior of Singapore Island, 'for it must be a great blessing to the poor people to have a man among them to whom they can go in any trouble or distress, who will comfort and advise them, who visits them in sickness, who relieves them in want, and who devotes his whole life to their instruction and welfare. My friend at Bukit-tima [Wallace stayed with this particular Jesuit several weeks] was truly a father to his flock. He preached to them in Chinese every Sunday, and had evenings for discussion and conversation on religion during the week. He had a school to teach their children. His house was open to them day and night. If a man came to him and said, " I have no rice for my family to eat today", he would give him half of what he had in the house, however little that might be. If another said, " I have no money to pay my debt", he would give him half the contents of his purse, were it his last dollar. . . .' (*The Malay Archipelago*, tenth ed., reprinted London, 1898, p. 18. Might not this have been written of St. Francis Xavier?).

[2] Macassar Town is well over a thousand nautical miles from Malacca.

Ever since the arrival of the Portuguese in the Great Archipelago, attempts had been made by brave men, priests, soldiers, or traders, to Christianize the native peoples. The Moslems had got the start of them and pre-empted the ground in many places, such as Malacca City and the whole of historic Java, but the Christians did not despair of the contest. They even beat the agile foe in the race for some. of the remoter islands, such as weird Halmaheira and Amboina. In the most northerly part of Halmaheira, called also Gilolo to keep us awake, there is a district now named Galela, which was known to the Portuguese and to St. Francis as Moro or Omoro or the Islands of Moro. The fact is that the early navigators could not get the hang of this queer, four-armed, star-shaped product of earthquakes, and thought bits of it to be separate islands, like as in the case of that other marine monster, Celébes. But there *are* islands about, a sheer mob of them, satellites attendant on the star, including five to the west of it which in Xavier's time were the most coveted parcels of land on this earth. Two others that no nation particularly wanted stood at the north of Halmaheira, a large one named Morotai and a little neighbour named Rau. Up there in the years 1533-4, that is, to mainland Moro and island Morotai, went two gallant and zealous men, the priest Simon Vaz and the merchant Francisco Alvares. By some wizardry of their own, they gained the trust of the local barbarian chieftains and won them and from five to six thousand of their people to the faith, baptizing them all. This was nearly as great a feat as St. Francis was to perform in Travancore, but he gave his converts some elementary instruction and dispatched Mansilhas and others to carry on the work, whereas the heroic pair in Halmaheira, and Fernan Vinagre who appeared later, could apparently do nothing except baptize and hope for the best. Father Vaz was killed on Morotai in 1535 and his companion Alvares barely escaped with his life.

In a similar fashion to those heroes, Antonio de Paiva, a merchant, worked among the more civilized, or anyhow more accessible, natives in the Macassar area of Celébes and gained to Christianity the *tres grandes señores* whose conversion so much excited St. Francis when Paiva himself brought him the news, together with four young specimens of the neophytes for the College of Holy Faith in Goa. It may be doubted whether the ' señores ' were much more than glorified headmen, but in Portugal, where all things Eastern loomed huge in a magnificent haze, they took on the majesty of potentates as splendid as King John himself. King John, in fact, conferred on the brave fellows, whose fathers, and likely enough themselves too when young, had hunted heads as industriously as any Dyak, the royal and jealously guarded title of *Dom*. Following Paiva's achievements, a good secular priest named Viegas had been sent from Malacca to the Macassar territory, and it was from him that St. Francis expected a report on the missionary prospects in southern Celébes. But the Padre did not return, and then, in early December, a change in the monsoon winds made his coming impossible for months. Others, however, had arrived and brought Francis disturbing news of trouble in his land of dreams. What it was is by no means certain, but it may have been an incident with a pleasantly Gretna Green flavour that had happened recently in Celébes. A young daughter of one of the converted ' señores ' fell wildly in love with a Portuguese gentleman named Eredia, and he reciprocated her sentiments, but her father, for reasons unknown, forbade the banns. However, Padre Viegas, good romantic soul, was a stalwart supporter of the match and, persuasion failing with the parents of the girl, counselled flight as the best expedient. He himself accompanied the runaway lovers over the stormy emulous seas to Malacca, where they lived happily ever after.[1]

Whatever it was that had disturbed Macassar, apart, of course, from such familiar and accepted occurrences as earthquakes and volcanic eruptions, it completely changed the plans of Francis Xavier. On December 16 he wrote from Malacca to his brethren at Goa in the following terms:

[1] A son of the marriage, Godhino de Eredia, told the story in a book he wrote about Malacca, which has had the honour of being translated into English: J. V. Mills, *Eredia's Description of Malacca*. In the *Journal of the Malayan Branch of the Royal Asiatic Society*, vol. viii, Singapore, 1930.

My dearest Fathers and Brothers, In my last big letter I told you that I was on the point of departure for Macassar. Well, we received news from there which was not so good as we expected, so I did not go, and am now preparing to go to Amboina instead, where there are already many Christians and bright prospects of making more. When I reach my destination I shall write to you again telling you, out of my experience at Cape Comorin and Goa, as also, please God, in Amboina and the Moluccas, how I think He can best be served and our holy faith advanced in those parts. . . .

At last, Francis has mentioned the magical name, Moluccas, the land of spices, mere pin-heads in the sea, over which two continents had been wrangling and contending for centuries. It is extraordinary that so small a thing as a clove should have made so much history[1]. The clove grew originally nowhere in the world except on five tiny islands off the west coast of big, flailing Halmaheira or Gilolo, their names, which should be sacred in all kitchens, Ternate, Tidore, Mutir, Machian and Bachian. Ternate, tri-syllabic, minute, consisting almost entirely of an ever-active volcano, played the most spectacular rôle in history. There must be many to ask themselves why human beings with any sense will persist in living at the foot of dangerous volcanoes, Etna, Vesuvius, Mount Lamington—Ternate. The answer is that volcanic ash makes splendid soil, such as the clove and the grape appreciate. The cloves and nutmeg of the Moluccas were to a large extent the magnet that attracted Columbus, Vasco da Gama, and Magellan over uncharted seas, it being the cherished ambition of Spain and Portugal to wrest the lucrative trade in those articles out of the hands of the Moslems.

The first thing that Albuquerque did after his conquest of Malacca was to send an expedition under Antonio Dabreu and Francisco Serrano to explore trading possibilities in the Moluccas. Serrano was exactly the right man for the purpose, a friendly capable person who liked the East Indians so much that he

[1] Cloves, nutmeg and other spices were coveted in China and the Western world primarily to give zest and flavour to unappetizing food, but also for use in medicine and the making of perfumes.

decided to settle down for good at Ternate where he became captain-general of the local sultan's forces in his never-ending wars with his brother sultan of Tidore.[1] The excellent man thus prepared at a long remove for the coming of St. Francis Xavier, but Francis had a more immediate precursor, and one truly worthy of him, in the person of Antonio Galvão, whose name the Reverend Richard Hakluyt, eponymous hero of the Hakluyt Society, naturalized in English as Galvano. Galvano arrived as Captain at Ternate in 1536. The previous fifteen years, since the death of Serrano, had been a period of strife and anarchy in the islands, to which the Portuguese, especially Captain Tristan de Ataíde, heavily contributed. Just before Galvano replaced him, Ataíde had deposed the Sultan of Ternate, Tabarija, and sent him a prisoner to Goa, where the half-baked Moslem, with an eye on the main chance, became a Christian. That complicated the situation for the Portuguese authorities, all the more because the

[1] Serrano was an intimate friend of Ferdinand Magellan. Both of them had taken part in the siege of Malacca, and it was Serrano's letters from Ternate which induced Magellan to attempt to reach the Moluccas by sailing west-wards, as Columbus had done. Magellan and Duarte Barbosa both lost their lives in the Philippines, but sixty of their men, survivors of the complement of 230 who had sailed from Spain, reached their goal. The thrill of the moment can be felt in the words of Antonio Pigafetta, the historian of the great voyage: ' The pilot told us that four rather high islands we came upon were the Moluccas, for which we gave thanks to God, and to comfort ourselves discharged all our artillery. It need not cause surprise that we were so joyful, since we had passed twenty-seven months less two days always in search of the Moluccas.' They put in at Tidore and were well received by Raja Sultan Manzor because, as servants of the King of Spain, they would presumably be no friends of the Portuguese gentry on Ternate. Serrano had died at Ternate less than eight months earlier, leaving behind ' a little son and daughter that he had of a lady he had taken to wife in Java, and two hundred bahars [close on thirty-five tons] of cloves '. Of themselves Pigafetta says that they ' bought cloves like mad ', by barter, of course. Then they sailed away home in the only one of their five ships left, the *Victoria*, under the command of the Basque pilot Sebastian del Cano, and reached their starting point of San Lucar on September 6, 1522. Cano was ennobled and on his coat of arms there figured two cinnamon sticks in saltire proper, three nutmegs and twelve cloves. His crest was a globe bearing the motto, *Primus circumdedisti me*—'You were the first to circumnavigate me '. The twenty-six tons of cloves they brought back more than paid for the loss of four ships and all their articles of barter, 20,000 bells, 1,000 looking-glasses, etc. (Crofton, *A Pageant of the Spice Islands*, London, 1938, p. 47).

Captain had given the vacant throne to a certain hearty infidel named Hairun, half-brother of the deposed sultan, who allowed himself the fullest latitude of the Koran in the matter of wives and other perquisites.

Riot and revolution followed the change of rulers, and Ternate Town was as effectually destroyed as if its own volcano had done the damage. At that point Galvano came on the scene and transformed it. With but 130 white soldiers at his back, he ended the internecine strife of the Moluccan sultans and gave the islands the only honest and enlightened administration they had ever known. Hakluyt could hardly contain his admiration for this Latin Catholic, his predecessor as a recorder of voyages, and spoke with enthusiasm to Sir Robert Cecil of his ' pietie towards God, equitie towards men, fidelity to his Prince, love to his countrey, skill in sea causes, experience in histories, liberalitie towards his nation, vigilance, valour, wisedome and diligence in restoring and settling the decaied state of the Isles of Maluco '.[1] This man after the heart of St. Francis Xavier speaks of himself only rarely in his books and in the third person:

In the yeere 1538, Antonie Galvano, being chiefe captaine in the isles of Maluco, sent a ship towards the north, whereof one Francis de Castro was captaine, having commandement to convert as many as he could to the faith, having been asked to do so by many of those parts. He himself, Galvano, christened numerous inhabitants of Celébes, Amboina, the Isles of Moro and Morotai, and divers other places. When Francis de Castro arrived at the Island of Mindanao and other islands north of it [the Philippines], six kings received the water of baptism, and most of them Antonie Galvano gave commandement to be called by the name of John, in remembrance that King John the Third raigned then in Portugall. . . .[2]

[1] The Discoveries of the World. Briefly written in the Portugal tongue by Antonie Galvano, Governor of Ternate. Published in English by Richard Hakluyt, Londini, 1601. Epistle Dedicatorie. This work was reissued with the Portuguese original by the Hakluyt Society in 1862. The original was published in Lisbon in 1563, six years after the author's death.

[2] The Discoveries of the World, p. 208.

That passage is very important as setting the course for St. Francis Xavier up to, but not including, the islands afterwards named the Philippines.[1] Galvano's noble character made a great impression on the native peoples who became ' so affectioned to the Portugals that they would venture for them their lives, wives, children and goods ', but his term of office was only three years, and he had to return to Lisbon, as poor as when he left it, without being able to make any provision for the future of his Christians. It is a terrible reflection on the gratitude of kings and their ministers that this selfless servant of his country was allowed to die in a charitable institution, without enough money to buy himself a winding-sheet. Francis Xavier probably never heard of him at all, as he nowhere mentions him, but he did know of the isolated groups of Christians, and it was primarily to find and succour them that he sailed from Malacca ôn New Year's Day, 1546.

The voyage of at least 1,740 nautical miles took a month and a half and was made either in a Portuguese merchant ship or in a Malay *prau*, which is shaped somewhat like a large Chinese junk with an immense bamboo mainyard carrying an oblong sail. The route lay through the South China, Java, Flores and Banda Seas, the strangest, most beautiful, perilous waters in the whole world. Even as late as the times of the indomitable Alfred Russel Wallace, to thread those seas was regarded by the Indonesian peoples as ' a rather wild and romantic expedition . . . the unachieved ambition of their lives ', but St. Francis had not a single word to say of the experience, which was carrying taciturnity to lengths unforgivable by a biographer. Surely he might have spared a line for the Line of all lines as he crossed it coming out of Malacca Strait, and what was there to prevent him paying

[1] The Philippines had been discovered by Magellan and his men, acting for the King of Spain. Into Spanish territory St. Francis was careful never to intrude. But the Spaniards were not so careful of Portuguese rights and claimed the Moluccas on the ground that they were on their side of Alexander the Sixth's famous line. The Philippines and the Moluccas are almost in the same longitude, but the geographers of the two countries shifted Alexander's line east or west as best suited the national interest. Spaniards and Portuguese, though at peace in Europe, fought a brisk little war under the rival banners of Ternate and Tidore, as will be seen below. The Portuguese prevailed but Spain got the Moluccas eventually by annexing Portugal.

a tribute to the wild beauty of Java as he coasted it from end to end? There he was, sailing among faery lands forlorn, hundreds of them, coming up out of miraculous dawns, garbing themselves in the sun's splendour, and fading into skies tinted as by the artistry of seraphim, and not a comment has he to make. The truth seems to have been that he could no longer give his mind to anything but the desperate condition of his fellow-men, still worshipping stocks and stones, or a god as adaptable to human passions as the aloof deity of Islam. Before leaving Malacca and again at his long journey's end he wrote to his men in Goa, urgent, imploring, peremptory letters, brimming over with the solicitude which tormented him for the poor fisher tribes of India he had won, or partially won, to the worship of the true, the only God. ' I beg, I pray you, my loved brothers Juan de Beira and Antonio Criminali, to hasten as soon as you have read this to the help of Father Francis Mansilhas at Cape Comorin. . . . For the love of God, let nothing, nothing hold you back. . . . Padre Juan and Padre Antonio, for your greater merit I order you in virtue of holy obedience to join Francis Mansilhas, Juan Lisano, and the three Indian priests at Cape Comorin. . . .'[1]

Though he arrived at Amboina on February 14, Francis had to wait until May 10 before he could dispatch a letter to Europe, as no ships sailed west during the interval. Meantime, a Portuguese armada of eight warships put in at Amboina with numerous Spanish prisoners captured in the northern islands. Francis discreetly omitted to mention the Spaniards when writing to Europe, but told his brethren in Goa.

> The fleet [he said] kept me busy from morning to night, hearing an endless stream of confessions, visiting the sick, absolving and comforting the dying, preaching. In and out of Lent I was at it the whole time. . . . This island of Amboina is from twenty-five to thirty leagues in circumference,[2]

[1] Schurhammer, *Epistolae S. Francisci Xaverii*, i, 309, 339. For men vowed to obedience an order such as Francis gave binds under serious sin.

[2] ' The island consists of two peninsulas, so nearly divided by inlets of the sea as to leave only a sandy isthmus about a mile wide near their eastern extremity. The western inlet is several miles long and forms a fine harbour, on

populous, with seven villages of Christians. Immediately on arrival here I visited those villages and baptized a large number of children who had not received the Sacrament. One hundred and thirty leagues from Amboina there is another country called the Coast of Moro where, I am told, there are many totally uninstructed Christians. I am going there as soon as ever I can. I give you this account that you may see how sorely you are needed in these parts. Well do I know that you are needed in India too, but these islands require your help even more, so for the love of Christ our Lord I earnestly beseech you, Father Francis Mansilhas and Father Juan Beira, to come to their rescue. For your greater merit, I order you in virtue of holy obedience to come, and should either of you die before being able, then another Father, Antonio Criminali, for instance, will take his place. If some of our Society arrive in India this year, I beg all of them for the love of God, and I order them likewise, to repair to Cape Comorin to teach and help the Christians there. Send me detailed news of any that may be coming. . . . I am afraid you will not receive this letter until February of next year [1547]. As soon as it reaches you, leave Cape Comorin for Goa to make ready for your voyage to the Moluccas on one of the King's ships that departs at the beginning of April. . . .

---

the southern side of which is situated the town of Amboina. . . . Hills and mountains form the background in almost every direction, and there are few places more enjoyable for a morning or evening stroll than these sandy roads and shady lanes in the suburbs of the ancient city. . . .' (Wallace, *The Malay Archipelago*, pp. 223–4. Wallace had a terrifying experience with a twelve-foot python while on the island. He grows lyrical over the harbour and its denizens: ' The clearness of the water, twenty to fifty feet deep, afforded me one of the most astonishing and beautiful sights I have ever beheld. The bottom was absolutely hidden by a continuous series of corals, sponges, actiniae. . . . In and out among the hills and valleys moved numbers of blue and red and yellow fishes, spotted and banded and striped, while great orange or rosy transparent medusae floated along near the surface. It was a sight to gaze at for hours, and no description can do justice to its surpassing beauty. For once, the reality exceeded the most glowing accounts I had ever read of the wonders of a coral sea. There is perhaps no spot in the world richer in marine productions than the harbour of Amboina.' If only St. Francis Xavier would speak like that now and again, remembering the *Benedicite*, we would love him even more than we already do).

Bring with you everything necessary for saying Mass, but let
the chalice be of copper, as it is a safer metal than silver to go
around with in this unholy land of thieves. . . . Give the
Augustinian friars of New Spain who are proceeding to Goa
news of me. I pray you to do everything in your power for
them and to show them all love and kindness, as they well
deserve. . . . Try, won't you, please, my brothers, for the service
of God our Lord, to attract into your company some men of
good life to help us teach the Christian doctrine in these islands.
I earnestly beg each of you to acquire at least one recruit, priest
or layman, who is out of patience with the world, the flesh, and
the devil, and longs to have vengeance on them for their
dishonour to God and His Saints. . . .[1]

According to all the books, Francis Mansilhas, so long the
patient mule of God, suddenly dug in his heels and refused to
obey the call to the Moluccas, for which recalcitrance he was
subsequently dismissed by St. Francis Xavier from the Society of
Jesus. There are two brief references to the matter in contemporary

[1] Schurhammer, *Epistolae S. Francisci Xaverii*, i, 339–43. This document refers
to the Sultan of Ternate, Hairun, who also had been deposed and sent prisoner to
Malacca by a high-handed Portuguese Captain, Jordan de Freitas. The idea
was to reinstate the former Sultan, Tabarija, now that he had become a
Christian, but the plan did not work because Tabarija died before he could be
given back his throne. Evil-living Moslem though he was, Hairun had then to
be accepted, and to smooth the way for his return de Freitas himself was
cashiered and sent back in disgrace to India, which served him right. Hairun
was in Malacca at the same time as St. Francis, but they did not become friends
until later at Ternate. Hairun reigned at Ternate as a vassal of Portugal until
1570, always at war, cold or hot, with his next neighbour, the Sultan of Tidore.
These two between them controlled all the trade of the Moluccas and were
courted successively or simultaneously by the Portuguese, the Spaniards, the
Hollanders and the English. Sir Francis Drake was among those who paid his
respects at Ternate, and received from the Sultan of the time ' a ring with
a faire emerald stone in the same ' for presentation to Queen Elizabeth. In the
year of the Gunpowder Plot, the ' kings ' of Ternate and Tidore exchanged
letters with His Majesty, James I of England, Tidore appealing for succour
against Ternate, and Ternate craving pardon for having called the Dutch
rather than the English to rescue them from their ' auncient enemies the Portin-
gals '. (*The Voyage of Sir Henry Middleton to the Moluccas*. Ed. Foster, London,
the Hakluyt Society, 1943, pp. 61–4.)

Jesuit letters, one from Malacca saying that Mansilhas *no se alló dispuesto para ir*, and the other from Goa saying, *Padre Francisco de Mansilhas se hallo indispuesto*. That word 'dispuesto' is as ambiguous in Spanish as it is in English, but in English 'indisposed' can, and most usually does, mean 'unwell'. In Spanish, the verb *hallar*, of which 'alló' or 'halló' is the third person singular in the past absolute, often means 'to feel, as to health'. Whatever may be thought of such linguistic considerations, the only begetter of the tradition that Mansilhas rebelled and was expelled was Father Francisco de Sousa in a huge uneven work which he published at Lisbon in 1710 (162 years after the event) under the grandiose title, *Oriente Conquistado a Jesu Christo pelos Padres da Companhia de Jesus*.[1] There, after an accurate citation from the letter of St. Francis, Sousa interpreted events in the following way. The summons of Francis was to Beira and Mansilhas. If either happened to die before he could come, another Father was to replace him. ' That was just how things turned out,' wrote Sousa, ' for Father Mansilhas refused to undertake the journey and, if he did not die, he disobeyed, and was afterwards given his dismissal, and might accordingly be regarded as dead to the Company.' All very well, but the historian provides not a shred of proof that St. Francis dismissed his old friend, the man to whom he had opened his heart as to no one else in the world. There exists no such proof, and consequently we are entitled to hold that Mansilhas left the Society of Jesus purely for reasons of health, as many a good man has done since. One thing is certain, that he remained on the friendliest terms with the Jesuits up to his death at Cochin in 1565. Of all the witnesses, sixty-five in number, who were summoned to give evidence about the life of Francis Xavier at the canonical investigations held in Goa, Bassein, Malacca and Cochin in the years 1556–7, Mansilhas stood out as the only priest. The others were laymen, soldiers, merchants,

[1] The Padre did not mean by his title that his Jesuits had conquered the whole of the Orient, but that he was writing of the tiny part of it which they had conquered. Other religious orders produced histories with similar titles, which were the fashion of the day. De Sousa was a fine man and sometimes a fine writer. He spent forty-seven years under the Indian sun and left his bones in Goa.

officials. And the evidence of Mansilhas, for its moderation and the love and reverence implicit in it, was the most precious tendered:

> I knew Father Francis in Portugal and I went about with him for six or seven years on the Fishery Coast. No human being could have done what he did or have lived as he lived without being full of the Holy Spirit. Indeed, his life was more that of a saint and angel than of a man. . . . Many a time, out of his love for God and our holy faith, he offered himself to martyrdom in the midst of his incessant labours and sufferings. . . . If he could find time in the night, as he never could during the day, he gave himself completely to prayer and contemplation. Day and night, he consoled men, hearing their confessions, visiting them when sick, begging alms for them when they were poor. He had nothing of his own, and on himself never spent a penny. As much as one could dream of a man doing he did, and more. . . .[1]

Sousa himself could not forbear from casting a flower on the grave of the man whose reputation he had ruined, and quoted a letter to Rome from the rector of the Jesuit house in Cochin, Father Jeronyme Rodriguez, at the time Mansilhas died :

> As soon as he felt himself to be dying, he made a general confession to a Father of our Society, and begged him with great emotion not to leave him at the last hour. To content him, one of our Fathers remained with him constantly. He wanted no others about him, and said that his greatest comfort was to be able to look at, to speak with, someone of our Society. He spoke of nothing but God during his last illness, and begged the Fathers to keep reminding him at the end of the sufferings of our Lord in His Passion. Truly, he gave us a wonderful example of patience and devotion. When the Father read to him some passage of the Passion, he would burst into

[1] *Monumenta Xaveriana*, ii, 316–7.

violent weeping and beat his breast, and so he continued to do until he died.

Assim morreo o primeyro expulso da Companhia na India, wrote Sousa, with a certain smugness which rather suggests, as the good man certainly did not mean, that it might be a very good thing for one's soul to be thrown out of the Society of Jesus! Francis Mansilhas was, in fact, among the greatest benefactors the Jesuits have known, for he bequeathed to them the little treasured bundle of letters written to him by Francis Xavier, almost equivalent to the legacy of Xavier's heart.[1]

By the same ship that carried the orders which Mansilhas is alleged to have disobeyed, St. Francis wrote also to his brethren in Europe and to the King of Portugal. He mentioned that, by the help of God, he ' had brought together in friendship many soldiers who never live peaceably on this island of Amboina ', but tactfully forbore to say that the brawling was between the warriors of Portugal and their rivals of Spain. Then he went on to speak of Morotai, his Omoro, the deadly island north of Halmaheira which had recently swum into his ken:

On this island many years ago a large number of people became Christians who, owing to the death of the clerics, their first apostles, have been left abandoned and without instruction. Omoro is a most dangerous place because the natives are full of treachery and put various poisons in the food and drink which they offer strangers. For this reason, people who might have looked after the forsaken Christians have stopped going there. I have made up my mind to go there myself to help them in their spiritual needs and to baptize their [children]. I feel it incumbent upon me to sacrifice my temporal life for the sake of the spiritual life of my neighbour, and so,

[1] Speaking strictly according to canon law, it may be doubted whether, at the time when he wrote from Amboina, May 10, 1546, St. Francis, as a Jesuit superior, had the power to order Mansilhas *in virtute sanctae obedientiae*. There is no record of Mansilhas having taken vows in the Society of Jesus, or, if he did, they were certainly simple ones, and these *at the time* did not constitute a man either a religious or a Jesuit (*vide infra*, p. 256, note 3).

putting all my trust in God our Lord, I have offered myself
to danger and death in whatever shape it may come, longing
as I do to be conformed in my own small and feeble way to
that saying of our Redeemer, *Qui enim voluerit animam suam
salvam facere, perdet eam; qui autem perdiderit animam suam
propter me, inveniet eam.* It may be easy to understand the Latin
and the general meaning of that saying of our Lord, but when
a man gets down to particulars in trying to come to a decision
about losing his life for God in order to find it again in Him,
and the dangers present themselves which will probably bring
about his destruction, then his thoughts grow hazy and even
the clear Latin becomes obscure. In such circumstances, it seems
to me, nobody can understand, no matter what his learning,
except one to whom God in His infinite mercy makes his particular case plain. It is then that we learn to know our flesh and
its infirmities. Many of my devoted friends have endeavoured
to dissuade me from going to such a perilous country, and
seeing that they could not prevail were for giving me numerous
antidotes against poison. They were offered to me with tears
but, while thanking my friends with all my heart for their love
and kindness, I did not take their *defensivos*, as I did not want to
burden myself with [the tokens of] a fear which I did not feel,
and still less to lose anything of the trust which I had placed
entirely in God. I besought them instead to remember me
constantly in their prayers, which are the surest remedy against
poison that can be found. . . .[1]

In all this, St. Francis was once more a law unto himself, as
when, in the hospital at Venice, he had swallowed the deadly
stuff from the hideous sores of a patient. On that occasion, his
sensitive, fastidious nature revolted at having to rub the man's
back, and he did his outrageous deed in order to subdue his
rebellious feelings. So too, at Amboina, it is perfectly plain that
his friends had given him a horrifying picture of what he might
expect on the nightmarish Morotai, and that he had been visited
by very definite qualms of natural terror at the prospect. They

[1] Schurhammer, *Epistolae S. Francisci Xaverii*, i, 325–6.

must be suppressed at all costs or they would hinder his work for souls and tarnish that absolute dependence on God which was his only palladium. Therefore, he must not accept the antidotes against poison offered him *con tanto amor y lágrimas*. He knew that his refusal might have the appearance of rashness or even of tempting God, and so his letter to his brethren bears the stamp of an *apologia*. There can be no doubt at all that the danger which he faced was great. The Indonesian islands, and isolated Morotai in particular, had acquired a sinister reputation, one to make the legendary Borgias jealous, for native skill in the manufacture and use of poisons. This deplorable habit, like that of head-hunting, was closely connected with the magical rites whereby the unhappy peoples hoped to placate spirits, to control the extremely un-dependable weather, to give fertility to the soil, and to achieve distinction in tribal warfare. In his lively book, *An Exact Discourse of the Subtilties, Fashions, Policies, Religion, and Ceremonies of the East Indians, as well Chyneses as Javans, there Abyding and Dwelling*, the robustious Elizabethan Edmund Scott, who sailed the Indo-nesian seas for over two years, has the following remarks to make: 'The people of those parts are given much to poysoning; which is the cause they hold their beazer stones in so high esti-mation that there is not any of account but they will alwaies have some ready in their house; and the noblemen doe horde them upp for great jewells. And surely I do hold that to bee the thing, next under God, that hath preserved the moste of our lives that have been long resident there.'[1] We may be sure that a bezoar stone was among the *defensivos* pressed on St. Francis Xavier, for the Portuguese believed in its efficacy as much as did the English.[2]

[1] In *The Voyage of Sir Henry Middleton to the Moluccas*, p. 128. Few books give a more vivid picture than Scott's (first published in London in 1606) of the rivalries and endemic violence which used to characterize native and European life in Indonesia in the sixteenth and seventeenth centuries. 'And now,' he writes at one point, 'to beginne the new yeare 1604, my pen affordes to speak of little else but murther, theft, warres, fire, and treason.'

[2] The word is from the Arabic *bazahr*, meaning poison-expelling, and the thing was a hard concretion found in the bodies of certain animals. The method of use was to drink it powdered in water. The Sultan of Bantam in Java sent King James I two of the stones, as a suitable present from one monarch to

This world of Molucca [St. Francis continued for the enlightenment of his European brethren] is composed entirely of islands, and no mainland has yet been discovered.[1] The islands are beyond numbering and nearly all of them populated. They are not Christians for lack of anybody to gather them into the fold. If our Society only had a house in Molucca many of the people would become Christians, and my fixed resolve is that there *shall* be such a house, for the great service of God our Lord. The gentiles of these parts are more numerous than the Moors and there is no love lost between the two parties. The Moors, who have been here for seventy years, offer the islanders a choice of Mohammedanism or slavery, and the islanders want neither. They would prefer to be Christians rather than Moors, and if only there was someone to preach the truth to them, they would all be converted.[2] Two or three Moslem priests from Mecca, where the Moors say is the body of Mohammed, converted a great number of the gentiles out here to his sect, but the best thing about those convert Moors is that they know nothing whatever of that perverse sect. . . . I give you these details so that you may feel and keep in mind how great a number of souls is lost because there is nobody to come to their rescue. Men who have not sufficient education and talent to be members of the Society,[3] have more than

another. A fragment of the horn of a rhinoceros, well ground, was also considered a good remedy. ' Had you no unicorn's horn nor bezoar stone about you? ' asks a character in Ben Jonson's *Every Man out of his Humour*.

[1] The Portuguese had blundered on New Guinea by accident, but no western eyes saw Australia until the following century. Geologically, and by their flora and fauna, Celébes and all the islands to the east of it belong to the Australian world; all to the west were originally part of Asia.

[2] Here again, as so often, the indestructible optimism of St. Francis outsoared his evidence. The fact that ninety per cent of the Indonesian population is today Moslem, in spite of the most heroic Christian missionary effort through the centuries, does not evince any native preference for Christianity.

[3] At first, the Society of Jesus was restricted by Papal authority to sixty members, all of whom had to be solemnly professed. All not so professed, such as Francis Mansilhas, did not qualify canonically as religious and might be regarded only as helpers. By a bull issued on June 5, 1546, Pope Paul III withdrew the restriction, so that priests taking final simple vows (spiritual coadjutors) and lay brothers doing the same (temporal coadjutors) would become

enough of both for this part of the world, were they willing to come and live and die among these peoples. If twelve such men came annually, they would soon destroy that evil sect of Mohammed and make all the people Christians. . . .

Possibly it might have been so if each twelve and all twelves had been Francis Xaviers.

Francis has not yet finished with the islands and the islanders:

The people are a very barbarous lot and full of treachery, brownish-yellow in complexion rather than black, and extremely disagreeable.[1] There are islands whose folk eat the bodies of enemies killed in their tribal wars. When one of them dies from sickness his hands and heels are eaten, and considered a great delicacy. Such barbarians are they on some islands that a man, wishing to hold a great feast, will ask his neighbour for the loan of his father, if he is very old, to serve him up as a dish, at the same time promising to give his own father when ripe for the purpose and the neighbour is desirous of having a banquet.[2] Within a month, I hope to go to an island where such things happen, as the people want to be

full religious and members of the Society of Jesus. This great concession, which, among other things, made Jesuit schools possible, remained unknown to St. Francis until much later.

[1] A sentiment heartily endorsed by Edmund Scott. 'The Javans and Chyneses,' said he, meaning most Indonesians, 'from the highest to the lowest, are all villaines and have not one spark of grace in them. . . . Amongst all other of the Divells instruments heere upon earth there was one of the King's bloud. . . .' (*The Voyage of Sir Henry Middleton*, p. 124 sq.). Though he frequently invokes the name of God, Scott himself, like many Elizabethans, was a brutal person and tortured offending natives as savagely as Jesuits were tortured in the Tower of London.

[2] The story that natives obliged with their aged fathers for the neighbours' pots was current among the Portuguese at least from the year 1510, but was denied as an invention of Moslem traders by several writers, including the well-informed Jesuit and biographer of St. Francis, Manuel Teixeira. But, in spite of Teixeira's correction, so tactfully administered, Pedro Ribadeneira apparently thought it too good a yarn to excise from his *Vida del P. Ignacio Loyola*, where it is still to be found with other exaggerations (e.g., in *Historias de la Contrarreforma*, Madrid, 1945, p. 280).

Christians. There are abominable fleshly vices among them, such as you would find it hard to believe and such as I dare not put on paper. The islands, which are full of great and dense forests, have a temperate climate and an abundance of rain. So mountainous are they and difficult to traverse that in time of war the people climb them out of danger's way, as they constitute natural fortresses. There are no horses available, even if it were possible to ride on the islands. There are constant earthquakes out here and similar commotions under the sea. Earthquakes are alarming enough but not as bad as seaquakes. If you are on a ship in one of these you feel as though the vessel had struck a rock. Many of these islands [have mountains that] cast forth fire with a noise greater than any artillery on earth could make, and with the fire are vomited huge masses of rock. For lack of anyone to preach in these islands the torments of Hell, God permits Hell itself to open for the confusion of the infidels and their abominable vices. . . .[1]

While on Amboina, St. Francis had an experience in the animal world which appears to have excited him far more than volcano or earthquake. It was an experience to make even such a hero of natural history as Alfred Russel Wallace violently jealous, for though he visited the island three different times he

[1] Indonesia has the distinction of being the most volcanic and earthquaking region on earth. Mount Lamington, so grimly in the news in 1951, belongs to a belt of volcanoes, active or quiescent, which stretches almost the whole length of Sumatra, right through Java (between those two, in the Sunda Strait, was famous Krakatoa) and all the islands following it up to Halmaheira, and then north again through the Philippines, and east, through New Guinea, to New Britain. Alfred Russel Wallace had his first experience of an earthquake while on Célébes: ' As I was sitting reading, the house began shaking with a very gentle but rapidly increasing motion. I sat still enjoying the novel sensation for some seconds; but in less than half a minute it became strong enough to shake me in my chair, and to make the house visibly rock about, and creak and crack. Then began a cry throughout the village of "Tana Goyang! Tana Goyang!" (Earthquake! Earthquake!) Everybody rushed out of their houses—women screamed and children cried—and I thought it prudent to go out too. On getting up, I found my head giddy and my steps unsteady, and could hardly walk without falling. I felt as if I had been turned round and round, and was almost sea-sick. . . .' (*The Malay Archipelago*, pp. 192–3).

never saw what Francis saw, a *billy*-goat which could be milked and bore lots of kids! 'In all my life,' wrote Francis, 'I have never seen what I have seen here, a he-goat [*un cabrón*] which is continually in milk and bears young regularly. It has only one teat and gives enough milk daily to fill a large bowl, which its young drink. A Portuguese gentleman has taken it to India to have it shipped to Portugal as something quite new. I myself with my own hands extracted milk from it. Otherwise, I would not have believed the story, considering it to be impossible.' That was certainly news for the brethren beyond the seas, and it did not remain entirely unconfirmed, for the Sultan of Tidore told Antonio Galvano, when he was governor of Ternate, about the remarkable billy-goat of Amboina.[1]

Leaving the goat, on whose masculinity he was highly competent to pronounce after spending the nineteen years of his youth in Navarre among sheep and goats, Francis for the first time directed his brethren's attention to the Celestial Empire:

In Malacca, I met a Portuguese merchant who had come from a land of great traffic called China. He told me that a distinguished Chinaman from the Emperor's court at Peking had put many questions to him, and in particular asked whether Christians ate pork. The merchant replied that they did and inquired why the other wanted to know. The Chinaman answered that in his country there lives a class of people in a mountainous part, segregated from others, who do not eat pork and celebrate many feasts. I do not know who these people are, whether Christians who keep the Old and New Law, as do those of Prester John, or the lost tribes of Israel. There is general agreement that they are not Moors. Every

[1]Galvano, *The Discoveries of the World* (Hakluyt Society, 1862), p. 120. Another contemporary of St. Francis, Gabriel Rebello, also refers to the goat in his *Informaçao das cousas de Maluco*. After this brief but glorious appearance on the stage of natural (or should we say, unnatural?) history, the animal disappears from view. It must have been a hermaphrodite goat of some sort, but this question is outside the province of a mere biographer. Père Brou and the numerous modern biographers dependent on him ignore the goat altogether, perhaps thinking milking operations to be beneath the dignity of a great apostle.

year, several Portuguese ships ply between Malacca and the
ports of China, and I have requested many sailing on them to
find out about this people, urging them in particular to make
inquiries as to their ceremonies and customs, so that it may be
possible in this way to determine whether they are Christians
or Jews. It is often said that the Apostle St. Thomas went to
China and made a large number of converts, and that the
Greek Orthodox Church, before the Portuguese mastered India,
used to send bishops to teach and baptize among those Chinese
Christians. . . . If I learn anything definite on the subject, by
personal experience or otherwise, I shall let you know next year.

The story that St. Thomas made converts in China derives
from a *lectio* in the Chaldean Breviary used by the Malabar
Christians, one of whose bishops, Mar Jacobus, was afterwards
to become a friend of St. Francis. Breviaries, however, have a
traditional style and convention of their own, and their lessons
may not safely be pressed into service as historical evidence.
Nestorian monks from Syria under a leader named Olopen
certainly penetrated into the heart of China in the year 635, and
the mission which they started continued to be fed by others of
their heresy from the Eastern Roman Empire until the year 980.
But, though enterprising men and, to judge by the famous
monument which they erected to themselves at Singanfu,
pleased with their accomplishment, they seem to have won very
few Chinese to their brand of Christianity. A second wave of
them came to China from the west early in the eleventh century,
but they too eventually merged with the Moslems, Jews or
pagans around them, retaining of Christianity only the symbol
of the cross and a few other traditional usages. Thus diluted, they
came to be known as ' Adorers of the Cross ', and very likely it
was of some such group that the Portuguese merchant brought
news to St. Francis Xavier.[1]

[1] In his magnificent edition of the works of Father Matteo Ricci, one of the
supreme achievements of modern scholarship and book production, Father
Pasquale M. D'Elia, S.J., Professor of Sinology at the Gregorian University
and the University of Rome, goes into the question in many places (*Fonti
Ricciane*, vol. i, Rome, 1942, liv–lxiii; vol. ii, 1949, 314–25).

The letter which St. Francis dispatched to Europe with his bulletin of information had a moving valediction:

> I pray you, my most dear Brothers and Fathers, by the love of Christ our Lord and of His most holy Mother and of all the saints that are in the glory of Paradise, to have special remembrance of me and to commend me to God continually, as I live in such sore need of your good offices and help. My great spiritual need of you has been brought home to me by many experiences of help in travail of body and soul given me by God through your intercession. Let me tell you what I have done so that I may never forget you. For my own great comfort and that I may have you constantly in mind, I have cut from your letters to me your names written in your own hand, and these I always carry about with me, together with the vow of profession which I made, to be my solace and refreshment. Thanks be to God and after God to you, *Hermanos y Padres suavissimos*, whom God made such that just to have your names about me puts me in good spirits. I say no more, as we shall soon be seeing one another in the next life, with a peace and restfulness unknown to this. Your least brother and son, Francis.[1]

That passage illustrates one aspect of the Saint's character, his capacity for affection. The following paragraphs from his letter to King John of Portugal, sent by the same ship, bring out another, his sympathy for all souls in trouble:

> Senhor, . . . With the fleet of Fernan de Sousa which sailed from India to the rescue of the fortress at Malluco [Ternate] threatened by Castilians from New Spain [Mexico], there came three captains, loyal and faithful vassals of your Highness. The Moors of Gilolo slew one of them, João Galvão, by a cannon shot. The two others, Manuel de Mesquita and Lionel de Lima, served your Highness greatly by the way they helped to deliver the fortress from the straits to which it was

[1] Schurhammer, *Epistolae S. Francisci Xaverii*, i, 321–30.

reduced, giving of their substance and that of their friends to feed the poor lascars, and to provide lodging, food and clothing for the Spaniards, as though they were neighbours rather than enemies. Those captains, being more gentlemen than traders or merchants, could not avail themselves of the cloves God gives that land to make good their expenses, and so look in the first place to God for the reward of their services and then to your Highness. And they served you well, undertaking that hard voyage to Moluco with so much peril of body and soul. Remember, your Highness, Manuel de Mesquita. He is sailing on a ship with many Spaniards and Portuguese whose maintenance he provides out of his own pocket. . . . Lionel de Lima has also been at great expense in the same way. Remember them, your Highness, in order to show them thanks which they so well deserve. . . .[1]

It was during his stay at Amboina, while on a flying visit from that island to its big northern neighbour Ceram or Serang,[2] that the most picturesque and popular of all the many miracles attributed to St. Francis Xavier is supposed to have happened. The traditional story, as told, for instance, by Francisco de Sousa in his reasonably sober *Oriente Conquistado*, runs thus:

> Voyaging one day from Amboina to another island, Xavier in his boat was assaulted by furious headwinds. He took from his breast his crucifix, which was about a finger in length, and from the side of the boat dropped it into the sea by its cord. But the cord slipped from his hands and the waves swallowed up the crucifix. He was greatly distressed by the loss and made no secret of his grief. The following day, twenty-four tempestuous hours after the disaster to his crucifix, he reached the Island of Veranula [old Portuguese name for Ceram].

[1] Schurhammer, *Epistolae*, i, 347–8. After ten years in the East, marked by much fighting and adventure, Lionel de Lima returned to Portugal to enter the Society of Jesus in 1550. He founded the Jesuit college in Bragança and was its first rector. The variations in the spelling of the place-name in this extract are typical of St. Francis.

[2] Amboina is almost exactly equal in area to the Isles of Wight and Man taken together. Ceram is more than eighteen times larger.

Accompanied by a man named Fausto Rodriguez born at Viana de Alvito [Portugal], he had walked about five hundred paces along the shore towards the village of Tamalo when both he and Rodriguez saw a crab come out of the sea with the crucifix held upright in its claws or pincers. The new standard-bearer of Christ crawled towards the Saint and stood before him with the divine banner hoisted. Xavier went on his knees, and the crab waited until he had taken the crucifix, whereupon it immediately returned to the sea. The Saint kissed his re-covered treasure a thousand times and pressed it to his heart. He remained on his knees in prayer for half an hour, as did his companion also, both giving God their profoundest thanks for so illustrious a miracle. That, and nothing more, is known of the sworn testimony taken from Fausto Rodriguez.[1]

Rodriguez, the only authority for the crab story, certainly bore witness under solemn oath to the truth of his experience, as an authenticated copy of his deposition was sent to Rome at the time and still exists. He was expelled from Amboina when the Dutch captured the island from the Portuguese in 1605, and made his way to the Philippines, where eight years later, just before his death in extreme old age, the Bishop of Cebu instituted a canonical process to obtain his evidence.[2]

When Xavier was canonized by Gregory XV on March 12, 1622, the bull customary on such occasions failed to appear owing to the illness and death of the Pope shortly afterwards. But the missing document was supplied at great length and with much Ciceronian rotundity by his successor, Urban VIII, on August 6, 1623, and in it the story of the crab and the crucifix

[1] *Oriente Conquistado a Jesu Christo pelos Padres da Companhia de Jesus*, first ed., i, 370–1.

[2] As Rodriguez was born in Portugal and Portugal did not permit emigration of families to its eastern dominions, he must have reached man's estate by the year 1546 when he met St. Francis in Amboina, especially as he is recorded to have been a gunner in the Portuguese navy. He must therefore have been *mui antigo*, as a letter from Goa to Rome in 1614 says (*Monumenta Xaveriana*, ii, 144), in fact, close on ninety, when he gave his testimony. That does not invalidate it but it raises the question why he did not speak up during all the intervening sixty-seven years. An obituary notice of him, telling of his holy death, was sent to Rome and is still extant.

figured prominently. The crab, in fact, became world famous and has remained so, but that does not in the least mean that Catholics are precluded from questioning, with due respect, the crustacean's right to be in the Bull or the miraculousness of its feat. It is entirely a matter of evidence, and any small boy, busy among the rocks by the sea-shore, will readily testify that crabs big and small seize bits of stick or other objects thrown to them and scurry off with the prize. In other words, the crab at Ceram may simply have behaved as crabs do everywhere, and the restoration of the crucifix to St. Francis, though providential, need not have been strictly miraculous. St. Francis himself nowhere speaks of this incident and gives not the slightest hint that he ever voyaged to Ceram or other islands near Amboina. It is difficult, in any case, to fit such a journey into his closely packed time-table, and that and the general vagueness of the evidence has led to a much more radical solution of the problems raised, namely, the denial that ' the new standard-bearer of Christ ' had any existence outside the realms of mythology. Père Delehaye, the Jesuit scholar who was for many years director of the Bollandists, declared without the slightest reservation or hesitation in his *Légendes Hagio-graphiques* (1905) that ' the story of the crucifix dropped into the sea by St. Francis Xavier and brought to land by a crab is simply borrowed from Japanese mythology '.[1] That the reader may judge for himself, here is the myth to which Père Delehaye referred, without himself, it would seem, having read it:

Meguro is one of the many places round Yedo [the old name for Tokyo, changed in 1868] to which the good citizens flock for purposes convivial or religious, or both; hence it is that, cheek by jowl with the old shrines and temples, you will find many a pretty tea-house. . . . In one of the tea-houses a thriving trade is carried on in the sale of wooden tablets, some six inches square, adorned with the picture of a pink cuttlefish on a bright blue ground. These are ex-votos, destined to be offered up at the Temple of Yakushi Niurai, the Buddhist

[1] The invaluable and fascinating *Légendes* appeared in English as *The Legends of the Saints* (London, 1907), and the words cited are on p. 30.

Aesculapius, which stands opposite, and concerning the foundation of which the following tale is told. In the days of old
[A.D. 833] there was a priest called Jikaku who was suffering
from disease of the eyes. In order to be healed, he carved a
figure of Yakushi Niurai, to which he used to offer up his
prayers. Five years later he went to China, taking with him the
figure as his guardian saint. . . . There he passed his time in
studying the sacred laws, . . . and after nine years set sail to
return to Japan. When he was on the high seas a storm arose. . . .
Yakushi Niurai appeared and said to him, ' Take my image,
which thou carriest in thy bosom, and cast it into the sea, that
the wind may abate. . . .' So with tears in his eyes, the priest
threw into the sea the sacred image which he loved. Then did
the wind abate, and the waves were stilled, and the ship went
on her course as though she were being drawn by unseen hands
until she reached a safe haven. . . . For three years the priest
prayed that the image which he had cast away might be
restored to him, until at last one night he was warned in a
dream that, on the sea-shore at Matsura, Yakushi Niurai would
appear to him. In consequence of this dream he went to the
province of Hizen and landed on the sea-shore at Hirato, where
in the midst of a blaze of light, the image which he had carved
appeared to him twice, riding on the back of a cuttlefish. Thus
was the image restored to the world by a miracle. . . . That
these things might be known to all posterity, the priest established the worship of Tako Yakushi Niurai—Yakushi
Niurai of the Cuttlefish. . . . Such is the story, translated from
a small ill-printed pamphlet sold by the priests of the temple,
all the decorations of which, even to a bronze lantern in the
middle of the yard, are in the form of a cuttlefish. . . .[1]

There is an obvious superficial resemblance between the
stories of the sidling crab and the jet-propelled cuttlefish, but the
difference is much greater. The crab story is straightforward,
natural, and decidedly possible; the other is wholly in the realm

[1] Mitford (A. B., second secretary of the British Legation in Japan),
Tales of Old Japan, London, 1871, vol. i, pp. 40–3.

of marvel and myth. The theory that the Japanese folk-tale gave rise to the Christian story is riddled with improbabilities. Japanese foreign relations in the early seventeenth century did not extend to the Malay Archipelago or the Philippines, so how was it possible for Catholics resident in those areas to have become aware of the cuttlefish legend, in order to apply it, suitably transformed, to St. Francis Xavier? Coincidence proverbially has a broad back and is perfectly adequate to explain the common elements in the two stories, without it being in the least necessary to resort to the theory of dependence.[1] When the life and miracles of St. Francis Xavier were being officially investigated at Quilon in 1616, the one hundred and fifth witness, a civil servant named Christopher Semedo, retailed the story of the crab and added that it was and is *publica et notoria* in India. If a mythical basis must be found for the story, India is far more likely to have provided it than Japan, as the crab figures very prominently and with high distinction in the folk-lore of the sub-continent. The crab is a model of domestic virtue. A girl falls in love with a very decent, hard-working, humorous crustacean. In the folk-tales the crab takes the place of the conventional mongoose as the traditional foe of snakes, saving many human lives. But among the numerous good deeds attributed to the benevolent creature, the restoration of lost property is conspicuously absent.[2] So much, and perhaps altogether too much, for the crab of St. Francis.

[1] ' I fully admit,' wrote Père Delehaye, ' that one must beware of raising a cry of plagiarism on the strength of a mere resemblance. The most disconcerting coincidences do occasionally occur, and I am willing to quote a noteworthy example. If one were to read that on the same day the Church celebrates two saints, who both died in Italy, whose conversion in both cases was effected through the reading of the Lives of the Saints; that each founded a religious order under one and the same title, and that both these orders were suppressed by two popes bearing the same name, one might feel justified in declaring . . . that a single individual had been divided into two. . . . And yet there exist two saints, strictly historical and even comparatively modern, of whom all these particulars are true, St. John Colombini who died at Siena, July 31, 1367 . . . and St. Ignatius Loyola who died in Rome, July 31, 1556 ' (*The Legends of the Saints*, pp. 99–100).

[2] Elwin, *Folk-Tales of Mahakoshal*, Oxford University Press, 1944, pp. 134–8, 153–7. Dr. Elwin refers to St. Francis, but is mistaken in thinking that his crab resided in the Gulf of Manar. Mahakoshal is a name applied by Indian nationalists to most of the eastern States and Districts of the Central Provinces.

CHAPTER XI

THE PERILOUS ISLES OF MORO

THE eight ships which had kept Francis so busy composing differences between their Portuguese and Spanish complements, wooing the soldiers and sailors from their vices, nursing them in their tropical illnesses, and committing them to their graves when they died, at length sailed away from Amboina on May 17, 1546, two months and eight days after their stately arrival. He had been himself just over three months on the island then, and is reckoned ·to have performed at least four hundred baptisms each month, with all the attendant ceremonies.[1] Even a very robust priest with no other engagements might find thirteen or fourteen separate baptisms a day a strenuous programme, but St. Francis had his daily instructions also to think of, and his sermons in fluent Portuguese or Spanish, or halting Malay, on Sundays and feast-days of obligation, those latter being then ten times more frequent than they are now. There are indications that the seven Christian villages he speaks of were in a jungle dense and perilous, though perhaps we need not take too seriously the picture of him based on the experience of later travellers, ' scaling steep declivities, plunging into deep ravines, slipping on the sodden ground, always in danger of falling into mountain torrents, or again lost in the midst of gigantic grasses, plodding on under the clove trees in an atmosphere of heady perfumes, and stirring up at every step clouds of insects '.[2] About the insects there is no doubt whatever. They are the prime curse of Indonesia and St. Francis must have been one of the most thoroughly bitten human beings then alive. The old travellers, except Francis himself, are eloquent and maledictory on the subject and hardly

[1] The estimate, carefully worked out, is Father Schurhammer's (*Epistolae*, i, 375, n. 6).
[2] Brou, *Saint François Xavier*, 2ième éd., Paris, 1922, i, 376.

less so are the moderns. Speaking of the Aru Islands east of Amboina, the valiant Russel Wallace wrote: ' Ever since leaving Dobo I had suffered terribly from insects. . . . My feet and ankles especially suffered, and were completely covered with little red swollen specks which tormented me horribly. . . . After a month's incessant punishment, my poor feet . . . broke into open insurrection, throwing out numerous inflamed ulcers, which were very painful and stopped me from walking. . . . Wounds or sores in the feet are especially difficult to heal in hot climates, and I therefore dreaded them more than any other illness. . . .' Nearer our time, an American traveller writes: ' Ants, termites, spiders, scorpions, and a host of insects marvellous in their variety swarm everywhere. . . . Mosquitoes particularly are infuriating pests, and freedom from their insistent attacks is perhaps the greatest single relief one feels in getting away from the Indies.'[1] Things must have been a good deal worse four hundred years earlier, and St. Francis Xavier, whose letters are as free from the drone of a mosquito as they are from the trumpet of an elephant, may be said to have passed his laborious days and prayerful nights in the circumstances of the Fourth Plague of Egypt.

Having set Christianity in Amboina on its feet and made all arrangements for other shepherds to cherish that flock, Francis felt the abandoned neophytes in the *Yslas de Moro* tugging insistently at his heart-strings. Towards the middle of June, two *coracoras*, small craft special to the islands, put to sea for Ternate. On one was Francis, his black hair rapidly greying, and on the other a Portuguese friend of his named John Galvano, unrelated apparently to the good and great Antonio. A second merchant, by name Araujo, with whom the Saint was not on the best of terms because he had shown himself less than generous to the sick, desired to travel also, but could not find a place in the small boats packed with native oarsmen. On one occasion, when he had refused wine from his ample store for the comfort of some poor dying fellow, Francis told him plainly that his hoarding would

[1] Wallace, *The Malay Archipelago*, p. 353; Kennedy, *Islands and Peoples of the Indies* (1943), p. 3.

avail him little, as he and his wine would soon be parted.[1] Away went the two boats, sometimes propelled by oars, sometimes under sail, as the winds decided, while two stalwarts of the crew banged heartily on wooden drums to help the rhythm of the rowers and to keep prowling demons at a distance. Russel Wallace enables us to get the feel of this little voyage of St. Francis by his description of one which he made in 1859 in exactly the same area:

> The boat was of the kind called Kora-kora, quite open, very low, and about four tons burthen. It had outriggers of bamboo about five feet off each side, which supported a bamboo platform extending the whole length of the vessel. On the extreme outside of this sat the twenty rowers, while within was a convenient passage fore and aft. The middle portion of the boat was covered with a thatch-house in which baggage and passengers are stowed; the gunwale was not more than a foot above water, and from the great top and side weight, and general clumsiness, these boats are dangerous in heavy weather, and are not unfrequently lost. A triangular mast and mat sail carried us on when the wind was favourable, which (as usual) it never was, although, according to the monsoon, it ought to have been. . . . There was a little cook-house in the bows, where we could boil our rice and make our coffee, everyone, of course, bringing his own provisions, and arranging his meal-times as he found most convenient. The passage would have been agreeable enough but for the dreadful tom-toms or wooden drums, which are beaten incessantly while the men are rowing. Two men were engaged constantly at them, making a fearful din the whole voyage. . . .

Though Wallace's voyage was only from Batchian to Ternate, a mere hundred miles, it took seven days. From Amboina to Ternate is three times that distance. Francis had nothing to say of his journey, though the necessity of replenishing the small bamboo water containers must have involved calls at many of

[1] For all the statements made here, *Monumenta Xaveriana*, ii, 112, 246, 261–2.

the picturesque islands strewing the route, and it is known that the boat containing Galvano was swept out of sight of its consort by a sudden storm.

St. Francis stepped from the noisy, battered *coracora* on to the shore of smoky Ternate one day early in July. It is a very small island, only twenty-five square miles, and the whole of it, except a narrow strip at sea level, is occupied by the forest-clad volcano, always in business.

> The island of Ternate where our fort is situated [wrote Antonio Galvano, its governor six years before St. Francis arrived] is one of the most sublime objects known in the world; it throws out fire from its summit, a thing so marvellous that its like is not to be found.[1] There are some princes of the Moores and courageous Portugals who determined to goe neere to the firie place to see what it was, but they never could succeed. Antonie Galvano undertooke to go up, and did so, with the help of God and our Lady, and the thing that most astonished him in this journey was a river so extreme cold that he could not suffer his hand in it, nor put of the water in his mouth. And yet this place standeth under the Line, where the sun continually burneth.[2]

Ternate has been lucky in its infrequent visitors. Like St. Francis so long before, Mr. H. M. Tomlinson stepped ashore there on a bright day in 1923 and promptly made the fortunate island, as his great forerunner had so signally failed to do, a place that any lover of beauty and solemn mystery must hanker to see:

> We came alongside a jetty in deep water where the bottom could be seen in the way we should see fields if the air was a tinted and pulsing lens. I stood on the old planks of that jetty, with lucky barbaric figures about me—Malays, of course. . . . Between the planks I could see the tide under our feet, but if a swarm of fish had not passed below like blue arrows, and like

[1] He must have heard of Vesuvius and Etna, and what he probably meant was that Ternate outclassed them altogether as an awe-inspiring spectacle.
[2] *Discoveries of the World*, 119–20.

globes of yellow light, the water would not have been there. Crimson lories were perched on the rail of the jetty, and on the shoulders of the barbarians. There was an unusual liveliness and sparkle in the air. I knew perfectly well my ship would have to leave without me. . . . It was long past noon. . . . I felt, as did Robinson Crusoe, that I must go out to take an inventory of my fortune. The lane led upwards the impending declivity, but as though that ascent were far too steep it turned lazily northward among the easy groves parallel to the beach. There were many smells. One had to stop and try them again. Once it was frangipani, and once it was vanilla, and once it was cloves. . . . The great breadfruit tree, with its extravagant leaves, the slight and delicate areca palm under the crowns of stalwart coco-nuts, may all some day get the verses they demand. But not here. When I looked at them that afternoon I felt in the mood for singing them. . . . I turned off through a plantation of palms to find the sea. . . . The sky was ready for the sunset. The Malay women, in colours which would make Monte Carlo seem like an outing of Calvinists, were gossiping in the streets of the village. . . . The sea, that deceptive sea of tide-rips and reefs, was as radiant and benign as though it had confessed its sins, and peace was now in its ancient heart and not sharks. Gilolo and Tidore were built of lapis-lazuli, but Ternate was of olivine, and about its head were clouds which . . . became bright gold after sunset. . . . The beach of Ternate . . . changed thus every day. I never saw it repeat itself. Why should it, with all those colours?[1]

[1] *Tidemarks*, XXIV, XXV. At Ternate Mr. Tomlinson experienced a tremor of the great earthquake which wrought such havoc in Tokyo in 1923. Like Antonio Galvano, he climbed to the crater of Ternate's volcano, and conveys the terror and sublimity of the veiled Moloch as only such an artist as he knows how: 'It was clear that Milton had wrongly reported his expulsion from Heaven. He still dwelt there. In fact, he had it to himself. He was solitary in the sky, monstrous and fuliginous under his lovely canopy, with a desolate court about him, and a footstool of blackened ruin from which the angels had fled. . . . When the natives of Ternate prudently assemble their canoes at signs more violent than usual, and even abandon their nutmeg groves, they are not showing timidity, for on the summit I got the impression that in the belly of the island there was a power latent which could lift it bodily from the sea.'

In spite of, perhaps, in the queer way of mankind, because of, the fiery menace impending over their heads and the suspense of the unquiet earth under their feet, the people of Ternate, Europeans and natives alike, gave themselves to the deadly sins with a kind of hectic determination. Let us eat, drink, be merry, and make a fortune, for tomorrow we die. The pungent tang of the clove seemed to have got into their blood, driving them not only to fleshly depravity, but to envy, hatred, malice, and all uncharitableness. The Portuguese authorities in Goa unwittingly exacerbated the evil by their habit of transporting to the Moluccas such bold spirits as they could not control at home, perhaps hoping that a few earthquakes and volcanic eruptions might subdue them. Antonio Galvano had stayed the corruption for a time, but that was six years ago, and when St. Francis arrived all was to do again. Never would the devil throw down the gauntlet to him with more assurance than in that ' perfumed gem of the seas ' which concealed in its loveliness ' an impassable region of mangroves, an aqueous wood holding only shadows, where grisly stems projected from the sludge like the elbows and knees of the drowned ' (*Tidemarks*). St. Francis accepted the challenge with a will, using his old weapons which might seem as silly as David's pebble but were, in fact, a thousand times more effective than Goliath's sword. As usual, he enlisted the children to be his shock-troops, and with that debonair and devastating smile of his wore down the resistance of their elders, abashed them by the sheer power and invincibility of his goodness. Not even the Sultan Hairun, with his hundred concubines, could entirely stand up to him. Nobody could. He was irresistible.

There was a hospital of sorts in Ternate Town and Francis made that his headquarters. He must be close to the sick by day and by night. Almost every day he preached a sermon, in the morning at Mass to the Portuguese masters, with bills of lading in their pockets and Malay beauties in their heads, then, after his dinner of sago, with perhaps a few cloves in it to give it life, to the native converts and slaves of the white conquerors. For two hours each day he could be found at his favourite task, drilling his shock-troops in the Creed and the prayers out of the little Malay manual which he had put together with so much toil at Malacca. On these occasions, he was as much choirmaster as catechist, for with the vivacity natural to him he taught the children to *sing* their lessons, to make of them a grand new game. And his tunes must have been attractive, for they caught on to such an extent with young and old alike that they quite displaced the traditional island melodies. Francis himself is our informant.

Thanks be to God it has become the custom in Ternate for the boys in the streets and the girls and women in the houses, day and night, for the toilers in the plantations and the fishermen at sea to sing, instead of vain songs, holy chants such as the Creed, Pater Noster, Ave Maria, the Commandments, the Works of Mercy, the General Confession, and many other prayers, all in a language understood by all, whether recent converts to the faith or people still pagans. It was the good pleasure of God our Lord that I should find in a brief time great favour in the eyes of the Portuguese on the island, and no less in those of the native people, both Christian and pagan.[1]

The first time Francis preached to the Portuguese in Ternate, he paused of a sudden, and became still and abstracted, as though seeing something far off. Then he said to his startled listeners, ' Let us offer an Our Father for the soul of John Galvano who has been drowned.' Three days later the wreckage of the *coracora* in which poor John had been was washed up on Ternate's coral strand, as Alfonso Teixeira, an eye-witness, testified. A little later, the same thing happened again, but during Mass, at the Offertory. Francis turned to the people and said: ' John Araujo has died this moment in Amboina. I offered Mass for him yesterday and this Mass is for the repose of his soul. I beg you to commend him to God in your prayers.'[2] These are but two of a dozen well-authenticated stories told on oath by men who either heard

---

[1] Schurhammer, *Epistolae S. Francisci Xaverii*, i, 377–8.

[2] *Monumenta Xaveriana*, ii, 441, 446, 381 (Araujo). There were twenty-two different witnesses for the Araujo incident, which became celebrated and is mentioned in the Bull of Canonization.

the Saint speak themselves or learned what he had said from others who were present. The facts seem beyond dispute, however we choose to interpret them. They did not involve trance or any other abnormal condition, but were matter-of-fact announcements of happenings at a distance which later evidence proved to be true. Thus, in the case of Araujo, a certain Rafael Carvalho arrived at Ternate from Amboina ten or twelve days after St. Francis made his announcement and confirmed that the man had died at the precise moment indicated. That might be accounted for by a natural gift of second sight or clairvoyance, which seems now to be scientifically proven, but there was an element of precognition or prophecy also in the Araujo story, which no laboratory experiments so far have determined conclusively to be within the unaided powers of the human mind.[1] A Catholic authority has written on the subject as follows, mentioning six saints, including Xavier :

The gift of clairvoyance or second sight, however suspicious among the somnambulists. . . , assumes a wholly different character among our saints. In this case the gift cannot be judged apart from the virtues and other supernatural gifts which precede it, accompany it, and follow it, and make up its whole meaning. . . . These gifts, even though they be natural in themselves and arise from secret forces of nature, are none the less a supernatural favour from God, either through the

[1] Dr. J. B. Rhine's well-known books on the subject, *New Frontiers of the Mind* (1937) and *The Reach of the Mind* (1948), both the result of long years of most patient and scientific experiment, are bound to convince any open-minded reader that extra-sensory cognition, knowledge of present events not derived from the senses, is possible and happens, even frequently happens, perfectly naturally, and without somnambulistic tricks, in the case of specially endowed persons. *How* it happens is another question, on which this most cautious investigator refuses to commit himself, though he is persuaded that no wave theory, regarding the brain as a kind of radio receiving-set, is adequate as an explanation. Similarly, after a wealth of delicate experiments often pointing in that direction, he concludes that precognition, involving ' the place of mind in time—or the place of time in the mind, to put it another way—cannot yet be represented as demonstrated by any procedure which we and other research workers have been able to devise *beyond all possibility of an alternative explanation* ' (*New Frontiers*, Chap. XV, italics in original).

supernatural end which He assigns to them, or the physiological conditions in which He permits these forces to be exercised. . . . It is always in a state of waking and in full possession of themselves that the saints see the most hidden secrets and foresee the future. In this they have nothing in common with the neuropathic somnambulists of our amphitheatres, the unbalanced hysterical subjects in our hospitals. Moreover, there is nothing that authorizes us to think that they might have become clairvoyants without a divine mission and intervention. The more clairvoyance is deemed insufficient of itself to prove the sanctity of the seer, the more the sanctity of the seer, once demonstrated, suffices to prove the providential and supernatural character of the clairvoyance. If the mysterious forces of nature may be awakened naturally in certain pathological cases, or by the power of the devil, there is nothing to prevent them from being so through divine intervention, when God judges it useful for the saint's mission or for the manifestation of his sanctity.[1]

The months of August and September were the time of the clove harvest in Ternate when the whole town turned out to gather the unexpanded flower-buds of the trees of good and evil which brought fortune and ruin to the little island. The absence of his neophytes in the scented groves gave St. Francis some unwonted leisure, which he devoted to the writing of his only book, a very little book, less than five thousand words, but still authentically a book. Its subject was an exposition of the Apostles' Creed in the simplest, most concrete terms, such as could easily be grasped and retained by children or adult converts from heathenism. A great deal of the heart of St. Francis went into its composition. He used all the little devices he could think of, sometimes borrowing them from other writers, in order to fix attention and ease the burden on memory. Thus, each article is rounded off by being attributed to a separate Apostle, and the

[1] Farges (Mgr. Albert), *Mystical Phenomena compared with their Human and Diabolical Counterfeits.* English trans. of French 2nd ed., London, 1926, pp. 437–8. This work received the special commendation of Pope Benedict XV.

Portuguese, wherever possible, is versified or at least given a rhythmical form. That this was deliberate is indicated by the way the author changed the traditional order of the words, or added to or subtracted from them in order to get a rhyme or assonance:

> *Movidos os fariseos de emveja, foram a* Pilatos,
> *Que entam era juiz, e com rogos e com medos. . . .*

> *Padeceo sob poder de Pontio* Pilato
> *Foi crucifidado, morto, e sepuldado.*

> *Jesu Christo e a Virgem sus may e Sam* Josefee
> *Se tornaram a sua terra, à cidade de Nazaré.*[1]

The whole composition is full of echoes of the *Spiritual Exercises* of St. Ignatius Loyola which St. Francis must have known largely by heart, as they had not then been yet printed and he certainly did not possess a manuscript copy. The *Declaration* begins in the following fashion:

Christians! Rejoice to hear and learn how God in creating made everything for the service of men. First, He created the heavens and the earth, angels, sun, moon and stars, day and night, all green growing things and fruits, the birds and beasts which live on land, the great creatures and fishes which inhabit the sea. And when all these things had been created, He finally made man in His own image and likeness. The first man that God created was Adam and the first woman Eve, and soon after creating them in the terrestrial paradise, He blessed and married them, and commanded them to have children and to people the earth. From Adam and Eve we and all the generations of mankind descend; and since God did not give Adam more than one wife, it is clearly in opposition to God that Moors and

---

[1] Father Schurhammer gives several other instances pointing to a preoccupation of St. Francis with rhymes and rhythms (*Epistolae*, i, 353–4), but he is not dogmatic on the subject and prints the Portuguese text in prose form (l.c. 355–67).

heathen and bad Christians have many wives. Similarly, it is obvious that persons living with women whom they have not married are in opposition to God, since God first married Adam and Eve before telling them to increase and multiply and have children of benediction. Those who worship in pagodas as do the infidels, and such as believe in sorcery and divination, greatly sin against God, for they adore and believe in the devil, taking him for their lord, and forsaking the God who created them and gave them soul and life and body and all they have. . . . But true and loyal Christians believe in and gladly and heartily adore the one only true God, Creator of Heaven and earth, . . . going on their knees in the churches and lifting their hands to Heaven where is the Lord God, their whole good and consolation, and confessing, as did St. Peter, *I believe in God, the Father Almighty, Creator of Heaven and earth.*

So St. Francis proceeds, telling of the creation and fall of the Angels, and of the subsequent fall of Adam and Eve through the envy of the devil and the pride of their own hearts.

O Christians! [he exclaims] what is to become of us, unhappy creatures that we are, if the demons for one sin of pride were thrust from Heaven to Hell, and Adam and Eve for another sin of pride were driven from their Paradise? How shall we, wretched sinners, climb to Heaven burdened with so much iniquity and clearly in a state of perdition?

That fervent note is struck again a few lines further on when St. Michael, tutelary angel of Castle Xavier in the youth of Francis, comes to the front:

Our true and trusty friend St. Michael and all the angels of Heaven, moved to pity and compassion for us poor sinners, besought the Lord God to have mercy for the evil that has come upon us through the sin of Adam and Eve. With united accord they prayed, ' O good God and merciful Lord, Thou Father of all peoples! Even now, Lord, has come the time for their salvation. Open the gates of Heaven to Thy children, seeing that now is born of holy Anna and Joachim that Virgin without Adam's stain, Mary, blessed above all women, peerless in sanctity! Now, Lord, Thou canst form a human body from her virginal blood, . . . and in that body create by Thy power the holiest soul that ever came from Thy hands, that Thy Son may descend from Heaven at the same instant and become incarnate, . . . in fulfilment of the promises made by Thee to the Prophets and Patriarchs, Thy friends, who await in Limbo Thy Son Jesus Christ, their Lord and Redeemer. . . .

St. Francis had come to the end of the Ninth Article, in St. Matthew's charge, when the winds whistled him away. Soon, they would veer from south-west to north-east and bar all approach to ' the perilous islands of Moro '. So his labour of love was never completed, because a greater labour of love called him. It is pleasant, and no harm, to think that little parrots, the lories, plumed as with the rainbow, perched on his shoulders, as he sat under a tamarind tree in that lotus-land, trying to find word-endings that would chime in children's memories and bring them closer to Him who said, ' Suffer little children to come unto Me '. He put to sea in a *coracora* as before, coasted mountainous, volcanic, frightening Halmaheira, until he reached its northern extremity and the shore of Galela, where many Malays and possibly some aboriginal Alfuros, too, had been baptized and abandoned. Opposite this strip of Halmaheira, twenty-five miles out to sea, lay the two islands, little Rau and large Morotai, or Morty, as the English adventurers called it. There also some thousands of natives had accepted baptism, probably as the price of Portuguese protection against the ubiquitous, slave-snatching Moslems. Far from keeping their part of the bargain, the Portuguese soldiers sent to Galela and the islands behaved worse than any Moslems and caused the reversion to complete heathenism of many who, when properly instructed, might have made good Christians. St. Francis is scanty and vague, as usual, with geographical details, but he mentions that he visited all the Christian localities and baptized a great number of babies. Summing up his three months' labours among the wild people, the mere thought of whom made other men, and they no cowards, shiver in their shoes, he wrote: *'Consoléme mucho con ellos y ellos comigo*—they were a great comfort to me and I to them.'

But he had no illusions about the islands and the islanders.

They are very dangerous places [he continued in his letter to Rome] by reason of continual strife between the barbarous tribes, who possess nothing in the nature of writings and can neither read nor write. It is their habit to poison anybody towards whom they feel ill-disposed, and in this way they kill large numbers. It is a very craggy part of the world, with mountains everywhere which make journeying a real misery. There is a dearth of some foods, and the people do not so much as know what wheat and wine are. They have no cattle or other source of meat, except, for a wonder [they being mostly Moslems], some domesticated pigs and plenty of wild ones. Many of the villages are without good drinking water. Trees called sago-palms grow in great profusion and yield both bread and wine, while from the inner bark of another species of tree the people make all the clothes they wear.[1] . . . There is a heathen tribe called the *Tabaru* in these parts which makes a pastime of murder. I am told that when they can find nobody else to kill they slaughter their own sons or wives. They have also slaughtered many Christians.[2] One of these islands is in an almost constant state of tremor caused by a mountain which continually ejects fire and ashes. Often, rocks as big as the biggest trees are hurled out of the flaming mountain. When

[1] The bread-fruit tree, about which Russel Wallace has a lyrical page. It produces not only a fruit, the size of a melon, which Wallace considered superior to any vegetable known to him in either temperate or tropical countries, but a fibrous inner bark which, beaten and prepared, makes the common utility cloth used in the islands. Wallace noticed also the abundance of wild pigs in the islands.

[2] The *Tabaru*, a people still existing in the north-west part of Halmaheira, were dependent on the fanatically anti-Christian Sultan of Gilolo, a town of Halmaheira straight across from Ternate, who employed them in his raids on the Christian villages in the north. They had also the reputation of being head-hunters in Morotai. Their murdering propensities may have had some connection with the practice of human sacrifice.

there is a strong wind it carries down so much of the ash that
men and women working in the fields become covered with
it, nothing showing but their eyes, noses, and mouths, so that
they look more like devils than human beings. I learned this
from the natives, not having seen the sight myself, as there were
no storms during the time of my stay. They told me too that
the ashes carried by the winds choke and kill great numbers of
the wild pigs, and that after a storm they find quantities of dead
fish on the beaches, for the ashes in the salt water poisons them.
They asked me what this awful mountain was, and I told them
it was a hell to which went all those given to the adoration of
idols. I was saying Mass in the place on the Feast of St. Michael
[September 29] when there was such a violent earthquake that
I feared the altar would collapse. Perhaps at that moment St.
Michael, by the power of God, was punishing the devils of
these parts who impede the service of God, and ordering them
back to Hell. . . .[1]

[1] Schurhammer, *Epistolae*, i, 379–83. St. Francis had his earthquake on the
mainland of Halmaheira, at some point on that northern arm of the queer
island facing Morotai which the Portuguese navigators thought to be a separate
island on its own account, but which is in fact a peninsula joining the other
three arms by a narrow isthmus. The volcano there which so much impressed
the Saint used to be called Mount Tolo. At the present day, it seems to be
reasonably quiescent, but has so radically altered the lie of the land since the
sixteenth century that it is impossible now to determine where any town or
village lay then. An eminent Jesuit scholar of Spain, Padre Pablo Pastells, who
died in 1932 after putting at the disposal of other scholars a vast collection of
documents from various Spanish archives bearing on the history of South
America and the Philippines, endeavoured to prove that, not Halmaheira, but
the Philippines owned the volcano which nearly upset the altar of St. Francis.
The idea was, of course, to claim St. Francis himself for the Philippines, once
a proud part of the great Spanish Empire, and still Spanish-speaking and marked
indelibly with the seal of Spain. Padre Pastells maintained that Mount Apo in
Mindanao was the disputed volcano, but in 1936 an American Jesuit, an expert
seismographer on the staff of Manila Observatory, proved fairly conclusively
that Apo, if a volcano at all, had not erupted or disgorged any ashes or rocks for
well over a thousand years. The writer, William C. Repetti, S.J., brought
several other arguments to bear, and established for good and all that St.
Francis never set foot in the Philippines, in spite of cherished traditions to the
contrary (*Archivum Historicum Societatis Jesu*, Roma, 1936, pp. 35–56). Apart
from volcanic dialectics, his *coracora* would never have survived a voyage to
the Philippines.

St. Francis has favoured us with hardly a single detail of his activities on this most dangerous of all his expeditions. No doubt, the Malay crew who managed his *coracora* and knew some Portuguese, acted as interpreters with the Christians of the islands, and he had probably memorized by then his catechism lessons in Malay. His daily round would have been much the same as in Malacca or Amboina or Ternate, baptisms, sermons, constant instruction of the children, marryings, funerals, care of the sick, the appointment of intelligent natives to act as catechists, and over all, through all, guiding all, incessant communion with God. To judge by what Russel Wallace has to say of *his* adventures by sea and land in that same area, Francis assuredly took his life in his hands every time he put off in a *coracora*, for the winds, Wallace protests, are never anything but anarchists, owning no law, and the coral reefs, edged like great knives, standing invitations to come and be drowned, and the currents completely diabolical. It is detracting nothing from the glory and courage of the hunter of butterflies and birds of paradise to suggest that his adventures, splendid as they were, did not match in sheer daring those of the hunter of souls. For one thing, he went about always well provisioned and with a gun in his hand. Two hundred years of Dutch rule had tamed the wild men of the islands and cured the bad habits even of the murderous *Tabaru*. Wallace paid a few brief visits to Halmaheira, but left Morotai severely alone, though it has fifty-six species of land birds, some of them unique. Francis Xavier made light of the *peligros y trabajos* which he faced unsupported and unprotected. Never was he more happy than then, when daily up against death in a dozen shapes.

These islands [he wrote to his Jesuit brethren in Europe] are very well fitted and equipped to make a man lose the sight of his eyes in a few years through the abundance, the excess, of *lagrimas consolativas* which he sheds. Never do I remember to have been so greatly and continually comforted by God, nor to have felt less the burden of physical hardship, of going about all the time surrounded by enemies and in places peopled by not very secure friends, without any remedies for illnesses of the body or indeed practically any help from secondary causes for the preservation of one's life. It would be more appropriate to call these places Islands of Hope in God than Islands of Moro. . . .

Three months Francis spent in his Indonesian Ultima Thule, until he had visited every one of the thousands of scattered and menaced Christians, inspiring them with new hope by the sheer transfusion of his own invincible trust in God, and promising them that they would not in future be forgotten and left to their own devices, that he would send priests to live and die in their midst. Then, in December, he took leave, reluctantly, we may be sure, of the little island world where he had been so happy, and headed south through the treacherous shallow sea for Ternate, where he found the deposed Sultan, Hairun, restored to his throne and his populous harem. He gives an interesting and rather touching pen-picture of this good-natured reprobate whose spirit was willing enough but flesh exceedingly weak:

The King of Maluco is a Moor and vassal of the King of Portugal, a position of which he is extremely proud. When speaking of it he says, ' The King of Portugal, my Lord.' His Portuguese is very good. . . . If he fails to become a Christian it is not because of any devotion to Mohammed, but because he is in thrall to carnal sins. The only thing Moorish about him is that he was circumcised as a child, and then as a man took unto himself a hundred principal wives and many other less important ones. The Moors who abound in these Moluccan islands do not hold the tenets of Mohammed's sect. They have few priests of that religion, and those nearly all foreigners who know next to nothing. The King showed me so much friendship that the principal Moors of his dominions took it badly. He wanted me to be his friend and gave me hope that in time he would become a Christian. He wanted me to love him, even though he was a Moor, and would say to me that Christians and Moors have one and the same God and some day we would all be united.

He took great pleasure in my visits to him, but I could never persuade him to become a Christian. He promised me, however, to have one of his numerous sons brought up a Christian, with an express understanding that this son should be king of the Islands of Moro.

Alas, the poor fellow, whose good resolutions were strangled at birth by the tresses of his ladies, did not keep his promise and himself died in old age unbaptized.

As Ternate was far the most important town and island in the Moluccas, St. Francis lingered there another three months and more, until after Easter of the year 1547, and when at last he had done all that mortal man could do, *confessando continuadamente por la manana y por la tarde y a mediodía,* preaching twice a day on most days, incessantly instructing children and native women, it was not to forge farther into the untraversed and unknown, but to turn about and go back on his tracks, to Amboina, to Malacca, to India, for more than two years. So much for the theory of his restlessness, of his itch to be anywhere but where he was, of his hankering after new worlds to conquer, of his surrender to the *vertige de l'inconnu.* He was given the chance to make the voyage to Amboina in the relative comfort of a large merchantman, but it would have meant leaving his flock just a week before Lent, and that he declined to do. In any case, a *coracora* was good enough for him. How greatly he was loved by the people of Ternate became apparent at the moment of his departure.

When the time came to leave Maluco [he wrote] I embarked about midnight so as to avoid the weeping and mourning of my devoted friends, men and women. But it was no good, and I did not escape the tears, for my friends found me out and I could not hide from them. The night and the parting from these my spiritual sons and daughters helped me to feel my unworthiness, and the thought came to me that perhaps my absence might contribute to the salvation of their souls.

He mentioned also that before leaving he had made arrangements for the teaching of Christian doctrine twice a day, and for
the use of his own *Declaration of the Creed* in the instruction of
converts, which the official chaplain of the Portuguese garrison,
his very good friend, guaranteed to see done. He had introduced,
too, as in Malacca, the ingenious custom of sending a small
procession through the streets at nightfall, headed by a member of
the Confraternity of Mercy in his sky-blue robes and carrying a
lantern and bell, to pray *con grandes vozes* for the souls in Purgatory,
and for all persons in the town in a state of mortal sin.[1] What
with this and the volcano, it is no wonder that he was wanted for
confessions morning, noon and night.

Francis came to Amboina this second time to join a merchant
ship bound for Malacca. He must have been absolutely worn out
from fatigue and lack of food and sleep, because how could any
mortal man sleep in a *coracora*? But instead of resting until his
ship sailed a fortnight later, he set to and built a little church, an
affair of bamboo poles and palm-leaves, where he said Mass and
sat all day listening compassionately to the long, sad, sinful tales
of several hundred men from the four large ships in the harbour.
Hize muchas pazes, he wrote afterwards—' I was able to effect
many reconciliations'. A Portuguese official named Gaspar
Lopez who arrived just then in Amboina testified that, after his
day with the sturdy sinners, Francis could always be found by the
couch of some poor fellow who was dangerously ill. Once, after
a man's death, he heard the Father say in a voice choked with
tears, tears of gratitude, ' Blessed be Thou, O Lord, who didst
bring me here so opportunely to help this man's soul'.[2] During
the two months voyage through the Great Archipelago, under the
Equator, Francis says, with unconscious meiosis that he ' did not
lack occupation '. One of his principal occupations was to keep

[1] Schurhammer, *Epistolae S. Francisci Xaverii*, i, 384–5.
[2] *Monumenta Xaveriana*, ii, 175–6, 191–3, 371–2. ' Making peace ' was a
considerable part of Xavier's apostolate among the uncommonly pugnacious
soldiers and traders. Fernam Mendez Pinto alludes to this trait in his famous
Peregrination: ' It is the quality of us Portuguese to abound in our own sense
and to be obstinate in our opinions. There arose amongst us so great a con-
trariety about a thing that we were ever on the point of killing one another.'

the soldiers and sailors, maddened by the tropical sun, from each other's throat, and there were sick and dying men by the score to be tended, and dead men to be committed with the Church's maternal rites to the sea. This time, St. Francis tarried at Malacca close on six months, from June to December, which was longer than white traders, however tough and determined, chose to stay, for reasons given by the Dutch traveller Linschoten, writing at the end of the sixteenth century:

> Mallacca ... hath great trafficke and dealing with all shippes which sayle to and from China, the Molucos, Banda, the Ilands of Java, Sumatra, and all bordering thereabouts, as also from Siam, Pegu, Bengal, Coromandel and the Indies: whereby a great number of shippes goe and come thither, and doe there lade and unlade, sell, buy, and barter, and make great trafficke out of all the Orientall countries. Therein also dwell some Portingalles, about a hundred households. . . . The cause why so few is because it is a very unholesome countrie, and an evil ayre as well for the natural countrymen as for straungers and travellers, and commonly there is not one that cometh thither and stayeth any time, but is sure to be sicke, so that it costeth him either hide or hair before he departeth from thence. And if any escapeth with life it is holden for a wonder, wherby the countrie is much shunned, notwithstanding covetousness and desire of gaine. . . .[1]

It was more than two years since Francis Xavier had seen one of the brethren whom he loved so intensely, and his joy was therefore great to be welcomed at Malacca by three of them, two priests, the Spanish Juan Beira and the Portuguese Nunus Ribeiro, and the very young and brilliant graduate of Coimbra, Nicholas Nunes, who was not yet ordained. Nicholas had had the world at his feet, but he turned from it without a regret to answer the challenge of St. Francis and to die before he was fifty for love of the Islands of Moro. Father Ribeiro met a martyr's death in

---

[1] *The Voyage of John Huyghen van Linschoten to the East Indies.* English translation 1598. London, the Hakluyt Society, 1885, vol. i, pp. 104–5.

the Moluccas after two years of heroic labour, being poisoned out of hatred for the faith. As for Juan Beira, once a lordly canon of Corunna cathedral, his story is not shamed in the article of valour by that of the later John who conducted the famous and terrible retreat. Indeed, he sacrificed more than the great soldier did, more than his life. He made the ultimate, the hardest of all sacrifices, that of his mind. He spent no less than nine years in those deadly islands where the most intrepid trader hesitated to spend a week, and it was said of him by a historian that ' it would be easier to count the hours of his death than the days of his life '. At one period of Moslem persecution he was nine months on the run, hiding in the wild mountains and dense forests of Halmaheira, living as best he could on roots and grasses, sleeping in the arms of a tree, and stealing out at dead of night to visit and comfort such Christians as had not been slaughtered. Twice he was betrayed by renegade Christians, sold as a slave to the Moslems, and tortured, to make him abjure his faith, within an inch of his life. He was too valuable a hostage to kill outright, but his brutal masters did everything short of that to wreck his mind and break his heart. Thus, they compelled him to watch while they snatched babies whom he had recently baptized from their mothers' arms and dashed out their brains against rocks. Both times he escaped and made his way again through a thousand hazards to the little scattered groups of his persecuted children. Visiting Rau and Morotai in a boat hardly bigger than a canoe, he was wrecked a dozen times. On one occasion, he spent two days and nights clinging to a plank in the depths of the sea, which eventually cast him up on a desolate rocky shore in the territory of the bloodthirsty *Tabaru*. He had lost his Breviary, and that was the hardest blow, his small stock of rice, his clothes, indeed everything except his great heart. He hid among the rocks by day and crept out at night to make a meal of seaweed. He got back to his Christians, and ever undaunted challenged a hundred times more the worst that winds and waves could do to him. Nine years' exposure to the equatorial sun, nine years of semi-starvation and of daily deadly peril by land and water, gradually took their toll of him and unhinged his mind. It was, however, the gentlest derangement, sweet bells jangled indeed, but hinting of harmonies so beautiful that men felt awed and uplifted by the mere sight of him when he returned to India. Dead martyrs were gloriously common in the Church, but a living, breathing martyr, with all his insignia upon him, was a rare phenomenon. Often, his mind cleared so that he could say Mass with his mutilated hands, and he died in perfect lucidity, believing himself to be the most abject of sinners.[1]

The worst of Beira's experiences were on the sea, and so too, we may reasonably conclude, were those of St. Francis, even if his letters are mostly blank on the subject. But he was willing to express himself in general terms and, apropos of Beira, wrote as follows to Simon Rodriguez:

I know not whether anywhere else in the whole world men zealous for the glory of God and the salvation of souls have as much toil and hardship to face and perils of death to brave as in the Isles of Moro. I beg you to intercede with God for the ones who have gone thither and for those who are later to go. I think that those islands will bring forth many martyrs to our Society and that soon the right name for them will be Islas de Martirio rather than Islas de Moro. Let, then, such of our brethren as long to give their lives for Christ be of good heart and rejoice, for there is prepared a seminary of martyrdom where they may fulfil their desire. . . .[2]

Francis had just one happy month in which to brief the dedicated three. 'Their company was an immense joy to me,' he wrote, 'for I recognized them to be true men of God who would royally serve His Divine Majesty in the Moluccas.' He saw them off on their long voyage at the beginning of August, and then reverted, a little lonely at heart, to his daily routine of confessions, sermons, instructions, hospital service, and all the other odds and

---

[1] Sousa, *Oriente Conquistado*, 1st ed. (1710), pp. 428–35. Sousa is here at his very fine best. He brackets Juan Beira with Francis Xavier, and ends the story with a sigh: 'If only all the men of foreign nations helping on our Portuguese missions had been of the stature of those two Spaniards. . . .'

[2] Schurhammer, *Epistolae S. Francisci Xaverii*, ii, 78.

ends of a life completely surrendered to God and his neighbour. The pressure on him for confessions was so great that it became physically impossible to meet all the demands, and the thwarted penitents at the end of the queue gave him an occasional black look. ' I was not shocked, but rather edified by their anger with me,' he said, ' as I saw that it proceeded from abhorrence of their sins.'

He carried on his work this time in a town encompassed by fierce enemies and frightened out of its wits, for the Moslem powers of Achin, Johore and Bintang had combined with the aim of destroying the small Portuguese garrison in A Famosa, ' the famous ' citadel built by Albuquerque. An impressive list of Portuguese officials or merchants, all resident in Malacca at the time, bore witness on oath to the main events, and their testimony is not much affected by a certain discordance and vagueness as to dates and geographical details. If one man says that a naval battle took place a hundred leagues north of Malacca and another that the distance was sixty leagues, it simply means that neither of them knew the precise scene of the engagement, but only that it was a long way off, at the mouth of a certain river. What happened was this. The Achinese Moslems, who were the most efficient and dreaded pirates of the Eastern seas, assembled a fleet of *fustas*, swift vessels of light draught, fitted with lateen sails, and one night late in August of that year, 1547, crept into Malacca Bay to plunder the shipping in the harbour. There is a story that they caught seven unfortunate Malay fishermen, cut off their noses, ears and feet, and sent Simon de Mello, Captain of A Famosa, a challenge written in their blood. Though a very brave man, the Captain had to refuse the challenge through lack of warships, and to content himself with salvoes of A Famosa's big guns, which had little effect in the darkness. The whole city was in an uproar until the pirates, having done all the mischief in their power, retired. But everybody knew that they would return unless pursued, and meantime another menace had developed. The Sultan of Johore, descendant of the last Sultan of Malacca whom Albuquerque had dispossessed, joined forces with the Sultan of Bintang and sailed up the estuary of the River

Muar to threaten Malacca by land. It was then, when all around him was panic and despair, that the spirit of Navarre awoke again in the heart of St. Francis Xavier. Though he probably had evidence no longer available, Valignano may have somewhat heightened the colours when he wrote in the following strain: 'Padre Maestro Francisco worked might and main for the equipment of a fleet to be sent speedily in pursuit of the Achinese enemy. He was so insistent and his authority with all parties was so great that the Captain himself declared him to be the creator of the armada, which without the Father's help he could not have got together.'[1] Francis as a kind of First Lord of the Admiralty is a startling idea, but he had played a similar rôle in India when he endeavoured with all his might and eloquence to raise a fleet for the punishment of Raja Sankily, the mass-murderer of Jaffna. He has been censured for these occasional ventures into the realm of power-politics, but what about the saints who preached crusades, and what about the reactions of any good, brave man, however meek, when confronted with tyranny that would destroy lives more precious to him than his own?

The fleet, a small one of some ten indifferent ships but manned by stout-hearted Portuguese who had Malay wives and children to fight for, set off confidently in search of the elusive foe. They were expected back in a week or so, but two and three weeks passed and there was still no sign, while all the time the fleets of Johore and Bintang lurked in the Muar, waiting their chance and carrying on a war of nerves against the timorous Malaccans. The Sultans sent spies into the city to spread rumours of disaster, which the long absence of the little armada seemed to render only too probable. A great cloud of gloom and terror descended on the city, and when the numerous *ballams* or small craft driven by paddles which Simon de Mello sent up the coast to investigate returned without news, the brave Captain himself began to lose

---

[1] *Monumenta Xaveriana*, i, p. 80. The Saint's influence was certainly great in Malacca. Father Francis Perez, a gallant soul who took up his station there the following year, 1548, said that he was regularly referred to, by Malays and Portuguese alike, and even by the Moslems and pagans, as 'El Padre Santo' (Wicki, *Documenta Indica*, i, 367).

heart. Indeed, only one heart in that city of a hundred thousand hearts still continued to beat calmly as the year wore on into December. A Portuguese nobleman named Bento Gomes was in Malacca then and bore the following witness: ' Father Francis encouraged and consoled the terrified people. He urged them not to mourn, but to put their trust and confidence in God, praying to Him earnestly for the fleet. As for himself, he said that he felt sure our men were safe and would be victorious over the foe.' His exhortations were not invariably heeded and some of the Malay Christians even turned from him to sorcerers and diviners for comfort which they did not get, being told, after the incantations, that the fleet had perished. Then came Sunday, December 4, when a great throng of frightened and sorrowing people crowded into the large church of Our Lady of the Assumption to hear St. Francis preach. He had finished his sermon, as usual a burning exhortation to trust in God, when suddenly he seemed to be rapt out of himself as by a glorious vision. After a few hushed moments he spoke again:

There are women and others here who practise divining and consult fortune-tellers, only to hear from them that our fleet has been destroyed and that their husbands are dead. Rather ought they to lift up their hearts to God in thankfulness, and to say a Pater Noster and Ave Maria in gratitude, for *I* tell you that today, this very day, our fleet has won a great victory and scattered the enemy.

That evening, while preaching at the church of Our Lady of the Mount to a congregation of native Christian women, St. Francis repeated his statement and told his thrilled audience the precise day on which they might expect news of the victory and of the safe return of their husbands. Everything fell out exactly as he had said. One of the first of the victors to return was a certain Alfonso Fernandez who quickly found himself surrounded by a crowd of eager questioners. At what date and on what day and hour had the victory been won? He told them, and they all cried excitedly that that was exactly the date and the day and the hour when Father Francis had made his announcement.[1] The only reference of Francis himself to those stirring events was in a letter to the King of Portugal pleading for the reward of Diogo Soares, Diogo Pereira, and Alfonso Gentil, three gallant gentlemen who had risked their ships and their lives in the battle, at heavy cost and without any compensation.[2]

At this juncture in his history, Malacca, December, 1547, St. Francis Xavier heard, with a great thrill of heart, the first definite news of Japan and met the first men of that recently discovered, mysterious land who had ever ventured so far west in their travels. Europe had learned of the existence of Japan from Marco

[1] There is no incident in the whole life of St. Francis better attested than this. No less than fifty references to it, taken from the official investigations held at Goa, Cochin and several other places in 1556, will be found in *Monumenta Xaveriana*, vol. ii. Most of the witnesses cited were present at the famous sermon on December 4, and heard the words with their own ears. The historian Do Couto who continued the *Decadas da Asia* of Barros gives a very good account of the famous victory and of the part played by St. Francis (*Decada*, VI, lib. v, cap. 1–2). Quite recently, Sir Richard Winstedt gave a vivid rendering of the story, in which, if anything, he assigns too much of the glory to St. Francis (*Malaya and its History*, 1948, p. 44). The reason why the fleet was so long away, a good forty days, was that the enemy had to be found before he could be engaged, and pirates are notoriously clever at making themselves invisible. The western coast of Malaya with its continuous mangrove swamps and countless streams and rivers, ' part of the most lavish water system in the world ', offers perfect hide-outs, and the Portuguese admiral, Francisco de Eça, had to explore many river estuaries before at length cornering the enemy about sixty miles north of Kedah. The Moslems had fifty ships to his ten, but a detail like that never worried the Portuguese. They loved to be outnumbered, especially when they had the advantage in weight of metal, because it enabled them to account for a larger proportion of the foe. This time, they almost wholly destroyed or captured the Achinese fleet, and so made the sea safer for trade than it had been for years. But the power of Achin was not finally broken until 1907, when the Dutch finished it after thirty-four years of costly war.

[2] Schurhammer, *Epistolae*, i, 411–17. Diogo Pereira was the very finest type of Portuguese merchant adventurer, a noble Christian soul, ready to sacrifice himself and his fortune, which was great, for any good cause. He became one of the most intimate friends of St. Francis and stood by him as nobody else in the last tragic and glorious months of his existence. Besides the three men named, Francis also recounted to the King the services of seven others, loyal vassals of His Highness, who deserved to be remembered and rewarded. None of them had asked for his intervention, which was entirely spontaneous, and probably unknown to them. The letter was like a dispatch from a battle front, recommending decorations for valour.

Polo in the Middle Ages, and ever after yearned for more knowledge of a land so wonderful and wealthy.

> Chipangu [wrote Marco] is an Island towards the east in
> the high seas, 1,500 miles distant from the Continent ; and a
> very great Island it is. The people are white, civilized, and well-
> favoured. They are Idolaters, and are dependent on nobody.
> And I can tell you the quantity of gold they have is endless. . . .
> I will tell you a wonderful thing about the Palace of the Lord
> of that Island. You must know that he hath a great Palace which
> is entirely roofed with fine gold, just as our churches are roofed
> with lead. . . . Moreover, all the pavement of the Palace, and
> the floors of its chambers, are entirely of gold, in plates like
> slabs of stone, a good two fingers thick ; and the windows also
> are of gold, so that altogether the richness of this Palace is past
> all bounds and belief. . . .[1]

Marco himself did not claim to have seen Japan, nor was its
coast ever sighted by European eyes until a bare five years before
St. Francis Xavier met the Japanese in Malacca. Japan would
appear to have been discovered by the Portuguese in three
successive stages, none of them premeditated. First, in 1542, they
found themselves, probably as the result of a storm at sea, on an
island in the Ryukyu Archipelago, which may have been the
now for ever famous Okinawa. Then, the following year, another
storm cast a few of them up on the island of Tanegashima, close
to Kyushu, the southernmost part of Japan proper. The names
of the three heroes who made history without at all meaning to
were probably Francisco Zeimoto, Antonio da Mota and Antonio
Peixoto, traders all and men of high spirit. The illustrious Fernam
Mendes Pinto claims in his *Peregrination* that he, too, was in the
party, and, indeed, its outstanding member, but there are good
reasons for denying him this particular feather in his already well-

[1] Yule, *The Book of Ser Marco Polo*, ii, 199–200. Marco often exaggerated
in his efforts to convey an impression of the real wonders which he had seen.
He was nicknamed *Il Milione* by the wits of his native Venice from his frequent
use of that sizable number.

fledged cap, though he was not long behind the pioneers.[1] There
was a daimyo or feudal lord on Tanegashima at the time and he
showed much interest in the castaways when he learned that one
of them had an implement or weapon which made a loud bang
and could bring down wild-fowl on the wing. They made his
lordship a present of the arquebus, and thus was friendship sealed
without the necessity of words, and Japan opened to trade with
the strange white barbarians who had come up out of the sea.
The great news soon spread among the Portuguese merchants
doing business with China through Canton, and from May to
August, 1544, there was a positive stampede of junks and all other
available craft across the East China Sea to Kyushu, where, for
anything known to the contrary, might be situated that Palace
roofed and paved with gold which Marco Polo had dangled
before the eyes of the Western world.

Pinto, to do him justice, was among the first in that ' Gold
Rush ' of 1544, but another admirer of Francis Xavier who
entered into commercial relations with Japan at this time is
much more to the purpose here, the shipmaster George Alvares,
a kindly, observant man, unvexed by romantic notions and
exaggerations. While this merchant's vessel was at the port of
Kagoshima, capital of Satsuma Province, southern Kyushu, in
1546, a Japanese gentleman name Anjiro, with two attendants,
took refuge on board one night. In some brawl or other, Anjiro
had killed a man, probably accidentally, and thought it wiser to
disappear for a while. A Portuguese of his acquaintance named
Alvaro Vaz had directed him to the ship. From the psychological

[1] In 1926, Father Schurhammer contributed a lengthy and profoundly
learned study of Pinto's *Peregrinaçam* to *Asia Major*, a journal published at
Leipzig and devoted to the study of the languages, arts and civilizations of the
Far East and Central Asia. His conclusions were not very favourable to Pinto's
claims in detail, and he more or less proved that Fernam could not have been
at Tanegashima in 1543, the accepted date for the Portuguese discovery of
Japan. This fine piece of destructive criticism (the conclusion alone runs to
seventy-three large pages!) was necessary because Pinto has much about St.
Francis Xavier, whom he knew and reverenced, in his book and most of it is
imaginary. .More popular writers such as Maurice Collis hold that the old
traveller was also a very truthful historian, but they cannot have studied
Schurhammer to any purpose.

and religious angle, this first Japanese to throw himself upon the mercy of Europeans and to sail away with them from his native land is a most interesting study. The Japanese are as human as the rest of mankind. They look before and after, and pine for what is not. Anyhow, Anjiro did. He belonged to the Shingon Buddhist sect whose religious teachings entirely failed to give him the peace of soul for which he yearned. He had a strongly developed sense of sin, the sins of his own youth—he was thirty-five—and longed to meet some master of the spiritual life who would help him to cope with his troubled conscience. After the manslaughter he had sought sanctuary in a Buddhist monastery for a time, but came out unsatisfied by the same door wherein he went. He is called a nobleman by some of the old writers, and may well have been of the samurai class, the military retainers of the daimyos, which meant as little as it did in old Europe that he was necessarily an educated man. He was unable, for instance, to read the Chinese ideograms in which the sacred books of Japanese Buddhism were written, so his knowledge of that great religion was extremely circumscribed and even parochial. There were about thirty-five different varieties of Buddhism competing for the adhesion of the Japanese, and by all the indications Anjiro's variety did not rank high among them. Of the others he appears to have known nothing. But he was a clever man in his own fashion and very quickly learned to speak a certain amount of Portuguese, sufficient at any rate to understand George Alvares when that good merchant told him about the great and holy bonze of the West, Francis Xavier.

It is a long way, more than three thousand miles over pirate-infested and typhoon-ridden seas, from Kagoshima to Malacca, and it speaks well for the determination and sincerity of the untravelled Anjiro that he made the voyage twice over in his attempts to find St. Francis. The first time he travelled with his two retainers in the ship of Alvares, which, after the usual tribulations of the East and South China Seas, brought him to Malacca towards the end of 1546, only to learn that the man he sought had departed for the Moluccas nearly a year earlier. To hunt for him in that part of the world would have been as unprofitable as looking for the proverbial needle in a haystack. By then, Anjiro had learned enough about Christianity from Alvares to want to be baptized, but when the Vicar of Malacca, a worthy named Alfonso Martinez who appears to have had the Pauline privilege much muddled in his honest head, learned that the prospective catechumen proposed to return to his pagan wife and family, he refused him the sacrament out of hand. The idea of a Christian man wanting to resume married life with a Buddhist woman! Sadly, with the next favourable winds, which blew from April to August, Anjiro turned aboard some Portuguese or Chinese ship towards his far-away home. It was just about the time that St. Francis set sail from Ternate in his *coracora* to catch a ship at Amboina for the return voyage to Malacca. However, a typhoon, sent by the providence of God, presently took a part in the affairs of the two men. Somewhere close to Japan, it laid hold of Anjiro's ship and drove it spinning back to the Chinese coast, where once again he encountered his friend Alvaro Vaz and other Portuguese merchants. They told him that the Santo Padre whom he had sought but not found in Malacca would by that time almost certainly have returned. They were themselves bound for Malacca, a month's voyaging away, so why not come with them to fulfil the purpose for which he had suffered so much and so long on the sea? He gladly accepted the invitation, and this time the fateful meeting took place which was to have such extraordinary consequences for St. Francis, for the Catholic Church, and for Japan. All those details are provided by Anjiro himself who, at the prompting of Francis Xavier, wrote a brief account of his life and adventures for the benefit of the Jesuits in Europe. It was dated from Goa, November 29, 1548, by which time the hero had become reasonably proficient in Portuguese.[1]

[1] The Portuguese original is no longer extant, but Spanish copies of the letter were made as soon as it reached Europe, and one of these, well larded with Portuguese words and expressions, has recently been edited and published in the most scholarly fashion by Joseph Wicki, S.J., in his *Documenta Indica* (Vol. i, 1948, pp. 332–41). It was first published at Coimbra in 1570, and subsequently in other places many times, but Father Wicki's text now supersedes all the earlier ones.

On my voyage home to Japan [he wrote] we were about twenty leagues from the coast and in sight of it, when there rose against us such a violent storm accompanied by darkness so complete, which lasted for four days and nights, that nobody knew what to say or do except cry out for mercy in that terrible extremity. There was nothing for it but to turn and run before the tempest back to the port of China from which we had set out. . . . Coming thence to Malacca, I met George Alvares who brought me the first time, and he took me immediately to Father Francis. We found him in the church of Our Lady of the Mount performing a marriage. I fell completely under his spell and gave him a long account of myself. He was so delighted to see and embrace me that it was clearly God who had brought about our meeting. I felt that more strongly in my soul every time I looked at him, and I was abundantly comforted and contented by merely watching his face. . . .

So much for Anjiro's first impressions; now for those of St. Francis:

When I was in the City of Malacca, some Portuguese merchants of high standing brought me great news of certain very large islands recently discovered to the east called the islands of Japan. In the opinion of those men, there would be better opportunities for the increase of our holy faith there than anywhere in India, because the people have an eager desire for knowledge and instruction, which is not the case with the Indians. There came with the merchants a Japanese named Anjiro seeking for me, as the Portuguese who had been to his country from Malacca spoke to him about me. He came with the desire of making a confession to me, for when he met the Portuguese he told them of certain sins committed in his youth and asked them how he was to obtain pardon from God for such grave offences, whereupon they had advised him to travel with them to Malacca to see me, which he did. But at the time of his arrival, I had gone to the Moluccas, and, hearing this, he embarked to return to Japan. When he was within sight of his native land, he and his shipmates were caught by such a terrible storm that they all seemed like to perish. They turned the ship about and took once more the route to Malacca, where I had meantime arrived. He found me and was delighted, as he had come with an eager desire to learn about our religion. He speaks Portuguese moderately well, so that he understood all that I told him, and I what he told me. If all the Japanese are as keen to learn as Anjiro, I think they must have the most inquiring minds of any people in the lands hitherto discovered. When he attended the Christian doctrine classes, he wrote down the articles of faith in Japanese. He used to go to the church to pray very frequently, and he was constantly putting questions to me. He is most anxious to learn, and that is the mark of a man who will profit greatly and quickly come to a knowledge of the truth. . . . I asked him whether, if I went back with him to his country, the Japanese would become Christians, and he said that they would not do so until they had first asked me many questions and seen how I answered and how much I knew. Above all, they would want to observe if I lived in conformity with what I said and believed. If I did those two things, answered the questions to their satisfaction and so demeaned myself that they could not find anything to blame in my conduct, then, after knowing me for six months, the king, the nobility, and all other people of discretion would become Christians, for the Japanese, he said, are entirely guided by the law of reason.

Poor Anjiro and poor St. Francis! While entirely sincere, the Japanese obviously knew next to nothing about the political condition, mental qualities and religious mood of his countrymen outside the narrow bounds of his own Buddhist sect and the confines of his native Kagoshima, which, though a pleasant city and populous, was then and still is very much off the Japanese map, remote from the great centres. The only time that it emerged into the light of international history was when it received a few token shells from the British Navy in 1863. The ruler of Satsuma Province in Anjiro's time, Shimazu Takahisa, was not a king in any proper sense of the word but a daimyo, one of some 260 military leaders, and far from the most important, who at that period of political anarchy divided an unhappy Japan between them. The daimyos corresponded closely enough to the great feudal barons who bedevilled the histories of France and England until quelled by the strong monarchies that arose in those countries. Japan had to wait many years after the days of Francis Xavier for such deliverance. From time immemorial the country rejoiced in the possession of an emperor lineally descended from the gods, but in the twelfth century he had been shorn of all temporal power by military adventurers and kept as a mere symbol of the nation's pride. These were matters apparently quite unknown to the honest backwoodsman Anjiro. Even St. Francis, who was only too apt to believe what he was told, seems to have suspected that the account of Japan given him might be too rosy, for he mentioned in his letter that he had asked his friend George Alvares to give him in writing ' some information about Japan and its people based on his experiences there and on the views of Japanese persons worthy of credence'. Alvares complied to the extent of a small pamphlet, which is almost certainly the first European account of Japan ever written.[1]

He commented on the pride and sensitiveness, the instinctive generosity and hospitality of the people, their propensity for asking questions and learning all they could, their sobriety, their calmness in conversation, which ' makes them despise us foreigners because we raise out voices '. Like Anjiro, Alvares had little idea of the complexity of politics in Japan. The daimyos were to him all kings, powerful persons whom one approached on hands and knees. The Japanese impressed him as a distinctly religious people, though very much given to a kind of domestic idolatry such as flourished in Ancient Rome. He noted that they made great use of beads on which to count their prayers, a common custom in

[1] A Spanish rendering of the Portuguese original manuscript was published in 1894 at Lisbon by Jeronymo da Camara Manoel in his *Missões dos Jesuitas no Oriente nos seculos XVI e XVII*, pp. 112–25. Still better is the German version, furnished with a valuable commentary, given by the Protestant scholar, Hans Haas, in his *Geschichte des Christentums in Japan* (Vol. i, Tokyo, 1902, pp. 269–79).

nearly all Eastern lands. The women he considered to be especially devout, excellent housewives, with charming manners, but too submissive to their husbands for his taste. He observed that the people were monogamous, but that divorce on the husband's part could be easily obtained, indeed, that the husband was an absolute despot, with power of life and death in certain circumstances. The good merchant must have visited some of the Shinto temples, for he noted accurately the ceremonies that went on in them and the lay attire of the ministers, in contrast with the distinctive robes of the Buddhist priests. For a complete stranger, his account of Buddhism as practised in Japan was astonishingly precise, and he did not miss the great social and political influence exerted by the bonzes, which afterwards, in the days of Oda Nobunaga, was to have surprising consequences for the Catholic Church in Japan. All this information profoundly impressed St. Francis. He told his European brethren to whom he dispatched Alvares's report:

I have a strong feeling in my soul that before two years are out either I myself or some other of our Society will go to Japan, though it is a very perilous voyage both by reason of terrible storms and of Chinese pirates who haunt those seas, with the consequent loss of many ships. So, dearest Fathers and Brothers, pray to God our Lord for those who will make the dangerous venture. Meantime, Anjiro will be able to improve his Portuguese, see something of India, and become acquainted with the European art and mode of living. We shall ground him in the Christian doctrine and then have him put it all into the Japanese language, which he writes very well, together with a lengthy declaration on those articles of faith that deal with the coming of Jesus Christ our Lord.[1]

[1] Schurhammer, *Epistolae S. Francisci Xaverii*, i, 390-2.

CHAPTER XII

BANDÉ MATARAM

S T. FRANCIS XAVIER baptized thousands of Indians
and East Indians after very sketchy instruction and without
inquiring too closely into the motives which inspired his
converts. But he made no move to baptize Anjiro, though the
man came to him in the best dispositions and already fairly well
versed in Christian doctrine. He had his reasons, much deeper
ones than a mere courteous desire to save the Vicar of Malacca's
face. Anjiro and his companions were in a class apart, civilized
pagans, very different from the lowly pearl-fishers or the Macuas
of Travancore, who needed rescuing from vice and idolatry
almost by a kind of holy violence and precipitation. To have
missed the one chance with them might easily have meant
missing everything, and the full Catholicizing of them, necessarily
a gradual and long process, would have to wait on the patient toil
of the priests whom he had planned to send into their midst.
Anjiro, on the other hand, had to be carefully shaped to be an
apostle himself, as any priest going to Japan with him would be
almost completely dependent on his services, and, besides, it was
important to invest his baptism with as much ceremony and
publicity as possible, in order to stimulate Catholic interest in the
great new venture about to be made at the world's end. The Bishop
of Goa, whose diocese would include Japan, was obviously the
person to baptize the first Japanese Christians. St. Francis could
afford to spend only a week in Anjiro's exciting company. He
must get back to India to clear up huge arrears of missionary
business, to assign posts to eight new Jesuit arrivals, to visit all his
Christians, to try again to bring about the conversion of Ceylon,
to concert various measures for the good of the Church in India,
Malacca, and the Moluccas with the new viceroy, John de
Castro, to write twelve letters, some immensely long, to Europe,

including three to the King of Portugal, and, of course, to make preparations for the mission to Japan.

St. Francis spent just over fifteen months in India this time, figuratively stormy months which began with a storm in good earnest. This particular effort of the monsoon winds is memorable for having really frightened Francis, a most unusual triumph of the elements. He had no fear of death, but he did not want to die, if God willed, before he could satisfy to some extent the great new ambition of his heart, the evangelization of Japan. When he set sail from Malacca towards the end of December, 1547, he had hoped that Anjiro might come with him, but that courteous man felt an obligation to wait for the ship of George Alvares, his benefactor, which meant a few days delay. Francis could not afford even that little postponement, but he appreciated the other's motive and esteemed him more highly than ever. Let him tell us himself what befell him on the sea:

On that voyage from Malacca to India we underwent manifold perils from a great storm which lasted three days and nights. I never experienced a worse storm at sea. The people aboard wept and wailed for their own deaths while still alive, and mighty were the vows they made never to put to sea again, should God deliver them. We jettisoned all the cargo we could to save our lives. While the tempest was at its height, I commended myself to God our Lord, taking for my first intercessors on earth all those belonging to the Company of Jesus, and the friends of the Company, blessed of God. With that great help, I gave myself completely to the loving prayers of the Spouse of Jesus Christ, Holy Mother Church, who, still on earth, is unceasingly heard in Heaven. Nor did I neglect to have recourse to all saints in the glory of Paradise, beginning with those who here below were of the holy Company of Jesus, especially the blessed soul of Father Favre.[1] I could never convey

---

[1] As mentioned earlier, Pierre Favre died on August 1, 1546, and the news was brought to St. Francis at Malacca just over a year later. Seven other Jesuits had died since Francis left Europe.

to you the consolation I received from thus commending myself to God our Lord through the intercession of my brethren of the Society, living and dead. While the danger lasted, I also put myself in the hands of the angels, praying to them choir by choir, and under the protection of the patriarchs, prophets, apostles, evangelists, martyrs, confessors, virgins—all the saints in Heaven—and to strengthen my hope of obtaining pardon for my infinite number of sins, I took for my protectress the glorious Virgin, our Lady, because in Heaven everything she asks of God our Lord is granted. Finally, I put all my trust in the infinite merits of the Passion and death of Jesus Christ, our Redeemer and Lord. With all this protection and help about me, I think I felt happier in the thick of the storm than afterwards when delivered from it. That a *grandissimo pecador* should have shed tears of joy and consolation in so great an extremity seems to me, when I think of it, matter for the deepest self-abasement. So I begged our Lord during the storm that, if I came out of it alive, it might only be to endure others as bad or worse for His greater service.

The battered ship carrying St. Francis put into Cochin harbour between the sea and the long lagoon on January 13, 1548. There were seventeen Jesuits in India then, but none of them had as yet come to this centre of the pepper trade which had been in Portuguese hands for forty-five years. The purpose of Francis in making a brief stay there was to find out what had been happening to the Indian Christians since last he saw them more than two years before. It was his fortune, not good but stern, to find the Bishop of Goa in the city, the gentle, devout, greatly perplexed old man, John de Albuquerque, O.F.M., saddled with the most difficult diocese in the world, and also the superior of the Franciscans, poor martyrs, to whom had been committed the mission of Ceylon. Sad indeed was the tale which they poured into the ears of St. Francis. Miguel Vaz, the Bishop's Vicar-General and main support, the strong arm of the Christians in India, a layman invested by the King of Portugal with full inquisitorial powers, an admirable person in many ways, selfless and bent only on the

protection and diffusion of the faith, even if too muscularly
inclined in the matter, had died, very suddenly at Chaul, twenty-
five miles south of Bombay, just a year ago. Many gave out that
he had been poisoned, and some, even among the Portuguese,
hinted darkly that Bishop Albuquerque was responsible. Poor
Bishop, of whom Cosmas Anes, the great friend of St. Francis
and main prop of the College of St. Paul in Goa, said: ' Why, he
wouldn't kill a flea for his own convenience ! ' Diogo de Borba,
the founder of the College and a Christian in a million, was so
shattered by the news of the Vicar-General's death that he collapsed
and followed his friend a fortnight later. The valiant were fallen
and the weapons of war had perished. The bright hopes centred
on the two princes of Ceylon who had fled their country to
become Christians at Goa were also extinguished in death.
Bhuvaneka Bâhu, King of Kottê, and his unloving brother
Mayadunnê continued their everlasting bickering and intrigue,
while the King of Kandy, on his menaced throne, bargained his
shifty soul with the Portuguese for the price of a hundred soldiers.
The Franciscans were at their wits' ends to find a grain of sincerity
or straight dealing in the abominable politics of these Buddhists,
each of whom aspired to be the ruler of all Ceylon. That island
paradise, on which there is good reason to think that he never
set foot, was one of the darkest disappointments of St. Francis
Xavier. Nothing, he learned, had been done to curb the anti-
Christian violence of Sankily, the Raja of Jaffna, and Iniquitriberim had been antagonized by the broken promises of the
Portuguese, with evil consequences for the Saint's humble converts at Cape Comorin. The viceroy, John de Castro, a good,
honest man and great soldier, had saved Portuguese India by his
splendid victory at Diu in 1546, but he showed no anxiety to be
a colonial reformer on the grand scale, as the times demanded.
No more than his predecessors did he control his officials, many
of whom continued to be as rapacious as ever, at the expense of
the Indian Christians. Brahmans, Jews and even Moslems were
given more or less a free hand in Goa itself, in Cochin, in Bassein,
in Tuticorin, and in other places where Portugal had control, and
it is not surprising that they used their immunity, granted in the

sacred interests of trade, to thwart or undo conversions to Christianity.[1]

Having heard the sombre news, St. Francis sat down to write hastily his big budget for Europe, including the enormous letter detailing his experiences in Malacca and the Moluccas, from which so many excerpts have already been given. It is about five thousand words long, and was meant for the Jesuits in general. To St. Ignatius he wrote separately, telling his love, appealing for advice, setting out the desperate need of men to preach the Gospel to the heathen, men so well imbued with the spirit of the Gospel that they could be trusted to venture forth alone without stay of father or of son to meet whatever dangers or death Almighty God might send them. As for Japan, this is what he said: ' I have not yet completely made up my mind whether I myself, accompanied by one or other of the Society, shall seek Japan in six months time, or whether to send two of our brethren ahead there. But it is quite certain that either I go or send others. As things now stand, my inclination is to go in person. May God our Lord make clear to me His divine will in the matter. . . .' He mentioned also that it was his intention to designate superiors at every point of the huge watery world where two or more of his men were working together, thus giving the missions a tentative form of organization.

---

[1] Nearly all the documents and letters published by Schurhammer and Voretzsch in their two volumes, *Ceylon zur Zeit des Königs Bhuvaneka Bâhu und Franz Xavers* (Leipzig, 1928), dating from 1546, reflect the confusion of Portuguese affairs in India and Ceylon at that time. The King of Portugal's instructions to Miguel Vaz, dated March 5, 1546, are particularly significant. He ordered the complete suppression of idolatry in the Portuguese dominions, and a whole series of measures to be taken for the protection and encouragement of the Indian Christians, but not much attention was paid to his directions after the death of Vaz (Document 57). Some grand characters appear in those teeming pages, for example, the gallant, hard-bitten old soldier Miguel Ferreira who, when told by the Viceroy that he need not appear for the impending struggle at Diu owing to his bad health, replied immediately: ' Senhor, the moment your letter reached me [at San Thomé] I forthwith made a testament that, did I happen to die before setting out, they were to put me in a coffin and thus take me to that armada of your Lordship ' (Document 70).

His third letter of the same date, January 20, 1548, was to King John III of Portugal, and a startling document. His Highness, he began, who was the principal and faithful protector of the whole Society of Jesus both in love and deed, would know from the detailed letters sent to Europe by himself what was being attempted for the service of God in Malacca and the Moluccas. As for Christianity in India, ' the holy Franciscan Fathers returning to Portugal would give His Highness the news ', and Friar John de Villa de Conde, a true servant of God experienced in the affairs of Ceylon, was writing to him a full and accurate account of that country.

Many a time [he continued] I have reflected anxiously whether it would be well for me, too, to write to your Highness about what I feel in my soul to be best for the promotion of our holy faith. On the one hand, I thought it might be to the service of God, but, on the other, I judged that such things as I wrote ought not to be ventilated. However, by not writing I felt I would burden my conscience, since God our Lord gave me to understand these matters for some purpose, which could not be other than that I should write to your Highness. So I write to you what I am painfully feeling in my soul. If the measures set out are not taken, it may be that my letter will be your Highness's accuser at the hour of death, before God, when the excuse of ignorance will not be accepted. Believe me, your Highness, that it pains me to speak in this fashion, since my only desire is to labour and die out here that I may help to discharge your conscience, in return for the great love you bear our Society. So in coming to the conclusion that I ought to write to you, I found myself in a state of great confusion. Eventually, for my own peace of mind, I determined to tell you what I know through experience gained in India, Malacca and the Moluccas. . . .

Plainly, Francis was perplexed in the extreme, torn between duty to the King and duty to the suffering Church in the King's dominions. He next spoke with charitable euphemism (or was it irony?) of the 'holy jealousies' or rivalries, the *sanctos ciumes*, which greatly hindered the service of God in India:

One says, 'I will do it'; another says,' No, leave it to me '; a third, 'Since I'm not to do it, it gives me no pleasure to watch you trying '. Again, there are people to be found saying, 'I do all the work and another gets all the thanks and advantage'. So the time goes by with each striving in the pursuit of his own aims till there is no place left for pursuit of the service of God. Moreover, much that might be done for the honour and service of your Highness in India is neglected for the same reason. If there are to be many converts to Christianity here, and if those who are already Christians are to be shown all friendship, without anyone daring to oppress or defraud them, whether Portuguese or pagans, then I know of only one measure adequate to meet the situation. It is that your Highness inform and direct the Governor in office here at present, or any other you may send here, that in no religious persons [Franciscans or Jesuits] now in this country do you confide as much as you do in him for the increase of our holy faith in India, naming all of us here, and telling him that, after God, his is the supreme responsibility for unburdening your Highness's conscience of the heavy load it bears, because through the failure of other Governors India has not become more Christianized. Order the Governor to give you an account of the Christians already converted, and of the prospects there are for the conversion of many more, and tell him that you will credit his reports to the exclusion of all others. But should he neglect to carry out your Highness's intentions by greatly promoting the growth of our holy faith, assure him that you are determined to punish him, and tell him with a solemn oath that, when he returns to Portugal, you will declare all his property forfeit to the work of the *Santa Misericordia*, and besides put him in irons for several years. Disabuse him of the idea that excuses or pretexts will be accepted, such as they allege for not actively promoting the faith being worthless. I cannot say all that I know in this respect for fear of grieving your Highness, nor must I think of my own past and present sorrows for evils that appear to be incurable. If the Governor is brought to understand that you certainly mean what you say and intend to fulfil your oath, the whole island of Ceylon will be Christian in a year, and so also will be many kings, as those of Malabar, Cape Comorin, and several other places. But so long as Governors do not live with this fear before their eyes of being disgraced and punished, your Highness need not count on any increase of our holy faith nor on the perseverance of those at present Christians, no matter how many appointments and dispositions you make. No more effective means exists to make all Indians Christians than for your Highness to punish a governor severely. As I have no hope that this will be done, I am almost sorry to have mentioned it. I assure your Highness that I would not have written thus about the governors if, with a good conscience, I could have held my peace. I am not as yet, Sire, completely determined to go to Japan, but I think I shall, for I almost despair of any real chance or encouragement to increase the faith in India, or even to preserve in the faith the existing Christian communities. . . .

It is difficult to know what to say about that outburst, except that it ought not to be judged out of its context, apart from its historical background, or by the standards of another age. St. Francis was by no means the only man of his time and place to express similar views, though he must have felt more deeply than others did the heart-ache and disenchantment of seeing the things he held dearer than life thwarted and negatived by the godless conduct, the rapacity and injustice of Portuguese officials responsible to the King and to his Governor. As for John de Castro himself who held the higher authority of Viceroy, he was one of the best appointments made by the King, just and chivalrous in all his dealings, but his *métier* was war against the Moslem foe, and he appears to have entirely neglected the root and branch reform of his civil service, which was so gravely needed. Politically also, he failed to exploit the many opportunities offered by kings and rajas in distress who appealed for Portuguese military assistance. True, the motives of those rulers in offering to become Christians themselves or to let their subjects be baptized, were highly questionable from a theological angle, but it should not be forgotten that France obtained her faith originally on similar terms and so did Hungary, Poland and other countries. At any rate, if John de Castro and his successors had lent the aid for which they were asked, instead of promising it and then doing nothing, there was a good chance that Iniquitriberim, two rajas in Travancore, the brother of the Raja of Jaffna, and the King of Kandy, would all have accepted baptism, perhaps with as much right in the matter as Clovis or the Jutish King of Kent. After listing the ills of India with which he was sadly familiar, the great Portuguese historian, Gaspar Correa, a contemporary of St. Francis, recommended that ' the King should order the public beheading of a governor on the wharves of Goa, with a proclamation that he was being executed for failing to carry out the duties to which he was bound '. Returning to the point in the last of his big volumes, Correa wrote: ' There will never be improvement in India until Portugal has a king prepared to cut off the heads of captains and governors for the great evil they do against God and against the royal interest.'[1] However much we may deplore from our twentieth-century armchairs the appeal of this sixteenth-century man to a familiar and accepted religious policy of his moment, almost coincident with the Battle of Mühlberg, we must allow for the selfless passion that consumed him to bring India into the light of the living God, and we ought to notice at the height of our indignation that he did not cry for anybody's head on a charger.

[1] *Lendas da India* (Lisbon, 1858), ii, 752; iv, 338–9. Though this vast history of Portuguese conquest was finished in India in 1556, it did not find a publisher for more than three centuries, because too full of scandalous revelations. Correa was a very admirable Christian himself and disgusted by the conduct of his countrymen, on whom at times he is definitely too severe. M. Bellessort would appear to have forgotten Clovis and his mass-converted Franks when he wrote in the following strain: ' *On voudrait effacer ce passage des lettres de François. Il n'est ni d'un apôtre, car un apôtre n'abdique pas ainsi entre les mains de l'autorité civile, ni d'un organisiteur, car, si le Roi et la Compagnie l'ont envoyé dans l'Inde, c'est afin d'organiser les missions et non pour en remettre le soin au vice-roi. Rien n'est heureux de ces conseils que lui dictent bien moins son expérience, comme il le dit, que son impatience et son irritation,*' etc. (*Saint François Xavier*, pp. 203–4).

The rest of St. Francis's letter to the King consists of a petition that more preachers be sent out, ' for lack of whom neither the Portuguese nor the Indian converts live as Christians ', of a warm defence of the Bishop of Goa, that true pastor, paid for his charity and good works in the world's usual coin, but as guiltless of the death of Miguel Vaz, ' as am I myself who was in the Moluccas when it happened ', and of a typically Franciscan appeal for the recompense of two good men, loyal vassals of the King. The second letter written the same day to the same majestic address has already been mentioned as containing appeals from Francis on behalf of nine merchants, officials and soldiers who had served the King well and been overlooked in the distribution of rewards. A large part of this dictated letter was occupied with the affairs of the Confraternity of Mercy at Cochin in whose hospital Francis probably stayed. The devoted members needed money for their church, for the support of their orphanage, for the extension and repair of their hospital, and the dear Saint is as urgent about those matters as if he had himself the mouths to feed and the sick to accommodate. A third letter to the King, now lost, was a plea for a dowager Sultana of Ternate who had become a Christian and lived in reduced circumstances. To conclude his correspondence, written at top speed to catch the ships whose sails were already set, Francis wrote to the one he addresses as *Hermano mio dilectissimo Maestre Simon*, imploring Rodriguez to send him more men qualified to teach the Indians. He had been given seventeen, but what were they among the teeming millions? He was one indeed to have compassion on the multitude, the humble peasants scraping and scratching from morn till night to wrest a pittance from the sun-baked ground, the fishermen in their bobbing *catamarans*, the ragged children swarming everywhere, mirthful though starved, the desolate negro slaves pining for their African kraals, the huge anonymous crowds in the cities who had no crucifix to assuage their sorrows or give their deaths a meaning, these were the parishioners of Francis, and the thought of his impotence to help them made his daily Gethsemane. Let us frown on him if we like for invoking the secular arm, but let us also remember India and give him an alms of understanding. He returned to the King's matter in this letter to Rodriguez, knowing that the good Simon was a power at Court:

If the King only realized the faithful love I bear him, I would ask for a favour at his hands, which is that he should daily, for a quarter of an hour, beseech God to bring home to him the meaning of our Lord's words, ' What doth it profit a man to gain the whole world and lose his own soul?' It is time, dearest Simon, to wake up his Highness. The hour is nearer than perhaps he thinks when God will demand an account of his stewardship. Therefore, see to it that he provides India with spiritual foundations.

He goes on to speak once more of the only course which he considered to be of the slightest use, the throwing of all the responsibility for the Christianization of India on to the Governor's shoulders: ' This would stop at once the injuries and plunderings to which the poor Christians are subjected, and those who contemplate being Christians would be greatly emboldened to go ahead.'[1]

Immediately after the departure of the ships for Europe (January 22), St. Francis left Cochin for Manapad on the Fishery Coast, presumably by sea. He was back in Cochin again before the end of February, and then early in March made the long voyage to Goa, and from Goa to Bassein, twenty-five miles north of Bombay. By April 2 we find him in Cochin for a third time, which means that in ten weeks he had sailed one thousand six hundred miles or more, in ships heavily outclassed for amenities by the grimiest tramp steamers of today. In Manapad he assembled all his men working in the south for a kind of family reunion, which lasted a fortnight. They made a small but gallant company, Antonio Criminali from the Duchy of Parma, aged only twenty-

---

[1] Schurhammer, *Epistolae S. Francisci Xaverii*, i, 397–422. The first letter to King John, the one with the shocks for liberals and democrats in it, ended its considerable travels in Berkeley Square, London, at the famous bookshop of Maggs Brothers.

eight, but so saintly, lovable and wise that the others had by
common consent chosen him their superior; the veteran Spaniard,
Alfonso Cyprian, soon to be a sexagenarian, a vehement character
of the Bobadilla class, whom Simon Rodriguez, five years earlier,
described as ' so great a satrap that he would force his advice on
the Emperor ', but a grand missionary all the same; Manuel de
Moras or Morais, another ' original ' difficult to control, who
worked hard in Travancore and, owing to his impetuosity, had
the distinction of being captured by Moslems and sold as a slave;
Francis Henriques, a man of much the same stamp, endlessly
courageous but not very prudent; and finally, his namesake,
Henry Henriques, a young priest of Jewish blood and very bad
health, who gave to the poor a large fortune in order to suffer
heroically and labour marvellously for twenty-five unbroken
years under the cruel Cape Comorin sun. He was the second-self
of St. Francis, a master of Tamil such as Francis never became,
the first Jesuit to study the sacred books of India, and thus the
forerunner of Robert de Nobili, Thomas Stevens, Joseph Beschi,
and other scholars who revolutionized missionary methods in
that country.

Francis, of whom Manuel Morais said that merely to look at
him made one feel a happier and better man, wrote for the
guidance of the united Fathers a long instruction bearing on every
aspect of their activities. Their greatest care must be for children
and the sick. The instruction of the children was stressed as nothing
else. On it everything depended. The Indian boys ought to be
associated with all the Fathers' spiritual ministries, going with them
to say prayers over the sick, accompanying them in procession
to bury the dead, helping with the baptisms. The children should
have the best part of their love, and they ought to be slow to
punish them, even when they deserved it. As infant mortality was
so rife in India, the Fathers must make sure by constant visiting
of homes that no babies died unbaptized. St. Francis directed that
all baptisms, whether of children or adults, might be performed
without the ceremonies, a fact which gave the good Henry
Henriques a scruple. He strongly emphasized the importance of
harmony between the missionaries and the Portuguese captains

and traders, and begged his men to exercise all forbearance in dealing with them.

> But be careful [he wrote] never to criticize the native Christians in presence of the Portuguese. Rather must you take their part and speak up in their defence, for they have been so short a time Christians and have so small a grasp of the faith that the Portuguese ought to be surprised to find them as good as they are. Try with all your might, Fathers, to win the love of your people, doing whatever you do for them with words of love. . . . Any alms we receive from men or women, or offerings made in church, we must give entirely to the poor, reserving absolutely nothing for ourselves.

The document was signed, ' Todo vosso, Mestre Francisco '. And he was all theirs, and they knew it, and so did the Japanese Anjiro who said this same year: ' I would lay down my life a hundred times for the love I bear him.'[1]

The holiday at Manapad over, the Fathers dispersed with new heart to their several posts, and St. Francis took the weary way round the Cape to Cochin and Goa to seek help from the Viceroy for his poor Christians in the south, troubled by various dis-appointed rajas, as well as for the infant Church in Malacca and the Moluccas. Legends die hard, but surely the one which repre-sents this man as a born globe-trotter, ever itching for pastures new and little regardful of the humble flocks he had gathered only to abandon, ought to be mouldering in a dishonoured grave by now. He did not find John de Castro at Goa. John had had a Roman triumph there after his splendid victory over the Moslems at Diu, and then was off again on crusade to harry the ancient foe in the north-west, round the Gulf of Cambay. Only recently, on December 21, 1547, he had worsted a powerful sultan at Broach, twenty miles north of Surat, and was at the pinnacle of his glory. He made Bassein his headquarters, that now long dead city of beautiful Baroque churches untenanted and roofless within the still standing fortifications, which Moslem might could not penetrate

---

[1] Schurhammer, *Epistolae*, i, 426–35 ; Wicki, *Documenta Indica*, i, 340.

but which the Mahrattas and the all-conquering mosquito did.[1] At Goa, St. Francis had the joy of meeting again his first and long-lost companion, Paul of Camerino, and the brave pessimist Nicholas Lancillotto, dedicated to the peculiar task of imbuing Indian youth with the mind of Virgil and Terence, and another but cheerful schoolmaster, Francis Perez, destined to do great things in Malacca. With them they had four men who aspired to be Jesuits, one of them a priest from Barcelona, aged thirty-eight, named Cosmas de Torres. For ten years Cosmas had been roaming the world searching, as he said himself, for he knew not what—*buscando o que nao sabia*. He had spent four years wandering in Mexico. Then, in 1542, he joined as naval chaplain the fleet of Roderigo Lopez de Villalobos which set out to explore the Pacific. After fifty-five days without sight of anything but salt water, they blundered into the archipelago which subsequently became known as the Marshall Islands. Finding nothing to eat there, they sailed on through the Caroline Islands to Mindanao, where they made a silent pact with the native tree-dwellers in the following picturesque fashion. Using a knife, the local chief-tain drew blood from his chest and arm, mixed it with some kind of wine, and offered the beverage to Villalobos, indicating that the Admiral was to do the same by him. They then solemnly drank and became brothers, while Padre de Torres looked on awe-stricken. They stayed in the Philippines forty unhappy days, during which it rained the whole time and they were very hungry as well as wet. Their project was to sail north, but the winds and currents drove them south to the Moluccas, where the Sultan of Tidore welcomed them as a counterpoise to the Portuguese backers of his rival, the Sultan of Ternate. But as already mentioned, the Portuguese won the private little war that followed, and brought the Spaniards prisoners to Amboina at which place

---

[1] Bassein is now one of the national monuments of India, and a group of Franciscans, indomitable as ever, has been allowed to brave the mosquito and live within it. A fervent Catholic population of fishermen and farmers, number-ing about 45,000, live close to the beautiful dead city. The Jesuit church in it where St. Francis used to say Mass has been re-roofed and is occasionally the scene of divine services.

Father Torres met Father Xavier. It was a case of love at first sight. ' There and then I wanted to follow in his footsteps,' said the good man, who had been round the world looking for peace and inspiration, and at last had found them.[1]

St. Francis spent only nine days in Goa, mostly concerned with the affairs of the College of St. Paul, that seminary for Asian youth which was presently to become by its directors' wishes a Jesuit responsibility. Then, towards the end of March and in the teeth of the prevailing winds, he took a ship of some sort to Bassein, where, it is said, he was at once called upon to preach a Lenten sermon and had among his auditors the much laurelled John de Castro, in a critical, appraising mood. John, the story goes, was completely won over by the strange priest who understood so little of a viceroy's difficulties and had backed up that late disturber of the peace, Miguel Vaz. It is a probable story, for there is no doubt at all that the great soldier and the great saint became very good friends. De Castro had worn himself out in the defence of his country's Indian empire. He had premonitions of death, and, being a thoroughly devout Christian, it is entirely likely that he would have wanted such a one as Francis at hand to see him safely out of this world. At all events, he begged Francis, as Francis himself reported, to stand by him at Goa, whither he was returning, during the rainy season then approaching. A few days later, the Saint, back in Goa, wrote to his great friend, the wealthy merchant Diogo Pereira, at Cochin:

> God knows, Sir, how I would love to see you before you depart to China, but his Excellency the Governor has asked me to spend the winter months in Goa and I cannot do other than comply, though I wanted to go to Cochin and thence to Cape Comorin, where my companions are. It would, besides, have given me so much pleasure and contentment to discuss with you, my very good and true friend, a number of things concerning a voyage and pilgrimage which, a year from now, I hope to make to Japan. . . . I would also have rejoiced to see

[1] Wicki, *Documenta Indica*, i, 471–6.

you before you sail in order to recommend to you a very rich kind of merchandise which the traders in Malacca and China regard as of little account. It is called a man's conscience, and so little esteemed in those parts that all the merchants believe they would go bankrupt if they invested in it! I hope in God our Lord that my friend Diogo Pereira will do good business with a big cargo of conscience where those others lose, not their traffic but their souls, for want of it. In my poor prayers and in my Masses I shall continually beg our Lord to bring you safely through, richer in soul and conscience than in fortune.

It is typical of its writer that more than a third of this charming letter is taken up with an appeal for a poor unknown fellow, a Spaniard named Ramires, who pined to go home to his father and mother, but had no money to pay his passage. 'I am so poor myself,' said Francis, 'that much as I want to help him home, I find it impossible. So I beg you for the love of our Lord and our Lady His Mother to take him into your employment and pay him enough to enable him to go home. You will do God a service and put me under a lasting obligation.'[1]

Very probably it was at this time, while he waited on the stricken Viceroy, dying in all his glory at forty-eight by the devilry of mosquitoes, that St. Francis composed, or compiled from various sources, a whole series of prayers and considerations for the morning and evening use of devout souls. His own soul is revealed in them, and all the pieties, strong yet tender, of which it was abundantly full, his profound devotion to the Most Holy Trinity, his horror of sin and compassion for sinners, his love for little ones, the *meninos e meninas* so constantly in his thoughts and plans, the realism of his attitude towards death as the most tremendous moment of life, his fervour of affection for his two

---

[1] Schurhammer, *Epistolae S. Francisci Xaverii*, i, 436–8. Francis mentioned that he was sending Father Perez and Roch Oliveira to Malacca to preach and teach, and made a joke and untranslatable pun about the style of education common in Spain and Portugal and their colonies at that time. It seems that the children in the schools were taught to read by means of law reports, as it were, out of the Police Gazette! Roch Oliveira, a first-rate schoolmaster, was sent out to reform all that.

mothers, Holy Mother Church and 'Minha Senhora Sancta Maria, Hope of Christians, Queen of all the Angels and Saints'. The following prayer of his own composition to be addressed to one's Angel Guardian gives an idea of the spirit in which all the prayers and counsels are written:

I beg thee, Blessed Angel, to whose providence I am entrusted, to be always at hand to help me. Present my petitions to the merciful ears of God our Lord that of His clemency and by thy prayers He may pardon my sins of the past, give me to know truly and repent heartily of my present sins, and counsel and warn me that I may shun sins in the future. Through thee may He give me grace to do good and persevere to the end. Drive away from me by the power of Almighty God every temptation of the Devil, and that which my own deeds, mixed as they always are with some evil, merit not, do thou obtain for me by thy prayers before our Lord. And if at times thou seest me straying from the paths of goodness to follow the errors of sin, procure that I may turn again speedily to my Saviour in the way of justice. When thou beholdest me in tribulation and anguish, obtain for me help from God by thy sweet advocacy. I beg thee never to forsake me, but ever to shield, help and defend me from all troubling and assaults of the demons, watching over me day and night, at all hours and moments. And when this life draws to a close, do not permit the demons to frighten me, and let me not fall into despair. Leave me not, my Guardian, until thou hast conducted me into the blessed vision of God, in the glory of which I with thee and God's Blessed Mother Mary and all the saints may rejoice for ever. Amen.[1]

On Whitsunday, May 20, 1548, St. Francis had the joy of seeing his three Japanese friends baptized with great solemnity by the Bishop of Goa in his Cathedral. Anjiro received the new

[1] Schurhammer, Epistolae, i, 447–62. The 'Oração ao aujo custodio' is on pp. 452–3. It is unnecessary to reproduce here the 'Prayer for the Conversion of the Gentiles' which St. Francis composed, as it is well known and to be found in many manuals of devotion.

name of Paul of Holy Faith, his servant that of John, and the
third man, who seems to have had an independent status until he
became entirely attached to Xavier, that of Antonio. As for Paul,
he said : ' I love Padre Francisco so dearly that I want to serve
him always and never part from him again.' The Viceroy, John
de Castro, died less than three weeks later, on June 6, and Francis,
the expert quartermaster of souls, was with him to his holy end.
The great soldier, second in glory only to Albuquerque, made no
will because he had nothing to bequeath, but he charged the
Saint and two of his Franciscan friends with a commission they
loved, which was to write to King John on his behalf, supplicating
for the reward of six veterans, as poor in everything except valour
as himself. The conquistadores have many dark deeds to their
account, but sometimes they touched the very summits of moral
grandeur.

The chief concern of St. Francis in Goa after de Castro's death
and while he waited for a change in the monsoon to waft him
south appears to have been the extraordinary College of St. Paul,
which had nothing like it on earth. There were some sixty
students ranging from the age of thirteen to twenty-one, and by
race Malabars, Bengalis, Malays, East Indians, Siamese, Ethiopians,
Kaffirs, Malagasies, Chinese, and Burmese. Between them, they
spoke nine widely differing languages, and it was hoped that,
when given some European culture and adequate religious
training, they would return to their several countries as priests or
catechists to spread the Catholic faith. The Africans and natives of
Madagascar on the College roll were the children of slaves, either
presented by their Portuguese owners or bought from them and
then manumitted. It was strangely fitting that those boys should
have been taught Latin by the rather bewildered Lancillotto out
of *The Maid of Andros* and *The Eunuch* of Publius Terentius the
African, once himself a boy-slave in Rome.[1] From the time of his

[1] Wicki, *Documenta Indica*, i, 136. Lancillotto mentions that he also
expounded the Eclogues of Virgil, ' some Fables and two Epistles of Ovid ',
and the *De duplici rerum et verborum copia* of Erasmus. During Lent, out of
regard for the season, he went over to an epistle of St. Jerome. He liked his
boys and said that if only ' they were given a competent master, they would
soon become learned men '.

first meeting with St. Francis Xavier in 1542, Diogo de Borba, founder and mainstay of the seminary, had desired him to take over its management. Francis could not do that, but he gave to the College half of his human assets in the person of Father Paul of Camerino. As the years went by and more Jesuits arrived from Portugal—three in 1545, nine in 1546, ten in 1548—the Saint assigned an increasing number of them to the same institution where they functioned purely as teachers and spiritual directors, without any voice in the general management, in the selection or dismissal of pupils, or in domestic arrangements. These things were the concern of four lay majordomos or school managers, presided over by Cosmas Anes, Controller of the King's Revenue and second most important man in the King's Indian Government. The double jurisdiction did not work very well, as the Jesuits were expected to sing the liturgy and attend processions and funerals, things dear to the Latin heart but not to the Constitutions of St. Ignatius Loyola, while the majordomos, on their side, proved to be inadequate housekeepers. In 1545, Father Lancillotto complained that the boys were being half starved, partly to save expenses, and partly with the mistaken idea of hardening them for their future apostolate. Cosmas Anes, busy with many other things, showed an increasing desire to be free of all responsibility for the College and looked hopefully to St. Francis. St. Francis, conditionally on the King's assent, accepted the burden, which was to weigh heavily on his remaining few years, and Simon Rodriguez, who had recently been made superior of all Jesuits in Portugal and her colonies, sent out as first rector Father Antonio Gomes, one of the most distinguished subjects under his command. Gomes, who was not yet thirty, had already won fame in his own country as a mover of hearts. It is said that when he appeared in a town, the crowd would abandon the bull-ring and flock to listen to him. In India, a Jesuit who heard him reported that he not only made the congregation weep by his eloquence, but himself, the preacher, also. Tears in the pulpit can be immensely effective, but the power to shed them and draw them is not the only quality necessary in a religious superior. He must be a humble man, not too strongly wedded to his own ideas, ready to be advised by others more experienced than himself, full of patient, understanding charity towards those under him, and with a mind big enough to be keenly aware that his order is not the Catholic Church, but only a tiny derivative part of it whose interests are ever to be subordinated to the good of the whole. In all those respects, and despite his zeal and other virtues, Antonio Gomes appears to have lamentably failed. He suffered, it seems, from some sort of *folie de grandeur*, an over-weening self-confidence that exasperated men familiar with the almost insuperable difficulties of the Church in India. He had been a brilliant student of the Jesuit college in Coimbra, and he quickly let the world know that he proposed to turn St. Paul's College, Goa, into a second Coimbra. But to do that it would be necessary to get rid of those Kaffirs and wild men from the Moluccas, substituting for them the sons of Portuguese gentlemen and Portuguese ladies, who would in due course join the great Society of Jesus and carry all before them. ' No doubt but we are the people and wisdom shall die with us,' about summed up his attitude.

That year, 1548, a much larger fleet than usual, containing eleven ships, set sail from Lisbon for Goa, and for the first time brought entire Portuguese families to India. It also brought the first contingent of Dominicans to arrive in the East since the Middle Ages. The Jesuits came in two parties, five on the *São Pedro*, and five, including the new rector, on the *Gallega*, which became separated from her consorts at the Canaries and arrived at Goa a month late, after St. Francis had left the city. But though he missed Antonio Gomes and his party, Francis had the deep satis-faction of greeting the other contingent on September 4. ' Our joy at seeing Padre Maestro Francisco was inexpressible,' wrote one of the new arrivals, ' and his charity past all understanding.' That was said by Father Gaspar Berze, a Netherlander aged thirty-three, born on an island at the mouth of the Scheldt. He was a man of heroic mould, formerly a soldier in the armies of Charles V, then a hermit at Montserrat, and finally a Jesuit in Coimbra. In a long and vivid letter to Europe Gaspar told of the eventful voyage which he and his four hundred fellow-passengers had, especially as they rounded the Cape and ran into the most terrible storm that the captain and pilot, seasoned mariners, had ever experienced. The captain took the Father aloft and bade him *conjurar la mar*, which he did with a right good will, making the sign of the cross three times over each of the huge billows as they crashed on the staggering ship, and shouting into the gale, *Christus vincit, Christus regnat, Christus imperat, Christus ab omni malo nos defendat*. At Mozambique, Gaspar spent all his nights at the hospital in attendance on six score of men and women desperately ill with contagious diseases, cooking little meals for them as best he knew how, mixing and administering their medicines, hearing their confessions, and easing by his loving, bracing counsels their passage to eternity. Ships of lighter draught than the big carracks often passed between Mozambique and Goa, so Berze's reputation went ahead of him and the first thing St. Francis did after their warm accolade was to ask him to preach on September 8, the feast of our Lady's Nativity. ' He charged me very earnestly to speak up,' wrote the good Father. ' The church was packed, as many people had heard of our adventures on the voyage, but Father Francis got no joy of my sermon because large numbers failed to understand me through being unable to catch what I said. He left for Cape Comorin shortly afterwards, giving me a parting order that I was to practise my voice in the church at night with a view to amplifying it. I did this till my brethren were satisfied with the results, and then the people began to relish the sermons.'[1]

In Father Berze's company there was a young Spaniard from Cordoba named Juan Fernandez. He had been a dandy in his day, a leader of fashion, wealthy and accomplished. It appears to have been a sermon of the fiery and cantankerous Jesuit orator, Francisco Estrada, that startled Juan out of his aesthete's dreams. The sight of other men, exquisites like himself, heartily flogging themselves in public in the good old mediaeval fashion after the sermon put his frivolous thoughts away for ever. He journeyed

---

[1] Wicki, *Documenta Indica*, i, 386–93. Berze was an M.A. of Louvain and a genuinely learned man, especially in scripture. He had the candour and open-heartedness of a child.

to Coimbra and offered his life to Simon Rodriguez on condition that he be accepted as a lay brother. Simon, always something of a fantast, ordered him as a test of his sincerity to don his latest fancy in suits and to ride through the main street on a donkey with his head to the animal's tail and holding the tail in his hands. Neither St. Ignatius Loyola nor St. Francis Xavier liked those methods of the Egyptian Desert any better than might a sophisticated man of today, but in this as in other respects the King's confidant, Rodriguez, was a law unto himself. As for Fernandez, he did not in the least mind being made a public show. He had got beyond all that nonsense, had escaped Vanity Fair, to find his Beulah-Land in Japan and there to die contentedly of hardship, persecution and overwork at the age of forty-one. At Goa, St. Francis looked upon him with love and marked him for his very own.

Having saluted his newly arrived brethren, Francis embarked once again to make the long tedious voyage to the Fishery Coast where so much of his heart seemed permanently fixed. Caravel, toni, fusta, catur (whence our cutter), nobody knows what he sailed in, but they were all of much of a muchness for discomfort and they all certainly precluded the possibility of saying Mass. About a month after his departure a rumour reached Goa that he had been shot at with arrows by enemies of the Christian name, that they had several times set fire to huts in which he rested a little at night, and that finally they had succeeded in killing him by some cruel means. 'His friends here,' wrote Gaspar Berze, 'and that means nearly everybody, were plunged into sorrow. Some desired to go in search of his body with a view to his canonization, saying that even if it cost them thirty thousand ducats it must be brought about. They spoke of miracles which they knew him to have wrought, but which he concealed. As to that I say nothing, for I do not think it to be a proper subject of discussion, but rather of great thankfulness to God from whom all good proceeds. We tried as well as we could to keep going, though there was a great void in our hearts, and would be in India.' Then suddenly Alfonso Cyprian and Manuel de Morais arrived from Cape Comorin and sorrow was turned into joy.

Father Francis, they announced, was very much alive. He had sent them to make ready for a mission to the poor abandoned Christians of Socotra. On the Fishery Coast he was received like a conqueror, *con grandissima alegría y fiesta*. Punnaikâyal, which he made his centre this time, burst into bunting and he was carried shoulder high to the church by his beloved Paravas. No saint ever longed more ardently than he to give God the testimony of his blood, '*mais la mort fuit encore sa grande âme trompée*', and instead of martyrdom he was accorded an ovation. ' We have a living martyr among us,' is what the Goan Fathers said of him, and they greatly preferred it that way.[1]

At Punnaikâyal, as before at Manapad, St. Francis brought the missionaries of Cape Comorin together for a brief reunion, half a holiday and half a retreat. One Father, the ex-barrister Francis Henriques, who was trying to shield the fifteen thousand Christians of Travancore from the hostile attentions of Mârtanda Varma, could not come to the meeting. The Raja, who had originally given St. Francis permission to baptize the Macuas in hopes of obtaining Portuguese trade and protection, turned on the neophytes when he saw his hopes unrealized. He summoned Henriques to his court and strictly forbade him, on pain of expulsion or even death, to make any more Christians, but that

---

[1] Wicki, *Documenta Indica*, i, 312, 402. Goa made festivity for a week when Gaspar Berze argued a prominent Brahman named Locu into the Church. His wife dutifully came with him and they were baptized with great ceremony by the Bishop at St. Paul's College, the Governor, Garcia de Sá, acting as godfather. Afterwards, there was a splendid procession through the decorated streets, while all the church bells of the city rang a joyful paean for this victory over the pagan gods. Other Brahmans who had no intention of being argued away from Vishnu and Shiva entered into the spirit of the thing and rode in the procession themselves. It was not against their principles, for they held, and still hold, all religions to be aspects or phases of one fundamental religion, a religion which includes millions of Indians, perhaps even a majority of Indians, believing in and devoutly worshipping a personal, infinite, only God, in the guise of Krishna, an avatar of Vishnu, and other millions of polytheists and animists, bowing down to stocks and stones, and yet other millions of pantheists, though they repudiate the name and weave shimmering webs of metaphysics over what to all intents and purposes is a void and abyss of nothingness. The last group must be comparatively small, for Indians are too profoundly religious by nature and nurture to be satisfied with absorption into an impersonal Brahma or Absolute.

fearless man answered him in the best forensic style that the sea belonged to Portugal and that if he harmed the Christian fishermen he would account to Portugal for it. Portugal, however, was very busy with the Moslems of the far north at the time, so the persecution went on in the south, and the disheartened Henriques, never celebrated for patience, moved to a more promising field of action at Châliyam, a town and fort on an island a little to the south of Calicut, whose raja had shown a leaning towards Christianity. Though so great a rover himself by the disposition of God, St. Francis Xavier strongly opposed any tendency of his men to stray from their assigned missions, no matter how good might be the intention, and accordingly, when he learned of Henriques's adventure, he ordered him back to Travancore. Then, from Punnaikâyal, he wrote him the following letter :

God our Lord knows how much better pleased I would be to see you and to console myself with the sight of your labours than merely to write to you. Compared with you and that hard work of yours undertaken solely for the love and service of God, the voluptuaries who enjoy at their ease the delights of this world are to be greatly pitied, and you and others of whom St. Paul said the world was not worthy are to be greatly envied. I am sending Balthasar Nunes to help you with the work in Travancore and to be a comfort to you while you wait to receive from the hand of God your ultimate reward. I am returning to Goa to do some business on behalf of the Christians here, which I hope will succeed and be the means of bringing many others to the faith. Will you please commend it to God and beg Him that, in spite of our great sins and unworthiness to be His instruments, He would yet be pleased in His infinite goodness and love to make use of us for the increase of His holy Church. Padre Antonio Criminali will come to see you soon. If you are unwell and find the work too hard, do as he shall tell you, whether it be to stay where you are or to go to Goa for a cure. Do not be despondent because you have not succeeded as well as you desired with your Christians. After all, they were born idolaters and now the King is opposed to them.

Remember too that you are bearing more fruit than you think in giving the divine life to new-born babes by your diligent and careful baptizing of them. For if you reflect on the matter you will find that few people, whether white or black, go from India to Paradise, except such as die in a state of innocence at the age of fourteen or under. Take notice, then, my brother Francisco Henriques, that you are doing far more good in your kingdom of Travancore than you imagine. Think how many children have died in their baptismal innocence and are now in the glory of Paradise who would never have had the vision and joy of God but for you! The Enemy of human nature heartily hates you and would have you away from where you are, so that nobody might go to Heaven from Travancore. It is a habit of the devil to represent to the servants of Jesus Christ that they might be doing better work for God elsewhere than where they are, his evil purpose being to disquiet and unsettle a soul in order to lure and drive him away from his post. I fear me that the enemy has you under just such assault, creating trouble and affliction for you that he may rid Travancore of your presence. . . . No wonder he wants you away, seeing that you have saved more souls in your eight months in Travancore than you did in Portugal or elsewhere since you have been a priest. . . .

A man might surely have been tempted to break the law deliberately to obtain such an admonition as that![1]

While on the Fishery Coast, St. Francis learned that the old oppression of the Christian Paravas by Portuguese officials still went on. Captain de Paiva, who used to mulct the pearl-divers in the past, had been succeeded at Tuticorin by a man even more predatory and cruel. He treated the Indians like slaves, uprooted them from their villages, forced them to work for him, taxed them mercilessly, and compelled them to purchase from him licences

[1] Schurhammer, *Epistolae S. Francisci Xaverii*, i, 465–8. At the end of the letter Francis mentioned that he was sending Cyprian and Morais to Socotra, but politics frustrated his design. The Portuguese had made a pact with the Turks and the local sultan, and did not want the good trade relations disturbed by intruding Jesuits.

to buy the necessities of life or to engage in any other transaction. By law the Paravas were required to pay a tribute of their
pearls only to the King of Portugal, but this swindler snatched
a good proportion of them as private loot. The fleet that put out
for the oyster beds in March numbered usually four hundred
ships and boats of various kinds, and of these three hundred
belonged to the Paravas, who also supplied the seven thousand
divers. When the pearls were marketed at Tuticorin, as many as
a hundred thousand buyers from Bengal and other places would
appear and fortunes would quickly be made, but not by the poor
Indians who, often through *force majeure*, had risked their lives and
ruined their health to harvest the oysters. It was robbery and
exploitation on a colossal scale, and it made the generous heart of
St. Francis Xavier rage with anger. He was ready for almost any
expedient to bring those thieving white officials to book. Four
years earlier he had petitioned for the appointment at Tuticorin
of a man with dictatorial powers exceeding those exercised by
governors or viceroys, and then had strongly urged the highly
Erastian remedy of making the governor or viceroy personally
responsible, under dire threats of punishment, for all spiritual as
well as temporal affairs, including complete control of the thirty
Jesuits serving in the King's eastern dominions. Now, he returns
to Cochin and Goa from the land of his first love with an even
more surprising plan, the dead opposite of the other, maturing in
his head. It is that Father Simon Rodriguez, charming, lovable,
wayward Simon, possibly, as Francis well knew, the most
influential priest in Portugal, should be sent to India by his great
admirer the King, to whom he was as Joseph to Pharaoh, furnished
with supreme temporal as well as spiritual jurisdiction in the
affairs of native converts to Christianity. All civil appointments
would be made by Simon, and without his nod no wretched,
money-grubbing official would dare to move hand or foot in the
whole mission-land of India.[1] It was a Utopian scheme, a dream of
a bygone, less sophisticated world, and it never came to anything,
probably much to the relief of Simon Rodriguez.

Francis spent nearly two months at Cochin on his way back

[1] Schurhammer, *Epistolae*, ii, 47–54.

to Goa, as there was much business to be done in connection with Jesuit missions and colleges soon to spring into vigorous existence along the Malabar coast. St. Ignatius, Rodriguez, the King, were each addressed letters which reveal the sorrows, the fears, the frustrations, the prejudices, the indomitable hopes, the sympathies, the pity, the tenderness of his bruised but always buoyant heart. To Ignatius he wrote as follows on January 12, 1549:

> *Padre mio in Christi visceribus unico.* By the principal letters which all of us your least sons in India have transmitted through Master Simon, your holy Charity will have been informed of the results obtained in the service of God our Lord out here. All is done and will be done through His divine assistance and by the merit of your holy Sacrifices and prayers. Let me give you now some details of this land so remote from Rome. First, with regard to the native peoples, as far as my experience of them goes and speaking in a general way, they are decidedly barbaric. Those of them already Christians and the new converts we make daily give us of the Society a great deal of trouble. So it is necessary for your Charity to have a special solicitude for all your sons in India and to commend them to God without intermission, knowing as you do how burdensome it is to come to an understanding with and live among people devoid of knowledge of God and led by their ingrained habits of sin to disobey their reasons.

That dreadfully summary judgment of India and Indians calls for a word of comment. It proceeded from the ignorance of Francis and closely resembles such famous foreign pronouncements as that England is a nation of shopkeepers, or Ireland a country of bog-trotters, or America a confederation of gangsters and Hollywood divorcees, or Spain a geographical expression inhabited exclusively by fascist vermin. St. Francis knew next to nothing of the real India, no more than did any of his European contemporaries. Rabindranath Tagore said with great justice that ' the West did not send its heart to conquer the man of the East, but only its machine '. St. Francis assuredly brought his heart, but the machine was there first and got in his way. The mystery and majesty of India eluded him altogether. He, the man of uttermost prayer, never guessed that he was in the most religious land in the world, a land which had taught countless millions of men to pray, Chinese and Japanese no less than Hindus. How tawdry and insignificant the brief histories and imperial ambitions of Spain, Portugal, France, Holland and England appear when set over against India's three thousand years of ceaseless, passionate search for the eternal and the divine. The gross superstitions and popular idolatry which St. Francis witnessed are not, as he seemed to think, the whole of the story, but its least significant part and, all aberrations considered, it remains true of India, as it was of Francis himself, that God is its entire adventure. If he could have met his great contemporary in Northern India, the poet of Bhakti or tender devotion, Tulsi Das, he would have revised his views on Indian religion.

Continuing his letter to Ignatius, he said:

Life in these lands is rendered very hard by the extreme heats of summer and the winds and rains of winter, which, however, is not cold. Sustenance for the body is scarce in the Moluccas, in Socotra, and at Cape Comorin, and dealing with the people of such places is a toil and torment of prodigious heaviness for both soul and body. The languages of India are difficult to acquire, and the dangers to life temporal and spiritual difficult to avoid.[1] . . . All the Indians whom we have so far seen, Moors and Hindus alike, are extremely ignorant. Those who have to go among them to convert them need many virtues, obedience, humility, perseverance, patience, love of the neighbour, and great chastity, for there are many occasions of sin. And they must be men of good judgment, sound in wind and limb, if they are to bear the toil and hardship. I tell you this because of the necessity, in my opinion, of proving the mettle of those you intend to send out here. If your Charity cannot test them yourself, let it be done by persons who have your fullest

[1] St. Francis wrestled, not very successfully, with only two of India's 179 languages and 544 dialects.

confidence. It is very necessary. Padre mio, the man you will have to send to take charge of the College of Holy Faith at Goa, with its native students and members of our Society, must have two qualities in particular, apart from others required in every good superior, in the first place, a great spirit of obedience, so as to make himself loved by all our leading ecclesiastics and by the secular authorities who rule the country, they seeing him to be not a proud but a truly humble man. I say this, my Father, because our ecclesiastical and secular rulers out here are very insistent on being obeyed, and when they find us obedient they are satisfied and love us, whereas disobedience scandalizes them. The second thing necessary is that he should be affable and peaceable in his dealings with others, not stiff and rigorous, but using every means in his power to win the love of those under his command, whether Indians or members of our Society now here or yet to come, so that they may have no grounds for believing him to want to exact their obedience by strictness or servile fear. If they thought that, many would leave our Society, and we should get few recruits, whether Indians or others. I tell you this, Father of my soul, because our brethren here were little edified by an order emanating from N. [Antonio Gomes] that certain of his subjects whom he did not consider exemplary should be seized and transported in irons to Portugal. Never to this moment did it seem right to me to keep anyone in our Society against his will by forcible means, if it were not the force of love and charity. Rather did I dismiss those who wanted to stay when I found them unsuitable, and those I considered to have a true vocation I dealt with in all kindness to make them the stronger in it, seeing that they endure great hardship out here for the service of God our Lord. Besides, to my way of thinking, the Company of Jesus means the Company of love and harmony of hearts, not of rigour nor servile fear. . . .[1]

Francis went on to tell Ignatius, his *Padre mio unico*, that ne did not think the Catholic Church or the Society of Jesus could or

[1] Schurhammer, *Epistolae*, ii, 5–10.

would be perpetuated in India by the Indians themselves. The disadvantages of becoming Christian were too great for many to make the necessary sacrifice. It meant excommunication from one's caste and adhesion to the detested *Prangui* or Western barbarians who polluted the sacred soil of India. Never was there a religion at once more syncretistic and more nationalistic than Hinduism. St. Francis divined that hard fact very accurately and said that ' it bores the Indians to extinction to be asked to become Christians '.[1] But a worse deterrent than social ostracism was Portuguese oppression of those who had the courage to apply for baptism. The fact was that the Portuguese tended to despise the low-caste Indians from whose ranks most of the converts came, and did nothing to improve their temporal lot or to make acceptance of the faith less of a burden.

For these and many other reasons too long to set down [Francis continued] and because of much information I possess about Japan, which is an island near China containing no Moors nor Jews but only gentiles of a very inquisitive turn of mind, desirous of new knowledge both of God and of natural things, I have decided, with considerable satisfaction of heart, to go to that country, as there, I think, the results we of the Society may achieve during our earthly course can be maintained and developed by the Japanese themselves. . . .

His election of Japan did not in the least mean that St. Francis had given up India as hopeless. He never gave up India, and when he lay dying off the coast of China less than three years later he was still trying desperately to hoist on his broken back that symbolic Indian of his dream in Venice long ago. He mentioned to Ignatius that he had designated four of his thirty-two men to care for the abandoned and persecuted Christians of Socotra, and it was no fault of his that they could not reach the desolate island. Four more were at work in the Moluccas, two at Malacca, six in the Cape Comorin area, two in Quilon, and the same number in Bassein. In each of those widely separated places he

[1] ' *Les pesa mortalmente quando les hablamos y rogamos que se agan christianos.*'

had appointed a superior and given elaborate instructions as to the missionary methods to be followed. Only Goa where Antonio Gomes, the protégé of Simon Rodriguez, ruled over the remaining twelve Jesuits caused Francis anxiety, as he turned his face towards the land of the rising sun. He admired the zeal and ability of Gomes and spoke of him in warm terms to Ignatius, but he had been given plenty of reason for doubting his aptitude as a superior, especially in such a complicated place as Goa. The thorny problem of ' accommodation ', which later, in the days of Robert de Nobili, led to the endless and disastrous controversy about the Malabar Rites, arose for the first time in 1549. The Raja of Tanur, a small principality south of Calicut, had secretly become a Christian, not, it appears, for purely religious reasons. The point then came up whether this important convert, in whose honour the Goans staged a bull-fight, could be permitted to continue wearing the sacred cord and other caste marks of a Brahman. Bishop Albuquerque argued strongly that he might, for he would be in no worse case than Joseph of Arimathea and Nicodemus who were both friends and disciples of Christ, but secretly, for fear of the Jews. Besides, caste in India is a social rather than a religious institution, and there was really no compelling theological reason why the Raja should have been obliged to renounce the badges of his nobility. But Antonio Gomes was determinedly opposed to the concession. The Raja must declare himself openly and wear Christian dress, by which the uncompromising Rector undoubtedly meant Portuguese dress. He seemed to want to have everything done in India as it was done in Portugal, and that narrow parochial attitude of mind, so conspicuously absent in St. Francis Xavier, did more than anything else to hinder the progress of Christianity. Portuguese pride roused Indian pride and the result was stalemate.[1]

[1] Wicki, *Documenta Indica*, i, 535–47. Letter of Bishop Albuquerque to King John III. The situation of the Catholic Church in India today belies some of the misgivings of St. Francis. Of five thousand Catholic priests there 3,480 are of Indian blood and so are twenty bishops of the Indian hierarchy. Of nine thousand nuns six thousand are Indians. More than that, since India became a sovereign state European missionaries have been encouraged by ecclesiastical authority to take out papers of nationalization, and have done so on a large

While brooding on the problems of India and worrying about the fate of his brethren at St. Paul's College under their ruthless Rector, St. Francis conceived a little plot to get Gomes out of Goa without hurting his feelings. He pointed to rich and romantic Ormuz on its island at the mouth of the Persian Gulf, one of the most famous of Portugal's conquests, and stressed the need of a great preacher there to put the fear of God into the garrison and the traders, who were sunk in depravity, and even abandoning Christianity for Islam. Who better qualified than Father Antonio for this vitally important mission which so intimately concerned the honour of Portugal? But Antonio had become far too powerful a person in Goa to be side-tracked so easily, and at the mere suggestion of his going his influential friends created a clamour. St. Francis resigned himself to the situation and sent the rector he had in mind for St. Paul's, Gaspar Berze, to Ormuz, where that stalwart of God spent two and a half sweltering years working with ferocious energy, until he had achieved a veritable religious revolution among the devotees of mammon who swarmed there from every quarter of the globe. Ormuz was then the greatest horse-market in the world, and horse-traders are a class apart. Even they, and the Moors and Spanish Jews, learned to respect and indeed love the utterly selfless and fearless Gaspar and used to press him to accept bales of precious silks and other presents, which, however, he always graciously declined, poverty being with him a passion. He helped the Arabs, to give them their rightful name, and the Turks, who interested him greatly, and the fire-worshipping Persians, and the Sikhs, in their dealings with his devoted friend, the Portuguese Captain, Manuel de Lima; he disputed courteously in the Synagogue with the Jews' out-standing champion, Rabbi Solomon; and he thundered day in and day out, mightily assisted by a succession of earthquakes, at the wicked Portuguese until they came crawling on their knees

---

and ever increasing scale. This is magnificent and something that would have enthralled the heart of St. Francis Xavier. They are Indians now, no longer Belgians, Italians, Spaniards, Germans, French or English, and they could surely have made no nobler reparation for the imperial pride and aggression of Europe in the past.

for absolution. He was a strong man and still well on the right side of forty, but he died within four years of sheer physical exhaustion.[1]

The inspiration of Berze's life, as he himself plainly indicates, was Francis Xavier. Before he set out on the two months' voyage to his abominable island, St. Francis, on the eve of his own departure for Japan, gave him in writing a long *Lembrança* or memorandum concerning the work to be done and the methods to be followed in Ormuz. The intensity of the Saint's care for the missions he was about to leave behind is marvellously reflected in this eleventh-hour document, and it provides a perfect answer to those who say that he had grown tired of India and was itching to be away to a fresh and more congenial field of operations.

First and foremost [he begins] be mindful of yourself and of your relations with God and your conscience, because on these depend your power of being much use to your neighbour. Be quick and eager for lowly and obscure tasks, so that you may learn to be humble and ever to grow in humility. To this end, see that you and no other teach the prayers to the children of the Portuguese, to their slaves, men and women, and to the freed Christians of the island. Visit the poor in the Hospital, and exhort them to go to confession and Holy Communion, hearing them yourself when you can, and help them in their temporal needs also by putting in a good word for them with those in authority. Do the same for those in gaol, and try to get them to make a general confession of their whole past lives,

[1] Schurhammer, *Epistolae*, ii, 36; Wicki, *Documenta Indica*, i, 502–6, 597–698 (this being two drafts of an enormous and most interesting letter which Berze addressed to his Jesuit brethren in India and Europe from Ormuz on December 1 and 10, 1549). The text of his Disputation with the Jewish Rabbis in their Synagogue is given with the letters (l.c. pp. 700–25). It turns chiefly on the Blessed Trinity and reveals a very remarkable knowledge, not only of the Old Testament and Jewish history before and after Christ, but also of the Mishna, the Talmud, and the works of Origen. It was a truly impressive feat for a man without reference books of any kind and so busy that he never had a moment to himself from morning to night, and often through the night. The confessions alone would have broken any man less completely self-sacrificial than he, and all done on that terrible little furnace of an island, dry as a bone, *triste, sem refrigerio.*

as many of them never go to confession. Commend them to the
Confraternity of Mercy whose particular care they are, and who
have the means to help any poor suffering fellow.[1] You will
serve the *Misericordia* in every way you can and be a close
friend of the Brothers, helping them in all their good work.
When you find penitents obliged to make restitution but unable
to do so because those they wronged are unknown to them or
dead, tell them to give the whole sum to the *Misericordia*,
unless, indeed, you know of deserving cases on whom the alms
might safely be conferred. Not all the poor are deserving
and cadgers are to be found among them sunk in vice and sin.
The Brothers of Mercy know those gentry well, so whatever
alms you have to distribute, give them to the Brothers for
people in real need. Another advantage of this is that when it
becomes known that you have no help to give except spiritual,
you will not be approached by those seeking only for money.

The next piece of counsel may appear somewhat cynical,
especially coming from a man whose temptation throughout life
was to give his friendship and trust too easily. It runs:

In all your dealings, conversations, and friendships with
others, so conduct yourself as if they might one day be your
enemies. . . . Use such prudence with this wicked world and
you will live always at peace within your soul, and so have
greater fruition of God. The suspicions of friends that they
may be forgotten or neglected affords them many pretexts
for ceasing to be friendly, and that can be a cause of scandal to
our enemies and to those who do not know us.

That piece of stoical wisdom was certainly the result of St.
Francis's own experience and not borrowed from a book, though

[1] Wherever the Portuguese conquerors went they set up a branch of the
Confraternity which was devoted entirely to doing the Corporal Works of
Mercy. The Dutch and the English empire-builders had nothing even faintly
resembling this great Catholic institution, and it is to the lasting glory of little
Portugal that even in her proudest hours she never forgot the claims of the
unfortunate, whether poor, sick, imprisoned, or dead.

Publilius Syrus, who once won a prize for his mimes from Julius Caesar, has it in black and white: *Ita amicum habeas, posse ut facile fieri hunc inimicum putes.*[1] It is not as cynical as it looks, or all exercise of the great cardinal virtue of prudence would have to be so described. In any case, a little cynicism is a healthy thing in a world as full of romantic nonsense and political humbug as the one into which we had the misfortune to be born and, besides, it gives a certain pleasant spice to life as well as to literature, provided that it be genial and without malice, except of the merry French kind. St. Francis next returns to his first and fundamental point:

> Do not forget to make the particular examination of conscience at least once a day, if you cannot make it twice. Let your own conscience be your care and concern much more than anybody else's, for if a man is not solicitous to be good and holy himself, how is he going to make other people such?

After that very fair question, he turns to the subject of preaching:

> Preach as often as ever you can, ... but eschew altogether in your sermons subjects of controversy and subtle theological questions. Be very clear, and teach the people what is right and what is wrong. Reprove vice, and show your sorrow that men should offend God and condemn themselves to the everlasting pains of Hell. Treat of sudden death which takes men off sadly unprepared, and touch on some point or points of the Passion, by way of a colloquy between a sinner and God. Do everything in your power to move your listeners to contrition, sorrow and tears, and incite them to go to confession and Holy Communion. ... Take particular care never in your sermons to denounce any man who holds a public charge, for there is a danger that such people may become worse instead of

[1] So regard your friend as though you thought that he might easily become an enemy.

better if reprehended from the pulpit. The place to admonish
them is privately in their own houses or in the confessional,
when you have become friends with them. The better friends
you are, the straighter you can talk, but while you are only on
nodding terms be slow to scold. Deliver your strictures with a
pleasant front, and in gentle, loving words rather than harshly.
Now and again, you might embrace the culprits and humble
yourself before them, so that they may take your correction
in better part. If you rebuke important or rich persons in good
round terms, I am afraid they only lose patience and turn hostile.

In his advice about the hearing of confessions, St. Francis is
almost amusingly insistent on the necessity of closely questioning
the King's officials as to the source of their wealth. It is no good
asking them, 'Have you acquired any property that rightly
belongs to others?' for to this they will reply readily, 'Of
course not,' it being so habitual with them, so much a part of
the established order, to gain their living by wicked means that
they no longer give it a thought. And here is another piece of
the Saint's humorous 'cynicism': 'Some people suffer no
remorse of conscience because they haven't got a conscience.'
Father Gaspar must therefore put captains, factors, and other civil
servants through a searching inquiry to discover whether they
are bound to make restitution, asking them, for instance, whether
they have helped themselves from the King's revenues, or taken
a slice from the wages they were supposed to pay others, or
reserved for private bargaining goods which ought to have gone
on the free market. Francis, through long and sad experience,
was wise to all the tricks, and could he have prevailed, the
Santa Misericordia's finances would have greatly benefited. The
traders of Ormuz were not to be lightly absolved. Father Berze
must stimulate them into carefully examining their laden consciences for two or three days before he hears their confession, and
then he is to defer absolution for an equal time, during which to
give them some meditations from the first or purgative part of
St. Ignatius's *Spiritual Exercises*, dealing with such fundamental
themes as the purpose of man's existence, death, judgment, Hell

and Heaven, and concurrently to see that they restored ill-gotten gains or handed them over to the Misericordia, that they resumed friendly relations with neighbours not in their good books, and that they withdrew from occasions of fleshly and other sins of their addiction. ' Make sure that they do these things before you absolve them, because they are very ready with promises in confession, but very slow afterwards to carry them out.' With sinners in general Francis, who counted himself among the worst of them, was nothing if not compassionate. Father Berze is told not to be rigorous with the poor souls nor to frighten them, ' but rather to speak to them of the great mercy of God and to make easy for them what is at best a difficult task.' With one class of penitents he must be especially gentle, those who out of shame have not the courage to confess the ugly things they have done. ' Put heart into them as well as ever you can. Tell them that whatever they have to say will be no news to you, for you have knowledge of much graver sins. Make everything as easy as possible for them. Sometimes, in such cases, as I know from experience, people are helped by your telling them in general terms about your own lamentable past.'

In the giving of penances the Saint entirely deprecates extravagant and grotesque mortifications, such as Simon Rodriguez, following some of the ancient Desert Fathers, believed in. ' They lead only to mockery and derision,' he said, ' and it is far more edifying to have the penitent serve in the hospital or at the Casa da Misericordia or in the capacity of prison visitor.' Berze is to be particularly careful to keep on good terms with the official garrison chaplain and any other secular priests who might appear at Ormuz:

You will defer to the Father Vicar in everything and obtain his permission to preach, hear confessions, and perform other sacred ministries, always striving to be his good friend and never for any reason breaking with him. . . . To the Captain you will be obedient *em grande maneira*, and you must stick by him too, even though you observe him to be up to mischief. When you and he have become friends it will be time enough to express

to him with great love, humility and gentleness the sorrow
you feel that he should so soil his soul and his honour. . . . In
your dealings with all and sundry be pleasant and cheerful.
Avoid stiffness and surliness, for a gloomy face will deter
many from approaching you and profiting by your counsel.
So, let your looks and words speak welcome to every comer,
and if you have to admonish somebody, do it with love and
graciously, giving no reason whatever for him to think that
you find his company distasteful.

There is much more of this document, which is saturated
throughout with the teaching of the *Spiritual Exercises* of St.
Ignatius, but sufficient of it has now been given to indicate its
scope and character. It might almost be called an autobiography
of the soul of St. Francis Xavier.[1]

Since he could not, without raising a storm, have Gaspar
Berze as his deputy in Goa, to that modest man's exceeding relief,
St. Francis did his best to save as many of the brethren as possible
from the scorpions of Antonio Gomes by a division of authority.
Gomes might continue to rule as he listed at Goa, because there
was no way of stopping him, but all Jesuits outside that city, at
Cape Comorin, for instance, were withdrawn from any jurisdiction which he might attempt to exercise over them. St. Francis
had quickly noticed Antonio's proclivity for expanding his
empire, and countered it by making his first companion, the
veteran Father Paul of Camerino, superior of all Jesuits not
directly connected with Goa's polyglot seminary. For the poor
martyrs there, he could do nothing as yet, and many months

[1] Schurhammer, *Epistolae S. Francisci Xaverii*, ii, 86–101. Francis counsels
Gaspar never to accept presents of any value because they destroy a man's
independence. ' How is he to find his tongue to rebuke the fault of somebody
from whom he has just accepted a substantial gift? But I do not mean that
you must refuse absolutely everything. You can take a gift of water or fruit or
such small things as it would be ungracious to decline.' The word *agoa* here
puzzled some of the old writers, so they omitted it, not knowing that Ormuz
was entirely without water, except such as could be caught during the rainy
season in the vast cisterns built by the Portuguese, or else brought in tanks from
the Persian mainland. The ruins of the cisterns and of Albuquerque's fort are
still to be seen on the now practically abandoned island.

later Father Nicholas Lancillotto had to write as follows to
St. Ignatius:

> Antonio Gomes is a good man, so full of knowledge, zeal
> and fervour that he considers it necessary for all the brethren
> in India to be born anew before they can even understand what
> our Society is for. He therefore began his rule by laying his
> hands on our eating, drinking, sleeping, reading, praying, even
> saying Mass, quantitatively and qualitatively, as though he had
> taken for his maxim *Recedant vetera, nova sint omnia*. We were
> not the only ones to suffer, for he constrained and harassed the
> Indians of the College also with a variety of orders and constitu-
> tions, fixing hours of prayer, contemplation and examination of
> conscience. I had been familiar with those students for years and
> knew them to be incapable of following such a régime. I
> accordingly told Father Gomes that new wine ought not
> to be put into old bottles, that we should proceed step by
> step with the young men, and be satisfied that they are
> Christians. But he would not listen to me, and after I had
> departed for Cochin by the direction of Father Francis, the
> Indians of the College began to leap over the walls and
> run away. . . .[1]

That was the situation, and St. Francis must look on helplessly
from afar while the new broom from Europe swept away much
of the Indian good will which he had so patiently and laboriously
won. He had every reason to be aggrieved with Simon Rodriguez
for appointing such a man, but instead wrote him a series of
letters in which was no shadow of complaint but only ardent pleas
that something be done for the maltreated Christians of Socotra,
that his *muy gran amigo*, the Franciscan Frei Vincente, be helped
with the running of his excellent college for the sons of the St.
Thomas's Christians at Cranganore, and above all that Simon

---

[1] Wicki, *Documenta Indica*, ii, 170–1. The Latin line quoted by the dryly
humorous Nicholas, ' Let old things retire, let all things be new ', is from the
well-known Corpus Christi hymn composed by St. Thomas Aquinas, *Sacris
solemniis*.

himself should rejoice his Jesuit sons by coming to India and taking complete charge of their affairs.[1] Like Gaspar Berze, Father Paul of Camerino received a memorandum of instructions and advice from Francis, delimiting his authority and pleading passionately for union and harmony between him and Antonio Gomes. Francis knew his Paul, and that, with all his virtues and considerable practical ability, he tended to be somewhat stubborn and crotchety in his conduct of affairs.

First and before all things [he began], I charge you by the love you bear to God our Lord and to Father Ignatius and to all of the Company of Jesus that, with deep lowliness of heart and careful tact, you live in love and charity with Antonio Gomes. . . . Again, I beg you, I order you in virtue of your vow of obedience to Father Ignatius, to see to it that there be no discord nor dissension between you and Antonio Gomes, but rather great love and charity. . . . Continue, my Brother, to progress in virtue and to set the good example which you have always done. Write to me in great detail about the affairs of St. Paul's College, and tell me of the love and charity that

[1] Schurhammer, *Epistolae*, ii, 35–46. St. Francis at this time wrote several letters to King John pleading, as before, for a greater assertion of his authority over officials in India and asking for help to be given to the Franciscan College, and that his Highness should write a letter ' *de muito amor* ' to Jacob Mar Abuna, head of the St. Thomas's Christians. This good old man (he had been at work in India for forty-five years) was a bishop from Mesopotamia, the land that had supplied the Malabar Christians with their prelates for a thousand years. Technically, from the Catholic point of view, he was a schismatic, though not in the least schismatically inclined and on terms of intimate friendship with the Franciscans and St. Francis Xavier. The Malabar Christians, who were a real phenomenon of Church history, had been cut off from all contact with the West by the rise of Islam and took to themselves the only bishops available. Christological problems passed over their heads and they probably had no idea that their bishops were out of communion with the Church of the West. Neither, very likely, had the bishops themselves, as Nestorianism had long ceased to be a live issue. It seems a pity that the admirable Frei Vincente and others should have persuaded Mar Abuna to adopt the Latin liturgy instead of his own venerable Chaldean rite. The matter caused trouble and real instead of nominal schism later on, but that was all happily cleared up by the Popes of our own time, and the great majority of the Malabar Christians, now in complete communion with Rome, retain their ancient liturgy.

subsists between yourself and Antonio Gomes. . . . Entirely yours, Francis.

Francis was not nearly so much of a *Divino Impaciente*, a heavenly hustler, as he has often been represented. He first heard of Japan in December, 1547, when he was at the half-way house of Malacca, and could easily have gone there with Anjiro immediately. But he did nothing of the kind. He, as it were, boxed his compass and turned right away from the tempting vision to give another sixteen solid months of the few years that remained to him to the service of the imperilled souls of a few hundred brave, unscrupulous white men, and to thirty or forty thousand of their humble brown dependants, least regarded children of the great land now lovingly greeted by them and by all her millions, *Bandé Mataram*, Hail, Mother! Mother India.

CHAPTER XIII

JAPAN AND THE WAY THITHER

TENS of thousands of Europeans and Americans alive today have been to Japan. The journey there can be made in a few days and very comfortably by aeroplane. A man who has seen Tokyo, or even Hiroshima, unless, indeed, he happened to be there when the bomb fell, is no longer lionized by the ladies' clubs or the lecture societies, but finds himself reduced to the ranks of the uncountable Toms, Dicks and Harrys who have been to New York. Japan, in fact, has unveiled herself, or has been compelled to unveil, with a vengeance. She is as trite as the Riviera. It was a very different story only a hundred years ago, and four hundred years ago there was no story at all, but only a surmise in people's minds caused by reading Marco Polo. Even the bold makers of maps, who hesitated at little, hardly dared to sketch Japan in their lucubrations, for they had no notion as to where it was, or what was its shape, or, indeed, whether it was at all. We have seen St. Francis Xavier, who was as well briefed as any man, for had he not a genuine Japanese to instruct him? describing the mysterious country to St. Ignatius as *una isla cerca de la China*. Apparently the untravelled Anjiro imagined Kyushu, on which stood his native Kagoshima, to be the whole of Japan, but it did not take St. Francis very long to learn on his two tired feet that a second, and very much larger island named Honshu, at least by foreigners, was also involved. Whether he ever learned of the existence of Shikoku and Hokkaido is doubtful, as he makes no mention of them, but he seems to have been the first Western man to pluralize Japan into 'islands', which was itself something of a geographical discovery. The sketchiness of the information given him by Anjiro is evident in the letter to St. Ignatius from Cochin: ' I have made up my mind to proceed at once to the place where the King resides, and then to visit the

341

universities where the Japanese make their studies, with a great
hope that Jesus Christ our Lord will help me.' It would be many
a weary day before Francis reached Miyako, the great and attractive city that was capital of Japan for more than a millennium
prior to 1868,[1] and then only to find that the ' King ' he sought,
Go-Nara-tenno, one hundred and fifth descendant of the sun
goddess, Amaterasu, was a monarch such as Spain and Portugal
never knew, *quasi*-divine and the fountain of honour, but without
a shred of political power or authority. That was not the sort of
king Francis believed in or wanted.

It was to be the same disillusion with regard to the ' universities ' which he fondly imagined as Eastern equivalents of Paris
or Coimbra, but found to be merely large Buddhist monasteries.
He went on to tell Ignatius some more of the remarkable information imparted to him by Anjiro, alias Paul of Holy Faith:

> Paul says that the Japanese acquired their religion from a
> country named Chengico,[2] which, according to him, lies
> beyond China and Tartary, and takes three years to get there
> and back, starting from Japan. I shall write to you from Japan
> and give you the fullest information about the customs of the
> country, its literature, and the doctrine taught at that great
> university of Chengico. Paul tells me that in the whole of China
> and in Tartary, a huge country between China and Chengico,
> no other doctrine is held except that taught at Chengico. After
> seeing the writings of Japan and consulting the professors at the
> universities, I shall give you a full account of all that I learn,
> and I shall not neglect to write to the University of Paris which
> will inform the other universities of Europe. I am taking with
> me Father Cosmas de Torres, a priest from Valencia who
> joined the Society here in India, and also the three Japanese
> young men. With the help of God, we shall set sail in April of
> this year, 1549, our route lying by Malacca and China, and then

[1] It is the present Kyoto, meaning ' capital ', which has a population of over
a million and is still a great religious and cultural centre.
[2] In the copies made of St. Francis's letter in Europe, the semi-mythical
Chengico appears variously as Chiugico, Chimguinquo, Chynguinco, Chem-
singho, and Chinzinquo !

on to Japan, which is one thousand three hundred leagues or more from Goa. I could go on writing endlessly about the great comfort I get out of the thought of this voyage, so full of the peril of death from terrible storms, shoals, and abundant pirates that it is marvellous luck if two ships out of every four survive. I would not give up going to Japan even if I knew for certain that dangers awaited me more formidable than I had ever before encountered, such and so strong is my trust in God our Lord that our holy faith will grow there mightily. . . . I greatly desire, my Father, that for the space of a year you would get some one of the Society to say a monthly Mass for me at San Pietro in Montorio, in the chapel marking the place where, according to tradition, St. Peter was crucified. For the love of our Lord, I beg your Charity to commission some one in the house to write me news of all the professed of our Society, their number and present stations, also how many colleges you have and what are the particular obligations of the professed, as well as much other news about the work the Society is doing. I am leaving instructions at Goa that the letters are to be sent to Malacca where they will be copied and dispatched to me in Japan by various routes. And so I come to an end, begging your holy Charity, *Padre mio de mi anima observantissimo*, kneeling on the ground as I write as though I had you here present before me, to commend me earnestly and much to God our Lord in your holy Sacrifices and prayers that He may give me to know His holy will in this present life and the grace to fulfil it perfectly. Amen. And I make the same petition to all of our Society. From Cochin, January 12, 1549. Your least and most useless son, Francis.[1]

[1] Schurhammer, *Epistolae S. Francisci Xaverii*, ii, 10–12, 15–16. Anjiro's geography was as vague and misleading as the rest of his information, which St. Francis had painfully to unlearn. By his Tartary must be understood Tibet and by his Chengico, otherwise Tenjiko, the fatherland of Gautama the Buddha, which lay somewhere on the Indian border of Nepal. It seems that a great Buddhist monastery grew up there with a school attached which exercised wide influence in China, and through China and Korea on Japan. The place had disappeared centuries before the time of St. Francis when Hinduism prevailed over Buddhism in India, but the memory of it lingered in Japan, a country of very long memories. It was quite erroneous to assert, as did Anjiro,

St. Francis often wrote his long letter to Europe in triplicate, sending the original and copies by different ships as a precaution against all being lost. The drafts were substantially the same, but there might be some such pleasant addition as the following to one or other of them: ' I am sending you [Ignatius] the alphabet of Japan. They write very differently from the way we do, beginning at the top of the page and going down perpendicularly to the foot of it. I asked Paul why his people did not write in our fashion, to which he riposted, " Why do you not write in ours, seeing that men's heads are above and their feet below and so it is natural for them to write up and down? " ' Francis mentioned also that, though Paul wrote the Japanese characters beautifully and had even transcribed the Gospel of St. Matthew in them, he could not read Japanese books because they were invariably composed in Chinese ideographs, which were not understood except by the learned world of Japan. Francis remarked very acutely that the language of the books was to everyday colloquial Japanese speech much as ancient Latin is to modern Italian or Spanish, which is precisely the illustration given by Captain Frank Brinkley, in his day the foremost English authority on Japan. The characters used by Anjiro and the language they stood for were abbreviations of Chinese ideographs evolved in Japan to represent not ideas or letters but syllables, a system of writing which came to be known as *kana* and had two forms, *katakana* (square, with forty-eight syllables) and *hiragana* (cursive), both equally diabolically difficult to memorize, to pronounce, to understand, or to use.[1]

---

that the Buddhism of Chengico was the only doctrine taught in China, there being also the wholly different Confucianism and Taoism, not to speak of riotous polytheism and animism, while in Japan Shinto, a primitive religion based on ancestor and nature worship, continued to live on side by side with Buddhism after that great cult had peacefully conquered the whole country and taken over the Shinto temples. In this letter of Francis to Ignatius there is a charming tribute to the Jesuit of Jewish blood, Father Henry Henriques, whose health was very bad. ' For the love of God our Lord,' says Francis, ' write to him and console him, because he is such a good man and doing such wonderful work.'

[1] The Japanese syllabary which St. Francis caused to be transmitted to Rome caused a great deal of wonderment there. Polanco sent a specimen to St. Peter

In a letter to Rodriguez from Cochin, January 20, 1549, St. Francis expressed a hope, apparently naïve, but later, through the power of his example, fulfilled abundantly: ' Please God, in the course of time many of our Society will go to China, and from thence to the great schools of Chengico situated beyond China and Tartary.' Less than a week later, he wrote again to Rodriguez: ' The ships have just arrived from Malacca bringing news beyond possibility of doubt that all the ports of China have been closed to the Portuguese, but that is not going to stop me going to Japan, as I told you in my last letter. There is no better rest in this restless world than to face imminent peril of death solely for the love and service of God our Lord. . . .'[1] Six days later, Francis addressed Simon for a third time:

So many people ask me to write to you on their behalf, and it is such a pleasure to write to you in any case that I think I get as much consolation from the exercise as I do from reading your letters. The bearers of the present are two married men from Malacca, excellent fellows and good Christians, who have certain obligations to fulfil in Portugal. . . . They will give you all the news of China and Japan. All my good and devoted friends are frightened and astonished at the prospect of my going on such a long and such a perilous voyage, but I am even more astonished at their little faith. God our Lord is master of the tempests that blow in the seas of China and Japan, even

---

Canisius at Ingolstadt, but called it an alphabet, which was a great mistake. St. Peter showed the weird drawings to his friend Johann Albrecht Widmanstadt, the Chancellor of Lower Austria, who was an Orientalist and excitedly asked for more. But, alas, Polanco appears to have disposed of all his specimens in the meantime, and the poor Chancellor had to go without. He consoled himself by bringing out at Vienna a Syriac version of the Gospels.

[1] The Portuguese merchants had been forbidden access to the Chinese mainland since 1522, but they continued to trade furtively from the islands close to Canton with that city, and also from other coastal islands with Chang-chow in Fu-kien Province and Ning-po in Che-kiang. Those various chinks in the Celestial armour of exclusiveness were forcibly and firmly blocked in 1548, but pirates will not be denied, and the Portuguese, whom the Chinese authorities regarded as such, crept back to at least one island near the mouth of the Canton River which the Mandarins called Shang Ch'wan, but which the Catholic world has known and venerated for four hundred years as Sancian.

though they be the worst known to man, and He rules over all the winds and the shoals which, they say, cause the destruction of many ships, and He has in His power and control all the robbers of the sea, appallingly numerous though they are, and most cruel pirates likewise, who torture their victims, principally the Portuguese, in many wicked ways. As the Lord God is omnipotent over all these things, I am afraid of none of them, but only that I may be chastised by God for my negligence in His service, for my impotence and incompetence to increase the glory of the name of Jesus Christ among a people who know Him not. As for all the terrors and tribulations conjured up by my friends, I reckon them as naught, and have fear only of God. The fear inspired by created things operates only to the extent that their Creator permits. I beg you for the love of our Lord to be good to the two men going with this letter to Lisbon during the few days they are there. Please give them hospitality and help them willingly in every way you possibly can. When they return, would you send me by them a very big letter telling me about all of our Society in Italy, France, Flanders, Germany, Spain, Aragon, and the dear College of Coimbra. The letter will be sent from India addressed to the Fathers of the Society in Malacca, who will keep the original and dispatch three copies of it by various ships plying between Malacca and China and between China and Japan—this that I may receive at least one copy. May God reunite us in the glory of Paradise. Your loving brother, completely yours in Christ, Francisco.[1]

From Cochin St. Francis returned to Goa on a whirlwind visit, the last he would see of the city for many a day. One of the Fathers at the College there said that they had the pleasure only of a glimpse of him, though he wanted with all his heart to be in their company. He had a thousand things to do and a hundred people to

---

[1] Schurhammer, *Epistolae*, ii, 39, 56–7, 65–6. It is noticeable that Francis distinguishes Aragon, which incorporated Navarre, from the rest of Spain. Practically every letter he wrote at this time contains an appeal on somebody's behalf.

consult, so that the Church in India might flourish when he was gone. ' We all desired to go with him,' they wrote from the College, ' but as that could not be, he left us with the hope that, should God open a way in the Far East, he would send for us all to come out to him. He took us away with him in his heart and consoled us, saying that if we did not meet again in this world', the scattered Society of Jesus would be reunited in the Heavenly Jerusalem. . . .' His equipment for at least the first part of the tremendous journey consisted of ' a Mass outfit and a few needed books, though Father Francis read and studied in only one book ', namely, that Scriptural and Patristic Anthology of the Dalmatian Marcus Marulus, which he had brought with him from Europe and took with him on all his wanderings, as faithfully as he did the other Scriptural and Patristic Anthology, his Breviary. During the first stage of the voyage, which began on April 15 and involved a brief halt at Cochin, made memorable to Francis by the immense kindness of the Franciscans, the Jesuits aboard the merchantman bound for the Moluccas numbered six, three for those islands, including a great priest, Alfonso de Castro, who witnessed to Christ our Lord with his Jewish blood out there, and three for Japan, Francis himself, Father Cosmas de Torres, and Brother Juan Fernandez. Besides these in the party were the three convert Japanese, a Chinaman christened Manuel, and a Malabar Christian named Amador, so Asia had fair representation. This time the monsoon was on its best behaviour and wafted them to Malacca as sweetly as a zephyr. Francis appears almost to have enjoyed his thirty-seven days on the deep, among the prodigious stinks and fearful assortment of noises which were part and parcel of ocean travel in those days. ' We arrived in great form,' he reported back to Goa. ' Not a man of us was sea-sick, the weather was excellent, without a single thunder-storm to make us feel queasy, and the pirates of Achin left us alone, praise be to God our Lord for ever.'

The Captain of Malacca at this time was Dom Pedro da Silva da Gama, one of the six sons of the celebrated Vasco. Portugal at her magnificent best, this good man and great soldier gave the travellers such a welcome and exerted himself to such an extent on their behalf that St. Francis felt he must sit down and tell the King about it:

> Senhor, . . . God has put it into my heart to go to the islands of Japan to spread our holy faith, and I arrived here at Malacca with two companions of my order and three Japanese Christians on May 31, 1549. The Japanese are very devout men, especially to the Passion of our Lord. They made the Spiritual Exercises with great recollection and came through them to a deep knowledge of God. They often go to confession and Holy Communion, and are returning to Japan full of zeal and desire to convert their countrymen to Christianity. The Captain of the fortress received all six of us with exceeding love and charity, . . . and has done everything in his power to give us good dispatch, as he promised immediately on our arrival. He has worked so hard on our behalf, and with so much love and willingness, that we could never repay the immense debt we owe him. He could not have done more for us if we had been his blood brothers. For the love of our Lord, will your Highness take over and pay our great debt to Dom Pedro da Silva? He made the most liberal provision for our voyage, and gave us the wherewithal to maintain ourselves during the first stage in Japan and to build a chapel there in which to say Mass, this by a present of thirty *bars* of the finest pepper marketed in Malacca. In addition, he put aside bales of rich material and other objects for us to take as gifts to the King of Japan, that he might give us better welcome to his country. I tell your Highness this in so much detail that you may know how generously and charitably I have been treated by your loyal vassals in India. It is the truth, Senhor, that no man was ever treated better, and I owe it all to your Highness's patronage and recommendation of me to your servants in India. Dom Pedro, in particular, has been so good to me that I again beg you, having nothing of my own, to recoup him on my behalf. . . .[1]

[1] Schurhammer, *Epistolae*, ii, 117–19. Francis really did love the King and so, in the way of a saint, was most concerned about his eternal welfare, which is the explanation of the little lectures he was in the habit of reading his Highness. This letter concludes with one also, so anxious that it might have been the

The *bars* of pepper mentioned in the letter are often mistakenly supposed to have been an inducement, very warm at that, for the mysterious Emperor of Japan, but they were, in fact, a present to Francis himself, and one that he assuredly did not take with him, for the following good reason. The Arabic word *bahar* represented a measure of weight employed in India and the Far East, which fluctuated in value, according to time and place, between 223 and 625 pounds avoirdupois. Taking 400 pounds as an average, thirty *bahars* would have weighed 12,000 pounds, or more than five tons. Now, five tons of pepper would be extremely awkward personal luggage even on the *Queen Elizabeth*, let alone a Chinese junk, and, besides, Francis could not have sold the pepper in Japan, for that would have been trading and contrary to canon law. What the Captain must have done, then, was to sell the pepper, no mean part of his private fortune, on the Malaccan market and put aside the proceeds as a fund for the assistance of the mission in Japan. On that fund St. Francis and his companions lived during the whole of their time in the country.[1]

From Malacca as from Cochin Francis wrote a whole bundle of letters, starred with the names of men and places, and all indicative of his overwhelming solicitude for the ' churches ' he was leaving behind. It might have been St. Paul in person, dreaming of Spain and at the same time eating his heart out with anxiety for Thessalonians, Galatians, Corinthians, Colossians, Ephesians. One of the first letters was to the heroic Beira, struggling with two men for his army to keep the flame of faith alive in the Moluccas, over which the shadow of Islam crept relentlessly.

---

soul of Francis rather than the soul of the King which was in question. It may have been noticed that at the beginning of this letter Francis speaks no more of the ' island ' but of the ' islands ' of Japan. He was learning quite fast.

[1] St. Francis himself said that while in Japan he ' received in alms more than a thousand *cruzados* ', which would have been the price obtained for the pepper. A *cruzado* at the time was worth 360 *reis* (plural of *real*) and 30 *reis* went to make a *fanam*, for which could be purchased, in India, at any rate, three plump chickens. Francis could therefore have purchased 36,000 such chickens with his thousand *cruzados*, though in Japan prices were higher and 24,000 would probably be nearer the mark. That amount of poultry gives some idea of the money values prevalent at the time. Most of the money went in charity, for the Saint and his men lived like the poorest Japanese, on a little rice and fish.

Francis could not be sure that he was still alive as rumour had spoken of his martyrdom. The three auxiliaries for the Moluccas who carried his letter would discover the truth, and if Beira had indeed been killed Alfonso de Castro, straight from his first Mass at Malacca, would replace him as superior, open the letter and carry out its minute instructions. These were principally to keep in touch, to be a true band of brothers on their separate islands, to write to him *muito particularmente* about their successes and failures, as well as about the prospects in other places of the Great Archipelago still unreconnoitred, such as Tontoli in the far north of Celébes and Macassar at the other end. The Saint's undiminished interest in Ternate, where the best of the three new men, Alfonso de Castro, was to reside, comes out movingly in a long letter addressed to Paul of Camerino and Antonio Gomes at Goa. They are to keep closely in touch by letter with the brethren in the Moluccas, and Antonio Gomes is specially charged to provide for the needs of two distressed ladies in Ternate, both converts from Mohammedanism and for that reason deprived of their property by the Moslem Sultan, Hairun.[1] Francis begins the letter by saying that he is writing them ' these few lines ' to tell them of the safe arrival of himself and his party in Malacca, ' where the whole town, big and little, turned out joyously to greet us ', and then the few lines go on till they become three hundred and five. They are largely a plea for letters, letters, letters. His thirst for news of the

---

[1] The story of those two Indonesians is complicated. One, *née* Niai Chili Boki Radja, was daughter of the Sultan of Tidore and second wife of Baiang Ullah, Sultan of Ternate, in which capacity she became mother of Tabarija whom the Portuguese prefect, Fonseca, made Sultan on the death of his father Baiang Ullah. But the next prefect, Tristan de Ataíde, deprived him in favour of Hairun and sent him and his mother prisoners to Malacca. There he became a Catholic but died before he could regain his throne. His mother returned to Ternate, fell in with St. Francis, and was baptized by him as Doña Isabel. The other lady was a daughter of Sultan Baiang Ullah who had married a gallant Portuguese soldier named Balthasar Veloso and become a Christian. Though she was his half-sister and though her husband Veloso was one of the dearest friends of St. Francis whom he so greatly liked, the unpredictable Hairun treated her very harshly for her desertion of Mohammed, probably to increase his credit with his Moslem subjects. Francis wrote to King John on behalf of both ladies, and begged that some special favour should be shown to Veloso for the generous way in which he had befriended the missionaries.

brethren was insatiable. They are please to write *muito particular-mente*, a phrase that now becomes a kind of slogan on his pen. In the space of fourteen lines he uses it or its equivalent *muito largamente* five times. He wants to know how every Father and Brother at St. Paul's College is getting on, and asks each of them to write to him separately, ' on two or three sheets of paper ', telling him how he feels about life and what work he is engaged on. A young African from Mozambique christened Diogo is to give him a detailed account of himself and all his schoolfellows at St. Paul's, saying whether they are contented and quiet and serving God our Lord. There is a special message for Antonio Gomes, the Rector, who is earnestly begged to cultivate the most friendly relations with the Friars of St. Francis and St. Dominic, and with the Bishop, and with his fellow Jesuits, making it his ambition to be loved by them and to provide for them in every fatherly way. Nobody and no place is forgotten. Antonio will send a preacher as soon as he can find one to Bassein and another to Cochin. He will ask the Governor to help Father Lancillotto in his struggle to start a house at Quilon, and he will of his goodness be a providence to the Fathers at Cape Comorin. Balthasar Gago, destined for nine years of hard labour in Japan, is commissioned, and that under order of holy obedience, to keep Francis supplied with news from Coimbra and Rome and to tell him how the affair of Prester John proceeded and whether that Lion of the Tribe of Judah had yet received the Jesuit Patriarch for whom he had applied.[1] There is a postscript of twenty-six lines to the letter in praise of Father Francis Perez at Malacca: ' I have been astounded since coming here at what he has achieved. . . . He works so hard that often he finds no time to sleep or eat. . . . Confusion seizes me when I think of all that this sick and suffering man has done with God's assistance. . . .' To Simon Rodriguez

---

[1] Great efforts were being made at this time to bring about the union of the schismatical and heretical Church of Abyssinia with the Catholic Church. Father Paschase Broet, one of the finest of the early disciples of Ignatius Loyola, was chosen for the exceedingly difficult office of Patriarch, but because he was a Frenchman King John of Portugal refused to accept his nomination, a good example of the way absolute monarchs treated the Pope.

he wrote: ' How happy I would be if all the missionaries you sent out were of the stamp of Francisco Perez! '

The Saint followed up his long letter to Goa with a second one which shows him in the unexpected rôle of matchmaker.

> Here in Malacca [he said] I ran into a great friend of mine named Christopher Carvalho. He is a bachelor in easy circumstances, of excellent character and education. In my zeal for the salvation of souls and considering the strong friendship between us, I begged him to adopt a more settled manner of life that would be to God's service and his own peace. . . . He told me that he greatly desired to settle down, . . . and as we conversed there came vividly to my mind remembrance of the immense kindness and charity shown to all of us by nossa May.[1] I spoke to him about marriage with a girl I knew and told him of her good qualities and virtues. The idea and the girl appealed to him very greatly and he gave me his word to carry out the project, which I believe he will keep, both because he is my good friend and because the marriage is to his advantage and peace of mind. I have accordingly written to nossa May on the subject. As I think that your help will be very necessary in the matter, I beg and beseech you to remember the hospitality and kindness which we have ever received from nossa May, and to join forces with the Controller of the Revenue [Cosmas Anes] to bring the marriage about, so that this honoured widow may be relieved and her daughter sheltered and supported.

Francis goes into many more details, but that is the gist of the story, which is surely a charming and revealing one, whether Christopher and the girl played the parts designed for them or not, especially as the letter was written on the day before Francis embarked for Japan. Such a leap in the dark as that might have

---

[1] Mai is Portuguese for mother. The Jesuits at Goa in the early days called an elderly widow named Violante Ferreira ' our Mother ' because of her extreme kindness to them. She had an unmarried daughter, and St. Francis had it in mind that this girl would make an excellent wife for his unattached friend Christopher, whereby three birds would be brought down with the one stone, the girl being provided for, her good mother's poverty relieved from Christopher's wealth, and Christopher himself safely anchored.

excused even a saint from taking up his pen, but it was not the only sweet word he wrote on ' the Eve of St. John '. He also sat down to compose with great love a set of detailed spiritual instructions for a new novice, Juan Bravo, aged twenty, whom he had received into the Society of Jesus there in Malacca. The instructions show how completely Francis had assimilated the teaching of St. Ignatius:

> Labour to overcome yourself in all things, ever denying your own appetites and inclinations, while enduring and embracing whatever they most abhor and recoil from. In all the ways of life look and long to be humiliated and treated as of no account, for without true humility you will never be able to grow in spirit or to profit your neighbour or to be approved by the saints and acceptable to God or to persevere in this least Company, which cannot suffer proud, arrogant men, in love with their own opinions and personal dignity, for such people never do any good to anybody. . . . *Vosso amigo de alma*, Francisco.

Meantime the friendly and generous Captain of Malacca had been endeavouring to find a ship that would take Francis and his companions safely and swiftly to Japan. The Portuguese ships in harbour belonged to daring merchants who, in spite of all threats and prohibitions from Peking, still continued to trade secretly with their opposite numbers in China, and for that purpose were accustomed to winter in some hidden cove of the fringe of islands stretching along the Chinese coast. No doubt, they would have been glad in their isolation and danger to have the company of such a one as St. Francis, provided that he was willing to lay up for the winter, too. After August, it became impossible for a sailing ship of that period to make Japan from the coast of China, owing to the winds being contrary, and as much as a year might pass before they became favourable again.[1] Francis could not possibly spare all that time, and gladly accepted when a Chinese shipmaster,

---

[1] At least so says St. Francis (Schurhammer, *Epistolae*, ii, 224: ' *Si de la China no parten a Japan primero de Agosto, no hay monçón hasta de hai un año* ').

hearing of his predicament, offered as a business proposition to take the whole party direct to Japan on his large junk.[1] A Jesuit writer of the period says that the man's name was Avân, but St. Francis mentions that he was more commonly known, at least in Portuguese circles, as *Ladrão* or Pirate, a sobriquet which he appears to have honestly earned. Captain da Silva was deeply suspicious of the old heathen who luckily, however, had given him a hostage by marrying a Malay wife in Malacca and starting a business there. He was very firmly told and required to sign an agreement that if he failed in any way to abide by his bargain, he would never see his wife again and his property would be confiscated. These details are from St. Francis himself who does not seem to have been unduly perturbed at the prospect of sailing under a known pirate on a completely heathen ship.

Two days before he climbed aboard the lumbering, flat-bottomed, three-masted junk, strangest of all his many transports, Francis wrote a hasty letter of farewell to the brethren in Europe. It somehow gives the impression of a brave man whistling in the dark, and, goodness knows, darkness was all around him. The Portuguese merchants told of ghostly experiences they had had in an abandoned Japanese house, of invisible presences that plucked at their garments and of a hideous phantom that had frightened the life out of one of their servants. Francis saw the Devil in all this. The Devil, he said, had worked hard to keep him out of Japan, but there were two things which helped him and his men to overcome the many impediments put in their way by the Enemy, the first being that God knew their intentions, and then that all creatures, the Devil included, depended on God, and could do them no hurt without God's permission. Some might think, he went on, that it was tempting God to commit oneself to such obvious dangers, but he had come to regard them as of no account:

I have nearly always before my eyes and my mind some

---

[1] Sea-going junks might require as many as two hundred mariners. They were sturdily built, with triple planking of pine, had sweeps, each requiring several men to pull it, as well as huge square sails made of bamboo laths woven into a kind of mat, and they boasted several private cabins.

words that I often heard our blessed Father Ignatius repeat, namely, that those to be of our Company must strive mightily to conquer themselves and cast from their hearts all fears and anxieties which would impede the growth of faith and hope and loving trust in God. . . . Great is the difference between the man who trusts in God, having all that he needs about him, and the man who trusts in God with nothing to his name, having despoiled himself even of life's necessities to be more like Christ. So too, it is one thing to put faith and hope in God when safe and out of danger's way, and quite another to trust Him completely when for His love and service a man faces gladly imminent and evident peril of destruction. It seems to me that those who walk in continual danger of death solely for God's sake will soon come to be sickened of life and to want to die that they may reign with God for ever in Heaven. For this mortal condition of ours is not life but a drawn-out death, and exile from the glory for which we were created. . . .[1]

It was on the afternoon of June 24, the feast of the Nativity of St. John the Baptist, that the long, eventful voyage of about three thousand nautical miles began. As a last precaution, Pedro da Silva appointed one of his men, Domingos Dias, to act as escort of St. Francis and his party, to keep Ladrão under observation, and to do any interpreting that might be necessary. The chief object on the junk was the shrine of some Chinese sea-god presiding from the high stern, round which the life of the heathen crew centred. Simple, superstitious men, they looked to their idol for guidance in every emergency, and Francis looked on them with sorrow and great compassion. At first the weather was good and Ladrão, a skilful pilot, got his lumbering old tub through the very narrow and dangerous Strait of Singapore without mishap. But no sooner was he in sight of the open sea, the ominous South China Sea, than Francis observed in him a tendency to linger unnecessarily at islands on the route, as though he designed to be late for the last of the South-East monsoon, blowing towards

[1] Schurhammer, *Epistolae S. Francisci Xaverii*, ii, 111–15, 117–19, 123–35, 145–51.

Japan. In one of the most vivid of his letters, addressed from Japan to the Jesuits at Goa, Francis told the story of the voyage:

Two things on it distressed us above all others, first, to see that the good weather and wind given us by God our Lord were not being used to advantage, with the consequence that we might miss the monsoon for Japan and be obliged to wait a year off China for another favourable monsoon; and second, the incessant and gross idolatry practised by the captain and his heathen crew in presence of an idol brought on their ship, to which they offered sacrifices. We were powerless to prevent it, or to stop the constant casting of lots and questions put to the idol whether or not the good wind would last to enable us to reach Japan. Sometimes, as they believed and told us, the omens were good and sometimes bad.[1] A hundred leagues from Malacca, we fetched up at an island where we took on a supply of wood for rudders and purposes of repair, in view of the great storms and heavy seas to be expected off the coast of China.[2] Then there was more casting of lots, preceded by many sacrifices, offerings and adorations, that the idol might tell whether we should have favourable winds or no. The lots foretold good weather and advised that we should delay no longer, so we weighed anchor and hoisted sail in a happy mood, the heathen confiding in that idol of theirs on the poop, which they worshipped with lighted candles and incensed by burning before it sticks of sweet-smelling wood, while we put our trust in God the Creator of Heaven and earth and in Jesus Christ His Son, for whose love and service we had come out to these parts to spread His holy faith.

[1] The various Chinese methods of divination by casting lots before an idol are described in Doré-Kennedy, *Researches into Chinese Superstitions*, vol. iv (Shanghai, 1917), pp. 349-52. This learned work, with a wealth of fascinating coloured illustrations, is by two Jesuits. The joss on the poop was the Chinese Neptune. ' Chinese sailors carry him along with them in all their voyages, and make great vows to him when they are in danger. . . .' (Kaempfer, *The History of Japan, 1690-92*, Eng. trans. 1727, vol. ii, p. 256).

[2] From the distance given by Francis and the woody nature of the island, it would appear to have been Pulo Timon, off the Malay coast, in latitude 2' 52" north.

There goes the fighting, crusading Francis, with Roland's cry deep in his heart if not on his lips, *Paien unt tort, e chrestien unt dreit*. His sense of God's paramount rights was so piercingly acute that he could never have the slightest patience with idolatry. For him, to give to a creature, and a mere stock or stone at that, the honour and homage due to the Living God alone, was the sin of sins, the awful inversion of hierarchies for which there was no forgiveness, but only inevitable damnation. Yet he yearned over his Pirate, who was an honest good fellow according to his lights. When the Christian Portuguese had failed him, this ' heathen Chinee ' came to his assistance. They were brothers under the skin, both of them kindly and daring souls, though in different fashions, and but for that execrable idol they might have been the best of friends. Before the year was out, Francis wrote from Japan to Dom Pedro da Silva to say that poor Ladrão was dead. ' All through the voyage,' he continued, ' he was good to us, and we were unable to be good to him, for he died in his infidelity. Even after death we could not help him by our prayers to God, for his soul was in Hell.' That was the harshest thing Francis ever said, and he said it, as is obvious, with deepest sorrow, but whether he had any right to say it may well be questioned. The Catholic Church, by her canonizations, has declared thousands of men and women to be in Heaven, but she has never pronounced a single human soul to be in Hell. She has not the competence to do so, and neither, decidedly, had her great son Francis Xavier. We must take Francis as we find him and that is how he was made, a man of few nuances, intransigent, authoritative, in a way even merciless, very Iberian, in fact, and at the same time one of the most loving and beloved of the children of men.[1] On the spiritual

[1] All the qualities which Ramón Menéndez Pidal finds characteristic of his people are to be observed markedly in St. Francis, material and moral austerity, detachment, energy, brotherhood, traditionalism, a longing for death as the gateway to God, the superimposition of the religious ideal on political life, a kind of transfigured Senecan stoicism, which appeared also in St. Ignatius Loyola, in St. Teresa, in St. John of the Cross, in many other Spanish saints and influential men not saints, such as Pedro Ribadeneira (*The Spaniards in their History*. Translated by Walter Starkie. London, 1950, pp. 103, 119–45. ' It was Ganivet who explained the essence of the Spanish conception of justice. The Spaniard aspires to pure and absolute justice, and he insists that it should be

plane, he largely resembled the best of the conquistadores, for instance, the tenderly devout, the selfless, the chivalrous, the ruthless Albuquerque, who held his own life at a pin's fee, and the lives of other men also.

Continuing his narrative of the voyage, St. Francis reported that the Chinese cast lots to determine whether the junk would get back safely to Malacca after reaching Japan. The answer given by the chips was that it would not return, which made the Captain and his men more reluctant than ever to keep on their promised course. Still a little irate, he writes:

> You can see the anxiety we were caused, being dependent on the whim of that devil of an idol as to whether or not we should attain our goal. . . . While sailing slowly along off the coast of Cochin China [Annam], which is close to China itself, we met with two disasters on a single day, the eve of St. Mary Magdalene [July 21]. It became very stormy and the sea rough, so we hove-to. The bilge of the ship had been carelessly left uncovered and as our companion, Manuel the Chinaman, was passing it the vessel gave a great lurch and threw him in. We all thought that he was killed, as it was a considerable drop and the bilge was full of water. But it pleased God that he should not die, though he was a long time submerged and had received a severe wound on the head. We had great difficulty in getting him out and he remained unconscious a good while. As he was coming round, the storm being still at its height and the ship rolling abominably, a daughter of the Captain fell overboard. The swell was so great that we could not save her, and she drowned there under the eyes of her father and of all of us. It was heart-rending to witness the sorrow of those poor heathens and to listen all that day and night to their loud lamentations, and it was piteous, too, to think of the plight and peril in which all aboard that ship stood. The following day, great sacrifices of slaughtered birds and other offerings were

---

rigorous, even implacable. But at the same time the Spaniard is always ready to pity the fallen, and he will take as much trouble to raise him up as he did to overthrow him. This characteristic, according to Ganivet, sprang from the stoicism of Seneca, and was a genuine Spanish trait ').

made to the idol, and lots were cast to learn why the Captain's daughter had died. The answer came that she would not have fallen into the sea to drown if our Manuel had died. You can see how our lives hung on those lots of the devil, for we were in the power of his servants and ministers. What would have become of us if God had permitted the devil to work us all the mischief he desired?

At this point Francis launches into seventy lines of counsel how to deal with the Enemy of God and man. He says that before the storm came down on them, he had begged God not to permit men whom He had made in His image and likeness to be guilty of such dreadful superstition, or if He did permit it that He would greatly increase the torments of the Devil its author every time he moved and persuaded the Captain to cast losts and adore him as God. The storm appears to have been a typhoon, and Francis was once heard to say that, in his opinion, typhoons were not caused so much by the winds as by demons on the prowl. The way to meet the terror which the devil sought to inspire was to show him a bold front, to distrust oneself completely, and to put all one's hope and confidence in God, so great a defender and protector, taking care to show no sign of cowardice, and never doubting of the victory.

Resuming his account of the voyage after this long spiritual parenthesis, he wrote:

As the storm had abated we raised anchor and, continuing on our way, all very sad at heart, reached in a few days [some islands adjacent to] the port of Canton. Captain and crew seemed of a mind to winter there. We alone opposed the idea, entreating them to go on, and also threatening them that we would write to the Captain of Malacca and tell the Portuguese [on the islands] how they had deceived us and broken their promise. By the good pleasure of God they changed their minds and went on to the port of Chang-Chow.[1] They were about to take the

[1] This was the famous Zayton which Marco Polo declared to be ' one of the two greatest havens in the world for commerce '. A later traveller, the Arab Ibn Batuta, said it was the greatest harbour on earth, and that in the superb city itself was manufactured a rich stuff called after it *Zaituniah*, which is to say, satin.

junk into the port with a view to wintering there, as the wind favourable for a voyage to Japan already showed signs of veering, when a sail approached us bringing news that the harbour was full of pirate ships, and that we would be lost if we went in. Indeed, they could be seen only a league away and they frightened our Captain who would have returned to the Canton islands but for having the wind on his bow, whereas there was a following wind to Japan, and, however reluctantly, he was compelled to ride before it. So neither the devil nor his disciples could hinder our progress, and God brought us to the land of our hearts' desire on the feast of our Lady's Assumption, in the year 1549. What is more, Captain and crew were unable to make any port of Japan but Kagoshima, the native place of Paul of Holy Faith, where his relatives and many others not of his kin received us with great love.

Seven weeks of stress and storm had passed since Francis left the known world behind him and now, as the battered brown junk ploughed through fifty miles of the great land-locked bay to harbour, his Odyssey entered on its climax. He was not a man much given to noticing such things, but volcanoes refuse to be ignored even by abstracted saints, and there on an island at the head of the bay, to remind him of Ternate, was majestic Sakura-jima, smoking with great dignity, like an old gentleman in a club, with just an occasional hint of flame. Opposite, on the mainland, at the foot of a range of low green hills lay the myriad thatched or tiled roofs of Kagoshima, capital of the province of Satsuma and southernmost city of Japan. The arrival of a big junk was an event in the life of Kagoshima which had none of the wealth and magnificence of Chang-Chow and eked out a frugal existence by strenuous toil in the paddy-fields or the terraced groves of cherry and orange trees mantling the ashen flanks of Sakurajima. If man could live by beauty alone, those people, lithe little men, often tattooed with bright blue dragons, and demure little women in graceful kimonos, would have been well off indeed, but as it was and is they were desperately poor. Those of them who flocked to the quays on that memorable August 15, '*une heure solennelle dans l'histoire de l'Asie*' (Bellessort), came certainly with no thought of welcoming Francis Xavier and his men, for they could hardly have had the slightest inkling of his approach. No doubt, the poor wife and relatives of Anjiro used to turn out, hoping against hope, whenever a junk arrived. Family affection is famously strong in Japan, and the good Paul would have been sorely missed. It would seem that his relatives must have made some composition with the family of the man he had killed or otherwise secured his pardon, for the affair is not mentioned any more.

The European peoples had long known a good deal about China through the writings of Marco Polo and other travellers, but their first real as against fanciful knowledge of Japan came to them from the letters of St. Francis Xavier, which also contributed the word *bonze* to their dictionaries. After less than two months in Kagoshima, the guest of Anjiro's family, it seems, St. Francis had fallen in love with the Japanese people.

> They are the best race yet discovered [he wrote in the same letter to Goa], and I think that among non-Christians their match will not easily be found. Admirable in their social relationships, they have an astonishing sense of honour and esteem it above all other things.[1] In general, they are not a wealthy people, but neither among nobles nor plebeians is poverty regarded as a disgrace. A very poor nobleman would not dream of marrying a woman not of his own class, however wealthy she might be, for he thinks he would lose his honour by so doing, and he esteems honour far above riches, which is something, so far as I know, that cannot be said of Christian peoples. The Japanese are full of courtesy in their dealings with one another. The men set great store by weapons, and nobles and plebeians alike always carry sword and dagger from the

[1] As did the Spaniards. Before his conversion Ignatius Loyola once nearly killed a man who accidentally jostled him in the street. Honour is largely the theme of the dramas of Calderon and Lope de Vega. On one occasion the French, who were no cowards, refused to fight the troops of the Great Captain, Gonzalo de Córdoba, saying: 'Those mad Spaniards value a little honour more than a thousand lives.'

age of fourteen. They will not endure to be treated slightingly or addressed in contemptuous terms. The ordinary people hold the military class [samurai] in great respect, and they for their part glory in serving their lord [daimyo] on whom they greatly depend, not, I think, from fear of anything he could do to them, but because it would mean loss of honour to fail in duty to him. They are a moderate people as regards food, but they indulge a good deal in an intoxicating liquor made from rice [saké], as the vine does not grow in Japan. They never play games of chance, considering them to be a form of theft and therefore highly dishonourable. Swearing is little heard and when they do swear it is by the sun. A good proportion of the people can read and write, which is a great help towards teaching them quickly the prayers and the things of God. They are mono-gamists, and they abominate thieving and punish robbers invariably with death. Of all the peoples I have seen in my life, Christians included, the Japanese are the most rigorously opposed to theft, and there are few robbers in the country. They are a well-meaning people and very sociable and anxious to learn. They take pleasure in hearing of the things of God, especially such as they can understand, and they have no idols made in the shape of beasts, but believe in men of ancient times who, as far as I can make out, lived as philosophers.[1] Many Japanese adore the sun and others the moon. They like to be appealed to on rational grounds, and are ready to agree that what reason vindicates is right. In my view, the ordinary lay people commit fewer sins and are more obedient to reason than those they call Bonzes and regard as their spiritual fathers. The Bonzes are addicted to unnatural vice, and readily admit it, for it is so notorious and well known to everybody that men

[1] As later letters show, St. Francis is here referring to the original founder of Buddhism, and to a purely Japanese development of his doctrine expounded by the Jodo sect (founded in 1175). According to this, individual salvation is attained by meditating and relying on a personal Buddha, imagined as a com-passionate being, Amida Buddha, who has acquired so much merit through innumerable rebirths that he can pass it on to his worshipper. It is not surprising that St. Francis was puzzled, and he was to be much more puzzled before he had done with the many intricate varieties of Buddhism excogitated by the questing Japanese mind.

and women of every condition take it for granted and show no abhorrence to it. Still, the laity are very pleased to hear us denounce this abominable sin. . . .[1]

The letter of St. Francis to Goa, which is close on ten thousand words long and the largest he ever wrote, was dated November 5, 1549, so in a brief time he had learned a great deal. But he had very much more to learn—and unlearn—about Dai Nippon, Great Sun-source Land, and its extraordinary people. Padre Alexandro Valignano, his successor out there twenty-five years later, wrote:

The Japanese have rites and customs so different from those of other nations that it looks as if they studied of set purpose to be unlike any other race on earth. It can safely be said that Japan is a world the reverse of Europe. Hardly in anything do their ways conform to ours. They eat and dress completely differently. Their obsequies, their ceremonies, their language, their methods of doing business, their manner of sitting down, their buildings, their domestic arrangements, their medicine, their education of their children, and every other mortal habit of theirs are so unlike ours as to be beyond description or understanding. What I could not get over in all this was that a people so utterly unlike ourselves should yet be so highly civilized. Even in their feelings and natural tastes they are so much our opposites that I would hardly dare to assert it had I not lived long among them. For instance, we hold white to be a joyous

[1] Schurhammer, *Epistolae S. Francisci Xaverii*, ii, 179–88. The adorers of sun and moon were Shintoists, followers of the very ancient indigenous nature religion based on the worship of deified tribal ancestors and heroes. It became to a large extent amalgamated with Buddhism when that conquering system was brought in from Korea and China, and remained so for a thousand years, until in the nineteenth century the Meiji revolution made it the national cult, centring round the Emperor or Tenno, restored to all the powers human and divine shorn from him by the great feudal families in the Middle Ages. Its practice was declared illegal by the Constitution of 1946. As for the bonzes, St. Francis says that they had ' many boys, sons of the warrior class, in their monasteries for education in reading and writing, *y con éstos cometen sus maldades* '.

and festive colour, but with them it is the colour of mourning and sorrow, and when they want to celebrate and be merry they put on black or purple, our mourning colours. As of the eye so of the ear. Our instrumental and vocal music offends their sensibility, and their music, which they love, is an absolute torment for us to listen to. Again, we take off our caps or sombreros and stand up to greet a visitor, but they remove their shoes and sit down, considering it the gravest discourtesy to receive any one standing. . . . The way they eat is equally astonishing, neatly and elegantly, with much composure, and their table service like their clothes is always immaculately clean. They do not use napkins, and have no knives, forks or spoons, but only two little sticks with which they manipulate the food so dexterously and cleanly that, though they never touch anything with their hands, not so much as a crumb falls from the plate to the table. . . . Until a foreigner gets the knack of this he has many tribulations at his Japanese dinner.

While with Anjiro's family and the many times he was the guest of other families or of the Buddhist monks, St. Francis had to endure the torture of the chopsticks. And there was another discipline to which, not his hands, but his legs once so lithe, had to submit, daily, for hours at a time.

The foreigner suffers much when he sits down in the Japanese fashion [writes Valignano] for they put their knees on the ground and sit on their heels, or as we say squat, a posture of ease for them, but to others most wearisome and painful, until little by little in the course of time they become used to it. It is astonishing to observe the importance they attach to certain usages which by us Europeans would be regarded as trivial or childish. Thus, it is a universal custom in Japan to drink a beverage made with hot water and the crushed berries of a little bush which they call *chaa*. This is held for a great thing among them, so much so that all gentlemen have a special room set aside in their houses for the purpose of drinking the beverage. As hot water in Japanese is *yu* and the name of the bush *chaa*, they call the salon *cha-no-yu*, and it is the most esteemed and venerated thing in Japan. . . . As a result of their addiction to the *chaa*, they greatly treasure certain pieces and vessels used in the *cha-no-yu* [tea-ceremony]. . . . The cups in which they serve the brewed *chaa* are very small, but if made of a certain quality, recognizable only by the Japanese, they are prized beyond belief. . . . The Daimyo of Bungo showed me an earthenware cup for which he paid nine thousand silver taels, which amounts to about fourteen thousand ducats. Now, to speak the truth, I would not have given for it more than a couple of *maravedis* [farthings], and we would not know what to do with it in Europe, except to put in a song-bird's cage as a drinking-trough. . . . To be esteemed, these cups and vessels must have been made by certain ancient masters, and among a thousand similar cups the Japanese immediately recognize the one with the master's touch, a gift which I think no Europeans could ever acquire. . . . In the same way they are ready to pay three, four, and ten thousand ducats for a little bird or a small tree painted in black on a sheet of rice-paper by the hand of an ancient master, a thing which we would regard as valueless. . . .[1]

What a Philistine! we may think, but the matter is not as simple as that. The Padre was an Italian, used to the well-filled canvasses of his native land, and could not fairly be expected to

[1] *Monumenta Xaveriana*, ii, 103–8. This account of Japan and its usages is the first based on direct observation to come from a European pen. The relation drawn up by George Alvares for St. Francis Xavier must have been based on information obtained at the ports, as Alvares never ventured more than a few miles inland. Only a small portion of Valignano has been cited, and he gives also, without comment, a very accurate description of suicide by harakiri and of many other customs good and bad. He opines that in certain respects the Japanese are altogether superior to Europeans, though their ' vicios ', which he lists under five headings, are more widespread and vile, expecially sexuality and cruelty, than anything on the same scale in Christian lands. He bears out St. Francis on the whole but is much more complete. Thus, speaking of marriage, he says : ' The Japanese can have as many wives as they like, though they usually regard one woman as their principal and proper wife. They can divorce her at pleasure and take another, without bad feelings on either side. All is done with wonderful decorum, and the repudiated wife and her relatives visit and treat the former husband with exactly the same regard and courtesy as before.'

have appreciated the exquisite economy of the Kakemono in which so much of the space is left blank. He felt this type of art, as his words about the small bird and small tree imply, to be a species of cheating on the artist's part, similar to that practised by the tradesman who gives short weight or puts ground rice in the sugar. Moreover, Valignano learned fast. One of his missionaries wrote to Rome in 1594 that ' God had given the Father an incredible love for the Japanese '. He became the great apostle of conformity and accommodation, and ruled that his Jesuits, in so far as was possible, and compatible with their religious profession, must thoroughly ' Nipponize ' themselves. They must build their churches and houses in the Japanese style, not on their lives forgetting the *cha-no-yu* sanctum, where a *Dôyuku*, meaning a native catechist, or other person skilled in the brewing and serving of tea, is always to be present. They are to have two or three kinds of tea, *una molto buona e altre più mediocri, per ricevere le persone che vengono secondo loro grado.* As the Japanese are the most punctilious and ceremonious people in the world, the Jesuits must diligently study and acquire all the intricacies of their etiquette, so as to be able to address each visitor by his correct title, give him the exact bow, and there were many kinds, which was his due, and to stand to the right or left of him, or before or behind, as his quality required. The ceremonies used by lay people were quite different from those observed by the Buddhist monks who were to be the Jesuits' models in matters of etiquette.[1] All this was merely a variation on the standing maxim of courtesy and good breeding, ' When in Rome do as the Romans do.' At the same time, Rome did not approve of the Jesuit superiors in Japan having themselves conveyed around in litters, in imitation of the head Bonzes or of their garbing themselves in silk kimonos !

If a poor connoisseur of Japanese art, Valignano acquired a remarkable understanding of Japanese politics, such as St. Francis Xavier, his ideal, never attained. Perhaps Valignano, coming from a country of republics, was readier than Francis, the out and out monarchist, to believe that Japan was not governed in the

[1] *Il Ceremoniale per i Missionari del Giappone.* Edizione critica di Giuseppe Schütte, S.J. Roma, 1946, pp. 182–282.

manner of Spain or Portugal. Francis found it difficult to conceive of a civilized country, such as Japan plainly was, without a central authority and he underwent a great deal of suffering and hardship in his attempts to find the non-existent potentate. When at last he became cognizant of the real state of affairs, we observe him turning his thoughts towards China, the millennial tutor of Japan, where there reigned the emperor of his dreams. The idea at the back of his mind was perfectly sound and remained the guiding principle of later great men such as Matteo Ricci. Life was brief and eternity was long. The Kingdom of God must be established in the whole world, and the only swift and effective means to achieve that glorious and passionately desired end was to win to Christ the man at the top, the ' King ' of Japan or the Emperor of China, or, if that proved impossible, at least to render them friendly to the Christian message.

Long ago in Japan [writes Valignano] there used to be a monarch called the *Dairi* who ruled over the whole of the country by means of his governors and captains, and in those days there was great peace. But five or six hundred years ago certain lords rose in rebellion against the *Dairi* and his nobles, who had become effeminate and unsoldierly through soft living, and dispossessed him of all his estates and power, leaving him only his dignity and his title. Thus did Japan lose her peace and incessant war became and still is to this hour the lot of the country. The *Dairi* continued to be the dispenser of social honours, and the war-lords themselves show him external reverence and obeisance, but they take no orders from him and give him no help, except a very small pension allowed him by the principal among them. So he and his nobles are very poor. . . .[1]

Japanese history is almost as fascinating as Japanese art. It began in a mist of gods and heroes long before the Christian era,

[1] *Monumenta Xaveriana*, ii, 96–7. This edition of Valignano's work has recently been superseded by a most admirably learned one due to the labours of Joseph Wicki, S.J., editor of the *Documenta Indica* and co-editor with George Schurhammer of the Letters of St. Francis.

and emerged as a patriarchal society, each tribe or clan having its separate chief and guardian deity, the sun, the moon, the winds, the rivers, the rocks, the trees, the flowers, all the powers of nature. From this refined animism Shinto, or The Way of the Gods, was developed, a simple but not ignoble cult, pantheistic in character, which gave the Japanese the feeling for nature so marked in their art. When a great Japanese master painted birds on the wing or trees in bloom, he gives the impression, not of having set down something apart from him lovingly studied, as might a Western artist, but of having *become* the bird or the bloom. Having no script of their own, the gifted people borrowed the Chinese characters at an early date, and slowly, subtly adapted them, as they did all that they borrowed, to their particular temperament and purposes. The move prepared the way for the coming of Buddhism and Confucianism, and the Chinese language was accepted as the proper and only vehicle for the study of those systems. Shinto at first strongly resisted the invasion, but the astute bonzes got round the difficulty by assimilating the Shinto gods as Buddhas in their own right. Buddhist monasteries sprang up all over the land and from them, as from the Benedictine monasteries in Europe, the country people learned not only a new and higher religion but also the arts and crafts of civilization. Meantime, from inter-tribal wars there arose a supreme chieftain who consolidated his power by diligently fostering the myth of his and his clan's descent from the sun-goddess. Thus came into being the ' O ' or Tennô, the semi-divine priest-king best known to other peoples as the Mikado. The curse of Japan, as of Europe at the same period, was the rise of great baronial families and clans which, in alliance with the powerful Buddhist monasteries, dominated the Emperor. The rivalries of four such families, the Fujiwara, the Taira, the Minamoto, and the Hojo, all strictly aristocratic and claiming descent either from the sun-goddess or from some other Shinto deity, form the complex and bloody pattern of Japanese history for hundreds of years. It was then that the institution and office of shogun or generalissimo came into being, its holder making elaborate pretence of deriving his authority from the powerless

Emperor (retained merely as a focus of national religious sentiment and unity) but in effect promoting quite independently the ambitions and policies of his clan.

The last great conflict between the rival families, Japan's Wars of the Roses, was fought out in the Middle Ages by the survivors of earlier rounds, the Taira bearing a red banner and the Minamoto a white. As in England, the white one prevailed, and the head of the Minamoto clan, Yoritomo, a great soldier and statesman, but also a monster of cruelty, succeeded for some years in imposing his will on the whole of Japan. In the provinces he appointed military governors, the daimyos or 'great names', who were to bedevil the subsequent period of Japanese history. At this time the stern military code called *bushido* came into existence, its chief principle being loyalty to the feudal lord, the daimyo, rather than to the emperor. When Yoritomo died, the fourth family of divine descent, the Hojo, which had been biding its opportunity, seized control of both shogun and emperor. The family had the distinction of defeating the Mongol Emperor, Kublai Khan on the sea, but became so tyrannical, that a final clan, not of imperial blood, the Ashikaga, succeeded in usurping the shogunate and destroying such national unity as had been painfully attained. This was the epoch when Europe had her Great Schism of the West, and at the very same time Japan suffered her Great Schism of the East, also a religious disaster, as two rival emperors claimed the devotion of the people. The result was the political anarchy and endemic war of which Padre Valignano spoke as still persistent in his time, though the two emperors had patriotically merged again into one before the dawn of the sixteenth century. Among the chief contestants for power were successive daimyos of the great House of Shimazu, lords of Satsuma province, to which St. Francis Xavier had come with his high hopes of finding Japan as united as Spain, under a strong philosopher king, ripe for the message of Christianity.

CHAPTER XIV

TRIAL AND ERROR

ST. FRANCIS XAVIER helps very little or not at all to enable any one to picture him in his Japanese environment. Some have thought that to plant a few beds of chrysanthemums and azaleas around him or to trail wistaria and convolvulus from the eaves of his house might serve a useful purpose. But the house itself is the real trouble, and not one of the myriad books written to his glory gives it a thought. For all they have to say, he might still, in Kagoshima, be resting under a roof in Lisbon or Rome. During his first months in Japan, it must be presumed that he and his two Spanish companions, Torres and Fernandez, were guests in the house of their convert Paul, though none of them says so explicitly. In that world reversed which left them dumb and helpless, they could not have moved out of sight or hearing of their one familiar landmark, *nuestro buen y verdadero amigo Paulo*, without becoming hopelessly lost. So it is necessary to study briefly the subject of Japanese domestic architecture, for otherwise St. Francis will be left suspended in mid-air, with damage to his three dimensions.

There is some difference of opinion among the experts on the merits of middle-class Japanese homes, such as was Paul's. They agree, indeed, that the houses, whether of today or of four centuries of yesterdays, could not be too highly praised for their good taste and spotlessness (except in the matter of fleas, which have beaten the best washers in the world), but when it comes to the point of *comfort* there is schism. In 1885, Edward S. Morse, Director of the Peabody Academy of Science and once Professor of Zoology in the Imperial University, Tokyo, produced a large and fascinating book entitled *Japanese Homes and their Surroundings,* from which may be learned all about the formal garden with its dwarfed trees and hints of hidden streams, leading up to the verandah of the one-storeyed house built entirely of wood, usually pine, and with a pleasantly curving roof of thatch made from a special kind of Japanese grass. The house, unlike that of the Western world, is not built into the earth, but rests about a a foot above it on strong stone supports, and it has no windows in the Western sense but is open on one or every side to all the winds of heaven, for the Japanese never can have too much fresh air. The open sides may, however, be closed at will by a most ingenious system of screens which themselves are works of art. St. Francis, remembering perhaps the solid walls of Xavier or the fine stone buildings of a Europe· now so remote, may have thought the structure uncommonly flimsy, as he was taken ceremoniously up the steps and through the verandah to the most important division in the house, the guest-room, for the Japanese are a sociable and hospitable race. He would have learned from Paul that a well-bred guest invariably removes his boots or shoes before entering the room, which is not strictly a room but a place partitioned off from others by sliding screens. The reason for the removal of footwear is that the floor is entirely covered with soft mats or *tatami*, two inches or more thick and six feet by three in size:

Upon these mats the people eat, sleep and die; they represent the bed, chair, lounge, and sometimes table, combined. In resting upon them the Japanese assume a kneeling position— the legs turned beneath, and the haunches resting upon the calves of the legs and the inner side of the heels; the toes being turned in so that the upper and outer part of the instep bears directly on the mats. . . . This position is so painful to a foreigner that it is only with a great deal of practice he can become accustomed to it. Even the Japanese who have been abroad for several years find it excessively difficult and painful to resume this habit. In this attitude the Japanese receive their company. Hand-shaking is unknown, but bows of various degrees of profundity are made by placing the hands together upon the mats and bowing until the head oftentimes touches the hands. In this ceremony the back is kept parallel with the floor, or nearly so. At meal-times the food is served in lacquer and porcelain dishes on lacquer trays, placed upon the floor in front of the kneeling family; and in this position the repast is taken. At night a heavily wadded comforter is placed upon the floor; another equally thick is provided for a blanket, a pillow of diminutive proportions for a head-support—and the bed is made. In the morning these articles are stowed away in a large closet. . . .[1]

Mr. Morse defends the Japanese house against all critics, particularly those of his own country and of England, and has sharp things to say to them. To the Americans: ' I found the Japanese house in winter extremely cold and uncomfortable; but I question whether their cold rooms are not more conducive to health than are our apartments with our blistering stoves, hot furnaces or steam-heaters; and as to the odours. . . .' To the Englishman: ' The glaring absurdity of a house that persists in remaining upright without a foundation, or at least without his kind of a foundation, makes him furious.' To critics who complain of the want of privacy in Japanese dwellings: ' Privacy is only necessary in the midst of vulgar and impertinent people—a class of which Japan has the minimum, and the so-called civilized races, the English and American particularly, have the maximum.'

In his classical and delightful book, *Things Japanese*, Mr. B. H. Chamberlain is a little more tender to the foreigner's point of view:

The Japanese genius touches perfection in small things. No other nation ever understood half so well how to make a cup, a tray, even a kettle, a thing of beauty, how to transform a little

---

[1] *Japanese Homes*, 2nd ed., London, 1888, pp. 124–5. Mr. Morse was enthusiastic about the beds—' the whole floor, the whole house, indeed, is a bed, and one can fling himself down on the soft mats . . . and find no creaking springs, hard bunches or awkward hollows awaiting him, but a bed-surface as wide as the room itself, and comfortable to the last degree'. He was not so much enamoured of the very hard cylindrical pillows, sometimes made of porcelain! and admits that at first they give the foreigner a stiff neck, but goes on to say that ' the neck is kept free for the air to circulate beneath, and the head is kept cool '. The book has 307 admirable drawings to illustrate all the virtues of a Japanese house.

knob of ivory into a microcosm of quaint humour, how to express a fugitive thought in half a dozen dashes of the pencil. The massive, the spacious, the grand, is less congenial to their mental attitude. Hence they achieve less success in architecture than in the other arts. . . . Japanese houses are supremely uncomfortable to ninety-nine Europeans out of a hundred. Nothing to sit on, nothing but a brazier to warm oneself by, and yet abundant danger of fire, no solidity, no privacy, the deafening clatter twice daily of the opening and shutting of the outer wooden slides, draughts insidiously pouring in through innumerable chinks and crannies, darkness, whenever heavy rain makes it necessary to shut up one or more sides of the house—to these and various other enormities Japanese houses must plead guilty. Two things, chiefly, may be said on the other side. First, these houses are cheap—an essential point in a poor country. Secondly, the people who live in them do not share our European ideas with regard to comfort and discomfort. They do not miss fire-places or stoves. . . . They do not mind draughts . . . . Furthermore, the physicians who have studied Japanese dwelling-houses from the point of view of hygiene, give them a clean bill of health.[1]

St. Francis Xavier had had more than eleven weeks of the squatting, draughts, chopsticks, neck-dislocating pillows, and other features of Japanese domestic life, before he wrote his first letter from the country on November 5. He made no reference to them, but a long digression in the letter on the subjects of fortitude, self-abnegation and confidence in God would seem to indicate that they had severely tested even his iron resolution. He warned the men at Goa:

[1] *Things Japanese*, 1901 ed., pp. 36–7. Mr. Chamberlain first went to Japan in 1873 and lived there throughout the transition stage of the nation, an experience that ' makes a man feel preternaturally old; for here he is in modern times, with the air full of talk about bicycles and bacilli; and yet he can himself distinctly remember the Middle Ages. The dear old Samurai who first initiated the present writer into the mysteries of the Japanese language wore a queue and two swords. . . .' Besides being authoritative, this book is a perfect joy for its humour and beautiful style.

The worst hardships you have hitherto endured are trifling compared with what awaits you when you come to Japan. . . . Believe me, the metal of those who come out here will be well tested. . . . I do not say this as though to give you the impression that the service of God is hard. Indeed no; it is light and easy on condition that a man seeks God by the conquest of his own inclinations. But if he is not resolute in the time of trial, he will never know the infinite bounty of God nor have peace in this weary life, which to live without the intimate realization of God is not life at all but protracted death. . . .

The greatness of that poor Saint, exhausted and soon to die, comes out magnificently in the pages of profound spiritual direction which he wrote for his sons at Goa. He was fifteen degrees nearer the North Pole than they, but he had only the same featherweight cotton soutane, made for the tropics, to protect him against the icy November winds which whistled round Anjiro's house and stabbed at him from every direction, as he crouched shivering in the *chigai-dana* or alcove of the guest-room where writing was done, at a table no more than a foot high. In another briefer letter to Goa, dated also November 5, he wrote: ' The Fathers coming to Japan must be well provided with clothes made of Portuguese wool. And they must come well shod, for here we are dying of cold—*aqui morremos de frio.*' But he momentarily forgot his troubles, forgot the draughts, the fearful aches in his legs and thighs, the dainty but inadequate food, the diabolical appliances for eating it, the bonzes and their incipient hostility, and the language, the terrible language. He was transported back to Goa again and yearned over each of his dear ones there, Antonio Gomes in the front, as though Japan and its dark mysteries were still only a dream of Marco Polo. He must warn them against the devil's wiles, the way he turns himself into an angel of light to make men imagine that they could serve God more grandly elsewhere and otherwise than at the humble place and post to which obedience assigned them. The great thing is to learn by resolute self-conquest to wait patiently on the will of God, meantime confiding their hopes and aspirations to the one God has put over them, namely, Antonio Gomes, without importuning him or endeavouring to wrest from him a permission which he is reluctant to give:

> For the love of God, Brothers, let us not be that type of Jesuit, but rather ones that work with all their might at whatever domestic task the superior tells them to do, no matter how lowly it be, . . . for it is not the actual physical exertion that counts towards a man's progress, nor the nature of the task, but the hearty readiness and spirit of faith with which it is undertaken, to the confusion of the devil. Let nobody deceive himself by imagining that he is going to be a signal success in great things if he has not first shown his quality in little, lowly things. . . . I am greatly afraid that the devil may trouble some of you at the College by suggesting that you are wasting your time and could have far greater fruit of souls and profit for your own souls if you came out into the wider world. . . . And I fear too that possibly some may come to India from Coimbra full of illusive fervour engendered by their self-chosen mortifications, who, cured by the stormy sea, may wish that they were well out of the ship and back at Coimbra. . . .[1]

The gist of all the counsel was that each should strive to win the battle of his own heart before crusading farther afield, that the way to conquer fear was to find courage *totalmente en Dios*, and that the road of true progress was for a man to show himself great in little things—*en las cosas pequeñas, grandes*.

Reverting to his rôle of reporter, Francis tells that their appearance at Kagoshima, ' Bonzes out of Portugal ', set the whole

[1] Schurhammer, ii, 194–8. The quotations given are little more than a paraphrase, as the passage is too long and too complicated for exact translation. Father Schurhammer gives references throughout to parallel passages in the Spiritual Exercises of St. Ignatius, but that must not be taken to mean that St. Francis merely borrowed from his ' only Father '. He, too, had been through the Dark Nights and had acquired his wisdom in the same hard school—where all the saints acquire it. He spoke from his own experience and became a master of the spiritual life in his own right, but there was a marvellous affinity of soul between the two men, which gave their thoughts the same supernatural resonance.

town talking, that the *bugyô* or civil governor and likewise the military captain gave them a good welcome, and that nobody reproached their friend Paul for becoming a Christian. Until he enlightened them they no doubt took Christianity to be just another of the ever proliferating Buddhist sects which it was quite in order for a man to adopt if he felt so inclined. Those were busy days for Paul and difficult ones for his guests, as the town, where nothing much ever happened except earthquakes, tended to lionize her remarkable son, home again after travelling so far and seeing such amazing things, elephants, for instance. The mats in the guest-room must have been nearly worn out by the procession of visitors all day long, and Francis must have been worn out too, squatting in that tormenting posture for hours on end and listening without understanding a word while Paul explained to successive waves of invaders the marvels of Goa and the splendid things he had seen in the world's market of Malacca. But there were more important matters to be discussed in the daily sessions at home or out of doors, for Paul, under the wing of Father Cosmas de Torres, had become a very earnest and well-instructed Catholic, even to the extent of having made the Spiritual Exercises of St. Ignatius in their completeness, for a month on end, as the Jesuits themselves do only twice in a lifetime. ' Paul,' says Francis, ' obtained a great hold on many of his kinsmen and friends. He preached to them day and night, and was instrumental in bringing his mother, his wife, his daughter, and several of his relatives and friends, both men and women, into the Christian fold. As the majority of them can read and write, they readily learn the prayers. . . .'

In his strong castle at Kokubu, about fifteen miles from Kago-shima, the powerful Daimyo of Satsuma, Shimazu Takahisa, one of Japan's ' big six ' in that anarchical time, heard of the stir in his capital and commanded Paul to his presence. The castle must have been an impressive sight, for George Alvares, who was familiar with Portuguese methods of fortification, had visited it and declared it to be the most impenetrable-looking place he had ever seen. The Daimyo shared that quality of his castle, but being a Japanese nobleman was extremely polite.

He was very pleased with Paul and did him much honour [wrote St. Francis]. He asked him many questions about the customs and influence of the Portuguese, to all of which Paul replied in such a way as to satisfy the ' Duke ' completely. Paul had taken with him on his visit a very devotional picture of the Madonna and Child which we had brought to Japan, and this gave the Duke the most wonderful pleasure when he was shown it. He prostrated himself before it and adored it most reverently, and then bade his courtiers do the same. Afterwards, the picture was shown to the Duke's mother who marvelled to see it and showed the greatest pleasure. A few days later, when Paul had returned to Kagoshima, this lady sent a nobleman to obtain a copy of the picture for her, but the materials necessary to make a copy are unobtainable in Japan, so we could not comply with her wish. She asked also to have in writing a statement of Christian belief, and Paul has been engaged for some days now in preparing this for her. . . .

The Daimyo of Satsuma had reason to be interested in the Portuguese. It was in his province that the first European dis-coverers of Japan had landed, bringing the famous arquebus, the remote ancestor of all Japanese guns, which was presented to his Highness, together with the secret of gunpowder, and soon multiplied a thousandfold by the cleverest copyists, and usually improvers, of other people's ideas in the whole world. Shimazu also desired to develop trade relations with the adventurous Western Barbarians, who, for all their barbarism, had things to sell which he coveted and could not obtain from China. It is reasonable to think that Paul spoke to the Daimyo of St. Francis and of the purpose for which he had come to Japan. Paul loved Francis and there is nothing merely fanciful in supposing that he gave a glowing account of his friend, his goodness, his power with God, and the great reverence in which he was held by the Portuguese merchants. There is no indication that Shimazu ever explicitly invited Francis to his castle, but neither did he display any unwillingness to see him, which was quite sufficient invitation as far as Francis, the world's boldest intruder, was concerned!

Besides, Shimazu, who is known to have been uncommonly astute, even for a Japanese, for those were the days before ' Dull as a Daimyo ' became a proverb in the land, very probably calculated that Francis might prove a useful type of bait to attract Portuguese ships to Kagoshima, a port the stupid barbarians tended to neglect in favour of more accessible anchorages to the north. As for religion, the Daimyo, himself a Zen Buddhist of the mild Soto school, displayed a very common attitude of mind among the cultured classes in regard to the supernatural, which has been neatly defined as ' politeness towards possibilities '. Had Paul unrolled before him a makimono showing a small black bird on a flowering branch, it is highly likely that he would have given it the same deep bow as he gave to the picture in oils of our Lady. *Toujours la politesse!* Or perhaps he thought that it was an unusual representation of a popular deity in the congested Olympus of Japan, Kwannon, the Goddess of Mercy, most attractive of the country's eight million deities.[1]

As St. Francis considered all the gods of the Gentiles to be demons, he chose the day for his visit to the Daimyo carefully— September 29, feast of St. Michael Archangel, under God the demons' most redoubtable foe, whom he had constituted patron of Japan. He must have taken with him either Paul or some other interpreter, as he knew no Japanese, and the reason for his going at all would appear to have been that he might obtain official sanction to preach Christianity in Satsuma. His account of the audience is very brief and bald: ' On the day of St. Michael we spoke with the Duke of that land, and he did us much honour, telling us to protect carefully the books in which was written the law of the Christians, because if the law was true and good it would arouse the opposition of the devil.' That was all our laconic man of Navarre had to say about this great occasion, try the biographers as they may to spin it out and give it a more regal

---

[1] ' The little lady Kwan-Yin [Japanese: Kwannon] is one of the loveliest forms of Buddhist mythology. She has not a trait one could wish absent or altered. In the heart of the Chinese [and Japanese] Buddhist she holds the place which the Madonna holds in that of the pious Catholic ' (Pratt, *The Pilgrimage of Buddhism*, p. 297). Perhaps, but with the somewhat important difference that the Madonna is no myth.

air. If the addiction of Rodriguez and Bobadilla to the dukes of Portugal and Italy used to make Francis smile, he would not have been much overawed by a Japanese version of the same article. What mattered to him was that the Daimyo, a few days later, ' gave all his vassals permission to become Christians, if they so desired '. That was indeed *buenas nuevas* to tell the men at Goa for their consolation, even if it meant, as it probably did, that Shimazu considered Christianity to be merely yet another development of Buddhism. The fact that Francis assigned him the title of duke rather than king shows our man to have been still nursing the illusion created by Anjiro and the Portuguese merchants of a Tennô or Heavenly Emperor who held sway over all Japan. That was the man he must see, whatever it cost him, and he may have mentioned his dear ambition to Shimazu. But Shimazu, who knew the truth as well as any man, being himself no little part of it, did not enlighten the odd and new type of bonze, did not by word or gesture give him a hint that the O had long since been transformed into a mere figurehead, a symbol without substance, exercising no political power and removed altogether from human sight behind the walls and screens of his vast crumbling palace in Miyaco, a poor bird of fine feathers imprisoned in a gilded cage. Nor does Francis seem to have heard of the dynasty of shoguns who had stripped the Tennô of all but his heavenly dignity, and then in course of time had been stripped themselves of their earthly power by the ambitious clan-chieftains, the daimyo, each sovereign in the territory he had carved out for himself from the body of Japan.

Here is St. Francis speaking on the situation with a confidence little justified by the facts:

We reached Kagoshima[1] at a time when the winds were

[1] He invariably writes the name Cangoxima, which is almost correct since medial *g* in Japanese, as in ancient Greek, has the sound of *ng*. To complete this piece of erudition, derived, of course, from the best, the most impartial, and the merriest book ever written on Japan, Chamberlain's *Things Japanese*, the reader should know that *Kago* (pronounced *Kango*, as he has already been informed) means generically a basket, but became specialized to one form of basket, a wickerwork sedan-chair, much used in Old Japan. Perhaps those

contrary for a voyage to Miyako, the principal city of Japan
and the residence of the king and the greatest noblemen of
the land. There will not be a favourable wind for another five
months. Then, with the help of God, we shall go to Miyako,
which is three hundred leagues from here. They tell us great
things about that city, for instance, that it has ninety thousand
dwelling-houses, a fine university with five principal colleges,
and more than two hundred Buddhist monasteries and
nunneries. . . .

Francis goes on to mention five other important ' universities '
of Japan, each catering for 3,500 students, but those places had
almost nothing in common with what the Western World meant
by universities and were in fact merely large Buddhist monasteries
dedicated to the study and diffusion of one or other of the many
sects derived from the Buddha's original doctrine, recorded or
invented in Ceylon, four hundred years after the Enlightened
One's death. The students, who were never as many as St. Francis
was told, resorted to the monasteries to be taught reading and
writing that they might thus become fitted for instruction in the
particular sect's teachings, but in absolutely nothing else. Francis
appears to have been a little sceptical about the tales with which
Anjiro, and others through Anjiro, regaled him.

Before being able to guarantee to you [he wrote] that these
great things they tell me are true I shall need to see them, and
then if my own experience bears out the descriptions, I shall
let you have full details. . . . Also, when I have investigated the
possibilities for bearing fruit of souls in those places, I shall not
find it burdensome to write to all the principal universities of
Christendom, thus discharging my conscience and laying the
responsibility on them, who with their great virtues and

exceedingly uncomfortable means of transport were manufactured at Kagoshima. Shima, as any one could guess for himself after studying a map of Japan,
means an island or islands, the Japanese language having no special form for
the plural of nouns, just as it has no genders, though the student may be able
by a profound study of the clues provided to decide whether a lady or a
gentleman is in question, or whether one daimyo or the whole 262 of them.

learning could remedy a dreadful evil by converting this vast mass of unbelief to the knowledge of its Creator, Redeemer and Saviour. . . . And if things are promising I shall write to His Holiness the Pope, too, Christ's Vicar on earth and Pastor, not only of all believing souls, but of all souls disposed to belief. . . . Nor shall I forget to communicate with the friars, those good men blessed of God, so full of holy desires for the glory of Jesus Christ in souls that know Him not, that many may come to this great Kingdom, and to the other even greater which is China. For travel to China may be accomplished in all security by means of a safe-conduct from the King of Japan, whom I have confidence in God will be our friend and readily grant us this favour. He is a friend of the King of China, possesses the latter's seal as a token of their good relations, and is empowered to use it in the granting of safe-conducts. The crossing to China is a matter of only ten or twelve days and many Japanese ships make it regularly. If God gives me another ten years of life I have high hopes of seeing great things achieved in this part of the world by men coming from your part. . . . Before the present year is out, two bonzes who studied at the universities of Miyako and Kwanto are going to India accompanied by other Japanese to learn about our holy faith. . . .

Was there ever a man who staked his all on God more sublimely than Francis? There he was, barely arrived in Japan and already dreaming of the conquest of China, Japan's Athens and Rome. What he was told about the seal of the Chinese Emperor had a certain amount of fact mixed up with much fancy. Not the seal itself but papers stamped with it had in the past been sent to shoguns with a view to promoting trade between the two countries, and Ouchi Yoshitaka, ruler of seven provinces and the most powerful daimyo in Japan, with whom St. Francis had an exciting audience, also enjoyed the privilege. Francis was brought into contact with the Buddhist monks of Kagoshima by his host Paul who, after killing a man, had taken sanctuary in one of their monasteries. There were a number of these in the district, each representing a different sect; the *Shingon*, founded by Kobo

Daishi in the ninth century, to which Paul himself appears to have belonged in his pagan days; the popular *Shin*, a kind of Lutheran version of Buddhism based on faith in Amida, which permitted its bonzes to have wives and made other concessions not to the liking of Western advocates of Nirvana; the highly influential *Zen*, introduced from China in the twelfth century, which dispenses with the ideas of God, the soul, and salvation, and is the type of Buddhism favoured by Englishmen and Americans in search of something deeper than apparently St. John of the Cross could give them; and finally the *Soto* sect, itself an offshoot of *Zen*.[1] St. Francis mentions that, speaking through Paul, he often reproached the celibate monks and begged them to desist from the ugly vice to which they were addicted: ' They took my words in good part and merely laughed, for they are not in the least ashamed to be chided on this score.' But not all the monks by any means stank of the Cities of the Plain. Some were noble characters, leading truly austere lives and faithfully practising the hard discipline of the Eightfold Path. From the first they showed a friendly interest in the priests from the West, and one, the greatest, gave them his affection, as St. Francis gratefully acknowledged:

I often held converse with some of their wisest monks, and with one in particular who is universally revered on account of his learning, the integrity of his life, his responsible position, and his age, for he is eighty years old. His name is Ninxit [Ninjitsu] which means in the Japanese language ' Heart of Truth '.[2] He holds, as it were, the office of bishop among them, and if his name squared with his profession he would be truly

[1] Mr. Christmas Humphreys, President of the Buddhist Society of London, has written extensively on Zen, and devotes many interesting pages to it in his recent excellent Pelican Book, *Buddhism* (1951). One surprising piece of knowledge which he imparts is that Zen deliberately uses laughter as a means to a spiritual end: ' Roars of laughter, cleansing, healthy, ferocious laughter, are part of the Zen monk's daily life and of those who practise Zen ' (*Buddhism*, p. 186). Roars of laughter, if not cleansing and healthy, at any rate ferocious, are heard in other institutions besides Zen monasteries.

[2] *Nin*, marrow; *Jitsu*, truth (Schurhammer, *Epistolae*, ii, 190, n. 50).

blessed. In many conversations we had together, I found him doubtful and unable to decide whether the human soul is immortal or dies with the body. Sometimes he would say yes and sometimes no, and I fear that the other learned monks have the same hesitations. It is astonishing how friendly with me Ninxit has become. Indeed, all the people, seculars as well as bonzes, are very pleasant to us, and marvel greatly that we should have come so far, the six thousand leagues between Portugal and Japan, simply and solely to speak to them of the things of God. . . .

Francis must certainly have taken Anjiro with him on those visits (quite unasked!) to the Buddhist monasteries. To supplement the little he has told us himself of what passed on those occasions, there are two other good and early sources, a history of Japan concluded in the year 1586 by a very able Portuguese Jesuit missionary named Father Luis Frois, and a letter written from Japan in 1562 by one of the greatest of the country's Christian apostles, Brother Luis Almeida.[1] Frois based his account of the happenings at Kagoshima on some papers of Brother Juan Fernandez, the companion of Francis Xavier, which he found at the mission established by the Saint in Hirado, an island and port off the north-west coast of Kyushu. The monastery, he says, over which Ninjitsu presided contained more than a hundred bonzes, all of the Zen sect whose doctrine runs: ' Birth and death, that is the whole story, for there is no other life, no chastisement for the bad nor recompense for the good, nor a Creator who governs the universe.' That is a simplification of Zen teaching but certainly not a travesty.

These bonzes [Frois continues] have the custom of making

---

[1] Père Cros gives many excerpts from Frois, whose work was still in manuscript at the time, in his *Saint François de Xavier: sa vie et ses lettres* (Paris, 1900), but the history did not get the honour it deserved for several years more, when Father Schurhammer edited it in his usual thorough and scholarly fashion, and published it in German, *Die Geschichte Japans von P. Luis Frois, S.J.* (Leipzig, 1926). Brother Almeida's letter saw the light in *Cartas de Japão*, a collection published at Evora in 1598.

one or two hours of meditation a hundred times a year, the subject of it being invariably the thought, There is Nothing.[1] . . . When gathered together for this meditation the monks assume a posture of such modesty and exterior recollection that they might be thought to be in ecstasy. One day that Master Francis found them thus occupied, he asked Ninjitsu, ' What are these monks doing? ' to which the old man replied with a smile, ' Some of them are reckoning up how much they have obtained from their parishioners these past months, others are thinking of clothing and food, a third group of amusement, none at all of anything of consequence.' . . . On another occasion the Father put the following question to Ninjitsu, ' Which period of life seems to you preferable, youth or the old age which you have reached? ' Ninjitsu replied, ' Youth ! For the body is then strong and a man can do as he desires.' Master Francis took him up, ' What do you consider the best time for those sailing from one port to another, when they are on the high sea exposed to the tempest or when they are about to reach their elected haven? ' Ninjitsu answered, ' I see what you are getting at, but it does not apply to me. For a man sure of his destination and that the port is open the best time is when he is approaching it, but I know not whither I am sailing nor how the goal is to be attained.'

How much of all that is Anjiro's gloss, or an interpretation of Brother Fernandez, or perhaps even the imagination of St. Francis, it is not possible to detect, but we know that the three men and Ninjitsu were at cross purposes from the letter of Brother Almeida, who was sent by Father Cosmas de Torres to help the Christians of Kagoshima, just ten years after the death of Francis.

[1] This *is* a travesty. ' *Samma Samadhi* [last stage of the Noble Eightfold Path] in its lower stages may be called Right Meditation, while its highest is the threshold of Nirvana. . . . It involves the attainment of that Universal Consciousness which mystics have described in a thousand ways. . . . It produces an immediate insight into the nature of the Universe and all that therein is, by a means of knowledge far transcending reason. The faculty involved is Buddhi . . . intuitive or direct cognition, by the use of which the evolving consciousness cognizes and unites itself with the All of which it is a part.' (Humphreys, *Buddhism*, p. 117).

I was aware [he wrote] that Father Master Francis had been on terms of intimate friendship with a bonze called Ninjitsu, superior of the principal monastery of Kagoshima. I went to see the old man [who lived to be a centenarian] and received a most friendly welcome. He told me all about his conversations with Father Master Francis in the past, and gave me the impression of a man very desirous to learn. For a Japanese he is humble and that is what endears him to us. Knowing that he suffered from an affection of the eyes I gave him a liquid salve, for which he thanked me warmly. He said to me that he had been anxious to know the doctrine preached by Father Francis, but could never understand him when he expounded it because he had not the language for the purpose.

The meaning here must be that Anjiro had not the language, the Japanese terms and names which might have conveyed some inkling of the Christian concepts to the bewildered old man, for Francis himself, *entre ellos como una statua*, knew no Japanese, theological or other kind. At a second Zen monastery called Nanriji which Francis had visited, there had been the same friendliness and the same lack of understanding. The Tôdô or abbot of this place, a disciple and close intimate of Ninjitsu, invited Brother Almeida to stay with him and they used to talk long into the night about the relative merits of Buddhism and Christianity. The Tôdô had studied seven thousand books dealing with the doctrine of Gotama, the Buddha, called also Sakyamuni or sage of the Sakya, his native clan, but had conceived doubts about it after the visit of Father Francis. He told Almeida that Francis had been unable to explain the Christian teaching owing to his ignorance of Japanese, but that nevertheless his mere presence, his face, his character, his obvious sanctity, preached better than words the truth of his message. From that time the Tôdô remained convinced, and even learned by heart the prayers which Anjiro had put into Japanese. Both he and his friend Ninjitsu begged Almeida to baptize them secretly. They would have to go on teaching the Zen doctrine, they said, to their monks and others who came to learn but would gradually mould and adapt it until it conformed entirely to the law of the Gospel. Of course Almeida could not accept such a condition, and it is unknown whether the two good old men ever became Christians.[1]

Padre Valignano, as usual, has a shrewd and compassionate comment on the situation in which St. Francis and his two brother-Jesuits found themselves:

> Everything served to bewilder them in their complete inexperience. Though Paul, who was uneducated, knew enough to translate the Christian doctrine into Japanese, he did it all so badly that it became a matter of mockery and laughter among the people. He did not express himself accurately when interpreting the truth which Father Francis preached, and as for his writing, it could only be read with a smile by educated men. But as nothing could cool the ardour of the Father's charity, as difficulties only added fuel to its flame, so the sanctity of his life and the spirit given him by our Lord brought greater conviction to people that what he desired to say was good and true than did the interpretations of Paul or his readings from the book he had written.

Valignano was highly complimentary to the Japanese language which, he said, expressed its concepts better than did Latin, but shockingly disrespectful to the Buddha, ' that Xaca [Sakya], a perverse and ambitious natural philosopher, full of wiles, and eager to ennoble and exalt his name in this world, since he knew so little about the next '. The Padre obviously did not know too much about that Xaca! As for the Japanese language expressing its concepts, a far greater authority than he has given an example of how this is done, which must now be copied for the reader's instruction and delight:

Kono goro ni itarimashite, Bukyô   ' At the present day,
This period at having-arrived, Buddhism Buddhism has sunk in-

---

[1] Cros, *Saint François de Xavier: sa vie et ses lettres*, ii, 77–81; Schurhammer, *Die Geschichte Japans von P. Luis Frois*, 122–3.

to môsu mono wa, tada katôjimmin
that [they] say thing as-for merely low-class people's
no shinjiru tokoro to natte
believing place that having become
chuto ijo de wa sono dôri
middle-class thence-upwards in as-for, its reason
wo wakimae-teru hito ga sukunaku;
discerning-are people being few,
shûmon to ieba sôshiki no toki
religion that if-one-says, funeral-rite's time
bakari ni mochuru koto no yô ni omoimasu.
only in employ thing's manner in [they] think.[1]

to being the belief of the lower classes only. Few persons in the middle and upper classes understand its *raison d'être*, most of them fancying that religion is a thing which comes into play only at funeral services.'

That, then, was the dragon of genuine Chinese stock standing in the path of St. Francis, and he spoke feelingly about it in his monster of a letter to Goa:

May God our Lord give us language to speak to the people of the things concerning Him, for then with His help and grace we might have great fruit of our labours. At present we are like statues among the people who speak and converse about us a great deal, while we stand by uncomprehending.[2] It falls to us now to become as little children in order to learn the language, and God grant that we may imitate them also in simplicity and innocence of soul. . . . God has done us a great

[1] Chamberlain, *Things Japanese*, p. 274. The writer who was for long a professor of Japanese in Tokyo goes on to point out that 'Japanese nouns have no gender or number, Japanese adjectives no degrees of comparison, Japanese verbs no person.' A student of this terrible language will hardly be consoled in his agonies by being told that, though the vocabulary is extraordinarily rich, 'it affords absolutely no means of cursing and swearing'.

[2] The famous Japanese politeness had its limitations, as that great but not blind lover of Japan, Basil Hall Chamberlain, readily admitted: 'In some exceptional particulars this most courteous nation does offend glaringly against the canons of courtesy, as understood in the West. Japanese will dog your footsteps in the streets. They will answer in English when you have addressed them

ST. FRANCIS XAVIER

and signal mercy in bringing us to this Gentile land full of
idolatry and of the enemies of Christ, for we are left with
nothing in which to put our trust and hope except God alone,
having here no relatives or friends or acquaintances. . . . In
other places where our Creator, Redeemer and Lord is
known, creatures are wont to make men forget and neglect
God. Thus it can be with love of father, mother, relatives,
friends, ay, and the love of one's own native land. And to
possess all that is needed of temporal goods or spiritual comfort
in health as in sickness works the same way. What above all
else forces us to rest our hopes in God is the lack of anybody to
help our souls in this strange land where God is unknown. . . .
Judge for yourselves now how imperturbably, contentedly and
happily we might pass our days, if only we were the men we
should be. . . .

Francis goes on to dilate on two other favours shown them by
God, first the impossibility in Japan of ruining one's health and so
' putting oneself in the power of the doctors ' by over-eating:

Even if we tried to pamper the body with superfluities the
very soil of Japan would not permit it. They do not kill or eat
any bird or animal, but subsist on a little fish and rice and
wheat. There are plenty of vegetables and some fruits, but they
use them sparingly. The people are marvellously healthy withal
and many among them are advanced in age, so it is easy to see
from the case of the Japanese that but little is necessary to keep
the body in good shape, although it may not much care for

in their own language. They will catechize you about your plans: " Whither
are you going? Whence do you come? What is your business? Are you
married? If not, how extremely odd of you ! " If you turn them off, they will
interrogate your servant, and that to your very face. At other times, seeing that
you speak Japanese, they will wag their heads and smile condescendingly, and
admit to each other that you are really quite intelligent—much as we might do
in presence of the learned pig or an ape of somewhat unusual attainments '
(*Things Japanese*, pp. 378–9). It amounts to this, that the Japanese people are
afflicted with the most shattering superiority-complex ever evolved by the
proud human race.

the things it is given. We, too, are in excellent health of body, and God grant that the same may be said of our souls!

The second favour, strange to tell, was the prevalence of bonzes in Japan, for though they smiled on him at first, Francis sensed a latent hostility:

> Our views about God and the salvation of souls are so completely opposed to theirs that we may easily suffer sore persecution from them, and not in words only. . . . We seek no controversy with them, but neither are they going to frighten us into leaving off speaking of the glory of God and the salvation of souls. . . .

To speak of the glory of God was meat and drink to Francis, and now his great problem was to learn how to do it in Japanese. ' I think,' he wrote towards the end of his colossal letter, ' that we shall spend this winter drawing up a lengthy declaration on the articles of faith, with a view to having it printed and widely diffused. As the majority of the people are literate, we may thus be able to extend a knowledge of our holy faith in many places, since we cannot ourselves be everywhere. Our dear brother Paul will carefully put into Japanese all that men must believe and do in order to save their souls. . . .' But dear brother Paul was himself no mean part of the linguistic problem, and perhaps all the more dangerous as a mentor and interpreter because the Christian doctrines had become so familiar to him. He certainly was not familiar with the Buddhist doctrines and his temptation, to which he often succumbed, was to read a Christian meaning into Japanese words and names which they did not and never would bear. St. Francis had come up against the same problem when trying to get his sacred message put into Tamil and to find terms in that language for such un-Indian ideas as creation, redemption, the resurrection of the flesh, and so on, but, if tinged with pantheism, Tamil at least went from left to right in lines, like the languages of Europe, whereas Japanese, steeped in pantheism, went from right to left in columns, like nothing a European could have imagined outside a nightmare. The *Hiragana* or cursive syllabary of Japanese writing runs in a certain order called *i-ro-ha* from the first three syllables, as we name our order of letters, alphabet, from the first two letters, but whereas our alphabet is merely a list of disparate symbols, the *i-ro-ha* is a Buddhist lyric commenting on the illusions and vanities of phenomenal existence! A Japanese child is therefore indoctrinated with a main tenet of Buddhism from the days when he first toddles to school.[1] No specimens of Anjiro's Japanese writing have survived, but it is very likely that he used this popular *Hiragana* syllabary, said to have been invented by the Buddhist saint Kobo Daishi, founder of the Shingon sect in the ninth century A.D., when he made his numerous translations for St. Francis Xavier. Possibly he was able to write the *Katakana* syllabary also, which consists of fragments of Chinese characters, but the Chinese characters whole and entire he could neither write nor read and so was excluded from the vast realm of Buddhist doctrine and speculation locked away from profane eyes in erudite books. Before leaving India, St. Francis had learned that, just as the theology of the Western Church used Latin as its medium, so Buddhist 'theology' in Japan employed the ideograms of China, which Anjiro did not understand. He therefore from the start rather doubted the good fellow's competence as an exponent of Buddhist teaching and determined to investigate it personally when he reached Japan—an ambition which Japan ruthlessly nipped in the bud.

Francis, in fact, remained tied hand and foot to Anjiro. He had no one else in the wide world to whom to turn and must needs accept what that perfectly honest but sadly deficient oracle propounded. The oracle did not lack self-assurance, which is the way of oracles. While they were all still in India, St. Francis had instructed Father Nicholas Lancillotto to interrogate the great man from Japan, and then on the basis of the information received to

[1] One of the earliest and best authorities on the new Japan of the nineteenth century tells of the shock he received when he heard small children in a Japanese school reciting the frightful piece of pessimism, which makes *The Shropshire Lad* seem cheerful by comparison: ' *En verité, cet abécédaire national m'en dit plus sur le fond du caractère du peuple japonais que beaucoup de gros volumes* ' (Aimé Humbert, *Le Japon illustré*, Paris, 1870, t. i, p. 103).

draw up a report on the country for the enlightenment of the Jesuits in Rome. This report still exists and gives Anjiro away completely as a know-all who knew next to nothing. The Japanese, he informed the delighted Lancillotto, all adored one only personal God, Creator of all things, who rewards the good and punishes the wicked, to whom Xaca, the Buddha, ordered men to pray and whom the bonzes preach and proclaim. Asked the Japanese name for God as thus described, Anjiro answered without a moment's hesitation that it was *Dainichi*, but that Dainichi was sometimes represented with three heads and under that form called *Cogi*. Lancillotto must have been more than ever thrilled by that revelation of Unity and Trinity in Japan. As for the statues to be found in Japanese pagodas, Anjiro assured him that they represented the saints who were worshipped in Japan exactly as Christians worshipped them. Now, there was and is a god in Japan named Dainichi, meaning the Great Sun, and a most important god, too. His temple at Nara, about twenty miles due east of Osaka on the Main Island (Hondo or Honshu), is the largest wooden building in the world, and his bronze statue therein, ' the unveiling of which by the Emperor of the day in 752 was a notable event in Japanese religious history ' is fifty feet high.[1] The appalling trouble which this Dainichi with his bowels of brass was to bring on the innocent head of St. Francis Xavier will be unfolded as the story proceeds.

It may be refreshing after such a dusty farrago of syllabaries and gods to permit Francis now to conclude his long letter to Goa, for the farewell is beautiful:

So I come to an end who can never come to an end of writing the great love I bear you each and all. If the hearts of those who love one another in Christ could be seen in this present life, believe me, dearest Brothers, you would be clearly visible in mine. If looking there you did not perceive yourselves, it would be your humility that veiled your eyes, for the image of each of you is stamped on my heart and soul. I entreat you to have true love for one another and never to let any bitterness

[1] Humphreys, *Buddhism*, p. 171.

grow in your souls. Put part of your fervour into your mutual love, and part of your desires to suffer for Christ into suffering for that love's sake, conquering in yourselves all the repugnances and dislikes that stop love growing. As you know well, Christ said that His disciples were to be recognized and distinguished by their love for one another. May God give us intimate understanding of His holy will and grace to fulfil it perfectly. *De Cangoxima a cinco de Noviembre de* 1549 *annos. Vosso todo en Christo Hirmão carissimo, Francisco.*[1]

With that letter, the mammoth of his correspondence, Francis dispatched four others bearing the same date, which does not necessarily mean that all were written on the same day. One went to the three Fathers, Berze, Gago and Carvalho, summoning them to Japan, which, however, only Balthasar Gago reached, to fight it out with Dainichi and all his company and thrust them ignominiously from the Japanese Christian catechism, but that was after the time of St. Francis. A second and very charming letter went to Father Paul of Camerino: ' If you remember me as well as I remember you, then we are as good as together all the day long.' Paul is to send him very detailed news—*muy menudamente nueva*—of each and all the brethren in India, and of the boys at St. Paul's College, how many they are and how getting on. ' Do your best above all for any Chinese and Japanese boys there, instructing them carefully in Christian doctrine, taking great heed that they progress in spirit, and seeing that they learn to read, write and speak Portuguese so that they may be able to act as interpreters to the Fathers who, please God, will be coming to Japan and China before long.' Paul is to find a preacher to replace Father Berze at Ormuz or, if he cannot find a treasure of eloquence, to send some holy, humble Father who will preach by his life

[1] Schurhammer, *Epistolae S. Francisci Xaverii*, ii, 211–12. The giant letter begins on p. 179. It is in Spanish but peppered with Portuguese words or turns of phrase. Throughout he used the Spanish *hermano*, brother, but in the very last line switched to the Portuguese *irmão*, perhaps for the benefit of that brother of his from Coimbra, Antonio Gomes. Francis was equally fond of adding initial *h*'s to words that did not have them, and of subtracting them from words that did.

better than is done in pulpits, for to work is a grander thing than to talk—*pues más es obrar que hablar*. Francis sends greetings to many by name, especially to the lady the Jesuits called *Nossa May*, Our Mother, and to a French priest who had been chaplain to Governor de Sousa and gave himself airs. ' Remember me to him,' wrote Francis, ' and tell him from me that as he is vicar of the Church of our Lady of Light he must obtain much light for himself, because at the time when I knew him he had mighty little of it!' Paul is to see that all the Fathers teach the Christian doctrine daily to the children and slaves, and to speak while doing so the kind of Pidgin Portuguese which the slaves used. ' That was the dialect I used myself when I taught at Goa,' added Francis. He then told his old friend about the two bonzes who were making a pilgrimage to India: ' Do your very best to ensure that they get a good welcome from the Portuguese. Dance attendance on them and show them much love, for they are a people that love alone can win.'

The third letter was to Antonio Gomes:

I have exhausted my news and there is only one thing to add, which is that you are always before my eyes. It could be that my desire and longing for your spiritual good is greater than your own. To you more than to all the brethren of India I would commend a special care of yourself, for if you neglect it how am I to commend to you anything else? Were I sure that you did not forget or neglect a matter of such importance, then I would have high hopes of one day writing to tell you to come to Japan to fulfil your holy desires at [the universities] of Miyako and Kwanto.

Antonio is to ask the Governor to write to the King of Japan and to send him by the next batch of Fathers coming out some bales of precious stuffs and other presents. It would be a great day for Portuguese trade if the King became a Christian because they could then establish a factory at the fine port of Sakai and become as rich as Croesus. ' From my experience of them in India,' added Francis, with an almost perceptible shrug, ' I am not so sure that the merchants would provide a ship to bring the Fathers here for the love of God alone, without any other consideration. Perhaps I misjudge them, in which case no one would be better pleased than myself.' To tempt the merchants, he made out and enclosed a list of all the things that could be traded at Sakai for its abundant silver and gold. Sakai figures again in the fourth letter, which is one of deep thanks and gratitude to Dom Pedro da Silva, the Captain of Malacca, for providing them with ' so good a ship ' (the junk!), so many presents for the Japanese lords, and such abundance of all things necessary on the voyage. When Japan is converted, the greater part of the merit and glory will be Pedro's who will thus have crowned the great work initiated by his illustrious father, Vasco da Gama. And Portugal will be the richer because God has been put first. Sakai awaits the Portuguese ships, and only two days journey by land from Sakai lies Miyako, the capital of Japan and a bigger city than Lisbon. ' I live full of hope that before two years have passed, I shall be writing to tell you, Sir, that the Church of Our Lady of Miyako has been opened in the city, to which the merchants exposed to the tempests of the sea may come to commend themselves to the protection of the Mother of God. If you had enough confidence in me, Sir, to appoint me your business agent out here, I could secure you a return of more than one hundred per cent.' So Francis rambled on, shocking by his last remark some people who read him too hastily. ' It is a little surprising,' wrote one, that he proposed himself as agent and guaranteed a profit of a hundred per cent on any investment.[1] It is still more surprising that the writer did not read the very next words of the letter:

There is a certain way of acquiring that dividend which no captain of Malacca has yet tried. It is by giving the entire proceeds of trade to relieve the poverty of those who will become Christians in Japan. You would not run the slightest risk with your money and your profit is guaranteed by Christ Himself who promised that anything given for His sake in this life will be rewarded a hundredfold in the next. But I have my

[1] Maynard, *The Odyssey of Francis Xavier* (New York, 1936), p. 262.

doubts whether captains of Malacca appreciate that kind of interest!

Pedro is next told that some Japanese shepherded by two bonzes are converging on Malacca, attracted thither by the eloquent propaganda of Paul of Holy Faith who had expatiated to them on the beautiful character of the Portuguese. Would Pedro see to it for God's honour and his own that the same Portuguese lived up to expectations so that the Japanese might be drawn to the Church? This the good Captain must have thoroughly done, because four of the daring travellers were baptized at Malacca and returned to Japan good Christians. All the letters, including ones from Father de Torres and Anjiro, who pirated the diction of St. Francis! were entrusted to Domingos Diaz, the escort given them by Pedro da Silva, and taken to Malacca on the junk of poor dead Ladrão. The last word of them was a little panegyric of Diaz, 'the best of good companions and my excellent friend'.[1]

During the winter of 1549–50 the three Jesuits at Kagoshima set about the task of mastering the Japanese language, without benefit of grammar or dictionary or help of any kind except the tuition of their friend Paul, who was certainly not born to be a schoolmaster. We may picture them squatted by the hour in front of him, endeavouring with fingers stiff from the cold to copy in their notebooks in Latin characters the baffling sounds for the familiar things around them, windows, doors, floors, roofs, mats, flowers, trees, men, women, children, but how to write the 'man opened the door or what stood for a door', or 'the woman arranged the flowers', or 'the child squatted on the mat', there is the rub. Balbus builds his wall in Japan by rules that an ancient Roman or a sixteenth-century Spaniard or even a modern Englishman would consider extremely odd, if not entirely crazy. The task of mastering Japanese has been described by a gallant Englishman who succeeded as 'almost Herculean', and he went on to say that 'the oldest resident—for all that his hair has grown grey in the land of bamboo and the jinrikisha

[1] Schurhammer, *Epistolae*, ii, 214–31.

[rickshaw]—may still to the end of the chapter, be pulled up sharp, and forced to exclaim that all his experience does not yet suffice to probe the depths of the mental disposition of this fascinating, but enigmatical race '. A brave Frenchman who tried earnestly to learn the language wrote despondently that *une vie entière y suffit à peine*.[1] And St. Francis Xavier thought of it as just a winter's task ! Well, he learned a great deal that winter, though not Japanese. Brother Fernandez, barely twenty-three years old, was the most promising of Paul's pupils, and eventually, after about two years' hard struggle, could make himself understood, or almost understood, provided that the Japanese whom he was addressing listened carefully and exercised their wits. St. Francis considered him a marvel and told the world that he spoke the language beautifully—*muito bem*—which was an exaggeration. But that the humble, self-effacing, self-sacrificing Brother, who died worn out in Japan at the age of forty-one, should have learned to speak it even badly, under the circumstances, the first European ever to do so, was truly marvellous. The years tell in this matter, and Father Cosmas de Torres, who had turned forty, succeeded no better for all his striving than did his defeated elder, St. Francis. The Japanese love courage, and what a picture some great artist of the nation might have made of the three poor foreigners breaking their hearts daily over the language, but grimly holding on !

St. Francis himself says that it took him forty days to memorize the Ten Commandments in their Japanese dress, and he had an excellent memory. His principal work that winter in Kagoshima was the drafting of a lengthy exposition of Christian doctrine in Portuguese for the good Paul to translate into Japanese, using the Hiragana syllabary, and then for all four of them to transliterate as best they might into Latin phonetics. In that final form the work, St. Francis says, took more than an hour to read right through, which gives some indication of its size. As for its contents, he tells that it dealt succinctly with the creation of the world and then with Scriptural history down to the Incarnation, after which

[1] Chamberlain, *Things Japanese*, pp. 276, 301–2; Tessan, *Par les Chemins Japonais* (Paris, 1918), p. vi.

the mysteries of our Lord's life were amply expounded from His nativity to the Ascension. A declaration on the Last Judgment brought the little book to an end. Francis added to his account the somewhat superfluous words: ' It cost us a great deal of hard work.' Two years after his death another Jesuit in Japan read the work aloud to a Christian family on Christmas Eve, and from him we learn that it dealt with the six traditional ages of history from Adam to the end of the world, significantly harping on the destruction of Sodom and Gomorrah. Francis had brought with him from India the ' Shorter Catechism ' containing the prayers, the Creed and the Ten Commandments, and that too was done into Japanese by Paul and then transliterated. Not a trace of either work in its Japanese form has survived, but from other sources it is known that the false god Dainichi usurped the place of the true God in both, through poor Paul's ignorance of what the name really stood for in Buddhist mythology and specu-lation. So for more than a year there was the extraordinary situation of a Christian saint preaching the worship of a heathen idol! The proof of this did not come to light until ten years after the death of Francis and was then hushed up as though it were a stain on his memory, whereas, rightly understood, it serves rather to enhance his greatness by bringing into clearer light the appalling nature of the difficulties which he so gallantly confronted and magnificently overcame.[1] A visionary he has been called, but there was hardly one of his apparently extravagant dreams which did not eventually, in greater or less measure, come true.

There is some evidence that the Daimyo Shimazu gave Francis a house of his own in Kagoshima where he and his two brethren and Paul could work and pray more peacefully than in Paul's congested home. From there, as soon as the famous translation was completed, he used to sally forth twice a day

[1] The whole highly interesting question has been investigated by Father Schurhammer with his usual thoroughness and competence in his brilliant study, *Das kirchliche Sprachproblem in der Japanischen Jesuitenmission des 16 und 17 Jahrhunderts*, Tokyo, 1927, pp. x–132. It was in Japan rather than in India or China that the tremendous and ruinous ' Rites Controversy ' began and St. Francis himself was innocently the origin of it.

carrying the notebook into which he had copied Paul's transliterated Japanese and betake himself to the terrace of one of the
Buddhist monasteries, where he would squat on the steps and
begin to read aloud from his book. The terrace seems to have been
in a public place and to have done duty as a kind of local Marble
Arch. Naturally people gathered round, as Francis must have cut
as strange a figure as would the Dalai Lama squatted and holding
forth on the steps of Eros in Piccadilly Circus. Some laughed at
and made sport of his atrocious accent and bad grammar, others
felt sorry for him, and yet more were queerly impressed, even if
they could not understand what he was trying to say. Among
those friendly ones was a young Japanese gentleman who soon
fell completely under the spell of Francis and was his very first
convert, apart from the large number brought in by the eloquence
of Paul. He baptized him as Bernard and kept him by his side all
through his time in Japan where he proved of the greatest help as
an interpreter. Later, at his own wish, Francis sent him to Portugal
where he was received into the Society of Jesus and became the
apple of several eminent Jesuits' eyes. They could not say too
much in praise of his bright intelligence, his tender piety, his
humble, docile spirit, his simplicity. Once, some one in his hearing
spoke of a Father who had become very proficient in Hebrew.
Much astonished, Bernard asked : ' How could a priest study the
language of the people who put our Lord to death? ' St. Ignatius
summoned him to Rome and he went there in the distinguished
company of Father Jerome Nadal to have as his confessor and
intimate friend for a whole year the no less distinguished Father
Pedro Ribadeneira, who saw in him the ' living image [retrato
vivo] of the Christians of the primitive Church '. They used to
talk together about Francis Xavier. ' For seven months,' said
Bernard, ' I slept in the same room as he. He took only a very little
sleep during which I frequently heard him sigh and invoke the
holy name of Jesus. When I asked him why he sighed like that in
his sleep, he answered: " I don't know. I was not aware that I
sighed." With my own eyes I have seen Father Francis deliver
many sick people from their maladies. He would make the Sign
of the Cross over them or sprinkle them with holy water and they

would be immediately cured.'[1] The bright hopes centred by the Jesuits on their first Japanese member were quenched by his death at Coimbra, still in the flower of his youth.

Another Japanese who fell to the charm of St. Francis was hardly less remarkable, the steward of a Samurai with the fine resounding name of Niirô Ise-no-kamidono who lived patriarchally in a castle called Ichiku, about six or seven hours walk north-west of Kagoshima. Francis gave the steward in baptism the name of Michael and with it some of his own apostolic spirit, for on his return to Ichiku the good man at once communicated his marvellous discovery and the joy it brought him to the Samurai's wife and children and to the castle retainers. He gave them the instructions which he had himself received and persuaded his master to permit St. Francis to come to heavily fortified Ichiku. Then on one day Francis baptized fifteen persons there, including the Samurai's lady and daughter, but not himself. He put the little community in charge of the devoted Michael and carefully showed him how to perform the ceremony of baptism in case others of the castle might wish to become Christians. He preached to them sweetly and lovingly from his book of instructions on the justice and mercy, the greatness and infinite goodness of— Dainichi! Either at that time or on a second visit made later in the year he left with them papers on which he had written in Latin the formula of baptism, the holy names of Jesus and Mary, and some litanies, and to Michael he gave as a memento one of his disciplines. For eleven years after that no priest nor Christian from the world without came near isolated and lonely Ichiku, but Michael guarded and inspired his little flock with his own great, strong faith and fervour. Perhaps only in Japan, the land of surprises and profound loyalties, are such things possible. When at last Brother Almeida visited the castle in December, 1561, he received an enthusiastic welcome from the Christians and even from the Samurai, who avowed that he would be a Christian himself were it not for fear of his overlord, the Daimyo of Satsuma. He was plied with questions, especially about St. Francis,

[1] *Las Obras del P. Pedro Ribadeneyra*, Madrid, 1595, i, pp. 146–7. Also, MHSJ, *Litterae Quadrimestres*, ii, 496 ; iii, 93, 678.

then nine years dead but living always in the hearts of those good people who proudly produced the prayers he had written for them and told of the many cures they had effected when laid upon the sick. Michael, then an old man, brought in the discipline St. Francis had given him. ' Once a week,' he said, ' I gather the Christians of the castle together and hand them the discipline so that each may give himself three strokes, not more. If any one tries to go beyond that number I stop him, for fear that the discipline might become worn . out. By this exercise we keep ourselves in good health.'[1]

One cold evening during Almeida's visit, the Christians and the Samurai himself came and squatted round an *hibachi* or brazier containing glowing charcoal to hear from the Brother an instruction on the things of *Deus* or *Dios*, the God of the Christians and only true God. He had not long been speaking when one of his attentive listeners suddenly broke in with a question: ' Is the *Dios* of whom you tell us the same as Dainichi? Father Francis preached to us that Dainichi was God and that it was to him that we must address our prayers.' Momentarily taken aback though he was by the unexpected interruption, Almeida went on to explain very carefully that Father Francis had preached Dainichi to them because he had been given incorrect information about Japanese religion. Dainichi, he was told, was the creator and first principle of all things existing so he concluded that he must be identical, under a Japanese name, with the *Deus* whom the Christians worship. What he did not learn and had no means of discovering was that the Buddhist priests meant something totally different by creator and creation from what Christians mean. For them, Dainichi was not a person nor even any specific thing but, as it were, the potentiality of all things, in fact, the *materia prima* of Aristotle and the Scholastics.[2] This is obviously

---

[1] Almeida's letter in Cros, *St. François de Xavier*, ii, 82–3.
[2] Schurhammer, *Das kirchliche Sprachproblem*, pp. 27–30. The passage referring to Dainichi in Almeida's original letter so greatly startled and puzzled the European Jesuits to whom it was addressed that they suppressed the name of the Japanese god altogether when they gave the letter to the printers. The result has been that in the books of Cros, Brou and all others who wrote before Schurhammer made his investigations no hint is given that St. Francis himself

pure pantheism. Nothing is made by Dainichi but all things are made out of him. He is all in all and all is in him, and the End of Man, his purpose and bliss, is to merge again into Dainichi, to become one and identical with him, the Absolute, through knowledge of him, who is Truth itself, achieved by moral self-discipline. Such was the esoteric doctrine of the Shingon sect which Kobo Daishi brought to Japan from China at the beginning of the ninth century A.D. In that system Dainichi, the Great Sun, the Illuminator, entirely superseded the historical Buddha, who became merely one of four Go-chi (Anjiro's Cogi), his attendant satellites. Doctrines so rarefied and difficult to grasp would not have been likely to appeal to the common man whom the Shingon apostles aspired to win, so they tempered their winds to the shorn lambs, of whom Anjiro was decidedly one, by allowing for ten ascending grades of enlightenment, by introducing many elements of popular Hinduism, by making Dainichi, alias Vairocana, visible and tangible in brass, and finally by welcoming all peoples and their gods into their fold. There was a variety of Shingon to suit all tastes, and if Anjiro, with his *anima naturaliter Christiana*, understood Dainichi to be God, personal and alone, Creator of the universe, not from His own substance nor from any pre-existing formless material, but out of nothing, he ran no danger of being excommunicated by the bonzes who would merely have been sorry for him as one still only on the lower rungs of the ladder of enlightenment. Vulgar persons had an esoteric theory of their own about Dainichi which made him to be a phallic god, symbolizing the human organs of reproduction.[1] That is enough, and perhaps more than enough, of the Great Sun, for the moment.

The first bright promise of the mission in Kagoshima did not last. Paul's little Pentecost had no sequel and Paul's confident prophecy in Malacca that six months might see the whole of

---

was deceived, though they have much to say about the true nature of Dainichi, derived from Luis Frois's *History of Japan*.

[1] Lloyd, *Developments of Japanese Buddhism*, in *Transactions of the Asiatic Society of Japan*, 1894, 388–92, a classical article on the subject; Humphreys, *Buddhism*, 172–4 ; Schurhammer, *Das kirchliche Sprachproblem*, 30.

Japan converted must have seemed to Francis almost a mockery when they had passed. No danger of his arm becoming paralysed with baptizing in this town where people were so different from the humble unquestioning crowds in India ! There, as the often vivid old history, *Oriente Conquistado*, said, he was able to fish with a net, but in Japan he had to fish with a line. And week after week would go by with never a rise to repay his patient angling. Always in the front of his mind was the thought of the Emperor in Miyako on whom he had pinned his hopes. He had intended to appeal to him immediately on his arrival in Japan, but the Daimyo and the monsoon had spoilt that plan. Now spring had reversed the monsoon, but the Daimyo still remained reluctant to let him go, saying that there was war in the north, as though Francis would have minded. But while he angled for souls in vain, the Daimyo angled just as unsuccessfully for ships. Plainly, thought Shimazu, this foreign bonze is not as important as I was given to understand, for he has not attracted a single merchantman to my harbour. Gradually, then, as the months brought beauty to the gardens and hills, Francis fell from favour, a process which the bonzes were happy to hasten. They had come to see as time passed that he was not a joke but a danger, that his doctrine and theirs could never be reconciled, that their power and prestige might be damaged by this persistent stranger who knew too much and openly denounced them.

The Buddhist monks, ' Friars ' of Orders Grey or Black according to their sects, had acquired an enormous ascendancy over the people and rulers of Japan at this time. The Emperor himself, once the only power in the land and venerated as divine, had sunk to the position of a bonze. The *kami* or familiar deities, almost the lares and penates, of Shintoism, had been tactfully and skilfully adopted into the Buddhist system, and that religion, with its professed respect for life even in its lowliest manifestations, actually took over and made its own the god of war *Yahata* whose shrine was at Usa in Kyushu. To this god the Buddhists gave the name of *Hachiman* and extended his worship to the whole of Japan, a development gratifying to the instincts of a bellicose race. To explain away the inconsistency, the bonzes invented the very popular ceremony of *hôjôe*, which consists in freeing birds from their cages, tortoises from tanks, and so on, and gave out that thus to release captive life compensated for any destruction of life in battle with enemies. By such arts, those clever clients of what was really a foreign, imported religion gradually became the effective masters of Japan, to whom even the warring daimyos had to bow.[1] For the bonzes, with all their pretensions to pacifism and non-resistance, did not for a moment hesitate to take up the weapons of this evil world of illusion. Their monasteries, which multiplied until they covered the whole land, were generally situated on mountain-sides or in other strategic positions and became, as time went on, fortresses and arsenals.

They formed orders half religious and half military, of the same kind as the Templars and the Teutonic Knights. Skill in the use of weapons was the best sign of a vocation. So all the samurai without masters and all social misfits and vagabonds felt an attraction to the rich monasteries where they were welcomed with open arms. The prestige of these bonzeries became such that no dispute was settled nor business transacted without an appeal for their support. Even the emperors and shoguns at the height of their power could do nothing against the redoubtable bonzes who were everywhere numerous and strong enough to bend all persons and events to their wills. ... The Emperor Shirakawa (1073-86) avowed that there were three things over which he had no power—the waters of the Kamogawa, the cast of the dice, and the bonzes of Hiei-zan. . . .[2]

[1] This 'Buddhification' of Shinto is very learnedly and genially described by the Abbé J.-M. Martin of the Société des Missions-Etrangères de Paris in his fine work, *Le Shintoisme, Religion Nationale du Japon*. Hongkong, 1927, ii, 325-9. The Buddhists made a liberal use of private 'revelations' in the course of their campaign.

[2] Steichen, *Les Daimyô chrétiens*, Hongkong, 1904, p. 11. This classical work is based largely on Japanese records. The Kamogawa is a river which flows through Kyoto (Miyako) and in old times used frequently to cause disastrous inundations. Hiei-zan is the highest of the hills around Kyoto and was almost entirely covered with monasteries of the Tendai sect of Buddhists. 'By the reign of Shirakawa the warrior monks (*sohei*) had become a positive menace

The bonzes of Kagoshima did not proceed to violence to get rid of St. Francis Xavier because it was not necessary. They had merely to encourage the growing suspicions of the Daimyo, himself a good Buddhist, that the *Nambanjin* or Barbarians of the South, meaning India, were unlikely to attract foreign trade to Satsuma, and that the wrath of the native gods might fall on his dominions if those strangers were permitted to lure people away from their worship. St. Francis in a subsequent letter to Europe mentioned that he and his companions were a little more than a year in Kagoshima and made during that time '*perto de cem christãos*', about a hundred Christians, mostly through the preaching and persuading of the Japanese Paul:

> Practically all the people would have become Christians had not the bonzes prevented it. They told the Duke of that land that if he allowed his vassals to accept the law of God he would lose his territories and have his pagodas profaned and destroyed by the people, because the law of God [*Deus*] was contrary to his laws, and people who accepted it would lay waste and desecrate all that they formerly regarded as holy. The bonzes prevailed with the Duke to the extent that he forbade any more conversions to Christianity under pain of death, and likewise prohibited further preaching. . . . The Japanese are singularly clever men and very obedient to reason, so if they failed to become Christians it was from fear of their temporal Lord and not because they did not recognize the truth of the Christian law and the falsity of their own. . . .[1]

There is much of Francis in those few bald lines. The bonzes have beaten him when he has gathered barely a stook of the harvest which he thought was going to be so great. It was such a poor return, and Anjiro's rather than his, for the shivers and the aches, the interminable intrusions, the weary hopeless struggle

---

to the capital, descending upon it and laying it waste until their demands were satisfied ' (Ponsonby Fane, *Kyoto, its History and Vicissitudes since its Foundation in 792 to 1868*, Hongkong, 1931, p. 114).

[1] Schurhammer, *Epistolae S. Francisci Xaverii*, ii, 258–9.

with those demons of syllabaries, through a year that must have dragged like ten years. But he is not at all dispirited. He has lost a battle, not a campaign. His enthusiasm for Japan and the Japanese shows no sign of waning. Give them a chance, he would say, and then see what the future will bring forth among this gifted people who prize honour more than life. It brought forth the sublimest epic of Christian heroism in the entire history of the Catholic Church. Francis, who might be said to have spent the whole decade of his apostolate in the catacombs, saw piercing the darkness gleams of great days to be. Even among the bonzes had he not found a Nicodemus and Gamaliel? And there was the young Bernard, a saint in the making, of whom a devout Jesuit afterwards said that the antipodes had come to Coimbra to shame him into piety. Michael of Ichiku belonged also to God's small aristocracy, in whom the divine *fidelitas*, the substance of the Psalms, was so beautifully mirrored.

But perhaps greater even than those two by Heaven's standards was the Japanese girl, daughter of St. Francis's hostess at the house made over to him by the Daimyo in the first bright days of the mission, so soon to be dimmed. She had wished to be a Christian and Francis, with Anjiro's help, instructed and baptized her, giving her the name of Mary. Then, within a couple of years the mission, so small and helpless, was at the mercy of the bonzes, yet when Brother Almeida came in the winter of 1561 he found two hundred Christians or men wanting to be Christians, whom he baptized. They were so grateful that they would have given him all that they possessed. ' Had I been a son of theirs returned after long absence,' he wrote, ' they could not have done more for me. . . . It is plain to see the working of the Holy Ghost in their souls, . . . for they live as sheep among wolves.' At this period there were still very few Jesuits in Japan and they were strained to breaking-point to keep going other larger missions which St. Francis had started or adumbrated. Sixteen more years went by before the forlorn Christians of Kagoshima had another visit from a Jesuit, and he had to tear himself away in a hurry. Six years later, in 1583, the indomitable Almeida, then near the end of his long heroic apostleship, arrived back in Kagoshima to find Mary the only Christian left. Many had died, others had reverted to Buddhism under bonze persecution, and perhaps a number had lost their lives in the fierce war between rival daimyos of Kyushu, out of which pagan Satsuma emerged victorious, but only itself to be smashed in due course by the brilliant soldier and statesman, Ieyasu, founder of the Tokugawa Shogunate. Father Almeida, as the great missionary had meantime become, endeavoured with Mary's help to win back lapsed Christians and convert new ones, but the bonzes secured his banishment from Kagoshima and he went away to die, the once wealthy merchant who had given his whole fortune to Japan and twenty-seven years of his fifty-nine.[1]

The following year, 1584, Mary of Kagoshima, lonely, desperately poor, and growing old, was visited by Brother Damian, a Japanese Jesuit. She wept with joy at sight of him, and each time he called on her during his brief stay in the dangerous town, she contrived to have some little present for him, if only a few cherries. On one of those occasions the Brother asked her whether she had no fear that by openly professing her faith and going through the streets with her rosary round her neck she might not suffer death or grievous bodily harm from the bonzes and other bitter enemies of the Christian name. ' Everyone here knows me to be a Christian,' she replied. 'Would to God that the bonzes might kill me for my confession of His holy Name, for then would my soul speed to the bliss of God's presence and the sight of my blessed Father, Master Francis, who baptized me. I would much prefer to die a martyr for the love of God than here in my room.' As she spoke, the Brother reported, tears trickled down her wrinkled cheeks. She then told him her two great sources of grief and anxiety, first, that in times of illness her heathen relatives were in the habit of visiting her and pestering her to invoke Amida and the Kamis for the recovery of her health. ' But I stop my ears so as not to hear them, and beg them to leave me alone that I may pray to God and die

---

[1] After Almeida's death it was said by one who knew him well that ' he who would recount his whole life, his voyages, labours combats and persecutions, need only have recourse to what St. Paul says happened to himself.'

as a Christian.' Her second and greater trouble was that when she died they would bury her in the common Buddhist graveyard, with the bonzes performing the funeral rites. ' I want none of their water and roses on my grave, and I have many a time begged my relatives to take my body outside the town and bury me among the pine-trees with my rosary around my neck, leaving me to make my own way to Heaven. Please pray to God, Brother, that this may be done and I shall die in peace.' For a good thirty years Mary had, single-handed and sorely pressed, kept the Christian flag flying in Kagoshima. So deeply affected was the superior of the Jesuits in Japan at the time by the story that he found means of bringing the valiant little woman, an unsung Barbara Fritchie, into the flourishing Christian community at Nagasaki. There she passed the remainder of her days holily and happily, with the love and veneration of the Christians, European as well as Japanese, around her. When she died the great Father Coelho himself sang her solemn Requiem and laid her to rest with the Rosary which St. Francis had given her about her neck. Not quantity but quality is what Heaven prizes, and here was a masterpiece from the hand of Francis, his abiding Kakemono, that will still be living and lovely when all the other famous ones are dust.[1]

St. Ignatius Loyola was so keenly interested in the fortunes of his sons, wherever they might be, that he once said he would like to know how many fleas bit them at night. Plenty of fleas bit his dearest son Francis Xavier while he snatched his brief slumbers on the matted floor, for though the cleanest people in the world beat and shake the mats incessantly the fleas still thrive in such excellent cover and are, or used to be, a chief curse of life in Japan. If anything, St. Francis, as his letters so plainly show, was ever even more agog than St. Ignatius for news of the brethren. It is not an exaggeration to say that he hungered and thirsted for such news. At this time he gave a notable proof of how much it meant to him. It was towards the end of June, 1550,

[1] Schurhammer, *Kagoshima*, an article based on the contemporary sources, published and unpublished, in *Die katholischen Missionen*, 48 Jahrgang, nr. 3, December, 1919, pp. 45–6.

and he lay prostrated by a fever, unable to swallow a mouthful of the rice or tea which Mary anxiously and lovingly prepared for him. Suddenly a rumour reached the town that a Portuguese ship had put in at the port of Hirado, lying on an island about two hundred miles away to the north-west of Kyushu. It was nearly two years then since India had sunk beneath the sick man's horizon, and he had a fever in his soul to know how the brethren were faring there stronger than the one in his blood. He must get to Hirado immediately, for the ship might sail again and perhaps take back the letters for which he longed, through ignorance of his whereabouts. Immediately he was away into the mountains with one companion, Bernard or another, to interpret for him. How he lived and bore up on that long forced march God alone knows. At fifteen miles a day, surely the limit for a sick man in wild country, the journey must have taken a fortnight. If some of us made such a journey even today, we might be tempted to write a book and call it *On Foot through Unknown Japan*. St. Francis Xavier made it four hundred years ago when there was war and anarchy in the land and never so much as mentioned it in his letters.[1] There are a few towns and villages along the route, so the two wayfarers may sometimes have been able to put up at an inn. It would be interesting to know whether they found a boat to take them across Shimabara Bay into the province of Hizen where Hirado lies, because Shimabara is the promontory where 40,000 Christians made their last stand in the days of the Great Persecution and were wiped out to the last man, woman and child by the pagan Japanese and the artillery of the good Calvinists from Holland.[2]

[1] The story comes from Father Frois's *History of Japan* as edited in German by Father Schurhammer, pp. 7–8. Frois was a junior contemporary of St. Francis and himself spent twenty-four years in Japan.

[2] Speaking of the sinister part played by his countrymen, Engelbert Kaempfer, that most remarkable early historian of Japan, whose book first appeared in an English translation in London in 1727, and then was republished in several volumes in Glasgow in 1906, castigates those responsible for lending aid to the persecutors in the strongest terms at his command. It was the *auri sacra fames*, the accursed lust for gold, that made them behave in a way, he says, that shocked even the nobler-minded Japanese pagans. Thus did this brave and excellent physician redeem his country's credit.

The Portuguese merchants at Hirado gave Francis a very good welcome, but letter for him they had none. However, his journey was not entirely in vain, for he learned that the local Tono or Lord, a piratical young person of twenty-eight named Matsura Takanobu, had been overjoyed by the coming of the Southern Barbarians to his port. He wanted foreign trade, the weapons, the cloths, the spices of those clever white devils, and was ready for any concessions to get them. Here, it seemed to Francis, God had indeed opened a great door for him to the real Japan, the Mainland, as the Japanese call the Island of Honshu, Japan of the Emperor. His hands, tied in Kagoshima, would here be absolutely free, and besides Hirado was a half-way house to Miyako. He must collect his frustrated men in the south and bring them to Hirado. There was still plenty of mirage included in his vision, but of what great pioneer cannot the same be said, Columbus, Magellan, Cabot, Raleigh, de Soto, Cook, even Captain Scott? A month later, Francis was back in Kagoshima and daringly asking the hostile Daimyo for some means of transport by sea to Hirado. He had been a disappointment and source of embarrassment to Shimazu who, no doubt to speed his departure, put at his disposal a *navicula perexigua*, the least valuable junk of his fleet. The word *navicula* means by itself a little ship and the adjective *perexigua* means very small, so the two in harness must have stood for a thing of the meanest dimensions.[1] Into it Francis, Father Torres, Brother Fernandez, Bernard, Anjiro's two Japanese companions, and Amador, the Malabar helper, had to pack themselves and their properties, including the presents for the Emperor given by Pedro da Silva, which had been stored in a *kura* or fire-proof outhouse, a very necessary adjunct to the highly inflammable Japanese home.

Francis left Anjiro in charge of the Kagoshima Christians, so largely his converts, until such time as he could provide a priest for the little flock. 'They saw us off with many tears,' he wrote, and there may well have been tears in his own eyes too, for he must have known in his heart that he would never see those

[1] They are from Polanco's *Chronicon*, ii, 140, and he must have had the description from the Japanese Bernard, who was among the *navicula's* victims.

firstlings of Japanese Christianity again. There is some indication of a farewell visit to the Christians of Ichiku, but the old writers have made such a hash of the Saint's itineraries at this time that it is difficult to be sure of any details. On general principles, however, it seems legitimate to say that the voyage in the *navicula* must have been a terrifying experience, for the indented coast was a favourite haunt of pirates and the winds made the cockleshell dance like a cork. So Polanco gathered from his informant Bernard. While the travellers contend with winds and waves, we may be permitted to bid good-bye to Anjiro, the dear friend of St. Francis and his perfectly innocent will-o'-the-wisp, who started the whole great epic of Japanese Christianity. Again, the old writers, the men on the spot or near the spot, throw us into confusion. One story is that Paul was driven from his home and country by the bonzes five or six months after the departure of St. Francis and died, equivalently a martyr, at the hands of pirates. That pleasing version of events had a distinguished origin, for it came from the celebrated *Peregrination* of Fernam Mendez Pinto, the sixteenth-century Marco Polo who had in him also by anticipation a good strain of the Baron von Münchhausen, as well as of the delightful Baron de Marbot.[1] Fernam was undoubtedly in Kyushu in 1551, as St. Francis, whom he helped, bears witness, and there is no particular reason why he should have given way to his well-known penchant for romance in relating the good sad end of Anjiro. But, alas, a much sorrier tale is told by the careful writer Luis Frois, S.J., in his *History of Japan*, to the effect that poor Anjiro was driven by want into becoming a pirate himself and perished miserably in some obscure affray with Chinese fishermen. Frois did not come to Japan until ten years after the event nor begin his history for twenty years. He may have had special information or he may have been deceived by Buddhist propaganda. Many things in his *History* are incorrect and there is no particular reason why he should be regarded as infallible in this instance. He is careful to say that Anjiro's piracy did not necessarily imply Anjiro's apostasy, and expressed a hope that the poor fellow had time to make an act of contrition before

---

[1] *Peregrinaçao*, cap. 208, Lisbon edition of 1711, p. 330.

he died. All very well, but piracy in those seas and times was not regarded as disreputable but as a substitute for the greater evil of open war. The best people went in for it, as later in Elizabethan England. St. Francis Xavier regretfully consigned his own pirate, Ladrão, to Hell, not on account of his peculiar profession but because of his unbelief. Frois gives no explanation of the penury into which Anjiro had fallen, whereas Mendez Pinto provides an excellent one, and his story in general is much truer to experience, much more credible, than the cataclysmic revelation of the Jesuit.[1]

---

[1] In the formidably learned article of great length already mentioned, entitled *Fernāo Mendez Pinto und seine ' Peregrinaçam '*, contributed to the German review, *Asia Major*, in 1926, Father Schurhammer dealt Pinto some very damaging blows, but left sufficient of the romancer's history standing to enable him to retain his niche as the best-travelled man of the sixteenth century. He was not, as he claimed, one of the three original discoverers of Japan, but he did visit Japan three times, and sailed the Red Sea, and was at Ormuz and Malacca, and travelled widely in Siam, and explored the Moluccas, and traded in China— glory enough for one man, without inventions.

Chapter XV

KAKEMONOS

AMONG the Portuguese merchants at Hirado was one Francisco Pereira de Miranda, destined for a terrible captivity in Canton, whom Xavier referred to as ' *meu especial amigo* '. Francis had told him that he would be returning with his companions soon, so when their toy ship heaved in sight the merchants ran up all their flags and saluted it with a thunderous salvo, nicely calculated to impress the Japanese authority. That person, Matsura Takanobu, was not a man to be attracted by Christianity, but he concealed his sentiments for the sake of trade and received Francis with a great show of friendliness—' *com muyto prazer* '. It would be time enough later when he had got all he wanted out of them to kick those barbarians and their bonzes into the sea. Francis spent two months in the town, during which time a hundred of the Japanese became Christians, largely, he implies, through the efforts of Brother Fernandez. But though he could not manage the language half as well as Fernandez, Francis himself also took part in the street-corner meetings, reading as best he could the Christian message in the strange music of transliterated Japanese. And here as at Kagoshima he continued to preach the glory and love of Dainichi. It is likely enough that the converts, who stood to gain nothing in this world by their change, would not have minded had he preached Mumbo Jumbo, because he was himself the best advertisement for the true and only God, by whatever name invoked, that any sincere man, open to the influence of divine grace, could have listened to. But he was not in Hirado, any more than in Kagoshima, to settle down. He wanted the freedom of all Japan for Christ, and that, he fondly imagined, could be secured most expeditiously by appeal to the Emperor, of whom the people everywhere and of every rank spoke with so much reverence. As at Kagoshima, the trickle of converts soon dried up but not before Francis had baptized his host, a man named Kimura, whose grandson, Leonard Kimura, a Jesuit lay brother, was burnt, or rather roasted, alive for his Christian profession at Nagasaki in 1619 and beatified by Pope Pius IX in 1867. Leaving Father Cosmas de Torres in charge of the neophytes at Hirado, the Saint began at the end of October, 1550, the most affecting, soul-subduing and agonizing of all his life's journeys. In length it was moderate enough, only about five hundred miles, but the weather and other circumstances combined to make it as brave an expedition as was ever undertaken and carried through by human beings. Francis himself admitted to perils on the way and to terrible cold, but otherwise used his familiar formula, ' We went to such and such a place.' Luckily, however, he had Juan Fernandez with him, and from that faithful soul Luis Frois afterwards obtained a first-hand account of their adventures, though Frois, to his lasting shame, failed to ask several obvious questions that would have lightened the labours of biographers. Bernard the Japanese was also of the party and afterwards gave his reminiscences to Polanco in Rome. The indications are that the three men went by sea to the port of Hakata, a voyage of only a couple of days but one made very dangerous by the presence in every hidden cove or river estuary of piratical junks, so many cats waiting for one defenceless mouse. After a brief halt at Hakata, the journey was apparently resumed by land to the port of Moji and there a crossing made of the narrow strait between Kyushu and the Main Island (Honshu) to the busy port of Shimonoseki, from whence the travellers pursued their way on foot to the great wooden city of Yamaguchi, hoping to find there some means of getting to their distant goal, Miyako.

Twelve or more years passed before Frois met Fernandez at Hirado and obtained from him the following account, a little confused in places, as is to be expected, of the nightmare journey:

Neither the bitterness of the cold, nor the snow nor the dread of unknown and unpredictable populations were able to hinder Father Francis from the pursuit of his designs in the service of God. While sailing on the sea we had pirates all around us and were often obliged to hide in the hold of the ship to escape their attentions. The journey by land was even worse. We carried in two bundles, similar to the wallets of the Friars Minor, all our baggage, which consisted of a surplice, three or four shirts, and an old rug to cover Father Francis and myself at night. There are no beds in Japanese inns, and it was a great thing if we could sometimes acquire a straw mat to sleep on and a wooden pillow. Arriving at one of those places in the evening, frozen to the bone and famished with hunger, we were more than once turned away and refused even a little shelter. On other occasions, when striving over rough mountain tracks, we were overwhelmed by fierce snow-storms and the icy wind. Our legs swelled under us and we collapsed where we stood. We were poor, badly clothed, obvious strangers. At some villages we were given a welcome frostier than the air, for the children ran after us yelling insults and pelting us with stones. At Hakata, which is a populous trading centre in the kingdom of Hizen, the Father paid a visit to a large monastery of bonzes of the Zen sect who believe in no life except this one on earth.[1] Those bonzes maintain many boys in their monastery with whom, according to public report, they commit unnatural sin. Imagining that the Father came from Tenjiku [native place of Gotama, the Buddha], they received him with great demonstrations of joy and took him to their Tôdô, who holds something like the rank of bishop among us. It gave him much pleasure to see us and he directed that we were to be served with fruit. But from the first moment the Father loudly reproached both the superior and the monks in

---

[1] Fair enough, to judge by Mr. Humphreys' glossary: ' Zen. One of the two main schools of Japanese Buddhism. The " sudden " or direct approach to Reality, transcending the intellect. Satori. The goal of Zen Buddhism. A state of consciousness which varies in quality and duration from a flash of intuitive awareness to Nirvana. Nirvana. The summum bonum of Buddhism. A state of supreme Enlightenment beyond the conception of the intellect. Annihilation of all we know as the personal, separative self.' But if there is no personal, separative self left, what is it that receives the supreme Enlightenment?

strong terms for the abominable vice of Sodom which prevailed among them, for teaching the people that there was
nothing beyond this life, and for exhorting them nevertheless
to make offerings for the dead, to the advantage of nobody
but the monks themselves. The listening bonzes were dumb-
founded that a man whom they had never seen before should
reprimand them so vigorously. A few of them laughed, but
the majority could only stare in amazement. Without other
compliment the Father strode out of the monastery and we
went on our way. The following five or six days were indeed
hard, but the Father added to what we were all three suffering
on that terrible journey a continual voluntary mortification
To form some idea of the details of this mortification you would
have needed to watch him, as I did, with your own eyes. Even
his manner of praying as we trudged along bore the stamp of
penitence. Meditation and contemplation were to him the most
familiar of things and there was nothing about us to cause a
moment's distraction, just mountains and valleys blanketed in
snow. Yet, during all the time of his prayer he never once
raised his eyes from the ground or glanced aside. He kept his
arms and hands absolutely still. Only his feet moved and they
very gently. By his reverence and modesty of demeanour he
showed very plainly that he was in the presence of God our
Lord. It was the same at the inns, which were little better than
stables. Though weary with walking, he was so gentle and
deferential in manner as he ate his poor meal that you might
have thought him a slave admitted as a favour to the table of
some great lord and never forgetting how unworthy he is to
eat the food provided by his master.[1]

Though Japan is in the same latitude as the Mediterranean, it
is also on its west coast completely open to the malign influences
of Siberia and when it gets snow does it in style. ' In the towns
near the Sea of Japan it lies three or four feet deep for weeks, and
drifts to a depth of fifteen to eighteen feet in the valleys '

[1] Cros, *Saint François de Xavier: sa vie et ses lettres*, ii, 99–101; Frois, *Die
Geschichte Japans*, übersetzt von G. Schurhammer, 8–10.

(Chamberlain). This was what St. Francis ran into on his expedition without map or guide, but the weather made only a part of his troubles for there was war also on the Main Island, daimyo endeavouring to swallow daimyo. Armed bands roamed the country, menacing lonely travellers who might have something to be robbed. Francis appears to have received warning of this danger, for he travelled very light. In Goa afterwards, Manuel Teixeira, who wrote a brief but vivid sketch of his life, heard him praise the Japanese Bernard and say that it was he who had kept them alive in the snow by dealing out to them rations of toasted rice, the Japanese *yakigome*, from a bag hung at his girdle.[1] It seems likely that Francis meant this visit to Miyako to be merely exploratory, for he left behind in Hirado those gifts which were intended to put the Emperor in a complacent mood. He left behind also, and it must have been a hard thing to do, his cheap chalice, paten, vestments and all else necessary for saying Mass, for he would not risk them to the brigands. The poorer they were, he reckoned, the better chance they would have of getting through, according to the old tag, *Cantabit vacuus coram latrone viator*. But he took his small well-worn Breviary and also the stout little anthology of Marcus Marulus, to which he was so much addicted.[2]

White is the colour of woe in Japan but the white journey of the three did not much dispirit them for they made three converts on the way, an aged samurai and a man of the people and his wife. The inns, about which Professor Morse waxes lyrical, made a painful impression on Brother Fernandez, he being young and gifted with a healthy appetite. After a hard day's contention with the snow, he said, all that they were given to eat at those places was ' a little rice boiled in water, some salt

---

[1] MHSJ. *Monumenta Xaveriana*, ii, 877-8. It is curious that Fernandez did not mention the presence of Bernard at all. Perhaps he did, and Frois omitted him as irrelevant. But he was far from being irrelevant, the only one of them with a reassuring Japanese face and an understandable Japanese tongue.

[2] His copy of Marulus, a very precious relic, was destroyed in 1931 when the ebullient spirits of the Spanish revolutionaries celebrated their victory by burning the Jesuit Professed House in Madrid. The Breviary, an even more sacred thing, was destroyed in an air-raid on Nantes in 1943.

fish, boiled or fried, and a tasteless soup made of herbs, which smelt abominably. Father Francis left the fish and contented himself with the soup and rice.' Francis had his reasons. The three Japanese who came to Malacca in 1549 had told him that the bonzes would be scandalized were they to see him and his companions eating meat or fish, and so, he informed the Roman Jesuits, ' we are going determined to live always on a diet rather than give scandal to anybody '.[1] The first of The Five Precepts of Buddhism is, ' I promise [not God, there being no God, but myself] to abstain from taking life '. Now, fishes have life, no less than hares or cows, so according to strict Buddhist tenets Isaac Walton would never attain Nirvana. But the teaching of gentler masters allowed fish to be eaten and fleas to be killed as a concession to human weakness, and a few pious frauds also came to the rescue. Our great authority, writing fifty years ago, stated: ' One may even now see the term " mountain whale " (*yama-kujira*) written up over certain eating-houses, which means that venison is there for sale. The logical process is this: A whale is a fish. Fish may be eaten. Therefore, if you call venison " mountain whale ", you may eat venison.'[2] At Kagoshima, it appears that St. Francis occasionally partook of a little fish and even of meat.

The bonzes [writes Fernandez] preach that this is a grave sin, though the majority of them do it themselves when sure of not being seen. We gave those who objected to our eating fish or flesh reasons justifying our conduct, but they were only half satisfied with them. So, during our journeys, if we were served fish or meat at the inns, Father Francis used to

[1] Schurhammer, *Epistolae S. Francisci Xaverii*, ii, 151.

[2] Chamberlain, *Things Japanese*, pp. 175–6. Mr. Chamberlain shared Brother Fernandez's sentiments on the subject of Japanese dishes: ' Imagine a diet without meat, without milk, without bread, without butter, without jam, without coffee, without salad or any sufficient quantity of nicely cooked vegetables, without puddings of any sort, without stewed fruit and with comparatively little fresh fruit—the European vegetarian will find almost as much difficulty in making anything out of it as the ordinary meat-eater. ... The food is clean, admirably free from grease, often pretty to look at. But try to live on it—no ! '

give a little explanation of the lawfulness of eating these things which God has provided for our sustenance. He would then add example to his lesson by consuming a tiny morsel of the food, after which he pushed it aside and ate something else.

Francis was not going to allow himself to be taken for a Buddhist if he could help it!

Eventually, bedraggled and half starved, the three men came to Yamaguchi, the 'mountain-mouth', a pleasant city of ten thousand homes and a hundred rich temples and monasteries, the headquarters at the time of Ouchi Yoshitaka, perhaps the most powerful daimyo in all Japan. Only Miyako, the capital (in Chinese Kyoto, as it is now called), surpassed Yamaguchi in size. Yamaguchi had become opulent on trade with Korea and China, and many of the *kuge*, descendants of younger sons of ancient Mikados and attendants on the living Emperor at Kyoto, deserted that poverty-stricken court for the flesh-pots of the other place, bringing with them their hereditary contempt for the profession of arms and the frivolous amusements that had helped to while away the boring hours in Miyako, elaborate dandyism, poetry-meetings, tennis parties, dancing, and above all the *cha-no-yu* or tea-ceremonies, to which the blood-and-thunder Daimyo and his samurai took like ducks to water. He and his guests at the tea parties reclined on couches spread with tiger and leopard skins:

The walls of the spacious apartments in which the guests assembled were hung, not only with Buddhist pictures, but with damask and brocade, with gold and silver vessels, and swords in splendid sheaths. Precious perfumes were burnt, rare fishes and strange birds were served up with sweetmeats and wine, and the point of the entertainment consisted in guessing where the material for each cup of tea had been produced; for as many brands as possible were brought in to serve as a puzzle or *jeu de société*. . . . Every right guess procured for him who made it the gift of one of the treasures that were hung round the room. But he was not allowed to carry it away himself. The rules of the tea ceremonies, as then practised, ordained that all things rich and rare exhibited must be given by their winners to the singing and dancing-girls, troupes of whom were present to help the company in their carousal. Vast fortunes were dissipated in this manner.[1]

How closely that picture resembles the habits of the pagan Roman aristocracy in decline!

Into that shining, decadent world of wealth and sensuality walked St. Francis on his two tired and swollen feet to preach Christ and Him crucified. It is a contrast difficult for the imagination to seize because so overwhelming, as of our Lord Himself before Herod or of His humble collateral relatives dragged from their peasant farms in Palestine to Rome to be questioned by Domitian.[2] Francis and his companions put up at the hostelry of a man named Uchida whose guardian angel might have whispered to him, ' This day is salvation come to thy house ', for he and his wife were the first two people of Yamaguchi to be baptized. It was not the express purpose of Francis at this time to evangelize the city, but while he waited for some chance of going on to Miyako, which had to be done in armed company owing to the prevalence of bandits, he could not desist from preaching his Divine Master. He and Fernandez started operations immediately.

[1] Chamberlain, *Things Japanese*, p. 451. The best that Mr. Chamberlain has to say of the tea ceremonies is that they are perfectly harmless, ' which is more than can be affirmed of tea and tattle '. He is speaking of the way the ritual is performed in modern Japan. It was by no means harmless as Ouchi Yoshitaka practised it, but the occasion for debauchery. A leading Japanese authority, Inazo Nitobe, lectured amusingly on the *cha-no-yu* in French: ' *La preparation et la manière de boire le thé, le théisme, si j'ose dire, ont été depuis longtemps élevées à la dignité d'un art, un véritable art de société. Les adeptes de cette cérémonie vont jusqu'à la considérer comme un acte de religieuse dévotion. Lorsque nous parlons de quelqu'un qui n'a ni éducation, ni goût, nous disons qu'il n'a point de thé. C'est un a-théiste! Inversement, un homme posé, reservé, distingue, est* cha-jin, *c'est un théiste. Un philologue pourra un jour s'exercer sur les dérivations du mot thé et sur le théisme* ' (quoted in Tessan, *Par les Chemins Japonais*, p. 98). What the ceremony teaches is social poise and that is not a bad thing.

[2] Eusebius, *Ecclesiastical History*, iii, 20, citing Hegesippus. Eng. trans. Lawlor and Oulton, London, 1927, p. 80.

We decided to hold forth in the streets twice a day [Francis reported to Europe later on], reading from the book we had brought with us and then giving a sermon on the subject. . . . Crowds gathered to listen to us, some of whom seemed pleased to hear the law of God, while others derided it, and a certain number pondered over it. On our way through the streets, children and their elders also harassed us a great deal, making a mock of us and shouting: ' These fellows say that we have to adore *Deus* to be saved and none other can save us but the Creator of all things [Dainichi?].' Others cried: ' These men teach that nobody can have more than one wife.' And there were some who said: ' Look at the two who tell us that sodomy is a sin ! ' for it is a very common vice among them. In a similar way they named other Commandments in order to make us a laughing-stock. . . . We continued thus to preach in the streets and houses of the city for many days, . . . and we made a few Christians.[1]

Not much style and colour in that report, but luckily Fernandez, who admits to having been several times terrified, is more communicative:

We preached in the streets without any licence or permission of the King, taking up our position at cross-roads where people thronged. I first read from the book in a loud voice about the creation of the world, and then in stentorian tones denounced the three chief sins committed by the Japanese, their neglect of God their almighty Creator, who had drawn them out of nothingness and kept them in existence, in order to adore wood and stone and inanimate things, and in them the Devil, enemy of God and man; next, their addiction to the abominable vice of Sodom, and here I expatiated on the shame-fulness and ugliness of this sin, and on the awful chastisements that have fallen on the world on account of it; and thirdly, the crime of women who to spare themselves the trouble of bringing up children kill them at birth or even before birth,

[1] Schurhammer, *Epistolae*, ii, 260–1.

which is a horrible cruelty and inhumanity. While I harangued in this fashion, the Father, standing beside me, gave himself to prayer, begging God to bless my words and my listeners. Thus we acted every day, until there was not a street or a crossing ot streets in the whole of this great city which had not seen and heard us. We did the same in many houses of the *kuge* or noblemen who invited us to come and discourse to them, some, merely in order to kill time, others to have their ears tickled with novelties, and many just to make sport of us. A few showed us marks of affection and pity. One of those nobles had us in, I believe, for the fun of the thing. I read to him out ot the book the story of the fall of the angels, how Lucifer for his pride was cast from Heaven into Hell, and told him that all proud persons will suffer the same fate and be delivered over to the demons to be tormented for ever. The man displayed his contempt for what I had read, whereupon Father Francis, with myself for interpreter, rebuked him sharply, saying, ' However powerful you be, if you do not practise humility and bewail your sins, God will bring you low, ay, as low as Hell.' The man then advanced on us, despising the Father's words, but he, inflamed with zeal and his eyes blazing [*com rosto vermelho e abrasado*], said, ' It's no use your disbelieving. If you do not become humble, to Hell and its torments you will go.' Then we left the house, and as we were going out the Father said to me, ' I am very sorry for that nobleman. The higher they rise, the less people of his class profit from the grace of God.'

In the year 1603, an old Japanese who was baptized as a boy in Yamaguchi by St. Francis remembered him as ' a man comely and spirited who did not know the language of the country but preached through an interpreter, and when he preached his countenance became suffused with blushes and glowing '.[1] Dear Francis went on fire altogether the memorable day when he and Fernandez were summoned by the Daimyo Ouchi Yoshitaka,

[1] Cited by Father Schurhammer from the report of a Jesuit named Rodrigues Giram.

who controlled twenty of the seventy principalities of Japan. Fernandez describes the scene as follows:

We went to the palace escorted by one of the courtiers, who took us to the hall where the King received ambassadors and all other strangers. When we came into his presence we went on our knees and made him two profound bows. There was no one in the hall except the King, one of his principal bonzes and the *kuge* who introduced us, but in the ante-chambers and on the terraces a large number of nobles had congregated. The King received us very benevolently and asked us many questions about our voyage, and about India and Europe. Then he expressed a desire to be told what was this Law which we desired to preach in his states. Father Francis bade me read from our note-book the account of the creation of the world and the explanation of the Ten Commandments which we had translated into Japanese. After dealing with idolatry and other aberrations there followed a section on the abomination of unnatural vice. In the book it is said that men who practise such things are filthier creatures than swine and much below dogs and other irrational brutes. When I read this passage, the King appeared to be thoroughly roused by it and betrayed his anger in his face. However, the *kuge* signed to us to go and we left without the King saying a word. As for me, I was afraid that he might order our heads off there and then.[1]

It is highly probable that Yoshitaka took them to be preachers of some eccentric form of Buddhism, as they had come from India where that peculiar way of regarding human life originated. Perhaps it was his reason for letting them go unscathed or, alternatively, he may not have understood half of what Fernandez said, through faultiness in his diction and accent, which are known to have been very imperfect.

Father Melchior Nunes Barreto visited Japan in 1556 and there met the two men whom St. Francis Xavier had moulded, whom he utterly loved and trusted, and to whom he bequeathed his

[1] Cited in Cros, *Saint François de Xavier: sa vie et ses lettres*, ii, 102–4; Frois-Schurhammer, *Die Geschichte Japans*, 10–11.

mantle when God called him away for ever in a fiery chariot very different from Elijah's. The visitor was awed by the spiritual greatness of Cosmas de Torres and Juan Fernandez. Cosmas had been once, before he saw Japan, a fine, tall, portly figure of a man. Japan had wasted him to such an extent with its short commons of tasteless rice and salt fish that Nunes doubted whether any of his old friends would recognize him:

In my own mind I thought of him as being the image of one of the Desert Fathers, only that they were wrapped up in God alone and could sweetly discourse together of things divine, while he, with one Brother for all his company, stood in the midst of persecuting enemies, half-starved and often nearly wholly frozen, labouring day and night for the good of men's souls. He had been through such terrible experiences that his face was furrowed with weeping, and yet he told me that never in his life had he been so completely happy as during those years in Japan. . . . His companion, that *persona rara* Juan Fernandez, told me how severely the blessed Father Francis used to rate the Japanese for their vices and idolatry. He said that he himself used to tremble with fear at the liberties taken by the Father in addressing whomsoever it might be, even the daimyos. To the good Brother it seemed as though he were asking to be killed for the faith and honour of Christ our Lord. In particular, he ran a great risk one day by his objurgation of the King of Yamaguchi for the *peccatum nefandum*. Some of those Lords of Japan spoke to them as they would to servants or persons of mean condition, whereupon the Father ordered Brother Juan to answer them in similar style, which he did, shaking with fright and expecting to have his head off his shoulders any moment. The Father said to him afterwards that unless those nobles learned to esteem them more than they did their bonzes, whom they hold in high honour, they would never accept the faith, and the way to win their esteem was to show them how little afraid one was to die.[1]

[1] *Nuovi Avisi dell' Indie di Portogallo, tradotti nell' Italiana.* Venetia, 1558, 45–52. Nunes felt that he too should sample a little of Japanese missionary life,

The missionary ideal of St. Francis Xavier had never been just to win a group of converts here or there but to Christianize whole countries, and in pursuing this great aim he was acting in accordance with the millennial tradition of the Church. To achieve it in his age, or perhaps in any age, it would have been necessary to convert or at least to render benevolent or neutral the men who controlled other men's destinies, the kings, the maharajas, the daimyos, the shoguns, the mikados. Eight days before Christmas of the year 1550, St. Francis, accompanied by Juan Fernandez and the Japanese Bernard, with a blanket and a few spare shirts for luggage, set out from sterile Yamaguchi to appeal to the Son of Heaven at Miyako, some two hundred zig-zagging miles away. The first stage of this winter journey consisted of about forty penal miles to the port of Iwakuni on the shore of the Inland Sea. They were the hardest miles St. Francis ever trod. Fernandez told Luis Frois that the snow came above their knees and that the icy, paralysing water of the many mountain torrents which they had to wade often reached to their waists. St. Francis, Fernandez mentioned, often walked the whole day barefooted, perhaps because it was the best way to plough through the white desolation, and the good Brother gives a little picture of him in an inn at night staring in woeful astonishment at his swollen and torn feet which had left tracks of blood in the snow. He says that he used the *tatami* or mat assigned to him in the inn, not to lie on, but as a covering to try to keep out the intolerable cold.[1]

At Iwakuni the exhausted travellers may have rested a little while before buying humble accommodation on a ship bound for the lovely island and sanctuary of Miyajima, one of the most popular pilgrim resorts of Japan, and thence for Sakai, the

---

' so I went,' he says, 'with Brother Fernandez into the interior of the country and was overjoyed to see the numbers that were being converted. But I was not worthy to have any part in the great work. The miserable food and the wretched beds, which consist of a mat on the floor and a piece of wood for pillow, caused me to become very sick. . . . I was ill for three months, burning with fever or shivering with cold, and so bad that I entertained little hope of surviving. But God gave me back my life. . . .'

[1] *Die Geschichte Japans* (1549–78) von P. Luis Frois, übersetzt von G. Schurhammer und E. A. Voretzsch (Leipzig, 1926), 11–12.

country's most thriving port in those days, at the eastern end of the Inland Sea. No voyage in the world is more fascinating than that stretch of calm waters studded with uncountable islands that turn with the sun to purple or silver or gold, but January is not the right month to relish the beauty nor was Francis Xavier the right man. It took the ship about a fortnight to thread its careful way through the maze, and now and again it would call at some quiet island haven. At one such place, perhaps Tomotsu, an eminent Buddhist was told that the three poor strangers had come all the way from Tenjiku where his religion had originated, and immediately took compassion on them. To Francis he gave a letter for a friend of his in Sakai, asking him to help the little party on their journey to Miyako by securing for them the patronage of some nobleman travelling there. That was about the only courtesy shown them since they had left Yamaguchi. On the boat they suffered terribly, not only from the biting winds against which they had no protection, but also from the biting words, the scoffing and scorning of young merchants addicted to the good old Japanese sport of baiting the stranger. One of them in particular made Francis the butt of his coarse jests, treating him, says Fernandez, now as a fool, now as a brute beast. ' Once Master Francis said to this fellow, with an expression of sweet sadness on his face, " Why do you speak to me in this way? I love you very much and I would greatly like to teach you the way of salvation." But the young man only scorned him the more.'[1]

[1] In Frois, *Die Geschichte Japans*, as before. In the 1880's Rudyard Kipling sailed through the Inland Sea and left his impressions: ' We have for the last twenty-four hours been steaming through a huge lake, studded as far as the eye can reach with islands of every size, from four miles long and two wide to little cocked-hat hummocks no bigger than a decent hayrick. Messrs. Cook and Son charge about one hundred rupees extra for the run through this part of the world, but they do not know how to farm the beauties of nature. Under any skies the islands—purple, amber, grey, green, and black—are worth five times the money asked. I have been sitting for the last half-hour among a knot of whooping tourists, wondering how I could give you a notion of them. The tourists, of course, are indescribable. They say, " Oh my ! " at thirty-second intervals. . . . Now we have come to a stretch so densely populated with islands that all looks solid ground. We are running through broken water thrown up by the race of the tide round an outlying reef, and, apparently, are going to hit an acre of solid rock. Somebody on the bridge saves us, and we head

In Sakai with its sixty thousand souls bent on the acquisition of wealth the three poorly clad strangers were as good as lost. The day of their arrival was spent in a fruitless search for the street and house of the merchant to whom they had been directed. Rich proud Sakai had rarely seen such nondescripts as they, cassocked scarecrows babbling a laughable attempt at Japanese. Even Bernard's countrified accent, up from that ridiculous place, Kagoshima, would have been thought funny in Sakai. The crowds in the streets hooted after the three as they sought anxiously for the address on their precious letter, and as night began to fall not an inn in the town would give them shelter. To avoid the stones and other missiles which the urchins hurled at them, they took refuge in a pine-wood on the confines of the town, but were pursued there by the terrible children and given a final salvo of stones before the darkness hid them. There can have been little sleep for them that mid-winter night. Next day, hungry and half-frozen, they stole into the inhospitable city again and to their immense relief found the elusive address. It was a fine house, the home of a rich Japanese merchant named Kudô who did credit to Sakya-Muni. He gave his unkempt and unexpected visitors good welcome, settled them in, and proceeded at once to make arrangements for their journey to Miyako, a short but dangerous undertaking owing to the prevalence of bandits and marauding soldiery in the neighbourhood. His plan was to find a place for the three men among the servants and mounted body-guard of some nobleman proceeding to Miyako in a palanquin. The bearers went at a trot, and so also did St. Francis and his young companions, each carrying on his back a share of the great man's baggage. All three appear to have gone barefooted through the deep snow, perhaps because their boots had worn out.[1]

---

out for another island, and so on, and so on, till the eye wearies of watching the nose of the ship swinging right and left. . . . Yes, it is a sea of mystery and romance, and the white sails of the junks are silver in the moonlight. . . . Today being the seventeenth of April, I am sitting in an ulster under a thick rug, with fingers so cold I can barely hold the pen. . . .' (From Sea to Sea, London, 1900, pp. 329–30).

[1] St. Francis in his letters is silent about everything except the robbers and the cold, which he mentions merely as an aside. All the details given or to be

The palanquin journey was made in two stages of about nine miles each, with a night's rest for the weary occupant of the litter at some hostelry between. The physical stamina of the running St. Francis must have been quite extraordinary, and it was joy that made him so strong. Both Juan Fernandez and Bernard are emphatic on the point. He had acquired some sort of Siamese cap or turban and went attired in this out of sheer good spirits, like a man wearing a paper hat at a Christmas party (*atada a cabeça com hum birro de Siao*). 'Never at any time did I see him display more gaiety than on this occasion,' testified Fernandez, and Bernard told Father Palmio in Rome that Francis, the happiest man he ever knew, used every now and then to leap and skip like a frolicsome child as he trotted along behind the horsemen and bearers. He had brought an apple with him, Bernard added, and this he would sometimes throw into the air and deftly catch as it came down. The kind Kudô had given him a letter of introduction to a merchant friend of his at Miyako, so why should he not be merry? This was the day he had dreamed of ever since his arrival in Japan. He was going to the Capital, the

---

given come from the oral reports or the letters of Juan Fernandez, and from the accounts given to the Fathers in Rome by Bernard. The oral reports are embodied in Luis Frois's *Die Geschichte Japans* and details from Fernandez's letters not mentioned by Frois are given in a later *History of the Church in Japan* written in Portuguese by a most interesting and attractive character, Father João Rodriguez Tçuzu, S.J., who came to Japan from his native Portugal in 1576, when he was barely sixteen years old, and remained in the country as one of its greatest missionaries for forty-five unbroken years. He was called Tçuzu, meaning in Japanese, interpreter, to distinguish him from another João Rodriguez, also on the Japanese mission, but all Western writers until Father Schurhammer have made the two men into one. The first Rodriguez deserved his title of Tçuzu, for he became so proficient in Japanese that he attracted the attention of the great military leader, Hideyoshi, Japan's Napoleon, who made use of his services in dealing with foreign nations. Even when Hideyoshi turned persecutor and ordered the crucifixion of the twenty-six canonized martyrs of Nagasaki, including three Japanese Jesuits, in 1597, he still remained on good terms with Father Rodriguez. So did the formidable genius Ieyasu who brought the whole of Japan under his sway and founded the dynasty of shoguns which lasted until the Meiji revolution in the mid-nineteenth century. Father Rodriguez Tçuzu's *History* has never been published, but Père Cros gives extracts from it in French, which unfortunately are not always completely accurate.

holy city of Japan, where dwelt the Tennô, the Son of Heaven, who would surely in his wisdom submit himself to the King of Heaven and bring all his people to the feet, the wounded feet, of Christ.[1] This dream would soon prove to be as frail and unsubstantial as others that had already faded, but he would not repine among its ruins nor think for one moment that the mercy of God had forsaken him. There was nothing of personal ambition in his many dreams. They all flowered, however impermanently, from the root of his overwhelming love of God, and that remained when the dreams drooped and fell, like the exquisite blooms of the tree which he had seen in Ternate, in glory for a day and then only a carpet of blanched petals under men's feet.

Miyako, or Kyoto as it is now named, both words, Japanese and Chinese, meaning the same thing, capital or metropolis,[2] is still the most interesting city in Japan, ' happy, lazy, sumptuous Kyoto '. It is a phoenix city and has risen from its ashes times without number. The streets are laid out on the gridiron pattern, in rectangular blocks, and perhaps it was from Kyoto that the Americans borrowed the idea to apply it so successfully at home. St. Francis must have noticed many burnt-out gaps in the long straight streets, for the monks of the great monastery on Hiei-zan mountain three miles away were much better fire-raisers than contemplatives and often raided the city. Hiei-zan was one of the so-called universities which Francis had designed to visit and he appears to have asked his host in Miyako, by name Konishi Ryusa and a close friend of Kudô in Sakai, how best to approach the monastery, which was obviously not too popular with the peaceful Buddhists of the capital. A brief interpolation may be permissible here to say that Konishi Ryusa became a devout Catholic eight years after the death of St. Francis, and that Kudô's son, Hibiya Ryôkei, followed him into the Church four years later to become an apostle on his own account at Sakai. At any

[1] Bernard's details were incorporated in a dialogue composed in the classical manner, but in French, by Père Emond Auger who received them from Padre Palmio. As mentioned earlier, extracts from the Dialogue, including Bernard's witness, were published in the French Jesuit journal *Etudes* (Tome CIX, December 5, 1906).

[2] Tokyo at this time was a mere fishing village called Yedo.

rate, those blooms on Francis's tree of hope did not fall to the ground. Konishi Ryusa appears to have thought that the most promising plan for obtaining admission to the Hiei-zan monastery would be for Francis to proceed, with one of the merchant's retainers as guide, to Sakamoto on Lake Biwa, and there, at the foot of the mountain, to bide his opportunity as the guest of Konishi's son-in-law. Francis gratefully followed the instructions, but soon discovered beside the beautiful lake, which is as large as that of Geneva, the disadvantages of being a poor man. The precincts of the three thousand Buddhist temples and seminaries on Hiei-zan were barred to all but noblemen with retinues or rich men bearing valuable gifts for the monks. He had only his little bundle containing the inevitable Marcus Marulus, that highly privileged anthology, his Breviary and a spare shirt, and his only robe to match the shimmering silks of the bonzes was always the same thin, black, sleeveless cassock worn threadbare by long use. Only the ruins of the once famous ' university ' and the myriad shrines remain today and few except Japanese archaeologists know anything of their history, but the name of the poor man at the gate who could not gain admission, a Lazarus hoping in vain for a crumb of instruction from the table of Dives, is known and revered throughout the world.[1]

His exclusion from Hiei-zan put an idea into the head of Francis. If those proud masters of Japan would not have him nor respect him unless he came splendidly attired, he would show them, back in Yamaguchi, what a gentleman of Spain could produce from his wardrobe. Poverty, in dress as in all else, was his love and his bride, but he was quite prepared to apparel himself as grandly as a daimyo or maharaja, if his pocket could stand it and his business with the souls of men required it. As soon as he was certain that the monks of Hiei-zan would have none of him, he returned to Miyako to seek audience of the O, the Dairi, the

[1] The fruitless visit of St. Francis to Sakamoto, which is only about three hours' walk from Miyako, has been closely studied by Father Schurhammer, first, with a wealth of references, in an article entitled *Der hl. Franz Xaver in Miyako*, contributed to the German periodical *Stimmen der Zeit*, 51 Jahrgang, März, 1921, pp. 440–55, and then in an invaluable brochure, *Der hl. Franz Xaver in Japan*, published at Schöneck-Beckenried, Switzerland, in 1947.

Mikado, the Emperor, again without result, except as a new and important chapter in his Japanese education. The O, the descendant of the Sun-goddess, was sadly in eclipse, mouth-honoured by all his people but shorn of every vestige of power and utterly neglected. He appeared in public only on the occasion of certain festivals and otherwise lived completely secluded from the world in a ramshackle wooden palace enclosed by a crumbling bamboo stockade. The allowance made to him by the real rulers of Japan, the daimyos and war-lords, was pitifully inadequate, and it is said that the poor godling used to write verses and endeavour to sell them to keep the wolf from the door. Also, and for this the poor man is hardly to be blamed, he would not grant audiences except at such a price as St. Francis Xavier was then unable to pay. Francis, stationed with his two companions at a gate in the enclosure, promised the tattered and hungry-looking *Kuge* who passed in and out, often perhaps in search of a square meal, that he would return with rich presents for the Emperor if his divinity would spare him just a few minutes conversation. But one look at the petitioner must have been enough to make the most ravenous courtier smile. What a tall story, just the sort of yarn an obvious beggarman would spin! After a number of rebuffs, Francis began to feel that Japan was decidedly not governed like Spain. The Emperor was the merest figurehead, a man whose permission to preach the Gospel throughout the country would have been absolutely worthless a mile from Miyako. Nor was the Shogun, who also had his palace in Miyako, of much more account. It was the shoguns who in the long past had deprived the Emperor of his temporal powers, and then the daimyos, whom they had created and ennobled, proceeded to clip the wings of the shoguns. So came anarchy to Japan, but even at this time the first of the saviours was alive, a boy named Oda Nobunaga who would crush the power of the Buddhist monks and greatly help the successors of St. Francis Xavier as a counterpoise to them. Francis would certainly have learned from Konishi Ryusa that the Shogun of the day, a boy of sixteen, was absent from Miyako, so he wasted no time at the gates of his dilapidated palace.

The real wielder of power in the central Japanese provinces of

Yamashiro and Omi was a blood-and-thunder war-lord named Miyoshi Chôkei who, shortly before the coming of St. Francis to Miyako, had defeated his rival Hosokawa Harumoto in a battle fought at Otsu on Lake Biwa, and had then entered the half-destroyed capital in triumph to prepare for new victories. This condition of politics and the strict veto of the Hiei-zan monks on all unlicensed preaching and teaching ruled out Miyako just then as a centre of Christian propaganda. St. Francis, like the good realist he was, in spite of his dreams, decided to cut his losses and return the way he had come after only eleven days of exploration. Twelve years later, there would be many Christians in the capital and its environs, and from among them would come many glorious martyrs, all because Francis had once gone there, *a galope*, in a ridiculous Siamese hat, juggling with an apple. The first Catholic church to be built in Miyako was called the Church of the Assumption because it was on that feast, a happy augury, St. Francis landed in Kagoshima. From the southern end of Lake Biwa emerges a river which has acquired the bad Japanese habit of changing its name three times on its relatively short journey to the sea, the Setagawa, the Ujugawa, and the Yodogawa, *kawa* or *gawa*, of course, meaning a river. It is navigable from a short distance below Miyako, and on it St. Francis and his two companions embarked in order to avoid the dangers of the land route in those troubled times. On their way to the boat, Fernandez told Frois, Francis purchased a quantity of dried fruit which he bestowed upon any children he met in the streets, with his blessing. It would seem that he had made an impression during the eleven days, for men and women approached him to tell of their infirmities or of the sickness of their children, and to these he gave, as in India, a scrap of paper on which he had written some verses from the Gospels, telling them to wear it on their breasts and they would be cured. An open boat in February, with the whole countryside, including the famous tea-plantations of Uji, under snow, is not the acme of comfortable travel and Fernandez for one considered that their run to Miyako eleven days earlier had been very much pleasanter than this frightful ordeal by water when a man could not move a limb to keep himself from freezing.

So they came to Osaka, ' the Venice of Japan ', with its one thousand eight hundred and ninety-four canals, rivers, dams and lagoons.[1] From Osaka the three travellers went on to Sakai to bid farewell to their kind host Kudô, and then bought tickets as steerage passengers on a ship about to make the long weaving voyage right across the Inland Sea and through the narrow Shimonoseki Strait to their starting-point of Hirado. They arrived at the beginning of March, 1551, after more than four months absence, during which they had suffered and learned a great deal. They set up a record, too, a thing they would have scorned to mention, by being the first Europeans to penetrate so far into Japan. Father de Torres holding the fort at Hirado must have often anxiously wondered through that winter whether the strange land had not swallowed up his beloved Master Francis altogether. And here he was, thinner perhaps than before, but as gay and sanguine as ever, with a grand new plan to put into operation.

After carefully weighing such evidence as he had been able to gather, Francis reached the conclusion that the gentleman in Yamaguchi, Ouchi Yoshitaka, was probably the most powerful prince then reigning in Japan, even if he by no means controlled the whole country. He would do for a Mikado, and to him Francis would now proceed in ambassadorial pomp, silk-clad and with a retinue consisting of Juan Fernandez, once a leader of fashion in

[1] That is more or less the number today and there may not have been so many in the sixteenth century. Historical truth requires it to be said that Osaka, now a city of three million souls, has been described, not only as the Venice of Japan but also as its Pittsburg and Manchester. A famous but foolish writer once said of the Japanese: ' They have the nature rather of birds or butterflies than of ordinary human beings. . . . They will not and cannot take life *au grand sérieux*.' He certainly can never have seen the ruins of Hideyoshi's fortress at Osaka which absolutely stunned Rudyard Kipling: ' Fifty feet was the height of the wall and never a pinch of mortar in the whole. Nor was the face perpendicular, but curved like the ram of a man-of-war. They know the curve in China, and I have seen French artists introduce it into books describing a devil-besieged city of Tartary. . . . The stone was granite, and the men of old time had used it like mud. The dressed blocks that made the profile of the angles were from twenty feet long, ten or twelve feet high, and as many in thickness. . . . " And the little Japs built this ! " I cried, awe-stricken at the quarries that rose round me ' (*From Sea to Sea*, p. 354). They built it in two years. Butterflies indeed !

the Old World, Bernard and another Japanese Christian, both no doubt in beautiful kimonos and possibly with swords in their sashes, and finally, in all likelihood, the Indian Amador whose extremely swarthy countenance greatly interested the Japanese, so that they would walk as much as twenty miles to see the phenomenon. An authentic fellow-countryman of the Buddha, and black as a coal at that, would be sure of a welcome at Ouchi's inquisitive court. Then there were the gifts provided so thoughtfully by Pedro da Silva and all well calculated to astonish a people who retain an attractive amount of the small boy in their adult characters. They included a grandfather clock which chimed the hours day and night, a musical box, a fine glass mirror, an elaborately worked musket with three barrels, bales of brocade, two pairs of spectacles or goggles, books richly bound in the European style, some beautiful crystal vases, various pictures in oils, and an unstated quantity of port wine, nearly all objects until then unknown in Japan.[1] With them and bearing two beautifully illuminated letters of greeting on parchment from the Governor of India, as representing King John III, and from Bishop Albuquerque, as representing Pope Julius III, St. Francis and his train embarked once more at Hirado for the Inland Sea. It is very probable that he landed at the beautiful little port of Mitajiri which is only three miles or so from his destination and there hired sumpter horses for his baggage and perhaps palanquins for himself and his companions. At all events he entered Yamaguchi in state and was immediately granted audience by the Daimyo, who had been advised of his approach.

How greatly impressed, in fact, how enthralled, Ouchi Yoshitaka was with the letters and presents is indicated by St. Francis himself in a letter to the European Jesuits dated January 29, 1552:

The Duke in his delight offered us all sorts of things and a

[1] Valignano guarantees the port and Frois the musket with three barrels, which must have been an uncommon sight even in Europe—' Hua espingarda de tres canos.' The other gifts are mentioned by Frois who obtained his information from Fernandez or by Cosmas de Torres, who did not think much of them.

large amount of gold and silver,[1] but we declined any of his gifts and asked only one favour, that he would give us permission to preach the law of God in his territories and allow those of his subjects who so wished to embrace it. He very willingly (*com muito amor*) gave us the permission and also ordered that written notices bearing his signature were to be posted in the streets of the city declaring the fact, that it was his good pleasure to have the law of God preached in his dominions, and that any who desired to follow it were hereby granted the faculty. At the same time, he made over to us for a dwelling an unoccupied Buddhist monastery, and there we held forth twice a day to a large crowd of visitors. At the end of each sermon there was invariably a discussion which lasted a long time. We were continually taken up with answering questions or preaching. Considerable numbers of Buddhist priests and nuns came to hear us, as well as noblemen and other people, so many in fact that the house was nearly always full and often could not contain all who wanted to come in. The questions they put to us were such and so many that by our replies they knew the laws of the holy men in whom they believed to be false and the law of God to be true. They kept up their questioning and arguing for several days and then we began to make converts among them, the first being those who had shown themselves most opposed to our sermons and arguments. A large proportion of our neophytes were of the samurai class and since their baptism have become our most devoted friends. They disclosed to us with great detail and accuracy the doctrines held by the various sects of [Buddhists]. As I said before, there are nine of these sects.[2] After obtaining

[1] Ouchi was a generous soul in his fashion and it was he who paid the coronation expenses of the penurious Emperor.

[2] In 1933 there were eleven sects but the three oldest among them numbered less than 100,000 adherents. The greater sects were all founded in the Middle Ages, as St. Francis rightly said, by Buddhist saints who made reforms in both doctrine and discipline. Numerically by far the most important is the Shin-shu, with more than thirteen million adherents and nearly twenty thousand temples (in 1933). Its founder Shinran (1173–1262) stressed faith in Amida Buddha as the all-sufficient and only essential necessity for salvation and discarded the celibacy of the monks and all other ascetic practices. This was a convenient

this true information about them we thought out reasons to prove the falsity of their doctrines and made daily onslaughts on them, to which neither the bonzes nor nuns nor sorcerers nor others on their side were able to answer a word. The Christians were delighted by the discomfiture of the bonzes and their faith in God increased every day, while the heathens present lost belief in their false sects. It made the bonzes very sad to see how many were becoming Christians and they took the converts to task for abandoning their traditional religion. Those already baptized and others under instruction replied that they went over to the law of God because it seemed to them more in accordance with reason than the doctrines of the sects and also because we were able to answer the difficulties put to us by the bonzes, whereas they could not answer our objections to their teachings. . . .

No doctrine taught by St. Francis in his monastery more greatly disturbed the audience than that of creation, because such

---

doctrine but spiritually negligible. Very different is the theory of the Zen-shu or Contemplative sect, founded by Eisai (1141–1215) and Dogen (1200–53) which seeks salvation by meditation and a certain ' divine emptiness '. Each believer (and there were nearly ten million of them with more than twenty thousand temples in 1933) must find the Buddha within him, working out his salvation by austere discipline, bodily and mental. This is the type of Buddhism, by no means ignoble, favoured in Europe and America. St. Francis Xavier came into contact with what appears to have been a degenerate form of it at Kago-shima. The monasteries on Mount Hiei which refused to admit St. Francis were the headquarters of the pantheistic Tendai sect and at perpetual war with their rivals, the equally bellicose monks of the esoteric and complicated Shingon sect whose camp was on Mount Kôya, south of Nara. In 1933 there were nearly nine million disciples of Shingon-shu, but little more than two million of Tendai-shu. The sect, or rather the radical reformation of Buddhism, inaugurated in the thirteenth century by the great outspoken patriot and fascinating man, Nichiren, whose theories bore a curious resemblance to the Apocalyptic speculations of Abbot Joachim of Floris, numbered just over three million in 1933. The gist of Nichiren's teaching was ' Back to Buddha ! ' and he utterly rejected and cast out Amida and Dainichi who had usurped the place belonging to Sakya-muni, the eternal Buddha, alone. On all these matters there is no better book than The Creed of Half Japan (London, 1913), a classic of the subject, written with immense learning and absolute fairness by a devout Christian, Arthur Lloyd, who spent many years teaching at the Imperial University and other academic institutions in Tokyo.

an idea was entirely foreign to Buddhism. The bonzes objected that if all things, including the human soul, had their origin from God, the Chinese sages would certainly have known it. Japanese Buddhism had come originally from China via Korea, and the priestly class and samurai entertained the highest regard for Chinese wisdom. The Mongols, masters of China under Kublai Khan, might attempt to subjugate Japan, and the Japanese under Hideyoshi, with a Catholic admiral commanding his fleet, might invade and conquer Korea, but those episodes and others like them in no way diminished the veneration of the bonzes for their Chinese masters in the spiritual life. This fact was to have a very important bearing on the last of the great missionary ideas conceived by St. Francis Xavier. One of the questions put to him in his daily sessions at the monastery touched on the problem of evil:

They questioned us closely and often about the Creator who made all that exists and desired to know whether He was good or evil, or whether there were two principles from one of which proceeded good and from the other evil. We told them that there was only one principle, entirely good and with no admixture of evil. This, they said, could not be so, for demons existed, malicious beings and enemies of the human race, and if God were good He could not have created such evil things. We replied that God created them good but that they made themselves evil, for which reason God will punish them for ever. They switched to a fresh objection, saying that a God who punished so severely must be without mercy, and, besides, if it were true, as we maintained, that God created the human race, why does He permit the evil demons to tempt us, and why also if He made us to serve Him does He create us so weak and full of sinful inclinations? If Himself good would He not rather have created us without evil in our composition? But He cannot be good or He would not have made something so bad and merciless as an eternal Hell nor would He, if good, have given the Ten Commandments, since they are so difficult to keep. In the mythology of their religion it is taught that

even should they go to Hell they can be delivered out of it by
calling upon the founders of their sects, and they consider it
exceedingly merciless and evil of God not to have provided
for a similar redemption. Their sects, they maintained, were
thus rooted in pity and mercy much more than was the law
of God. . . .

It is plain to see that those objections were not frivolous.
The bonzes had a case and their arguments pierced deep. Today,
four hundred years later, they are still good objections and take
a deal of answering. It would be highly interesting to know how
St. Francis answered, through Fernandez and Bernard, but he
says only that the critics were completely satisfied. He himself
was the best answer. God created him too, and he reflected God,
proving at the very least by the selfless sacrificial love and pity
of his heart that if there is a problem of evil there is equally a
problem of good. He may have been too rigorous in his interpretation of the theological maxim, *Extra Ecclesiam nulla salus*,
and too ready to believe, erroneously, with St. Augustine that
unbaptized persons necessarily went to Hell, but he yearned over
them with more than a mother's tenderness and killed himself
trying to rescue them from their peril. He regarded the quick
intelligence of the Japanese as a manifestation of the mercy of
God and was only too delighted that they should bombard him
with questions from morning to night. From him who had sailed
so much of its surface they first learned that the earth was round,
their Buddhist cosmography telling a different story, and he gave
them also in answer to their inquiries the latest ideas of Paris on
comets, lightning, rainfall, snow, and similar matters. ' They
were highly pleased with our explanations,' he wrote, ' and held
us for learned men, which helped not a little to gain credit for our
sermons.' He mentioned that in the space of two months they
had baptized about five hundred converts at Yamaguchi and
that baptisms continued daily—excellent Christians who showed
their apostles ' an extremity of love '. The principal trouble of
those men of good will before they received the light of faith
was inability to reconcile the infinite goodness and mercy of God

with the fact that He had not made Himself known to them and to their ancestors before the coming of St. Francis. If it was true, as Francis taught, that all who did not adore the true God went to Hell, then their ancestors must have gone there, even though they had been given no opportunity by God of realizing their duty to Him.

Our Lord helped us to deliver them from this terrible misgiving [said Francis]. We gave them very good reasons for holding that the law of God was imprinted on men's hearts from the beginning. Before ever the law of the Buddhists came from China to Japan, the Japanese, their ancestors, knew that it was wrong and wicked to commit murder, to steal, to bear false witness, or to break any other of the Ten Commandments, and their consciences smote them if they did so, proving that they knew the commandments of God without having been taught them except by the Creator of all peoples.

St. Francis instanced the case of a ' wolf-child ', a sort of Romulus or Remus nurtured in the wilds, who yet when found and taught human speech would instinctively know the difference between right and wrong, would, in fact, recognize Kant's *Categorical Imperative*, even if he were not awed by the starry heavens above him. Like Kant and Newman so long afterwards, Francis recognized in the moral law an implicit revelation of God to all men, by keeping which they would obtain light and grace to render God explicit worship and so to save their souls. In that way he overcame the misgivings of the Japanese about the fate of their ancestors, which was in itself a generous sentiment.[1]

There were no less than 102 Buddhist temples in Yamaguchi at this time, distributed among the various sects. One important point which the Saint learned from his converts was that the other sects detested the powerful and numerous monks of Zen-shu because they denied the immortality of the human soul, as do earnest and high-minded disciples of Zen, such as Mr. Christmas Humphreys, at the present time. With the men of Zen Francis

[1] Schurhammer, *Epistolae S. Francisci Xaverii*, ii, 262 -7.

and his disciples had many sharp disputations, but it may be doubted whether either side had much understanding of what the other was trying to say. All the sects possessed an esoteric core of doctrine intelligible only to initiates, and for the rest, the *profanum vulgus*, provided a liberal supply of gods and goddesses, magical incantations, invocations, praying-beads, and large quantities of other mechanical devices for wheedling benefits or averting dangers at innumerable shrines. The consequence was an absolute riot of superstitious beliefs and practices which the bonzes condoned because they were fruitful in revenue. Against such a travesty of true religion St. Francis declared immitigable war. He told St. Ignatius that the disputations and the constant stream of visitors from early morning until late into the night, as well as summonses to the houses of nobles and other important people who could not be denied, left ' no time for prayer, meditation, contemplation, even, at least at the beginning, for saying Mass or Office, or for eating a meal or finding some sleep '.

The war, which was waged out of doors as well as within, produced some startling results. According to Father Rodriguez Tçuzu who knew personally some of the actors in the drama at Yamaguchi but is inclined to embellish the facts with which they supplied him, Francis used to emerge in company with Fernandez twice a day and sit or squat in the Japanese fashion by a well in one of the streets, weary as his Lord and God was that day by Jacob's Well. There he would wait for his Samaritan Woman, who was not one but a legion of both men and women, even more argumentative than the much-married lady with the jar. Ten weeks had gone by since the Daimyo had given him the complete freedom of the city, ten weeks of almost interminable argument and not a single convert to show. Spring had passed with its glory of cherry-blossoms, tree-peony, azalea and wistaria, and high summer had come, heralded by the iris, but St. Francis must have thought that the ice would never thaw in the hearts of this people whom he loved. They had talked the sun up to the July meridian when all of a sudden the great thing happened. Fernandez was preaching to a considerable crowd, while St. Francis prayed. An ill-conditioned fellow shouldered his way

through the crowd and spat full in the Brother's face. It may be
remembered that Juan was very much of a Spanish gentleman
and that Spanish gentlemen through the ages have killed offenders
for insults a thousand times less grave than that. But Fernandez
merely drew from his pocket his Japanese paper handkerchief,
wiped the spittle from his face, and continued his sermon.
'There was in the crowd,' writes Tçuzu, 'a man of breeding
(*homem de honrado*) known to be a great adversary of Father
Francis, who came to the meetings for the sole purpose of gainsaying him. The gesture of Brother Fernandez was like a flash of
lightning in this man's soul. At the end of the sermon he followed
the two strangers to their abode and there begged Francis to
prepare him for baptism. He was the first Christian of Yamaguchi.'[1]

Among the five hundred men and women, many of them of
the samurai class, who separately asked to be instructed and
baptized during the two months following that dramatic breaking
of the ice, none was more remarkable than a certain strolling
minstrel who made his living by singing at street corners to the
accompaniment of his *biwa*, a stringed instrument shaped like
a mandolin.[2] This public entertainer and half-mountebank was

[1] Cros, *Saint François de Xavier: sa vie et ses lettres*, ii, 140–1. Père Cros had
been unable to identify Tçuzu as author of the manuscript history and always
refers to him as 'the Annalist of Macao'. Tçuzu was in error in saying that the
man of the above story was Yamaguchi's first Christian. St. Francis himself
explicitly says, referring to his earlier visit to the city: '*Ffaziao-se pouquos
cristãos.*' Among the few on that occasion, the first of them, were the Saint's
landlord and his wife who bore the Japanese name of Uchida and were baptized
as Thomas and Maria.

[2] It must have been a *biwa*, as the subsequently very popular *samisen* or
three-stringed guitar had not at this time been yet introduced into Japan from
southern China. Here is what a very honest lover of Japan had to say about
Japanese music at the turn of last century: 'Be the scale what it may, the effect
of Japanese music is, not to soothe, but to exasperate beyond all endurance the
European breast. . . . Japanese music employs only common time. Harmony
it has none. It knows nothing of our distinction of modes. . . . One never hears
a party of Japanese talking seriously about music. . . . A Japanese Bayreuth is
unthinkable. Men on the spree send for singing-girls chiefly in order to ogle
and chaff them, and to help along the entertainment with a little noise. . . .
Before another century elapses, may all the [*biwas*], *samisens*, *kotos* and other
native instruments of music be turned into firewood to warm the poor, when—

not a prepossessing sight. Frois who knew him well says that he was ' *de muy ridiculosa fisionomia* ', entirely blind in one eye and myopic in the other. Nevertheless, he was popular not only in the streets but in the houses of noblemen, for he had a very ready wit and a fine gift as a reciter of ballads and tales of long ago. He had also an inquiring mind and shuffled along regularly, his *biwa* slung over his shoulder, to pose highly intelligent questions to St. Francis and Fernandez. Behind his engagingly ugly face there functioned a brilliant mind and underneath his superficial buffoonery lay a great earnestness and passion to discover the purpose of his existence, if it had a purpose. Like Cosmas de Torres and many another, he found, not so much in St. Francis's answers as in St. Francis himself, the polarization of his restless and unsatisfied aspirations. Frois says that ' the charity of Father Francis ravished him, that the greatness of his designs awed him, that he, the public clown, became lost in admiration of these strangers who had come thousands of leagues through untold perils and hardships, for no personal advantage whatever but simply and solely to win men to the service of God, so casting away his *biwa* and abandoning his songs, his stories, his witty sallies, he begged to be allowed to share their labours that he, too, according to his capacity might glorify God our Lord and help to save souls '. St. Francis received him with open arms, gave him in baptism the Christian name of Laurence, and forthwith employed him as interpreter and catechist.[1] Never in his life did Francis make a greater convert than this grotesque, misshapen, entirely uneducated harlequin, who, as a Jesuit lay brother, evangelized his country with devouring zeal for thirty years. Not a bonze in Japan could stand up to him in argument and even the bellicose

---

if at no previous period of their existence—they will subserve a purpose indisputably useful! ' (*Things Japanese*, pp. 339–41). That is more or less what has happened and Japan has now many symphony orchestras which interpret the European masters to appreciative audiences. She has also many abominable jazz bands. St. Francis had a sensitive musical ear and must have suffered much from the frightful Oriental caterwaulings that stood for music in the Japan of his day.

[1] Frois in Cros, *Saint François de Xavier: sa vie et ses lettres*, ii, 146–7; Tçuzu, *ibidem*, p. 141; Frois-Schurhammer, *Die Geschichte Japans*, 16-17.

brethren of Hiei-zan who had excluded St. Francis learned to respect and esteem him. Their great enemy, the dictator Oda Nobunaga, who was a complete sceptic, appreciated his good company and used to invite him to tea. Once, in the presence of that ruthless person who caused the monks of Hiei-zan to be massacred to the last man, Brother Laurence entered into argument with a leader of the Zen Buddhists named Nichijô on the subject of human immortality. Beaten all along the line, the bonze in a rage seized a sword and made a dash at the Brother, shouting to the three hundred samurai present, 'I'll show you how immortal his soul is!' But he was restrained, and the great-hearted blind minstrel on whom so marvellous a light had dawned outlived a thousand such perils to die peacefully on his *tatami* at Nagasaki in 1592, breathing the name of Jesus.

In contrast to the illiterate genius Laurence was another convert of St. Francis who had studied for years at the greatest centre of Chinese learning and Confucianism in Japan, Ashikaga Gakkô, situated about seventy miles north of Tokyo. This man, whose name Francis does not supply, was regarded as being the finest scholar then living in Yamaguchi. He had been a bonze in his time, but became dissatisfied with Buddhist teaching, abandoned his orders and took a wife. He attained to belief in God as the Creator of the world by processes of reason, and so was ripe for Christianity when St. Francis appeared. His conversion caused a sensation in Yamaguchi, delighting the Christians and no doubt filling the eager heart of their shepherd with fresh hopes of bringing the land of Confucius to the feet of Christ. He nowhere in his letters refers to Confucianism which supplied the native Japanese religion, Shintô or The Way of the Gods (eight million gods, in fact), with its ethics of loyalty and filial piety, but he would certainly have learned about it from his new friend, the distinguished graduate of Ashikaga. Already Francis is planning an assault on that celebrated Academy and he will later write urgently to Simon Rodriguez in Portugal specifying the type of men to be sent from Europe for the purpose. They must be men of great experience, well tried and proved, for the bonzes will fight them to the death, and they must be sturdy men, sound in wind and limb, so as to be able to endure the intense cold and short commons of Ashikaga, which Francis thought to be uncomfortably near the North Pole, though it is in fact in the same latitude as Gibraltar.[1] He suggested that some Germans and Flemings might be the men for the situation, ' since they are born to cold and hardship '! To Rodriguez he repeated what he had said to St. Ignatius, that Japan devoured a man's time, leaving him no room for set prayer, the food of the soul, nor for a snatched meal of rice and herbs, the body's humble sustenance, either. The Japanese, inquisitive by nature, had no mercy on the strangers with ideas as rare and wonderful as their clocks and spectacles, the fame of which is recorded in the annals of Yamaguchi and penetrated, as Frois discovered, even to the Buddhist fastnesses of Hiei-zan. A man must be strong indeed and a miracle of self-control to stand up to the daily and nightly fusillade of questions. No longer will Francis be content with men of small learning and average goodness for the missions. He pleads to be sent men of the finest grain, worthy to stand beside his two heroes, Cosmas de Torres and Juan Fernandez. How Francis himself must have missed his morning Mass, he whose every Mass became an ecstasy! But there it was, a sacrifice of God for God which is at the heart of all true mystical experience.

At the court of Ouchi Yoshitaka where he had graduated into being a welcome visitor, the Saint encountered Buddhist priests of the Shingon sect which was of Indian origin but took root in China and thence leaped the sea to Japan at the beginning of the ninth century A.D. Its Japanese apostle and chief saint was a greatly gifted man named Kobo Daishi who believed in catering for all religious tastes and in welcoming all varieties of religious opinion. The esoteric doctrines of Shingon are almost impossibly complicated, ' extremely difficult to comprehend and more difficult to put into intelligible language ' (Sir Ernest Satow). But provision was made also, as in the old Gnostic systems, for the uninitiated, the unmetaphysical man in the street, by the use of *hôben* or pious devices, that is, by the presentation of abstruse doctrines under a form suited to the capacity of simple people.

[1] Schurhammer, *Epistolae S. Francisci Xaverii*, ii, 275, 297-8.

It astonished St. Francis Xavier to find so many practices and institutions in Buddhism which closely resembled those of the Catholic Church, as the use of sacraments and symbols, of elaborate ritual, of praying-beads, of sacred vestments, of bells and chant, of incense, of holy water, of images, and the prevalence of monasticism for both men and women, the addiction to the making of pilgrimages, the invocation of saints, and much else. These interesting parallels made Francis wonder whether the religion of China and consequently of Japan had not been influenced either by the preaching of the Apostle St. Thomas or by contact with the later Nestorian missions. After careful investigation with the aid of learned converts, he decided that in Japan at least there had hitherto been no knowledge of the true God nor of His Son, Jesus Christ. The Shingon priests in the Daimyo's entourage questioned him about the God whom he worshipped, for instance, whether He had any form or colour. ' The Father answered,' writes Frois, basing his account as usual on the letters of Juan Fernandez, ' that He had no colour nor form nor accidents of any kind, for He is pure substance, separate and distinct from all elements of which He is the Creator. The bonzes then asked from what source this God derived His being, to which the Father replied that He was self-existent, the principle of everything else in existence, infinitely powerful, wise and good, without beginning and without end '. The answers delighted the Shingon priests. Why, they said to the wondering Francis, ' those are the very attributes of our Dainichi. You and we may differ in speech and custom, but in theology we are absolutely at one.' ' So the bonzes of that sect,' continues Frois, ' warmly invited the Father to their monasteries,[1] feasted him and showed him high honour, not indeed for love of him personally but because of the

---

[1] There were six Shingon monasteries or *thera* in Yamaguchi. The Zen-shû sect had many more and the Jôdo-shû which, like the Shin-shu, worships the entirely imaginary Amida, were well represented also. St. Francis came to the conclusion that the Buddha himself, or Xaca, as he called him (i.e., Shaka, the Japanese form of Sakya-muni) was no less a fictitious person than Amida, in which he was wrong. ' For the love and service of our Lord,' he wrote to Europe on January 29, 1552, ' I beg all those who read this letter to beseech God to give us victory over those two demons, Xaca and Amida. . . .'

advantages which they looked to obtain from their disciples and the King through the dissemination of their sect by this foreign bonze.' His sudden popularity and the fact that the Dainichi whom he had until then been preaching as the true God was the god of this Buddhist sect gave Francis pause. He must find out more about the Great Sun. The good Anjiro, then, unknown to him, in a watery grave, had already led him a pretty dance in Japan and perhaps Dainichi too, was part of the unintended mystification.

With the aid of his converts, and particularly, we may assume, of the learned man from Ashikaga, who was proficient in the Chinese sacred books, Francis discovered that Dainichi corresponded to the Indian Vairocana, not a personal god at all but a purely pantheistic conception of Brahmanism. He also learned that in the popular mind the name bore an obscene connotation. Thereupon he returned to one of the Shingon monasteries with the light of battle in his eyes. What, he demanded of the suave priests, were their views about the Blessed Trinity, and did they believe and teach that the Second Divine Person had become man and died on a cross to redeem mankind? The bonzes showed their consternation. They had never heard of such ideas, regarded them as ludicrous and laughed them to scorn. That was how Francis lost his illusions about Dainichi. He and Fernandez at once went forth to their usual pitches and warned the crowds that they were never again to pray to Dainichi nor to regard him as God, since he was only an invention and imposture of the devil foisted on men by the false deceiving Shingon sect. So ended the tea-parties at the monasteries, and so, in the opinion of Frois, might the life of Francis have ended, had not the enraged monks been deterred from violent measures by fear of his protector, the Daimyo. Those clocks and that barrel of port proved a very effective armour.[1] Having utterly repudiated and reprobated the Great Sun of Shingon, which he had once innocently interpreted as meaning Christ, the Sun of Justice, St. Francis felt no inclination to explore farther in the Japanese pantheon in search of a

[1] Frois-Schurhammer, *Die Geschichte Japans*, pp. 15–16; Schurhammer, *Das kirchliche Sprachproblem in der Japanischen Jesuitenmission*, pp. 32–3.

native name for God. He took the only safe course open to him and from then on employed the completely Christianized Latin name *Deus*. He had already used that name, or its Spanish equivalent, *Dios*, on his first visit to Yamaguchi as an alternative to Dainichi, and mentioned that the children in the streets used to sing out after him mockingly, ' Deus! Deus! Deus! ' Now he would use it exclusively, which gave the Shingon monks also a chance to mock. When they preached, he said, they pronounced the name *Deusu* and said it was the same as *Daiuso*, meaning Dai, great, and *uso*, lie ' and so they tried to keep back people from the worship of our God '.[1]

In the midst of his daily debates and constant battles with the men of Zen and Shin and Shingon, St. Francis received a letter from the Daimyo of Bungo in Kyushu, a young man of twenty-two named Otomo Yoshishige, asking him to come to his capital, Funai, now the large and thriving city of Oita, as a Portuguese ship had arrived at the city's port of Okinohama and he wished to discuss with him certain business. Francis was not the one to miss such a God-given chance as this of meeting a prince who controlled not only Bungo but the adjoining provinces of Chikugo, Higo, and Southern Chikuzen, that is, more than one third of the nine provinces comprised in Kyushu. He hastily summoned Father Cosmas de Torres from his lonely outpost in Hirado, left him and Juan Fernandez in charge of the Yamaguchi Christians, and was away ' to discover whether the Daimyo desired to be a Christian and to see the Portuguese '. He left in the middle of September, accompanied by three Japanese Christians, namely the man baptized with Anjiro at Goa and given the name John who knew Portuguese and could act as interpreter, Bernard of Kagoshima who desired to go to India and Europe, and a convert made at Yamaguchi named Matthew who nursed the same ambition. Antonio, Anjiro's former henchman, remained with Father de Torres. The journey of about sixty miles was completed in less than a week, partly by land and partly by sea. At this point in the story the celebrated romancer Fernam Mendez Pinto reappears to supply us with a certain amount of picturesque misinformation. It is quite

[1] Schurhammer, *Epistolae S. Francisci Xaverii*, ii, 270.

true that he was on the Portuguese ship which had come to the daimyate of Bungo, but that did not entitle him to concoct and subsequently embody in his *Peregrination* a completely spurious letter of St. Francis, nor to say that Francis had been ' a little more than a year ' in Yamaguchi and had made three thousand Christians there. Fernam, as is his wont, multiplies the number of months by three and the number of Christians by six. The captain of the Portuguese ship, Duarte da Gama, was one of the best of his kind, a genuinely devout and zealous man. He had known and revered St. Francis in India and it is altogether likely that he gave him a very fine reception, but whether it was the stagey kind related by Pinto, a cavalcade to meet him, a thunder of guns, and the rest of it, who shall say?[1]

After he had heard their confessions and said Mass for them, which was one of his chief reasons in coming, St. Francis, according to Pinto, was taken from the port of Okinohama, long since washed away by the sea, to Funai or Oita in a gaily beflagged sloop, with all the Portuguese merchants and mariners in festive attire as his retinue. They walked in procession through the streets of the great city filled with gaping crowds to the Daimyo's palace. Francis himself says that the young prince, whom Japanese chroniclers accuse of having reached his shaky throne by the murder of his father, gave him a very good welcome, chiefly, no doubt, because the Portuguese merchants held him in such high regard and Yoshishige wanted the merchants' trade. According to Pinto, one of the Portuguese anticipated the gesture

[1] Pinto devotes twelve consecutive chapters of his book (207–18 inclusive) to St. Francis, but it is a waste of time to try to sift the few grains of wheat from his mountain of chaff. He deceived the uncritical Tursellini, the first biographer of St. Francis, who had access to his manuscript, and helped himself liberally to his inventions in the second edition of his book. But he did not deceive the Jesuits working in Japan at that time who pronounced the letters and speechifying supposed by him to have passed between the Daimyo and the Saint to be ' false and ridiculous forgeries, entirely unlike the usage and style of Japan ' (Schurhammer, *Fernão Mendez Pinto und seine ' Peregrinaçam '*, in *Asia Major*, Leipzig, 1926, pp. 209–10. This is a devastating piece of ' debunking ' and makes Maurice Collis's recent attempt at rehabilitation look really foolish. It is impossible to rehabilitate Pinto for he has given himself away too often. Father Rodriguez Tçuzu, not himself the most accurate of writers but one who knew Japan extremely well, described the *Peregrination as a ' livro dos fengimentos '*).

of Sir Walter Raleigh and spread his magnificent cape over a mat in the Daimyo's reception hall for Francis to squat upon it. That is a typically Pinto touch which the Saint would surely have scorned as an insult to his host. The host is a most difficult person to assess. In many ways he seems to have borne a curious resemblance to King David, being a man of generous impulses and terrible passions, capable of the gravest sin and of the heartiest repentance. He belonged to the Zen sect of Buddhists and there can be no doubt at all of his strongly religious bent, though it took him twenty-seven years to break with his vices and make up his mind to become a Christian. He chose the name of Francis at his baptism in 1578, but this was not because the Saint had wielded any particular influence in the long process of his conversion, despite Mendez Pinto's rubbishy pretences to the contrary. Shortly before he was received into the Church to become responsible, by the sheer force of example, one hopes, for the conversion of seventy thousand of his subjects, the Daimyo told a Japanese Jesuit brother that the man who had helped him most was a Portuguese merchant named Diogo Vaz. St. Francis he did not mention at all, and the brave Fernandez, who went to Funai in 1553, only to say that the excellent Juan's Japanese was beyond his comprehension![1] Nevertheless, Fernandez and his companion Father Gago increased the number of native Christians in Bungo from the half dozen or so made by St. Francis himself to between six and seven hundred.

The happiness caused to Francis by the Daimyo's friendliness and unconcealed interest in the Christian faith had one great flaw in it. Duarte da Gama's ship had brought him no letter from India or from Europe. Not since he landed at Kagoshima more than two years earlier had he heard a word from his Jesuit brethren in those other far-off countries, though he had implored them to write frequently and had given careful instructions as to how the letters were to be dispatched. His post must come from Malacca

[1] Schurhammer, *Das kirchliche Sprachproblem in der Japanischen Jesuitenmission*, pp. 10–11. Yoshishige said that Diogo Vaz, who was with him for five years, spoke good Japanese. Vaz was a friend of St. Francis and interpreted for him during his brief sojourn in Bungo.

and for various reasons connected with war and weather Malacca remained almost entirely cut off from Japan during the period. Francis did not know this circumstance and was greatly puzzled and troubled by the silence of the men he loved and who loved him. Almost immediately after arriving in Japan he had summoned three of his men in India to come out to him and he might just as well have summoned Iniquitriberim or Vettum Perumâl. What on earth could have happened to cause this deathlike stillness from Goa to Cape Comorin and all the long way round to Malacca and the Moluccas? There was only one thing for it— he must journey back and see. At Funai he determined not to return to Yamaguchi, as he had intended, but to sail with the Portuguese merchants for their trading-station off Canton and there, with luck, find another ship to take him to Malacca and India. The evidence is as clear as it could be that he meant his Indian visit to be temporary, a tour of inspection and regulation, after which he would fare eastwards again to the land where he had left his heart. He reckoned that within a year he could be back in Yamaguchi. At the first chance of a messenger he wrote to tell Cosmas de Torres of his decision and sent him three hundred *cruzados* borrowed from the good Mendez Pinto, who is likable in spite of his much nonsense, to enable the Father to build a small church and house. At the end of October, Antonio the Japanese arrived in Funai with letters from both Torres and Fernandez announcing dreadful news.

Shortly after the departure of St. Francis from Yamaguchi, the most powerful vassal of Ouchi Yoshitaka, a certain Sue Takafusa, rebelled against him and plunged the whole daimyate into a state of war. Ouchi, softened by a life of luxury and vice, lost his nerve and fled from Yamaguchi which was rapidly invested and captured by the rebels, to be given over to slaughter and destruction. The unhappy Daimyo tried to escape by sea but was cut off and then committed harakiri, after ordering his son to be killed lest he fall into the hands of the enemy. As his protégés, Father de Torres and Juan Fernandez knew themselves to be in deadly danger. They had carried on their disputations as usual until the war drew near, when their audience faded away in terror of what was to come.

Then, gathering their few effects into a bundle, the two men quitted their cloister and sought refuge with one of the most eminent Buddhists in Japan, a devout member of the Jôdo sect who had built several monasteries to the glory of Amida. This man, Naitô Takaharu, and his excellent wife had been from the first on the most friendly terms with St. Francis.

They did everything in their power [he wrote] to help us to spread the law of God, which they venerated as true and good, though we could never persuade them to embrace it. The reason for their reluctance was that they had built and endowed a large number of monasteries where the monks might pray on their behalf to Amida, to whom they were extremely devout, begging the god to preserve them from evil in this life and to bring them to his paradise in the next. They produced for me many reasons why they should not become Christians, saying that they had shown long and signal service to Shaka and Amida, and would lose, by becoming Christians, the fruits of so many years of devotion, of all the alms they had given and of all the monasteries they had built out of their love for the gods. Moreover, they held for certain that Amida would reward one crown given for his sake in this world with ten in the world to come and so they looked to receive a very great recompense hereafter which they could not sacrifice by becoming Christians. . . . All those errors were put into their heads by the bonzes.[1]

Whatever we may think of Naitô's sugar-plum notions of immortality, he and his wife felt and practised a compassion

[1] Schurhammer, *Epistolae S. Francisci Xaverii*, ii, 269–70. The Jôdo sect, like the Shingon, was of Indian origin, and the name is the Japanese equivalent of the Sanskrit Sukhavati, meaning the 'Pure Land' or paradise in which worshippers of Buddha and Amida will be rewarded after death for their faith and good works. As St. Francis correctly points out it is a very materialistic paradise in which there will be great feasting and beautiful clothes and shoes to wear, something much more like the Norse Valhalla or the Islamic paradise than the Christian conception of Heaven. But Jôdo, in contrast to Shin-shu, the other sect worshipping Amida, does insist on the necessity of good works and of becoming worthy by self-abnegation and compassion of Amida's salvation. That is why Jôdo has remained a relatively small sect, while Shin, which dispenses with good works, has flourished exceedingly.

worthy of Him who said, ' I was a stranger and you took me in, hungry and you fed me, naked and you clothed me '. They hid the two refugees and their man Amador in one of the monasteries which they supported where the bonzes gave them a distinctly cool welcome. ' For two days and nights,' reported Cosmas de Torres to Francis, ' we lay concealed in a recess of their pagoda, with plenty of fear in our hearts but nothing whatever in our stomachs. During that time, many indeed were the houses of samurai and monasteries which went up in flames.' The super-stitious Shintoists of the city sought for them everywhere to put them to death, regarding them as the authors of all the trouble through their preaching against the cult of the *kami* and *hotoke*, the multitudinous native godlings of Japan. When their sanctuary itself was threatened, Naitô hid them in a small room of his house for five days. By that time the murder and pillage had somewhat subsided, so Torres determined to beard the new authorities and ask them to confirm the dead Daimyo's permission to preach, as well as to give them a new residence instead of their burnt-out monastery. Failing that, he said, they would preach and teach in secret until such time as Yamaguchi had a new daimyo and Father Francis had returned from India. The sublime daring of the man backed by the great influence of Naitô pulled them through. In his letter, Fernandez gave a lengthy specimen of the kind of disputation carried on by Father de Torres with the bonzes. Nearly all the elements of it are in the accounts given by St. Francis of his own disputations, but it brings into clearer light points in his answers which he left obscure. Those big strong men did not wear their hearts on their sleeves, but Fernandez could not refrain from a sigh in his letter: ' It will be a sore trial to me to have to be deprived of your holy company for a whole year.'[1] Before the siege and destruction began the brave pair had added another fifty converts to the five hundred made by Francis

[1] The letters of Torres and Fernandez are given in a French version in Cros (*Saint François de Xavier: sa vie et ses lettres*, ii, 157–63). Father Schurhammer published the original Spanish text of the letters together with a German translation and a most admirable commentary in his brochure, *Die Disputationen des P. Cosme de Torres, S.J. mit den Buddhisten in Yamaguchi in Jahre 1551* (Tokyo, 1929, pp. x–114).

himself, but when he received their news he must have thought
that the little flock of Yamaguchi which was to him as the apple
of his eye had reached the limits of its growth. He had liked the
luckless Daimyo, in spite of his addiction to practices unmention-
able and considered that it was the devil who had inspired the
rebellion, but the good angels must have been working too, for
a delegation arrived one day in Funai from the rebels to offer
the vacant throne to Haruhide, the younger brother of the
Christianly inclined Otomo Yoshishige. The offer was accepted
and both Otomo and Haruhide promised faithfully to protect and
support the missionaries.[1]

It was accordingly with an easier mind that St. Francis made
preparations for the long voyage before him. The Daimyo
Yoshishige said farewell to him reluctantly, having had time to
appreciate his character even if he could not understand his
Japanese. He appointed an ambassador to accompany the Father
and bring his greetings to the viceroy of India, together with a
letter and presents of Japanese weapons and armour for the King
of Portugal. Francis would dearly have liked to bring a few learned
bonzes also, just to show the brethren in India the new style of
antagonist, so different from the pearl-fishers or Macuas or third-
rate temple Brahmans, whom they must be prepared to meet.
But the bonzes felt no itch for foreign travel and declined his

---

[1] Frois-Schurhammer, *Die Geschichte Japans*, p. 50. Haruhide kept his word
until, in 1557, he too was overthrown by another powerful vassal and committed harakiri. During his friendly reign, Father de Torres built the church
and house for which St. Francis had sent him the money and brought the total
of Christians in Yamaguchi and its environs up to two thousand, including a
number of former bonzes. But the new master of the city, Môri Motonari,
absolutely banned any further preaching of the faith. The new church and house
went up in smoke and Cosmas de Torres and his companions had to fly for
their lives to the safety of Bungo where they were soon joined by Brother
Laurence and St. Francis's first Yamaguchi convert, Uchida Thomas. Uchida
brought with him two altar-stones and a crucifix which he had rescued from
the ruin of the church, and gave himself and his son entirely to the service of the
missionaries. Scattered far and wide, persecuted, reduced to beggary, condemned
to cruel deaths, the marvellous Christians of Yamaguchi remained steadfast to
the end in the faith brought to them by St. Francis Xavier. A brief but excellent
account of events is given by Sir Ernest Satow in his article, *Vicissitudes of the
Church at Yamaguchi from 1550 to 1586* (Transactions of the Asiatic Society of
Japan, vol. vii, 1879, pp. 137-66).

invitations, as also did some of his more distinguished converts, dreading the perils of the sea. So he had to be content to take Bernard, Matthew, John and Antonio, all excellent specimens of Japanese manhood, but not products of the famous ' universities '. Mendez Pinto was in the company too, which meant that the voyage was bound to be exciting, at least on paper. And by the trident of Neptune, what a storm he invented for the occasion, such a storm, he said, as land-lubbers ' could never even imagine '! They sailed from Funai about the middle of September and this typhoon from the land of dreams caught them seven days after Japan had faded out of sight. It whirled them ' nor'-nor'-east through an unknown sea never before traversed by a ship of any nation ', and then, changing direction, drove them a thousand miles before it into the Indonesian Archipelago![1] Pinto's fantasies do not prevent us from believing that there may well have been some reasonable kind of storm. St. Francis, who heartily disliked storms and frequently mentioned them in his letters, is silent about this one, but another man on the ship named Galeotto Pereira bore testimony to the typhoon, at Cochin in 1557, long before Pinto's book saw the light. The same witness, speaking only six years after the event, told also the story of the ship's long-boat, which went into the Bull of St. Francis's canonization. It had been lowered in the storm as a precaution, with two Moslem seamen and much victuals aboard, broke from its moorings and soon disappeared in the murk. While all were bewailing the mishap which put their own lives in jeopardy, Francis bade them lower sail and be of good heart, for within three days God would bring the skiff and its occupants back to them. So it punctually happened, and Francis had the comfort, rare in his life, of instructing and baptizing the two sons of the Prophet whom his pity and prayer had snatched from the merciless sea.[2] Pinto says that they arrived at Sancian Island near the mouth of the Canton River on December 17, which was good sailing after their

[1] *Peregrinação*, re-edited Lisbon, 1711, p. 345.
[2] *Monumenta Xaveriana*, ii, 327–8, 712. Pinto tells the story also, but with plenty of trimmings. He even obliges in italics with the very words and prayers which he deemed St. Francis might be expected to have uttered on the occasion.

imaginary divagations to Kamtchatka and Celébes. There St.
Francis found his old and faithful friend, Diogo Pereira, waiting
for a favourable wind to take his ship, the *Santa Cruz*, back to
Malacca. The Portuguese at Sancian were, strictly speaking,
smugglers, as normal trade with the merchants of China had been
forbidden by the emperor of that country under pain of death
or life imprisonment. Several of the foreigners had been caught
and languished in the gaols of Canton. By some means or other,
probably a heavy bribe, one of those brave unfortunate fellows
managed to spirit a letter through to Diogo Pereira begging that
good man to get himself officially appointed Portuguese ambassador to the court of Peking, for only by some such move could
the prisoners be saved from their terrible fate and the ports of
China reopened, perhaps, to commerce with the West.

Pereira showed the letter to St. Francis in whose thoughts it
caused a revolution. Though he had been for long deeply
interested in China and felt the attraction of the mysterious
empire, his mind appears to have been made up to return to
Japan until the fateful letter of the poor captive in Canton was put
into his hands. What he had so often observed, the way religious-
minded Japanese looked to the Chinese as reverent pupils to their
masters, struck him then with the force of a new revelation. In
religion Japan had always gone the road China had taken, and
might not China now, after millenniums of straying, be persuaded
by the mercy of God to take the right road? In China all power
rested safely in one strong pair of hands, and could those hands
be brought to make the Sign of the Cross the countless humbler
hands might easily make it too, without in the least having to
repudiate the best lessons of Confucius. In that case the conversion
of Japan would follow almost automatically. So St. Francis and
his friend appear to have argued as the *Santa Cruz* ploughed her
uneasy way south to Singapore. ' You might have heard them of
an evening on the vessel's deck and think you were listening to two
romantic adolescents giving rein to their fancies of an assault on
the Dragon's cave and of conquering the world with his treasure.
But the one was a business man and the other a proficient missionary, and they counted between them twenty or thirty years of

sobering experience in the Far East.'[1] Both men were hard-headed as well as tender-hearted and their plan was not purely quixotic, for three successors of St. Francis, Ricci, Schall and Verbiest, put it into operation with the most startling success. Pereira had the means to make himself an extremely persuasive ambassador, and Xavier, given the chance as his secretary or chaplain, could be depended on to captivate even an emperor. Pereira testified at Goa in 1557 that the first thought in the mind of Francis was to deliver the unhappy prisoners at Canton but that he feared lest the devil should make their embassy impossible. 'When he had repeated this misgiving to me many times,' continued the witness, 'I made a warm protest which had no effect on him, for he simply answered, " You will see. You will see ".'[2]

At Singapore, whose narrow Strait had to be traversed cautiously and in daylight by big caravels such as the *Santa Cruz*, St. Francis wrote a hurried note on Christmas Eve to his greatly loved Father Perez at Malacca and dispatched the Japanese Antonio with it on a light Siamese *balon*, a rowing boat not dependent on winds and untroubled by shoals. ' If there is a ship in harbour trimmed for the voyage to India,' he said, ' would you ask the captain to delay sailing for one day more. I hope to be in Malacca by Sunday the 27th. . . . And would you also obtain for me such things as are needed on the voyage to India. As we are so soon to meet and to be a great comfort to each other in the Lord, I say no more. *Todo vuestro in Domino*, Francisco.'[3] It was an urgent little scrap of correspondence. The bells of Malacca would soon be ringing in the new year, 1552, and before it closed St. Francis would be dead.

---

[1] Bellessort, *Saint François Xavier*, 13ième, éd., p. 310.
[2] *Monumenta Xaveriana*, ii, 262.
[3] Schurhammer, *Epistolae S. Francisci Xaverii*, ii, 239–40.

CHAPTER XVI

FOR THE PEACE OF JERUSALEM

TO Antonio's delight he observed a tall ship with sails set for departure in the Malacca roads as his *balon* came scudding to the quay. There was just time for Father Perez to have a signal sent from the shore and to row in hot haste with St. Francis's petition to the captain. This man, one of ten Pereiras who had come East to make their fortunes, for our confusion, bore the name of Antonio also and was in many respects an excellent good fellow, only too pleased to defy the monsoon's vagaries yet a while for the honour and pleasure of having St. Francis on his ship, the *Gallega*. The fact is that, like Mendez Pinto, he had too high an opinion of St. Francis, and wildly exaggerated plain facts in order that the Father, and himself too, of course, might have the greater glory. He says, for instance, that Francis came on board with a train of fourteen or fifteen Japanese, and that the Saint, while still in the Strait of Singapore ninety miles away, knew by divine inspiration of his, Antonio's, presence in Malacca, though in the ordinary course of events he should long since have sailed for India.[1] Now, all this is demonstrably untrue. Francis had only five Japanese with him, the four Christians and the unaccompanied ambassador from Bungo who was received into the Church at Goa later on. Nor did he know that the *Gallega* was at Malacca but merely hoped that there might be *some* ship there, as his note to Father Perez makes perfectly plain. Antonio had the effrontery to pretend when giving evidence before an ecclesiastical tribunal at Goa in August, 1557, that Francis had sent the note to him personally and even provided a purely imaginary version of it, exactly in the manner of Pinto. Those facts have to be set down here in their place, even if they momentarily break the thread of the narrative, because one

[1] Schurhammer, *Epistolae S. Francisci Xaverii*, ii, 236–7.

man and one man alone was responsible for creating the hoary
and still persistent legend that St. Francis possessed the gift of
tongues, and that man was Antonio Pereira. Here is what he
testified on oath before an ecclesiastical court at Malacca in
November, 1556, as taken down at the time by a secretary in
Portuguese: ' He said that wherever Master Francis turned he
acquired and could speak the languages of those parts in a very
few days, as was the case in Malabar, the Moluccas and Japan.
He, the witness, was skilled in those languages, as also in Malay,
and used to converse with the Father in them.'[1] What a picture
it conjures up, the two men pacing the deck of the *Gallega* and
trying out their Japanese, Tamil, Malayalam and Malay on each
other ! So far as is known Pereira never set foot in Japan and it is
highly likely that his proficiency in Eastern languages was confined to a smattering or even mere *baragouinage* of Malay. Sixty
years passed without Antonio's story receiving any recorded
confirmation, but then, in 1616, a pearl-fisher, ' aged eighty and
upwards ', boldly stated that when a young man ' at the port of
Temanapattanam on the Coromandel Coast ' he had heard Francis
preach in polished Tamil and moreover that when he spoke many
persons of diverse nations and tongues heard and understood him
perfectly, each in his own language.[2] All that need be said about
this piece of evidence from the Sand Waste is that no such town
as Temanapattanam ever existed on the Coromandel Coast or
anywhere else.[3] Yes, indeed, Antonio Pereira started a wonderful
ball rolling that day at Malacca, and it is rolling still, and will
probably be rolling at the fifth century of the death of St. Francis
in the year 2052.

The *Gallega* arrived without incident at Cochin on January 24,
1552, and the Viceroy of Portuguese India, Dom Alfonso de
Noronha, who was in the city, gave St. Francis a very hearty
welcome. Indeed, he was so overwhelmed with welcomes from
all quarters that he found it extremely difficult to get a few neces-

[1] *Monumenta Xaveriana*, ii, 418.
[2] *Monumenta Xaveriana*, ii, 546–7.
[3] A careful inspection of the many towns and villages beginning with the
letter ' T ' in Hunter's all-inclusive Gazetteer of India, vol. xiii, reveals no
place even faintly resembling Temanapattanam.

sary letters to Europe written in time to catch the ships about to sail thither. To the one addressed to his brethren in general, he added a disarming last paragraph:

I disembarked at Cochin as the ships were about to leave and was so constantly interrupted while writing to you by the visits of friends that I had to finish the letter in a great hurry, leaving the things I tell you in a disorderly jumble and the arguments I used [against the bonzes] inconclusive. Take me in good part! There is so much to say about Japan that I could never come to an end of it. I fear that you will grow wearied with what I have written, there is such a lot of it, but console myself with the thought that the ones I bore have the remedy in their own hands, which is to stop reading me! And so I end, without being able to come to an end, writing to my Fathers and Brothers, so dear and beloved, and telling them about such wonderful friends as are the Christians of Japan.[1]

During his brief stay in Malacca on the way back Francis had received from Father Perez a considerable post, consisting of letters and documents of an official character, sent from Rome, chiefly by St. Ignatius Loyola, more than two years earlier. One of these was a diploma appointing him Provincial, in place of Simon Rodriguez, ' of all those in India and other transmarine territories subject to his Serene Highness the King of Portugal, as well as places beyond [e.g. Japan], who live under obedience to the Society of Jesus '.[2] Thus did India become the third Province of the Jesuits, thus was abolished the double jurisdiction whereby Rodriguez, a poor judge of men, made the principal appointments in India, while St. Francis, who loved him, had the thankless task of trying to shield the missions and missionaries from his

---

[1] Schurhammer, *Epistolae S. Francisci Xaverii*, ii, 279. A good deal of this long letter, which runs to 783 lines, has been already cited in the foregoing pages. As Francis said, it is certainly a jumble and his answers to Japanese difficulties lack the finish he might have given them but for being so greatly rushed.

[2] The diploma and the accompanying letter of Ignatius are given in Wicki, *Documenta Indica*, i, 508 -15.

mistakes. His biggest blunder, one which had made the heart of the Saint ache as he departed for Japan, was the selection of Father Antonio Gomes, with all his brilliance, for the post of rector in Goa. These pages have already shown how Francis tried to protect as many of the brethren as possible from the slings and arrows of the Apollo out of Coimbra by giving as much authority as he dared to Fathers Paul of Camerino, Lancillotto and Henriques. Now that he was back in India he had to meet the full blast of the troubles caused by the imprudence and imperious temperament of Gomes in his absence.

To Ignatius he wrote on January 27:

My true Father, I received a letter of your holy charity at Malacca on my way back from Japan, and God our Lord knows what a comfort it was to have news of the health and life of one so dear to me. Among many other holy words and consolations of your letter I read the concluding ones, 'Entirely yours, without power or possibility of ever forgetting you, Ignatio.' I read them with tears, and with tears now write them, remembering the past and the great love which you always bore towards me and still bear, while at the same time calling to mind the many trials and perils of Japan from which God delivered me through the intercession of your holy prayers. I could never put down in writing all that I owe to the people of Japan, for through them God our Lord gave me a deep understanding of my infinite sinfulness [*infinitas maldades*]. Being out of myself I was not aware of the amount of evil that lay hidden within me until I found myself up against the hardships and dangers of Japan. God then gave me to understand the extreme need I stood in of some one to keep anxious and most careful watch over me. Now your holy charity may reflect on the charge which you have given me of so many devout souls of the Society who are in these parts, for by the sole mercy of God I recognize plainly my utter inadequacy. I lived in hopes that it was I who must be commended to those of the Society, not they to me. In your letter you tell me how greatly you desire to see me before this life closes. God knows the profound impression that those words of great love made on my soul and the many tears they cost me every time I thought of them. I felt that I could rejoice over them too, for to holy obedience nothing is impossible. . . .[1]

From the last line cited, Francis would appear to have cherished a hope of being called home and of seeing Ignatius again, but the cruel sea balked his chances. His letter took two years and three months to reach Rome and Ignatius replied almost immediately, calling him back, but by then he had been seven months in his grave. Continuing his letter, he came at once to the chief problem which confronted him: ' For the love and service of our God I beg a favour of you, and would beg it on my knees at your feet were I before you. It is that you would send out here a person well known to you to be rector of the College of Goa, as the College stands in the direst need of such a benefit from your hands.' The Jesuits in India were unanimous on the subject of Antonio Gomes. He was quite impossible as a superior, though a good man and a good preacher, zealous for the promotion of Jesuit interests. Bishop Albuquerque, that most kindly old man, said that he preached ' like an angel ', but Nicholas Lancillotto, with Italian realism, would only allow him to be a ' satis bonus concionator '. Nicholas is a refreshing soul, always ill and always working like fury, while feeling himself to be absolutely useless. ' In the opinion of us all,' he told St. Ignatius, ' Antonio Gomes is the last man in the world to be a superior. He will write you letters full of fervour and rhetoric, but I have no doubt that you possess the spirit of the Lord which investigates all things.'[2] Just a year before the return of St. Francis, the Viceroy, Alfonso de

---

[1] Schurhammer, *Epistolae S. Francisci Xaverii*, ii, 286–8. The letter which drew such a loving reply from Francis has unfortunately perished, with two others from Ignatius that awaited him at Malacca. Only the fourth, a purely business one appointing Francis Provincial of the East, survived. It was high honour for India to be constituted a Jesuit Province before even Italy, France or Germany, before any countries except Spain and Portugal. The words of Ignatius which brought tears to the eyes of Francis were in the latter's peculiar spelling, ' *Todo vuestro, syn poderme olvydar en tyempo alguno, Ygnatyo* '.

[2] Wicki, *Documenta Indica*, ii, 172.

Noronha, addressed himself to Simon Rodriguez in the following terms: ' Father Antonio Gomes is a very good man and as such I regard him, but he has given scandal to the people of this country for the following good reason. . . . One day, without the consent of the Bishop or any secular person, and solely with the conni-vance of Jorge Cabral,[1] he dismissed all the pupils of the College of St. Paul and left the place as desolate as a land struck with the plague. Great indeed was the consternation of Goa at such a change. The Bishop and other gentlemen begged Antonio Gomes to change his mind but he refused, saying that it was his wish and determination to have at the College only the sons of Portuguese families. . . .' Antonio also set about great building operations, for it was his ambition to raise a new Coimbra on Indian soil. The Viceroy ordered him to stop this nonsense which was entirely contrary to the constitutions of St. Paul's and to the wishes of the King. He was therefore obliged to have back the Indian boys, the Indonesians, the Chinese, the Kaffirs, and the other varieties who made the College an historic institution as the first, though not eminently successful, effort to create an indige-nous clergy. The good Rector became so disgusted with the frustration of his grandiose plans that he resigned his post and went off on an expedition to Ceylon. In a letter to King John the Viceroy expressed his sentiments fairly plainly: ' Before the coming of Antonio Gomes to this country, the Apostles, meaning those of the Company of Jesus, were held in the highest respect. . . . Since his coming they have lost their reputation. . . .' It was not only at Goa that the high-flying Antonio made grave trouble for his brethren. In Cochin also he felt that the Jesuits, those vessels of election, ought to have a fine college and church, worthy of their eminence in the world. The site was chosen and the ambitious plans devised. Now, adjoining the site, the gift of the city, stood the Church of *Madre de Deus*, belonging to that best of all Portuguese institutions, the Casa da Misericordia. The

---

[1] The previous Governor, with whom Gomes was on such intimate terms that people laid on him the blame for all the mistakes and injuries of which Cabral was guilty. At least so says Noronha, but it has to be remembered that viceroys and governors were in the habit of blackening the reputation of their predecessors, so that their own virtue might shine the more brightly by contrast.

next thing we learn is that the church has passed into the hands of the Jesuits, having been granted to them for their exclusive use by a deed of Bishop Albuquerque.[1]

Bishop Albuquerque was old and easily swayed. The question arises, Who swayed him? Valignano plainly thought that it must have been Gomes, 'using his excessive influence with Governor Cabral who helped him in the affair, so that the Brothers of Mercy were ordered out of the church none too gently, to the anger and scandal of the City of Cochin '.[2] To replace Gomes after his resignation, the Jesuits of Goa, of whom there were thirty-six at the College, elected Father Paul of Camerino as their new rector. Shortly afterwards, Father Melchior Nunes Barreto was sent from Portugal to fill the post, but the brethren, content with their own chosen man, refused to acknowledge his authority. Nunes, whom by anticipation we have seen in Japan, did not mind, being a good and peaceable man, but another good, indeed saintly, man minded very much, Father Gaspar Berze, as his highly significant report to St. Ignatius from Goa, December 12, 1551, clearly shows:

Having been summoned by Father Master Francis to Japan, I arrived here from Ormuz to find Father Micer Paul substituted Rector of the College in place of Father Antonio Gomes who had resigned. Father Paul was elected by the unanimous vote of the Brethren at the College, in spite of the fact that another man, Father Melchior Nunes, had been dispatched from Portugal by Father Master Simon to fill the post of Provincial. The Brethren were not disposed to give Father Melchior their obedience until they had word from Father Master Francis in Japan. In explanation of their attitude, they told me that Father Francis did not wish anybody to be given a post of authority until his capacity had been tested for some time, because India is very different from other parts of Christianity and demands great perfection of spirit, especially in the matter of humility, as the Indians are so much given to pride. I could

[1] The Bishop's deed is given in Wicki, *Documenta Indica*, ii, 135–7.
[2] *Monumenta Xaveriana*, i, 144.

find no fault with the action taken by so many virtuous men
on those grounds, being myself the vilest creature, made to
obey rather than command. Wary indeed must I be after my
own brief experience as a superior, a post for which I was not
fitted and from which Father Francis had to withdraw me.[1]
However, in my feeble judgment the following steps seem
necessary, though your Reverence should not be influenced
by what I say until you have better information on the subject.
In the first place, Father Master Francis, whether or no he is
Provincial, ought not to pass beyond the limits of India. His
fame here is so great and he is so greatly loved by everybody
that we, as it were, subsist solely on the reputation of his
virtues. He is necessary here for the conservation of the work
which he built up, and God will provide another to take his
place in Japan.[2]

St. Ignatius was very much of the same opinion as Gaspar
Berze. The letter of St. Francis to him hinting that an order of
obedience summoning him back to Europe would be welcome
took an unconscionable time to reach Rome, as Ignatius explained
in his answer, dated June 28, 1553. In the gentlest way the one
Saint, who had not moved a foot out of Rome for twelve years,

[1] He had been rector at Goa for a short while in 1549.
[2] Wicki, Documenta Indica, ii, 242–3. Berze's apostolate in the terrible island
of Ormuz, subject to the Shah of Persia, is one of the outstanding events in
missionary history. It consisted largely of conflict with Jews, Moslems, renegade
Christians who had become Moslems for the sake of trade, and evil-living
Portuguese. But the very men he trounced in fiery sermons deeply respected
him and when he was called away from the island he had to steal off secretly for
fear of being forcibly retained. He had the simplicity of all great souls and told
St. Ignatius with charming candour about the methods he employed in his
ministry. ' Before I became a priest,' he wrote on January 12, 1553, ' I had
learned all sorts of tricks, and stratagems [manhas] and I have used them out here
to see whether I could not render God as much service by them as before I had
done Him injury. I do my best to laugh with those who laugh and I try at times
to sing with those who are in a mood for singing. When people are in a merry
mood I enter into the spirit of their fun, and when they become sad and weep,
I follow their example. . . . If anybody would be helped by seeing me dance, I
would dance for them. . . . There may be delusion in this, . . . but I comfort
myself because I have seen something of the same kind in Father Francis, whose
shoe-strings I am unworthy to untie. . . .' (l.c., ii, 595–6).

suggested to the other that perhaps it was time for him, too, to anchor himself, to stay in one place and go no more a-roving. Ignatius, a man of few words and sober, explained what was in his mind.

> We have heard [he wrote] of the door which God our Lord has opened for the preaching of His Gospel and for the conversion of the peoples of Japan and China by your ministry, and the news has given us great consolation. I think also that it was right and proper for you to send Master Gaspar [Berze] and others to China, and if you yourself have gone there (as you said you had a mind to do if not impeded by the affairs of India) I would likewise approve, being sure that it is the Eternal Wisdom which guides you. Nevertheless, from such understanding of the situation as is possible here, I think God our Lord would be better served by your remaining in India and sending and directing others to do the work which you would have done yourself. In this way you would extend to many countries the influence which you would personally have wielded in but one. What is more, looking always to the greater service of God and the help of souls in those parts and considering how much their good depends on Portugal, I have determined to order you in virtue of holy obedience to take, among so many other of your routes, the road to Portugal, at the first opportunity of a good passage, and so I order you in the name of Christ our Lord, even though it be that you return directly to India. . . .[1]

It was certainly from no mere desire of seeing again the man he could never forget, his long-lost Francis, that Ignatius issued his orders, and it is certain, too, that Francis would have obeyed them with equal alacrity if he had known that he would not be able to get to Rome at all. Ignatius felt, and said as much in his letter, that Francis was the one man in the world capable of really enlightening the King and the Pope on the position, the prospects and the requirements of the missions in the East. ' I have an idea

[1] MHSJ. *Monumenta Ignatiana*, vol. v (Madrid, 1907), p. 149.

also,' he continued, ' that you would kindle a new interest in the King's heart for the mission of Ethiopia which for so many years has been mooted in Portugal but never put into effect. And I think you could be of no little help to the missions of the Congo and Brasil. . . .'[1] Another argument that would undoubtedly have appealed to Francis ran as follows: ' You know how important it is for the welfare of the Indian mission that the men sent out from here should be of the right kind. Your coming to Portugal and Rome would be a great help in this respect, for you would not only inspire many more with eagerness for India, but would be able to see for yourself which of them had the right qualifications.' ＊ All this, however, is of the stuff of dreams and can scarcely be said to belong to the life of St. Francis, except as showing a little the way those two great Basques regarded each other. For, a year and more before the letter of Ignatius reached India, Francis had taken, of all his countless roads, the one along which no traveller returns.

In his letter to St. Ignatius Gaspar Berze, a shrewd, forthright Hollander, strongly hinted that Jesuit superiors in Portuguese India ought not to be Portuguese Jesuits. He had Antonio Gomes in mind, but he did not reckon with the rampant nationalism of that period of history. Portugal, however, was not more afflicted with the blight than other Christian countries, notably Tudor England, but she *did* suffer from it, and severely. Gomes and his champion in Europe, Simon Rodriguez, were notable victims, both men of real charm and goodness, but convinced beyond all argument that the axis of this earth passed straight through the lovely city of Coimbra. St. Francis, it may be remembered, had asked that Belgians and Germans might be sent out to him, and, perhaps to reinforce his request, the lovable Italian Nicholas Lancillotto informed St. Ignatius that ' Japan is a country lying

[1] It was one of the great dreams of Ignatius's life to bring Abyssinia into the Catholic fold. When appointing Francis Provincial of India and the East he expressly excluded Ethiopia from his jurisdiction, as he intended making it a separate Jesuit province if he could once get his men accepted and established there.

to the north, very near Germany, they say'.[1] When leaving India Francis had divided authority there between Antonio Gomes and Paul of Camerino, Paul having charge of all Jesuits not on the staff of Antonio at the Goan College. But the Italian was much too mild a man to stand up to the forceful Portuguese who had no patience with gentle methods of government and lost respect for those employing them. 'Micer Paul,' wrote Valignano commenting on the matter, ' was too humble and timid to want argument with Antonio, so he let him have his head and himself attended to his hospital, being content to serve and bring to health his poor sick folk. Father Gomes, therefore, not only ruled the College of Goa according to his own sweet will, but extended his arbitrary authority over all the other residences.'[2]

To Paul, Rector then at Goa, St. Francis wrote one of his few really disconsolate letters from Cochin on February 4, 1552:

> Micer Paul, Manuel de Morais and Francisco Goncalvez are proceeding [to Goa]. As soon as they arrive and you have read this letter, you will go to the house of the Lord Bishop and say to his Lordship that you deliver over to him the priest Manuel de Morais, I having told you that the Society puts the said Father entirely at his Lordship's disposal. And you will inform Manuel de Morais that I have instructed you to dismiss him [from the Society]. You will also dismiss Francisco Goncalvez. This I order you to do in virtue of obedience. You are not to permit either of them to enter the College and must further forbid all at the College to hold converse with them. . . .

Poor timid Micer Paul! The reason for those sudden Navarrese lightnings was obvious and adequate enough. The two men had

[1] Wicki, *Documenta Indica*, ii, 17: ' *Molto appresso Alemania, segun che dicono.*' No wonder that Ignatius wanted Francis to come home and enlighten their geographical darkness! Francis repeated his request for Flemings and Germans several times (Schurhammer, *Epistolae*, ii, 298, 349, 373-4).

[2] *Monumenta Xaveriana*, i, 114. Lancillotto's opinion of Paul of Camerino is worth giving: ' It is impossible to express how hard he works in the service of God. He has been so engaged all day long and a large part of the night for many years now, without ever a break. A man of few words but many works, his constancy is absolutely astounding' (Wicki, *Documenta Indica*, ii, 153).

been sent out to help the great and gallant Beira in the Moluccas in 1549, but after a year or so tired of the labours and perils, abandoned their posts, and returned without Beira's knowledge or consent to Malacca. It was the plainest piece of insubordination, made worse by a good deal of boasting on the part of Morais.

It is a heavy sorrow to me to have to dismiss them [St. Francis continued in his letter to Paul] and what makes it worse is that I fear they may not be the only ones who will have to go. God our Lord knows with how much reluctance I write this letter. I looked to find here some consolation after the many toils and hardships I have borne, and instead have encountered troubles which grievously distress me, such as disedifying complaints and discords among the people. As for obedience, I think from what I have been able to learn since my return that there is little or none of it, may God be praised for everything. . . .[1]

Several others, nearly all recruits made indiscriminately by Antonio Gomes, were required to go or went on their own account, for Francis, like Ignatius, heartily believed that quality and not quantity is what makes the religious life flourish. Ignatius, who came within an ace of dismissing even Simon Rodriguez for want of the essential virtue of good soldiers as well as of good religious, was somewhat disturbed by the rapid development of his order, and when he died had admitted only twenty of his sons out of a thousand to their solemn profession. In a letter to Ignatius written from Quilon in 1555, Father Lancillotto related what St. Francis had done to settle the trouble over the church in Cochin, three years earlier, an action exactly agreeing with Nicholas's own sentiments expressed pointedly in 1551:

With regard to the church called The Mother of God, I know that the people are in a ferment [about its transfer to the Jesuits] and that the Bishop is even more distressed. He has complained to me himself more than once. In view of the

[1] Schurhammer, *Epistolae S. Francisci Xaverii*, ii, 310–11.

amount of pressure brought to bear on the Bishop to make the transfer and considering also what people in general think, I would, were I in charge of this affair, not only refuse to accept the church for the Society but shake the very dust of it from my shoes. Master Francis will be of the same opinion, as he is most careful to avoid even a breath of scandal and for that reason is adored by everybody. . . .[1]

In his letter of 1555 the same Lancillotto wrote: ' About the church, *Madre de Deus* in Cochin, Master Francis, now with God, relinquished it absolutely and delivered a signed document to the heads of the Casa da Misericordia in which he stated that we had no rights whatever in that church and that our Fathers would say Mass and teach Christian doctrine there as mere visitors and with the consent of the Brothers of Mercy.' Padre Joam de Lucena, who came out with a Portuguese biography of St. Francis at Lisbon in A.D. 1600, six years after Tursellini's effort, livens up the picture. According to him Francis assembled the clergy and brethren of *Madre de Deus* in the cathedral church, and there, in the presence of the Vicar-episcopal, went on his knees and made a most edifying discourse which the good Lucena had carefully prepared for him. That done, he solemnly handed back the keys of *Madre de Deus* to the Brothers, and all went home rejoicing, all except Francis who had still the most distasteful of his reformatory tasks to perform.[2] He was in Goa by the middle of February and there had a sad encounter with Antonio Gomes who, according to Valignano, showed no regret for the undoubted mischief he had caused. It is extremely difficult to make out what happened between the two men, and to this day there are Jesuits who maintain a grudge against St. Francis for his harsh treatment of the gifted and debonair Antonio. He banished him from his

[1] Wicki, *Documenta Indica*, ii, 172—' *ob quam rem ab omnibus adoratur. . . .*' Nicholas begged Ignatius to excuse him for writing in Latin as he had forgotten his Italian.

[2] Valignano writing much earlier gives the same account of the restoration of the keys as Lucena and mentions also that Francis made a humble loving speech, though certainly not the one invented for him in Thucydidean fashion by his second biographer (*Monumenta Xaveriana*, i, 144–5).

beloved Goa where he used to keep congregations spell-bound with his eloquence to the obscure Portuguese fortress-town of Diu on a diminutive island of the same name, situated 180 miles north-west of Bombay. But that unhappily is not the end of the story. Early in April, 1552, Francis constituted Gaspar Berze rector of Goa and vice-provincial, at the same time leaving him sealed instructions which he was to open later on and put into effect ' *em virtude de obedientia* '. The actual text of the instructions has not survived but the tenor of them is plain from what Francis says in the covering letter:

> If Antonio Gomes leaves Diu at any time during the course of the present year on no matter what pretext, you will open the enclosed order, send him a copy of it while retaining the original, and at the same time write to him in conformity with the order. That is what you must do in the first place. Secondly, even though Antonio Gomes makes no attempt to leave Goa [during the year] you shall open the order as soon as the ships have sailed from India [in January and February, 1553], send him a copy certified by the Lord Bishop to whom you will have shown the original, and earnestly beg the Bishop to write and give him orders under obedience, as his subject, concerning his future work. In my opinion, it will be best to let him stay in Diu. . . .[1]

These are the unhappiest words St. Francis ever wrote. Why did he not dismiss Gomes himself instead of leaving the invidious task to Berze? Above all, why did he hold a suspended sentence over Antonio's luckless head until the ships had left India and there was no chance for him to appeal to Rome?

At first sight there appears to be a kind of vindictiveness in the procedure altogether unlike what we have learned to expect from St. Francis Xavier. Light is thrown on this dark episode by the parallel case in Europe of Simon Rodriguez. Simon had attached himself irrevocably to Ignatius when Ignatius was as yet only a poor vagrant much harassed by the minions of the Inquisition.

[1] Schurhammer, *Epistolae S. Francisci Xaverii*, ii, 382.

He possessed great ability and charm of character, and to him the Society of Jesus owed the finest and most heroic of her provinces, Portugal. Francis Xavier loved Simon to the last. Again and again he had angled for his company in India, and on this occasion had written to him from Cochin: 'How would it be, my Brother, Master Simon, if you were to join me in China?' Francis was aware of his little weakness for dukes and other people of high caste, but it made no difference to their enduring friendship. Alas, it seems to have made a disastrous difference to Simon himself. He became too much the darling of King and Court, too much a power in the land, to be content with the management of mere Jesuits. Discipline among them suffered so heavily that at last, in 1552, St. Ignatius, who loved him no less than did St. Francis, was most reluctantly obliged to relieve him of his post of Provincial. He made the change with infinite tact, appointing him to be Provincial of Aragon, which Spaniards at least would regard as definite promotion. Not so Simon. After about seven months in Spain, he returned, pleading ill health, and installed himself in the palace of an old friend, the Duke of Aveiro, at Lisbon. When the new Portuguese Provincial, Diogo Mirón, discovered where he was hiding, he ordered him under obedience to return to his post in Spain, but Simon refused to go and kept the Jesuits guessing as to his whereabouts by moving from one ducal establishment to another. Eventually, Mirón, a strong-minded person, discovered him and ordered him to leave Lisbon within eight days and Portugal within twenty, under pain of excommunication. Simon then repaired to Rome demanding trial and rehabilitation. He was given a very fair trial and a peppercorn penance, about which he made a great song for long afterwards. In his old age he became the lovable Simon again and was permitted to return to Portugal, where he died in peace, venerated by Jesuits as well as dukes as the last survivor of the little band of brothers who had gathered round Ignatius in Paris so long ago. Like Rodriguez, his protégé Gomes put his trust too much in princes or their equivalents. Valignano says that 'the Viceroy and the whole of the nobility' rallied to his defence in opposition to St. Francis. Such interference of secular authority, especially

when invited and welcomed from within as happened in the
cases of both Rodriguez and Gomes, would render the government of any religious order impossible, and that, in Valignano's
opinion, was why Francis, minded to stamp out the irregularity
for good, sacrificed the most brilliant of his men in India. The
sequel is tragic. Poor Antonio, too, decided to go to Rome to
rehabilitate himself, but his ship was wrecked and the sea relieved
him of all his troubles in this world. As for Xavier, he said that
God alone knew whether the combined sorrows and sufferings
of his entire missionary career matched the anguish of his brief
home-coming to India.

Luis Frois, aged twenty, was in Goa when St. Francis arrived
there and gave an enthusiastic account of the event to the Jesuits
of Coimbra:

He came when we were least expecting him, the elect of
God, our Father in Christ dear beyond all others, Master
Francis. . . . Soon he will be steering towards China. The
satisfaction, the transports [alvoroço] of spiritual joy expressed
by all of the Society and by the entire people at his coming, so
eagerly awaited, is something I know not how to convey. . . .
Since his arrival at this College of St. Paul of Goa great things
have been done for the glory of God which give a halo and
lustre to the Society. The flowers have appeared in our land,
the time of pruning is come, the voice of the turtle is heard, the
fig tree hath put forth her green leaves, the vines in flower
yield their sweet smell. . . .

Father Melchior Nunes Barreto, the first Jesuit to penetrate
into China, wrote to the same address in a similar vein:

At the beginning of February it pleased God suddenly to
bring us Father Master Francis from Japan. I am sure that his
coming was more the result of divine inspiration than of human
calculation, so great was the need of his presence to put the
Society's affairs in order in this part of India. Oh, what a joy
his coming brought to my soul! Imagine, my Brothers, what

it meant to see a man walking this earth whose conversation is wholly in Heaven. During the few days I had the privilege of speaking with him, what did I not observe—a heart on fire with the love of God, burning with the love of men, a devouring zeal to help the sick and the souls of the dead, an incessant diligence to restore sinners to the state of grace, and this all with so much affability, so cheerful and serene an address! He seemed to be always smiling and yet somehow never to smile. The charity and jubilee of his spirit overflowed on to his countenance and lit it up with joy which gave him the appearance of always smiling, and yet he was so recollected, so deeply withdrawn from created things, that one could say he never smiled. It made me marvel, even frightened me, to observe his passion for the honour of God, and the sharp way he felt the least imperfection in one of the brethren. On the other hand, he was all patience and loving kindness with even the greatest of sinners, stooping to the level of their capacity that they might profit by his admonitions and teaching. . . .

The holy, humble Nunes ended his long letter by picturing St. Francis as 'the good standard-bearer' who went forward discovering new lands where the young and fervent men of Coimbra might follow to plant the faith. 'Remember, Brothers,' he said, 'that the peoples of Japan and China are sighing for you. . . . Get ready, then, with desires enkindled in the fire of divine love, ever increase in all self-denial and humility, as in the wisdom from above and the hunger for God and for souls, so that God may grant you the privilege of seeing India in this life and His glory in the next.'[1]

The activity of St. Francis during his two months in Goa might be likened to one of those typhoons which he did not greatly

[1] Wicki, *Documenta Indica*, ii, 449–50, 494–5, 505–6. Luis Frois became one of the heroes as well as the historian of the Eastern missions. Melchior Nunes daringly made his way to Canton in 1555 to redeem the Christian captives held in the city's gaols. It is disputed whether he was the first European since the Middle Ages to penetrate into China and he has a Dominican rival for the honour. A plethora of ' Oh's ! ' in the extract given from him has been pruned, without, it is hoped, damage to the sense.

enjoy. In that brief time when he had visitors all day long and was very busy, besides, preaching and teaching, he managed to write or dictate some 21,280 words, which are extant, and perhaps as many more, which have perished. They are words that dispose completely of the legend of a Francis who disliked India, for they were inspired by an overwhelming desire to bring India out of her dark forest of gods and demons into the radiance of Christ. All places that the eye of heaven visit were in very truth to him ports and happy havens if they permitted him any sort of approach to the human family, no matter what the colour of its skin nor how drab the furniture of its mind. He had longed to stay on the bleak rock of Socotra, in sweltering Malacca, at the poison-island of Moro, on fuliginous Ternate. Now back in India and bound for China, he is as much concerned for the poor pearl-fishers of Cape Comorin and for the lowly tribes of Travancore as he is for the daimyos of Kyushu or the mandarins of Canton. When appointing Melchior Nunes Barreto superior of the Jesuit house in Bassein just north of Bombay, which had been well endowed by King John, he bade him to remember carefully the many needs of his brethren at Goa, at Cochin, at Quilon, and at Cape Comorin. Bassein, which appears to have been a favoured spot, must share its revenues with those others struggling all the time to make ends meet. 'Always keep before your eyes,' he wrote, 'the great indigence of the men at Cape Comorin, and remember how many babies die unbaptized because there is no one to baptize them owing to the fewness of the Fathers who can be supported in that area. . . .'

The Portuguese Captain at Tuticorin, Manuel Rodrigues Coutinho, was a very different person from the acquisitive de Paiva with whom St. Francis had had his contention in the past. The Jesuits and their flock loved Coutinho and their one dread was that he might be changed. In a typical letter written from Cochin to King John, pleading, as he had often done, for the reward of no less than thirty-one of the King's good servants in the East, including Fernam Mendez Pinto, Francis took up the matter of Coutinho: 'I have had splendid news from the Christians of Cape Comorin. . . . Of the good being done there a great part is to be attributed to Manuel Rodrigues Coutinho. . . . For the love of God, and if you wish there to be a Christianity in that land, order Manuel Rodrigues Coutinho to remain at his post for the rest of his life. . . .'[1]

The practical, businesslike element in the son of Navarre comes out strongly in his instructions to Nunes, as in many other places. His conversation was indeed in Heaven, but that did not prevent his much-travelled feet from being very firmly planted on this earth. It is pleasant to find a saint giving a lesson in accountancy and requiring, as he did of Nunes, ' to be minutely informed ' of the debits and credits in his books. The mission at Bassein apparently depended on some kind of local tax. Nunes was not to collect this himself, but to get friends among the lay Christians, ' really good men who go to confession and have the fear of the Lord in their hearts ', to do it. Nunes will give them the First Week of the Spiritual Exercises as a preparation for their tax-gathering activities. It would be an advantage if they were wealthy as well as good, for then they would be more tender towards little and poor people who had to pay their small quota.

Above all, I recommend you to beware of giving scandal [Francis continues], which you can best do by being truly humble. In the beginning you will employ yourself heartily in all lowly tasks, for that is what people like to see. . . . It would please me very much to find you closely associated with the Father Vicar and the Brothers of Mercy, for then you could attribute to them whatever good work you do for God our Lord, . . . and the people would not curse you [*não praguejasse tanto de vos!*] so heartily when things went wrong. . . . When you write to the King, beg his Highness to address a letter expressing his thanks to the Misericordia and to the Father Vicar, seeing that they so nobly help the progress of the faith. Be careful always to make great account of the Father Vicar and of the Brothers of Mercy, as well as of the Captain, if that

[1] Schurhammer, *Epistolae S. Francisci Xaverii*, ii, 318–19, 303. Tuticorin was a coveted appointment, so no one need waste his sympathies on Coutinho for being ordered to remain there.

is within the bounds of possibility. . . . It would be wonderful if you could rouse the Captain to action. . . .[1]

Perhaps some people may frown on those wiles of Francis, but surely they can no more be branded as insincere than the ordinary workaday keeping up of appearances without which social life would be impossible.

In April, a fortnight before he took ship for China, Francis addressed himself to Nunes again in a letter from which one could never gather that such a place as China existed. Bassein was China enough for Francis just then. He sends men to Melchior ' to edify and doctrinate and preach and teach ', not only in Bassein, but in the big pagan centre of Thana on the island of Salsette where Bombay became mighty. He would be very pleased to hear about Melchior's preaching. ' Exercise yourself in it as much as you possibly can,' he says, ' for I have good hopes in God our Lord that, if you remain humble, you will make a great preacher.' He comes back to the question of scandal which obsessed him. Any Jesuits who might be responsible for it are to be dismissed from the order immediately by Nunes himself. Monies coming in may be used when absolutely necessary to build small churches, but for the most part should be spent on the fashioning of ' spiritual temples ' by the Christian education of Indian boys. If Melchior could send him a few bales of the white cotton material for the weaving of which Bassein and Thana were famous, he would be doing a corporal work of mercy to the scantily clad folk in Goa.

Work hard [Francis concludes] at your preaching and hearing of confessions. Go the rounds of the hospital, the prisons, and the Casa da Misericordia. Remember what I told you about being close friends with the Father Vicar, and with all the secular priests, the captain, the royal officials, and the people in general. So you will win their love and sympathy and be able to do them good. Write to me in great detail at Malacca in September about the progress you make, and

[1] Schurhammer, *Epistolae*, ii, 319–20. Francis was still obviously suspicious of captains, never having got over his experiences with de Paiva.

write often also to this College of Goa. May God our Lord bring the two of us together in the glory of Paradise. Amen.

But Nunes was not the only one to be so carefully and lovingly briefed. Gaspar Berze, the new rector of Goa and heir-apparent to the authority of Francis in India, received no less than five separate ' Instructions ', one of them running to the dimensions of a twelve-page pamphlet. If, as the legend pretends, Francis disliked India and was anxious to be away from it, he certainly took the most paradoxical pains to leave his spirit behind. Today, when no part of the world is more than thirty hours away from any other part, we find it difficult to imagine what a voyage from India to China involved in those old times, something, it may be surmised, such as the long and elaborate preparations for a modern polar expedition, or the ones described so well in that charming and inspiring book, *Those Greenland Days*. China had her ' Iron Curtain ' as impenetrable then as now, except at the price of death or a dungeon. She wanted no communication with the outer world, not even with Japan, though the Japanese pirates, the notorious *Wako*, including St Francis's Anjiro, murderously contested her claustral ambitions. It was a tremendous undertaking to penetrate into the Forbidden Empire and St. Francis knew it, yet there he was, within a fortnight of his last and greatest adventure, completely absorbed, it seemed, in the most humdrum tasks of administration. Not a detail escaped him, and not a Jesuit either, did he need admonishment or encouragement at his post maybe a thousand miles away. Gaspar Berze, whom he constituted superior of all Jesuits ' from the Cape of Good Hope to Goa, everywhere else in India, in Malacca, the Moluccas and Japan ', unless, as he expressly stated, ' our Father Ignatius sends some other particular person ' to take charge, might not last very long owing to the shattered state of his health after his labours in Ormuz, so Francis draws up a sealed codicil to the diploma of appointment legislating that, in case of Gaspar's death, Paul of Camerino is to govern temporarily until Manuel de Morais[1] has

---

[1] No relation of the Manuel de Morais whom Francis had dismissed from among the Jesuits.

been recalled from his hard labours in Colombo to take over the reins, and should Manuel also go to God then Melchior Nunes is to be summoned from Bassein to succeed him—all on the understanding that St. Ignatius had not in the meantime sent out any one from Europe to assume authority.[1] If Francis could help it, there would not recur on the missions such divisions of rule or doubts as to ruler as had troubled the brethren when Antonio Gomes was consul. Anybody who failed in strict submission to Berze was to be dismissed immediately from the Society of Jesus, ' no matter how great his abilities and good qualities, because he will be lacking in the better qualities which are humility and obedience '. Berze himself was put under obedience not to stir from the Island of Goa for the space of three years, but God thought otherwise and took Gaspar to Himself within two years.

The Instructions are full of details that come surprisingly from a man with China on his mind. Berze is taught how to deal with importunate beggars and put under an obedience to refuse them help until he has paid every penny of the College's debts, as well as provided for the needs of his own household and of the hospital close by. ' Be wary,' says Francis, ' of people who come to manifest to you their corporal rather than their spiritual necessities.' Again and again Berze is reminded to pay his debts. He is recommended to hire a laundry-man to do the College washing because that would probably be cheaper than sending it to public laundries, and he had better put a lay brother in charge of the garden, as hired gardeners are expensive and wasteful. ' Purchase two slaves to help him,' writes this saint of God who plainly did not consider slavery to be contrary to Christian principles. There he was wrong, but he erred with the rest of his world and would have cherished the slaves as his brothers, as he had always done. The second of the Instructions is about government:

> Treat the Fathers and Brothers under you with much love, charity and modesty, not gruffly and rigorously, unless indeed they try to take advantage of your kindness. In that case it would be good for them to show a certain severity, particularly

[1] Schurhammer, *Epistolae S. Francisci Xaverii*, ii, 336–42.

if you feel them to be opinionated and proud. . . . Do not be
too ready to receive many into the Society, for good men,
even if they be few, are what the Society needs. Always
exercise those whom you do accept in true abnegation and
interior mortification of their passions rather than in external
ascetic practices, and if, to help the interior mortification, you
test them also exteriorly let it be in ways that edify, such as
serving in the hospital and begging for the poor, not by
extravagances that only cause people to laugh and mock. . . .
If you are criticized either within or without the Society, pay
little heed provided that you are doing your duty and the
critics are not doing theirs. . . .

The third Instruction gives Berze some maxims for his
consideration, written partly in the first person and dealing
mainly with the subject of humility:

At some convenient time each day I shall occupy myself
for an hour or more with the following points. First, I am to
cultivate great humility in my preaching, attributing all the
good of it to God very perfectly. Secondly, I shall keep before
my eyes the good people who listen to me, remembering that
it is God who gives them the devotion to hear me out, and to
me the devotion to preach. Thirdly, I must strive to acquire
a great love for my people, remembering the obligation I
bear towards them. . . . Fourthly, I shall consider how the
grace of being able to preach comes to me through the prayers
and merits of my brethren in the Society who with humble,
charitable love beg God's blessing on the efforts of such as
myself, for the greater glory of God and the salvation of souls.
Fifthly, I must ever bear in mind my strict duty to cultivate a
humble heart, seeing that anything good in my sermons is not
mine at all but God's liberal gift to me. With love and fear
must I use His grace, as one bound to give a strict account of
it to God our Lord, and so I shall be careful to attribute nothing
to myself but my many faults and sins, my pride, my negligence, my ingratitude against God and my people and my

brethren of the Society. . . . I shall beg God earnestly to make me realize the obstacles which I put in the way of those who might make better use of me but have to refrain because I am what I am. . . . Before God who sees into the hearts of men I shall humble myself mightily, and take the very greatest care never to be a cause of scandal to the people in my preaching or my conversation or my work. . . .

Francis concludes the Instruction on a stern note:

For the love of God our Lord and by the heavy debt you owe to our Father Ignatius and to the whole Society of Jesus, I beg you again and again to exercise yourself in humility continually and as much as you possibly can, because if you do not I fear you may lose your soul. . . . Never forget that there are many preachers in Hell who were more eloquent and successful than you, men who converted sinners and were the instrumental cause of many people going to Heaven, while they, unhappy ones, went to perdition because they took to themselves what belonged to God, holding out their hands to the world and being delighted with its praises. . . .

The fourth Instruction is the longest and touches on a great variety of matters, especially the entrances and exits of members of the Society of Jesus. Berze is to beware of receiving persons too young, or others whose admission is forbidden by Father Ignatius, such as homicides, apostates, heretics, men branded by judicial sentence as infamous, excommunicates, any one previously given the habit of another religious order, slaves, married men, and men weak in the head. To this fairly inclusive list of impediments which barred admission to all orders strictly so called, St. Francis added one that did not become Jesuit law until forty years after his death, namely Jewish lineage. This is interesting because some of the men whom he most admired were 'New Christians', descendants of Jewish families which had accepted baptism in Spain and Portugal as an alternative to expulsion. Among such men were the great and saintly Diego Laynez, second General of

the Jesuits, Henry Henriques, one of the finest of the Indian
missionaries whom Francis made superior of all the brethren in
the Cape Comorin region, and Francis's own novice, Alfonso de
Castro, the heroic lieutenant of Beira in the Moluccas. Francis
personally felt no objection whatever to the presence of New
Christians in the Society of Jesus, no more than did St. Ignatius.
But not all minds were as large as theirs, and certain Portuguese
Jesuits, very much including Antonio Gomes, strove to have that
dear, holy, suffering soul, Henriques, ' tan buena persona ' in the
words of Francis, debarred from taking his final vows. When
his case was brought before St. Ignatius by the opposition, he
answered curtly: ' To be of New Christian lineage is not an
impediment to admission into the Society. . . . The Society
knows no distinction of Jew and Greek '.[1] But the opposition in
Portugal was very strong and included the King, on whom the
missions so greatly depended. That was why Francis gave way to
the pressure brought to bear on him, but neither he nor Ignatius
gave way in the case of Henriques who was admitted to his final
vows and made a truer Jesuit than any of the critics boasting
descent from Vandals, Visigoths and other murderous types of
gentiles.[2]

Another matter on which St. Francis dilates as though he had
not a care besides in the world is the Jubilee of 1550 which had
been extended for two years in India owing to the fewness of
confessors out there. Francis is as anxious that every poor pearl-
fisher and Travancore peasant should obtain its graces as he had
been to obtain them himself, and he is urgent with Berze to see
that all from the highest to the lowest are given their opportunity.
Berze is reminded again and again that charity begins at home,

[1] MHSJ. Monumenta Ignatiana, vi, 569.
[2] Henriques laboured under a genuine canonical impediment for he had worn
the Franciscan habit in Portugal for six or seven months. When the Franciscan
authorities discovered that he was of Jewish extraction they dismissed him, as
it was against their constitutions to admit descendants of Jews or Moors. St.
Ignatius obtained from the Pope a dispensation from the impediment of having
worn the habit of another order for this man ' whose virtue and kindness ',
wrote the saintly Lancillotto, ' were beyond all description ' (Wicki, Documenta
Indica, ii, 134).

that his first care must be for the Fathers and Brothers, the youth of Africa and Asia, and the Indian orphans, at the College of St. Paul, but he is told with equal earnestness that charity does not stop at home, that it must travel also to Cape Comorin, Quilon, Cochin, Bassein, Ormuz, San Thomé, Malacca, the Moluccas and Japan. ' If any Father arrives from Portugal, not much of a preacher, but of good quality and reasonably educated and eager for hard work, send him by the April monsoon to Malacca that he may join Father Cosmas de Torres in Japan. And seek alms that he may be able to bring something worth eating to the men out there.' Francis has not forgotten the everlasting rice and smelly soups of the Japanese inns! ' With all my heart,' he continues, ' I beg you to have a special care of the men in Japan both by your prayers to God for them and by seeing that their needs are supplied.' If Berze has not the means himself he is to apply to the King for assistance, ' as Japan is so poor a country that it cannot give us the necessities of life '. In this fourth Instruction Francis harps, as in the others, on a favourite string, the duty of Jesuits to do their utmost to remain on amicable terms with the secular clergy and with the members of other religious orders. ' Those of the College,' he said, ' are always to show themselves the very good friends of the Franciscan and Dominican Fathers and Brothers. Beware of any dissension, and above all, let no word ever escape in the pulpit which might shock or disedify the people. Let others say whatever their charity permits, it is your duty to be silent under criticism and to avoid scandalizing the people.' In India as in Europe the fine and fiercely anti-Jesuit Dominican theologian Melchior Cano had his disciples, and it is to them that Francis is referring with most careful tact. ' They and we,' he said, ' are bent on one common course, which is the glory of God and the salvation of souls. . . . Visit them from time to time, and let charity between you not only be maintained but ever grow.'

The fifth Instruction deals entirely with that matter so dear to the heart of Francis, the avoidance of scandal. Berze and his men are not to hold converse with women except in public, be they the highest ladies in the land or poor untouchables. If it is necessary to visit them in their homes to bring them the sacraments when they are sick, the priest must be accompanied by the husband, or if the invalid is unmarried, by some neighbour of hers known to be a good man. Berze is not to waste too much of his time in the spiritual direction of women, but rather to tackle their husbands and urge them to shepherd their wives towards God.

Should discord arise between wife and husband [Francis continues] and the marriage be threatened, always strive your best to bring about a reconciliation. Get them to make a general confession, and give them some meditations from the First Week of the Spiritual Exercises before you absolve them. . . . Put little trust in women's devotion when they try to persuade you that they would serve God better if separated from their husbands. That kind of devotion does not last long and is seldom indulged in without giving scandal. Be careful not to lay the blame for dissensions on the husband in public, even though he be responsible, but rather coax him into self-accusation and then you can chide him with much love and charity and meekness. With those men of India you can achieve a great deal by gentle persuasion but by force nothing whatever. I repeat, never blame the husband in public even though he be the guilty one, because women are such indomitable creatures that they seek out occasions for putting their partners in the wrong, and then brag of their own innocence. Innocent or not, don't listen to their excuses, but tell them of their duty to put up with their husbands, to whom they have often been insolent and therefore deserve whatever comes to them. Plead with them to be patient in their present trouble and encourage them to be humble and obedient to their husbands. Hear both parties before you pronounce against either, and remember that in these cases both parties are always to blame, though in different measure. . . . If you cannot prevail upon them to be reconciled, remit them to the Bishop or the Vicar-general, but on no account fall out with them. . . .[1]

[1] Schurhammer, *Epistolae S. Francisci Xaverii*, ii, 393–434.

The argus-eyed Francis missed little that was going on even in such places as Ormuz and San Thomé, with more than the whole breadth of India between them. To Gonçalo Rodrigues sweltering at Ormuz he wrote from Goa on March 22:

God our Lord knows how much better pleased I would be to have you here with me than to be merely sending you a letter, which is so often a bad second best to converse face to face. . . . My order to you under obedience is that you show the utmost deference to the Father Vicar, and only with his will and permission preach, hear confessions, and say Mass. You are under an obedience also, remember, never on any account to break with the said Father. . . . To the other secular priests you must be most respectful, looking down on none and being friends with all. Show them an example of obedience to the Father Vicar that they and the people, too, may learn from you to obey him in all things, and reckon that the good you are to do will come rather from your obedience and humility than from your preaching. . . . I write to you thus out of the love I bear you and the good I wish you. . . . Obedience and humility are so necessary for the service of God that I hereby strictly enjoin you to go to the Vicar, cast yourself on your knees before him, and most humbly beg his forgiveness for all past faults and want of obedience. . . . You may find the doing of this hard, but it is necessary in order to confound the devil, the lover of discord and disobedience. Be careful in your sermons never to shock anybody. I would get more joy out of your doing the amount of good represented by this line ———— without scandal of any kind, than from the amount represented by this line

if accompanied by some scandal. . . . Write to me in great detail about what God is doing through you in that city, and about the friendship between you and the Vicar, the other priests, and the whole people. Your letter will be sent on to me in China where I am now going, from this College, and I shall be delighted to get it. Japanese affairs are going prosperously under the guidance of Father Cosmas de Torres and Brother Juan Fernandez who will be joined this year by others of the Society. The hardships they endure are greater than I have power to describe to you, incomparably greater than those you endure yourself at Ormuz, . . . though they are bad enough. I tell you this that you may have them always in your Masses and prayers. When you write to the College write also, but briefly and with great respect and deference, to the Lord Bishop, giving him an account of your activities, he being our prelate who has shown us so much love and given us every favour in his power. This letter is addressed to you as to a man of virtue and perfection who will know how to read it aright, not as to a weakling in whom I have little confidence. You owe thanks to God who made you what you are, better pleased to be admonished as a strong, good man than to be cajoled as a weak one. . . . As by the mercy of God we shall soon see each other in the glory of Paradise, I say no more, except to ask you to remember with how much love I wrote you this letter. . . . Your brother, Francis.[1]

At San Thomé, the present Mylapore, adjoining Madras, there laboured Alfonso Cyprian, aged sixty-three, who had been received into the Society of Jesus by St. Ignatius in Rome. He was a headlong sort of Spaniard, given to leaping before he looked. In Portugal where he was stationed for a while Simon Rodriguez said that he had become so much of a satrap he would force his advice on the Emperor. But he possessed the virtues of his faults and worked with impetuous zeal and hardihood on the Indian missions until his death in 1559. Father Henriques marvelled that at his age he should be able to labour so strenuously and to put up with so much hardship. ' They say

---

[1] Schurhammer, *Epistolae*, ii, 323–6. Francis added a little postscript: 'You will show this letter to the Father Vicar.' The Vicar was a secular priest named Antonio de Moura. The Saint's Portuguese is sometimes excessively clumsy, as this, for example: ' *Por isso haveis de dar graças a Deos, que vos fez tal, e deo virtude e prefeição* [sic] *para folgardez mais de ser admoestado com reprehensoens, que serdes engando comdescendendo com fraqueza, com fraquezas humanas, como fraco.*'

that he is never idle and at San Thomé they call him a saint.'
Francis Xavier, however, was not wholly of that opinion and
addressed the satrap in the following lively terms from Goa just
before he set off for China:

> Right badly have you carried out the instructions I gave
> you as to your conduct in San Thomé, and it is clear to see how
> little remains to you of the spirit of our blessed Father Ignatius.
> It was very wrong of you to go to the Vicar with your lists
> of claims and complaints. You must always act according to
> your headstrong nature, and the result is that you undo with
> one hand whatever good you may have achieved with the
> other. Be it known to you that I do not like your way of
> acting nor its results. If the Vicar behaved as he should not have
> done, he was hardly likely to be converted by your repre-
> hensions, especially when delivered in your fashion, with
> little prudence. You are so accustomed to do as you like that
> wherever you happen to be you give scandal by your way of
> acting and betray your brusque character. Please God, you will
> some day do penance for these imprudences. For the love of
> our Lord I beg you to control yourself and to let the future
> amend the past. You would not be so irascible if you paid
> more attention to God, your conscience, and the love of your
> neighbour. Take it from me that at the hour of death you will
> see the truth of what I say. I do beseech you in the name of
> our blessed Father Ignatius that, in the few days remaining to
> you, you turn over a new leaf and become a patient, gentle,
> humble man. . . . By your love and obedience to Father
> Ignatius, I entreat you to go to the Vicar and beg his pardon on
> your knees for the past. Kiss his hand, though it would console
> me more if you kissed his feet, and promise him never to
> withstand him in anything again. Believe me, you will be
> glad to have done this when you come to die. I have the fullest
> confidence in God our Lord that when He sees your humility
> and it becomes known to the people all the merit lost to you in
> His service and in your work for souls will be restored and
> credited to you once more. Your error, and that of others also,

was to imagine that without deep humility you could get people to do what you required of them, merely because you were a member of the Society. You neglected to build on the foundation of those virtues through which God gave and gives our Father Ignatius so much authority with all men. I beg you above all things to avoid open discord with the Vicar, the clergy, the captains and others holding office in your parts, even when you see them misbehaving. If there is anything you can remedy in a genial, inoffensive way, remedy it, but do not risk everything by coming to a quarrel when you could save everything with humility and meekness.

So far, the letter was dictated by Francis, but at this point he added a codicil in his own hand :

O Cyprian, if you only guessed the love with which I write these things to you, you would have me in your mind day and night, and you might perhaps even weep remembering my great love for you. If it were possible in this life to see into the hearts of men, believe me, my brother Cyprian, you would be clearly seen in mine. Entirely yours, without my being able ever to forget you. Francisco.[1]

The picture that emerges from the foregoing instructions and letters is surely one of a born ruler of men, strong-minded yet very tender and considerate, loyal and lowly himself to the utter-

[1] Schurhammer, *Epistolae S. Francisci Xaverii*, ii, 388–91. Cyprian's age of sixty-three was regarded in those times as both advanced and dangerous. It was the grand climacteric, nine sevens, when anything might happen to a man. St. Robert Bellarmine made his will in preparation for it, and it was the reason why St. Francis Xavier attributed fewness of days to the satrap, though he outlived Francis by nearly seven years. The codicil did its work and he became a very gentle, humble, lovable satrap before he died. The Portuguese text is as follows: ' *O Cypryano, sy supyéssedes el amor con que os escrebo estas cossas, de dia y de noche os lembrarieys de mi, e por ventura lloraryais en lembrarvos do amor grande que hos tengo; y sy los coraçones de los hombres se pudiessen ver en esta vyda, cred, Hermano myo Cypryano, que os beryais* [sic] *claramente en mi anima. Todo vuestro, syn nunca poderme olbydar de vos.*' It may be remembered that the last words were first used by St. Ignatius and made a profound impression on St. Francis.

most and so a creator of loyalties in other hearts, who never asked for surrenders or sacrifices which he did not make on his own account in divinely extravagant measure. Even his failings leaned to virtue's side, and if a little of Navarre and its feudal intransigence came to the surface in his treatment of Antonio Gomes, he at least bore with him for a long time and gave him a very generous measure of rope with which to hang himself. Familiar lines apply to him so well that their quotation may be forgiven:

> In his duty prompt at every call,
> He watched and wept, he prayed and felt, for all.
> And, as a bird each fond endearment tries
> To tempt its new-fledged offspring to the skies,
> He tried each art, reproved each dull delay,
> Allured to brighter worlds, and led the way.

Now we may take a glimpse at Francis pursuing his favourite rôle of ambassador of peace in another direction. He was a true Spaniard, as appears so often in his ardent words and actions, but he had completely surmounted the spirit of expansive nationalism and decidedly wished his own countrymen to be content with their half of the newly discovered lands, leaving Portugal in peaceful occupation of the other half. But the Spaniards were by no means contented. Like the Portuguese, they continued to be dazzled by the vision of Zipangu, the island where the temples and palaces were paved and roofed with gold, which Marco Polo, in an evil hour for the peace of nations, had invented and dangled before their eyes. The learned who concern themselves with these matters are now disposed to think that Columbus had more than the Spice Islands in mind when he went west and blundered on Haiti, believing it to be Japan. But it was a disappointing Japan and other expeditions financed by Spain set off afterwards from Mexico or Europe to discover the real gold-plated island. But curiously by the time of St. Francis the vision had turned from gold to silver and Japan became known generally among the Spanish sea-dogs as ' las Islas Platarias ', the Silver Islands. In actual fact copper is the chief mineral product of

Japan. A manuscript in the British Museum written by a Portuguese the year Queen Elizabeth died speaks of ' *as Platarias por que os Castelhanos sempre sospirao* '. It really is extraordinary that those Castilians with Mexico and Peru in their possession should still be sighing after the silver of Japan, but such is the power of a myth and such is human nature. St. Francis had encountered his roving countrymen at Amboina where they had no right to be, and it took him all his time to keep the peace between them, captives though they were, and the victorious Portuguese. For the sake of the missions and for the Spaniards' own sake he was most anxious to keep them away from Japan.

In a letter to Simon Rodriguez written from Goa on April 8, Francis said:

The Castilians call Japan the Silver Islands. The Portuguese in Japan told me that the Spaniards who set out from New Spain to find the Moluccas passed very close to these islands and that, should they seek to discover them, they would be lost at sea. This they learned from the Japanese who gave as their reason that the only route open to the Spaniards is full of shoals, on which they would perish. I send you this information, my brother Simon, with a view to your imparting it to the King our master and to the Queen that, for the discharge of their consciences, they may counsel the Emperor or the King of Castile not to dispatch fleets from New Spain in search of the Silver Islands, as all such expeditions are bound to come to grief. Even if they survived the sea and reached Japan, they would be no better off, for the Japanese are such a bellicose and covetous people that they would seize all ships, no matter how numerous, coming from New Spain. In any case, food is so short in Japan that the Castilians would die of starvation, and besides that, unless they had some friendly port for refuge their ships would not have the slightest chance of escaping destruction in the terrible storms off the coast. Moreover, as I said above, the Japanese are so rapacious that for the sake of their weapons and clothes they would kill every Spaniard they encountered. I wrote to tell our lord the King so, but perhaps

he will have forgotten it in the press of business, and I am therefore writing to you to remind their Highnesses, as my conscience
obliges me. It fills me with pity to hear that many fleets leave
New Spain in search of the Silver Islands and are lost on the
way. . . .

With regard to all this it has been averred that Francis deliberately created bogies in an endeavour to preserve the commercial monopoly of Portugal in the Far East, and that, of course,
he was put up to it by his friends the Portuguese merchants. It
would have been entirely unlike him to lend himself to such a
manœuvre, but in any case the insinuation can be easily disposed
of. Francis invented nothing. The route to Japan from Mexico,
or New Spain as it was then called, was decidedly dangerous, as
Magellan and many another great captain found to their cost,
and Japan itself was a decidedly dangerous place unless approached
humbly and tactfully, which was never the Spanish habit. Even
the Portuguese who had learned to be extremely cautious and
subservient might have been massacred to a man when they first
came to Bungo but for the intercession of the Daimyo's son, the
friend of St. Francis. Francis did not fabricate the typhoons and
the low standard of living; he had suffered them, and he knew
better than most that the legend of temples roofed with silver or
gold was so much moonshine, for he had seen very many of
them.[1] He was moved by two considerations in writing as he did:
a perfectly sincere concern for the lives of his countrymen and a
deep anxiety for the future of his missions. The Portuguese
conquistadores differed greatly from the Spaniards in their
colonial aims. They did not seek to conquer foreign countries,
but merely to acquire footholds in them, towns or islands, for
purposes of trade, and even then, as in the Moluccas, often let
the local ruler, raja or sultan, retain his authority. The Spaniards,
on the other hand, were addicted to seizing whole states, Peru
and Mexico for instance, killing or banishing their rulers and

[1] In Kyoto there is to this day a famous temple called the Silver Pavilion,
because the Shogun who built it in 1479 intended to roof it in that metal, but
neither he nor any of his successors was able to achieve the ambition.

incorporating the entire territory in the Spanish Crown. To have tried that in Japan would certainly have meant utter destruction for the aggressors. Even Kublai Khan, with forces far more powerful than Spain could even muster, had been ignominiously defeated, and it required atom bombs to bring Japan to her knees for the first time in history. Within half a century of the death of St. Francis his forebodings were realized. Spain conquered Portugal, forced her way into Japan from the Philippines, and brought irretrievable ruin to the marvellously flourishing Christian missions.

While he was thus doing all that lay in his power to ensure the safety and prosperity of the missions in India and Japan, Francis was busily preparing to bring the knowledge of Christ his eternal Lord to the teeming millions of China, as he explained to his temporal lord, the Portuguese King:

I wrote recently to tell your Highness of my determination to go to China where I have been assured that the chances are good for the extension of our holy faith. In five days' time I am sailing from Goa to Malacca which is the route to China. In the company of Diogo Pereira I shall make my way to the court of the Chinese King. We are taking with us a very fine present for him, bales of precious stuffs which Diogo Pereira purchased out of his own money, and I am bringing besides from your Highness such a present as was never before sent by king or potentate to that King, namely, the true law of Jesus Christ our Redeemer and Lord.[1] This gift of your Highness is so great that if its recipient only knew its value he would esteem it more than all the immense power which he wields. My trust in God our Lord is that He will have pity on so vast an empire and mercifully open a way for His creatures made in His image to adore their Creator, and to believe in Jesus Christ, His Son and their Saviour. Besides myself there will be another Father and a lay brother going to China with Diogo Pereira, he as ambassador to petition for the release of the Portuguese

[1] Not entirely accurate, as missionaries had been sent to China by the Avignon Popes.

prisoners and to negotiate a treaty of peace and friendship between your Highness and the King of China; we Fathers of the Society of Jesus to start war and discord between the demons and those who adore them, with a great summons from God to the King and all his subjects that they adore only Him who created them and made the heavens and the earth, and Jesus Christ, the Saviour of the world, who redeemed them. It must appear extreme audacity to go thus into a strange land and to a king wielding such enormous power in order to admonish men and proclaim the truth, two things highly dangerous in our time even among Christians and how much more so among pagans! Still, there is one thing which puts us in good heart, that God knows the desires implanted by His mercy in our hearts. With them He has given us great confidence and trust in Himself who is incomparably more powerful than the King of China. Since all created things depend on God and operate only so far as He permits them and no more, there is nothing to fear except offending Him. . . . Indeed, the greater effrontery is ours as manifest sinners than as men daring to brave a strange land and a mighty king. . . . But we go confiding in the infinite mercy of God and knowing ourselves right well to be unworthy instruments. . . .

It is easy for us in our armchairs to say that Francis was deluded, and goodness knows his briefing and qualifications for such a tremendous enterprise could not be called adequate. For one thing, he knew hardly a word of any variety of Chinese and his knowledge of Chinese religion and civilization consisted of a few generalities picked up casually in Japan. Here he is, giving St. Ignatius a lesson on the Celestial Empire:

China is a huge country, very peaceful and governed by great laws. There is only one king and all render him the strictest obedience. It is an extremely wealthy country, only a short distance from Japan, and abounds in all manner of produce. The Chinese are a very clever people, desirous of knowledge, and much given to study, especially of the human laws by which the empire is governed. They are a white, beardless race, with very small eyes, liberal of disposition and remarkably pacific. War is unknown among them. . . . I am in great hope that by the labours of the Society of the name of Jesus both Chinese and Japanese will abandon their idolatries and adore God and Jesus Christ, the Saviour of all peoples. It is to be carefully noted that the Chinese and Japanese do not understand each other's speech because their languages are wholly different, but Japanese who know the Chinese letters can read Chinese writing, though unable to follow the spoken word. . . . Each Chinese character represents a specific thing, and when the Japanese write it they paint above it what it signifies. Thus, if the character means a ' man ', they paint above the figure of a man, and so with all the other letters which in this way become syllables. . . . We made a book in the Japanese language dealing with the creation of the world and all the mysteries of the life of Christ, and afterwards wrote the same book in Chinese characters to help me along in China until I learned to speak the language. . . .[1]

Francis signed that letter to his Father Ignatius with the words: ' *Menor hijo y en destierro major. Francisco* '—Your least and most exiled son.

St. Ignatius cannot have obtained much light on China from his explanations which, at least in the matter of the two languages, are not correct. The book to which Francis referred cannot, of course, have been written by himself as he was certainly not capable of painting Chinese ideographs. Perhaps one of his learned converts in Yamaguchi wrote it for him before he left

[1] Schurhammer, *Epistolae S. Francisci Xaverii*, ii, 361–2, 291–3. Both the letter to the King and that to St. Ignatius contain long and moving appeals for men, men of real quality, strong, humble, learned, to be sent to Japan. He begged the King to concert measures with Ignatius to this end. Japan was in his mind all the time and he was going to China in the last resort for the sake of Japan. The same was true of India and of every mission which he had started. They were dearer than life to him, those infant churches of the East, and he carried the thought of them all and his solicitude for them all to his lonely grave off the Chinese coast.

Japan, or maybe the ambassador of the Daimyo of Bungo did so on the voyage to India helped by those in the company who knew the Latin letters for transliteration purposes as well as the syllabary of Japan. But it matters little anyhow, for it was just another of the dear Saint's delusions that one could speak Chinese, as the man thought he could play the flute, not by sight nor by ear, but by main force. God be praised for great men's delusions, for where would the world be without them? Columbus suffered from them and Magellan and Galileo and Newton. And so, too, geographically speaking, did St. Paul, whose China was Spain. A man's reach should exceed his grasp, or what's a Heaven for? Delusions is not the right word at all, but dreams, and the dreams of Francis, as the subsequent history of Japan and China proved, had a way of becoming startlingly true.

CHAPTER XVII

THE LAST ADVENTURE

FRANCIS must have had a marvellous constitution. When he left Goa in the middle of April, 1552, it was close on ten years since his first arrival there, and they had been ten years of incessant toil in tropical heat or arctic cold, always ill-clad, and eating and sleeping barely enough to keep body and soul together. The only sign of what he had been through in Japan was a certain emaciation and the greyness of his hair, once as black as a raven's wing. In his own words, he returned to India ' in splendid physical condition but worn out spiritually '. Still, strong though he felt he appears to have had a premonition of early death. Just before sailing, he went to say good-bye to his old friend Cosmas Anes. ' And when shall we see your Reverence again?' asked Cosmas. ' In the Valley of Josaphat,' replied Francis.[1] Luis Frois, the historian, was then a member of the Goan community and recorded that all of them prayed fervently to God for the privilege of accompanying Father Francis, ' because of the many lands where he had been China was the one offering the best prospects of martyrdom '. Francis, he continued, worked so intensely to put the affairs of India in good order that he gave the impression of a man about to take his leave for ever. His whole dealings with people became a sort of unspoken farewell:

As the time approached for his departure he gave us a nightly exhortation in the choir of our church from which the Brethren received enormous consolation, for his words had such grace and power that they inflamed all hearts and transformed them into something new. His last words to us, after he had embraced each one with many tears and put him within his heart, were of constancy in the first fervour of our vocation, of deep

[1] This is well attested (*Monumenta Xaveriana*, ii, 260).

humility proceeding from self-knowledge, and above all of promptitude in obedience, a virtue so much loved and esteemed by God and so necessary to all in the Society of Jesus. On Maundy Thursday in the afternoon when the day's solemn ceremonies were over, he departed with his companions, and you can imagine, Brothers, how each of us felt at the separation from one so dear. But consolation prevailed over sadness because he was going on so great an enterprise and to [the glory of] certain martyrdom. Some of the brethren accompanied him to the shore, but most of us remained before the Blessed Sacrament praying with all our hearts to God for him. . . .[1]

The fortunate few chosen by Francis to go with him were the priest, Balthasar Gago, destined later for notable work in Japan,[2] the scholastic, or as yet unordained Jesuit, Alvaro Ferreira, pious but not valiant, taken probably because he gave evidence of some linguistic ability, a young Chinaman named Antonio who had been for eight years at the College of St. Paul and was to act as interpreter, and finally a Malabar Christian named Christopher in the capacity of servant to St. Francis. With them, *en route* for Japan, travelled the ambassador from Bungo who had become a

[1] Wicki, *Documenta Indica*, ii, 453–5.

[2] He became the reformer or expurgator of the book of doctrine compiled by St. Francis at Kagoshima and put into Japanese, with a transliteration in Latin characters, by Anjiro. This was the book which gave Dainichi his brief run as the personal God of Christianity. But Gago and Father Melchior Nunes, who was an excellent theologian, discovered in their contests with the Zen-shu bonzes that Anjiro had foisted several other dangerous terms, more than fifty in fact, on to the helpless St. Francis, e.g., the Japanese names for the soul, Heaven, Hell, angel, etc. *Tamashii*, the Buddhist term for the soul borrowed by Anjiro, does not mean a personal, immortal soul at all, but a mere transitory appearance, as it were, a wave on the ocean of the Absolute. So gravely infected was the book of St. Francis that Father Nunes decided to replace it with a Portuguese manual of doctrine done into Japanese by the brilliant Brother Laurence, the former clown, who had a profound knowledge of esoteric Buddhism and was not to be misled like poor Anjiro by the priests' crafty use of *hoben* or accommodations of doctrine to suit the capacity of the uninitiated. Portuguese or Latin terms were boldy introduced where no theologically exact Japanese term could be found (Schurhammer, *Das kirchliche Sprachproblem in der Japanischen Jesuitenmission des 16. und 17. Jahrhunderts*, Tokyo, 1927, pp. 46–90).

Christian at Goa under the name of Lourenço Pereira, two other Jesuit scholastics, Pedro de Alcaçova, and Eduardo da Silva, and the two Japanese baptized with Anjiro, Antonio and João. Perhaps the most memorable of them all was the Chinese Antonio, a loyal lovely character whom Luis Frois described as ' the saintliest man I have seen in this part of the world '. Indeed, Antonio had only one drawback as a companion to Francis, he had completely forgotten his native tongue! Frois gives an inventory of the gifts which Francis brought for the Emperor in Peking, as distinct from the other rarities purchased by Diogo Pereira. There were rich robes of brocade, velvet and silk, canopies and fine carpets, large altarpieces and the whole furnishings of a splendid chapel, this last, ' as it were to attest the Father's faith and hope that he would attain the end desired '. All the shining things came from fabulous Ormuz where they had been bought on a very happy shopping expedition by Gaspar Berze with a large sum of money given him by the Viceroy of India. That was two years back, when Gaspar was thrilled by his summons to Japan, but now Francis commandeered the hoard for a greater personage than any resplendent daimyo, leaving the other man appalled by the change in his fortunes. ' Father Francis,' he told St. Ignatius, ' has given me charge of this College and of all the brethren in India in his absence. Your Paternity may imagine my confusion when I think of my frailty. I had longed with all my heart to sacrifice myself for our Lord in Japan and that Scythian Sea, but I have always held that the sacrifice of obedience and of one's own will is more acceptable to God than any other.'[1]

The ship bearing St. Francis and his companions made a brief call at Cochin where a somewhat sombre post awaited the voyager at the college there, presided over by Father Antonio de Heredia. The news from Cape Comorin and Quilon was bad, and Francis, beset by callers, dashed off a hasty letter with three postscripts to Berze about it. Father Paul do Valle, ' a man of much perfection ' and only two years a priest, had died of hardship and harder

[1] Wicki, *Documenta Indica*, ii, 580. The Scythian Sea was part of the great geographical mythology of the sixteenth century, like Cathay.

work at Punnaikâyal, so the gallant Henry Henriques with the tainted blood remained the only priest on the Coast. ' For the love of God, see if you can help him,' wrote Francis, and suggested that Antonio Dias, another Jesuit child of Abraham and ' perfect Brother ', should be one of the two sent to the rescue. In Quilon, the dear Lancillotto, always ill and always active, was going through a very bad time at his College of San Salvador, built of mud and roofed with palm branches, trying to feed and educate fifty Indian boys on an income hardly enough to support five. Nearly all the missions except Goa itself were in a similarly parlous plight because King John had almost exhausted his treasury and was no longer in a position to help them. *Pardaos*, worth three testoons and three vintens for the reader's enlighten-ment,[1] became therefore a constant preoccupation and worry of St. Francis and he appealed to his men at wealthy centres such as Ormuz, Bassein and Malacca to send any of them they could spare to the destitute brethren in the south. But they were not to beg for help and must be sure to pay their own debts before they sent a single *pardao* to Lancillotto or Henriques. Every time Berze wrote to Francis in China, he must state how far he had settled with his creditors and how much he still owed them. He must also give news of each and every one of the brethren, saying how they are progressing in the way of God. Some time past, a Christian of Cape Comorin had sent money to Goa for the purchase of a silver chalice, but the money had been spent and the chalice not delivered. Berze will rectify this injustice as soon as he can and also in his charity send a second chalice to Japan, where they have only the one. Francis is full of gratitude to Gaspar. ' We should be in a nice predicament were it not for you,' he writes, referring to the gifts from Ormuz. A certain ' Padre de Evangelho ' or deacon named Estevan Borralho will be coming to Goa to decide his vocation. ' I love him very much,' says Francis and begs Berze to see the Bishop on his behalf, as also to be good to another Stephen ' who always was a great help to me when I required his assis-

---

[1] Let us be helpful and reckon in chickens. With one *fanam* a man could buy in India three chickens for his pot. The *fanam* in 1550 was worth 30 reals and there were 300 reals or ten *fanams* or thirty chickens to a *pardao*.

tance '. These are odd trifles to be preoccupying a man with the Emperor of China looming on his horizon, but they are typical of this man who in default of other titles might be called St. Francis the Thankful.

During his few days ashore in Cochin, the traveller, with half the town knocking at his door, managed to find time to write a little tract of counsel and encouragement for Antonio de Heredia:

> Try above all things to win the love of the Franciscan Fathers, the Brothers of Mercy and the people generally. In everything that you do and in your way of doing it show that you are eager to be at one with them. . . . When the poor tell you of their corporal necessities, seek alms for them from the Brothers of Mercy, . . . and at the same time speak to them of their spiritual needs, of their need to draw near to God by confession and Holy Communion. . . . Do not put on solemn airs when you speak with the people and beware of being dictatorial or of giving them an impression that you regard them as dependent on you. Be pleasant and genial when you talk with them, and only severe when they persist in evil ways. Even so, you must not cause them to despond but encourage them by recalling God's mercy. Be very lowly and modest in all your dealings with others, rendering each the deference due to him, be he priest or layman, and giving them the credit for any good work done. . . . In your sermons avoid conceits meant to tickle people's ears and get you a reputation as a wit, for that is but a vanity which dishonours God and does no good to souls. . . .

Francis was heartily of the opinion of the poet who said that axioms in philosophy are not axioms until they are proved upon our pulses. Here in this scribbled note he expresses the same thought in humbler language, namely that the ' sentimento interior ' of a man is what makes the maxims of the saints, meaningless and dry as a stick to the unlit heart, put forth leaves and flowers.[1] Letters of comfort to Lancillotto and Henriques con-

---

[1] Schurhammer, *Epistolae*, ii, 449–52. The haste in which Francis composed this little document is indicated by the fact that his handwriting entirely baffled the copyists in numerous places.

cluded the business of Francis with India but, as said before, he metaphorically took away in his heart Ormuz, Diu, Bassein, Goa, Cochin, Quilon, Cape Comorin and San Thomé, when he sailed on April 24 to his final defeat and everlasting victory.

The voyage to Malacca occupied a month and was not without incident, if we may believe the sober Valignano who went to considerable pains to find out the truth. This is his story:

> On the way to Malacca the ship ran into such a terrible storm that much of the cargo had to be jettisoned. All aboard were in consternation, some running to confession and others bracing themselves like men with death before their eyes. Seeing them thus, full of dismay and grief, the Father rallied and heartened them, looking very cheerful the while and telling them not to be afraid because our Lord would save the ship. Then mounting the poop, he took a reliquary which he had with him and, in the name of Father, Son, and Holy Ghost, cast it into the sea, beseeching the most Holy Trinity to have mercy on them all. He continued to be rapt in prayer until the winds abated and the storm died away altogether. . . .[1]

Valignano reports also, as do others closer to the event, that Francis was troubled on the voyage with forebodings of disaster in Malacca. He felt, as he had told Diogo Pereira when they first planned the expedition, that the devil would be sure to try and frustrate their hopes. He carried with him a diploma from the Viceroy appointing Diogo ambassador of Portugal to the Court of China, but left behind at Goa unfortunately the precious parchment brief of Pope Paul III which had constituted himself apostolic nuncio in the East, as also copies of various bulls extending to Jesuits the Church's protection as they went on their lawful occasions.

Pereira had remained at Malacca with his ship the *Santa Cruz* to fit out the expedition when Francis had gone on to India, and

---

[1] *Monumenta Xaveriana*, i, 147. This is suspiciously like another storm in which Francis had been implicated earlier. But storms at sea are much of a muchness, anyhow.

spent from four to five thousand gold crowns, no inconsiderable part of his fortune, purchasing pepper in Java and other merchandise, as well as presents for his Celestial Majesty, whom his friend always persisted in calling King because he would not allow to any pagan, however mighty, the sacred title of Emperor. For Francis there could be but one Emperor as there was only one Pope. His good friend Pedro da Silva da Gama was still Captain of Malacca, but his younger brother, Alvaro da Ataíde da Gama, the same who came to India originally with St. Francis and suffered imprisonment unjustly at the hands of Francis's friend, Governor Martim Affonso de Sousa, had arrived from Goa to share his authority as Grand Captain of the Malaccan Seas. That office gave Alvaro separate command of the harbour and roadstead with all their shipping, including the *Santa Cruz*. As he was to succeed his brother in command of the Fortress also in a few months, he easily drew into his following traders with an eye on the main chance and fickle Malays. When he learned of Diogo Pereira's ambassadorial elevation he became violently jealous that a mere trader should have been preferred before himself for so honorific and lucrative a post. He gave out that the King's interests would not be promoted by the Chinese project and flatly refused the good merchant permission to sail. He even requisitioned his ship for a time and impounded the rudder and tiller. His brother Pedro and some other eminent men protested against this violence, but to no purpose, and seeing how little he prevailed the good Captain resigned his authority into the hands of a royal judge named Francisco Alvares. When his representations also were flouted by the man with the mob at his back, St. Francis felt it to be time to intervene. He drew up a little document stating that he had been appointed apostolic nuncio by a brief of Pope Paul III, and that this brief had been delivered to him by the King's own hands, who confirmed all its provisions. On arriving in India he had presented his Papal and Royal credentials to the Bishop, Dom João de Albuquerque, his ecclesiastical superior, who approved them, and later on approved also his going to China, as the letter enclosed from the Bishop to the King of China showed. The Viceroy, for his part, seeing that his going to

China would be of great service to God, appointed Diogo Pereira ambassador to the Court of the Chinese King, as the diploma accompanying the present document testified. Next, Francis addressed himself directly to the Vicar of Malacca, João Soares, for whom the document was intended.

Now [he continued] the Senhor Grand Captain of the Sea is preventing this embarkation and voyage, . . . wherefore I require your Reverence on the part of God and of the Bishop whom you represent that you make known to the said Captain the Decretal *Super Gentes* and explain to him that it pronounces accursed and excommunicated all who hinder apostolic nuncios in the performance of duties laid upon them by their ecclesiastical and secular superiors. Beg him in the name of God and of the Bishop not to thwart my expedition nor hinder me from carrying it out in the manner arranged by the Senhor Viceroy, for if he does, he will be excommunicated, not by the Bishop, nor by your Reverence nor by me, but by the holy Pontiffs who made the canons. Tell the Captain that I beg him by the Passion and death of our Lord Jesus Christ not to incur so grave an excommunication, entailing, let him have no doubt, the terrible chastisement of God. . . . Will your Reverence let me have the Captain's reply as quickly as you can, as the monsoon is ending. . . . It is impossible that he should refuse me once he has seen the Decretal. . . .[1]

Francis was entirely wrong in his last assumption. Father Perez, his excellent adjutant in Malacca, took the document to the Vicar and they both in company with the judge, Alvares, went to point out to the Grand Captain the error of his ways and its consequences. The judge was careful to rub in that he not only incurred ecclesiastical censure but also had made himself liable to be charged with high treason for his disobedience to the express injunctions of the King and Viceroy. It was no good. India and Portugal were a long way off and the tough Captain had all the

---

[1] Schurhammer, *Epistolae*, ii, 454–6. The Decretal was one of those known as *Extravagantes*, that is, 'wandering outside' the main *Corpus Juris*, like an Order in Council.

cards in his hands, especially the backing of the timid and subservient population who wished to ingratiate themselves with the
master of their fate for the next three years. ' After the documents
and letters had been read to him,' reported Perez, ' he jumped up
from his chair and burst into a flood of imprecations such as my
pen dare not write. Then he spat upon the ground and, stamping
his foot, said, " That's what I think of the Viceroy and his
instructions ".' As for the intruding priest, the old crony of his
enemy de Sousa, let him prove his nunciature by producing the
brief. He might go where he listed, and to the devil at that, but
Pereira, he swore, would not accompany him. At the investigations held in Cochin in 1556, a number of witnesses came
forward to tell the sequel. ' The adherents of Alvaro da Ataíde,'
said one, ' used to wait for the Father in the streets and yell after
him " Drunkard ! " and other opprobrious terms. . . . But he
said Mass every day for Alvaro. . . .' Another reported that
eventually Francis hardly dared to stir abroad at all, so violent
had the feeling against him, fanned by Alvaro, become.[1] On
June 25, while they were both still in Malacca, he addressed a sad
little letter to his unhappy friend Pereira.

> Your sins and mine [he said] have been so great that God
> does not wish to be served by us. For our disasters we have
> only our sins to blame. Mine were of such magnitude that they
> have brought my projects to naught and caused your destruc-
> tion. With good reason, Senhor, you can lay at my doors
> the ruin of yourself and of all those who came with you in
> your ship. It was for my sake that you spent four or five
> thousand *pardaos* on gifts for the King of China, so I am
> responsible for the loss of that money, and now also for the
> loss of your ship and your whole fortune. I beg you to
> remember, Senhor, that my intention was always to be of
> service to you, as God knows and as you know too. If this
> were not so, I would die of sorrow. Please do not come to
> visit me, for the sight of you would break my heart. I am going
> to take refuge on the *Santa Cruz* so as not to see the accusing

[1] *Monumenta Xaveriana*, ii, 326, 341.

tears of men whose ruin I have brought about. As I said, if my good intentions did not save me I would die of grief. I have done with Senhor Dom Alvaro since he has chosen to prevent our going together. My only way of making amends to you would be for me to write to our lord, the King, tell him that I had ruined you . . . and beg him to make good the losses which you incurred through your efforts to serve him. . . . But I am unable to do this through being so much persecuted and thwarted by Senhor Dom Alvaro. . . . It grieves me to think of the heavy punishment which awaits him from God. . . . *Vosso tryste e desconsolado amyguo, Francisco.*[1]

The mind and heart of Francis are reflected in other letters which he wrote at this time of darkness and frustration. He had a dear friend named Affonso Gentil who was also a notable sinner. Many a time Francis had tried to persuade him to marry the woman he was living with, but he always put him off on some pretext or other. Francis wrote from Malacca begging Bishop Albuquerque to inquire whether Affonso, then resident in Goa, laboured under some matrimonial impediment from which he might be dispensed and enabled to make an honest woman of his mistress. Gaspar Berze was called in also to use his persuasive charm on the reluctant scapegrace. Another letter to Berze, dated July 13, ran as follows:

Master Gaspar, I would have you know that I owe more to Senhor Dom Pedro da Silva than I could ever repay. Not since I came from Europe have I met a man more generous than he was to me while he was Captain of Malacca. . . . Would to God that he were still Captain, for then I would be going to China in quite another style. Very different has been the attitude of his brother, Dom Alvaro, towards me. God

[1] Schurhammer, *Epistolae S. Francisci Xaverii*, ii, 461–3. According to Manuel Teixeira, an ocular witness, the wretched Alvaro was stricken with leprosy in Malacca and died of the disease when removed thence to Portugal (*Monumenta Xaveriana*, ii, 893). He had been imprisoned for his many injustices while ruling in Malacca, and he was the only one of Vasco da Gama's four sons who did not add lustre to an honoured name.

forgive him, he has spoiled the whole expedition arranged by the Senhor Viceroy. . . . Just now, Dom Pedro has done me a great service most willingly by lending me three hundred *cruzados* to repay the sum advanced to me in Japan for the construction of a church in Yamaguchi. . . . Will you please reimburse him out of the College revenues or the two thousand *cruzados* which the King assigns to the College annually, and see that you do so immediately, for I would be distressed if Dom Pedro had to ask you for the money. . . . God bring us together in the glory of Paradise. Entirely yours in Christ, Francisco.[1]

Wanting to be rid of St. Francis, and fearing, perhaps, that he had already gone too far in contradiction of superior authority, Dom Alvaro at last permitted the *Santa Cruz* to sail, but without her master Pereira and chiefly manned by officers and sailors of his enemy's choosing. As the embassy on which he had counted so much was ruined and he would have to find some method of

---

[1] Schurhammer, *Epistolae*, ii, 467–8. This letter proves that Mendez Pinto must then have been in Malacca. It also tends to show that he was a mean kind of person, for he was rich and could surely have made Francis a present of the money. Pedro da Silva, on the other hand, was poor, having been too upright a man to enrich himself out of the spoils of office. In 1554 Pinto was worth 12,000 *pardaos* and regarded as one of the wealthiest merchants in the East. In that year he offered himself·to the Society of Jesus at Goa but left it before completing his novitiate. In his recent book, *The Christian Century in Japan* (C.U.P., 1951), Professor C. R. Boxer quotes a remark of the Portuguese scholar Armando Cortesão, 'With the same ease with which he [Pinto] entered it [the Society of Jesus] when rich, he left it when poor,' the implication being, of course, that the Jesuits had hung on to his fortune. Boxer mildly comments: 'This taunt is perhaps not altogether deserved.' This taunt can easily be proved to be a brazen lie. From the very first the Jesuit Constitutions forbade the disposal or alienation of property, even to the Society of Jesus, until a man came to take his final vows, after ordination. Until then he retained the complete ownership, though not the use of, his property, and when the time came to dispose of it, he might do so in any way he wished, to the poor, to relatives, to hospitals, etc. Pinto was less than two years a novice and did not take even his first vows. If he brought his wealth in with him, he certainly took it all out again. His later poverty, as he says himself, was due to mishaps at sea and unsuccessful business ventures. If he demanded back his three hundred *cruzados* from St. Francis, is it likely that he would have allowed other Jesuits to retain his twelve thousand *pardaos*?

his own for breaking into China, Francis travelled lightly, leaving behind in charge of Perez the brocades and silks and ' *todo o aparelho de capelo em pontifical*'. He also relinquished to Japan his one priest companion, Father Gago, and took with him only the Jesuit scholastic, Alvaro Ferreira, who was of little use, the faithful lay Chinaman, Antonio, and his Malabar domestic, Christopher. By July 21 they were baking in the Straits of Singapore. One friendly soul on board, Estevan Ventura, bore the following testimony: ' On the voyage, many, both Christians and Moslems, fell sick, and it was the Father's only recreation and delight to attend on them and to pray. Thus did he spend all his time. He used to buy chickens for the sick at half a crown each . . . and when his own exiguous meal was put before him, he reserved most of it for his patients. Anything else they needed he begged for them, as I know because I offered him money, and with his own hands he ministered to their every want. . . .'[1] Among the worst casualties were Ferreira and Antonio who gave Francis, in his own words, ' more anxiety, more toil in nursing them, than I could well express '. From the Straits he wrote again to Gaspar Berze.

You would hardly believe [he said] how much I was persecuted in Malacca. . . . I have told Father Perez to give you the particulars. He will let you know about the excommunications incurred by Dom Alvaro for preventing the expedition to China . . . and for gainsaying the bulls conceded to our Society by Pope Paul III, and Pope Julius now reigning. . . . I want you to use all diligence in bringing these matters to the Bishop's attention, so that through him the excommunications may be made public and Fathers of our Society going to Japan or China not thwarted on other occasions. When his Lordship writes to the Vicar of Malacca, ask him to mention that Pope Paul appointed me nuncio to the Indies for the greater service of God. I showed his Lordship the brief of Pope Paul and he endorsed it. . . . I think you have it at the College and if necessary you can produce it for the Bishop's perusal again. I want

[1] *Monumenta Xaveriana*, ii, 278.

this done purely to prevent impediments being put in the way of our Fathers in the future. I would never ask a prelate to excommunicate anybody, but neither would I make any bones about telling those who are excommunicated by the holy canons and the bulls conceded to our Society the plain fact, so that they might repent of the evil they had done and not repeat it in the future. This is my reason for being so insistent. I charge you to write in detail to Father Juan Beira,[1] and to send him a mandate from the Lord Bishop ordering the Vicar of Malacca to promulgate the excommunication against Dom Alvaro for having prevented a voyage so serviceable to God and advantageous to our holy faith. I am going on to the islands off Canton divested of all human help, but hoping that some Moor or gentile will take me to the Chinese shore. . . .

Few of Francis's letters are more involved and repetitive than this one, reflecting as it does the trouble in his soul. The thought of Alvaro da Ataíde haunted and horrified him, and the phrase about the ruined Embassy, ' *de tamto serviço de Deus e acrecemtamento da nosa samta ffee* ', recurs again and again like the tolling of a somewhat unmelodious bell for the death of a cherished dream. Gone now was the only chance of entering China lawfully, in an ambassador's train, but he might still be able to land furtively and bribe his way to the unhappy Christian prisoners rotting in the dungeons of Canton. Anyhow it was worth trying, and if he ended, as seemed highly probable, by sharing their fate, that might be the next best way of serving God. The thought of Japan brought him refreshment in the clammy tropical heat of the Straits.

Do try hard to send someone to Japan each year [he adjures Berze]. Balthasar Gago has gone there now with Eduardo da Silva and Pedro de Alcaçova. They went off in a fine ship and in excellent weather. God grant that they may arrive safely in Yamaguchi where Father Cosmas de Torres and Juan Fer-

---

[1] This heroic man had returned from the Moluccas to Malacca to find more helpers before St. Francis left on the *Santa Cruz*.

nandez are. If you have any alms to spare, try your best to send something to them every year by one of the ships that sail in April for Malacca. If it is quite impossible for you to provide a Father of good attainment for Japan any particular year, then dispatch some able and trustworthy layman with your alms and the assurance that you will send a priest the following year. But be careful to send only such as are well educated to Japan and China, and if the best you can offer is a Brother let him be one with an aptitude for learning the language. Strive every way you can, through the *Misericordia*, through devout persons known to you, through the Viceroy, through any agency you like, to acquire alms for the brethren in Japan. Father Francis Perez in Malacca will see that they reach their destination. Give Juan de Beira all the help in your power . . . but be careful to see that he returns to the Moluccas in April, as he will be sorely missed there. If a Father of small learning comes from Portugal meantime give him and some really virtuous Brother to Father Beira, because cultured persons are not needed in the Moluccas but men of sterling virtue and constancy. . . . Write to me in great detail, giving the letter to Father Beira when he returns to Malacca, from whence it will be forwarded to me in China. Should it happen that God does not want me in China, I shall return to India for the whole of the months of December and January, if He gives me health and life. Tell me in your letter all the news of India and Portugal, of his Lordship the Bishop, and of the friars of St. Francis and St. Dominic, to whom you will give my most affectionate good wishes and beg them earnestly to remember me in their Holy Sacrifices and prayers. At the College, make a particular point of commending me and the Fathers and Brothers in Japan to God, for I can assure you that we have the greatest need of His help. May our Lord bring us together in the glory of Paradise where we shall have more peace than in this weary world. *Do estreito de Symquapura.* Your friend and brother, Francis.[1]

---

[1] Schurhammer, *Epistolae S. Francisci Xaverii*, ii, 470–5.

As is now sufficiently plain, the C Major of this life was ever, at least in his letters, the favourite key of St. Francis. He will be humdrum to the end, dealing with administrative problems as long as he can hold a pen or has voice to dictate his orders and wishes. The ships in the Straits were obliged as a rule to wait four or five days for sunlight and wind combined to negotiate the tricky and dangerous passage which was then the only known route to China. Of course, the Portuguese traders should not have been going to China at all. China was strictly forbidden to them ever since others of their nation had roused the Celestial ire by their arrogance and high-handed behaviour, and the penalty, they well knew, if caught, would not be a swift, clean death but a loathsome and tortured existence. Their hopes rested on the activities of the Japanese pirates who kept the Chinese authorities so busy in the Yangtse delta that they had not sufficient junks and men to patrol the coast farther south. Even so, up to fifty of their fraternity had come to grief and lay buried alive in Canton. These poor wretches filled the thoughts of Francis as, wearied to death in the stifling heat, he cooked chickens for his sick ' Moors ' and Christians, and endeavoured to keep them and their stinking quarters clean. He had so much to trouble him, Juan de Beira for instance, the saintly valorous man whose mind was giving way under the intolerable strain of life in the Islands of Martyrdom. He had disconcerted Francis in Malacca with tales of apocalyptic visions, and now Francis writes begging him in the most tactful way ' never to tell another soul about the interior things ' which God had given him to feel. His very presence in Malacca marked a disappointment and defeat for Francis, for he had come with a story of promises broken and anti-Christian villainies done by a man whom the Saint had thought to be a friend and trusted, Sultan Hairun of Ternate. He is to be cautious in dealing with that perjured miscreant, to let the Viceroy decide the best medicine for him. And on no account is he to miss the April-May monsoon for his return to the islands where he is so badly needed. ' Keep this letter,' says Francis, ' so that nobody in India may try to deter you from going back, and remember, not a word to any one about those things you disclosed to me in *Nossa*

Senhora do Monte at Malacca. May God unite us again in Heaven.'

As mentioned above, Francis had brought with him to Malacca the two Japanese baptized with Anjiro at Goa, Anthony and John. Anthony he had sent back to his own country as Father Gago's interpreter, but he asked John to remain so that the Jesuit or Jesuits coming out the following year might have a spokesman in the wonderland of daimyos and cherry-trees. John, who had been the servant of poor Anjiro, was a simple good fellow and dear to Francis. From the Straits of Singapore he received the following little letter, almost the equivalent of a pension:

John of Japan, my son. I am writing to Father Master Gaspar to obtain alms to enable you to purchase merchandise at Goa so that you may have something to live on when you return to your own country. You will travel to Goa with Father Juan de Beira when the fleet leaves Malacca for India, and I want you to present the letter I enclose with this one to Father Master Berze. You must show yourself a very faithful servant of the Fathers going to Japan until they reach Yamaguchi. Go to confession and receive our Lord frequently, so that God may help you. Cast yourself upon God and beware of all sin, because if you offend God in this world you will assuredly suffer heavy punishment in the next. So mind that you avoid doing evil things which would bring you to Hell. Remember me with all kindness to Mark and Paul when you get back to Japan. May God make you holy and happy, and take you into the glory of Paradise. . . . Keep this letter carefully and show it to Father Perez in Malacca and to Father Heredia when you reach Cochin. Tell Father Perez from me that he is to write to Father Heredia on your behalf. They will both do their best to assist you. Your affectionate friend, Francis.[1]

[1] Schurhammer, *Epistolae*, ii, 476–7, 482. The Paul referred to was Anjiro whom Francis thought to be still alive and with the Christians of Kagoshima. Berze in his letter was urgently asked to find up to thirty *pardaos* for John, besides what Perez and Heredia might be able to get for him. Francis suggested that John should use the money to buy goods in Goa which he could sell on the Japanese market very advantageously and thus make for himself a modest living that would not, however, turn him into a drone. He was very precise

ST. FRANCIS XAVIER

The last letters from the Straits were all dictated or penned on
July 22, to King John and his Viceroy Noronha on behalf of
Diogo Pereira and the Vicar of Malacca, though the latter person
had been far from helpful in the trouble with the obstructive
Captain, to the Bishop of Goa, to Father Francis Perez
recommending him ' to take great care of his physical health as
he had always done of his spiritual health ', and finally to Diogo
Pereira, whose men on the *Santa Cruz*, Estevan Ventura,
Francisco de Aguiar, and Tomas Escander were being so good
to him.

My longing for you, Senhor [he said], and the knowledge
that you are still in so sickly a place [as Malacca] keep you in
my memory all the time. All your good men on this your ship
have treated me, out of regard for you, with the greatest
respect and kindness. They have given me in abundance all
that I need for myself who am well and for the sick persons
who embarked. They get worse from hour to hour, and the
merciful God knows the anxiety and trouble they give me.
May He be praised in Heaven and on earth for ever and ever.
I am sending you unsealed letters for the King and the Viceroy
so that you may read what I have said in them. I would be
greatly pleased and relieved if the letter to the King could be
transmitted to Portugal this year by some very trustworthy
person, so that his Highness may speedily do what I am hoping
for.[1] You might show the letter to Dom Pedro da Silva for him
to see what I say about him to the King. . . . I earnestly beg

---

and practical, our man of Navarre. The alms for the Japanese missionaries, he
told Berze, ought to be in the Venetian gold coins which were in circulation
in Goa, because they were made of the purest gold and much appreciated in
Japan where the gold was not so fine. The Japanese craftsmen used them to
adorn the hilts and scabbards of swords and daggers. The letter closed with the
words: ' Your brother in Christ who loves you very much. Francisco.'

[1] To recoup Diogo for his losses, Francis sent a sealed copy of the letter by
another route, but this appears to have fallen into the hands of Alvaro da
Ataíde who is said to have opened and read it, but to his shame, for there was
not a whisper of complaint against him in it. Both the letter and its copy are
lost, perhaps through Alvaro's machinations.

you, Senhor, to do me the favour of taking great care of your health and life, being very prudent in your transactions and going cautiously the while with those who pretend to be your friends and are not. Above all, I beg you to come close to God that He may comfort you in this time of great affliction. For the love of our Lord do me this favour, a really big one—go to confession and receive our Lord and conform yourself to His holy will. Then will all that persecution turn to your advantage and glory. I have taken Francisco Davila with me as he will be needed in China to help your manager, Tomas Escander, to transact your business. He will return to Malacca, please God, by the first *bancam* that puts out from China. If God our Lord does not open to me the way into China I shall return to Malacca in any sort of boat available, and if I can then catch one of the King's ships I shall journey back to India. On the other hand, should God take me to China do not neglect to write me all the news of yourself because it will give me the intensest pleasure [*porque com ellas folgarei muito em estremo*]. . . . The Father Vicar asked me to write to the King on his behalf and I have done so, though I have been told that he did nothing to help our expedition, which was so much for the service of God and the increase of our holy faith, because he wished to be thought on Dom Alvaro's side, hoping apparently thus to obtain some temporal advantage. In what a fool's paradise they live who, leaving out of account God, the source of all good, busy themselves to obtain remedies at the hands of men! I take my revenge on those who are not my friends by doing them services. . . . I can truthfully say that I feel great compassion for them when they hinder the service of God, for I fear that you will see them punished more drastically than they could imagine. Will you please give the Vicar with your own hands the letter to the King in which I speak of him. If God brings me to China, as I trust He will, I shall tell the Portuguese [prisoners] there the immense debt of gratitude they owe you, recounting to them the great expense you went to in your desire of redeeming them. And I shall give them your kindest wishes and hearten them with the hope that your efforts will be suc-

cessful next time. . . . I beg you warmly, Senhor, to visit the
Fathers in the College at Malacca frequently that you may
find comfort in their company. *Vosso muito grande amigo,*
Francisco.[1]

At last the wind in the Straits blew the way it was wanted,
and the *Santa Cruz*, piloted by one of Pereira's men, moved
slowly and majestically into the open sea. The voyage was about
the same length as from Cape Comorin to Malacca, roughly
1,500 statute miles, but the going was far more uncertain and might
take double the time. This was the uneasy world of typhoons,
pirates, and police junks, but the *Santa Cruz* had the luck to
encounter no such things or persons and made an excellent swift
voyage, except that she overshot her mark and cast anchor at the
wrong island. The pilot had to confess that he did not recognize
the place, and the Captain, one of Alvaro da Ataíde's following,
was at a loss what to do until St. Francis, who had been in those
parts twice before and possessed, through long experience, a good
eye for landmarks, advised him to turn back. He was not prepared to do that but he sent a *bancam* southwards to investigate,
and sure enough it returned after three days with fresh provisions
from the right island. This we know from the report of the Chinese
Antonio, as good a witness as he was good a man, who went on
to say that they reversed course and tacked safely to their destination, 'with great joy and thankfulness to our Lord for giving
them such a prosperous voyage'.[2] The destination was a barren
and uninviting little island lying just six miles off the Chinese
shore a hundred miles south-west of Hongkong. Its situation, so
near the mainland and yet sufficiently distant from the huge,
fantastic capital of Kwangtung Province, Canton, to escape the

[1] Schurhammer, *Epistolae S. Francisci Xaverii*, ii, 485–7. Francis, we see, is
not now so confident of being able to break into China on his own account but,
as will appear, he had another card up his sleeve to trump whatever might be
produced by the Dragon Throne. A *bancam* was a small version of a junk
propelled by oars.

[2] *Monumenta Xaveriana*, ii, 787. The information comes from an invaluable
letter which Antonio wrote from Cochin in September, 1554, less than two
years after the death of St. Francis, to the Jesuit who first attempted a life of
him, Manuel Teixeira. It gives a full account of the last days of Francis on earth.

prying attentions of the mandarins, made it an ideal resort for the
Portuguese smugglers who wished to trade with their opposite
numbers from that City of Rams. Its Chinese name is Shang-
chwan which the Portuguese transformed into Samchoão and
Jesuits writing in Latin into Sancianum, whence the common
Western name Sancian. Since the death of St. Francis Xavier it
has been revered as one of the Holy Islands of Christendom, like
Lérins or Lindisfarne, but the Shang or Sam or San part of the
word is purely prepositional and has nothing to do with sanctity.
Fifty miles to the nort-east lay the estuary of the Chukiang or
Pearl River, a water-way which took ships of reasonable draught
right up to the walls of Canton, twenty feet thick, from twenty-
five to forty feet high, and six miles in circumference. In those
formidable walls were twelve heavily guarded gates with such
ambiguous names as The Great Peace and Eternal Rest, which
the traveller, according to his credentials, might interpret as a
welcome or a menace.

When the *Santa Cruz* cast anchor at Sancian in the calm waters
between the bosky island and the Chinese coast, there were other
Portuguese ships riding there and a number of junks laden with
silks and translucent glazed earthenware. These were exchanged
for the pepper and spice and all things nice which the Southern
Barbarians had brought from India and the Moluccas. The Chinese
dealers had not much to fear because they were usually doing
business for the mandarins of Canton, the guardians of the law,
but the Portuguese smugglers needed to be wary and so, for the
most part, lived on their ships which they kept in a state of readiness for instant departure, should pirates or police be announced
in the vicinity. Among the brave fellows whom St. Francis found
engaged in the ritual of barter was a certain Manuel de Chaves, a
first-hand authority on the subject of Chinese gaols. This was the
very man who, the year before, had got a letter through from his
dungeon in Canton to his fellow-countrymen at Sancian,
suggesting the embassy of Diogo Pereira. He had subsequently
escaped, and none better than he could have described to Francis
the hideous underground galleries to which the starved prisoners
were herded at night and so chained to the filthy ground that the

slightest movement became all but impossible.[1] It is likely that the fugitive did not spare Francis any of the grim details, for he and other friendly Portuguese were utterly opposed to his project and refused to have any hand in it. But they built him a small wooden hut covered with straw on the shore of Sancian and a similar frail structure to serve as a chapel. There he said Mass, heard confessions, preached, and looked after sick people brought to him from the ships, while he waited week after week, pleading in vain for a boat or raft or any sort of transport to take him the few tantalizing miles to the forbidden land whose craggy out-lines he could see from his hut. There were some slaves and children on the ships and these he tirelessly instructed, says Antonio, ' con muita charidade e amor ', begging from the merchants the food and clothing which they needed. One of the slaves was a Chinaman captured by the Portuguese in their famous engage-ment with the pirates of Achin, and through him Francis was able to converse with the polite, smiling and utterly undependable customers from Canton. On October 22, when he had been on the island perhaps a month, Francis wrote his first letter to give Father Perez at Malacca the news:

> By the mercy and goodness of God our Lord I and all those who came on the ship of Diogo Pereira arrived safely at this port of Sancian, where we found many other ships belonging to merchants. Sancian is thirty leagues from Canton and numerous merchants from the latter place come here to do business with the Portuguese. I tried hard to persuade one of them to take me to Canton, but [at first] they all begged to be excused, saying that their lives and fortunes would be put in jeopardy if the governor of Canton discovered my presence. Nothing I could offer would induce them to give me a passage on one of their ships. By the good pleasure of God our Lord, however, an honourable citizen of Canton eventually agreed to take me for two hundred cruzados in a little junk manned

[1] An intrepid Dominican, Gaspar da Cruz, succeeded in getting into contact with the prisoners in 1556 and gives a nightmarish account of what they suffered in his Tractado da China, published at Lisbon in 1562.

only by his sons and servants, so that the governor might not come to hear from mariners that it was a merchant who smuggled me in. More than that, he volunteered to keep me hidden in his house for three or four days, after which he would escort me before dawn, with my books and other little properties, to a gate of the city whence I could at once proceed to the governor's palace to tell him that we had come in order to make our way to the court of the King of China and to show him the letter of the Lord Bishop to His Highness. . . . According to other Chinamen this course involves two risks, first, that the man taking us, when paid his money, may cast us adrift on some desert island or dump us in the sea to make himself safe against discovery by the governor, and secondly, that, even if we reached Canton and appeared before the governor, he might order us to be tortured or consigned to a dungeon . . . , since the King of China had so stringently forbidden foreigners entrance into his territories without his express written permission. But there are other perils much greater than those two, which the Chinese would not understand and which would take too long to recount, though I cannot refrain from telling you something of them. The danger of all dangers would be to lose trust and confidence in the mercy of God for whose love and service we came to manifest the law of Jesus Christ, His Son, our Redeemer and Lord, as He well knows. . . . To distrust Him would be a far more terrible thing than any physical evil which all the enemies of God put together could inflict on us, for without God's permission neither the devils nor their human ministers could hinder us in the slightest degree. . . . We are therefore determined to make our way into China at all costs, and I hope in God that the upshot of our journey will be the increase of our holy faith, however much the devil and his ministers may persecute us. If God is for us who can overthrow us? When the Santa Cruz leaves here for Malacca I hope it will bring you news of how we were received in Canton and of what the governor did to us. . . . Alvaro Ferreira and Antonio the Chinaman have been sick all the time, but just now, by the mercy of God, are feeling better. Antonio will not do as an interpreter for he has forgotten how to speak Chinese, but a certain Pero Lopez, captured in battle by Antonio de Lopez Bobadilha, who can read and write Portuguese and knows Chinese sufficiently well, has offered himself with much good will to be my companion. May God reward him in this life and the next. . . . When I came to Sancian we made a little chapel where I said Mass daily until I went down with fever. I was ill for a fortnight, but now by the mercy of God am all right again. There is plenty to do here, what with confessions, care of the sick, and the task of making peace between persons at loggerheads with one another. I do not know that there is anything more to tell you except that we are absolutely determined to go to China. All the Chinese merchants I have seen here appear to be honourable men. . . . Either because they consider that we have some law written in our books superior to their own laws, or because they are lovers of novelties, they all make a show of great pleasure at our going to their country though none of them will take the risk of helping us on our way. . . .[1]

Father Perez, the postmaster-general of St. Francis, was much in his mind during those weeks of waiting on Sancian. Three years back he had spoken of that other Francis with accents of awe at his illimitable, indefatigable goodness in the poisonous climate of Malacca. Robust merchants had said that a few months of Malacca would bring death to any man, short of a miracle, yet Perez who never had any health worth the name had been there for more than three years, always working, always cheerful, and universally beloved. 'It fills me with confusion,' St. Francis had said, 'to see the amount of good he has done with the help of our Lord, while continually ill and suffering.' It was time that he had relief, and from Sancian, to make sure of it, Francis strictly ordered him under obedience to hand over *Nossa Senhora do Monte* and all other Jesuit responsibilities to the secular clergy, and to go to Cochin as superior in succession to Father Heredia

[1] Schurhammer, *Epistolae*, ii, 493–6.

who would at once make ready for the journey to Japan. Later on, when one was available, a Father would be sent out to reopen the suspended mission of Malacca. Francis would himself lie buried for a while in *Nossa Senhora do Monte*, whose ruins are still standing, but Malacca was definitely one of the very few places he did not like, and we could imagine him being grateful to Sir Stamford Raffles for overwhelming it with Singapore. The Chinese merchant who was to get two thousand pounds of Diogo Pereira's pepper for transporting him where he longed to be had gone back with his family to Canton. On October 22 he wrote to Pereira:

I am watching every day for the return of the merchant who has agreed for twenty *picos* of pepper to convey me to Canton. . . . If men knew as well as God does about my journey, they would see that it is all your doing, for you are paying all the expenses. Your manager, Tomas Escander, has carried out your instructions to the letter and given me everything I required. May God our Lord requite you for all your immense charity to me. My Chinaman is known to Manuel de Chaves and gave him refuge in his house in Canton for several days after his escape from prison, and that fact renews my hope every day that he will come for me. Manuel will write to tell you about my going and how I was received in Canton. If it should happen by God's permission that the merchant does not come for me and I am precluded this year from going to China, I know not what I shall do, whether to return to India or to sail to Siam, with hopes of being allowed to join the annual embassy of the King of Siam to China. If it is to India I go, it will be with no hope of anything being done in the matter of China while Alvaro da Ataíde da Gama holds sway, unless God provides otherwise. What I feel on this score I forbear to say. . . . Manuel de Chaves will let you know if I go to Siam in the junk which Diogo Vaz de Aragão bought out here . . . so that by some means or other you may get a letter through to me telling me what you have decided to do this year. Whether you come in the [Siamese] embassy or not, we might meet in Ke-moi or some other port,

but God grant that it may be inside China. . . . But if we do not
see each other again in this life, may the merciful God bring us
together in the glory of Paradise, where we shall see each other
always and for ever. Your true and affectionate good friend,
Francisco.[1]

That daily watch of Francis from his desolate island over the
empty sea has its parallels only in the great love stories of legend
or history, as when Dido waited on the Carthaginian shore or
Mary Magdalen outside the forsaken tomb, as millions of wives
and mothers have waited for ships that would never return. But
he had not yet given up all hope as October drew to a close and
the merchants, Portuguese and Chinese, concluded their
bargaining and one by one disappeared. On October 25 he wrote
to Gaspar Berze a sort of last testament of his love for the ' Companhia do nome de Jesus', which had been to him a mother, a
family, a country, a heaven upon earth. The well-being of the
beloved in the East now rested in Gaspar's hands, so let him daily
remember his responsibility to grow into the most humble man
alive. ' Wishing you and the others all the good I do,' he said,
' I would greatly prefer that you should dwell, not on what God
has achieved by your efforts, but rather on what He might have
achieved through you if you had not failed Him.' The letter is
one of sweetest charity and thunderbolts. Gaspar is to give his
love to each and every one of the brethren; he is to visit the
Franciscans and Dominicans and bring them his kindest wishes,
with a petition to be remembered in their holy prayers; he is
to dismiss from the Society of Jesus any Father or Brother who
gives the slightest cause for scandal and, in virtue of obedience,
on no account to receive them back, but at most, if they show
themselves truly penitent, to give them a letter for the Rector
of Coimbra, ' because they are not wanted in India but might do
some good in Portugal '. Finally, he is to admit very few, muito
poucos, into the Society and only such men as the Society has need
of. Yamaguchi, the one place where he had been supremely

[1] Schurhammer, Epistolae, ii, 498–501. Ke-moi is a little island opposite
Amoy in Fukien Province, about four hundred miles north-east of Sancian.

happy, *summamente consolado*, shines like a star in his gathering darkness, and he bequeaths the care of it and of the whole mission of Japan, largely for the sake of which he had come to his present pass, into the hands of his great lieutenant. He is still hoping against hope, waiting for the brown sail that is so slow to come. He has received some news that encourages him. The Emperor, or to him, the King, of China, Kia-tsing, of the Ming Dynasty, was a Taoist who liked to know how other nations were governed and by what laws they lived. He had even sent delegations abroad to inquire into those matters, so why should he not be glad to hear of the Christian law, as the Chinese merchants said he would be? Anyhow, Francis was going to test the possibilities, if necessary round by Siam. Pero Lopez, the volunteer interpreter, had withdrawn his offer when he heard about the dungeons in Canton. Alvaro Ferreira, the only Jesuit left to him, also began to shiver in his shoes. Better hire or buy some negroes to do the work of the College, he told Berze despondently, than to depend on such as he. Christopher the Malabar was merely a paid servant, there for what he could get, and ready to desert at the first hint of danger. Only the young Antonio, the child of China who had lost his Chinese, remained, but with him for company Francis would cheerfully affront all the mobilized dragons and demons of the huge weird world that beckoned to him and scowled at him, just six miles away.

October had been a hard month for the watcher on Sancian, with its fluctuations of hope and disappointment. Very probably the Portuguese merchants, practical men all, shrugged their shoulders and said something about the folly of attempting the impossible as they set their sails for the good markets of Malacca, until eventually only a single ship besides the *Santa Cruz* was left behind. The captain of that ship, a creature of Alvaro da Ataíde, would gladly have joined them but, like the Apostle who deserted his Master, he must perforce stay, though not out of love, to see the end. He dared not return to the Portuguese world without Francis alive or dead or, at least with news of him in a Chinese dungeon. The providence of God often works at long removes, and on the sixth day of that identical October there was born at Macerata in central Italy the gentle genius Matteo Ricci, destined thirty years later to be welcomed as a Christian mandarin and missionary at the Court of Peking. When he wrote his *History of the Introduction of Christianity into China*, Ricci said, referring to St. Francis: ' All the Blessed Father's stratagems for entering China fell to the ground, but we may well believe that if he could not obtain from God the privilege for himself, he obtained it in Heaven for us his companions who, against all human hope, succeeded when he was thirty years dead.'[1] Had there been no Xavier to attempt the impossible, there might never have been a Ricci to achieve it. November was nearly half over before Francis wrote again, almost jubilantly, to Father Perez and Diogo Pereira, by some ship bound belatedly for Malacca. He had increased his offer to the Chinese merchant from 200 to 350 *cruzados* worth of pepper, no doubt through one of the others returning to Canton, and he felt that such a mountain of the hot stuff, nearly two tons of it, enough to make every nose in Canton sneeze, would be bound to bring his canny customer at top speed to Sancian. ' I have been expecting him for a week now and he is certain to come if I do not die,' he told Father Perez. ' I owe it all to my good friend Diogo Pereira, may God repay him, as I have not the means.' Perez is to do everything in his power in India to prove his gratitude to Diogo, and if there is the slightest chance of Diogo being allowed to come to Canton as ambassador the following April, which Francis doubts; thinking again sadly and resentfully of that obstructive person in Malacca, he is to be given a priest for companion if at all possible, and to be entrusted with the treasures which Gaspar Berze had brought from Ormuz. The silk, the brocade, the damask meant for the pleasure of an emperor would be used eight months later by Juan de Beira and Diogo Pereira to embellish the casket in which they secretly and lovingly laid all that was mortal of Francis Xavier.

But Francis was not dead yet, nor in the mood to die. He dismissed Ferreira from the Society of Jesus as one not meant for it, forbade Perez and Berze to receive him in any Jesuit house,

[1] D'Elia, *Fonti Ricciane*, vol. i (Roma, La Libreria della Stato, 1942), p. 139. This is a volume learned and magnificent beyond all praise.

and at the same time urged them to help him in every way they could to become a mendicant friar. He gave no hint why he dismissed him at such a time and place, just as he kept strictly to himself the final reasons that led to his cashiering of Gomes. We shall never know them exactly, but from all we know of him we may guess that pride and insubordination were the gist of them.

I shall take good care [he told Perez] to write to you from Canton and let you know what kind of reception they gave me. . . . We go with God's help, Antonio, Christopher and myself. Pray much to God for us, as we run the very gravest risk of being made captives, but we comfort ourselves with the thought that it is much better to be a captive for the love of God than to be at liberty through fleeing from the labours of the Cross. In case our man does not come for us and has changed his mind, fearful of the risk, I shall go to Siam and thence to Canton in the fleet which the King of Siam sends to that city. . . .

The letter to Pereira of the same date, November 12, is largely an outpouring of gratitude.

May God our Lord requite you [he says]. All my life I shall feel strictly bound to beg God to protect you from every evil, to give you in this life grace and health for His holy service, and Paradise in the world to come. As I am personally incapable of thanking you as I should, I have earnestly commended you to the Fathers of the Name of Jesus in all India that they may hold you for their especial friend and never cease to remember you before God our Lord in their prayers and Holy Sacrifices. If the law of our Lord Jesus Christ is made manifest in China . . . the glory and joy of that holy work will be yours in this world and the next. Those who become Christians there and the Fathers serving God will feel a perpetual obligation to have you in their prayers. . . .

*   *   *   *   *

He mentions the ' *pobres captivos* ' of Canton, begging that their plight be remembered, and tells that his special friend, Francisco Pereira de Miranda, who had been very good to him at Hirado in Japan, and other Portuguese, had recently, through a terrible disaster, been added to their number. Finally, with a gesture of infinite pathos, he returns to Diogo the Viceroy's diploma constituting him ambassador to the Court of Peking. That dream had faded into the mists gathering about the vanishing Portuguese ships and the dilatory junk from Canton.

But Francis was fiercely determined that other dreamers, Ricci for instance, should never again be thwarted by the cupidity and jealousy of men calling themselves Christians. On November 13 he took up his pen for the last time and addressed himself jointly to Perez and Berze:

I strongly urge you to see that the Society's bulls and the parchment in which the Pope makes me nuncio to the Indies are shown to the Bishop and the Vicar General. And you will see to it that the mandate of the Bishop declaring Dom Alvaro's excommunication because he forcibly kept me from China, in contravention of the Viceroy's provisions and in disobedience to the orders of the Captain of Malacca, who was then Francisco Alvares, as you, Father Perez, know well, having been present throughout, that this mandate, I say, be sent to the Father Vicar of Malacca, with orders to publish it in the church. You will be diligent in this matter for two reasons only, first, that Dom Alvaro may recognize his sin against God, do penance for it, and seek absolution from his excommunication, resolving that he will never again treat others as he treated me. The second reason is that the Brethren of the Society who come to Malacca or the Moluccas or Japan or China may find no obstacles placed in their way at Malacca in future. Men without any fear or love of God in their hearts may yet be deterred from raising such obstacles to God's service by the shame of excommunication and dread of what the world may think and do. I order you under obedience to be diligent in this matter. Give the Bishop's or the Vicar

General's dispatch to Juan de Beira or to a Father going to Japan that he may transmit it to the Vicar of Malacca, and petition the Bishop or Vicar General as a favour to write to the Vicar of Malacca, ordering him in virtue of obedience and under pain of excommunication to make the sentence known publicly in the church. Write to me within a year to tell me how active you have been in the business. . . .

All this may sound strangely fierce as coming from a man so gentle and compassionate, but Francis had steel in him too and was acting only in mercy, as his Mother the Catholic Church does when she solemnly pronounces her anathemas on ruthless, godless men who lay violent hands on her prelates, corrupt her little ones, and endeavour in their insolence to blot the name of Jesus from the pages of history.

The letter went on:

> As this voyage to China is difficult and full of peril, I know not whether it will succeed, but I still have good hopes. As I told you, if I cannot get to Canton direct this year I shall go to Siam, and if within twelve months Siam also fails me, I shall return to India. Nevertheless, I am greatly hoping that I shall be able to make my way into China. Know this for certain and have no doubt that the devil will do all in his power to prevent our Fathers from entering China, . . . but also know equally certainly that with the grace and help of God our Lord the devil will be put to confusion. What great glory to God it will be if by one so vile as I am the vast presumption of the devil is brought to nothing! Master Gaspar, remember the counsels I left you on my departure and those I have written to you. Do not neglect to observe them as others have done, thinking me to be dead. For if it is the will of God I shall not die, though it is a long time since I felt so little inclined to live as I do now. . . .[1]

By this time there remained at Sancian only the *Santa Cruz* and one other ship, trimmed for departure, which took with her

[1] Schurhammer, *Epistolae S. Francisci Xaverii*, ii, 518–21.

the last letter of Francis and all but one of his few friends, the same Diogo Vaz who was afterwards to be the chief instrument under God in making a devout Catholic of the mighty and tempestuous Daimyo of Bungo. Diogo now acted host to Francis on the island, instead of George Alvares who had returned to Malacca. Some years, the weather on Sancian can be pleasant in November, but it was not so that year. It was bitterly cold. The huts put together by the Portuguese were mere temporary storage-places for their merchandise, very lightly constructed and always destroyed without trace when they sailed away. They afforded little protection against the biting winds which whistled round the island in November, 1552, and Diogo Vaz, good compassionate man, could do little to alleviate the discomforts of his guest who often went hungry and was always chilled to the bone. The whole story of splendour and sorrow is very simply told by the faithful Chinaman Antonio in a letter which he wrote from Cochin two years later to Manuel Teixeira at Goa, and which Teixeira embodied textually in his *Vida del Bienaventurado Padre Francisco Xavier*, the earliest of the many biographies, though unpublished until 1912. Having referred to the Father's occupations on the island while there were merchants or others to be helped, Antonio continued:

Every day and every hour of each day the Blessed Father looked with great desire and anxious longing for the return of the Chinese merchant who, according to their pact, was to take him to Canton. But our Lord ordained otherwise, having determined to bestow upon him at that time the reward of all the great labours and sufferings which he had borne for His love and service. When practically all the ships had sailed for India and with them the majority of the Portuguese merchants, including the Father's host, George Alvares, that man of benediction remained behind, almost without resources. There were times when he asked me to beg a little food from the remaining merchants for the love of God, as he had nothing to eat. Indeed, he lacked everything. What with this, and with his daily toil and his passionate longing to be in Canton, he fell ill on November 21, after saying Mass for a man recently dead on the island. . . . He asked me at the time whether I thought it would be a good idea for him to row out to the ship of Diogo Pereira, the Ambassador, which lay at anchor off the island. I said that it was an excellent idea, as the ship had ample stores, and perhaps also the sea would do him good, so he left on a Tuesday at midday. But he stayed on board the *Santa Cruz* only that one night, the heavy rolling of the ship being too much for him, with the fever ever mounting in his veins. Next morning he returned to the island where I had remained, carrying under his arm a pair of cloth breeches which he had been given on the ship as a protection against the great cold, and also a handful of almonds [*almendras*] as a remedy for his infirmity. He arrived in so dread a fever that a Portuguese merchant [Diogo Vaz] compassionately carried him to his hut as his guest and begged him to allow himself to be bled, as he was more seriously ill than he imagined. The Father replied that he was not used to being bled, but in that matter as in everything else pertaining to his illness, his friend was to do with him as he thought best. He was bled forthwith and fainted for a brief time under the knife, because, as you know well, dear Brother, he was of the choleric-sanguine temperament. It was a Wednesday, and there followed on the bloodletting so great a nausea that he was unable to swallow anything. Next day, he underwent the operation again, and again fainted. He asked to be purged when he came to, but the fever went on increasing, causing him the most grievous anguish. But he bore it all most patiently, without the slightest murmur or any appeal for relief. His mind began to wander at this time, and in his delirium his words, incoherent though they were, showed him to be thinking of his brethren in the Society of Jesus. . . . With eyes raised to Heaven and a very joyful countenance, he held long and loud colloquies with our Lord in the various languages which he knew.[1] I heard him repeat several times the words: *Jesu, fili David miserere mei; tu autem meorum peccatorum*

[1] Antonio did not understand any of the 'various languages' except the Latin exclamations. He knew Portuguese well and could probably have made

miserere. So he remained until Monday, November 28, which was the eighth day of his illness. On that day he lost the power of speech altogether and continued silent for three days, until midday on Thursday. During that time he recognized nobody and ate nothing. At noon on Thursday he regained his senses, but spoke only to call upon the Blessed Trinity, Father, Son and Holy Ghost, always one of his tenderest devotions. I heard him again repeat the words: *Jesus, Son of David, have mercy on me,* and he exclaimed again and again: O *Virgin Mother of God, remember me!* He continued to have these and similar words on his lips until the night of Friday passed on towards the dawn of Saturday, when I could see that he was dying and put a lighted candle in his hand. Then, with the name of Jesus on his lips he rendered his soul to his Creator and Lord with great repose and quietude.[1]

It was a poor and humble death, not unperplexed, such as befitted a poor and humble man who had no notion whatever that the world would want to remember him. He had brought thousands of others the comforts of the Church in their last moments, but he died himself without anointing or Viaticum. When they packed his frail exhausted body in lime and put it in the unconsecrated Chinese earth, there was no one to read over it the Church's last farewell to her children. Had he ever been so far untrue to his character as to give a thought to his obsequies, he would surely have been well content that his bones should remain there, as it were, keeping watch until the end of the world, if indeed, he would not have prayed to God with all his heart to be allowed the last privilege of the lowly, an unknown and forgotten grave.

---

out Spanish words, had the dying Saint spoken them. It is not certain, but psychologically nearly so, that the 'various languages' were, in fact, Basque, the tongue of Francis's childhood.

[1] MHSJ. *Monumenta Xaveriana,* ii, 894–6. Just as there was controversy at one time about the date of St. Francis's birth, to has there been about the date of his death. Antonio's letter has decided the question. St. Francis died in the small hours, probably 2 a.m., of Saturday, December 3, 1552, aged forty-six years and eight months.

THE APOTHEOSIS OF FRANCIS XAVIER

ANTONIO the Chinaman writing to the Jesuit Manuel Teixeira at Goa:

In death the blessed Father looked so happy and so fair that one might have thought him still alive. . . . I went at once to the ship [the *Santa Cruz*, still riding at anchor off Sancian] to obtain the vestments and all else necessary for his burial. . . . Some of those on the ship returned with me . . . and we made a wooden coffin in which we placed the body clothed in sacerdotal vestments. We then took it in a boat to another part of the island opposite to where the ship and its people lay. . . . It was very cold, so most of them stayed aboard and there were only four of us at the burial, a Portuguese, two slaves and a Chinaman. . . . Having dug a deep grave we lowered the coffin into it and were about to cover it with earth when one of the company suggested to me that it might be a good idea to pack the coffin with lime above and below the body, as it would consume the flesh and leave only the bare bones, in case anyone in time to come should wish to take them to India. This seemed to us an excellent suggestion, so we withdrew the coffin, obtained four sacks of lime [from the ship] and poured two underneath the body and two above it. Then we nailed on the lid again and filled in the grave. . . . I put some stones around it as markers, so that if I or any member of the Society happened to come to the lonely spot in the future and desired to see where the body of the blessed Father rested, we would be able to find it. Thus did we bury him, full of bitter sorrow, on the afternoon, of Sunday December 4, the day following his death.[1]

[1] *Monumenta Xaveriana*, ii, 897–8.

Apparently Antonio did not know of Alvaro da Ataíde's
intrigue and believed his minions on the *Santa Cruz* to be as much
the friends and admirers of St. Francis as he was himself, a delusion
which, for their own good name, they took care to foster. He
speaks of them as being stricken by the death of Francis, and it
plainly astonished him that they did not come to the funeral.
It is only when a writer is in great straits that he will trust anything
reported by Mendez Pinto, but in connection with the death of
Francis he cites a letter written by someone on the *Santa Cruz*,
' whose name for the sake of his honour I refrain from mentioning ', to Ataíde at Malacca, just a fortnight after the forlorn
funeral, and this extract, a *rarus natans in gurgite vasto*, does seem
to bear all the marks of authenticity. It runs:

> Master Francis has died out here, and with never a miracle.
> He is buried on the beach of Sancian, in the same way as the
> others who have died on the ship. If the body is in a fit state to
> be moved we shall transport it to Malacca at an opportune
> moment, so that the slanderers there may not be able to say we
> are worse Christians than themselves (*Peregrinação*, cap.
> CCXVI).

The Portuguese plainly were not too keen on the exhumation and
had given it no thought until Antonio pleaded with the captain,
who agreed to send one of his men to examine the state of the
body, shortly before their sailing date, February 17, 1553, more
than ten weeks after the burial. The body was found to be
exactly as when buried, completely intact and smelling only of the
lime in which it was resting. To convince the captain, his man
removed a small portion of flesh for examination on the ship,
after which a party was sent ashore to bring back the rough coffin
and its contents, including the lime. The captain does not seem
to have been much impressed, for he gave orders that the coffin
lid was to be securely nailed lest it come off during the voyage,
with unpleasant consequences. Malacca was reached on March 22,
and then Francis dead received a civic welcome such as would
have acutely embarrassed him when living. The largest procession

Malacca had ever seen accompanied the remains to our Lady's church where Francis had so often spoken his heart to good people and bad, to children, to negro slaves. A grave had been hollowed out of the rock near the high altar, and in it, after the solemn services, the body, removed from the coffin, was laid. It had no wrapping but the priestly vestments and a piece of linen over the beautiful face, so strangely untouched by the finger of death. The grave proved too short and could not be lengthened owing to the nature of the ground, so the body had to be gently pressed into it in such a way that the head was forced over the chest. That was not the last of the well-meaning indignities to which it would be subjected, nor did an element of scorn fail to show. One who was present at the obsequies reported three years later that Alvaro da Ataíde ostentatiously played draughts with a boon companion in full view of the funeral cortège as it slowly moved in a blaze of candle-light to the church.[1]

The body lay under and in full contact with the earth for nearly five months, until the Feast of the Assumption that same year, 1553. Meantime, rumour had reached India that Francis was dead. His old friend, the heroic Juan de Beira, there on business, hurried his return to the Moluccas in order to investigate the story and at Malacca discovered the sad truth. Overcome with a great longing to see again the face that had been his life's inspiration, he sought the help of Diogo Pereira, the friend of friends and organizer of the honours already paid to St. Francis. Secretly, and at dead of night by the light of a lantern, the two men, helped by a few trusted companions, exhumed the body again and found it still wearing the colours of life, as on the day more than nine months earlier when Antonio had committed it to the Chinese earth. The only damage appearing had been done, not by nature but by man, during burial in the inadequate grave. The nose was crushed, there were bruises on the face, and a sharp stone had made a wound in the left side. Otherwise, Francis might have been only asleep. The awed friends grouped around decided immediately that such a treasure ought not to be returned to the Malaccan earth. It belonged to Goa, the Rome of the East, and

[1] *Monumenta Xaveriana*, ii, 276.

thither it should be taken. The empty grave was filled in and the body of St. Francis taken secretly to Pereira's house, where he reverently and lovingly laid it in a coffin lined with Chinese damask and covered with the finest brocade. Not until December 11, more than a year after the death of Francis, did a ship sail for India, and it was a crank and battered old thing that had been too long at sea. Merchants hesitated to trust their wares on it, but Diogo Pereira felt perfectly sure that *his* cargo, the holy remains of his friend, would see the veteran through. Many tales are told · of the vicissitudes of that voyage over the ocean wastes that had so often menaced Francis when he was alive. Now dead, he appeared to have control of the elements, for, if we may believe some of the worthies aboard, the ship got into every sort of trouble and scrape of which ships are capable, tempests, shoals, sandbanks, reefs and rocks, yet limped safely home after taking twice the usual time to do it.[1]

The strange Odyssey of St. Francis's mortal remains ended at Goa in such a storm of excitement as that lively city had never before known. Everybody, from the Viceroy to the humblest Kaffir slave, seemed suddenly to realize the sublimity of the man whose body was being brought home. Had it been only a handful of dust or a few whitened bones instead of a soul's temple entirely unravaged by the grave, the enthusiasm would probably have been just the same. It was quite spontaneous, an upsurge of emotion which swept over the city in a mighty wave and almost drowned the solemnities of Lent, 1554. It shook the complacent Fernam Mendez Pinto, then in Goa, to such an extent that he temporarily renounced his grand standing as a merchant adventurer and became about the most unlikely Jesuit novice that ever was known. One friend of friends, the second self of Francis who yearned as he did to make the whole world his parish, was not there to share in the triumph. Gaspar Berze's flaming soul had burnt out his frail body six months before. The Dominican Father who preached at his funeral could not be heard for the sobbing of the huge congregation and had to leave the pulpit choked by his

[1] *Monumenta Xaveriana*, ii, 758–9, 901–902, 927–8.

own tears.[1] When Berze's successor as vice-provincial, Melchior Nunes Barreto, learned that the body of St. Francis had reached Cochin, he could not wait while the old tub bearing it laboured up the coast to Goa, but must obtain a swift sloop from the Viceroy to bring the sacred treasure back before Holy Week put the Church into mourning. Among those he took with him was the first historian of St. Francis, Manuel Teixeira, whose pages glow as he tells the story of how they met the ship flying all its flags and thundering salutes from its big guns. They had brought a small choir of boys from St. Paul's College, garlanded and carrying palm branches in their hands, who sang the *Gloria in Excelsis* and other festive canticles while Father Nunes and his companions stood in tears around the silk-covered catafalque where the body in its unlidded coffin lay. ' I saw and studied it with my eyes and handled it with my hands,' the Father reported to St. Ignatius, ' and I who had been incredulous till then cried in astonishment, *Memoriam fecit mirabilium suorum misericors et miserator Dominus. . . .*' It was midnight on Thursday in Passion Week, March 15, when the light *fusta* anchored opposite Goa, and the remains were taken to a little church on the shore for closer inspection. Manuel Teixeira who knew the living Francis tells what he saw and felt on this occasion:

He looked in stature and appearance exactly as we had formerly known him, lying there in his priestly robes complete and fresh as if he had been buried only an hour ago. Under the vestments next to the skin the body was clothed in a rich garment which the Father had taken with him from Goa to wear at his interview with the Emperor of China. Though it had been more than a year under the earth, it was so clean and intact that Father Nunes claimed it for his own to put on when later he paid visits to the kings of Japan. . . . At the College of St. Paul that Thursday night of Passion Week nobody went to bed, so busy were they adorning the church with flowers and banners for the reception of the holy body next day.

[1] *Monumenta Xaveriana*, ii, 922–3. A certain Jesuit named Aires Brandão who was present is the reporter here.

By dawn on Friday, Teixeira continues, there were thousands of
people on the beach, including the Viceroy and all his court.
That worthy, somewhat to the consternation of the Jesuits who
knew that Rome did not like her judgments to be anticipated,
had given orders that the many bells of the city were to be joyously rung as in welcome to some great prince or conqueror.
The Franciscan Fathers made other inroads into the rubrics of the
season by singing, instead of Requiems, Masses of joy and thanks-
giving. Altogether, it was just as well that the officials of the
Congregation of Rites were at a safe distance. For four days,
with never a break till midnight, the crowds thronged into the
church to kiss the exposed feet that had travelled so much and so
far on errands of mercy, through the busy streets of Indian cities
to prisons and hospitals, over the burning sands of Cape Comorin,
in the lovely dangerous Indonesian islands, and along the highways
and byways of Japan.

   Some good men in Goa suspended judgment or maintained
an attitude of healthy scepticism in the midst of the popular
excitement. They suggested that the body must have been em-
balmed. To settle the question the Viceroy instructed the chief
medical authority in the city to make a thorough examination of
the corpse and report, which he did in the following terms:

   I, Doctor Cosmas Saraiva, physician to the Senhor Viceroy,
   have been to examine the body of Father Master Francis,
   brought to this city of Goa. I felt and pressed all the members
   of the body with my fingers, but paid special attention to the
   abdominal region and made certain that the intestines were in
   their natural position. There had been no embalming of any
   kind nor had any artificial preservative agents been used.
   I observed a wound in the left side near the heart and asked one
   of the Society who was with me to put his fingers into it.
   When he withdrew them they were covered with blood which
   I smelt and found to be absolutely untainted. The limbs and
   other parts of the body were entire and clothed in their flesh
   in such a way that, according to the laws of medicine, they
   could not possibly have been so preserved by any natural or

artificial means, seeing that Father Francis had been dead and
buried for about a year and a half. I affirm on oath that what I
have written above is the truth. Doctor Cosmas de Saraiva.

Another doctor, Ambrosio Ribero, who was also Vicar General
of the diocese of Goa, examined the body independently. ' I felt
and kneaded the flesh of practically the whole body with my own
hands,' he testified, 'and I certify that the flesh is intact, covered
with its natural skin, flexible and in no way desiccated. There is
not the slightest trace of corruption. . . . I put my face right
against the body in order to test this fact. . . .'[1]

Those doctors made their tests in the year 1554. One hundred
and forty years later, in 1694, a French Jesuit, Père Joseph Simon
Bayard, was passing through Goa on his way to the mission in
China as secretary to the newly consecrated Vicar Apostolic of
the East, Bishop Espínola. The Bishop desired to see for himself
the state in which the body of St. Francis then was, and in great
secrecy, for fear the populace might swamp the church as they had
done on other occasions, the shrine was opened. For an hour and
a half Bayard and the Bishop closely examined the body, feeling
the flesh and flexing the limbs. It is an odd thing that Bayard's
account of this experience, written to his brethren in France,
should contain easily the best description of the appearance of St.
Francis Xavier ever written. After a compliment to Goa which,
he said, yielded nothing in magnificence to the proudest cities
of France, with the sole exception of Paris, and when he had
pictured the magnificence of the silver shrine gleaming with
countless jewels, he continued:

> The Saint's hair is black and slightly curling. The forehead
> is broad and high, with two rather large veins, soft and of a
> purple tint, running down the middle, as is often seen in talented
> persons who concentrate a great deal. The eyes are black, lively
> and sweet, with so penetrating a glance that he would seem to
> be alive and breathing. The lips are of a bright reddish colour
> and the beard is thick. In the cheeks there is a very delicate

[1] *Monumenta Xaveriana*, ii, 910–11.

vermilion tint. The tongue is quite flexible, red and moist, and the chin is beautifully proportioned. In a word, the body has all the appearances of being that of a living man. . . . It is so great a marvel that on seeing it, while I was present, the Commissary of the Dutch East India Company, Mynheer Vandryers, became at once a convert to the Catholic faith.[1]

Only fourteen years later the first signs of darkening and desiccation had begun to be noticed, and Father Francis de Sousa, the well-known author of *Oriente Conquistado*, who was then in Goa, wrote to petition the General of the Society of Jesus that the relics of St. Francis should be locked away in their shrine for good and the key ' cast into the depths of the sea '. This the Viceroy and Archbishop of Goa would by no means permit, and not so very long afterwards, in 1759, they themselves became guardians of the keys and of the shrine when the Marquis de Pombal expelled the Jesuits from all the Portuguese dominions. The shrine has been opened on many occasions since then, and in 1932 permission was given for the relics to be photographed. These show the body to have been at the time still in a remarkable state of preservation, considering the extent to which it had been handled, moved and even mutilated through the centuries. But it seems to be now no longer flexible and very definitely mummified, as is also the severed arm which has been venerated for more than three hundred years in Rome and was taken round the world and through Japan in 1949. The fact that the remains have shrunk and become dark and rigid does not preclude the possibility and likelihood of a miraculous preservation for a century and a half, for how else is a phenomenon so well attested to be explained? Because a miracle does not go on for ever is no proof that there never was a miracle. To argue in that fashion would be much like saying that the raising of Lazarus must have been non-miraculous, since Lazarus subsequently died again.[2] The bodies of many saints

---

[1] *Monumenta Xaveriana*, ii, 776–8.

[2] In his great work on the Beatification and Canonization of Saints Pope Benedict XIV has two long and fascinating chapters *De Cadaverum Incorruptione* in which with his usual thoroughness, serenity, and genuinely scientific spirit

displayed the same qualities as those of St. Francis Xavier for
long after death, e.g., St. Isidro, the Patron of Madrid, the Franciscan St. James della Marca, St. Catherine of Bologna, the two
Carmelites, St. Teresa of Jesus and St. Mary Magdalen de' Pazzi,
St. Luis Bertrand, o.p., but in every case they eventually became
desiccated.

Those who have had the patience to read this book will probably
agree that Francis Xavier might safely have been canonized
on the evidence of his letters alone, heroic sanctity is so plain to
read in almost every hurried paragraph of them. But the signs
from Heaven such as the Church in her wisdom requires did not
fail, either before or after death, though they were certainly not
so numerous nor so dramatic as some of the old writers in their
enthusiasm imagined. The legend that St. Francis 'spoke in
tongues' was traced to its source earlier in this book and shown
to be quite baseless. The story of the Crab and the Crucifix, which
Père Delehaye dismissed as merely a borrowing from Japanese
mythology, received even rougher treatment from his successor
as Director of the Bollandists, that great scholar and man, Père
Paul Peeters [died an octogenarian in 1950]. Pere Peeters maintained, even against the formidable authority of Father Schurhammer who still retains a lingering tenderness for the celebrated
crab, that the whole story was an invention of the seedy ex-gunner
and refugee, Fausto Rodriguez, a Portuguese living on Spanish
charity in the Philippines:

---

he investigates the whole question. Bodies of saints and others that had not
disintegrated but become rapidly mummified, he rules out altogether, attributing the phenomena to artificial or natural causes. The only cases he is willing
to consider miraculous are those of bodies that retain their flexibility, their
colour as in life, and their complete freshness for a long period after death,
without, of course, any artificial help such as the use of spices or embalming,
and even in such cases he would not admit miracle unless it could be clearly
proved that the persons whose bodies are in question practised virtue in a heroic
degree during their lives. The general impression left by the Pope's most
learned and finely discriminatory discussion is that the Church is very reluctant
to admit incorruption in the full sense of the word as a miracle of the kind
required for canonization, though it is often mentioned in the bulls issued on
those occasions.

*Comme ancien bombardier, il devait se connaître en artifices:
lui faisons-nous une bien gratuite injure en nous demandant si
peut-être il n'aurait pas imaginé celui-là pour attirer sur sa misère
désespérée la bienveillance des confrères et compatriotes de Xavier,
que l'on savait très avides en ce moment-là de recueillir des témoinages
en vue de sa béatification prochaine? La question se pose comme
d'elle-même; nous accueillerons volontiers toute réponse plausible.*[1]

The way the miracles of St. Francis, some of which, particularly
in the healing of the sick and in the prevision of future events,
undoubtedly happened, were multiplied and magnified by the
old writers is evident in such a classic of hagiography as Pedro
Ribadeneira's *Life of St. Ignatius*. That work was finished as early
as 1569 and, though Ribadeneira is himself moderate and reasonably accurate in his statements about St. Francis, he yet dropped a
few seeds which were destined later to grow into a substantial
tree of legend. Thus in the chapter of his great and indeed epoch-
making book of its *genre* which he devoted to the life and death
of St. Francis, he wrote: ' It is a certain fact that God honoured
him [Francis] by giving him the grace and gift to work many
and very illustrious miracles. . . . He cured infirmities of many
kinds, drove many demons from human bodies, restored sight
to the blind and raised the dead to life. . . .' Ribadeneira's first
draft of his biography, written in Spanish, failed to reach publi-
cation but was circulated privately among the author's Jesuit
brethren. They subjected it to severe criticism on various grounds

---

[1] *Analecta Bollandiana*, t. xlvi (Brussels–Paris,1928), pp.459–60. In the course
of his researches Father Schurhammer discovered some old Japanese parasols
with the crab story painted on their panels. Everything would, of course, depend
on the date of those objects. If they were painted before 1608 when Rodriguez
first made his announcement they might confirm his picturesque tale, but if
later, when the story had caught hold, through the Bull of Canonization in
which it figures and through intercourse between the Christians of the Philippines and those of Japan, they would be of negligible value as evidence. Now,
even if the date of the parasols and of the Japanese legend of the cuttlefish
were known, which is far from being the case, the objections raised by Père
Peeters on psychological grounds would lose nothing of their force. Besides,
granting the complete authenticity of the story, the fact, owing to crab nature,
could never be proved to have been miraculous.

and not until 1572 was Ribadeneira permitted to bring out a
much improved Latin version at Naples. This also was not regarded
as definitive but rather as a means of obtaining the views of
eminent Fathers in various parts of the world, including Alexandro Valignano and Manuel Teixeira in the East. From Goa
on December 8, 1584, Teixeira addressed a charmingly tactful
and deferential letter to Ribadeneira in which the following
passage occurs:

> It is said in Book IV, chapter vii, that our Lord by means of
> Father Master Francis raised the dead to life. His virtue and
> sanctity were indeed such that our Lord, of His infinite good-
> ness and power, could have wrought such miracles through him,
> but inquiry has revealed no certainty on the subject, only
> common report that they had happened. The clearest rumour
> was that our Lord had raised a dead person by his instru-
> mentality at Cape Comorin, but when the matter was investi-
> gated no one could be found who had seen the miracle. Father
> Henriques of our Society who was for forty years and more on
> the Fishery Coast told me that he had been ordered to make
> inquiries, but could not find any certain evidence. It is not from
> any doubt of the Blessed Father's sanctity and power with God
> that I write thus, but only because in a matter of such grave
> importance, certainty would appear necessary, or at least
> evident probability. As your Reverence well says in your
> prologue, if falsehood or exaggeration under any circumstances
> is unworthy of a Christian man it is far more so in dealing with
> the lives of the Saints. God has no need of our lies. . . .[1]

Padre Valignano, a plain, blunt man, did not strive excessively
to be tactful and pronounced statements in that same Franciscan
chapter of Ribadeneira to be variously *grande hiperbole, muy grande
hiperbole*, and *mucho mayor hiperbole*, which was about the truth of
the matter.

Francis Xavier was beatified by Pope Paul V on October 25,
1619, and canonized by Pope Gregory XV on March 12, 1622,
in the splendid company of St. Philip Neri, St. Ignatius Loyola,

[1] *Monumenta Xaveriana*, ii, 805–6.

St. Teresa of Jesus, and St. Isidro of Madrid.[1] Pope Benedict XIV constituted Francis patron saint of India and all the East, where he is now revered even by Hindus, Moslems and Buddhists as, so to speak, one of the family. Later, he was declared to be the patron of all the foreign missions of the Catholic Church. Every year throughout the world there is held immediately before March 12, the date of his canonization, a solemn novena in his honour, the Novena of Grace. This annual nine days of public veneration and intercession seems to have originated from a great and perfectly attested miracle worked by St. Francis at Naples on January 3, 1634, the instantaneous cure of Father Marcello Mastrilli, subsequently an outstanding martyr of Japan, who lay at death's door from a grave lesion of his brain. There were several eye-witnesses of the event, including the very distinguished future Jesuit General, Father Vincent Carrafa, and they set down their testimony in the most sober factual manner that could be desired.[2] Finally, for the sake of completeness, it may be as well to say that the beautiful Spanish sonnet beginning, *No me mueve, Señor, para quererte*, loosely Latinized in the familiar hymn, *O Deus, ego amo te*, is definitely not the work of St. Francis Xavier, however much it may reflect his spirit.[3]

[1] St. Isidro, or Isidore, is little known outside Madrid where they celebrate his feast every year with a magnificent display of fireworks. This married ploughman, who died as long ago as A.D. 1130, is one of the most winning of the whole bright company of Heaven and would make a perfect patron for the agricultural labourers of the world. His wife is also venerated as a saint in Spain, under the title of Santa Maria de la Cabeza, because her head is often carried in procession in times of drought. Isidro's body, like that of St. Francis Xavier, is still entire, though long mummified. How pleasant it is to know that the beautiful proud capital of Spain, the city of the grandees, has a humble, illiterate workman for its chief advocate in Heaven. If anyone considers this note to be irrelevant to the life of St. Francis he is quite justified and most welcome to his opinion.

[2] *Monumenta Xaveriana*, ii, 992–1005.

[3] The sonnet was written by an anonymous author in the seventeenth century, long after the time of St. Francis who, in any case, was no poet (Schurhammer, *Epistolae S. Francisci Xaverii*, ii, 526–35—a full and lucid discussion of the question).

INDEX

A

Achin, 233, 288

Alantalai, 175, 183, 185

Alcaçova, Pedro de, 496, 506

Albuquerque, Affonso de, 100 and n., 101; in Goa, 116, 117; in Malaya, 232-3; sends expedition to Moluccas, 244; citadel of, in Malacca, 288

Albuquerque, Juan de, O.F.M., Bishop of Goa, 118, 119-20, 203, 300, 302, 303, 309, 330, 460, 462, 466, 534

Almeida, Luis, 383, 384, 399, 405-6; ——Letter of, 385

Almeirim, Francis goes to, 90

Alonso, Nicholas, see Bobadilla

Alvares, Francisco, 242, 500, 501-2

Alvares, George, 293, 294, 295, 298-9, 301, 376, 524

Amboina, 242, 244; St. Francis arrives in, 248, 248 n., 253, 254; a remarkable goat on, 258-9, 262, 267, 283, 284; de Torres meets St. Francis, 313-14

Ancolina, Lady Faustina, 80 and n.

Anes, Cosmas, 203, 303, 318, 352, 494

Anjiro (Paul of the Holy Faith), 293-7; St. Francis on, 296-7, 298, 299, 300, 301; on St. Francis, 312, 316; baptized, 317, 341, 342, 344, 376-7, 389, 390-1, 404, 409, 410

Antonio, the Chinese, 495, 505, 515, 519, 521, 528; ——Letter from, to Manuel Teixeira, on St. Francis' death, 524-6, 527

Antonio, the Japanese, 317, 453, 455, 456, 496, 509

Aragon, Ferdinand, King of, 21 and n.

Aragon, Juan of, 216

Aragon, River, 13

Araujo, John, 268-9, 273, 274

Arrack, St. Francis attacks drinking of, 166, 169, 175

Artiaga, John, 160, 164, 165; St. Francis dismisses, 169, 171, 180, 181, 182

Ataíde, Captain Tristan de, 245

Ataíde, Alvaro da, see Gama

Augustinian Friars, 250

Azpilcueta, Maria de, 15, 16, 17; religious ordinances of, 18-19

Azpilcueta, Martin da ('the Doctor of Navarre'), 16; offers to join St. Francis, 89, 91; ——Letter to, from St. Francis, 89-90

B

Badagas, The, Christians persecuted by, 174-85

Badia, Thomas, O.P., 71

Baptisms, 'automatic', in Goa, 124-5; in Tuticorin, 136

Barbosa, Duarte, on Malacca, 232-3; on the Javanese, 237-8

Barbosa, Nicolas, 199

Barreto, Melchior Nunes, 422-3; appointed superior at Bassein, 473, 531; ——Letter from, to Jesuits at Coimbra, 471-2; ——Letter to, from St. Francis, 474-6

Barros, João de, on non-Christians, 117, 118

Basque language, 15

Bassein, 124, 303, 310, 312, 313 n., 314, 329, 473

Batchian, 269

Bayard, Joseph Simon, S.J., 533-4

Beira, Juan de, 248, 249, 285, 286-7, 349-50, 467, 506 and n., 507, 520, 529; ——Letter to, from St. Francis, 508

Benedict XIV, Pope, 538

Bernard of Japan, 398-9, 405, 408, 409, 410, 413, 416, 424, 433, 446

Berze, Gaspar, 319-20, 321, 331; on the rectorship of St. Paul's College, 462, 464, 465; rector of Goa, 469; St. Francis' instructions to, 476-82, 496, 497, 503, 530; ——Letter from, to St. Ignatius, 496; ——Letters to,